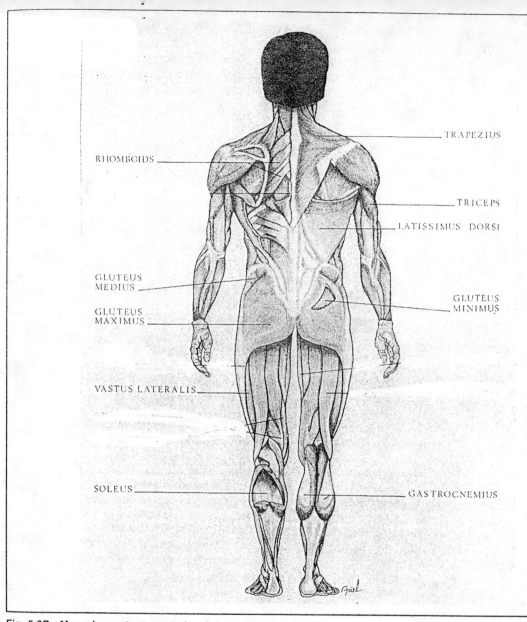

RHOMBOIDS

TRAPEZIUS

TRICEPS

LATISSIMUS DORSI

GLUTEUS MEDIUS

GLUTEUS MAXIMUS

GLUTEUS MINIMUS

VASTUS LATERALIS

SOLEUS

GASTROCNEMIUS

Fig. 5-3B Muscular system—posterior view

Cardiac muscle forms the walls of the heart. While cardiac muscle is striated

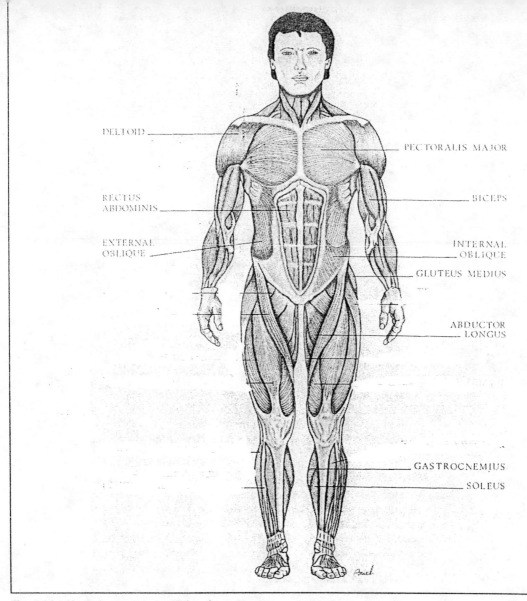

DELTOID

PECTORALIS MAJOR

RECTUS
ABDOMINIS

BICEPS

EXTERNAL
OBLIQUE

INTERNAL
OBLIQUE

GLUTEUS MEDIUS

ABDUCTOR
LONGUS

GASTROCNEMIUS

SOLEUS

Fig. 5-3A Muscular system—anterior view.

found in the human body: skeletal, smooth ar

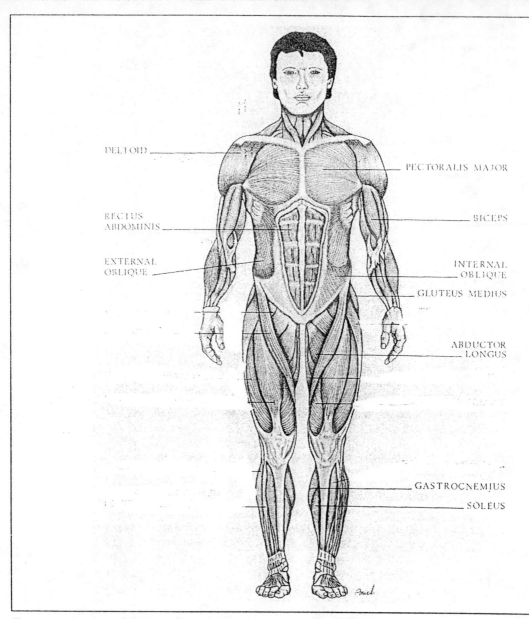

DELTOID

PECTORALIS MAJOR

RECTUS
ABDOMINIS

BICEPS

EXTERNAL
OBLIQUE

INTERNAL
OBLIQUE

GLUTEUS MEDIUS

ABDUCTOR
LONGUS

GASTROCNEMIUS

SOLEUS

Fig. 5-3A   Muscular system—anterior view.

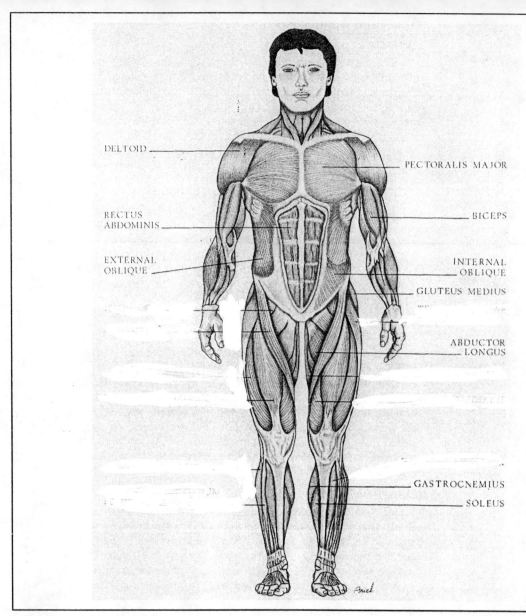

DELTOID

PECTORALIS MAJOR

RECTUS
ABDOMINIS

BICEPS

EXTERNAL
OBLIQUE

INTERNAL
OBLIQUE

GLUTEUS MEDIUS

ABDUCTOR
LONGUS

GASTROCNEMIUS

SOLEUS

Fig. 5-3A   Muscular system—anterior view.

Muscles

There are three types of muscle found in the human body: skeletal, smooth a
cardiac muscle (April 1984; Moore, 1985; Tortora, 1988). Skeletal muscle
attached to bone via tendons and allows voluntary movement of the boc
Because of its striped or band-like appearance under the microscope, skele
muscle is also known as striated muscle tissue. Smooth muscle is nonstriat
and is found in the walls of organs such as the stomach and intestines. Becau
it does not require conscious control for a contraction, smooth muscle is a
called involuntary muscle.

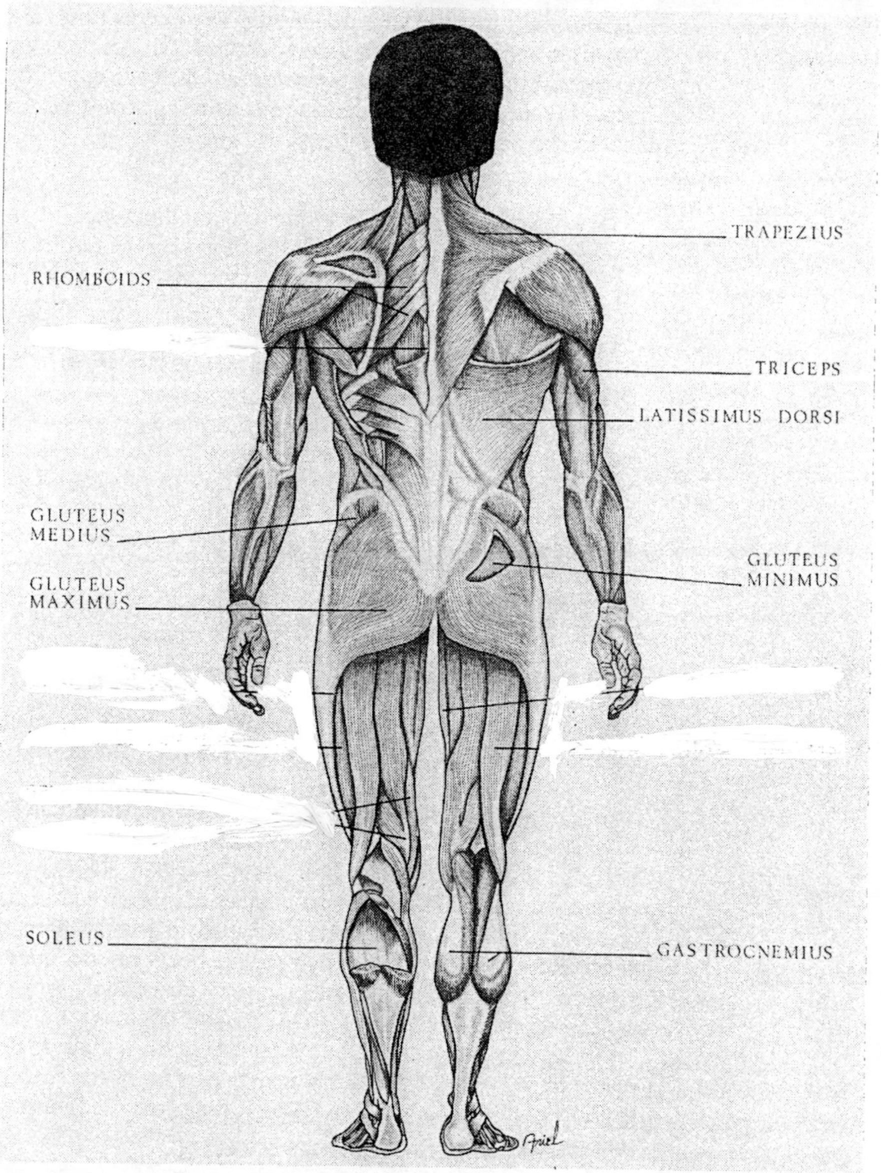

Fig. 5-3B Muscular system—posterior view

Cardiac muscle forms the walls of the heart. While cardiac muscle is striated in appearance, it does not require our conscious thoughts to contract and pump blood through the body.

Skeletal Muscle

Skeletal muscle makes up approximately 44-51% percent of total body weight in men and 35-42% total body weight in women (Komi, 1992; Tortora,

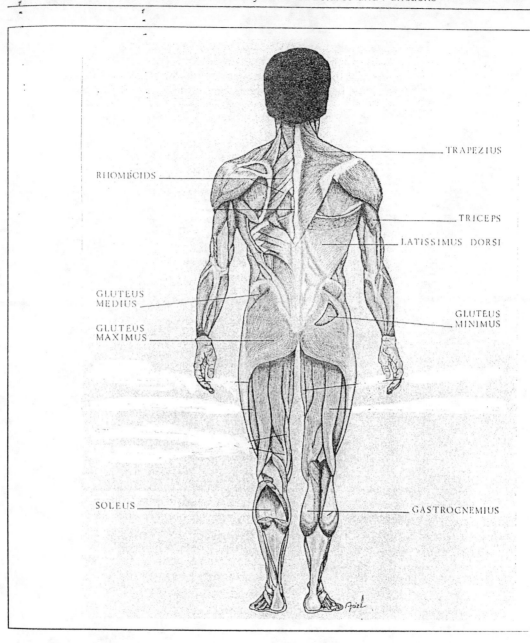

TRAPEZIUS

RHOMBOIDS

TRICEPS

LATISSIMUS DORSI

GLUTEUS
MEDIUS

GLUTEUS
MINIMUS

GLUTEUS
MAXIMUS

SOLEUS

GASTROCNEMIUS

Fitness
Theory & Practice

Second Edition

We dedicate this book to a powerful behind-the-scenes woman, an industry "rain-maker," visionary and unwavering tour de force—Linda D. Pfeffer, RN, president of AFAA.

Due to her expansive drive, enthusiasm and love of "big ideas," she carried this nearly impossible project through countless hurdles all the way to an impressive finish line.

We move and play
to keep pace with
the heartbeat of the earth,
and the music in our souls.

Fitness
Theory & Practice

The Comprehensive Resource for Fitness Instruction

Second Edition

Editor
Peg Jordan, RN

Aerobics and Fitness Association of America

Sherman Oaks, California 91403

Co-Publishers

Aerobics and Fitness Association of America
15250 Ventura Blvd., Suite 200
Sherman Oaks, CA 91403

Reebok University Press
100 Technology Center Drive
Stoughton, MA 02072

ISBN 0-9638168-4-5

Library of Congress Catalog Card No. 93-072944

10 9 8 7 6 5 4 3 2 1

Printed in the United States of America.

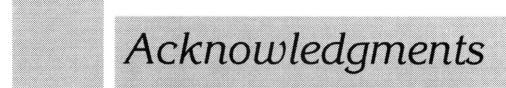

Acknowledgments

The editors wish to acknowledge the guidance and talents of the following in the creation of this book.

    AFAA President: Linda D. Pfeffer, RN

    AFAA Executive Vice President: Roscoe K. Fawcett, Jr.

    Former AFAA Senior Vice President: Marti West

    AFAA Board of Certification and Training: Robin Foss, Nancy Gillette, Laura Gladwin,
        Peg Jordan, Kathy Stevens, Carol Swett

    Former AFAA Board of Certification and Training: Linda Shelton and Marti West

Editorial Production:

    Managing Editor, Second Printing: Laura Gladwin, MS

    Text Editor: Mary Beth Ferrari

    Cover Art: Malcolm Farley

    Medical Illustrations: Michael Aniel, Andrew Bonsall and Gina Urwin

    Book Design & Production: Kendall/Hunt Publishing Company

    Assistant Production Editors: Rhonda J. Wilson, Jeanette Dvorak and Ayn Nix

    AFAA Photography: Dan Magus

Publishing a comprehensive resource of this size and scope could not have been done without the valuable assistance and generous support of AFAA's co-publisher, Reebok University Press. Special thanks to Angel Martinez, President, Fitness Division, and Bob Cole, Director of Reebok University.

Contents

Fitness: Theory & Practice

Foreword

IN 1985 THE AEROBICS AND FITNESS ASSOCIATION OF AMERICA (AFAA) provided a young, rapidly expanding profession of exercise instructors with its first textbook: *Aerobics: Theory & Practice.* That groundbreaking resource became the so-called "bible" of the industry, a much used, dog-eared, rarely-on-the-shelf resource serving instructors for the past eight years. Today, AFAA has grown into a widely respected international presence, serving the needs of millions of students and dedicated enthusiasts. AFAA Certified Instructors not only teach aerobics, they counsel clients on everything from strength training for older adults to post-partum exercises for nursing mothers. Today, an accomplished instructor may teach lateral training for elite athletes; tomorrow, imaginative play for pre-schoolers. They are, in fact, ***fitness practitioners,*** new advocates in the making—professionals who play a key role in the future of health promotion.

Fitness Practitioners™ fulfill a lifespan of fitness needs for a population that has come to count on them for guidance and accuracy. Because of that comprehensive coverage, they not only need a book that presents and deciphers the explosion of research and practical knowledge developed over the past decade—they need a book that clearly speaks their language, a book that takes the theory from the exercise laboratory and brings it where it is needed most—the exercise studio, the home gym, the street. It is in this spirit of theory-into-practice, of science-you-can-use, that we offer this book.

Welcome to *Fitness: Theory & Practice,* the second edition of AFAA's original text. Usually second editions maintain the original title, but due to the broadened scope of practice since publication of that first book, *Aerobics* was switched to *Fitness.* Over two years of planning and collaboration went into this anthology of 65 authors—all recognized leaders and authors in fields which impact fitness instruction: exercise physiology, research, sports medicine, nutrition, weight management, sports psychology, exercise adherence, anatomy, kinesiology, physical therapy, biomechanics, personal training, business, instructional presentation, and special populations guidelines. Contained in these pages is the most impressive "who's who" of the fitness industry. We offer their professional knowledge and hard-earned practical wisdom to you with the intention that you will use it to develop your own rewarding fitness career or perhaps simply to pursue your personal fitness dreams.

Fitness: Theory & Practice is the first textbook that offers a complete "How To Teach Exercise" section, with advice on every aspect of instruction, as well as an entire section devoted to holistic fitness and wellness concepts. Expert advice on personal training, fitness assessment, body composition counseling and professional responsibilities are also provided. Another unique feature is the section on "Special Populations." For the first time, practitioners have a valuable reference guide for addressing large exercisers, prenatal women, seniors, children, and those requiring adaptive fitness. Featuring the newly revised AFAA Standards and Guidelines, this text is the official preparatory guide for AFAA's Primary Certification Exam. And when it's time to quit studying, and simply move for the fun of it, there are over 14 different workout samples provided in "Specialty Classes & Trainings." It is our sincere hope that this resource becomes just as dog-eared and relied upon as the original. May it help you put all your fitness theory into practice!

—*Peg Jordan, RN, Editor*
—*Mary Beth Ferrari, Text Editor*

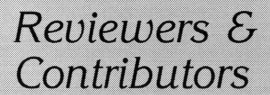

Reviewers & Contributors

Reviewers

LAUVE METCALFE, MS
Masters degree, Administration in Health Promotion from Florida State University; past president, Association for Worksite Health Promotion; president-elect, National Fitness Leaders Association; former director of program development, Campbell's Institute for Health and Fitness; recipient, Healthy American Fitness Leader; board member, National Governor's Council on Physical Fitness and Sports; consultant, President's Council on Physical Fitness and Sports; original contributor, *Aerobics: Theory & Practice;* private consulting practice based in Tucson, AZ.

CAROL OTIS, MD
Acting Director Specialty Clinics, University of California Los Angeles Student Health Service; UCLA Associate Professor, School of Medicine; key drafter of the ACSM Position Statement for committee on the Female Athlete Triad; *SHAPE* magazine board member; private practice in Los Angeles, CA; author and lecturer.

NEIL SOL, PhD
Preeminent international consultant and research pioneer in preventive health and wellness services; doctorate in Exercise Science from Kent State University; former general manager, The Houstonian; former president, Association for Worksite Health Promotion; author, *Presidential Sports Award Manual;* contributing editor, *Optimal Health* magazine; ACSM certification in Preventive and Rehabilitative Exercise; founding member, AFAA Advisory Board for the Fitness Practitioner; original reviewer, *Aerobics: Theory & Practice,* President, Health Vantage, Inc., Houston, TX.

Contributors

KEN ALAN
Owner, Ken Alan Associates; producer of music tapes for step and aerobic classes and senior workouts; international seminar presenter; National Step Reebok Trainer.

Exercise Adherence

KAREN ANDES-CARCAMO
Weight training and bodybuilding professional instructor; producer of "Muscles," strength training video workout; author of *The Beauty of Strength, a Mind-Body Manual;* co-producer of "The Aqua Jogger Workout Video."

Body Contouring With Elastic Bands
Deep Water Workouts

JUDITH BAKER, MEd
Health and wellness educator and teaching associate for Fitness Resource Associates in Needham, MA; co-author of AFAA's Personal Training Certification.

Lifestyle Questionnaire

DEBBIE BAN-PILLARELLA
Elementary school teacher, AFAA Lead Consultant and Certification Specialist; owner of BodyWorks Inc.; author of City KidZStep; creator of the "Power Moves" workout video and star of several others.

Training for Plyometrics and Power

WILLIAM C. BEAM, PhD
Professor, Department of Kinesiology and Health Promotion, California State University, Fullerton, CA; lecturer, member, AFAA Advisory Board.

Energy Production During Exercise
Developing and Maintaining Aerobic Fitness
Improving Health and Performance Through Aerobic Fitness

AMANDA J. BEAUDIN
Certified by American Red Cross in Standard First Aid, Responding to Emergencies, Adult, Infant and Child CPR instruction; teacher for the American Red Cross in Colorado; AFAA Certified Instructor and wellness counselor for Poudre Valley Hospital in Fort Collins, CO.

Emergency Protocol: Standard First Aid and CPR

DIAHANNE BEDORTHA
Creator of the Aqua Jogger and co-script writer in "The Aqua Jogger Workout Video"; hydrotherapy program designer for athletes with physical disabilities; certified by AEA and USWFA.

Deep Water Workouts

PAULA BESSON, MEd
Director of Educational Services and co-owner of Fitness Resource Associates in Needham, MA; co-author of AFAA's Personal Trainer and Fitness Counselors; AFAA Certification Specialist; adjunct professor at Leslie College.

Professional Scope and Responsibility
Counseling for Body Composition Changes

JILL BOYER
Technical Advisor at Be Some Body Women's Health Club in Bethlehem, PA; intramural coach at Lafayette College in Pennsylvania; ski instructor and amateur ski racer; AFAA Certified Personal Trainer, AFAA Consultant and Trainer.

Sports Conditioning Class

LYNNE BRICK, RN
Co-owner and founder of Brick Bodies; AFAA Consultant, AFAA and ACE Continuing Education provider; co-owner of a chain of women's health clubs entitled "Lynne Brick's Women's Health and Fitness"; star in over a dozen videos.

Building Aerobic Choreography

MERYN G. CALLANDER
Social worker; co-author with John Travis, *Wellness for Helping Professionals;* co-director, Wellness
Associates Network; facilitator.

Wellness: The Big Picture

SHARON CHENG, MS, PT, MBA
Occupation Health Services Manager, All Saints Hospital, Fort Worth, TX; AFAA Lead Consultant,
Certification Specialist, Personal Trainer Instructor.

Musculoskeletal System: Structures and Functions

BOB CHOQUETTE
Founder of Visually Impaired Program (V.I.P.) based in Londonderry, NH; pioneering fitness leader in
aerobics, weight training, and aqua programs for the visually impaired.

Fitness Programming for the Visually Impaired

JANIE CLARK, MA
AFAA Senior Fitness Consultant; author, *Seniorcise: A Simple Guide to Fitness for the Elderly; Disabled;
Full Life Fitness: A Complete Exercise Program for Mature Adults; The Wellness Way;* host of "The
Wellness Workout" television series; director of ABLE (Arthritis: Better Living through Exercise) of Volusia
County, FL; health/fitness instructor, Daytona Beach Community College.

Sample Workout for Active Seniors

NANCY CLARK, MS, RD
Nutrition counselor at SportsMedicine Brookline, Brookline, MA; AFAA Advisory Board Member; featured
columnist in *American Fitness* magazine; member of Sports and Cardiovascular Nutritionists and American
College of Sports Medicine; author of *Nancy Clark's Sports Nutrition Guidebook* and *The Athlete's Kitchen.*

Sports Nutrition

SUSAN COOPER, MA
Co-owner of BodyBusiness, Inc. and BodyBusiness Education Services and Training, Inc. in Austin, TX;
AFAA Lead Consultant; producer of four instructional videos for sculpting: "P.U.M.P," "P.U.M.P. Bench,"
"The Upper Cut" and "Below the Belt."

Muscular Endurance Training

TROY DE MOND, MA
President of Fitness On The Move; National Director of Education for SPRI Products; contributing author,
American Fitness magazine; international presenter; producer of "Just Pump I.T. with Troy DeMond" and
"Troy DeMond's TNT Workout."

Interval Training

JEANETTE DVORAK
Senior Editor of AFAA's *American Fitness* magazine and author of over 20 articles in the health and fitness
field.

Safe Foundations: Shoes and Floors

LISA ERICSON
Leader in field of seated aerobics; instructor at Craig Hospital, Englewood, CO; former professional ice skater; producer of "Lisa Ericson's Seated Aerobic Workout"; 1993 Healthy American Fitness Leader honoree.

Seated Aerobics: Creating Accessibility for All Interested Parties

DAVID ESSEL, MS
President, David Essel, Incorporated; author, lecturer, video and audio cassette producer, specializing in motivation; radio host for "David Essel Live!" on NBC's Radio TALK NET.

Marketing and Promoting Your Business

TERE FILER, MA
AFAA Lead Consultant, Certification Specialist with background in nutrition and exercise science; former Program Director for AFAA; owner, Actions Plus Consulting Services.

Circuit Training

LORNA FRANCIS, PhD
Assistant professor in physical education at San Diego State University; researcher in aerobic fitness; author of several fitness books and many magazine articles; workshop presenter; member, several advisory boards; founding member of the Step Reebok program development team.

Step Training

JUDITH GANTZ, MA
Visiting professor of dance at UCLA; contributing editor and former fitness editor to *SHAPE* magazine; member, AFAA Advisory Board; instructor of certification programs at the Laban/ Bartenieff Institute of Movement Studies in New York; member of the Educational Board for the *Journal of Kinesiology and Medicine for Dance.*

Training for Flexibility
Coordination: The Overlooked Fitness Concept

RONDA GATES, MS
Owner of Lifestyles health promotion company in Lake Oswego, OR; author; developer of many national health programs including Covert Bailey's Fit or Fat System and television series.

Body Image and Self-Esteem

NANCY GILLETTE, MA
Physical educator with California teaching credentials and background in adaptive physical education; co-author AFAA Adaptive Fitness Certification with National Handicapped Sports Association; AFAA Trainer and Lead Consultant; author and lecturer; owner of ATG International, a fitness consulting company; past International Vice President; AFAA Board Member and Director of Consultant Services and Education.

Advancing Your Fitness Career
Instructor Training

LAURA GLADWIN, MS
Physical educator; member, California State University, Fullerton Advisory Board, Department of Kinesiology and Human Performance and Department of Gerontology, senior fitness specialist program; AFAA Lead Consultant, Master Specialist, AFAA Board of Certification and Training; owner LGA Fitness Consulting & Training; primary author and Director of AFAA Senior Fitness Programming.

International Travel for Instructors
Senior Fitness

SANDY GREGER, MEd, ATC
Certified Athletic Trainer at Sports Medicine Lehigh Valley in Bethlehem, PA; ski racing coach and competitor; Alpine ski instructor; Certified level one ski racing coach with the U.S. Ski Coaches Association; member, Camelback Alpine Team.

Sports Conditioning

VICTORIA JOHNSON
Corporate aerobic program director at the Riverplace Athletic Club in Portland, OR; owner of Metro Fitness, Inc.; producer of several videos; L.A. Gear spokesperson; AFAA Continuing Education Provider.

Funk

GAIL JOHNSTON
President of Symmetry Systems and Curves Unltd.; pioneer in exercise systems for larger individuals; AFAA Lead Consultant, former AFAA Board Member, Director of AFAA's Specialty Certification, Teaching Fitness to the Large Exerciser; author of forthcoming *If I Know I Should Be Exercising, Why Aren't I?*

Trends in Weight Management
Teaching Fitness to the Large Exerciser

PEG JORDAN, RN
Health journalist; cardiovascular and psychiatric nurse; former director of cardiac rehabilitation programs at Los Angeles hospitals; founder and editor of AFAA's *American Fitness* magazine; co-author of *Aerobics Today* and author, *Aerobic Dance Injuries;* honoree, Healthy American Fitness Leader; member, AFAA Board of Certification and Training; FOX-TV health and fitness commentator; member of the National Fitness Leaders Association and the California Governor's Council on Physical Fitness & Sports.

Defining Fitness
Editor

FRANK I. KATCH, PhD
Professor, Department of Exercise Science, University of Massachusetts, Amherst, MA; co-author *Exercise Physiology: Energy, Nutrition and Human Performance.*

Evaluation of Body Composition

VICTOR L. KATCH, EdD
Professor, Department of Movement Science, Division of Kinesiology; Associate Professor, Pediatrics, School of Medicine; Director, Weight Control Clinic, University of Michigan, Ann Arbor, MI; co-author, *Exercise Physiology: Energy, Nutrition and Human Performance.*

Evaluation of Body Composition

SHEILA KING, MS
Exercise physiologist; ACSM Certified Program Director, program development consultant for the Personal Fitness program at the University of California, Los Angeles Extension.

Overcoming Client Dependency

SARA KOOPERMAN, JD
Attorney with practice in Chicago, IL; owner of Sara's City Workout, Inc.; founder of the MANIA Conventions; lecturer, trainer for ACSM; adjunct faculty member for the Kenneth Cooper Institute for Aerobic Research; author; international presenter.

Law and Exercise

PETRA LANSNER ROBINSON
AFAA Vice President, Marketing-Special Events; former co-owner of the Anaheim Hills Workout Fitness Studio; former corporate program director for the LA Fitness Health Club chain; former Wellness Director for Rockwell Corporation and Northrop Corporation-Saudi Arabia.

Competitive Aerobics

MADELEINE LEWIS
Choreographer for over 25 videos; producer of "Madeleine Lewis' California Calorie Burner"; international seminar presenter; Team Leader in the Nike Elite Network; national spokesperson for Quaker Rice Cakes; AFAA Lead Consultant.

Fat-Burning Class: What is it really?

CHARLES LITTLE
Program Director and trainer for Contours Exercise Studio near Washington, D.C.; international presenter; AFAA Consultant; producer and talent in "Pro Low Impact" and "Super Step" videos among others.

Funk Guidelines

CONNIE LOVE, MA
Owner of Love's Fitness Services and program coordinator of the Jamnastics Fitness Center in Chicago, IL; AFAA Lead Consultant and Certification Specialist; member of the Step Reebok National Instructor Training Team; producer of "Dynamic Definition/Chicago Funk"; former host of the "Shape Up Chicago" television show; competitive bodybuilder.

Resistance Tubing: Class and Guidelines

PAT LYONS, RN
Pioneering researcher in size acceptance movement; registered nurse, fitness instructor and Senior Health Education Consultant for Kaiser Permanente Regional Health Education, Oakland, CA; co-author, *Great Shape: The First Fitness Guide for Large Women.*

One Size Does Not Fit All

PATTI MANTIA, MEd
Master Certification Specialist for AFAA; Aerobics Director at the Brockton Athletic Club, Brockton, MA; Consultant for Fitness Resource Associates, Needham, MA.

Cardiopulmonary System: Structure, Function and Exercise Application
Common Aerobic Injuries: Prevention and Treatment

LINDA MASON, PT
Physical therapist specializing in pulmonary rehabilitation, orthopedics and sports medicine; AFAA Certification Specialist for the Personal Trainer/Fitness Counselor Program and Continuing Education Provider for Fitness Resource Associates.

Common Aerobic Injuries: Prevention and Treatment

DIANA MC NAB, MEd
Professor and sports psychologist at Seton Hall University; sports psychologist for the United States National Racquetball Team; member, Board of Advisors for *SHAPE* magazine and the International Dance Exercise Association; former member, Canadian National Ski Team; owner of Sports Vision consulting firm; author and lecturer.

Motivating for Behavior Change and Exercise Adherence

CYNTHIA MC NEILL
AFAA Lead Consultant, Certification Specialist; background in dance education; registered therapeutic recreational specialist; Program/Fitness Director at the Concourse Athletic Club in Atlanta, GA; recipient of the IRSA Fitness Director award, 1991.

Directing Fitness Programs

SANDRA NICHT
Aerobic Director at the Meadow Mill Athletic Club and Director of the reConstruction project, Inc., in Baltimore, MD; AFAA Certification Specialist, Continuing Education Provider and Consultant; Creator of BenchAquatix.

Aquatic Exercise

KATHY NORMANSELL, MS
Co-developer of adaptive fitness guidelines for AFAA in conjunction with the National Handicapped Sports in Washington, D.C.; Director, Adaptive Fitness Instructor Workshop, NHS.

Adaptive Exercise for the Physically Challenged

LAURA PAWLAK, PhD, RD
Registered dietitian; extensive background in biochemistry from the University of Illinois Medical Center and postdoctoral training in immunology from the University of California; ACSM and AFAA Certified Fitness Instructor; author; instructor, "Life Without Diets"; private consultant; founding member of the AFAA Advisory Board and an original contributing author to *Aerobics: Theory & Practice.*

General Nutritional Needs

PENNY REEVES-GOFF
Co-owner, Body Business and Body Business Educational Services and Training Inc., in Austin, TX; AFAA master certification; radio host and motivational speaker.

Basic Business Skills
Personnel Management

DONNA RICHARDSON
AFAA Consultant and Certification Specialist; owner of DonnAerobics Fitness Company; co-star of the "Stay Fit with Donna and Charles" video; choreographer and aerobics competitor; competition judge; spokesperson for the Rainbow Anti-drug Program; Dance for Heart chairperson.

Funk Guidelines

SCOTT O. ROBERTS, MS
ACSM Certified Exercise Program Director; clinical exercise physiologist at Lovelace Medical Center in Albuquerque, NM; task force chair and lead researcher for AFAA's Youth Fitness Guidelines.

Exercise Guidelines for Children
Working With Additional Populations
Low Back Protocol

DEBBIE ROSAS and CARLOS ROSAS
Authors, *Non-Impact Aerobics* and *NIA-Neuromuscular Integrative Action Body-Mind Training Manuals;* extensive background in the field of body/mind/spirit exercise; producers of NIA Wave; owners, NIA Fitness, Portland, OR.

Holistic Fitness

JO-ANN ROSS, MA, CCC
Licensed speech pathologist with private practice; co-founder of "Vocal Impact," a voice care program for aerobic instructors.

Voice Care and Injury Prevention

BONNIE B. ROTE, RN, BSN, NACES
Registered Nurse and Clinical Specialist, maternal/infant health; certified Lamaze instructor; AFAA Lead Consultant and Certification Specialist; Director, AFAA's Prenatal Exercise Educational Program and Childbirth Education Coordinator at Pascack Valley Hospital in Westwood, NJ.

Pregnancy and Fitness

LINDA SHELTON
Director of Technical Development and Consultant Training for AFAA; founding member, former AFAA Advisory Board; fitness editor for *SHAPE* magazine; producer and talent in "One on One with Linda Shelton" among other videos; owner of Professional Fitness Services in Thousand Oaks, CA; completed masters work in exercise physiology.

Glossary

ARTHUR J. SIEGEL, MD
Chief of the Department of Internal Medicine at McLean Hospital in Belmont, MA; original contributor to *Aerobics: Theory & Practice;* founding member of AFAA's Advisory Board.

Medical Considerations of Aerobics

MERRILY SMITH
ACSM Certified Exercise Leader/Aerobics; AFAA Trainer, Lead Consultant, Certification Specialist; National Step Reebok Step Trainer; Director of Fitness Seminar Services in Santa Barbara, CA.

Low Impact Aerobics

KATHY STEVENS
AFAA Board Member; AFAA Certification Specialist; Program Director, Gold's Gym; Educational Developer and Director for the Kneedspeed/Slide Reebok program.

Choosing Aerobic Equipment
Substitute Teaching
Slide Aerobics: Lateral Movement Training

CAROL SWETT, MA, CCC
AFAA Board Member; Lead Consultant and former Director of Consultants; licensed speech pathologist in private practice; co-founder of "Vocal Impact," a voice care program for instructors.

Voice Care and Injury Prevention

JOHN TRAVIS, MD, MPH
Research pioneer in the field of wellness; founder of Wellness Resource Center; co-author, *Wellness Workbook, Wellness: Small Changes You Can Use to Make A Big Difference;* co-author, *Wellness for Helping Professionals;* codirector, Wellness Associates Network; lecturer, group facilitator, international presenter.

Wellness: The Big Picture

DENISE TUCKER
AFAA Lead Consultant; Continuing Education Provider; Strength and Conditioning Coach for three varsity sports and Step Reebok Trainer, Reebok University.

Monitoring Aerobic Intensity

MARTI WEST
Former founding member, AFAA Advisory Board; Former AFAA Senior Vice President of Education; pioneer in competitive aerobics; international presenter; original contributor to *Aerobics: Theory & Practice.*

Competitive Aerobics

NEIL WOLKODOFF, MA
Director of Sport Sciences at the Cherry Creek Sporting Club in Denver, CO; numerous certifications; doctoral candidate in psychology; consultant to several professional teams and athletes; trainer for the Copper Mountain School.

Training for Strength

MARY YOKE, MA
Adjunct professor in Department of Human Performance, Adelphi University, Garden City, NY; AFAA Lead Consultant; Master Specialist; ACSM Certifications in Exercise Test Technologist and Health Fitness Instructor.

Fitness Assessment and Testing

Basic Exercise Standards and Guidelines

Aerobics and Fitness Association of America

THESE STANDARDS REPRESENT an ongoing process of research, critique and consensus by a multidisciplinary team of aerobic industry leaders. Introduced in 1983, AFAA's Basic Exercise Standards and Guidelines were the first nationally developed tools used by instructors. This revised 1995 edition reflects a higher level of sophistication and accuracy achieved by applying the most up-to-date research findings to the practice of aerobics.

I. Basic Principles, Definitions and Recommendations

All standards and guidelines outlined as follows apply to an average adult without known physiological or biological conditions that would in any way restrict their exercise activities.

A. Components of Physical Fitness

A complete physical fitness program should seek to improve and then maintain:

1. Cardiovascular efficiency and endurance
2. Muscular strength and endurance
3. Flexibility
4. Optimal body composition

B. Principles of Training

1. Training Effect

Improvement, or creating a TRAINING EFFECT, refers to the physiological changes that occur in the body as a result of exercise. Training should be: (1) consistent, (2) progressive and (3) specific. A training effect will occur if the exercise is sufficient in all of the following areas:

    a. frequency: number of exercise days per week

    b. intensity: degrees of physiological stress

    c. duration: length of time

2. Overload Principle

Training occurs when the body is regularly stimulated beyond its normal workloads by progressively increasing FREQUENCY, INTENSITY and/or DURATION of exercise. The body responds by increasing its capacity to perform work, allowing it to adapt to increasing physiological demands. This principle applies to all types of physical conditioning. This does not mean that you must go for the burn to create a training effect. A TRAINING EFFECT will occur when muscles are worked slightly beyond their point of fatigue on a regular basis, with periodic increases in FREQUENCY, INTENSITY and/or DURATION as a result of adaptation to the workload.

3. Specificity of Training

Specificity refers to training specifically for an activity or isolating the specific muscle groups and/or movement pattern that one would like to improve. For example, a marathon runner will train for the event by running distance, not wind sprints, because the marathon is an endurance event. To strengthen a muscle group such as the biceps, choose exercises that isolate the biceps muscle with the least amount of assistance from other muscle groups.

4. Mode of Exercise

Mode of exercise refers to the type of activity that an individual is participating in. Modes of exercise that maintain a consistent intensity level may be more beneficial in improving cardiovascular fitness compared to exercise modes of variable intensities, provided that frequency and duration are also considered.

C. Frequency of Aerobic Training

1. Improving fitness

Improving fitness is achieved by participating in a minimum of 4-5 aerobic workouts per week. Individuals beginning an exercise program should begin with 3 workouts per week as indicated by qualified exercise prescription. Additional workouts should be added only after an individual has become accustomed to the present level of exercise.

2. Maintaining fitness

Maintaining fitness is accomplished by a minimum of 3 workouts evenly spaced throughout the week. Detraining occurs within 2-1/2 weeks or less following cessation of exercise, depending upon training level and/or fitness level at the time of exercise cessation.

3. Overtraining

The body needs time to rest, recover and rebuild from the stress of vigorous exercise. Instructors and students should be aware of the following symptoms of overtraining:

    a. fatigue

    b. anemia

    c. amenorrhea

    d. stress related injuries

- stress fractures
- tendinitis
- bursitis

- shin splints or other persisting lower leg pain
- chronic knee pain

e. atypical changes in resting and recovery heart rates

f. other symptoms related to weight training
- decrease in strength and lifting performance
- constant soreness leading toward pain
- muscle tears

4. Teaching Fitness

As an instructor, be aware of the symptoms of overtraining as outlined above. Individual differences in the number of classes per week that an instructor can teach without risk of overtraining depends on the following variables:

a. level of fitness

b. length of time (experience) instructing any one particular type of fitness class

c. type of class one is teaching

d. degree of active demonstration

e. other fitness activities outside of teaching

Twelve classes per week, including no more than two high impact classes per day, should be the maximum for the experienced instructor.

D. Muscle Balancing

1. Principle

For every primary muscle worked (agonist), the opposing muscle group (antagonist) should also be worked. Example: biceps/triceps. By exercising opposing muscle groups, one lessens the possibility of muscular imbalance, thus reducing the potential for injury. Repeating the same exercise month after month works the muscles only through that range of motion, stressing the joint and its attachments in the same areas over and over. A variety of exercises that strengthen both the agonist and antagonist muscle groups will balance and improve joint stability.

2. Muscle Balancing and Posture

Many acquired postural problems, Low Back Syndrome being the most common, may be due to muscular imbalances. These imbalances are manifested by:

a. increased lumbar curve

b. shortened and contracted iliopsoas

c. shortened and contracted hamstrings

d. weak abdominals

e. hyperextended knees

f. rounded upper back and forward shoulders

g. supinated or pronated feet

3. Application

Muscular imbalance causes the stronger muscle groups to compensate for the work of the weaker muscles. For example, during a push-up, if the triceps are not equally as strong as the pectoralis muscles in performing the exercise, the pectoralis muscles will take over to perform the majority of the work.

1. Correct neutral

2. Incorrect posterior tilt

3. Incorrect hyperextension

Sometimes an agonist muscle can become so much stronger than the antagonist muscle, that injury can occur when both the applied stresses to and the support of the skeletal system are unequally distributed among the muscles. For example, in runners, the quadriceps can overpower the strength of the hamstrings, causing the hamstring to become injured due to poor strength ratio between the quadricep and hamstring muscles.

When muscle imbalances in flexibility and/or strength occur, particularly between anterior and posterior muscles, there is difficulty in maintaining a stabilized torso. To achieve a balanced posture and avoid the risk of Low Back Syndrome:

a. strengthen abdominals and quadricep muscles

b. increase flexibility of back and hamstrings

c. lengthen and release iliopsoas with posterior pelvic tilts and proper stretches for these muscles

d. stand and exercise maintaining proper body alignment (see following section)

e. perform exercises regularly for optimum strengthening/ lengthening training effect

f. include exercises that concentrate on balance, posture and kinesthetic awareness.

g. incorporate muscle isolation techniques to promote torso and pelvic stabilization

h. avoid hyperextension of the knee while standing because this tilts the top of the pelvis forward (anterior), causing the lower back to arch

i. avoid arching or back bends as these activities compress the lumbar spine, possibly resulting in pain and/or damage to the vertebral discs

j. incorporate exercises to functionally strengthen back muscles into weekly exercise program.

E. Body Alignment

When performing any exercise, be conscious of body alignment and posture. Stand tall, yet keep posture relaxed, not tense. Imagine a "midline" running from the top of the head down through the middle of the body. Keep body weight balanced and evenly distributed in relation to this imaginary "midline." Abdominal muscles should be contracted with rib cage lifted so pelvis is in neutral alignment with the "tailbone pointing down" (Photo 1). Shoulders are back and relaxed. Do not hyperextend (lock) knee or elbow joints. Hyperextension places excess stress on ligaments and tendons that attach at each joint, increasing potential for injury as well as decreasing the effectiveness of stretching or strengthening activities (Photo 3).

F. Speed, Isolation and Resistance

Exercises should be performed at slow to moderate speed that will allow full range of motion and concentrated work for the isolated muscles which are the focus of the exercise. Isolation of a muscle requires that an exercise be specific to the joint action (i.e. flexion, extension, abduction) that will cause a muscle to contract to perform work. In order to isolate a muscle group, it is important not to work a muscle beyond the point of fatigue so that other muscle groups compensate and take over to continue work.

Performing an exercise too quickly often relies on momentum, often making this desired type of controlled movement impossible and may lead to joint or muscle injury. Strengthening a muscle requires working the muscle against resistance in a controlled, deliberate manner. Resistance is supplied in one of two ways:

1. Through the use of hand-held weights (see AFAA's *Weighted Workout Standards and Guidelines,* c 1986, revised 1988, 1993), surgical tubing, elastic bands or other resistive equipment.

2. By concentrating the tension of muscular contraction in the most advantageous position against gravity.

G. Full Range of Motion

1. Normal Range of Motion

The full degree of movement that a lever is capable of is restricted by the joint and surrounding tissues. Full range of motion is desirable because (1) muscle strength will increase when taken through the entire range of motion of an exercise and (2) it maintains adequate joint mobility.

2. Application

The working muscle(s) should extend through the full range of motion dictated by the flexibility of the muscles and joint(s) involved. Proper form and body alignment should be maintained and hyperextension should be avoided. To work the muscles efficiently, move through the full range of motion required to complete each exercise.

II. Class Format

A. Sequence

This is a guideline to class design and format that is physiologically sound and effective, and can be appropriately adapted to fit most club policies or your personal preference. Only in certain exercise categories such as warm-up or cooldown are the specific exercise types important. The following is a recommended sequence used by AFAA for a one-hour class:

1. Pre-class instruction
2. Warm-up: A balanced combination of rhythmic limbering exercise and static stretching.
3. Exercises from the following groups, performed in a standing position, in order of preference:
   a. Aerobics and post-aerobic cooldown
   b. Upper body strengthening
   c. Standing lower body strengthening
4. Descending to the floor for the remainder of the class, exercises from the following groups may be performed in order of preference:
   a. Legs
   b. Buttocks
   c. Hips

  d. Abdominals

  e. Lower back

 5. Cooldown: static stretching

B. Purpose of Consistent Sequencing

  If the above sequence is followed in the order listed, it is effective because it will help to keep the flow of the class smooth. Getting up and down off the floor repeatedly creates "exercise gaps" and can cause rise and fall of heart rate within the aerobic segment, which could have some contraindicated effects. Strive for smooth transitions between exercise activities. Repeatedly stopping class is not only choppy and inconsistent but a sure way to lose the interest of the class. Keeping the class moving will maintain the energy and interest level. The following recommendations should be adhered to regardless of class format used:

 1. Always begin class with warm-up.

 2. During aerobic portion, movement should be continuous without abrupt stopping and starting, or peak high and low activity.

 3. Always follow aerobics with sufficient cooldown period, including hamstring and calf stretches.

 4. Upon completion of strengthening exercises within specific muscle groups, always stretch those muscles before proceeding to the next group.

 5. Always end class with static stretching.

C. Class Level

  Unless class level is specific, i.e., beginner or advanced, it is best to teach at an intermediate level and explain to the class how to adjust or modify the individual exercises to their particular level of fitness and experience. In other words, try to give both a beginner and advanced version of your exercises while performing at an intermediate level. Skill level, intensity and duration capabilities of individuals must be considered.

III. Instructional Methods, Concerns and Responsibility

A. Monitoring—Purpose

1. Maximizing exercise effectiveness
2. Injury prevention

 a. Monitoring your students for alignment or performance errors is important in preventing musculoskeletal injury.

 b. Know the following Exercise Danger Signs. Should you observe any one of these or should a class participant complain of any of these, he/she should stop vigorous exercise immediately. If necessary, refer to on-site procedures.

  • unusual fatigue

  • nausea

  • dizziness

  • tightness or pain in chest

  • lightheadedness

- loss of muscle control
- severe breathlessness
- allergic reactions, i.e., rash or hives
- blurring of vision

The individual should contact his/her physician or obtain immediate medical advice. It is important that instructors always maintain current CPR certification.

B. Cueing

It is essential that vocal commands are used while instructing. A routine seems to flow more smoothly when the class is verbally cued as to what the next exercise will be. ANTICIPATORY CUES are key words and small phrases which describe an exercise or a sequence which will be performed next. It is also important when teaching exercise, that you strongly concentrate on body alignment. An exercise that is done incorrectly may not only be unsafe, but may lack any real benefit. It is essential that you as an instructor give BODY ALIGNMENT CUES for every exercise and make the necessary verbal corrections during class. Hand and directional signals are equally important so you can VISUALLY CUE your class along with verbal cues for clarity.

C. Legal Responsibilities

1. Instructors should complete training and certification programs that test both theoretical knowledge and performance skills and should practice according to a nationally accepted standard.
2. Instructors should carry a personal liability insurance policy.
3. It may be advisable for instructors and club owners to consult an attorney to prepare a participant disclaimer and release that is in accordance with the state and local laws.
4. In addition, it may be advisable for fitness facilities and independent fitness contractors to seek program review by qualified fitness and medical professionals.

IV. Pre-Class Procedures

A. Medical Clearance

Before class, determine if there are any new class members and the level of their experience. Ask participants if they have a medical condition to let you know so that you can assist them in modifying their workout.

According to the American College of Sports Medicine, (ACSM), men under the age of 40 and women under the age of 50 with one risk factor or less and apparently healthy, can participate in moderate exercise without medical clearance.

Medical clearance from a physician prior to exercise participation is recommended for:

- Men above the age of 40 and women above the age of 50, regardless of current physical health or risk factors
- Anyone with a pre-existing medical condition
- Anyone with 2 risk factors or more

- Anyone with known cardiovascular or other related metabolic disease
- Anyone with symptoms suggestive of possible cardiopulmonary or metabolic disease, i.e., chest pain, known heart murmur

Diagnostic exercise testing may be recommended in any of these instances.

In most cases, if an individual exhibits one or less risk factors, medical clearance is not needed. However, each participant's health and risk factors should be considered individually when determining the need for a medical exam and/or diagnostic exercise testing. At any age, an exercise test results provide valuable information, useful in developing a safe and effective exercise prescription. AFAA recommends that an instructor use common sense in relation to risk factors and medical clearance recommendations as some risk factors may be more significant than others. For example, an individual with high blood pressure or diabetes may be more at risk beginning exercise without clearance than someone who is overweight. It is advisable that all individuals sign a health release and waiver form, indicating their current physical condition as well as medical history prior to exercising.

1. Risk Factors

Some medical limitation and lifestyle habits require modified programs and specific recommendations. An individual who demonstrates or acknowledges two or more of the following should be advised to have a medical exam and diagnostic exercise test prior to beginning an exercise program:

- diagnosed high blood pressure*
- high cholesterol*
- cigarette smoking*
- diabetes mellitus*
- family history of coronary or other atherosclerotic diseases in parents or siblings prior to the age of 55*
- sedentary lifestyle (physical inactivity)*
- obese or overweight
- high triglycerides and/or abnormal HDL ratio
- poor eating habits
- high resting heart rate
  Indicates a major coronary risk factor (ACSM).

When two or more risk factors are present, extra precautions must be taken prior to exercising as some activities may need to be modified.

2. Effects of Drugs and/or Medications

Certain prescriptions as well as non-prescription medications such as antihistamines and antibiotics will elicit side effects during exercise similar to the Exercise Danger Signs outlined in III A of this chapter. Some medications can alter heart rates. For example, beta blockers suppress heart rate activity. It is not recommended that individuals engage in vigorous activity when taking drugs or medication if not under medical supervision. Individuals desiring to continue their exercise regimen should be advised to consult their physician regarding possible side effects.

B. Introductions

Introduce yourself and announce the level of the class.

C. Attire

If some class members are without shoes, AFAA strongly recommends they obtain and use shoes designed for aerobic exercise as a means of reducing the risk of injury to feet, knees and shins. This should be explained to the class.

D. Level of Participation

Explain that the class is non-competitive and that all participants should work at their own level. Make sure the class is aware of Exercise Danger Signs. In case of any acute pain experienced while exercising, the activity should be discontinued and the instructor should be notified immediately. If any stress or discomfort is experienced by a participant during class, urge them to discuss this with the instructor following class.

E. Breathing

Breathing should follow a consistent rhythmic pattern throughout the class. The level of activity will reflexively dictate rate and depth of ventilation. Do not restrict inhalation to the nose. Inhale and exhale through the nose and mouth in a relaxed fashion. Holding your breath while exercising may induce the Valsalva maneuver, closing the glottis and creating an unequal pressure in the chest cavity which may cause a rise in blood pressure. By the same token, hyperventilating or breathing too hard while exercising can irritate the nasal passage as well as cause lightheadedness.

F. Orientation to Aerobics

Define aerobics for new members. Explain before class how they can calculate their own "estimated" training heart rate range for aerobic work and how and where to take a pulse count. Explain perceived exertion and how to correlate how one feels with actual exercise intensity.

V. Warm-up

A. Purpose

Prepares the body for vigorous exercise and may reduce the risk of injury.

B. Time

Class should begin with 8-12 minutes of a balanced combination of static stretches and smoothly performed rhythmic, limbering exercises.

C. Stretching

Correctly performed mild stretching will increase the capacity for full range of movement. This allows one to perform exercises more efficiently with less risk of injury to joint attachments and connective tissue.

    1. Muscle Length

        a. Resting length—length of a muscle at rest

        b. Maximum length—the degree to which a muscle length can be stretched at any particular time

        c. Increasing length—repeated stretching of a muscle over a period of time will gradually increase the resting length of the muscle fibers

2. Static Stretch

Stretches should always be static and non-ballistic. Static stretches are sustained in a supportive position which allows the muscle being stretched to relax and elongate. Ballistic movement is forcefully executed, causing muscle contraction. Ballistic movement, such as vigorous bouncing during a stretch, invokes the stretch reflex. Stretching is most effective if it is done slowly and gently without bouncing or pulsing.

Pulsing, though it is a small controlled movement, still elicits muscle contraction and the stretch reflex. Therefore, pulsing is an inappropriate activity to be included during the warm-up.

3. Stretch Reflex

The stretch reflex is a neurological response, activated as the body's automatic protective mechanism against sudden changes in muscle length, severe injury and abuse. Whenever a muscle is stretched quickly and with force, or beyond the limits of the body's flexibility, an involuntary reflex is initiated by proprioceptors located in the tendon of the muscle being stretched, which causes the affected muscle to contract to protect and prevent injury and overstretching.

4. Position

Always assume a position with the body correctly aligned and supported so that the stretch will occur along the muscle's longitudinal line. Example: in a calf stretch, do not rotate the hips and turn the back foot out. Both feet should face the same direction so hips are square to the front leg and a calf stretch can be performed.

5. How to Stretch

Begin slowly in an easy stretch, not taking the muscle to its maximum length. Stretch to the point of mild tension and hold the position. As the muscle relaxes, increase the stretch slightly until point of tension is reached again. If tension is painful, ease off slightly. Breathing should be slow, rhythmic and controlled. The length of time that a stretch is held will vary according to whether or not one is stretching at the beginning of class when the muscles are not thoroughly prepared, or at the end of class when the muscles are warm. For warm-up, hold each stretch approximately 8-10 seconds. Avoid stretching muscles that are cold prior to performing some preliminary rhythmic limbering exercises.

D. Sequence

In order to maintain a smooth flow to your warm-up, follow an order that will include all major muscle groups. Warming up from either head to the toes, or vice versa is an easy way to avoid omitting any muscle groups.

E. Muscle Groups

AFAA recommends that all of the following muscle groups be warmed-up at the beginning of class, depending on class type and format:

1. Head and neck (sternocleidomastoid, levator scapula, trapezius-occipital portion)
2. Upper back, middle back, rib cage, shoulders (trapezius, rhomboids, latissimus dorsi, teres major, serratus anterior, anterior, medial and posterior deltoid, and rotator cuff muscles)

4. Stretch back before moves like this

5. Don't do full head rolls

6. Unsupported forward flexion

3. Chest and arms (pectoralis major and minor, biceps brachii, triceps brachii, brachioradialis, brachialis)

4. Front of torso and lower back (rectus abdominis, external and internal obliques, erector spinae)

5. Front and back of thighs (quadriceps group and sartorius, hamstring group)

6. Buttocks (gluteus maximus)

7. Outer thigh and upper hip (tensor fascia latae, gluteus medius and minimus)

8. Inner thigh (adductors longus, brevis and magnus; pectineus and gracilis)

9. Calf and front of shin (gastrocnemius, soleus, tibialis anterior)

10. Feet and ankles (flexors and extensors)

F. Rhythmic Limbering Exercises

Rhythmic limbering exercises are multijoint exercises that incorporate large muscle groups and are performed at a smooth and moderate pace. They help prepare your body for more vigorous exercise by: increasing the range of motion of the joint and its attachments, raising muscle and body temperature, increasing circulation to the tissues surrounding the joints, and maximizing neuromuscular function. Rhythmic limbering exercises can serve as a rehearsal of similar moves that may be performed later at a higher exercise intensity.

G. Special Do's and Don'ts

1. Do rhythmically warm-up and static stretch the lower back before attempting lateral spinal flexion or spinal rotation in which one arm, straight or bent, would diagonally, by lifting or reaching, cross the sagittal plane or body's midline (Photo 4).

2. Don't do traditional toe touches to stretch the hamstrings as this places a strain on the lower back muscles and ligaments.

3. Don't do full deep knee bends (grand pliés), as this strains the cruciate ligaments in the knees. Do keep hips above knee level.

4. Don't do rapid head rolls or hyperextension of the cervical spine as this strains the neck muscles and places tension on the vertebrae and discs in cervical region (Photo 5).

H. Special Considerations

1. Spinal Flexion-Forward

Although the spine was meant to flex forward, hanging with the torso in an unsupported position with gravity pulling downward on the back can place stress on the vertebrae, discs and connective tissue, i.e., ligaments, in the lumbar region as well as increase potential for overstretching lower back muscles and ligaments of the spine (Photo 6). Ligaments have little elasticity. Once overstretched, they remain elongated, decreasing the stability and support in the lumbar region.

Follow these guidelines if you choose to perform exercises in the spinal forward flexed position:

a. When stretching, or performing rhythmic limbering exercises, all movements should be performed in a controlled manner.

7. Incorrect

8. Correct lateral stretch

b. Do not maintain any forward flexed position for an extended period of time as overstretching of the ligaments in the lower back may occur.

c. Always support the torso by flexing from the hip joint, placing hands on the upper leg above the knee joint, lower leg or directly on the floor, depending upon individual flexibility level. Avoid arching backwards (Photo 7).

d. Contract abdominals to protect the low back. By keeping the torso stabilized with a neutral spine, the internal organs are supported by the abdominal muscls to maintain a correct posture.

e. Keep hips above knee level when flexing at both hip and knee joints. Allowing the hips to drop below the knees places stress on the ligaments of the knee as well as the back.

f. Always roll up from a bent over position, with knees relaxed.

g. when stretching hamstrings from a standing or seated position, lead with the chest and bend from the hips. Do not bend from the waist or back, arch the back or drop the head. Head should always be in alignment with spine.

2. Spinal Flexion—Lateral

Stretching to the side unsupported for a long period of time can be just as stressful as anterior spinal flexion IF performed incorrectly. These positions can be potentially dangerous and can cause ligament damage. Individuals who can stretch sideways to a horizontal position are usually relying on ligaments that have been overstretched in past activities by forcing or bouncing to increase flexibility.

Follow these guidelines when performing any type of lateral stretch:

a. Support the torso with one hand on torso or thigh with hips squared (Photo 8).

b. Never lean so far over to the side that you are "hanging" and have to throw one hip out of alignment to support the back.

c. Do not perform lateral flexion with both hands extended over head (Photo 9).

VI. Aerobics

A. Aerobics

Aerobic exercise can be defined as a variety of activities which create an increased demand for oxygen over an extended period of time. Aerobic exercises train the cardiovascular and respiratory systems to exchange and deliver oxygen quickly and efficienfly to every part of the body being exercised. As the heart muscle becomes stronger and more efficient, a larger volume of blood is able to be pumped with each stroke and with fewer strokes, thus facilitating the rapid transport of oxygen to all parts of the body with less stress on the heart. An aerobically fit cardiovascular system will allow an individual to work longer, at a more vigorous pace, with a quicker recovery.

B. Time

A minimum of 20-30 minutes of continuous activity is recommended.

9. Don't raise both arms over head

10. Proper jog

C. Sequence

The aerobic portion should resemble a normal bell curve. Start slowly and gradually increase the intensity and range of motion of your aerobic movements. Avoid lateral high impact moves such as "pendulum leg swings," jumping jacks or high impact grapevines during the first three minutes to allow your ankles and feet to become sufficiently warmed up. Peak movements, which involve a larger range of motion using both arms and legs, require a greater amount of oxygen to be delivered to the muscles and should be interspersed with lower intensity aerobic patterns to maintain steady state. These peak movements should not be included during the first three minutes.

D. Position

Correct posture (refer to section I, E.), with the abdominals contracted rib cage lifted, should be maintained throughout the aerobic portion. For all exercises performed, heels should contact the floor with each step.

When jogging, follow these guidelines:

1. Don't jog on your toes, as this shortens the calf muscles and Achilles tendon.
2. Don't lean forward, as this can contribute to shin splints and knee stress.
3. Do keep body weight balanced over entire foot and not backwards on heels.
4. Don't kick heel up to touch buttocks, as this arches the lower back. Keep knees aligned under or in front of hips (Photo 10).

E. Types of Movements

Try to vary your movements in order to both maintain interest level and effectively involve as many muscles as possible. Combination moves requiring coordination of both arms and legs should be entered into slowly, starting with either the arms or the legs and then adding the other. Build upon your moves instead of trying to teach a complicated combination all at once. Choose moves that are appropriate for the fitness level of the class. Avoid extended periods of jumping or high leg kicks. Do not jump on just one leg for more than eight times in succession because of risk of injury caused by repeated impact. Avoid elevating the arms overhead for an extended period of time as this activates a pressor response (refer to glossary).

F. Breathing

Steady, rhythmic breathing through both the nose and mouth should be used. Breath holding should be avoided.

G. Surface

Aerobics should ideally be performed on a suspended wood floor, which provides a cushion of air between wood and concrete, or on high density mat-type aerobic flooring. If jogging on concrete is unavoidable, mats should be used or low impact movements should be utilized.

11. Radial pulse

12. Carotid pulse

H. Music Speed

AFAA recommends that music speed during the aerobic portion should range from 130-155 beats per minute, depending upon fitness level and type of activity, i.e., high impact, low impact, combo, low impact with weights. When selecting music speed, lever length, i.e., arms, legs and torso, needs to be considered so he/she can complete a full range of motion for an exercise at that given speed.

I. Heart Rate

Monitoring heart rate serves as a guideline recommendation, indicating the level of exertion (intensity) for each participant.

1. Where to take pulse
   a. **Radial artery:** Place the fingers on the inner wrist, just below the wrist bone, straight down from the base of thumb. This location is preferred to the carotid pulse due to the possible depressant effect on the heart rate during palpation at the carotid site (Photo 11).
   b. **Carotid artery:** Place index and middle fingers by outside corner of eye and slide them straight down to the neck. Do not press hard or place thumb on opposite side of neck at the same time as the blood flow could be impeded and accurate heart rate measurements would not be possible (Photo 12).

2. How to determine your heart rate
   a. Count—Count your pulse for 10 seconds, beginning with "1."
   b. Multiply—Multiply this number by 6, and you will know what your estimated heart rate is for one minute at that particular time.

3. Resting heart rate
   a. Averages—Average for women is 78-84 beats per minute. Average for men is 72-78 beats per minute. A person in good aerobic condition generally has a lower resting heart rate.
   b. How to determine your resting heart rate—Take pulse for three consecutive mornings while still lying down, but after heart rate has settled down if awakened by an alarm. Add these three numbers together and then divide the answer by 3. This number is your resting heart rate.

4. Maximum heart rate

Maximum heart rate is the theoretical maximum number at which your heart can beat at your age, based on the maximum heart rate of a baby at birth. The mathematical constant 220 minus your age equals your estimated maximum heart rate. Do not exercise at this level.

5. Training heart rate range
   a. Purpose: Provides an easily identifiable gauge of an individual's level of aerobic work and whether or not the intensity of aerobic activities should be increased or decreased.
   b. To determine your training heart rate range (THRR), subtract your age from 220 and multiply this number by .55 and .85. This is your training heart rate range or zone that you should "target" during aerobic exercise. Individuals with special needs (i.e., pregnant women or anyone with a

history of cardiorespiratory problems) should consult a physician regarding the recommended training heart rate range. When beginning an aerobics program, it is recommended that all individuals train at the lower end of their range for the first eight to ten weeks.

6. Application

The pulse should be quickly located after vigorous exercise. Keep feet moving, i.e. walking, and take a 10-second count. Multiply by six. This number should be in your individualized training range. If it is higher or lower than the recommended limits of your range, you will need to adjust the intensity of your exercise accordingly by being more or less vigorous.

7. Monitoring heart rate during exercise

In the most ideal of situations, AFAA recommends taking heart rate at three different times: (1) five minutes after the beginning of active aerobic work to determine if participant is exercising within his/her training heart rate range, (2) at the completion of the most intense aerobic work to see if he/she has maintained aerobic training level, and (3) at the completion of post aerobic cooldown to determine if he/she has sufficiently recovered from aerobic work. However, as taking heart rates at these times is not always feasible, heart rate should be checked at the completion of the most intense aerobic work rather than not at all.

8. Recovery heart rate

A recovery heart rate can indicate an individual's fitness level by the speed at which heart rate returns to a pre-exercise level. It is also an indicator of whether the cooldown period was sufficient, and if exercise intensity was appropriate. After five minutes, the heart rate should be 60% or less of the estimated maximum HR (220 minus age, multiplied by .6).

VII. Post-aerobic Cooldown

A. Purpose

A post-aerobic cooldown provides a transitional period between vigorous aerobic work and muscular strengthening exercises or stretches. Without a gradual cooldown period, the blood can pool in the extremities immediately after an aerobic workout and does not return to the heart quickly or efficiently if movement stops suddenly. Moderate to slow, rhythmic movements for the upper and lower body will enable the muscles of the extremities to pump the blood back to the heart and brain. Stopping motionless after an aerobic workout could result in lightheadedness and/or fainting.

B. Time

Approximately 2-3 minutes of decreased intensity aerobic work such as walking, marching or other rhythmic activities is recommended.

C. Breathing

Breathing should be relaxed with rate and depth dictated by physiological reflexes. Students should learn to be aware of their own oxygen requirements and learn to regulate their breathing accordingly.

D. Stretches

After 2-3 minutes, muscles that have been utilized during the aerobic portion, especially the calves, front of lower leg, quadriceps, hip flexors, hamstrings and the back should be statically stretched for 10-20 seconds before proceeding with other exercises or rest.

E. Heart Rate

As an added precaution, AFAA recommends that the heart rate be again checked before beginning floorwork. Heart rate should not exceed 60% of estimated maximum heart rate (220 minus age, multiplied by .6) five minutes after aerobic work ceases. If heart rate is too high, continue walking slowly until heart rate has lowered sufficiently.

VIII. Upper Body Exercises

A. Purpose

To strengthen and improve muscle endurance of the arms, chest, shoulders and back.

B. Time

Approximately 5-7 minutes is recommended.

C. Isolating Upper Body Exercises

Exercises may be performed with the lower body in a stationary position, with limited lower body movement, or may be incorporated with the aerobics. If performed during the aerobic portion, keep footwork simple so that the upper body muscle groups may be the area of concentrated work. Always include exercises that will work the opposing muscle groups for muscle balancing.

D. Method

Refer to Section I, F, 1 and 2 (Speed, isolation and resistance)

E. Position

In a standing, stationary position, maintain correct body alignment. Abdominals should be contracted, rib cage lifted, knees relaxed with pelvis in neutral alignment. The same upper body alignment should be applied when performing arm work during aerobics. Do not use momentum as this can alter both the effectiveness of the exercise as well as body alignment, placing unnecessary strain on the back muscles. Do not hyperextend elbow or shoulder joints, but do move through the fullest range of motion that is possible for maximum muscle involvement. Choose exercises that will work muscle(s) in the most advantageous position against gravity. Use alternate positions to standing; i.e. kneeling, lunge, sitting, supine, prone, for variety as well as torso stabilization.

F. Push-ups

Push-ups, performed with either straight legs or on the knees, can be excellent exercises for strengthening the muscles of the arms and chest. In order to perform push-ups safely, the following guidelines should be noted:

13. Correct start

14. Correct start

15. Incorrect sagging

16. Correct finish

1. In order to protect the lower back, it is advisable to slightly raise the buttocks, maintaining a neutral pelvic tilt, when the legs are fully extended.
2. Hands should be positioned on the floor, even with or slightly outside shoulder width.
3. Hand placement should be slightly forward of shoulders with fingers pointing straight ahead comfortably, following the natural curve of an individual's arms as they are extended. when hands are rotated inward or outward, it increases the amount of stress to wrist and elbow joints, and changes the muscle groups being exercised.
4. Elbows should not lock or overbend.
5. Head should be held straight in a natural extension of the spine.
6. Body weight should be evenly balanced regardless of position chosen by distributing support between arms and upper torso and the legs. This will minimize stress to the shoulder and wrist joints as well as the lower back.
7. Both the descent and ascent should be performed as a smooth movement, so the body's line remains straight without "sagging" in the middle. Lead with the chest, not the abdominals.
8. When push-ups are performed on the knees, knees should be directly under hips, or behind hips, depending on fitness level.
9. In any position, separate the legs for balance and lower body weight distribution (Photos 13-16).

G. Torso Stabilization

Mild to moderate lower back strengthening and conditioning will occur when back muscles are involved to directly stabilize the torso as exercises for other muscle groups are performed, i.e., squats, standing hip extension. It is important to strengthen these muscles because they hold the torso in pelvic neutral alignment. Strengthening back muscles that are not directly involved in holding the torso in neutral position but are utilized for all lifting and bending activities should also be performed as indirect stabilization exercises, i.e., bentover rows, lat pulls, reverse flies. Strengthening back muscles both directly and indirectly can aid in reducing the risk of back injury. Be aware of the following guidelines:

1. When performing exercises that utilize lower back muscles, be conscious of proper form and alignment.
2. Always maintain pelvic neutral alignment and an erect torso when performing any exercises.
3. When bending forward, flex at the hip joint, instead of flexing the spine which rounds the back as this will stress lower back muscles.
4. Don't hyperextend the spine in an unsupported position when the spine is not stabilized.
5. Individuals who experience back pain or have a history of chronic back pain should be advised from a medical professional as to which exercises are appropriate for them.

Back strengthening can also be performed in the prone position. (Photo 36, page 25).

IX. Legs, Hips and Buttocks Exercise

17. Outer thigh lift

18. Don't lean backwards

19. Don't do "L" position

A. Purpose
To strengthen the muscles of the legs, hips and buttocks.

B. Time
Approximately 10-15 minutes is recommended.

C. Hips and Outer Thigh, Side Lying Position

1. Primary Muscles and Joint Action

Gluteus medius and minimus, tensor fascia latae: hip abduction.

2. Alignment and Method

Body should be in a straight line, either lying fully extended on the floor or raised up on one elbow with supporting arm positioned squarely on the floor under shoulder; rib cage lifted so that the torso does not collapse. For either position, shoulders and hips should remain square during the execution of any of the exercise variations, with the hips neither leaning to the front nor rolled backward onto buttocks. Use top arm to help stabilize the upper body. Lower leg should be relaxed and both legs aligned so knees can "stack" when both legs are extended in a straight line. Position of the bottom leg is for support only and may change with different exercise variations. When extending the upper leg, extend directly to the side, without locking the knee (Photo 17).

To isolate the outer thigh and hip muscles, resistance should be on the upward lift against gravity and not the downward motion. Lift the leg as high as possible without altering alignment. The knee should face forward during the entire exercise. If the knee points "upward," either alignment base has altered by leaning backward onto hip, or hip rotators are actively involved in the movement (Photo 18).

a. Special Considerations: "L" position

The "L" position requires the upper leg or both legs to be placed in a position at 90 degrees in relationship to the upper torso. For this reason, AFAA does not recommend the use of the "L" position as this position strains the gluteus medius tendon and is very difficult to maintain if an individual has inflexible hamstrings. Place the legs, either bent or straight at a 45-degree angle to the hips for a more appropriate variation (Photo 19).

3. Common Problems
- rolling back on hip
- supporting elbow too close or too far out from shoulder
- low back arched
- "slouching" on supporting arm, causing the rib cage to collapse rather than be lifted
- lifting top leg too high to throw the body out of alignment
- using momentum rather than controlled resistance
- rolling hips too far forward
- twisting upper torso so shoulders are not square

20. Corrrect outer thigh

21. Don't lift too high

• intermediate position or couch potato (refer to glossary), which elicits an unsupported torso and/or cervical spine

D. Hips and Outer Thigh—All Fours Position

1. Primary Muscles and Joint Action

Gluteus medius and minimus, tensor fascia latae: hip abduction

2. Alignment and Method

On all fours, when working one leg to the side, knees should be separated and aligned under hips and hands under shoulders. Hands and fingers should face forward and elbows should be slighfly relaxed, not locked. Hips remain square, pelvis in neutral alignment and weight should be balanced evenly between supporting leg and leg to be lifted without leaning to the side to compensate for lack of strength, or to achieve greater height. Abdominals should be contracted with pelvis tilted so that the lower back doesn't arch. Head should be held in a natural extension of the spine, not hanging down.

Raise bent leg directly to the side. Knee remains pointing forward. Lift the leg only as high as possible with the hips square and without leaning over onto the supporting leg. Do not perform straight leg lifts directly to the side as this position stresses the lower back and supporting hip, and is difficult to perform and still maintain proper body alignment. All abduction work performed in this position should be slow and controlled without using momentum to gain height. Modifying this position to elbows and knees does not allow enough range of motion against gravity, nor does it effectively work primary muscles involved, particularly for an individual with long levers (Photo 20).

3. Common Problems

• leaning to one side
• using momentum to lift leg
• lifting leg too high and not directly to side (Photo 21)
• dropping head down
• using torso movement rather than isolating the leg that is being lifted
• sway back
• locking elbows

E. Inner Thigh—Side Lying Position

1. Primary Muscles and Joint Action

Adductors longus, brevis and magnus; gracilis, pectineus: hip adduction

2. Alignment and Method

Body should be in a straight line, shoulders and hips are square. The most effective position is to lie all the way down with head resting on forearm, top leg in a supportive position so that foot, ankle and knee are aligned. The top leg's knee position can either be placed all the way down on the floor or with the knee slightly elevated, depending on lever length and ability to maintain a position so that hips aren't rolled forward or leaning backward. This allows inner thigh to be isolated with the bottom leg extended directly to the side in a straight line with the torso.

22. Correct inner thigh

23. Correct inner thigh start

24. Don't separate too far

Movement of the inner leg is upward against gravity. If using a position where the torso is raised and supported by forearm, maintain this position without collapsing torso as the lower leg is lifted (Photo 22).

3. Common Problems

- rolling hips back so body weight is on buttocks
- holding bottom leg either too far forward or too far behind torso; should be extended directly to side
- turning toe of bottom leg upward so that the quadriceps are involved or turning the toe downward so that the hamstrings are involved
- top leg position places too much stress on ankle and knee joints
- intermediate position (couch potato), which elicits unsupported torso and/or cervical spine.

F. Inner Thigh—Supine Position

1. Primary Muscles and Joint Action

Adductors longus, brevis and magnus; gracilis, pectineus: hip adduction

2. Alignment and Method

Lie on back with legs vertically raised in air above hips, shoulder width apart (Photo 23). Knees can be bent or only slightly relaxed. If legs are too far apart, it requires the use of the hip flexors to bring the legs close enough together to isolate the inner thigh muscles, which may cause the back to arch off the floor (Photo 24). If legs are straight, don't lock the knee joint.

Bring legs together, resisting motion in towards body's midline. Place hands either on inside of thighs for added resistance, or relaxed at sides. It is important to control speed so that the exercise remains resistive without the use of momentum. If an individual places his/her hands under hips to lift pelvis, it is difficult to maintain vertical alignment of the legs over the hips if abdominals are weak. Placing hands under hips forces pelvis into an unnatural position if individual cannot naturally support lifted legs unaided. An individual should be able to maintain correct position required for this exercise with his/her own body strength and flexibility.

3. Common Problems

- arching back off floor
- using ballistic moves outward, rather than resisting in toward midline of body
- legs dropped too far forward, causing strain on lower back

G. Buttock—All Fours Position

1. Primary Muscles and Joint Action

Gluteus maximus: hip extension

2. Alignment and Method

On all fours, when working one leg extended to the rear, the hips should be square and the back straight, not swayed. Knees should be separated and aligned under hips with hands under shoulders. Abdominals should be contracted. Head is in alignment with the spine and elbows are slightly bent, not hyperextended. This position can be modified to elbows and knees; the same alignment applies. If using elbow and knee position, elbows should be positioned under shoulders (Photo 25).

25. Corrrect

26. Don't lift beyond hip

Leg lifts should be performed through full range of motion without lifting leg above hip height. Movement should be upward without torso involvement. Avoid jerking or throwing the leg upward as this can stress the lower back. Balance weight between supporting leg and leg that is extended. In either recommended position, emphasis is on the "upward" movement against gravity, contracting the gluteals with each lift. Avoid exercises which will arch and hyperextend the back, or use momentum, such as the donkey kick (Photo 26).

3. Common Problems
   - arching back
   - raising leg higher than hip in either position
   - torso movement
   - momentum
   - head dropped, abdominals not contracted
   - hip laterally rotated so toes point outward, involving the hip rotator muscles

H. Buttocks—Prone Position

1. Primary Muscles and Joint Action

Gluteus maximus: hip extension

2. Alignment and Method

27. Corrrect prone

Lying face down on stomach, with both legs extended, hips and chest should remain in contact with floor, pelvis in neutral alignment and abdominals contracted. To maintain this position, the pelvis must be tilted posteriorly to proper neutral alignment so that the lower back is protected. Head is in a comfortable position, either resting on forearms, chin on floor or neck laterally rotated to face sideways. Variations and movements are the same as recommended for the all-fours and elbow-knee positions. The range of motion in the prone position is limited to avoid hyperextending the back and to keep the hips in contact with the floor throughout the entire movement. For isolation of the buttocks, don't do double leg lifts as this stresses the vertebrae, ligaments and muscles in the lower back (Photo 27 and 36).

3. Common Problems
   - arching back
   - using the lower back muscles instead of buttocks to perform exercises
   - raising leg higher than hips
   - hips lifting off floor
   - using momentum

I. Buttocks—Supine Position

1. Primary Muscles and Joint Action

Gluteus maximus: hip extension

2. Alignment and Method

When lying on back, knees should be bent and feet flat on floor, a comfortable distance from body. Back should not arch but be in contact with the floor prior to initial movement. Pelvis should be tilted and abdominals

28. Correct supine

29. Correct squat

30. Don't lower hips below knees

31. Incorrect forward lean

contracted. Arms can be relaxed in any position that is comfortable, i.e. behind head or close to torso. (Photo 28).

The gluteal muscles should be contracted with the upward movement against gravity and released with the downward movement without jerking or bouncing the pelvis up and down. Lift only high enough to lift pelvis off the floor, keeping the midback and waist (mid-torso) area in contact with the floor throughout the entire movement.

3. Common Problems
- using back rather than pelvis for lift
- arching lower back of floor
- expanding rib cage
- feet too close to body, stressing knees, or too far from body, arching back
- knees not aligned with toes

J. Quadriceps—Standing Position

1. Primary Muscles and Joint Action

Quadriceps group: rectus femoris, vastus lateralis, vastus intermedius, vastus medialis; sartorius: hip flexion, knee extension

Hip flexors: psoas major and minor; iliacus: hip flexion

2. Alignment and Method

In a standing position, use basic guidelines for body alignment (refer to I, E): knees should be relaxed and aligned in the same direction as the toes, pelvis in neutral alignment, abdominals contracted and rib cage lifted. Shoulders should remain back in a relaxed position.

a. Squats

When performing a squat or any squat variations, feet can be placed about shoulder width apart, knees and feet aligned in the same direction. Squat in a controlled manner, lowering torso until thighs are parallel or slightly above parallel to the floor. Hips should never drop below knee level. Overbending or bending too low may cause stress to the ligaments of the knee. During the lowering phase of a squat, the tailbone points to the rear as an extension of the spine, without arching the back. From a squat, straighten legs without hyperextending knees to full extension of the hips to pelvic neutral alignment. Keep lower back in a fixed position without torso movement during entire descent and ascent to reduce overstraining back muscles. Keep heels on floor during entire exercise by balancing body weight evenly over foot. Don't lean forward; keep torso erect (Photos 29, 30 and 31).

b. Pliés

When performing a plié or "a modified squat," feet should be about or slightly more than shoulder distance apart in a comfortable position, with the toes turned outward and aligned with knees. The pelvis is stabilized in neutral alignment with the rib cage lifted and abdominals contracted. Knees should remain slightly flexed. During the lowering phase of a plié, the torso remains in neutral alignment with the tailbone pointing downward. Descend only as low as

32. Correct lunge

33. Don't project knee beyond toes

possible without changing alignment of the pelvis or overshooting the toes with the knees. From a plié, straighten legs without hyperextending knees to full extension of the hips to pelvic neutral alignment. The torso remains erect without leaning forward during both the descent and ascent. Variations with one or both heels lifted may be appropriate as long as proper body alignment can be maintained.

c. Lunges

When performing a lunge and any lunge variations, the front knee should never extend beyond toes. This places tremendous strain on the knee joint and its attachments. The lower front leg should be perpendicular to the floor on any lunge variation, whether stationary or moving. Don't step so far forward that the return move places a strain on the back and alters alignment. The depth of the lunge will depend on type of lunge performed. However, don't lunge so deep that the back knee touches the floor or so low that knee pain or strain is felt (Photos 32 and 33).

d. Standing Knee Extension/Hip Flexion

When performing standing knee extensions, do not hyperextend or lock the knee. This exercise should be performed in a controlled manner without any rapid jerky motions. Standing exercises can include any variety of knee extension and hip flexion movements in combination or isolation. Doing these exercises in a standing position requires good balance. When performing hip flexion, either with a straight or bent knee, maintain pelvic neutral alignment. Don't lift leg so high that the buttocks "tuck under." This is all hip flexor work with very little quadricep isolation and relies on momentum for leg height. Rotating the hip can isolate different muscles within the quadricep group. If performing exercises utilizing rotation, the same basic guidelines for standing alignment should be followed.

NOTE: Squats, pliés and lunges are multi-muscle exercises which additionally involve the gluteus maximus and hamstring group.

3. Common Problems
   - using momentum rather than a controlled lift in a standing position
   - hyperextension of the knee joint when performing extensions or straightening knees from a squat position
   - arching the back
   - dropping hips below knees during a squat
   - extending knees beyond toes when performing a squat or lunge
   - lifting heels off floor during a squat
   - loss of balance or leaning to one side when performing hip flexion/knee extension variations

K. Quadriceps—Sitting or Supine Position

1. Primary Muscles and Joint Action

Quadricep femoris group: rectus femoris, vastus lateralis, vastus intermedius, vastus medialis; sartorius: hip flexion, knee extension

34. Corrrect sitting quad

35. Incorrect sitting quad

2. Alignment and Method

Effective quadricep strengthening can also be accomplished by either sitting in a chair or on the floor, supported on elbows, or lying on the back. For any of these positions, the upper torso should be maintained in a supported position, shoulders back. Keep the non-working leg bent and foot flat on floor for support. If supported on elbows, don't slouch, but keep rib cage lifted, shoulders down and pelvis tilted to press lower back to the floor. Keep abdominals contracted. When lying supine, lower back should remain pressed to the floor for the entirety of the exercise being performed. Sitting upright on the floor and maintaining an erect posture is difficult, and the range of motion of the exercise is limited to decrease the amount of hip flexor work. Use the other alternative positions unless the sitting position can be maintained for desired number of repetitions and can accomplish muscle fatigue (Photo 34).

Use slow, controlled resistive movement to perform knee extensions or straight leg lifts. To work the entire quadricep group, both joint actions need to be included as part of a complete strengthening program. As in the standing position, don't lift leg so high that only hip flexors are utilized. Lifting the working leg to approximately knee height of the support leg will help to isolate the quadriceps and lessen hip flexor involvement. Going beyond knee height or a 45 degree angle is mostly hip flexor work. Note that rotation of hip will emphasize work of different muscles within the quadricep group (Photo 35).

3. Common Problems
- using momentum rather than a controlled lift
- hyperextension of the knee joint
- using hip flexors exclusively to lift leg
- slouching in the supported elbow position
- leaning backwards in the sitting position
- arching the back in supine position

L. Hamstring—Standing, All Fours and Prone Positions

1. Primary Muscles and Joint Action

Hamstring group: biceps femoris, semitendinosus, semimembranosus; knee flexion, hip extension

2. Alignment and Method

Hamstring strengthening occurs when performing straight leg lifts and bent knee curls behind the body. In order to strengthen the entire hamstring group, both joint actions, particularly knee flexion, need to be included as part of a complete strengthening program. When strengthening hamstrings in a standing position, follow the alignment guidelines outlined for quadriceps in a standing position (see IX, J). Hamstrings will also be strengthened as the opposing muscle group when performing squats. To strengthen hamstrings on all fours or prone, follow the guidelines outlined for buttocks (see IX, G, H). In either of these positions, strengthening will occur by curling the foot toward buttocks or with a controlled straight leg lift in a resistive manner against gravity. To protect the back and isolate hamstring muscles, do not the arch back or lift leg above hip level. Do not rotate the hips but maintain a "hips square" position.

3. Common Problems
- arching the back

- hips not square so one hip is too high
- no resistance with the curl
- rotating hip outward
- leaning on one leg in all fours position
- not fully extending legs to complete ascent on a squat

X. Lower Back Exercise

A. Purpose

To strengthen the muscles of the lower back

1. Primary Muscles and Joint Action

Erector spinae: extension

B. Time

Approximately 5-7 minutes is recommended

C. Alignment and Method—Prone Position

36. Correct prone

Lying face down on stomach with both legs extended, hips should remain in contact with floor. Maintain a pelvic tilt to keep pelvis in neutral alignment and abdominals contracted. Depending on the variations utilized, arms can either both be extended overhead, one arm extended overhead, extended close to torso or bent with forearms folded to support head. For all variations, the head must remain lowered and neck in good spinal alignment without any hyperextension. To protect the lower back discs and ligaments, the rib cage and chest should be in contact with the floor while performing exercises (Photo 36).

Variations for mild to moderate back strengthening include: (a) lift one straight leg at a time to hip height, (b) alternating straight leg lifts, (c) lifting one leg and opposite arm or (d) lifting both arms with torso slightly raised while legs remain in contact with the floor. Pelvic neutral alignment should be maintained throughout lifting and lowering phases of exercise so that hips remain in contact with the floor. Avoid lifting both legs at the same time as this variation can rely on momentum if the lower back muscles are weak, and can increase the risk of pressure to the intervertebral discs. Don't place hands under hips as these exercises should be performed only if an individual is strong enough to maintain alignment unaided. A modified cobra position supported on the forearms, held statically for 10-20 seconds can also be utilized. Move slowly and don't hyperextend back. Keep head aligned with spine.

D. Common problems

- using momentum on any variation to gain more height
- lifting head, shoulders and/or upper torso on floor when lifting leg
- double leg lifts
- lifting hips off floor
- arching back

XI. Abdominal Exercise

A. Purpose

To strengthen the abdominal muscles and provide support for the internal organs and the back.

1. Primary Muscles and Joint Action

37. Correct ab curl

38. Don't do full sit-ups

39. Correct reverse curl

40. Correct hip lift

Rectus abdominis: spinal flexion, external and internal obliques: lateral spinal flexion, spinal rotation, transverse abdominis: abdominal compression

B. Time

Approximately 5-8 minutes is recommended

C. Alignment and Method—Supine Position

In order to isolate and innervate all four of the abdominal muscles, an abdominal curl which flexes the spine approximately 30-45 degrees will contract these muscles sufficiently to improve strength and tone. Lie on the floor on your back, with knees bent, feet flat on floor a comfortable distance away from body. Tilt pelvis so that the lower back and torso maintain a neutral spinal position so the low back can be on the floor or as close to the floor as possible without creating an extreme posterior tilt.

1. A curl will bring the head, neck, shoulders and rib cage up and forward in a slow controlled motion without momentum so scapula clears the floor at the top of the lift. Do not lift with the neck and push the head out of alignment. Head should be fully supported without any neck movement (see arm positions). Return to starting position without dropping head and shoulders on floor. Maintain a consistent, moderate contraction of the abdominals throughout the exercises performed. Keep the lower back on the floor to stabilize the pelvis and protect the back (Photos 37 and 38).

2. Additionally strengthen the external and internal obliques by including exercises that involve rotation with the lower torso stable and motionless. Keeping the lower body stationary when rotating will help to isolate the oblique muscles because resistance will occur against the lower body as a stabilizing force. The hips should not roll from side to side as the torso is lifted. When rotating, lead with the shoulder, not the elbow so that the twist lifts the upper body in one fluid motion. Elbow motion does not guarantee that torso movement is also taking place.

3. When performing a reverse curl or pelvic thrust, both legs should be elevated with the thighs perpendicular to the hips so that the lift will occur as a result of reverse spinal flexion, not hip flexion. In this position, if these exercises are performed correctly, the hip flexors are deactivated to allow the abdominal muscles to contract, resulting in a curl of the lower torso toward the chest, or a vertical lift. Maintain no less than a 90-degree angle of the legs to the hips. Dropping both legs away from the torso below this angle will place stress on the lumbar spine, causing the back to arch. Use these variations only if individuals are strong enough to maintain alignment and can perform exercises without momentum to initiate the lift (Photos 39 and 40).

D. Arm Positions

When supporting the head, do not clasp and interlock fingers behind neck (Photo 41). This position does not offer support if you are pressing forward on neck or the head hangs down behind neck in a hyperextended position. Place open fingers on the back of the head for better support. Arms may also be extended up and/or out in front of the body as long as the head and neck are

41. Don't pull on neck

42. Don't lift both legs off floor

43. Ab work variety

aligned as an extension of the spine. Other arm variations may include but are not limited to: crossing arms in front of chest, fingers on forehead or top of head with elbows forward, forearms crossed behind head or extended behind head. Avoid "always looking up at the ceiling" as this position may not correspond to chosen arm position and abdominal exercise. Arm position should complement the abdominal exercise that is being performed along with modifications for fitness level.

E. Abdominal Work vs Hip Flexor Work

During a full sit-up, the first 40 degrees of movement relies on the abdominals. However, the remainder of the movement toward a full sitting position depends on the hip flexors (iliopsoas muscles). When lying on the back and performing any exercises that lift one or both legs the hip flexors will be involved in the work. Never lift both straight legs off the floor or lower at the same time as this can place tremendous strain on the lower back, even if the hands are underneath the buttocks or legs are bent (Photo 42).

F. Breathing

Breathing is especially important while performing abdominal exercises. Exhale while contracting the abdominals at the point of finishing your greatest exertion. Example: exhale as you sit up and inhale on the downward movement.

G. Variety

Vary your abdominal exercises. Exercises that include changing the position of the arms and legs, i.e. bent into the chest, lifted vertical in the air, elbow to knee twists, or reverse curls will work the abdominal muscles effectively and isolate these muscle groups without the use of momentum. While adding variety is important, performing only exercises that involve both torso and leg action will not isolate the abdominal muscles without using the hip flexors. A balanced combination of exercise variations that include exercises that stabilize the lower torso as well as adding movement is most beneficial (Photo 43).

H. Standing Abdominal Exercises

While exercises in a standing position can be performed, i.e. twisting or rotation, these exercises do not effectively isolate the abdominal muscles against gravitational force. While standing abdominal exercises may be utilized if proper standing alignment is followed, it is more advantageous to perform abdominal exercises in the supine position.

I. Common Problems
- arching the lower back off the floor
- arching the rib cage
- using neck motion only
- unsupported head
- using momentum
- not bringing shoulders and upper torso off the floor
- when breathing, pushing the abdominal muscles out
- rolling of the hips when performing rotation exercises

- using only elbow movement without a torso twist for rotation
- throwing the legs too far toward head on a reverse curl

XII. Cooldown Stretches

44. Correct low back stretch

45. Incorrect low back stretch

A. Purpose

To increase joint flexibility, relaxation and increase potential to reduce metabolic waste accumulated in the muscles from strengthening activities.

B. Time

Approximately 4-6 minutes at the very end of class is recommended.

C. Stretching

Follow the same guidelines as outlined for stretches at the beginning of class (refer to V, C). Static stretching is the most effective at the end of your class when your muscles are very warm and prepared to stretch a little farther than at the beginning of your class. Now is the time to work on increasing flexibility, holding stretches for a little longer, (a minimum of 20 seconds) without bouncing, stretching a little farther as the muscle relaxes. (Photos 44 and 46)

D. Muscle Groups

Stretch all major muscle groups that were used during the workout, especially calves, hamstrings and quadriceps. Stretches for the back and upper torso should also be included. Include exercises that will balance muscle groups, improve posture and body alignment. It is not necessary to follow a particular exercise order as long as all major muscle groups are included.

E. Position

Final cooldown stretches can be performed in any position, i.e. lying, kneeling, sitting or standing, as long as correct body alignment is utilized so that appropriate stretching technique can be applied to the muscle that is being stretched.

1. Stretching the hamstrings when in an upright sitting position may be difficult for individuals with inflexible hamstrings and/or weak torso strength. Modify this stretch by bending one knee and stretch one leg at a time or lie supine and stretch one hamstring at a time.

2. In a sitting position, legs should not be straddled to an extreme, but only to shoulder width or slightly more so that the angle of toe to shoulder will form a diagonal line. The adductors can be sufficiently stretched without flexing forward from the hips. This position may be painful or uncomfortable for individuals with uneven hips, weak hip rotators, inflexible hamstrings or weak torso strength. Modify this stretch in any of these cases by bending one knee and stretch one leg at a time.

   a. If stretching forward from the hips, hands should be in a supporting position on the floor so the stretch forward is hip flexion, not bending from the waist so upper torso collapses (Photos 46 and 47).

46. Correct supported straddled

47. Don't collapse torso

48. Don't do the plow

b. If stretching laterally, the torso should also be supported by placing one hand on the floor in front of you or to the side so that the torso does not collapse.

c. Placing elbows on floor or chest on floor to increase the degree of inner thigh stretch may stress the lumbar/sacral region. A safer alternative would be supine, knees bent with hands gently resisting outward on inner thighs.

F. Breathing

Inhale as you begin the stretch, then simultaneously stretch and relax the muscle as you exhale.

G. Exercises to Avoid

1. Don't do the "plow" as this position could cause injury to the neck. The vertebrae and discs in the cervical area were not designed to withstand this type of pressure. Modify with both knees into chest (Photo 48).

2. Don't do the "hurdler stretch" as it places extreme tension on the medial ligaments of the knee. Modify with the inverted hurdler stretch (Photo 49).

49. Don't do the hurdler stretch

3. Don't do the "cobra" as this position hyperextends the lumbar spine, placing stress on the discs and connective tissue as well as hyperextending the elbows. Modify to the forearm supported cobra position (Photos 50 & 51).

50. Modified cobra

51. Don't do full cobra

XIII. Final Heart Rate

A. Purpose

To determine if heart rate has sufficiently returned to normal pre-exercise ranges.

B. When

Heart rate should be taken as static stretches are finished and class members prepare to leave.

C. Heart Rate

Again, the recovery heart rate equals 60% of maximum heart rate (220 minus age, multiplied by .6) or less. If not below this level, the individual was probably exercising too intensely and should work at a less vigorous level during the next class. Cooldown stretches sufficiently should be continued until heart rate is lowered.

D. Saunas and Hot Tubs

Saunas, hot tubs and even hot showers should be avoided immediately following exercise. The heat causes the blood vessels to dilate and this, along with the fact that the blood tends to be pooled in the extremities following vigorous exercise, causes the heart and brain to receive less blood and can cause overheating.

E. Hydration and Rehydration

Overheating can be a serious problem and special precautions should be taken, particularly in hot weather. Individuals should be advised to hydrate before, during and after exercise in order to replenish necessary body fluids and to maintain electrolyte balance. For every twenty minutes of exercise, allow 3 ounces of water. Salt tablets are not necessary unless involved in heavy endurance events and should not be taken without consultation with a sports physician or nutritionist. Deliberate dehydration by wearing heavy, rubberized clothes to induce profuse sweating is not recommended. This weight loss is temporary and will be regained through appropriate hydration. The practice of deliberate dehydration is very dangerous as it can cause death or brain damage due to very high body temperatures.

Part 1

Essentials of Exercise

Defining Fitness

Developing Fitness

Energy Production

Improving Performance

Musculoskeletal System

Cardiopulmonary System

Strength

Power and Plyometrics

Flexibility

Coordination

Peg Jordan, RN

1 Defining Fitness

Ever-Changing Concept

THE THINKING ON WHAT FITNESS means has broadened since AFAA's first textbook was published in 1985. In the early days we were concerned with teaching aerobics, and that generally meant keeping a conventional dance exercise class safe and enjoyable. Fitness, as far as the fitness instructor was concerned, was defined as aerobic or cardiorespiratory endurance along with adequate muscular endurance and strength, but with a definite emphasis on the aerobics. Flexibility was also part of the definition, but in practice, it too was given a backseat to aerobic and strength workouts.

Today most people live increasingly hectic lifestyles with overburdened schedules and a shrinking amount of recreational time. In this high stress age, fitness is more important than ever, and its definition has shifted to include vibrant health and well-being for mind, body and spirit. As a result, people have come to expect more from their workouts than a fast-paced drill for their hearts. Supporting this higher expectation, researchers discovered that if you approach your exercise session with the same frenzied pace and "do or die" attitude that you might experience at work, then the high stress knots are never untied, and the health benefits stay out of reach.

Therefore, stress release, active relaxation and enjoyable diversions for body and mind have all come under the contemporary fitness umbrella. For the first time in Western history, the mind and the body have been reunited—and nobody caught on quicker to this ancient wisdom than fitness instructors. Conscientious professionals are learning how to include those elements within their programs as well as the traditional teachings from exercise science—and the result is an ever-expanding list of fabulous fitness pursuits.

New, Improved Varieties

Aerobic exercise as a form of exercise has now been around for over 25 years, evolving into a number of truly remarkable varieties. Today, aerobic workouts encompass everything from aqua to interval, step to pump, seated to slide. While our definition of "fitness" reaches out to broader horizons, instructors scramble for new research and emerging guidelines in order to maintain their vision of teaching the most effective and exciting class possible.

This book is the culmination of widespread efforts spanning several years to discover the leading developers and professionals in these expanding fields of fitness. You will encounter both the theoretical foundation which they draw from, and the innovative practices that spring forth. You'll even have a chance to put into action specific examples of those practices, with the examples given in Part 8, Special Populations and Part 9, Specialty Classes.

Part of the reason we have a new, stretched version of fitness is due to research. New findings add to the broadened picture everyday. After the 20-year study done by Dr. Ralph S. Paffenbarger, Jr., on over 16,000 Harvard University alumnae, we had a growing body of evidence that supports how activity and exercise help reduce the risk of heart disease, stroke and cancer, and how it may even extend the life span. We finally put to rest the objection that exercise was far too risky and could now convince people without a doubt to move their bodies. Also, since AFAA's first text was written, a new science of psychoneuro-immunology has emerged. This science addresses ways in which the psychological and emotional aspects of living can impact our immune systems. We've always taught that healthful nutrition and daily exercise keep a body strong, but now we're finding that a smile a day may keep the doctor away as well.

In regard to boosting immunity, researchers are also scrutinizing the role of toxic molecules called free radicals in tissue damage and premature aging. Free radicals combine with oxygen and attack any nearby molecules in the body, such as DNA, proteins, lipids (fats) and carbohydrates. Those who are most plagued with free radical development are people living in urban pollution, smokers, sun- worshippers, junk food addicts, and sadly, heavy-duty exercisers tend to produce an overabundance of free radicals. The good news here is that scientists have also discovered ways to minimize their cell-destroying impact. A rich supply of antioxidant nutrients such as betacarotene, vitamins C and E and the trace mineral selenium in your diet can protect you from free radical activity.

As a result of more research in the fields of exercise and nutrition, health professionals and fitness instructors began to shift their thinking about supplements. There was a time when AFAA instructors simply followed the well-intentioned advice of many registered dietitians to eat a nutritious diet based on moderation, variety and balance, and not bother with vitamin and mineral supplements. That advice still holds for the most part for people with enough time on their hands to select and prepare three healthy meals a day. But for the rest of you who tend to eat on the run, fly out of a part-time job, pick up a child at day-care, hurry to teach an evening class and collapse at home after a non-stop day—well, some supplemental "insurance" makes good sense. Regular supplementation of calcium for women may be helpful in preventing osteoporosis, just as zinc, other minerals and some vitamins may be very useful for endurance in athletes. One thing the researchers agree upon: stay within recommended doses of supplements; megadosing is a waste of money and in some cases a potential health hazard.

Be Open to New Findings

Our motto at AFAA has always been one of openness and accommodation to new findings. And for good reason—in this ever expanding field of health promotion, hard-and-fast rules are outdated faster than computer software! A prime example of being flexible in our teaching guidelines is the subject of exercise hydration. AFAA's first text clearly states that exercisers should drink plain, pure water before, during and after a workout. The rule of thumb at the time was to drink about 8 ounces of water for every 20 minutes of strenuous exercise.

It's still a good rule. Water hasn't gone out of style. However, two other styles have changed: life-style and style of workouts. Many instructors report overburdened schedules and in general, an increase in stress levels since they started teaching several years ago. They also report that classes have become much more physically taxing in their overall composition. We are overloading muscles more effectively, plus we are growing wiser in our elicitation of more muscle groups. To check this out, compare an early low impact class of 1985 with a step-plus-conditioning class of 1993. As the body of knowledge has grown about teaching techniques and ways to isolate muscles, new movements have evolved along with better equipment. We've actually become "smarter" in our workouts, and as a result, we've also become more demanding.

As the demand increases on the body and the energy output begins to grow, so too must the quality of our intake or we'll be depleting our physical engines. Therefore, getting more readily available nutrients into the body is a major challenge. This is how AFAA's thinking on sports drinks began to change. It all started with the "always-starving" complaints tossed around by instructors at conferences and workshops. They began reporting that there were not enough hours in their busy days to eat sufficient complex carbohydrates, the primary fuel for active exercisers and athletes.

Re-Fueling Systems

The instructors who tried new sports drinks (in addition to water) were reporting higher energy levels and vastly improved performance. Plus, they weren't undergoing endless carb cravings. As often happens in rapidly expanding fields, the scientists got to work proving in the laboratory what the instructors intuitively knew in the studio. New research in the area of performance nutrition found that the single greatest factor leading to fatigue is the depletion of carbohydrates stored as muscle glycogen. For the first time, we had instructors whose intake of carbohydrates solely from food sources was not enough to sustain their high-performance schedules.

Instructors who complained about losing their "cuts," or wasting their muscular definition, were actually undergoing muscle glycogen depletion, despite consuming a high carbohydrate diet (55-65% of total caloric intake from carbohydrates). The new emphasis on strength training in fitness classes probably has contributed to this breakdown in muscle tissue for energy—if the exerciser is not consuming enough carbohydrates or storing enough glycogen. At this point, the instructor was faced with the decision of either cutting back their teaching schedule or continuing to catabolize or self-digest! But, just in time, new findings begin to modify current hydration recommendations, and endurance exercisers have a bright solution: sports drinks in addition to water may be the hydration of choice during prolonged exercise.

It seems that bodies can "re-fuel" during exercise with a special combination of energy-producing carbohydrates known as glucose/fructose polymer drinks (GFPDs). Researchers compared the effects of a high carb diet with GFPDs and discovered that those consuming GFPDs had an amazing 126% performance improvement over the carbohydrate diet group. Another study simulating the Tour de France showed that GFPDs can also help prevent muscle catabolism. Instructors also began reporting that their body fat levels were shrinking on the sports drinks—probably due to their renewed energy levels, and their enhanced ability to sustain exercise longer.

Healthful living, proper nutrition, and good exercise are still the mainstay of AFAA advice. We're not banishing the gold standard of good sense, but we are suggesting that it is especially wise today to investigate new tools that may be particularly potent against the rigors of our "nanosecond" lifestyles.

Responding to Social Forces

Finding ways to exercise "more, better, faster" is only part of the fitness picture. The real revolution in the fitness world over the past few years has been directed at ways in which fitness professionals sought the new recruits—the under-served, the drop-outs, the unconverted. In the early days, aerobic dance definitely had its fans in a white, middleclass demographic, but three social factors have influenced how aerobics is practiced today.

First of all, a **multicultural** dynamic is alive and well in much of the world, especially the United States. This new multiculturalism has energized the aerobic class with fresh, downbeat sounds and rhythms of African dance, Salsa, hip-hop, funk, Caribbean movement and Eastern-oriented holistic movement. With these exciting additions, classes are teeming again in the major cities.

Secondly, the abundance of **new research** on the benefits of muscle strengthening, along with an aging population, has awakened the alert instructor to provide a variety of excellent conditioning choices: step-plus-weight, tubing classes, bands-plus-aerobics. Retaining lean muscle is not only great for body shaping but it's the latest advice for weight control. Strength training is being embraced by everyone from adolescents to the over-80 crowd, making a demand for personal trainers and well-informed instructors alike.

Lastly, the benefits of **cross-training** have been well documented in the past few years. Not only does it provide a much-needed motivational diversion, cross-training allows the neurological and musculoskeletal systems to be challenged. The rich bounty of classes and guidelines presented in the following pages is designed to present a cross-training challenge for professionals and enthusiasts.

Inactivity is a Definite Risk

By far, the biggest shot in the arm for the fitness profession has been the official recognition of physical inactivity as a serious risk factor contributing to our nation's most significant killers—heart disease and stroke. We've always known that exercise is beneficial for overall health and longevity, but now we know after a careful review of 43 studies that the *absence* of exercise is downright hazardous to your health. That was the joint announcement in the summer of 1993 by the Centers for Disease Control and Prevention, the American College of Sports Medicine and the President's Council for Physical Fitness which finally put to rest any last questions about the value of exercise.

From toddlers to seniors, from the overweight beginner to the wheelchair user—everyone deserves the right to wear a "fit" label, and be supported and taught with the latest, safest information. It requires a real shift in thinking to realize it's not that we have a host of unfit people out there—it's just that we haven't thought of the right fitness program to spark their imaginations and get their pulses racing. Every time we expand our definition of fitness, we get to flex our creativity and commitment within a wonderful profession.

Energy Production During Exercise

2

William C. Beam, PhD

Focus

HUMAN SKELETAL MUSCLE CONTAINS A VARIETY of fuels and enzymes that allow it to provide energy in a number of ways. Exercise physiologists have categorized these fuels and enzymes into "energy systems" and have described their importance for different types of exercise. Changes within the muscle itself, dependent on the duration and intensity of the exercise, control which of the energy systems is most active at any one time. As a result, energy is produced automatically, in the most efficient manner possible, to meet the energetic needs of the exercising muscle. The study of how energy is released and transformed in the body is referred to as energetics.

Basic Principles of Energetics

The term "energy" is most simply defined as the ability to do work. Various forms of physical or biological work that require energy include contraction of skeletal and cardiac muscle that allows us to move and to walk and to exercise; the growth of new tissue in children or healing adults; and the conduction through our bodies of electrical impulses that control heart rate, release hormones or constrict blood vessels. Ultimately, the source of energy for all of these bodily functions comes from the sun. It is hard to imagine, in the middle of an aerobics session, that the energy you are using to contract your muscles has actually originated in the sun, but it is true. You cannot simply exercise in the sunshine, however, and absorb the energy. The energy needs to be transformed from light into a form of chemical energy that can be used by the body.

Energy Flow to Humans

The transformation of light energy begins with its absorption by green plants through the process of photosynthesis. Plants begin with very simple forms of synthetic compounds, such as water and carbon dioxide, and in the presence of light, produce complex food molecules that contain a large supply of stored chemical energy. Plants can form and store various types of carbohydrates, fats and proteins. Animals and humans can derive energy by ingesting these plants and using them as sources of fuel (Figure 2-1). Vegetarians derive all their energy from plant sources alone. Those humans and animals who consume meat, derive a portion of their energy by consuming the protein, carbohydrate, and fat stored in the meat of other animals.

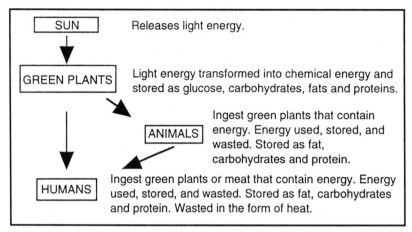

SUN	Releases light energy.
GREEN PLANTS	Light energy transformed into chemical energy and stored as glucose, carbohydrates, fats and proteins.
ANIMALS	Ingest green plants that contain energy. Energy used, stored, and wasted. Stored as fat, carbohydrates and protein.
HUMANS	Ingest green plants or meat that contain energy. Energy used, stored, and wasted. Stored as fat, carbohydrates and protein. Wasted in the form of heat.

Fig. 2-1. The flow of energy from sunlight, through green plants and animals, to humans.

During this energy flow from the sun, neither plants nor humans are creating the energy. It is being transformed by plants from light into a form of stored chemical energy. Humans, after ingesting the plants, then transform the energy again. At this point, it is used for biological work or it is stored, primarily in adipose tissue, skeletal muscle and the liver, for later use. None of these transformations are particularly efficient. In fact, humans use or store less than half of the original energy that was available from the food. The unused or lost energy escapes in the form of heat. When large amounts of energy are released, as is the case during exercise, the energy lost as heat is enough to increase body temperature. The following equation expresses the relationship or balance between the energy flowing into the body, and that which is used, stored and lost.

Energy in = Energy used + Energy stored + Energy lost
(food)   (work/exercise)   (adipose tissue)   (heat)

Significance of Adenosine Triphosphate

In most cases of biological work, the source of energy is specific. Energy must first be transferred into a compound called adenosine triphosphate (ATP) before it can be used. A molecule of ATP possesses a significant amount of stored energy. ATP possesses this energy largely because of its structure. The last phosphate group attaches to the remainder of the molecule by way of a "high-energy" bond. When the bond breaks, the phosphate group is released, and at the same time a substantial amount of energy is released. The end result is adenosine diphosphate (ADP) and phosphate (P), as seen in the reaction below. This breakdown of ATP provides the only source of energy for muscular contraction. Any energy stored in the body in the form of carbohydrate or fat, must first be converted into ATP before it can be used for exercise. As may also be observed, this reaction is reversible. That is, ATP can be replenished if there is a source of ADP, P, and energy.

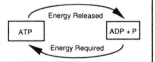

The actual amount of energy released from the breakdown of ATP can be estimated. When a specific amount of ATP, described as "one mole" of ATP, reacts in a test tube, it consistently releases about seven kilocalories (kcal) of energy. In the body, however, the amount of energy released from one mole of ATP is about ten kcal. To put this amount of energy in perspective, let us assume that walking one mile requires about 100 kcal of energy. One mole of ATP could supply enough energy to walk only about one-tenth of a mile.

Overview of Energy Production

The body possesses three separate systems for the production of energy. Each muscle cell in the body contains these energy systems. The systems differ considerably in their complexity, regulation, capacity, power and the types of exercise for which they are the predominant supplier of energy. They are called upon to provide energy at a rate dependent upon the intensity and duration of the exercise performed. The three energy systems are the phosphagen system, the lactic acid system and the aerobic system. The goal of each system is to release energy from chemical or food sources and transform that energy into ATP that can subsequently be used for muscular contraction and exercise (Figure 2-2).

The energy systems are discussed in this chapter beginning with the simplest and moving toward the most complex. The phosphagen system is a simple system of coupled reactions; the lactic acid system is more complex involving a sequence of reactions; and finally, the aerobic system is a complex and intricate combination of several pathways. In terms of their significance in everyday life, however, the order of discussion would be reversed. Most of our energetic needs throughout the day (and night) are met by the aerobic system alone. It is only activities that require a significant amount of muscular effort, such as moderate to intense exercise, heavy manual labor, climbing several flights of stairs, carrying a baby, or changing a tire, that require the recruitment of the lactic acid or phosphagen systems.

Anaerobic Energy Systems

There are two energy systems in the body—the phosphagen system and the lactic acid system—that can operate in the absence of oxygen. Because of this, they are frequently referred to as anaerobic energy systems. It is probably more important, however, to identify them as systems that are capable of producing ATP energy at a high rate. They are utilized when the rate of energy production demanded of the exercise exceeds that of the aerobic system alone. The main limitation of these systems is the relatively small amount of ATP that can be made before fatigue ensues.

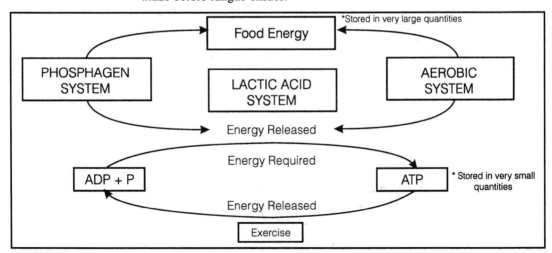

Fig. 2.2. **The common goal of all three energy systems is to release the chemical energy from food that can be used to make ATP, which subsequently breaks down and supplies energy to the muscle.**

Phosphagen System

The phosphagen system supplies energy very rapidly. It relies entirely on a chemical source of fuel, however, and because of this its total capacity for producing energy is severely limited. It is the primary source of energy for very high intensity exercise.

Description

The phosphagen system is by far the simplest biochemically of the three systems. Energy for the production of ATP comes by way of a coupled reaction involving the breakdown of creatine phosphate. The compound creatine phosphate (CP), also referred to as phosphocreatine, is similar to ATP. Because of this similarity, CP and ATP are referred to collectively as "phosphagens." The structure of CP consists of a creatine base molecule with one phosphate group attached by way of a "high-energy" bond. The splitting of CP into creatine (C) and phosphate (P) results in the release of enough energy to attach a phosphate onto an ADP molecule thereby producing ATP (Figure 2-3). During high intensity exercise, at almost the same instant ATP is produced, its terminal phosphate group is lost. The energy is then transferred into the contractile mechanism of the muscle. This mechanism transforms the chemical energy now available into the mechanical energy necessary for rapid or forceful muscular contractions.

The regulation of the phosphagen system—and the other energy systems—relies in large part on the activity of its specific regulatory enzyme(s). Enzymes are protein molecules that speed up a chemical reaction by lowering the amount of energy necessary for the reaction to initially occur. Every reaction in a biological system has an associated enzyme. An enzyme is considered regulatory if it possesses the ability to alter or regulate the rate at which an entire series of reactions occurs.

The enzyme most responsible for the rate at which the phosphagen system operates is creatine kinase (CK), also called creatine phosphokinase. Any condition that stimulates or speeds CK will increase the rate at which the phosphagen system produces energy. Conversely, any condition that inhibits or slows CK will reduce the maximal rate of energy production of the system. The most significant stimulatory factor is the rapid accumulation of ADP within

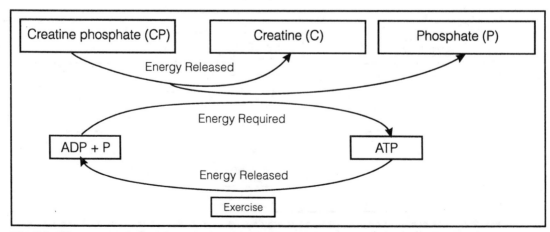

Fig. 2-3. The energy released from the breakdown of creating phosphate is coupled to the production of ATP, which subsequently breaks down and supplies energy to the muscle for exercise.

the muscle cell. This is a signal to the muscle that ATP is being consumed rapidly. In an attempt to maintain the concentration of ATP, creatine kinase is activated, and creatine phosphate is rapidly broken down. The energy released from CP is used to replace the ATP being consumed.

Capacity and Power

The capacity of the phosphagen system can be estimated by measuring the amount of fuel available in the muscle. Heavy physical exercise can be sustained only while CP and ATP are available. Once the level of phosphagen is depleted, fatigue will rapidly ensue. To determine the capacity of the system requires the measurement of the total amount of phosphagen stored in skeletal muscle. For years, the only way of making such measurements was through the use of a needle muscle biopsy in which a small piece of muscle is removed from the body for analysis. More recently a method of quantifying CP, ATP, ADP and P from outside the body has been developed. It is called nuclear magnetic resonance (NMR) spectroscopy.

Throughout this chapter, whenever estimates of the capacity or power of any of the energy systems are made, they are based on the following assumptions. The proposed subjects are a young male and female who are healthy, active and untrained. The male is assumed to weigh 70 kg (154 lbs) with 30 kg (66 lbs) of muscle. The female is assumed to weigh 57 kg (126 lbs) with 20 kg (44 lbs) of muscle. Any changes in body weight, muscle mass, or level of training will significantly affect the estimated capacities and powers.

It has been estimated, using NMR spectroscopy, that the average amount of phosphagen (combined CP and ATP) in a 70 kg male is about one mole. Therefore, the capacity of the phosphagen system would be limited to one mole of ATP, or equivalent to about 10 kcal of energy. This is a very small amount of energy. Barely enough to sprint 200 m (20-30 sec) before it is exhausted. The capacity in a 57 kg female is even less, about 0.7 mole of ATP or seven kcal, due to a smaller muscle mass.

The "power" of the system expresses its ability to produce energy at a particular rate, usually in moles of ATP per minute, or in kcal of energy expended per minute. Thus, a system that is characterized as possessing a high power is able to produce ATP very rapidly. To estimate the power of the phosphagen system another assumption must be made. Assume that with maximal exercise, the total phosphagen in the body would last for no longer than about 15-20 seconds. The power of the system then is equal to the total phosphagen used divided by the amount of time required to utilize the fuel. Therefore, the power of the phosphagen system in the male subject is 4.0 moles/min of ATP production, or 40 kcal/min energy expenditure.

With no frame of reference, this value has little significance. However, as will soon be seen, the power of the phosphagen system is twice that of its nearest competitor, the lactic acid system. A female, by producing 0.7 moles of ATP in 15 seconds, would possess a power of 2.8 moles/min with a corresponding energy expenditure of 28 kcal/min in the phosphagen system.

Types of Exercise

Because of its ability to supply energy immediately, the phosphagen system is most important in exercise in which energy is required immediately. Such exercises would include sprinting, jumping, throwing, kicking and lifting heavy weights. Sports that include these activities would rely at least in part on the phosphagen system. The common factor of analysis is the time involved. If the activity can be sustained for no more than 15 to 20 seconds, the phosphagen system is the primary source of energy (supplying over 50 percent of the energy).

Shorter exercise (1-5 second duration) that requires even higher energy production relies more heavily on the phosphagen system. Exercise sustained slightly longer (30-45 second duration) relies less on phosphagen metabolism. Good examples of specific events that rely on the phosphagen system for their primary source of energy include 100 and 200 meter running sprints, 50 meter swimming sprints, high jump and long jump, shot-put and discus and power lifting.

Many other activities and sports are more difficult to analyze due to their variable, intermittent nature. Even with these complicating factors, however, it can be concluded that the more intense sections of an aerobics routine: the sprinting and kicking in soccer; the jumping and spiking in volleyball; and the sprinting, jumping, and shooting in basketball, all rely heavily on the phosphagen system.

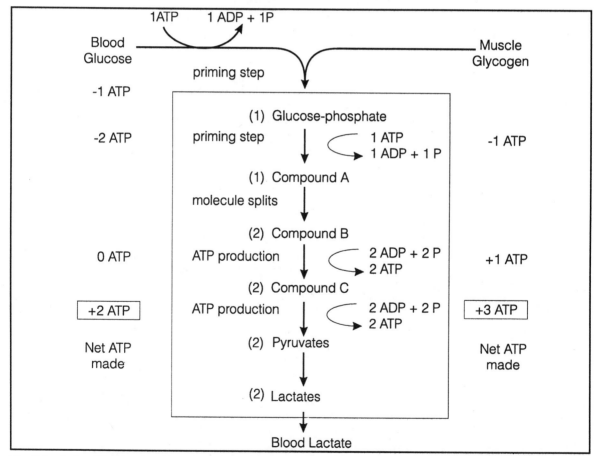

Fig. 2.4. A simplified version of the lactic acid system (fast glycolysis). Note that: (1) glucose can come from blood glucose or muscle glycogen; (2) priming steps are required; (3) the glucose splits into two equal parts; (4) ATP is produced; and (5) lactate is made in the muscle and diffuses into the blood. The increase in blood lactate indicates that the system is active.

Lactic Acid System

The lactic acid system also provides a rapid source of energy. Its fuel source is glucose, the usable form of carbohydrate in the body. Because the supply of glucose exceeds that of muscle phosphagen, the lactic acid system produces more ATP than the phosphagen system. But still, its capacity is limited because of the production of its end product, lactic acid, which is not tolerated well by the body. The lactic acid system is the primary source of energy for sustained high intensity exercise.

Description

Glycolysis is a process that occurs in the sarcoplasm or fluid portion of the muscle cell. It involves a sequence of reactions that partially breaks down glucose into a simpler compound called pyruvate. Once pyruvate is formed, it can take one of two pathways, depending on the need for energy or the presence of oxygen in the muscle. If the level of oxygen in the muscle is sufficient and the demand for energy is low, glycolysis operates in such a way that pyruvate enters the mitochondria and is combusted aerobically. This is referred to as "aerobic" or "slow" glycolysis. But if the level of oxygen is insufficient, or the demand for energy is high, the pyruvate is transformed into lactate (lactic acid). Under these circumstances, the process is referred to as "anaerobic" or "fast" glycolysis, and is also described as the "lactic acid system."

The foods that we typically eat can be separated into three categories: carbohydrates, fats and proteins. Carbohydrates are the only form of food that can be used as fuel in the lactic acid system. Furthermore, the only form of carbohydrate that can be used is glucose, a simple six-carbon sugar. The glucose used for fuel can come either from the blood glucose or from stored glycogen within the muscle. In either case, the glucose enters glycolysis initiating a sequence of nine or more reactions resulting in the production of lactate. A simplified version of glycolysis is presented in Figure 2-4. It is believed that this sequence, through evolution, has developed into the most efficient way of rapidly transforming food energy into ATP.

As mentioned previously, the source of fuel for glycolysis is provided by blood glucose through a phosphorylation made possible by the breakdown of ATP. This is considered a "priming step." It is analogous to priming a pump. Energy must first be added before any work can be done resulting in the flow of water. In this case, before any ATP can be made, one phosphate group is removed from ATP and attaches to glucose making glucose phosphate. This priming step is not necessary if glycogen is the source of fuel. (Keep in mind however, that the glucose had to proceed through this step to be stored as glycogen in the first place.)

Next, a second priming step occurs, with another mole of ATP donating its phosphate group. The compound then splits into two equal parts. Therefore, from this point on, every reaction actually occurs twice for every one glucose that originally entered glycolysis. The next step is the first reaction in the sequence in which ATP is produced. There is sufficient energy released during this reaction (10 kcal) to combine an ADP and P to produce ATP. There are actually two ATP formed from the input of one glucose. Another reaction now occurs in which ATP is formed. Again, two ATP are made since this reaction occurs twice.

The final step in glycolysis is the conversion of pyruvate to lactate. Also indicated below is the net production of ATP from glucose and glycogen, which is summarized in the second equation.

Blood glucose	+2 ADP +2 P + energy—> 2 lactate +2 ATP
Muscle glycogen	+3 ADP +3 P + energy—> 2 lactate +3 ATP

Regulation

The regulation of the lactic acid system is considerably more complex than that of the phosphagen system. It still depends, however, on the activity of regulatory enzymes, of which there are several. The most important regulatory enzyme in glycolysis is phosphofructokinase (PFK). Its importance lies in the fact that it exists in the lowest concentration and possesses the lowest activity of any enzyme in the sequence. Because of these characteristics, the reaction that PFK catalyzes is considered the "rate-limiting step" of glycolysis. It is analogous to the strength of a chain being determined by its weakest link. PFK, and hence the lactic acid system, is stimulated by the rapid accumulation of ADP and by the rapid depletion of CP that occur during very high intensity exercise.

The lactic acid system is inhibited under resting conditions due to an interaction effect with the aerobic system. Specific intermediates in aerobic metabolism that are in relatively high concentration in skeletal muscle at rest inhibit PFK and suppress the use of carbohydrate and anaerobic metabolism at rest.

Capacity and Power

The primary limiting factor in the capacity of the lactic acid system is not fuel depletion, but the accumulation of lactic acid. If used to its fullest extent, the lactic acid system would fatigue before using one mole of glucose. If it is assumed that the average male stores at least 2.5 moles of glucose, this means that as much as 50% of the fuel remains in the body at the time of fatigue. It does not seem likely, therefore, that the level of fuel limits the capacity of the system.

What is important to remember about this system is that while producing ATP, it simultaneously produces lactic acid. As the lactic acid is formed it rapidly loses a proton or hydrogen ion (H+) and becomes lactate. The problem is the neutralization or "buffering" of the excess hydrogen ions. The result is the muscle becomes too acidic to operate, many of the enzymes are inhibited and the actual mechanism of muscular contraction is affected.

The maximal capacity of a person's lactic acid system is determined by his or her ability to neutralize and tolerate lactic acid. Research suggests that the level of lactic acid that can be tolerated by an untrained 70 kg male corresponds to a total ATP production of about 1.5 moles, or to a total energy expenditure of 15 kcal. This amount of energy would allow for only about one minute of very high intensity exercise. Our 57 kg female could tolerate only enough lactic acid to produce about 1.0 mole of ATP.

The maximal power of the system again depends on the time required to produce a given amount of ATP. If it is assumed that the lactic acid system can be exhausted in as little as 45 seconds of intense exercise, the theoretical rate at which ATP energy is produced through the lactic acid system can be determined. The estimated power of the system in the untrained male turns out to be around 2.0 moles/min (20 kcal/min), and in the female about 1.5 moles/min (15 kcal/min).

Types of Exercise

Because of the relative simplicity of glycolysis, and because oxygen is not needed, the lactic acid system produces ATP rapidly. It provides the primary supply of energy for physical activity that results in fatigue in 45 to 90 seconds. Shorter, more intense exercise would rely to some degree on the phosphagen system, while longer, less intense exercise would begin to require aerobic metabolism. The lactic acid system is very important in prolonged sprints (400-800 meters running, 100-200 meters swimming or 1000-2000 meters cycling). It also provides much of the energy for sustained, high-intensity rallies in soccer, field hockey, ice hockey, lacrosse, basketball, volleyball, tennis, badminton and other sports. The floor routine in gymnastics relies in part on this system, with intermittent bursts of higher energy production from the phosphagen system. The common denominator in all of these activities is a sustained, high intensity effort lasting from one to two minutes.

Aerobic Energy System

The aerobic system is a complex collection of several different components. Because of its ability to use carbohydrates, fats and proteins as a source of fuel, and because it produces only carbon dioxide and water as end products, the system has a virtually unlimited capacity for making ATP. Its complexity and its need for a constant supply of oxygen, however, limit the rate at which ATP is produced. The aerobic system supplies all of the energy for low to moderate intensity exercise. It supplies energy for sleeping, resting, sitting, walking and other forms of low intensity physical activity. As the activity becomes more intense, to the point that it can only be sustained for a matter of a few minutes, the aerobic system can no longer provide energy at a sufficient rate. At this stage, ATP production is supplemented by the lactic acid and phosphagen systems.

Description

The term "aerobic system" refers to a complex series of reactions that, for the purpose of description, can be divided into three components (Figure 2-5). The first component can actually be one of three pathways depending upon whether the source of fuel is carbohydrate, fat or protein. When carbohydrate is used, the first component is glycolysis, which under these conditions operates slowly or aerobically. As a result, lactate is not formed and the end product is pyruvate.

When fat is used, the first component is a process called fat oxidation, in which large molecules of fat are made into

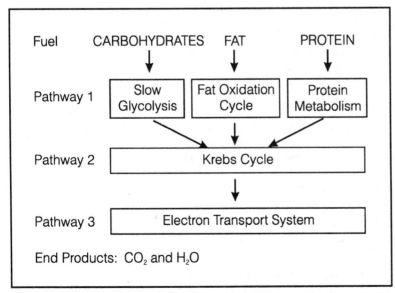

Fig. 2-5. An overview of the pathways involved in the aerobic system. Complex food molecules are broken down into much simpler molecules of CO_2 and H_2O. In the process, energy is released that can be used to produce ATP, which subsequently breaks down to provide energy for exercise.

much simpler molecules that fuel subsequent reactions in the system. If the source of fuel is protein, the first component pathway is protein metabolism. While a minimal amount of ATP is formed directly in each of these pathways, the main purpose of the first component is to produce acetyl groups (small two-carbon compounds) and a supply of electrons for subsequent reactions.

The second component is a cyclical process called the Krebs cycle and is common to all types of fuel. The main purpose of the Krebs cycle is to remove electrons and protons for subsequent reactions. The final component, also common to all types of food fuel, is the electron transport system (ETS). The electron transport system, because of a coupled process called oxidative phosphorylation, accounts for over 85% of the total ATP produced by the aerobic system. A good way to begin to understand the components of the aerobic system is to follow one mole of glucose from start to finish throughout the entire system.

ATP Production from Carbohydrates

The aerobic production of energy from carbohydrate begins with "slow" or "aerobic" glycolysis. The enzymes and intermediate compounds of glycolysis are simply dissolved in the sarcoplasm (fluid portion) of the muscle cell. Although they are not physically arranged in any particular order, the compounds react in the specific sequence described previously. The muscle cell is also composed of subcellular (within the cell) structures called mitochondria. The mitochondria are rod-shaped organelles, existing separately or possibly in the "networks," that contain the enzymes associated with the Krebs cycle and ETS. It is within the mitochondria that most of the ATP is produced aerobically.

The difference between "fast" and "slow" glycolysis is the utilization of the electrons and pyruvates produced. If the activity of the mitochondria (which relies in part on the supply of oxygen and the rate at which energy is being produced) is sufficient, the electrons and pyruvates formed enter the mitochondria (Figure 2-6). The electrons flow directly to the ETS, while the pyruvates are oxidized (lose electrons) and decarboxylated (lose CO_2) forming acetyl groups that enter the Krebs cycle. Because of the entry of the pyruvates and electrons into the mitochondria, there is no lactate produced under these conditions.

Krebs Cycle

The acetyl groups formed from the pyruvates enter into the Krebs cycle. The combination of the acetyl with other compounds results in the production of citric acid, the first intermediate in the Krebs cycle. Once citric acid is formed it goes through a series of reactions, including several oxidations in which more electrons are removed. These electrons are very important, because they are the driving force for the electron transport system (ETS). The electrons are actually shuttled into the ETS by something called coenzyme. A significant portion of the structure of the coenzyme consists of the B vitamin riboflavin. Severe vitamin deficiencies could lead to reduced aerobic function.

Electron Transport System

The final sequence of reactions in the aerobic production of ATP is the electron transport system. This system consists of a number of reusable electron-carrying compounds that can exist in either oxidized or reduced form. These compounds are arranged into specific "complexes" and are physically located within the mitochondrial membrane. They are arranged so that an electrical gradient (difference) exists between the beginning and the end of the system. The gradient created by this arrangement allows the electrons to pass from one intermediate to the next, or in other words to "flow" through the system. This flow, through a very complicated chemical process beyond the scope of this explanation, supplies the energy necessary to make a tremendous amount of ATP. The entire aerobic breakdown of glucose can be summarized by the following reaction.

$$1 \text{ glucose} + 38 \text{ ADP} + 38 \text{ P} + \text{energy} \longrightarrow 6 \text{ CO}_2 + 6 \text{ H}_2\text{O} + 38 \text{ ATP}$$

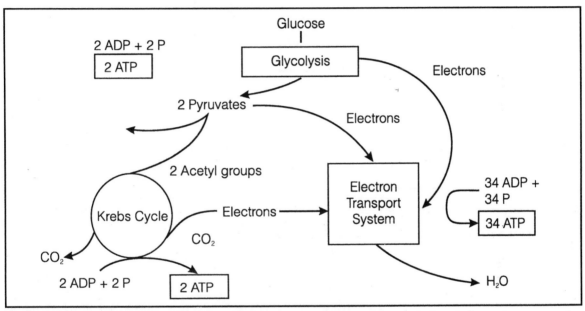

Fig. 2.6. Overview of the aerobic system using carbohydrates as a source of fuel. Glycolysis produces pyruvates that are converted into acetyl groups and enter the Krebs cycle. Electrons are sent from many sources to the electron transport system where most of the ATP is actually made.

ATP Production from Fat

Fats are stored in the body in adipose tissue and within skeletal muscle in the form of triglycerides. For fat stored in adipose tissue to be used for exercise, it must first be mobilized and transported to the muscle. The fats must then be converted into a form the muscle can use as fuel. This usable form of fat is called a free fatty acid. A fatty acid is a molecule much longer than glucose that can contain as many as 26 carbons in a long chain. Typical fatty acids used by humans for energy production include the saturated fats, stearic acid (18 carbons) and palmitic acid (16 carbons) and the unsaturated fats, oleic acid and linoleic acid (each possessing 18 carbons).

The utilization of fat as a fuel begins with a cyclical process called the fat oxidation cycle, which occurs within the mitochondria (Figure 2- 7). The fatty acid is first "activated" through a priming step involving the input of one mole of ATP. This priming step is not required for every revolution of the cycle, only for the initial entry of the fatty acid into the cycle. Three significant reactions occur during fatty acid oxidation. Two oxidations occur feeding electrons into the electron transport system, and the third involves the cleaving of an acetyl group from the carbon chain of the fatty acid. The fatty acid (less two carbons) then revolves a second time through the cycle.

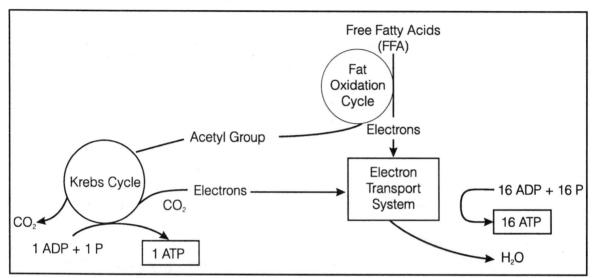

Fig. 2-7. Overview of the aerobic system using free fatty acids as a source of fuel. One revolution of the fat oxidation cycles produces an acetyl group that enters the Krebs cycle. Electrons are sent from many sources to the electron transport system where most of the ATP is actually made.

This process will continue until only two carbons remain in the skeleton of the fatty acid. At this point, the two carbon remnant (an acetyl group) enters the Krebs cycle leaving nothing of the fatty acid. It has been completely oxidized to carbon dioxide and water through the aerobic system with a considerable amount of ATP-energy produced in the process. When stearic acid (an 18-carbon fatty acid) is used as a source of fuel, the combination of eight full revolutions of the fat oxidation cycle and the remaining acetyl group remnant results in the production of nearly 150 moles of ATP (or nearly 1500 kcal of energy). A fatty acid with a longer carbon chain (>18 carbons), results in greater energy production, while a shorter carbon chain (<18 carbons) produces less energy. The aerobic breakdown of stearic acid can be summarized as shown below.

$$\text{Stearic acid} + O_2 + ADP + P + \text{energy} \longrightarrow CO_2 + H_2O + 147\ ATP$$

ATP Production from Protein

Finally, a brief word about the use of protein as fuel is in order. Protein usually does not provide more than 10 to 15% of the total energy requirement of an activity. As such, protein does not play as significant a role as carbohydrate or fat as a fuel for exercise. The main source of stored protein in the body is muscle. It is obviously not advantageous to use this source for fuel during exercise. Some dietary protein (from animal or vegetable origin) is used for fuel. It must first be broken down into amino acids, its simpler, more usable form. Typically, amino acids consumed through the diet include alanine, leucine, valine, and tryptophan. One mole of alanine, metabolized aerobically, produces one acetyl group and one pair of electrons, which result in the production of 15 ATP. In summary then, a mole of carbohydrate (glucose) produces 38 ATP; a mole of fat (stearic acid) produces 147 ATP; and a mole of protein (alanine) produces 15 ATP when combusted by the aerobic system.

Regulation

The regulation of the aerobic system is more complex than that of the lactic acid system. This complexity is understandable given the vast number and nature of the reactions involved in aerobic metabolism. The discussion of the regulatory factors focuses on the control of the Krebs cycle, fat and carbohydrate metabolism and the electron transport system.

Krebs Cycle

The rate at which the Krebs cycle operates depends primarily on the activity of its enzymes. All of these enzymes are stimulated by elevated concentrations of ADP, and inhibited by high concentrations of ATP. The enzyme that assumes the key regulatory role within the cycle is isocitrate dehydrogenase, which regulates the oxidation of isocitrate. Under resting conditions, the level of ATP in the mitochondria is high. To avoid the overproduction of ATP, which cannot be stored, the elevated mitochondrial ATP inhibits the regulatory enzyme and slows the Krebs cycle. During low to moderate intensity aerobic exercise, the amount of ADP entering the mitochondria rises. This has a stimulating effect on isocitrate dehydrogenase which speeds up the Krebs cycle.

Fat and Carbohydrate Metabolism

Determining which gets burned—fat or carbohydrate—has been a subject of much concern to fitness instructors. The control of fat and carbohydrate entry into the aerobic system is intimately involved with its overall regulation. Under resting conditions, fatty acids are readily available and provide the primary source of fuel. The presence of high concentrations of fatty acid and citric acid inhibit glycolysis by inhibiting PFK. Therefore, under these resting conditions, fat metabolism flourishes while carbohydrate metabolism is inhibited. During prolonged, moderate intensity exercise (<85% HRmax), subtle changes occur in the level of secretion of several hormones. The secretion of epinephrine (adrenaline) from the adrenal glands rises and the secretion of insulin from the pancreas decreases. These hormones influence the rate of fat and carbohydrate uptake by muscle in such a way that fat metabolism still predominates and is further enhanced naturally or endogenously during prolonged work.

With higher intensity exercise (>85% HRmax), changes occur that begin to inhibit the use of fats. The most significant inhibitor is the lactic acid produced. It reduces the availability of fatty acids by slowing their release from triglycerides. As a result, fat metabolism is inhibited and carbohydrate becomes the preferred source of fuel, used by the aerobic system and the lactic acid system.

> *Higher Intensities Inhibit Fat Usage*

Electron Transport System

The status of the electron transport system also influences the overall regulation of aerobic metabolism. Oxygen must be in constant supply for the proper functioning of the system. The increase in blood flow to the muscle during aerobic exercise ensures a sufficient oxygen supply and allows the aerobic system to increase its rate of energy production. The increased influx of ADP into the mitochondria during exercise also stimulates the enzymes associated with ETS, further enhancing its performance. The system is inhibited, on the other hand, by reduced blood flow resulting in reduced oxygen availability. A strong, isometric muscular contraction, caused by exerting pressure on blood vessels, causes a brief restriction of blood flow. This results in the temporary inhibition of the aerobic system so that the muscle relies more on the lactic acid and phosphagen systems.

Capacity and Power

If all fuels are considered, including the total carbohydrate, fat and protein stored in the body, the aerobic system has a virtually unlimited capacity for producing ATP energy. Its complexity and its need for oxygen, however, limit the maximal power at which the system can operate.

Capacity

The only practical limit to the capacity of the system comes when analyzing prolonged, continuous aerobic exercise. The best example of this type of exercise is a marathon completed in competitive time (under three hours). A marathon run at this pace requires significant reliance on carbohydrate metabolism. If the competitor is not careful, the carbohydrate within the muscle can be depleted before the end of the race, resulting in premature fatigue or "hitting the wall." The total amount of ATP that can be produced aerobically from stored muscle glycogen can be estimated. If the same assumptions are used regarding the level of training, body weights and muscle weights, a male subject may store about 450 grams (1 lb) of glycogen. This much glycogen would theoretically produce nearly 100 moles of ATP, equivalent to 1000 kcal of energy, or sufficient energy to walk or run about ten miles. A female subject, with a muscle mass of 20 kg and a similar glycogen concentration would have a capacity of approximately 65 moles of ATP upon glycogen depletion.

The capacity of the aerobic system grows tremendously if stored fat is included as a potential source of energy. For example, a 70 kg male of average body composition (15% body fat) possesses just over 10,000 grams of stored body fat. Since one gram of fat yields nine kcal of energy, the amount of energy available from the complete combustion of stored fat would result in over 90,000 kcal of energy, or 9000 moles of ATP. Theoretically, this would be enough energy to walk from New York City to Chicago (900 miles) without eating. A 100 kg subject with 31% body fat would have enough stored energy to walk from New York City to Los Angeles (2800 miles) without refueling!

Power

The power of the aerobic system depends on the maximal rate at which the body can transport and consume oxygen. The maximal rate of oxygen uptake (VO_2max) is determined by a graded exercise test to exhaustion. If done on a treadmill, the protocol usually consists of increasing the speed and grade of the treadmill every two to three minutes during the exercise test. Oxygen uptake and other physiological variables are measured throughout the test. Testing continues until the subject can no longer maintain the speed of the treadmill belt and voluntarily stops due to exhaustion.

An average value for maximal oxygen uptake in an untrained 70 kg male subject is about three liters/min. If it is assumed that for every liter of oxygen consumed, about five kcal of energy are expended, the VO_2max can be converted into a maximal energy expenditure of about 15 kcal/min. Finally, if one mole of ATP is required for each 10 kcal of energy expenditure, an estimated maximal rate of ATP production would be about 1.5 moles/min.

Thus, when producing energy at a maximal rate (15 kcal/min), the aerobic system produces energy 75% as fast as the lactic acid system (20 kcal/min) and less than 40% as fast as the phosphagen system (40 kcal/min). Following the same assumptions for the female subject with a body weight of 57 kg and an average VO_2max of 2 liters/min, the estimated power for her aerobic system would be about 1.0 moles/min or a maximal energy expenditure of 10 kcal/min.

Types of Exercise

The aerobic system, because of its limited power, provides energy primarily for low to moderate intensity exercise. Virtually all of the energy necessary for resting activities including sitting, reading, studying, watching television and sleeping comes by way of the aerobic system. With slightly higher intensity activity like walking, leisurely bicycling, shopping and office work, the aerobic system still supplies most of the energy. It is not until the intensity reaches a moderately high level (above 75-85% of maximum heart rate) that the limit of the aerobic system is reached and other energy systems need to be recruited to provide supplemental energy. Such activities would include aerobics, running, swimming, cycling, rowing, skating and others that are performed above 75-85% of maximum intensity. This intensity is such that the activity could be sustained continuously for at least five minutes without fatigue, yet requires a significantly elevated heart rate to accomplish.

The best examples of exercises relying primarily on the aerobic system for energy include 40-60 minutes of aerobics, distance running (>5000 m), distance swimming (>1500 m), distance cycling (>10 kilometers), cross-country skiing (>5000 m) and the triathalon. Any activity, providing it is sustained continuously for a minimum of five minutes, relies primarily on the aerobic system. This encompasses portions of several team or more complex individual sports including soccer, field hockey, lacrosse, basketball, tennis and squash, to name a few. All of these sports, however, also periodically require energy production from the lactic acid and phosphagen systems for more intense rallies and bursts of sprinting, jumping and kicking.

Summary

"Aerobic system" is a term used by exercise physiologists to refer to a complex system of metabolic reactions. The system is capable of using any form of food, including carbohydrate, fat or protein, as a source of fuel. The first component of the system, which is different depending on the source of fuel, begins with large food molecules and breaks them down so that pyruvates, acetyl groups and/or electrons are produced. This provides the fuel for the

Krebs cycle and for the subsequent reactions associated with electron transport and oxidative phosphorylation.

With a sufficient supply of oxygen, the aerobic system can completely catabolize these food fuels into carbon dioxide and water, while saving much of the energy released through the formation of ATP. (On the assumption that someone could utilize most of the carbohydrate and fat stored in the body, the aerobic system has a virtually unlimited capacity.) However, because of its complexity and the need for oxygen, the power of the system is somewhat limited. These characteristics make it an ideal source of energy for prolonged activity of a low to moderate intensity (<75-85 HRmax).

Summary and Comparison of Energy Systems

A full appreciation of the energetics of exercise requires a fundamental understanding of the energy systems. Conclusions can be drawn as to the significance of each system with regard to many sports based on the system's characteristics.

Summary of Energy Systems

Energy is produced within the body in response to demands placed on it. The body attempts to produce energy in the most efficient manner possible and at the necessary rate. When conditions permit, the body produces energy aerobically because of the efficiency with which this process is completed. However, when exercise is performed at an intensity that exceeds the capability of the aerobic system, the energy requirement is met through anaerobic metabolism.

Capacity and Power

The aerobic system produces a virtually limitless supply of energy through the catabolism of carbohydrate, fat and protein stored within the body. The combustion of these fuels occurs in such a way that the only remaining end products are easily removed by exhalation from the lungs. The lactic acid system is more limited in its energy producing capacity due to the disruption of the normal acid-base balance that it creates. Hydrogen ions produced by dissociation from lactic acid quickly saturate the body's buffer systems and fatigue ensues. The phosphagen system provides an immediate source of readily available energy. The amount of usable fuel is so limited, however, that the capacity is minimal and can be completely exhausted within a matter of seconds.

The significance of the anaerobic energy systems lies more in their ability to produce energy at high speed. The phosphagen system, because of its elegant simplicity, is able to provide energy immediately for forceful muscular contractions. It produces energy at least twice as fast as either of the other systems. Anaerobic glycolysis, the sequence of reactions constituting the lactic acid system, is similarly simple and as such provides a rapid source of energy as well. The complexities of the aerobic system and its reliance on oxygen as an acceptor of electrons limit its rate of energy production to below that of the anaerobic systems.

Types of Exercise

Any sport, exercise or physical activity that can be accomplished with a level of exertion not exceeding 80-85% of one's maximal capability (as indicated by heart rate for example) can be accomplished almost exclusively with aerobic metabolism. Frequently in sports, however, the athlete cannot exercise at a constant intensity but instead must alternate between low (<50% HRmax), moderate (50-85% HRmax), high (85-95% HRmax) and very high (>95% HRmax) intensities. When this is the case, the body frequently shifts between energy systems, taking advantage of the differing characteristics of each.

Comparison of Energy Systems

The characteristics of the systems are compared in Table 2-1. Based on these characteristics, conclusions are made as to the types of exercise for which each system is best suited. The basic facts contained within this chapter provide a foundation for developing a training program for any sport. Through proper training, the capacities and powers of each of the systems can be improved with the accompanying expectation of improved sport performance.

Table 2-1. Summary of the Characteristics of the Three Energy Systems.

Characteristic	Phosphagen system	Lactic acid system	Aerobic system
Fuel used	creatine phosphate	carbohydrate	CHO, fat, protein
Location	sarcoplasm	sarcoplasm	mitochondria
Fatigue due to:	phosphagen depletion	lactate accumulation	glycogen depletion
Capacity	very limited	limited	unlimited
Male	8-10 kcal	12-15 kcal	>90,000 kcal
Female	5-7 kcal	8-10 kcal	>115,000 kcal
Power	very high	high/moderate	moderate/low
Male	36-40 kcal/min	16-20 kcal/min	12-15 kcal/min
Female	26-30	12-15	9-12
Intensity	very high	high/moderate	moderate/low
%Max	>95% max	85-95% max	<85% max
Time to fatigue	very short 1-15 sec	short/medium 45-90 sec	medium/very long >3-5 min.
Running distance	<100 m	400-800 m	>1500 m
Swimming	<25 m	100-200 m	>400 m
Cycling	<175 m	750-1500 m	>3000 m
Rowing	<50 m	250-500 m	>1000 m

Note: Assume male is healthy, untrained with weight of 154 lb (70 kg). Assume female is healthy, untrained with weight of 126 lb (57 kg). Distances are estimated based on various published performance times.

References

Fox, E.L., Bowers, R.W., & Foss, M.L. (1993). *The physiological basis for exercise and sport* (5th ed.). Madison, Wi.: Brown & Benchmark Publishers.

McArdle, W.D., Katch, F.L., & Katch, V.L. (1991). *Exercise physiology: energy, nutrition, and human performance* (3rd ed.). Philadelphia: Lea & Febiger.

Powers, S.K., & Howley, E.T. (1991). *Exercise physiology: theory and application to fitness and performance*. Dubuque, Ia.: Wm. C. Brown Publishers.

Sharkey, J.G. (1990). *Physiology of fitness* (3rd ed.). Champaign, Ill.: Human Kinetics.

Wilmore, J.H., & Costill, D.L. (1990). *Training for sport and activity: the physiological basis of the conditioning process* (3rd ed.). Dubuque, Ia.: Wm. C. Brown Publishers.

Developing and Maintaining Aerobic Fitness

3

William C. Beam, Phd

Focus

There is little doubt that a conscientious program of physical activity, especially aerobic exercise, significantly improves the health and wellness of the exerciser. What is more, evidence is mounting that the benefits of regular and continuing exercise can be enjoyed over an entire life span. It has been proven fairly convincingly that individuals who maintain an active lifestyle may actually add years to their lives while significantly enhancing the quality of life in later years as well. Physical activity reduces the premature, deleterious effects of degenerative diseases, especially cardiovascular disease. Individuals of all ages, from children to the elderly, should be encouraged to exercise. It is never too late to begin a regular exercise program, but the best time to start is now.

General Principle of Aerobic Exercise

Aerobic exercise is generally recognized as exercise that is rhythmic, uses the major muscle groups and is maintained at a fairly continuous intensity for a prolonged period of time. Provided the intensity is such that the exercise is maintained without undue fatigue for at least 10-15 minutes, the aerobic system serves as the predominant source of energy. Because of the significant role the cardiovascular and respiratory systems play in aerobic exercise, adaptations occur in the heart, blood vessels and lungs with regular and continued aerobic training. These adaptations lead to significant health benefits and to an improvement in aerobic exercise performance.

Modes of Aerobic Exercise

Most authorities consider the best aerobic exercises to be those which consistently maintain intensity at a constant level. This is especially true for individuals who are just beginning an exercise program or for those individuals who may experience symptoms of cardiovascular disease including chest pain, abnormal heart rhythms or unusually high blood pressure. Many other exercise modes, in which the intensity is more variable, also provide significant aerobic benefits, but may not be recommended for all people.

Constant Intensity Exercise

Some of the best examples of aerobic exercise in which the intensity can be maintained at a constant level include walking, hiking, jogging, running, stepping, aerobics, step aerobics, stationary cycling, road cycling, mountain biking, rowing, roller skating, roller blading and cross-country skiing. All of these exercises, provided they are performed at the appropriate frequency, duration and intensity, improve the performance of the heart and lungs to an equal degree. However, some might be considered more beneficial than others because they train a larger portion of the body's muscle mass as well. The important factor is not which of these modes is used, but that any mode done consistently will result in beneficial health and performance changes.

Variable Intensity Exercise

Other modes of exercise, in which the intensity is less predictable and more variable, have the potential for providing aerobic benefits. These include recreational pursuits such as tennis, racquetball, squash, handball, soccer, basketball, street hockey and ice hockey. However, these sports must be played in a continuous manner. In the racquet sports, the time spent serving and receiving a serve must be intentionally reduced, and the players must have levels of skill which enable them to maintain longer rallies. In the team sports, penalties and play stoppages must be eliminated or severely restricted, so that the level of activity is more evenly maintained. For example, if basketball is played recreationally, if no free throws are taken, and the ball is quickly put back into play after each foul or basket, it can provide significant aerobic benefit. As it is played competitively at the collegiate or professional level, however, basketball is very highly anaerobic.

Before and After Exercise

To maximize safety, certain precautions should be taken before and after exercise. Adequately warming-up prior to the aerobic exercise session may prevent damage to skeletal muscle, connective tissue, and the heart. A sufficient cooldown is necessary after exercise to alleviate a potential rapid drop in blood pressure that could cause lightheadedness, dizziness, or fainting. Proper warm-up and cooldown are increasingly important when exercise intensity builds.

Warm-up

Prior to aerobic exercise, low-intensity, dynamic exercise is performed to gradually prepare the body for the exercise and to prevent damage to skeletal muscle, connective tissue and the heart. The main benefits of the warm-up are to increase blood flow to the previously mentioned tissues and to increase body temperature. Skeletal muscle and connective tissue become more pliable, stretching more easily, and thus become more resistant to tearing. The gradual increase in exercise intensity allows adequate blood flow to the heart. Without proper warm-up, especially in older adults, exercise can result in an inadequate blood flow to the heart which can lead to chest pain, tissue damage or an irregular heart beat. Inappropriate changes in blood pressure have also been observed with inadequate warm-up. Additional benefits of proper warm-up include increased oxygen delivery to muscles and improved nervous tissue conduction.

Typically, two different types of exercise are performed during the warm-up session. Mild, dynamic exercise is used to increase blood flow and body temperature. This exercise is usually of the same mode as the exercise used for the aerobic conditioning but is done at a lower intensity (30-50% of maximum). Static stretching exercises are a second type of exercise that can be included in the warm-up to increase flexibility and help minimize the risk of soft tissue injury. For instance, cycling should be preceded by static stretches emphasizing the muscles in the legs; swimming is preceded by stretches emphasizing the arms and upper body. While emphasizing particular muscle groups is a good idea, it should not be done at the exclusion of other muscles throughout the body. It is usually a good idea to precede any exercise, especially aerobics, with a general whole body stretch.

Cooldown

The cooldown period following exercise is used primarily to prevent a rapid drop in arterial blood pressure. Many arteries are fully dilated following exercise due to changes that have occurred in the skeletal muscle around them. This significantly reduces the resistance to blood flow. If heart rate, stroke volume and cardiac output are allowed to drop rapidly after exercise, the reduced blood flow in combination with the reduced resistance can result in very low blood pressure. As a result of inadequate blood pressure, an insufficient supply of blood reaches the brain which can cause lightheadedness, dizziness or fainting. To avoid rapid drops in blood pressure, it is important to continue some type of dynamic exercise during recovery. Due to the rhythmic muscular contractions, blood flow back to the heart is enhanced which maintains stroke volume and cardiac output. Standing or sitting still after exercise should be avoided because of the pooling of blood in the legs which will occur. The blood pooling reduces stroke volume which reduces cardiac output and thereby leads to a significant drop in arterial blood pressure.

Exercise Principles

In this discussion, aerobic training is assumed to consist of continuous aerobic exercise. It is generally performed at 55-85% of maximal intensity, a determination based on maximum heart rate range. The main purpose of aerobic exercise is to improve the ability of the cardiorespiratory system to deliver oxygen and to improve the aerobic endurance of the skeletal muscle used during the exercise. This type of training is highly recommended for the general public because of the associated health benefits. It is believed to facilitate a normalization of blood pressure, to lower body fat, to reduce psychological stress and to reduce the risk of heart attack and stroke.

Three important characteristics of exercise must be considered: The frequency, duration and intensity of the exercise are all interrelated and must be monitored and adjusted to provide maximal aerobic benefits. As discussed previously, to ensure the safety of the exercise, careful consideration must be given to the activity used in warming-up prior to the exercise and in cooling down afterward. Provided all of these principles are followed correctly, they may be applied to improve the aerobic fitness of any apparently healthy adult or athlete.

Frequency

In order to see improvement in aerobic power, the exercise should be performed from three to five times per week. Exercising only once or twice a week has been shown to maintain fitness for the most part, but does not provide enough stimulus to achieve significant gains in aerobic fitness. On the other hand, performing the same mode of exercise too frequently has a tendency to increase both the possibility of exhaustion and the risk of overuse injuries. It is recommended that one or two days per week be rest days with no hard training. Cross training, using more than one primary mode of exercise, has become a popular way of exercising more frequently with less risk of injury. It also relieves, for many people and athletes, much of the boredom associated with long months of training.

Duration

The duration of the exercise must be at least 15 minutes to achieve gains in aerobic endurance. More significant gains are observed when the duration is extended to 30 to 60 minutes per session. There is nothing wrong with exercising continuously for over an hour if it is tolerated well. Some individuals, however, become chronically fatigued and are prone to overuse injury due to exercising for too long with insufficient rest. Long training sessions, of over an hour in duration, should be divided into bouts of differing modes of exercise, or should be limited to two to three times per week. While exercise bouts of less than 15 minutes have not proven useful in improving aerobic endurance, there is recent evidence they may still result in health benefits such as psychological and emotional benefits. In other words, benefits can be gained by taking advantage of brief exercise breaks such as walking the dog, walking during your lunch break or riding your bike to work.

Intensity

The intensity of the exercise is more difficult to monitor than frequency or duration. With less experienced exercisers, intensity is best monitored by using heart rate as an indicator of stress. An added benefit of using heart rate is that it is sensitive to environmental changes the exerciser may encounter. To improve aerobic power, the intensity of the exercise should be maintained between 55% and 85% of heart rate range (HRrange).

HRrange is the number of beats between resting heart rate (HRrest) and a measured or estimated maximal heart rate (HRmax). Resting heart rate is simply the lowest palpable heart rate achieved while resting. It is usually suggested that HRrest be taken in the morning, but it can be measured at any time during the day provided the subject is well rested and free from stress. Although maximal heart rate is best obtained through the use of a graded exercise test, it can also be estimated based on the subject's age. Table 3-1 demonstrates the method for calculating training heart rates at 55% and 85% of heart rate range using a maximal heart rate estimated from age.

Table 3-1. Equations for Calculating Training Heart Rates at Various Exercise Intensities [Example is for a 40-Year-Old Subject]

Equations	Sample Calculations
HRmax = 220 - age	HRmax = 220 - 40 = 180 bpm
HRrange = HRmax - HRrest	HRrange = 180 - 80 = 100 bpm
HR60% = (HRrange x .60) + HRrest	HR60% = (100 x .60) + 80 = 140 bpm
HR85% = (HRrange x .85) + HRrest	HR85% = (100 x .85) + 80 = 165 bpm

*Assuming maximum heart rate of 180 bpm and resting heart rate of 80 bpm.

The minimum intensity believed necessary to produce significant cardiorespiratory changes in a healthy adult is about 55-65% HRrange. Increasing the intensity of the exercise to 70-85% HRrange causes adaptations to occur more quickly, resulting in faster increases in aerobic power. By increasing the intensity still further, however, to over 85% HRrange, the exercise now requires anaerobic energy production. Consequently, the exercise leads to fatigue too rapidly and, as such, is not suggested for inclusion in an aerobic program. More experienced exercisers usually do not need to monitor heart rate each time they exercise. Instead, they can eventually rely on their experience to perceive and maintain a level of exertion that produces the desirable heart rate within a minimal range of error.

The most appropriate exercise intensity is determined based on the fitness level and goals of the subject. Fitness level may be assumed based on the exercise history of the subject or can be measured using a graded exercise test. Intensity should be kept at the minimum (55-65% HRrange) for apparently healthy individuals who are in below-average condition. In certain populations, including elderly, previously sedentary or symptomatic subjects, even this level of intensity may be too high. In these populations it is generally recommended that more mild exercise (40-60% HRrange) be performed until the subject reaches a sufficient level of fitness. The main advantage of low intensity exercise is contained in the health benefits achieved. It can result in weight loss, an improvement in body composition, a modest reduction in blood pressure and possible improvement in blood lipids. Because of the low-intensity, however, it needs to be done more frequently, and for a longer duration, to obtain the desired benefit.

For those in average or good condition, a slightly higher-intensity (70-75% HRrange) exercise is recommended, but this intensity should not be attempted until some initial level of fitness is attained. Exercise of this type results in both health benefits as well as some adaptations that may lead to improvements in exercise performance. For subjects who are in very good shape, with a previous history of regular aerobic exercise, higher intensity exercise (80-85% HRrange) is required to ensure sufficient stress for continued improvement. Exercise of this intensity can lead to significant training effects in the heart, lungs and skeletal muscles that can improve aerobic exercise performance. A summary of determining training heart rates based on fitness level and goals is presented in Table 3-2.

Two other means of measuring intensity include the Talk Test and Rating of Perceived Exertion. Both of these methods, along with a discussion on finding and calculating heart rates, is covered extensively in the chapter on "Measuring Intensity."

Table 3-2. Choosing an Appropriate Exercise Intensity Based on Subject Description and Exercise Program Goals.

Intensity (%HRange)	Subject Description	Exercise Program Goals
40-60%	Sedentary, elderly, symptomatic, poor fitness	Health benefits and modest gains in fitness
55-75%	Healthy, active, average level of fitness	Health benefits and some aerobic training effect
75-85%	Active, above average to high level of fitness	Health benefits and improved aerobic exercise performance

Summary of Exercise Principles

To appreciate the relationship between frequency, duration, and intensity of exercise, a brief summary is necessary. When beginning an exercise program, it is best to maintain a conservative approach and start at the suggested minimums of three times per week, 15 minutes per session, at no more than 55-65% HRrange. Provided this level of activity is tolerated well, the next step consists of gradually increasing the duration to 30 minutes, while maintaining the same frequency and intensity. The intensity should not be increased until the subject can exercise for 30-45 minutes without becoming overly tired. At this point, the intensity can be increased to 70-75% HRrange.

The frequency may now also be increased to four to five times per week if so desired. Once the subject feels comfortable exercising 30-45 minutes, three to five times per week, at 70-75% intensity, the intensity may be raised toward the recommended maximum of 80-85%. If the purpose of the exercise is to maintain aerobic fitness in a healthy non-athlete, the previous recommendations of frequency (three to five times per week), duration (15-60 minutes) and intensity (60-85% HRrange) apply.

If the purpose is to increase the aerobic power and endurance of a young athlete, more appropriate recommendations might include exercising a minimum of 45-60 minutes per session, four to six days per week, at 80-85% HRrange. The same basic principles of frequency, duration and intensity apply to virtually any subject; it is only the level at which they are performed that differs, depending upon the purpose and application of the exercise program.

CHECKLIST

THE FIT(M) PRINCIPLE

An easy way to remember the requirements for achieving an aerobic training effect is the FIT acronym. Recently, the letter "M" has been added to the FIT principle and signifies Modality or Type of exercise.

F - Frequency   3 to 5 times per week

I - Intensity   55-85% age-predicted maximum heart rate

T - Time   Duration 20-60 minutes of continuous aerobic activity

M - Modality   Aerobic activities (running, swimming, biking, etc.)
using continuous rhythmic activity of large muscle groups

—Troy E. De Mond, MA

References

American College of Sports Medicine (1992). *ACSM fitness book.* Champaign, Ill.: Human Kinetics Publishers.

American College of Sports Medicine (1991). *Guidelines for exercise testing and prescription* (4th ed.). Philadelphia: Lea & Febiger.

Heyward, V.H. (1991). *Advanced fitness assessment and exercise prescription* (2nd ed.). Champaign, Ill.: Human Kinetics Books.

Hockey, R.V. (1993). *Physical fitness: pathway to healthful living* (7th ed.). St. Louis: The C.V. Mosby Company.

Howley, E.T., & Franks, B.D. (1992). *Health fitness instructor's handbook* (2nd ed.). Champaign, Ill.: Human Kinetics Publishers.

Improving Health and Performance Through Aerobic Fitness

4

William C. Beam, Phd

Focus

A SUFFICIENT DEGREE OF AEROBIC FITNESS provides numerous benefits. Many of these are health-related and result in an improved state of overall wellness. To achieve wellness does not require an excruciating, drop-dead workout regimen. Wellness can be achieved with a consistent program of regular, moderate-intensity exercise. However, some benefits of exercise, those that improve an individual's aerobic exercise performance, do require more vigorous workouts. Therefore, the benefits of aerobic exercise will be discussed first as they relate to improving health, and second as they relate to improving aerobic exercise performance.

Considerations Before Starting an Exercise Program

Before anyone starts an exercise program, several considerations should be made. The first is to assess whether the individual is a good candidate for an exercise program. The best candidates are individuals described by the American College of Sports Medicine (ACSM) as "apparently healthy adults." This phrase denotes an adult who has no documented cardiovascular disease, who has no symptoms of heart disease (such as chest pain or heart rhythm abnormalities) and who has no more than one primary risk factor for coronary heart disease (CHD). The ACSM recognizes the following primary risk factors for CHD including (1) high blood pressure (165/100 mmHg); (2) high serum cholesterol (240 mg/dl); (3) cigarette smoking; (4) personal history of diabetes mellitus; (5) family history of CHD (especially premature death of family members due to heart attack or stroke) and (6) physical inactivity. Apparently healthy adults may engage in a moderate exercise program with very little risk of cardiovascular complication.

Those adults who are free of known disease and symptoms, but who have two or more primary risk factors are classified as "higher risk" individuals. It is especially important that these individuals are evaluated thoroughly before engaging in an exercise program. A third classification includes those subjects who are known to have cardiovascular disease. They should only exercise on the advice of their physicians, preferably within some supervised exercise setting, such as a cardiac rehab program, or a corporate, community or commercial fitness program staffed by appropriately trained and certified personnel.

Other considerations include deciding on an appropriate exercise program, setting short- and long-term goals, creating a social support system of family and friends and developing a method of monitoring the effectiveness of the program. The exercise program must fit into an existing schedule that may very well include work, school, family, friends, church, hobbies, social commitments and more. The program must allow the participant to derive some personal, physical, psychological and social benefits. Goals may be set, including physical goals such as attaining a particular body weight, body composition, resting blood pressure or serum cholesterol; stress reduction goals such as feeling more relaxed; or social goals such as exercising twice a week with a spouse or friend. The early goals should be easily monitored and reasonably attainable.

Once the potential exerciser has been assessed as a good candidate for an exercise program, the most important goal is to begin and continue the workouts. The expected benefits of exercise will occur only if a regular habit of physical activity has been established.

Adaptations that Improve Health

Many adaptations that lead to improved health take place as a result of physical activity. Changes occur in resting blood pressure, serum cholesterol, body composition and other health-related factors that enhance the overall wellness of the participant.

Cardiovascular and Respiratory Changes

A significant adaptation to continuing aerobic exercise is an increased volume of the left ventricle, the main pumping chamber of the heart. This volume allows the heart to pump more blood per beat, so that it does not have to beat as often, thereby improving its mechanical efficiency. This improved efficiency results in the low, resting heart rates characteristic of aerobically trained individuals. Changes in the lungs allow oxygen and carbon dioxide to exchange more efficiently. Increased blood flow through the lungs and increased lung diffusion lead to improved oxygen delivery to various body tissues. Several other changes leading to improved aerobic exercise performance are described in a later discussion.

Changes that Lower Risk of Cardiovascular Disease

The main complication of cardiovascular disease is an increased risk of premature heart attack or stroke. Exercise has been found effective at lowering the risk of cardiovascular disease by affecting two primary risk factors including arterial blood pressure and total serum cholesterol. Exercise is most effective in lowering the blood pressure of those subjects who already have elevated blood pressure (systolic over 165 mmHg or diastolic over 100 mmHg).

Aerobic exercise may reduce blood pressure 10-20 mmHg and may also reduce the need for antihypertensive medications. Favorable changes have also been observed in blood lipids or blood fats. Regular, continuous aerobic exercise can lower total serum cholesterol, which is directly related to the risk of heart attack and stroke. By lowering total serum cholesterol, an individual may concurrently lower the risk of cardiovascular disease by the same degree.

A particular component of cholesterol metabolism called high-density lipoprotein (HDL), otherwise known as "good" cholesterol, actually serves to protect an individual from developing disease. The higher the HDL, the better protection provided. Aerobic exercise, especially in combination with a low-fat diet and weight loss, significantly increases the proportion of HDL in the blood, thereby lowering the risk of disease. It might be interesting to note that increases in HDL have also been observed in individuals who have stopped smoking and in people who partake of alcohol in moderation.

Body Composition and Metabolic Changes

Body composition can be improved dramatically through a program of proper exercise and dietary intake. Body composition is best improved by a combination of: (1) daily, prolonged (30-60 minutes), low-to-moderate intensity aerobic exercise; (2) mild caloric restriction (300-500 fewer kcal per day); (3) resistance exercise (2-3 times weekly); and (4) slow weight loss (1-2 pounds per week). Crash dieting and semi-starvation, especially without exercise, are not suggested due to the related loss of muscle and lean tissue. Weight loss can be estimated on the assumption that the loss of one pound of fat requires that a subject expend 3500 kcal more than he consumes over some given length of time, preferably about a week. The typical changes in body composition observed with appropriate exercise and diet include a loss of body weight, a loss of body fat and no change or an increase in muscle and lean weight. Weight loss, as previously discussed, may help promote a reduction in blood pressure and serum cholesterol. In diabetics, there is some evidence that weight loss may also improve glucose metabolism, reducing the dependency on medication or insulin.

Neuromuscular and Bone Changes

There may be modest changes in skeletal muscle, connective tissue and bone associated with regular and continuing aerobic exercise. The loss of muscle tissue and bone mineral content is a significant problem among the elderly. It leads to an increased likelihood of immobility and bone fracture and a reduction in the degree of independence the older adult is able to maintain. Active, older adults are generally more capable of maintaining their physical independence, and therefore maintain a higher quality of life. However, aerobic exercise may not be enough. The American College of Sports Medicine now recommends regular resistance exercise be included in the average adult's exercise regimen with the specific purpose of maintaining muscle mass and bone mineral content over the life span. The health benefits of aerobic exercise are summarized in Table 4-1.

Table 4-1. Selected Health Benefits of Aerobic Exercise

- Increased longevity (life expectancy)
- Reduced risk of premature heart attack and stroke
- Lower resting arterial blood pressure
- Improved blood lipid profile
    Decreased total serum cholesterol
    Increased HDL cholesterol
- Decreased body weight and body fat
- Modest improvement in bone density
- Improved control of blood glucose
- Improved psychological and social well-being

Interval Training

Aerobic training can be done either continuously or intermittently. When training for prolonged activities longer than 45 to 60 minutes in duration, such as the marathon or triathalon, continuous aerobic exercise can be used almost exclusively. Training for activities of shorter duration, however, should also include some higher intensity, interval training. Such activities might include running a 5 or 10K race, competing in a mini-triathalon or competing in an aerobic competition. All of these types of activities require a high degree of aerobic power that is maximally developed only by the addition of interval training.

Interval training generally refers to any type of training that is intermittent or discontinuous in nature. It consists of a bout of exercise of varying duration and intensity interspersed with varying periods of recovery. Interval training is not necessary for the non-athletic population, because most of the beneficial effects of exercise can be achieved with continuous aerobic exercise alone. Some subjects may still use interval training, however, to help minimize the boredom associated with long, continuous exercise. But then again, what some consider boring, others may find an enjoyable experience and a good way to relax and relieve stress.

If the interval training is being done simply as an alternative to continuous exercise and not to improve performance, there is no reason to highly structure the intervals. The subject runs, or swims, or cycles, or performs harder for two to five minutes until the exercise becomes stressful, then reduces the intensity for several minutes to allow a sufficient recovery. The recovery periods should be of a duration equivalent to the exercise interval. These intervals of alternating exercise intensity are continued for the same duration as discussed previously (15-60 minutes).

See chapter on "Internal Training" for specific exercise class models

In preparation for competition, interval training is used to maximize aerobic power, and when done at higher intensity, to increase aerobic endurance and anaerobic power. Interval training to improve performance is done with relatively long exercise intervals, lasting anywhere from a minimum of about two to three minutes to a maximum of four to five minutes. It should be done two to three times per week during the time leading up to the competition as a supplement to aerobic or distance training, rather than as a substitute or alternative form of training. Appropriate training intervals for events such as 5 and 10 kilometer runs include repeated runs of 800-1500 meters (about 1/2 to one mile), with a total distance per workout of around five-seven kilometers (three-five miles). Some general interval training guidelines for improving aerobic power are provided in Table 4-2.

Table 4-2. General Interval Training Guidelines

Intensity (%HRrange)	Number of intervals	Exercise duration (min:sec)	Recovery duration (min:sec)	% Contribution by aerobic system	anaerobic systems
80-85%	3-5	4:00-5:00	2:00-5:00	75-85%	15-25%
85-90%	6-8	2:00-3:00	1:00-5:00	50-60%	40-50%
*90-95%	10-20	0:30-1:30	1:00-3:00	20-25%	75-80%

* Results in more significant changes in anaerobic energy systems.

Adaptations that Improve Exercise Performance

Numerous adaptations occur in the heart, lungs and skeletal muscle that enhance the delivery of oxygen, speed the removal of carbon dioxide and thereby improve aerobic exercise performance. A laboratory assessment of the elite aerobic athlete demonstrates clearly that many physiological variables are significantly improved as a result of regular, continued aerobic training.

Increased Maximal Blood Flow

As discussed earlier, performing aerobic exercise forces the left ventricle to pump large volumes of blood which gradually causes an enlargement of the chamber. The heart, thus, pumps more blood each beat, or in other words increases stroke volume. The maximal stroke volume attained during exercise is increased as well, which increases maximal cardiac output, and therefore the maximal heart rate may actually decline somewhat with training. The increased stroke volume more than compensates, however, for the lower maximal heart rates.

Increased Oxygen Delivery and Carbon Dioxide Removal

While maximal heart rate frequently declines with training, the opposite is true of maximal breathing rate. Maximal breathing rates in trained aerobic athletes reach 45-55 breaths/minute compared to 40-45 breaths/minute in non-athletes. In combination with a larger tidal volume (the volume of air exhaled per breath) the increased maximal breathing rates allow trained athletes to possess pulmonary ventilation during maximal aerobic exercise. The cardiorespiratory system saturates blood coming through the lungs very efficiently. In fact, the blood fully saturates with oxygen in less than one second. The high pulmonary ventilation appears to assist more with the removal of carbon dioxide during exercise. If carbon dioxide is not removed, the acidity of the muscle increases which reduces the muscle's ability to contract. Trained aerobic athletes, by possessing very high maximal pulmonary ventilation, are able to remove carbon dioxide at a higher rate, thereby better maintaining appropriate acid/base balance.

Increased Maximal Oxygen Uptake and Aerobic Power

The adaptations that occur in trained skeletal muscle consist of two types: first, structural and functional changes that allow increased blood flow; and second, biochemical changes that increase the capacity and power of the aerobic system. These changes, observed with aerobic training, usually occur more frequently in slow-twitch muscle fibers than in fast-twitch muscle fibers.

Maximal blood flow during exercise in trained skeletal muscle is determined by the extent to which the vascular system or blood vessels have developed in that particular muscle. Regular aerobic exercise causes an increase in the number of capillaries per muscle fiber. Highly trained endurance athletes may possess 30% more capillaries per muscle fiber than untrained subjects. The increased vascularization provides a richer supply of oxygen and nutrients, removes carbon dioxide and other wastes more rapidly, and therefore allows a higher maximal rate of aerobic energy production. The higher maximal cardiac outputs in trained athletes are also due in part to the increases in total blood volume observed, which are approximately 20-25%.

The capacity and power of the aerobic system are increased by many biochemical changes resulting from regular, continuous aerobic training. Significant increases, as much as 50-100% or higher, in both carbohydrate (glycogen) and fat (triglyceride) storage in skeletal muscle have been observed. The increased fuel storage increases the total capacity of the system. Aerobic power increases primarily through an increase in mitochondrial volume and activity. The mitochondrial adaptations translate into a significant increase in many key enzymes associated with aerobic metabolism. The concentration and activity of all of the enzymes associated with fat oxidation, the Krebs cycle and electron transport are augmented by as much as 100% in comparison to untrained subjects. These adaptations are reflected in the superior maximal oxygen uptakes observed in elite aerobic athletes along with other related physiological variables (Table 4-3).

Table 4-3. Values for Untrained Subjects, Trained Subjects, and Elite Athletes Demonstrating the Adaptations to Aerobic Training.

Variable (units)	Untrained M / F	Trained M / F	Elite M / F
Max cardiac output (1/min)	24 / 20	27 / 21	38 / 30
Max pulmonary ventilation (1/min)	120 / 96	135 / 108	193 / 154
Max oxygen uptake (1/min)	3.2 / 2.3	3.9 / 2.9	5.3 / 4.0
Max oxygen uptake (ml/kg/min)	45 / 40	55 / 50	75 / 70

M: Male subjects; F: Female subjects

Summary

Those individuals who maintain a regular program of aerobic exercise and physical activity derive significant physical, physiological, and psychological benefits. When accomplished with sufficient regularity, exercise of even a relatively low intensity can promote health benefits and enhance wellness. Exercise performed at a higher intensity not only provides health benefits but can lead to structural adaptations in the body which can, in turn, result in improved aerobic exercise performance.

To maximize the benefits and enjoyment of exercise, it is recommended that many different types of exercise be used, including aerobics, walking, running, cycling, swimming and more.

References

Bowers, R.W., & Fox, E.L. (1992). *Sports physiology,* 3rd ed. Dubuque, IA: Wm. C. Brown Publishers.

Fisher, A.C., & Jensen, C.R. (1990). *Scientific basis of athletic conditioning,* 3rd ed. Philadelphia: Lea & Febiger.

Hockey, R.V. (1993). *Physical fitness: pathway to healthful living,* 7th ed. St. Louis, The C.V. Mosby Company.

Wilmore, J.H., & Costill, D.L. (1990). *Training for sport and activity: the physiological basis of the conditioning process,* 3rd ed. Dubuque, IA: Wm. C. Brown Publishers.

CHECKLIST

The Comprehensive Impact of Exercise

Cardiorespiratory

Increases
Circulation
Aerobic capacity
VO_2 maximum
Stroke volume
Cardiac output
Oxygen transport
Blood distribution
Lung capacity
Good cholesterol (HDL)

Decreases
Heart disease risk
Resting HR
Blood pressure
Bad cholesterol (LDL)

Musculoskeletal

Increases
Bone density
Lean muscle tissue
Functional strength
Functional endurance
Joint stability
Functional abilities of ligaments
Functional abilities of tendons
Resting length of muscles
Range of motion
Joint integrity

Decreases
Risk for injuries
Postural problems
Risk for osteoporosis
Inflexibility
Muscle/joint soreness
Body fat percentage

Neuromuscular

Increases
Reaction speed
Sensory awareness
Coordination and balance

Metabolic/Neuroendocrine

Increases
Basal metabolic rate
Balanced blood glucose levels
Number of mitochondria in cells

Decreases
Body fat
Need for insulin

Psychoemotional

Increases
Self-esteem
Self-confidence
Mental alertness
Enhances sleep
Sexual health
Relaxation
Stress management

Decreases
Premature aging
Mood swings
Anxiety
PMS symptoms
Effect of chronic stress

Immunological

Increases
Resistance to some illness and disease

Decreases
Risk of cancer

—Troy E. De Mond, MA

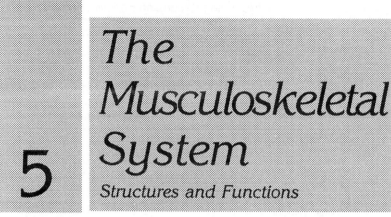

The Musculoskeletal System

5

Structures and Functions

Sharon Cheng, MS, PT

Focus

THIS CHAPTER WILL GIVE a comprehensive overview of the anatomy and kinesiology of the musculoskeletal system as it relates to human exercise. Your applied knowledge of structure and motion is the cornerstone of safe fitness instruction.

Background

Scientists have always been interested in the structure and movement of the human body. The ancient Egyptians are believed to be the first people to study anatomy (Moore, 1985). In the middle of the 4th century B.C., Hippocrates, the "Father of Medicine," continued these studies in Greece. Aristotle (384-322 B.C.), the "Father of Kinesiology," was the first scientist to describe and analyze the actions of muscles (Rasch & Burke, 1974). Galen (131-201 A.D.) is credited with introducing the concept of muscle contractions and terms such as agonist and antagonist muscles. Today, scientists continue to conduct research to learn more about how the human body works. Anatomy looks at the structure and function of the human body while kinesiology addresses human motion by applying information from other sciences such as anatomy, physiology, physics and neurology.

When looking specifically at human motion, it is the musculoskeletal system that allows the body to move through space. Voluntary movements occur when muscles contract and pull on bony levers to cause movement at joints or fulcrums. The skeletal system, composed of bones and cartilage, provides the site of attachment for the muscles. The muscular system refers to the tissue that contracts and moves the bones. To study how voluntary movement occurs, it is necessary to understand both systems.

The Skeletal System

The skeletal system is composed of the bones and cartilage in the body. The basic functions of this system are: 1) to provide a supportive framework for the body, 2) to protect its vital organs, 3) to act as levers in conjunction with muscles to cause movement, 4) to produce red blood cells and 5) to store minerals such as calcium and phosphorus (April, 1984; Moore, 1985; Tortora, 1988).

While bones are often thought of as lifeless, dry objects, they are actually living organs in the body that change as we age. They have an outer shell of compact bone encasing spongy bone which surrounds a medullar cavity (April, 1984; Moore, 1985; Tortora, 1988). The spaces in the spongy bone and the medullar cavity are filled with bone marrow. Red bone marrow is where blood cells are made in a process known as hematopoiesis (Gr. hemato-blood; poiein, to make). As we mature, much of the red marrow is replaced with fatty yellow marrow except in parts of the ribs, skull, sternum and vertebrae (Rausch & Burke, 1974). The red marrow in these areas will continue to produce red blood cells throughout our lifetime. Like other organs of the body, bones also contain blood vessels, lymph vessels and nerves.

To withstand the stresses of ordinary activities, bones must have a combination of elasticity and rigidity. Living bones are about 25-30% water, 60-70% mineral salts and a small percentage of collagen (Rasch & Burke, 1974). The collagen forms most of the organic matrix that provides elasticity and resilience (Guyton, 1986). The inorganic minerals that give bone its hardness and rigidity are primarily composed of calcium and phosphate. If the inorganic materials were removed from a bone, it would keep its basic shape, but it would be so flexible, it could be tied into a knot (Moore, 1985). If all the organic materials were removed, the bone would be brittle and crumble easily. Therefore, the collagen fibers provide tensile strength while the bone salts give compressional strength (Guyton, 1986). Bone strength can vary according to the changes in the amount of organic versus inorganic material as we age (Moore, 1985). The bones of a child have higher amounts of collagen and are slightly more flexible. As we mature, our bones become more rigid due to ossification (hardening) by an increase in salt crystals.

In addition to the changes in the amount of collagen and minerals, bones are constantly being broken down and repaired or remodeled throughout our lifetime. Wolff's Law states that bone increases or decreases its mass to adapt to functional stresses (Komi, 1992; Rausch & Burke, 1974). The continual remodeling allows bones to become thicker and stronger in response to resistive activities (Pollock & Wilmore, 1990; Guyton, 1986). Conversely, the bones will also become weaker and thinner without any stress. If a leg is in a non-weight-bearing cast, the bones could become 30% decalcified in only a few weeks. That is why load-bearing or resistive activities are recommended to help increase bone density (Komi, 1992). However, studies have also shown that if the exercise is excessive, fatigue or stress fractures may develop. The amount of exercise that is considered excessive varies from individual to individual (Komi, 1992).

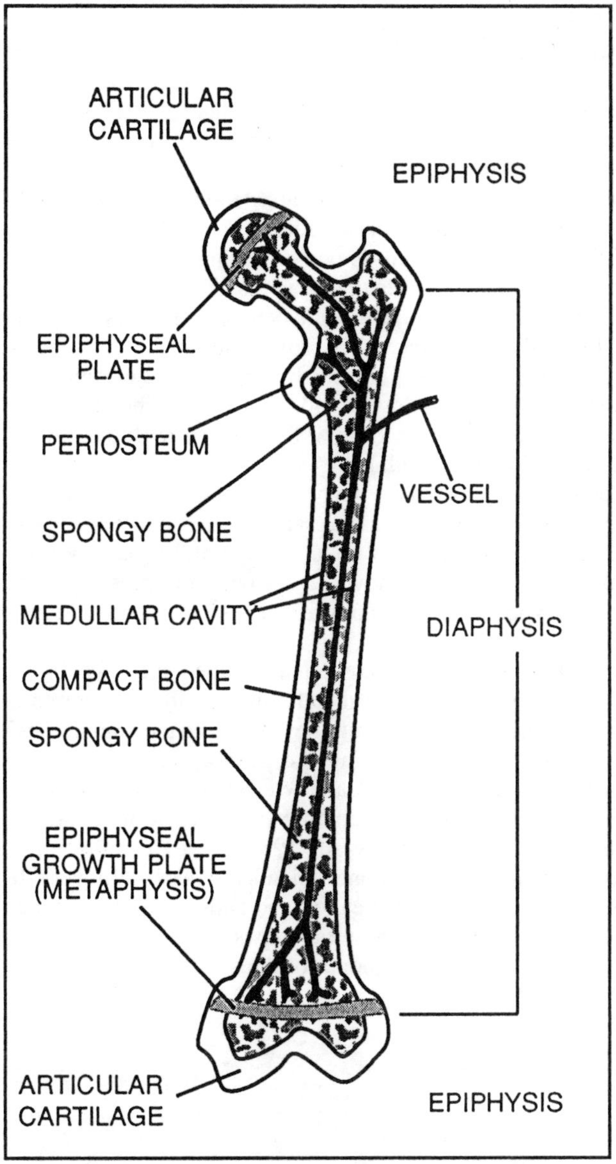

ARTICULAR CARTILAGE

EPIPHYSIS

EPIPHYSEAL PLATE

PERIOSTEUM

SPONGY BONE

VESSEL

MEDULLAR CAVITY

COMPACT BONE

SPONGY BONE

DIAPHYSIS

EPIPHYSEAL GROWTH PLATE (METAPHYSIS)

ARTICULAR CARTILAGE

EPIPHYSIS

Fig. 5-1. Anatomy of the Femur

Bone Replacement

As we age, the rate of bone replacement gradually becomes slower than the rate of breakdown; and our bones become less dense. In severe cases, **osteoporosis** (Gr. osteo-, bone; poros, passage; -osis, disease process) develops where there is a pathological decrease in both the collagen fibers and salt crystals. The osteoporotic bones become brittle, thin and may fracture easily.

Bone Replacement

The basic structure of bone can be studied by looking at the anatomy of a long bone such as the femur (thigh bone) shown in Figure 5-1. The main parts of the femur are the diaphysis (shaft or long portion), the epiphyses (ends of the bone, singular is epiphysis), the metaphysis (area between the diaphysis and epiphysis), the articular cartilage and the periosteum (April, 1984; Moore, 1985; Rausch & Burke, 1974). The articular (L. articulus, joint) cartilage covers the epiphyses (Gr. epi-, upon; phyein, to grow) and reduces the friction at a joint. The **periosteum** (L. peri-, around; L. osteum, bone) is a thin tissue-like covering around the surface of the bone that serves several purposes including serving as the point of attachment for ligaments and tendons. Blood vessels and nerves supplying the bone are in the periosteum.

The **metaphysis** (Gr. meta-, between) is one of the areas that changes as we age. In a child, the metaphysis is cartilaginous and is also referred to as the epiphyseal growth plate. This is the area where the bone lengthens as the child increases in height. Once the bone reaches its adult length, the metaphysis ossifies and connects the diaphysis and epiphysis. If an injury to the epiphyseal plate causes premature fusion of the diaphysis and epiphysis, the bone will not grow to its normal length (Komi, 1992; Moore, 1985; Rausch & Burke, 1974). This is one of the reasons why lifting with heavy weights is not recommended for children whose epiphyseal plates have not yet closed (Fleck & Kraemer, 1987). While the diaphysis and epiphysis fuse at varying rates in different parts of the body, most of the bones are fused by about the age of 20 years (Moore, 1982; Rausch & Burke, 1974). X-rays, however, provide the most accurate method of determining whether or not the epiphyseal plates have closed (Rausch & Burke, 1974).

Epiphyseal Growth Plate

206 Bones

The 206 bones in the human body are often grouped into two broad categories: the axial skeleton (the skull, vertebral column, ribs and sternum) and the appendicular skeleton (the upper extremities including the scapulae and clavicles, and the lower extremities including the pelvic girdle). The **axial skeleton** provides the framework for the trunk and head while the **appendicular skeleton** consists of both arms and legs including the bones which connect these extremities to the axial skeleton (April, 1984; Tortora, 1988). The appendicular skeleton contains trabecular bone which has a faster turnover rate than the cortical bone found in the axial skeleton and ends of the long bones of the appendicular skeleton. Anterior and posterior views of the human skeleton are shown in Figure 5-2A and B while the bones of the axial and appendicular skeleton are listed in Table 5-1.

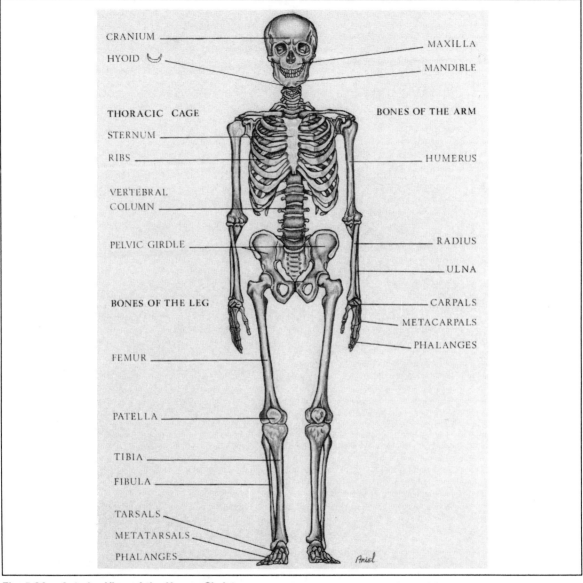

CRANIUM
HYOID
MAXILLA
MANDIBLE
THORACIC CAGE
STERNUM
RIBS
VERTEBRAL
COLUMN
PELVIC GIRDLE
BONES OF THE LEG
FEMUR
PATELLA
TIBIA
FIBULA
TARSALS
METATARSALS
PHALANGES
BONES OF THE ARM
HUMERUS
RADIUS
ULNA
CARPALS
METACARPALS
PHALANGES

Fig. 5-2A.   Anterior View of the Human Skeleton

Joints

Joints are the point at which two or more bones meet or articulate and where movement occurs. There are several different methods of classifying joints, but we will look at two general categories: nonsynovial and synovial (Moore, 1985). Nonsynovial joints are joints where little movement occurs, while synovial joints are freely movable joints.

Nonsynovial joints are classified according to whether they are held together with fibrous connective tissue or cartilage. The fibrous or synarthrodial joints are immovable. Examples of fibrous joints include the joints between

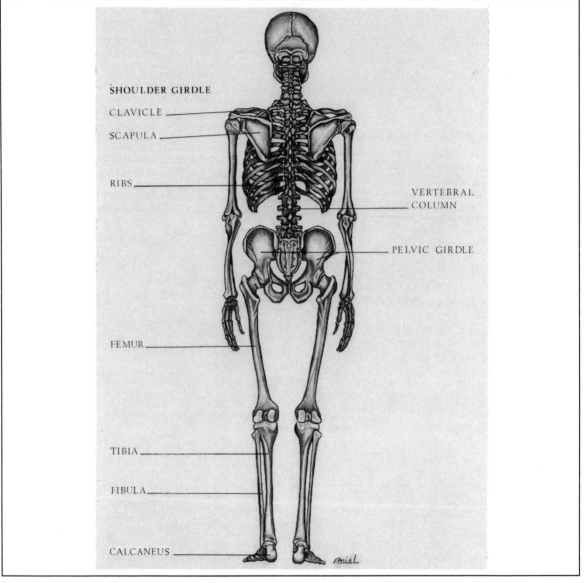

Fig. 5-2B. Posterior View of the Human Skeleton

the bones of the skull and where the teeth fit into the mandible (jaw bone). The cartilagenous or amphiarthrodial joints are slightly movable. The amphiarthrodial joints which are most important to the fitness professional are the intervertebral joints (between the vertebrae). While there is little movement at one intervertebral joint, the vertebral column as a whole has a wide range of motion.

Synovial joints, also known as diarthrodial joints, are the most common type of joint (Moore, 1985). They have a small space between the articulating bones that allows a greater range of motion. Cartilage covers the weight-bearing surface of the bones, and the entire joint is enclosed by a capsule (April, 1984; Hertling & Kessler, 1990; Moore, 1985; Rausch & Burke, 1974).

Table 5-1. Bones of the Human Skeleton

	# of Bones		# of Bones
AXIAL SKELETON	80	APPENDICULAR SKELETON	126
Skull	29	Upper Limb	64
Cranium (brain box)		Pectoral Girdle	
Parietal		Clavicle	
Temporal		Scapula	
Frontal		Arm	
Occipital		Humerus	
Sphenoid		Radius	
Ethmoid		Ulna	
Nasal		Carpal	
Lacrimal		Metacarpal	
Inferior nasal concha		Phalanges	
Vomer			
Face		Lower Limb	62
Zygomatic		Pelvic Girdle	
Palatine		Ischium	
Mandible		Ilium	
Others		Pubis	
Auditory ossicles:		Leg	
malleus		Femur	
incus		Patella	
stapes		Tibia	
		Fibula	
Vertebral Column	26	Tarsal	
Cervical vertebra (7)		Metatarsal	
Thoracic vertebra (12)		Phalanges	
Lumbar vertebra (5)			
Sacral vertebra (5 fused)		TOTAL BONES	206
Coccygeral vertebra (2-4 fused)			
Rib Cage	25		
Rib (24)			
Sternum (3 fused)			

There are six types of synovial joints. Plane joints, such as those found between the carpal (wrist) bones, allow gliding or sliding movements. Ginglymus or hinge joints are found in the interphalangeal joints of the fingers and allow only flexion and extension movements. Pivot joints permit rotation to occur at places such as the atlantoaxial joint where the first cervical (neck) vertebra articulates with the second cervical vertebra. Condyloid or ellipsoidal joints allow flexion, extension, abduction and adduction at joints such as the metacarpophalangeal (knuckle) joints of the hand. Saddle joints, characterized by the carpometacarpal joint of the thumb, allow flexion, extension, abduction and adduction. Spheroidal or ball and socket joints are highly mobile joints found in locations such as the shoulder and hip.

Joint Capsule and Ligaments

The joint capsule has two layers, the outer fibrous layer and the inner synovial membrane (Norkin & Levangie, 1989). The outer fibrous capsule is often reinforced with ligaments. The ligaments, which connect bone to bone, help prevent joint dislocation with the aid of the joint capsule. When injured or sprained due to excessive or continuous stress, ligaments can become permanently elongated. Once the ligaments across a joint are overstretched, the joint becomes less stable. The inner layer of the capsule, the synovial membrane, secretes synovial fluid. This fluid acts as a lubricant for the articulating surfaces and provides nutrients to the avascular (no direct blood supply) cartilage.

Range of Motion

The amount of motion that is available to a specific joint is referred to as the range of motion (ROM). In a healthy joint, the ROM is determined by factors such as the shape of the articular surfaces, musculotendinous connections, ligaments, and the joint capsule (Pollock & Wilmore, 1990). The ROM can be pathological when the range is either greater or less than normal (Norkin & Levangie, 1989; Rausch & Burke, 1974). A hypermobile joint is a joint where the available ROM exceeds normal limits. Conversely, a joint may have less than normal ROM or be hypomobile. This hypomobility may be due to many factors including scar tissue, arthritis, lack of flexibility exercises, or aging. As we grow older, our ligaments and joint capsules which are constantly being remodeled are slowly replaced with less collagen. This leads to decreased flexibility. Either hypermobility or hypomobility of a joint can lead to injuries at the affected joint or at nearby joints. Because our joints are linked together in series, an altered movement in one joint can lead to altered movement at another joint.

Cartilage

There are two types of cartilage found at joints: fibrocartilage and hyaline cartilage (April, 1984; Norkin & Levangie, 1990). Fibrocartilage is thick and heavy and forms structures such as the menisci at the knees for a better fit of the femur (thigh bone) on the tibia (shin bone). Hyaline or articular cartilage is found on the articular surfaces of mobile joints. Its purpose is to reduce the friction between the bony surfaces and lessen the impact of the applied force that occurs on the articular surfaces during movement. Cartilage is avascular and aneural. Because it has no blood supply of its own, it depends on synovial fluid for nutrition. The synovial fluid can be distributed to the cartilage during full ROM movements. Immobilization or lack of full ROM at a joint decreases the flow of fluid to the cartilage and can lead to degenerative changes. While the hyaline cartilage has no nerve supply, the bone directly beneath it has many nerves. Therefore, with disease processes like chondromalacia (Gr. chondro-, cartilage; malakia, softness) of the articular cartilage of the patella, pain is felt along the posterior surface of the patella since the cartilage has worn away to expose the nerves of the periosteum covering the femur.

Bone and Joint Disorders

ARTHRITIS

There are two basic types of arthritis (Gr. arthro-, joint; -itis, inflammation of): inflammatory arthritis and osteoarthritis (Gr. osteon, bone) (Andreoli, Carpenter, Plum & Smith, 1990; Tortora, 1988). Inflammatory arthritis such as rheumatoid arthritis often attacks synovial joints such as the metacarpophalangeal joints (knuckles). The disease primarily affects the membrane in the joint capsule that releases synovial fluid. The inflammation of the synovial membrane leads to joint tenderness. During this stage, the swelling also limits the available range of motion. In severe cases, joint damage can lead to a permanent decrease in the range of motion at the joint. The disease is relatively rare and primarily affects women of childbearing age. Osteoarthritis is the most commonly found joint disorder and is often described as either a result of trauma or a normal result of aging and "wear and tear" on the joints. The articular cartilage slowly deteriorates while bony overgrowths may also occur within the joint. As the space in the joint cavity decreases, joint movements become more painful and restricted. Studies have shown that by the age of 40, many people have some evidence of "wear and tear" osteoarthritis; and by age 75, almost everyone will have osteoarthritis in at least one joint. People who have injured a joint may develop osteoarthritis at an earlier age.

HERNIATED (SLIPPED) DISC

A common cause of low back pain is a herniated disc (Hertling & Kessler, 1990; Kapandji, 1974; Saunders, 1985; Tortora, 1988). The intervertebral disc, composed of the nucleus pulposus and annulus fibrosus (L. annulus, ring; fibrosus, composed of fibers), does not actually slip out of place. The gel-like center, the nucleus pulposus, may move posteriorly and either break through the annulus fibrosus or cause the fibrocartilage to press on structures such as spinal nerve roots. The pressure can lead to various signs and symptoms including low back pain, decreased sensation or muscle weakness in the lower extremities.

OSTEOPOROSIS

Osteoporosis refers to a condition where the bones have decreased calcium due to a decrease in osteoblastic activity to form new bone (Andreoli, Carpenter, Plum & Smith, 1990; Tortora, 1988). The bones lose enough mineral salts to become more susceptible to fractures. It seems to be more common among middle-aged or elderly white females. Some of the factors that may contribute to osteoporosis include decreased levels of estrogen, calcium deficiency or malabsorption, and inactivity.

SPRAIN AND STRAIN

Sprains refer to an overstretching of ligaments while strains indicate that the damage occurred to a muscle (April, 1984; Tortora, 1988).

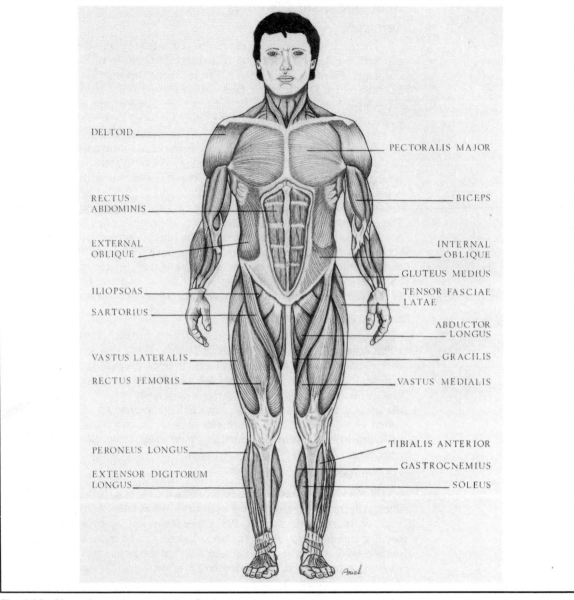

Fig. 5-3A Muscular system—anterior view.

Muscles

There are three types of muscle found in the human body: skeletal, smooth and cardiac muscle (April 1984; Moore, 1985; Tortora, 1988). Skeletal muscle is attached to bone via tendons and allows voluntary movement of the body. Because of its striped or band-like appearance under the microscope, skeletal muscle is also known as striated muscle tissue. Smooth muscle is nonstriated and is found in the walls of organs such as the stomach and intestines. Because it does not require conscious control for a contraction, smooth muscle is also called involuntary muscle.

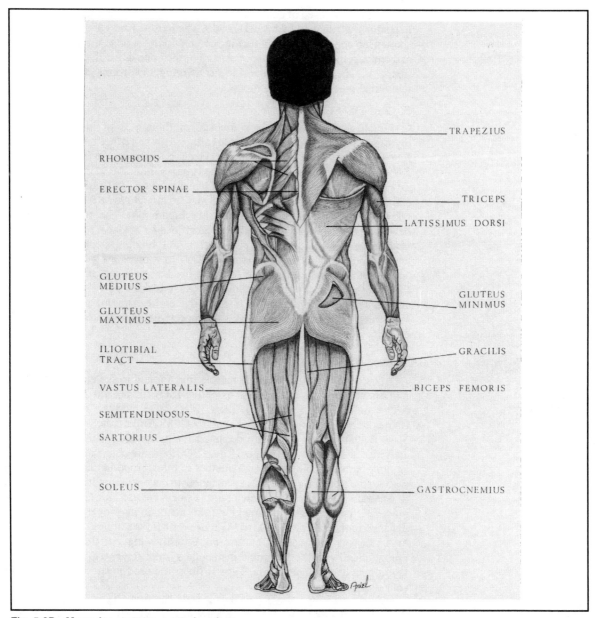

Fig. 5-3B Muscular system—posterior view

Cardiac muscle forms the walls of the heart. While cardiac muscle is striated in appearance, it does not require our conscious thoughts to contract and pump blood through the body.

Skeletal Muscle

Skeletal muscle makes up approximately 44-51% percent of total body weight in men and 35-42% total body weight in women (Komi, 1992; Tortora,

1988). It is composed of contractile tissue including muscle fibers and connects to tendons surrounded by fascial sheaths. The muscle fibers are the portion that shorten or contract during muscular contraction. Tendons are noncontractile and connect the muscle to the periosteum of the bone or cartilage by Sharpey's fibers. Fascia is the thin, translucent covering that forms a sheath for an individual muscle or muscle group.

SLIDING FILAMENT THEORY

Each skeletal muscle is composed of thousands of muscle fibers or myofibers (Gr. myo-, muscle). The myofibers can be further broken down into functional units known as sarcomeres (Fleck & Kraemer, 1987; Guyton, 1986; Komi, 1992; McArdle, Katch & Katch, 1986). Within the sarcomere are thick myofilaments, myosin, and thin myofilaments, actin. According to Huxley's sliding filament theory, these myofilaments are thought to be the structures that allow a muscle to contract or shorten (See Figure 5-4). The myosin filaments have tiny crossbridges with a swivel head located at one end. These swivel heads have both an actin-binding site and an ATP-binding site. During a muscle contraction, the myosin head attaches itself to a myosin-binding site on the actin. With the energy from the ATP, the head swivels and draws the actin in toward the center of the sarcomere. As multiple myosin crossbridges simultaneously pull the actin inward, the entire sarcomere shortens. The shortening of the sarcomeres causes the muscle fibers to shorten and a muscle contraction occurs.

Types of Muscle Fiber

There are two basic types of muscle fibers found in skeletal muscle. Type I fibers are slow twitch or slow oxidative (SO) fibers, and Type II are fast twitch or fast glycolytic (FG) fibers (Fleck & Kraemer, 1987; Groves & Camaione, 1975; Guyton, 1986; Komi, 1992; McArdle, Katch & Katch, 1986). Slow twitch muscle fibers are designed for prolonged, submaximal aerobic activities and are slow to fatigue. These SO fibers are characterized by a large amount of myoglobin and a high number of mitochrondria that give a reddish color to the fibers. Aerobic energy metabolism occurs within the mitochrondria to generate ATP. The slow twitch muscle fibers are used for long-term, low to moderate intensity activities ranging from maintaining proper posture to long distance running. Fast twitch or FG muscle fibers are able to generate quick, high intensity contractions but are more easily fatigued. Because they rely predominantly on the anaerobic metabolic system for energy, they have less myoglobin and mitochrondria. Type II fibers are used in short spurt activities such as sprinting.

In humans, there appear to be several variations of the Type II fibers. Type IIa fibers have the capacity to use both aerobic and anaerobic energy systems and are known as fast-oxidative-glycolytic or FOG fibers. Type IIb fibers are the FG fibers previously described. Type IIc fibers are rare, undifferentiated fibers. Some research indicates that fibers may be able to change from one type to another as an adaptation to aerobic or anaerobic training (Komi, 1992; McArdle, Katch & Katch, 1986). Therefore, with aerobic training, there may be an increase in Type I fibers; and with anaerobic training there may be an increase in Type II fibers. Among elite competitors, endurance athletes have a high percentage of slow twitch muscle fibers while the groups trained for anaerobic-type sports

| Slow Twitch |

| Fast Twitch |

exhibit more fast twitch fibers. What remains unclear, however, is how much was genetically predetermined, how much is due to increased efficiency of the original fibers from specific training, and how much is due to fiber transformation.

Muscle Innervation

The stimulus for a muscle contraction comes from a specialized nerve cell or motor neuron. Each motor neuron can transmit signals to a number of myofibers. One motor neuron and all the myofibers that it stimulates are called a motor unit (Brunnstrom, 1972; Fleck & Kraemer, 1987; Guyton, 1986; Komi, 1992; McArdle, Katch & Katch, 1986). In areas needing fine motor control such as the eye, a motoneuron may only connect with 5-10 muscle fibers. In larger muscles that require greater contractions, a single motor unit may have as many as 500 myofibers. Each motor unit follows the all-or-none principle. When the motoneuron is stimulated, all the muscle fibers in the unit will fire simultaneously. A contraction of only a portion of the fibers in an individual motor unit is not possible. However, to allow for smooth muscle contractions and to avoid fatigue, all the motor units in a muscle will not contract at the same time.

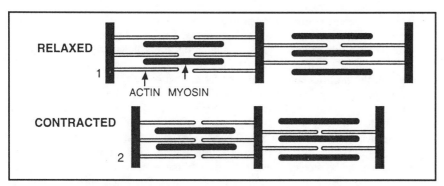

Fig. 5-4. Sliding Filament Theory

Recruitment refers to the number of motor units that are stimulated for a specific muscular response. The firing of the motoneurons will alternate to allow some motor units to contract while others relax (Guyton, 1986; Tortora, 1988). This system of recruitment allows the muscle to sustain a contraction for a longer period of time before fatigue sets in. It is also thought to contribute to muscle tone, where a muscle stays in partial contraction. In activities requiring power, where a high degree of force needs to be generated quickly, more motor units are fired simultaneously. However, since more of the units are being stimulated at any one time, fatigue will occur more quickly.

In a voluntary contraction, the brain sends a signal down through the spinal cord to the motoneurons to stimulate the appropriate motor units. According to the "size principle," the order of motor recruitment is usually from small to large (Fleck & Kraemer, 1987; Guyton, 1986; Komi, 1992). Therefore, the smallest motor units are normally recruited first. To recruit more motor units, it is necessary to increase the workload of the targeted muscles. When a muscle is overloaded or fatigued, assistor muscles will be recruited to help accomplish the task.

Proprioceptors

Proprioceptors in the muscle and tendon sense the degree of tension and the length of the muscle (Fleck & Kraemer, 1987; Guyton, 1986; Komi, 1992; McArdle, Katch & Katch, 1986; Rosse & Clawson, 1980). The muscle spindle, the proprioceptive receptor that attaches to the sheaths of the surrounding muscle fibers, is parallel with the muscle. It sends afferent information to the brain about changes in muscle length and the speed at which the changes are occurring. When stimulated, the muscle spindles relay a message to the spinal cord to cause a contraction in the same muscle. The afferent or sensory neurons in the muscle spindle communicate with the motoneurons of the target muscle through interneurons in the spinal cord without requiring any conscious thought. This spinal reflex is known as the stretch reflex (Grove & Camaione, 1975; Guyton, 1986). When ballistic movements are used, the muscle spindles will sense the quick changes in muscle length and cause a muscular contraction. A physician checks the spinal reflex of the quadriceps by tapping on the patellar tendon to cause the knee to extend (Bates, 1983; Moore, 1985). Physical therapists use the stretch reflex to stimulate a muscle contraction when the patient is too weak to complete the movement (Sullivan, Markos, & Minor, 1982).

The **golgi tendon organ**, located in the tendon, is described as being in series with the muscle fibers (Guyton, 1986; McArdle, Katch & Katch, 1986). This proprioceptor protects the muscle from excessive contractions or stretches. It senses tension caused by muscular contraction or extreme stretching. When stimulated by excessive tension or stretching, the golgi tendon organ inhibits contraction of the muscle from which it originates. This reflex inhibition is used in the proprioceptive neuromuscular (PNF) stretching technique known as hold-relax (Fleck & Kraemer, 1987; Pollock & Wilmore, 1990; Sullivan, Markos & Minor, 1982). With this PNF technique, the tight muscle is put on a light to moderate stretch. The client is asked to contract the target muscle isometrically for a few seconds. He or she is then asked to relax and to further stretch the target muscle by contracting the opposing muscle group. This technique can be repeated several times until there are no further gains in range of motion or the client experiences any discomfort. To avoid injuring the muscle, all the movements should be done by the client without any additional resistance from external sources such as a fitness instructor. When done properly, the muscle will relax and increase its length due to the reflex inhibition from the golgi tendon organ of the target muscle.

| Muscle Spindles |

| PNF Stretching |

Types of Muscle Contractions

The three types of muscle contractions are: 1) isometric, 2) isotonic and 3) isokinetic (Brunnstrom, 1972; Fleck & Kraemer, 1987; Norkin & Levangie, 1989; McArdle, Katch & Katch, 1986; Tortora, 1988). In an **isometric** (Gr. isos-, equal; metron, measure) contraction, no joint movement occurs. In physics, work is defined as force times distance. By this definition, no work is done because the bony lever has not been moved any distance. However, energy is expended and calories are burned to maintain the contraction. When using isometric contractions for strengthening, it is important to remember that the muscle will only be strengthened at the specific joint angle used in the exercise. To strengthen a muscle throughout its entire range, it will be necessary to do exercises throughout the full range of motion. Isometric contractions have also been found to increase blood pressure.

Isotonic contractions can be divided into concentric and eccentric work. In a concentric contraction, the muscle fibers are shortening and positive work is done against gravity or an external resistance. An eccentric contraction, or negative work, occurs when the muscle fibers lengthen and the bony levers move into the direction of gravity. Similar strength gains throughout the range of motion can be achieved with either concentric or eccentric exercises (Fleck & Kraemer, 1987). The difference is the amount of energy expended to perform the action. Eccentric contractions require the least amount of energy, isometric contractions use a moderate amount of energy and concentric contractions require the most energy. Eccentric contractions also appear to be associated with delayed onset muscle soreness. Newcomers to step or high impact aerobic classes sometimes experience delayed onset muscle soreness of the gastrocnemius and soleus. The soreness in their calves can be due to the repeated eccentric contractions of the gastrocnemius and soleus as the heel is lowered to the floor.

Isokinetic contractions cannot be done without the use of specialized equipment. Due to the changing resistance of gravity and the ability of the muscle to contract, certain portions of a full range of motion contraction are harder to perform than others. When working with free weights, the most difficult portion is often where a spotter is needed to assist with the exercise. Isokinetic equipment is designed to vary the resistance so that the speed of the movement is constant. Therefore where a person would normally require a spotter with free weights, the isokinetic equipment makes the exercise easier to complete.

Levers

When looking at the forces required to perform a joint action, it is necessary to understand the three basic types of levers (April, 1984; Brunnstrom, 1972; Norkin & Levangie, 1989). Levers are rigid rods that move about a fulcrum or pivot point. Acting on the lever are two different types of forces—resistance and effort. In the human body, the levers are the bones, the fulcrum is the joint, the effort force comes from the muscle and the resistance force comes from gravity. The resistance force may also be increased with the use of training aids such as weights or elastic bands.

The three types of levers are first-class, second-class and third-class (See Figure 5.5A). They are classified according to the placement of the fulcrum, the effort or applied force and the resistance force on the lever. A **first-class lever** occurs when the fulcrum is in between the applied force and the resistance. The classic example of a first-class lever is the see-saw. A **second-class lever** is when the fulcrum or axis is at one end of the lever, resistance is in the middle and the effort force is at the opposite end. The wheelbarrow is an example of a second-class lever. A **third-class lever** also has the axis at one end, but now the

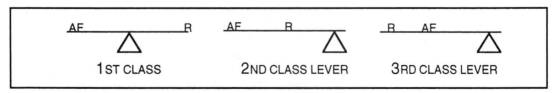

Fig. 5-5A. First-, Second-, and Third-Class Lever Systems

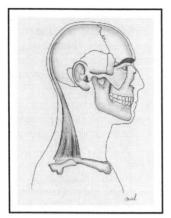

Fig. 5-5B First-class lever at skull and first cervical vertebra

applied force is in the middle and the resistance is at the end. Using a hammer to drive a nail into a piece of wood is an example of a third-class lever.

In addition to looking at the placement of the fulcrum, applied force and resistance force, it is also important to understand the concept of mechanical advantage (April, 1984; Brunnstrom, 1972; Guyton, 1986; Norkin & Levangie, 1989). The perpendicular distance from the pivot point to the line of action of the resistive force is known as the resistance arm. The effort or force arm would be the perpendicular distance from the fulcrum to the point of application of the applied force. Mechanical advantage refers to the relationship between the length of the effort arm and the length of the resistance arm. The equation for this relationship is Mechanical Advantage = Force arm ÷ Resistance Arm.

As the length of the force arm increases, or as the resistance arm decreases, the mechanical advantage increases. In other words, the ease with which a task can be accomplished increases as the length of the force arm increases. Conversely, more muscular force is required if the force arm is shorter than the resistance arm. The patella, located in the quadriceps tendon, lengthens the force arm of the quadriceps muscle to increase the effectiveness of the muscle (See Fig. 5-6).

In a first-class lever, either the resistive force or the applied force may have the mechanical advantage depending on the exact placement of all three items. The force arm will always be longer in a second-class lever while the resistance arm will always be longer in a third-class lever. Gravity will always have a mechanical advantage in a third-class lever system. However, it is possible to achieve a greater range of motion at a faster speed at the distal end of a third-class lever system.

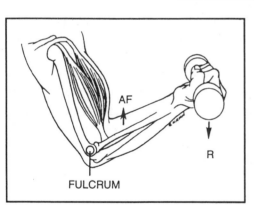

Fig. 5-5C Typical third-class lever system

There are few examples of first- and second-class levers in the human body. Experts in biomechanics disagree in the exact number and examples of first- and second-class levers in the human body. The atlanto- occipital joint, where the skull articulates with the first cervical vertebra, is an example of a first-class lever shown in Figure 5-5B. The weight of the skull pulls the head forward while neck extensors, such as the trapezius, extend the head to keep it balanced on the vertebral column. In a full-body push-up, the entire body acts as a second-class lever. The toes are the axis, the rigid body is the lever, gravity is the resistive force and the arms supply the effort force. While there is general discussion about the clearest examples of first- and second-class levers in the human body, it is agreed that most of the musculoskeletal system is composed of third-class levers. While it requires more muscle force to move the body in a third-class lever system, it allows for greater speed and range of motion (Fig. 5-5C).

When describing motions of the human body, it is common to assume that the movements are initiated with the body starting in anatomical position. **Anatomical position** is "standing erect with the head, eyes and toes directed forward, the heels and toes together, and the upper limbs hanging by the sides with the palms facing anteriorly" (April, 1984; Moore, 1985). Motions are also named by the movement occurring at the joint rather than the segment that is moving. Therefore, "flexing the elbow" is more accurate than "bending the arm." Movements may be further described by the planes in which they occur.

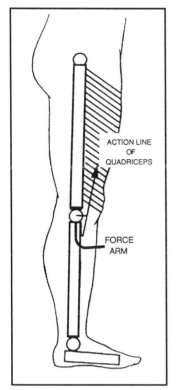

ACTION LINE
OF
QUADRICEPS

FORCE
ARM

FIG. 5-6. Action line

Figure 5-7 illustrates the **three cardinal planes: sagittal, frontal and horizontal** (or **transverse**). Table 5-2. indicates the joint, possible movements and the planes in which the movements occur.

A muscle has at least two points of attachment on the skeleton. The most **proximal** (nearest to the center of the body) attachment is called the origin, and the more **distal** (L. distans, distant) attachment is referred to as the insertion. Conventionally, a muscle is said to bring the insertion closer to the origin during a concentric contraction. This is because the insertion is often on the most movable bone while the origin is located on the most stable bone. However, when muscle fibers contract, they simply shorten the distance between the ends of the sarcomeres (Grove & Camaione, 1975). The least stable end of the joint will move toward the most stable end. In the arm, it is then easy to see how the insertion of the biceps on the radius (bone in the forearm) comes closer to its origin on the scapula during a biceps curl. However, in a pull-up, because the hands are fixed on an immovable bar, the rest of the body actually moves toward the insertion. Therefore, some fitness professionals will use the terms proximal and distal attachments rather than origin and insertion (April, 1984; Moore, 1985).

A straight line drawn between the centers of the proximal and distal attachments will indicate the direction of the muscle's line of pull or line of action. The power that a muscle can generate is partially dependent on its line of pull (April, 1984). Muscles with parallel fibers (fusiform muscles), such as the rectus femoris portion of the quadriceps, can lift a weight through a long distance at great speed (See Figs. 5-8A and 5-8B).

Some muscles have fibers that run obliquely to the long axis of the muscle. Because of their resemblance to a feather, they are called pennate (L. penna, feather) muscles. **Pennate** muscles may be unipennate, bipennate or multipennate such as the deltoid. The advantage of pennate muscles is that they can contract with greater force than fusiform muscles, but at the expense of speed (Groves & Camaione, 1975).

Muscles work together to accomplish a task. The muscle(s) performing the work are called **agonists** or primary movers. **Assistors** are muscles that help perform the same task. Stabilizers help prevent undesired or unnecessary motions. The muscle opposing the agonist is known as the **antagonist.** Because it has an action directly opposite to primary mover, the antagonist must relax and elongate to allow the agonist to move the joint. This occurs due to a spinal reflex known as reciprocal innervation (Rosse & Clawson, 1980). In a bicep curl, during elbow flexion, the brachialis, biceps brachii and brachioradialis are the agonists. The triceps must relax during elbow flexion since it is the antagonist. There is some disagreement among fitness professionals about the use of the word **synergist.** Some people use the word synergist to describe assistor muscles (Brunnstrom, 1976). Others

Table 5-2. Joints, Possible Movements and Planes

Joint	Movement	Plane
Vertebral Column	Flexion-Extension	Frontal
	Lateral Flexion	Sagittal
	Rotation	Horizontal
Shoulder	Flexion-Extension	Sagittal
	Abduction-Adduction	Frontal
	Inward-Outward Rotation	Sagittal
	Horizontal Flexion-Extension	Horizontal
Elbow	Flexion-Extension	Sagittal
Radioulnar	Pronation-Supination	Horizontal
Wrist	Flexion-Extension	Sagittal
Hip	Flexion-Extension	Sagittal
	Abduction-Adduction	Frontal
	Inward-Outward Rotation	Sagittal
Knee	Flexion-Extension	Sagittal
	Inward-Outward Rotation	Horizontal
	(when knee is flexed at 90 degrees)	
Ankle	Dorsi-Plantar flexion	Sagittal

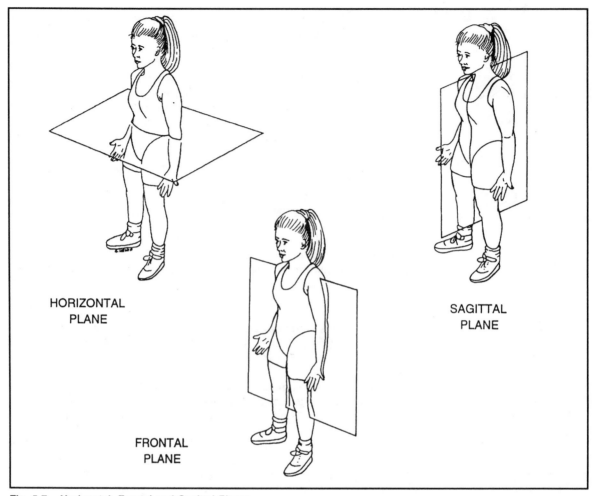

HORIZONTAL
PLANE

SAGITTAL
PLANE

FRONTAL
PLANE

Fig. 5-7. Horizontal, Frontal and Sagittal Planes

describe synergists as muscles that complement the action of the primary mover by preventing unnecessary movements (Tortora, 1988). For example, the anconeus prevents excessive supination by the biceps brachii as the elbow flexes. Fixator or stabilizer muscles steady the proximal joints to allow movement at distal joints (Moore, 1985). The deltoid is a fixator muscle that helps stabilize the humeral head during fine motor activities such as writing.

The amount of tension that a muscle can develop is affected by its length. The optimal length for creating tension is close to the muscle's resting length (Brunnstrom, 1972; Groves & Camaione, 1975; Komi, 1992). At this stage the actin and myosin filaments are capable of forming the greatest number of crossbridges to shorten the muscle. If the muscle is stretched beyond its normal limit, there is less overlap of the actin and myosin filaments to form crossbridges. When the muscle is in its shortened position, the crossbridges have already

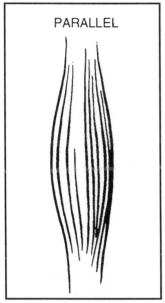

Fig. 5-8A Shapes of Muscles

been formed so there are no more available actin and myosin filaments to generate any additional tension.

When a muscle is in a shortened position where it cannot form any additional crossbridges, it is said to be in **active insufficiency** (Brunnstrom, 1972; Norkin & Levangie, 1989). The muscle cannot generate any additional tension because all of the crossbridges have been formed, and there are no additional actin and myosin filaments to slide across each other. Active insufficiency is easily demonstrated with biarticular or two-joint muscles. These muscles cross two or more joints and can cause motion at more than one joint. For example, because the hamstrings cross both the hip joint and the knee joint, they can extend the hip and flex the knee. However, when attempting to perform hamstring curls in the prone position with the hips extended, it is common to see people flex their hips near the end of the range of motion to bring their heels toward their buttocks. This is because their hamstrings are in active insufficiency since the hips are in extension and the knees are in flexion. In order to generate more tension, they flex their hips to allow more crossbridges to be formed to allow for knee flexion. Kreighbaum (1985) recommends strengthening biarticular muscles by shortening them over one joint while stretching them over the other and then vice versa or by shortening the muscles over both articulations at the same time. Table 5-3 shows some biarticular muscles and the joints they cross.

Kinetic Chains

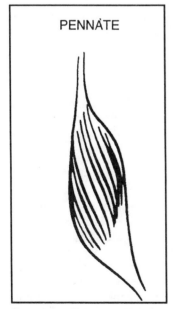

Fig. 5-8B. Shapes of Muscles

In engineering, kinetic (Gr. kinema, motion) chains are a series of rigid links interconnected by a series of pin-centered joints. Motion at one of the links will cause movement at the other joints due to their relationship to each other. In the body, it is possible to have open or closed kinetic chains (Brunnstrom, 1972; Norkin & Levangie, 1989). In an open kinetic chain, the terminal joint is free while it is fixed in a closed kinetic chain. Closed kinetic chains behave like the engineering kinetic chains in that movement at one joint will cause motion in all the related joints. For example, if you keep both feet on the floor and bend your knees, you will also flex at the hips and dorsiflex at the ankles. Because the feet are fixed on the ground, the legs are operating as a closed kinetic chain. If you allow your foot to leave the floor as you bend one knee, no other joint movement has to occur. This is referred to as an open kinetic chain. The concept of closed chain exercises is important because muscles at other joints in the chain can substitute for the target muscle. In a push-up, the triceps extends the elbow and the pectoralis major adducts the humerus to lift the body up against gravity. However, in this position, external rotation at the shoulders will also cause the elbows to extend and lift the body. The ability of the external rotators to assist in a push-up is easily demonstrated by first performing a push-up with both arms in the sagittal plane and the elbows close to the torso and pointed toward the feet throughout the entire exercise. Then, start with both arms in the horizontal plane and the elbows pointed away from the body and bring them in toward the torso as you lift.

The second exercise will be less fatiguing to the triceps because the external rotators have assisted the movement.

Table 5.3 The Biarticulate Muscles and the Articulations They Cross	
Muscle	**Articulations**
Biceps brachii	Shoulder/Elbow
Triceps	Shoulder/Elbow
Rectus Femoris	Hip/Knee
Semitendinosus	Hip/Knee
Semimembranosus	Hip/Knee
Biceps Femoris	Hip/Knee
Sartorius	Hip/Knee
Gastrocnemius	Knee/Ankle

We have now addressed the basic musculoskeletal anatomy and kinesiology of the human body. While a general understanding of how the body moves through space is useful, it is also important to look at specific joints that are used during exercise. A comprehensive look at the major joints of the body is beyond the scope of this book, but we will look at some specific details of the shoulder, the vertebral column, the hip and the knee.

The Shoulder Complex

The shoulder complex is composed of three bones: the clavicle (collarbone), the scapula (shoulder blade) and the humerus (arm bone). These bones, together with the shoulder muscles and connective tissue, perform the complicated task of allowing dynamic stability (Brunnstrom, 1972; Hertling & Kessler, 1990; Norkin & Levangie, 1989; Tortora, 1988). The shoulder complex has a larger range of motion than any other part of the body. At the same time, it has to provide a stable base for the rest of the upper extremity so the hand can perform fine motor skills.

The clavicles and the scapulae form the shoulder or pectoral girdle. The anterior portion of the pectoral girdle is formed by the clavicles while the posterior portion is comprised of the scapulae. The proximal end of a clavicle and the sternum (breast bone) form the sternoclavicular joint. This is the only bony attachment for the upper extremity to the axial skeleton. Muscles secure the shoulder girdle to the rest of the body.

The lateral portion of the scapula forms a small cup-like projection that is called the glenoid fossa (Gr. glene, a socket; L. fossa, trench or ditch). The head of the humerus (arm bone) articulates with the glenoid fossa and forms the glenohumeral joint. As a spheroidal or bail-and-socket joint, the glenohumeral joint provides a great deal of mobility to the upper extremity. However, the scapula can also move to further increase the available range of motion for the upper limb.

While the scapula moves along the thorax (rib cage), it is not a true anatomic joint because it has none of the characteristics of a joint. The movements of the scapula, however, are commonly described as motions of the scapulothoracic joint (Norkin & Levangie, 1989). The motions of the scapula include elevation/depression, abduction/adduction, and upward rotation/downward rotation (See Figs. 5-9A, 5-9B, 5-9C, 5-9D).

The dynamic stability of the shoulder complex can be demonstrated in the motions necessary to change a light bulb in the ceiling. In order to raise the hand over the head, the glenohumeral joint has to flex while the scapula rotates in an upward direction. Once the hand is in position, the muscles of the pectoral girdle have to stabilize the entire shoulder complex so the hand can unscrew the light bulb.

Because most motions of the shoulder complex involve both the scapulothoracic joint and the glenohumeral joint, a complete exercise program should include exercises for muscles that move the scapula and muscles that move the humerus. Table 5-4 shows the major muscles of the pectoral girdle and the glenohumeral joint.

The Vertebral Column

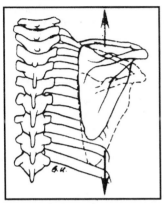

Fig.5-9A Elevation/ Depression

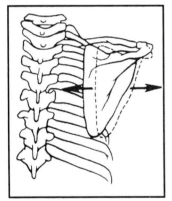

Fig. 5-9B. Adduction / Abduction

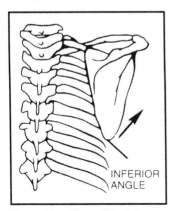

Fig. 5-9C. Upward Rotation

Figure 5-10 shows that the vertebral column is typically composed of 26 vertebrae: 7 cervical (neck), 12 thoracic (where the ribs attach), 5 lumbar (lower back), 5 sacral (fused to form the sacrum) and 4 coccygeal (fused to form the coccyx or tailbone) (Brunnstrom, 1972; Hertling & Kessler, 1990; Norkin & Levangie, 1989; Tortora, 1988). The majority of the vertebra have a body, a spinous process in the back, and transverse processes on either side. Behind the body is an opening or foramen through which the spinal cord passes. The spinal cord conducts **afferent** or sensory messages from the body up to the brain and **efferent** or motor signals down from the brain to various parts of the body. Certain afferent signals trigger specific motor responses in the spinal cord without going to the brain. These automatic responses that do not require our conscious thought are known as spinal reflexes.

Located between adjacent vertebral bodies to form the cartilagenous joints are the **intervertebral discs**. The discs have a soft, gel-like center called the nucleus pulposus surrounded by the annulus fibrosus (L. annulus, ring; fibrosus, composed of fibers). While the nucleus pulposus is usually found in the center of a disc, it is located more posteriorly in the cervical and lumbar regions (Hertling & Kessler, 1990; Kapandji, 1974). While each joint has limited movement, the intervertebral joints together contribute to the motions of the entire spinal column.

Table 5-4. Shoulder Joint and Pectoral Girdle Actions	
Shoulder Joint Actions	**Primary Mover**
Flexion	Deltoid
Extension	Lattissimus dorsi
Abduction	Deltoid, Supraspinatus
Adduction	Latissimus dorsi
Internal Rotation	Subscapularis
External Rotation	lnfraspinatus, Teres minor
Horizontal Adduction	Pectoralis major
Horizontal Abduction	Deltoid
Pectoral Girdle Actions	**Primary Mover**
Elevation	Trapezius, Levator scapulae
Depression	Trapezius
Abduction	Serratus Anterior
Adduction	Trapezius, Rhomboids
Upward Rotation	Trapezius
Downward Rotation	Rhomboids

As a major portion of the axial skeleton, it is important that the vertebral column be properly aligned to protect the spinal cord, to bear the weight of the body and to provide, with the ribs, a framework for the attachment of our internal organs. There are **four distinct curves** in the normal vertebral column. Two of them, the cervical curve and the lumbar curve, are concave posteriorly (open to the back of the body). The thoracic and sacral curves are concave anteriorly. The purpose of these curves is to provide flexibility and shock-absorbing capacity to the spinal column. The spinal curves allow the vertebral column to handle axial compressive loads up to ten times greater than what could be expected from a straight spine (Saunders, 1985). That is why

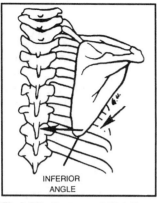

Fig.5-9D Downward Rotation

proper alignment through the trunk is important during all of our regular activities including exercising.

Several structures work together to help maintain proper alignment of the spine. The shape of the vertebral bodies and the intervertebral discs is primarily responsible for the four spinal curves (Hertling & Kessler, 1990). The muscles that can affect the curves of the spine should be balanced in strength and flexibility. Many ligaments also provide stability throughout the length of the vertebral column (See Fig. 5-11).

Along the front of the vertebral bodies is the **anterior longitudinal ligament**, which is considered by some researchers to be the strongest ligament in the body (Hertling & Kessler, 1990). Along with the spinal muscles, the anterior longitudinal ligament limits spinal hyperextension and provides strength to the anterior portion of the intervertebral disc during lifting activities. The posterior longitudinal ligament reinforces the posterior annulus fibrosus

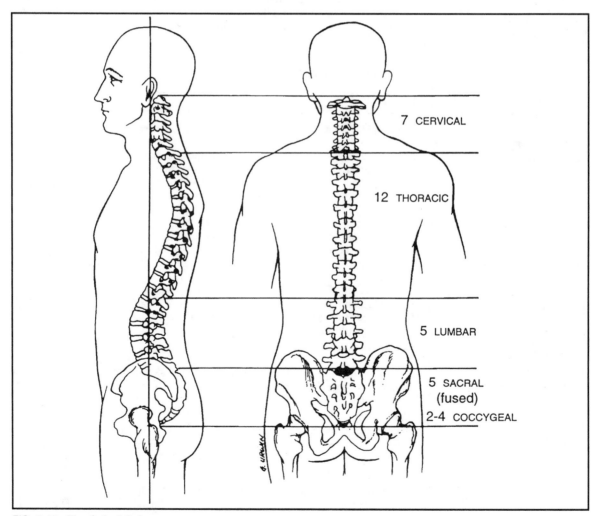

7 CERVICAL

12 THORACIC

5 LUMBAR

5 SACRAL
(fused)

2-4 COCCYGEAL

FIG. 5-10 The Spinal Column

and runs along the back side of the vertebral bodies. However, it is much narrower than the anterior longitudinal ligament and only attaches to the margins of the vertebral bodies to allow the blood vessels and lymph vessels to enter and exit the vertebrae. In the lumbar region, it is often narrowed to a cord-shaped filament and gives reduced support to the intervertebral discs. In the lumbar region, another posterior stabilizing ligament, the interspinous ligament, has been found to be weak or ruptured in 90% of the subjects studied who were over 40 years old (Hertling & Kessler, 1990). The posterior longitudinal ligament, along with other ligaments and spinal muscles such as the erector spinae, limit the degree of forward flexion.

In the United States, some studies have found that 80% of the general population will suffer from back pain (Hertling & Kessler, 1990; Saunders, 1985). **Back pain** is currently the most expensive ailment among people in the 30-60 year-old category. While many disease processes can produce low back pain, the primary causes of low back pain appear to be poor posture, faulty body mechanics, stress, decreased flexibility and poor physical fitness (Saunders, 1985). Examples of poor posture include sitting in a slumped posture, leaning forward while standing, and standing with an excessive lumbar curve. Faulty body mechanics include one of the most common mechanisms for back injuries: bending forward and lifting.

All of these factors do not allow the vertebral column to maintain its natural spinal curves. Therefore the flexibility and strength of the spine is compromised in these situations. While muscle contractions or spasms are commonly associated with low back pain, some professionals do not believe that muscle spasms are the primary cause of the pain (Saunders, 1985). These people believe that the back muscles tighten to prevent further movements that may aggravate the pain. Poor posture and faulty body mechanics can lead to back pain by causing intervertebral disc protrusions or herniations (McKenzie, 1985; Saunders, 1985). Because the nucleus pulposus is a gel-like substance, it can protrude through the annulus fibrosus and irritate the spinal nerves as they exit the vertebral column. The higher incidence of intervertebral disc problems in the lumbar area may be due to the posterior position of the nucleus pulposus and the decreased strength of some of the posterior ligaments in this area. Both of these factors increase the opportunity for an intervertebral disc to bulge or herniate posteriorly. When a disc

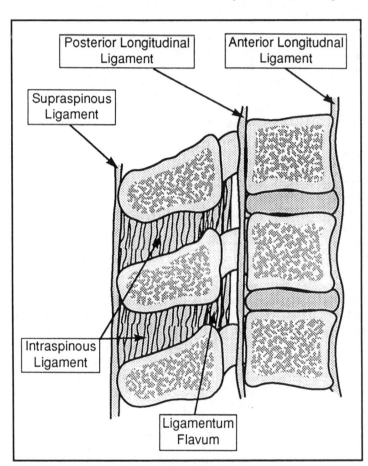

Fig. 5-11 Ligaments of the Vertebral Column

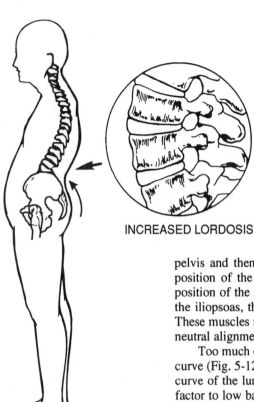

INCREASED LORDOSIS

Fig. 5-12A   Anterior Pelvic Tilt

protrudes posteriorly, it can cause many different signs and symptoms including low back pain if it puts pressure on the spinal cord or spinal nerves in the area.

There is considerable controversy among health professionals about how much muscle weakness contributes to low back pain. Some people feel that the erector spinae as well as abdominal muscles and other spinal muscles should be strengthened, others feel that muscle endurance is more important than strength, and still another group believes that there is not a clear cut relationship between muscle strength and endurance and low back pain (Hertling & Kessler, 1990).

It is also important to look at the other muscles that can affect the lumbar curve. Near the bottom of the vertebral column is the sacrum which is wedged between the two ileum (the posterior portions of the pelvic girdle). It is at this junction, the sacroiliac (SI) joint, that the weight of the head, upper body and trunk is transferred to the pelvis and then the lower extremities. Muscles that can directly change the position of the lumbar spine or indirectly affect the spine by changing the position of the pelvic girdle include the rectus abdominus, the erector spinae, the iliopsoas, the rectus femoris (part of the quadriceps) and the hamstrings. These muscles need adequate strength and flexibility to maintain the pelvis in neutral alignment.

Too much of an anterior tilt of the pelvis will lead to an increased lordotic curve (Fig. 5-12A) while a posterior tilt (Fig. 5-12B) can eliminate the normal curve of the lumbar spine (Fig. 5-12C). Either extreme can be a contributing factor to low back pain. Weak abdominals and hamstrings together with tight erector spinae and iliopsoas can cause an increased lordosis. Tight hamstrings with weak hip flexors and erector spinae can lead to a posterior tilt and lack of a normal lumbar curve. For muscle balancing, the tight muscles should be stretched and the weak muscles should be strengthened. AFAA's Basic Exercise Standards and Guidelines provide several recommendations for strengthening the erector spinae and stabilizing the torso safely and effectively. The recommendations are designed for participants with normal, healthy backs. Instructors may wish to refer people with a predisposition for back problems to a specialist for more specific exercise prescriptions.

Abnormal curvatures of the spine shown in Figure 5-13 include: scoliosis, kyphosis and lordosis (April, 1984; Tortora, 1988). Scoliosis (Gr. skolios, twisted) is the most common of the three conditions and is a lateral bending of the spine. Kyphosis (Gr. kyphos, a hump) refers to an exaggerated curve in the thoracic area. Lordosis (Gr. lordos, bent backward) is an increased concave curve in the lumbar portion of the spine. This condition is often accompanied by an increased anterior tilt of the pelvis.

The Hip

The hip is a spheroidal or ball and socket joint like the glenohumeral joint. the joint is formed where the pelvic girdle meets the femur (thigh bone), (See Figure 5-14.)

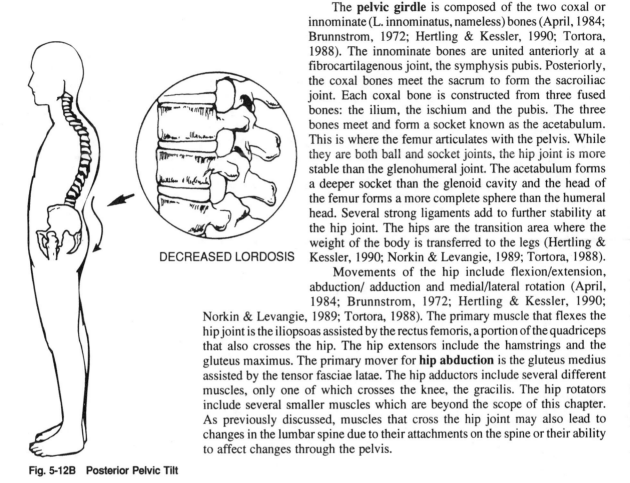

DECREASED LORDOSIS

Fig. 5-12B Posterior Pelvic Tilt

The **pelvic girdle** is composed of the two coxal or innominate (L. innominatus, nameless) bones (April, 1984; Brunnstrom, 1972; Hertling & Kessler, 1990; Tortora, 1988). The innominate bones are united anteriorly at a fibrocartilagenous joint, the symphysis pubis. Posteriorly, the coxal bones meet the sacrum to form the sacroiliac joint. Each coxal bone is constructed from three fused bones: the ilium, the ischium and the pubis. The three bones meet and form a socket known as the acetabulum. This is where the femur articulates with the pelvis. While they are both ball and socket joints, the hip joint is more stable than the glenohumeral joint. The acetabulum forms a deeper socket than the glenoid cavity and the head of the femur forms a more complete sphere than the humeral head. Several strong ligaments add to further stability at the hip joint. The hips are the transition area where the weight of the body is transferred to the legs (Hertling & Kessler, 1990; Norkin & Levangie, 1989; Tortora, 1988).

Movements of the hip include flexion/extension, abduction/ adduction and medial/lateral rotation (April, 1984; Brunnstrom, 1972; Hertling & Kessler, 1990; Norkin & Levangie, 1989; Tortora, 1988). The primary muscle that flexes the hip joint is the iliopsoas assisted by the rectus femoris, a portion of the quadriceps that also crosses the hip. The hip extensors include the hamstrings and the gluteus maximus. The primary mover for **hip abduction** is the gluteus medius assisted by the tensor fasciae latae. The hip adductors include several different muscles, only one of which crosses the knee, the gracilis. The hip rotators include several smaller muscles which are beyond the scope of this chapter. As previously discussed, muscles that cross the hip joint may also lead to changes in the lumbar spine due to their attachments on the spine or their ability to affect changes through the pelvis.

The Knee Complex

The knee has two distinct purposes: to provide stability in activities such as standing and to allow for mobility in movements such as sitting or squatting (Brunnstrom, 1972; Hertling & Kessler, 1990; Norkin & Levangie, 1989). The knee is actually two separate joints, the tibiofemoral joint (where the thigh bone meets the shin bone) and the patellofemoral joint (where the kneecap meets the thigh bone). The fibula, which is the bone at the lateral aspect of the lower leg, is not considered a part of the knee since it is not included in the joint capsule of the knee. Because the femur (thigh bone) and the tibia (shin bone) do not fit together particularly well, they are said to be somewhat incongruent (Hertling & Kessler, 1990). To increase the area of contact between the two bones, on the superior surface of the tibia are the two fibrocartilagenous menisci (Hertling & Kessler, 1990; Komi, 1992; Norkin & Levangie, 1989). Their purpose is to 1) serve as shock absorbers, 2) help lubricate and give nutrition to the knee, 3) decrease the friction and 4) increase the area of contact between the femur and the tibia.

When looking at the leg anteriorly, you can see that the femur and the tibia do not form a straight line. The angle formed by these two bones is known as the **Q-angle** (Fig. 5-15). To measure the angle, two lines should be drawn: 1) from the anterior superior iliac spine of the pelvis to the midpoint of the patella and 2) from the tibial tuberosity to the midpoint of the patella (Norkin & Levangie, 1989). Figure 5-15 shows a normal Q-angle, which is approximately 15 degrees.

Several ligaments and muscles that cross the knee joint also help provide stability (Hertling & Kessler, 1990; Norkin & Levangie, 1989). On either side of the knee are the medial collateral ligament and the lateral collateral ligament. Within the joint are the anterior cruciate ligament and the posterior cruciate ligament. The main muscles crossing the knee joint are the quadriceps anteriorly and the hamstrings posteriorly.

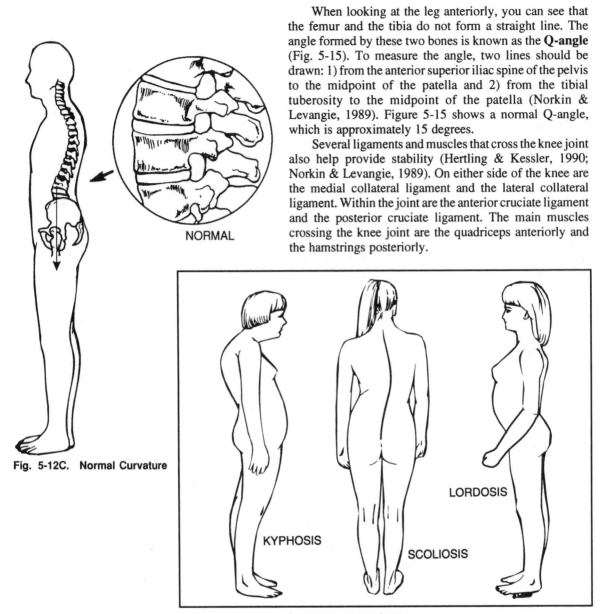

NORMAL

Fig. 5-12C. Normal Curvature

KYPHOSIS

LORDOSIS

SCOLIOSIS

Fig. 5-13. Abnormal Curvatures of the Spine*

*Note: Among some medical professionals, kyphosis and lordosis refer to the normal curvatures found in the vertebral column (Hertling & Kessler, 1990; Kapandji, 1974; Norkin & Levangie, 1989). Curves that open toward the anterior portion of the body are kyphotic curves and are found in the thoracic and sacral areas of the spine. Lordotic curves are concave posteriorly and are located in the cervical and lumbar spine. Abnormal curvatures would be referred to as an exaggerated or increased lordotic or kyphotic curve in a particular area of the spine.

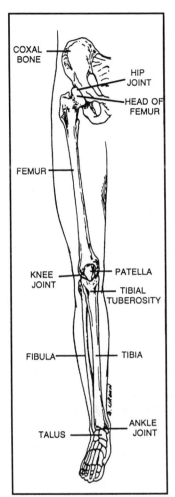

Fig. 5-14. Lower Extremity, (Anterior View)

Labels on figure:
COXAL BONE
HIP JOINT
HEAD OF FEMUR
FEMUR
KNEE JOINT
PATELLA
TIBIAL TUBEROSITY
FIBULA
TIBIA
ANKLE JOINT
TALUS

The **quadriceps** are composed of four muscles: the rectus femoris, vastus lateralis, vastus medialis and vastus intermedius (Brunnstrom, 1972; Moore, 1985; Norkin & Levangie, 1989). The rectus femoris (L. rectus, straight) runs down the front of the thigh and crosses both the hip and knee joints. As a biarticular muscle, the rectus femoris can flex the hip or extend the knee. The three vasti (L. vastus, large) muscles attach to the femur (thigh bone) and form the common quadriceps tendon that attaches at the tibial tuberosity (on the shin bone).

Embedded within the quadriceps tendon is the patella (L. patera, little plate), the body's largest sesamoid bone (Norkin & Levangie, 1989). Sesamoid bones are found in tendons and they serve as a pulley and protect the tendon from excessive wear and tear (April, 1984; Moore, 1985). The main purpose of the patella is to increase the effective strength of the quadriceps by increasing its leverage or mechanical advantage.

The patella fits into the femur along the patellofemoral groove. The vastus lateralis, along with other structures, tends to cause the patella to track laterally during knee extension. A small, oblique portion of the vastus medialis appears to offset the lateral tracking to keep the patella centered in the **patellofemoral groove** (Norkin & Levangie, 1989). A weak vastus medialis oblique can lead to abnormal tracking of the patella in the patellofemoral groove and result in irritation of the lateral aspect of the patella.

The entire quadriceps group is worked in exercise programs that include standing, squatting and stepping. They work concentrically to extend the knee from a squat position or to step up on a bench. They work eccentrically when lowering into a squat or stepping off of a bench. In both cases, they are working in a closed kinetic chain to support the weight of the body against gravity. It is important to balance the strength of the quadriceps with its opposing muscle group, the hamstrings. In an exercise program without additional equipment, it is difficult to strengthen the hamstrings as well as the quadriceps.

All three of the hamstring muscles cross the hip joint and help support the weight of the body against gravity in squats and stepping by concentrically extending the hips in a step up and eccentrically allowing the hips to flex in a squat. However, the short head of the biceps femoris does not cross the hip joint (April, 1984). Because it only crosses the knee joint, it is necessary to perform knee flexion against the pull of gravity to work this portion of the hamstring. Because this will be an open kinetic chain, you will only be lifting the weight of the lower leg against gravity rather than the trunk and upper extremities.

Research indicates that the trunk and upper extremities are about 60% of total body weight while the lower leg is only about 6%. Assuming that in a squat both legs work symmetrically, each quadriceps supports about 45 pounds while in a hamstring curl, the weight lifted is only about nine pounds in an individual weighing 150 pounds (Brunnstrom, 1976; Dempster, 1955). Because of the difference in resistance provided by body weight alone, knee flexion with additional external resistance would help balance the strength of the quadriceps and hamstrings.

Summary

By having a general understanding of anatomy and kinesiology, fitness professionals can plan effective exercise programs for their students and clients. It is easy to see why it is important that opposing muscle groups be balanced in strength and flexibility. Being able to understand how muscles work and the factors that affect their efficiency allow instructors to help design safe and effective muscle strengthening and endurance activities.

References

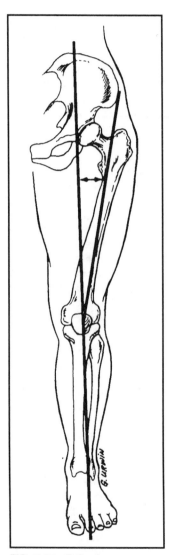

FIG. 5-15   Q-Angle

Andreoli, T.E., Carpenter, C.C., Plum, F., & Smith, L.H. Cecil (1990). *Essentials of medicine* (2nd ed.). Philadelphia, Pa.: W.B. Saunders Co.

April, E.W. (1984). The national medical series for independent study. *Anatomy.* New York: John Wiley and Sons.

Bates, B. (1983). *A guide to physical examination* (3rd ed.). Philadelphia: J.B. Lippincott Co.

Brunnstrom, S. (1972). *Clinical kinesiology* (3rd ed.). Philadelphia: F.A. Davis Company.

Dempster, W.T. (1955). *Space requirements of the seated operator.* WADC Technical Report. Wright-Patterson AFB, Oh.

Fleck, J.F., & Kraemer, W.J. (1987). *Designing resistance training programs.* Champaign, Ill.: Human Kinetics Books.

Guyton, A.C. (1986). *Textbook of medical physiology* (7th ed.). Philadelphia: W. B. Saunders Company.

Hertling, D., & Kessler, R.M. (1990). *Management of common musculoskeletal disorders: physical therapy principles and methods.* (2nd ed.). Philadelphia: J.B. Lippincott.

Kapandji, I.A. *The physiology of the joints: the trunk and the vertebral column* (2nd ed.). New York: Longman Inc.

Komi, P. V. (Ed.) (1992). *Strength and power in sport.* The Encyclopaedia of Sports Medicine, International Olympic Committee. Oxford: Blackwell Scientific Publications.

Kreighbaum, E., and Barthels, K.M. (1985). *Biomechanics, a qualitative approach for studying human movement.* Minneapolis: Burgess Publishing Company.

McArdle, W.D., Katch, F.I., & Katch, V.L. (1986). *Exercise physiology: energy, nutrition, and human performance* (2nd ed.). Philadelphia: Lea & Febiger.

McKenzie, R. (1985). *Treat your own back* (4th ed.). Waikanae, New Zealand: Spinal Publications, Ltd.

Moore, K.L. (1985). *Clinically oriented anatomy* (2nd ed.). Baltimore: Williams and Wilkins.

Moore, K.L. (1982). *The developing human: clinically oriented embryology* (3rd ed.). Philadelphia: W. B. Saunders Company.

Norkin, C., & Levangie, P. (1989). *Joint structure and function: a comprehensive analysis.* Philadelphia: F. A. Davis Company.

Pollock, M.L., & Wilmore, J. H. (1990). *Exercise in health and disease: evaluation and prescription for prevention and rehabilitation* (2nd ed.). Philadelphia: W. B. Saunders Company.

Saunders, H.D. (1985). *Evaluation, treatment and prevention of musculoskeletal disorders.* Minneapolis: Viking Press, Inc.

Steindler, A. (1977). *Kinesiology of the human body under normal and pathological conditions.* Springfield, Ill.: Charles C. Thomas.

Sullivan, P.E., Markos, P.D., & Minor, M.A. (1982). *An integrated approach to therapeutic exercise: theory & clinical application.* Reston, Va.: Prentice-Hall.

Tortora, G.J. (1988). *Introduction to the human body.* New York: Harper & Row, Publishers.

The Cardiopulmonary System

6

Structure, Function and Exercise Application

Patti Mantia, MEd

Focus

THIS SEGMENT EXAMINES THE CARDIOVASCULAR SYSTEM, the pulmonary system, and how they work together to maintain vital processes.

Location and Structure

The heart is a muscular organ located in the chest, or thoracic cavity, diagonally behind the breastbone, or sternum. Shaped and sized similarly to that of a clenched fist, this relatively small organ performs a tremendous amount of work to maintain life processes. Even at rest, the amount of blood pumped by the heart per minute (cardiac output) is an average of five liters.(5)

The structure of the heart allows for an efficient mechanism to perform vital processes. The heart is divided, anatomically and functionally, into right and left sides by a partitioning wall, or septum. The right side of the heart receives deoxygenated blood as it is returned from the body through the venous system and pumps the blood to the lungs, or pulmonary system. The left side of the heart receives the oxygenated blood from the lungs and pumps it, via the arterial system, throughout the body. Because the heart performs two distinct functions, this singular organ is often referred to as a double-pump.

The heart is further broken down into upper and lower chambers called the atria (atrium, singular) and the ventricles, respectively. The superior **atria** (right and left) are the blood receiving units of the heart. The blood is then forced through an efficient one-way system of valves, known as atrioventricular, or AV valves, to the inferior ventricles. The contraction of the **ventricles** forces blood through the semilunar valves and into the great arteries of either the pulmonary or systemic circulation. The familiar "lub-dub" sounds of the heart are produced by the closing of the atrioventricular and semilunar valves.

The heart is entirely contained within a loose yet protective sac, the pericardium, which prevents the beating heart from brushing against the chest wall. The heart itself is composed of three specialized layers of tissue; the epicardium, the myocardium and the endocardium. The epicardium is a thin membrane located on the outermost layer of the heart. The primary work of the heart is performed by the next layer of muscular tissue, the myocardium. The **myocardium** is thickest and strongest in the left ventricle, as the left ventricle is responsible for pumping blood against the resistance of the vessels to the extremities. The coronary arteries are the primary source of nourishment for the epicardium and myocardium, as only the endocardium is enriched by

the blood-filled chambers of the heart. The term myocardial infarction, or heart
attack, refers to a dysfunction of the tissues of the myocardium usually due to
ischemia or a lack of blood flow to the myocardium. The endocardium is a
smooth membrane which lines the cavities within the heart.

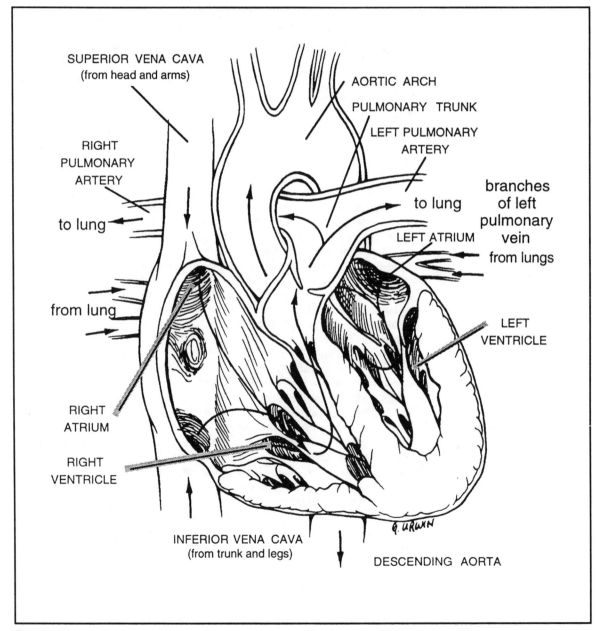

Fig. 6-1. Structure of the heart

Conduction System

The conduction system of the heart is "authorhythmic" in nature and controlled by a specialized nerve center in the brain. This center receives signals from the body and relays commands to the heart. Conduction begins with an electrical impulse of the **sinotrial (SA) node** within the right atrium. The SA node, because of its rapid and spontaneous impulses, dictates regulation of contractions of the heart and is therefore referred to as the "pacemaker." On an average, the adult's heart, at rest, beats 60-80 times per minute.(6) The electrical impulse of the SA node causes both atria to contract synchronously and, consequently, blood is forced into the ventricles. Almost immediately after the SA node fires, the electrical charge travels through specialized conduction tissue to reach the atrioventricular node. The AV node consists of slow conducting muscle cells and delays the impulse before it excites the ventricular conductors, through the bundle of His (Pronounced: Hiss). The conduction system continues through

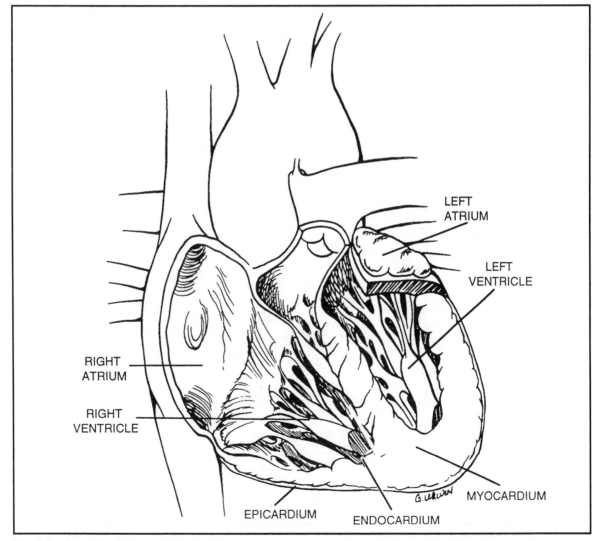

Fig. 6-2. Specialized layers of the heart

the branches of the bundle of His into the Purkinje fibers. This chain of electrical events results in a simultaneous and powerful contraction of the ventricles. The blood is then forced from the ventricles into the major arteries. It is the contraction of the ventricles that constitutes a heartbeat.

Cardiac Cycle

The contraction/relaxation pattern produced in the heart is known as the cardiac cycle. The contraction phase is called systole and the relaxation phase is diastole. Generally, these terms refer to the contraction/relaxation of the ventricles. It is important to understand that the atria have a separate contraction/relaxation phase. Fundamentally, atrial contraction (**systole**) occurs during ventricular relaxation (**diastole**) and ventricular systole occurs as the atria relax. The time interval of the

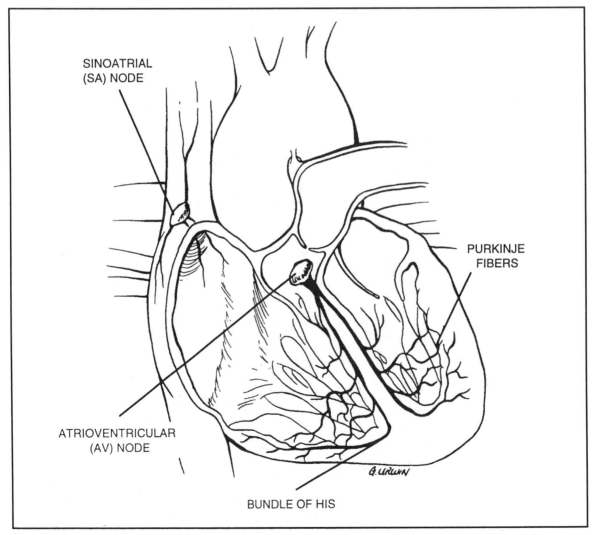

SINOATRIAL
(SA) NODE

PURKINJE
FIBERS

ATRIOVENTRICULAR
(AV) NODE

BUNDLE OF HIS

Fig. 6-3 Conduction system of the heart

cardiac cycle decreases as the cardiac rate increases, as would occur with vigorous exercise.

The contraction/relaxation phases of the cardiac cycle produce pressure changes adequate to produce blood flow through the arteries. Arterial blood pressure increases from 80 to 120 mm/Hg with the systemic circulatory system as a result of ventricular systole.(6) The pressure in pulmonary circulation is significantly lower. Simply stated, the contraction/relaxation of the ventricles causes a squeezing action which produces blood flow through the arteries.

Blood Pressure

Measurement of blood pressure provides significant information concerning heart function. With the use of a device called a sphygmomanometer, the qualified technician can easily record blood pressure. First, an inflatable cuff is fastened around the arm, just above the elbow. Air is then pumped into the cuff to apply pressure sufficient enough to cut off blood circulation. As the air is slowly released from the cuff, the technician listens for the first pulsing sounds with a stethoscope. When the first sounds are heard, the pressure within the arteries can be determined by the reading shown on the dial attached to the cuff. This is the systolic pressure. The diastolic pressure is viewed on the dial

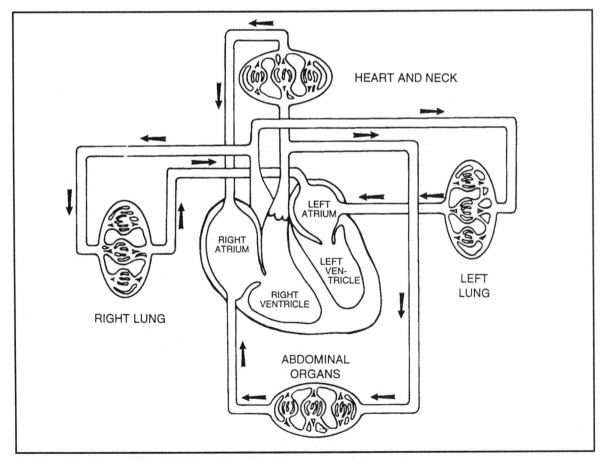

Fig. 6-4. Bloodflow pattern of the circulatory vessels

when the technician can no longer hear the pulsing sound on the stethoscope. These figures reflect pressure on the arteries as the blood flows through. The higher number, or systolic pressure, represents the minimum pressure needed to completely stop blood flow. The lower number, or diastolic blood pressure, indicates the pressure at which full blood flow is restored. Blood pressure of the healthy person averages around 120/80 mm/Hg. A pressure of 140/90 is considered to be high blood pressure, or hypertension, and often relates to serious health problems such as cardiac arrest, stroke, aneurysm and kidney failure.

The Circulatory System

The system which allows the blood to flow through the heart, lungs and body is called the circulatory system. The circulatory system consists of the blood carrying vessels: the arteries, capillaries and veins. As a unit, these vessels produce a circuit of blood flow throughout the body. That is, they work together as a closed system to provide a specific function in circulation. Arteries carry blood away from the heart to capillaries, which work as exchange vessels for nutrients and gasses, and veins transport blood from the capillaries back to the heart. Figure 6-5 illustrates the blood flow pattern of the circulatory vessels.

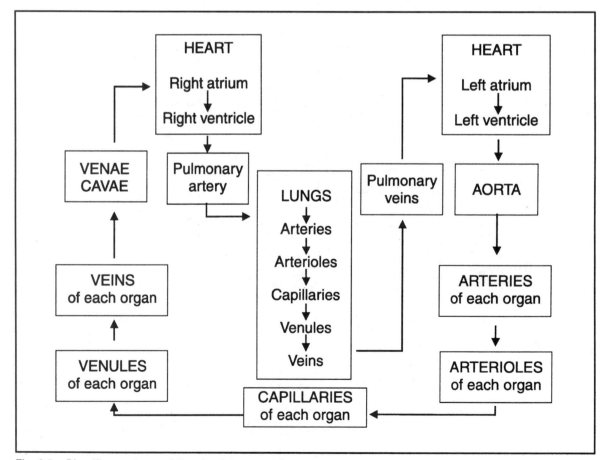

Fig. 6-5.   Bloodflow patterns of the circulatory vessels

Pulmonary Circulation

As previously stated, arteries constitute a major part of our blood transportation system and function to direct blood flow away from the heart. With each ventricular contraction, blood is pumped into the largest arteries (the aorta and pulmonary arteries). The pulmonary arteries receive **deoxygenated blood** from the right ventricle and direct it to the lungs where carbon dioxide is exchanged for fresh oxygen. This newly oxygenated blood leaves the pulmonary circulation, returns to the heart (left atrium and ventricle) and is then forced through the aorta, to the body, by a network of arteries. The primary arteries of this network are the carotid arteries in the neck and head, the abdominal arteries and the axillary and iliac arteries of the arms and legs, respectively. A great number of smaller arteries branch off the large arteries, each yielding smaller and smaller units until the blood passes into the smallest arteries, called arterioles. The elastic, muscular structure of arterial walls is capable of expansion and contraction to regulate a smooth continued blood flow.

Exchange Vessels

Once again, the purpose of the pumping action of the heart and transportation mechanisms of the circulatory system is to exchange oxygen and other nutrients for waste products. This exchange takes place in microscopic vessels, called **capillaries**, which connect the arterioles to the smallest branches of the veins, the venules.

The structure of the capillaries is significant in that the single-celled composition of their walls allows for an easy transfer of materials to nearby tissue cells. It is here, at the capillary level, that the blood gives up its oxygen, food and fluids to the tissues and the tissues give up carbon dioxide and fluid wastes to the blood. The blood leaving the capillaries, now laden with waste products and oxygen poor, returns to the heart through the venous system.

Venous System

The veins complement the arteries in function. Structurally, veins resemble the arteries, however they are thinner walled and less muscular. The venous blood is returned to the heart under low pressure and is often forced to move against gravity. To keep a steady blood flow to the heart, veins contain a one-way system of valves which prevent backflow of blood. Additionally, the massaging action of the muscles in the legs and arms helps move blood back to the heart (**venous return**). (**This is why we must include a cooldown period after vigorous exercise. The muscular action will help prevent the blood from pooling in the extremities.**) Blood return begins in the venules, the smallest venous unit. The venules gradually branch into larger structures facilitating blood return to the right atrium through the largest veins, the superior and inferior vena cava. The blood is now returned to the heart and the circulatory process repeats itself.

The Pulmonary System

Of all systems required to maintain life, the pulmonary system is one of the most crucial. We can survive for weeks without food, days without water, but live only a few minutes without oxygen. The exchange of gasses, such as oxygen and carbon dioxide, is of the utmost importance. It is the pulmonary, or respiratory system that provides these life-sustaining processes.

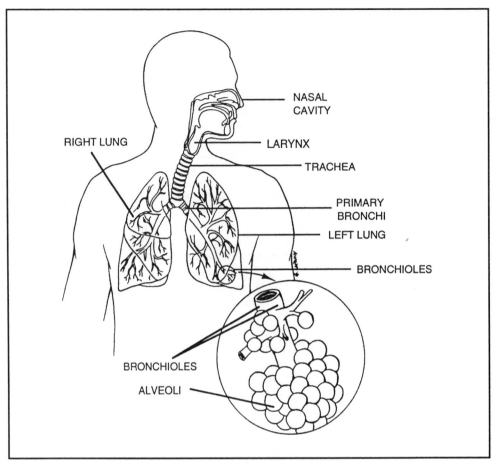

Fig. 6.6. Structures of the pulmonary system

Assisted by numerous integrated body systems, the pulmonary system is responsible for providing two major functions: **air distribution** and **gas exchange**. Additionally, the pulmonary system effectively filters, warms and moisturizes the inhaled air. Organs associated with the pulmonary system also produce sound, speech and provide us with a sense of smell.

The pulmonary system is divided into two major components: the conducting airways and the functional unit. The elements of these systems will be examined as we trace an inhalation through the pulmonary system. The conducting airways consist of the mouth/nose, pharynx, larynx and the primary branches of the bronchial tubes.

Air enters the body through the mouth or nostrils into the nasal cavity where it is warmed and humidified. The oral and nasal passages lead to the throat, or pharynx. The pharynx allows for passage of air into the lungs. After passing through the pharynx, the inspired air enters the larynx. The larynx is composed of pieces of cartilage, the largest of which is known as the Adam's apple. The larynx is often referred to as the voice box because the production of sound occurs as air passes the vocal cords which stretch across the interior of the larynx. Another cartilaginous structure found in the larynx is the epiglottis.

The epiglottis partially covers the opening in the larynx and closes during swallowing to prevent food passage into the trachea. The epiglottis, or glottis, is the structure involved in the potentially dangerous Valsalva maneuver.

Valsalva Maneuver

The Valsalva maneuver occurs when a person deeply inhales and then holds his/her breath during strenuous activity, as in lifting weights or shoveling snow. The glottis is closed **against pressure**. This causes an increased thoracic pressure which interrupts venous return to the heart, blood flow to the coronary arteries and oxygen supply to the brain. In healthy individuals, this may result in dizziness, slowing of the heart beat or a temporary loss of consciousness. For the individual predisposed to cardiovascular disease, the Valsalva maneuver could trigger cardiac arrest and result in death. Proper breathing techniques are, therefore, essential during heavy exercise.

Passage of Air

The air flows from the larynx into the trachea or windpipe which connects the larynx to the bronchi in the chest cavity. The trachea is structurally protected by cartilaginous rings. Sometimes, however, a blockage of the trachea occurs, such as in choking. The lifesaving Heimlich maneuver can be used to free the trachea of obstructions caused by food or other foreign bodies. The Heimlich maneuver is an easily acquired skill and, like CPR, should be learned by all professionals in the health/fitness field. (See Appendix.)

In the chest cavity, the trachea branches into two main bronchi, the right and the left bronchus, which travel into the respective lungs. In the lungs, the bronchus develops into smaller passageways for air known as the bronchioles. At this site, the functional unit of the pulmonary system begins.

The functional unit of the pulmonary system includes the bronchioles and alveoli, alveolar sacs within the lungs. The structure of this unit, as seen in Figure 6-6, resembles that of an upside down tree as it branches out into the terminal structures.

Pulmonary Airways

The bronchioles, found within the lungs, consist primarily of smooth muscle and elastic tissue in the walls. (Excessive spasm in the smooth **muscles of bronchioles** creates the breathing difficulties and associated diseases such as asthma.) Decreasing into respiratory units, the bronchioles lead to tiny tubes, or alveolar ducts. The ducts attach to a cluster of grape-like structures called alveolar sacs. The alveolar sacs are composed of millions of alveoli. The **alveoli** cover a large surface area and are extremely thin walled. The number, structure and proximity of the alveoli to the structurally similar capillaries allow for an efficient diffusion of gasses between air and blood. It is in the lungs that inhaled oxygen passes through the alveoli and enters the blood in the nearby capillaries. Some of the oxygen is absorbed in the blood, but most of it combines with the protein molecule called hemoglobin of the red blood cell. Oxygen is carried within the red blood to the tissues. Hemoglobin then releases oxygen to the tissues in exchange for carbon dioxide. Carbon dioxide is transported back to the alveoli for removal during exhalation.

| Pleura |

The lungs are a pair of pine-cone-shaped organs that lie within the chest cavity, one on either side of the heart. They are well protected by the surrounding structures; the ribs, intercostal muscles, sternum, spine and diaphragm.

A thin layer of moist membranes, called pleura, covers the lungs and lines the chest cavity which allows for smooth inflation/deflation of the lungs.

Intercostal Muscles

The protective structures surrounding the lungs also provide the mechanics of breathing. The breathing process begins with the respiratory center of the brain. Nerve impulses signal the muscles of respiration, the diaphragm and the intercostal muscles, to contract. The diaphragm is the pair of tent-like muscles that separates the lung cavity from the abdominal cavity like a bellows used to fan the flames of a fire. As the diaphragm contracts, it moves downward and increases the volume within the chest cavity. Contraction of the intercostal muscles pulls the ribs outward, causing further enlargement of the cavity. A vacuum is then created within the space and the negative pressure draws in the outside air. Exhalation occurs as the muscles relax and reverse the process, causing the lungs to contract and force air out.

The total amount of air exchanged between the body and the atmosphere per minute is referred to as minute ventilation. At an average of 12 ventilations per minute, approximately six liters of air is exchanged per minute.(6) During exercise, the demand for oxygen and amount of carbon dioxide to be removed increases. The respiratory center in the brain responds to the stimuli and consequently increases the rate and depth of ventilations accordingly.

Summary

After a thorough analysis of the components of the cardiopulmonary system, we can better comprehend how the system functions collectively.

In summary, air is inhaled from the atmosphere, through the conducting airways to the functional unit of the lungs. A gaseous exchange occurs between the alveoli and capillaries of the lungs. Carbon dioxide returns to the lungs and is exhaled. The newly inspired oxygen travels within the red blood cells from the lungs to the left side of the heart and is pumped throughout the body via the arterial circulation. Exchange of oxygen, carbon dioxide and nutrients in the tissues occurs throughout the body at the capillary level. Oxygen-poor blood is then returned through the venous system to the right side of the heart. The heart contracts and forces blood back to the lungs whereby the process repeats itself.

How The Cardiopulmonary System Meets the Demands of Exercise

1. Increased Heart Rate

Given an average resting heart rate (RHR) of 70 beats per minute (bpm), let's acknowledge that the heart can comfortably (assuming average fitness and without disease) perform at least twice its resting values. Aerobic exercise is generally performed between 60-90% of maximal values. (Maximal heart rate is estimated by subtracting your age from 220.) The average adult at 20 years of age, for example, can comfortably train between 120-170 bpm (Cooper or Simple Formula).(4) This is a remarkable performance for such a small organ.

2. Increased Stroke Volume

The amount of blood pumped by the heart per beat can increase as much as 50 to 60% above resting values to meet the physiological demands of exercise.(6) The tremendous increases in stroke volume are a result of fitness (adaptation) and are less significant in the untrained exerciser. That is, increased stroke volume is a training effect of aerobic exercise and allows the fit individual to pump more blood per beat, resulting in a lower heart rate for a given workload.

3. Increased Cardiac Output

Cardiac output, the amount of blood pumped by the heart per minute, is a product of heart rate times stroke volume, i.e., Q = HR x SV. The average adult heart at rest pumps approximately five liters of blood per minute. The cardiac output, as a result of adaptation to an exercise stimulus, can increase to almost eight times its resting values.(6) The increases are found within both the heart rate and stroke volume and depend tremendously on the efficiency of the system, that is to say, fitness. The sedentary individual will typically exhibit a cardiac output of 20-22 liters per minute (four times resting values), whereas the elite athlete is capable of increases almost eight times the resting values or 35-40 liters per minute.(2)

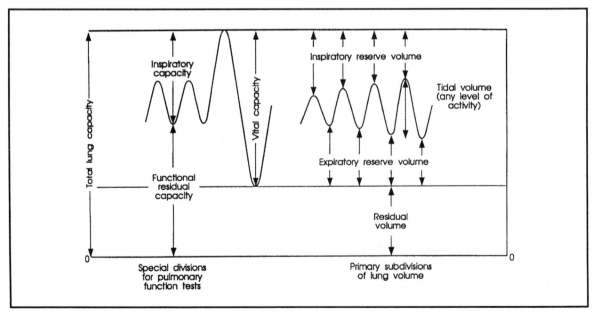

Fig. 6-7. Lung volumes

4. Vasodilation and Vasoconstriction

An extraordinary physiological adaptation of the circulatory system is the ability to regulate direction of blood flow. The vessels have the capacity to constrict or dilate in order to redistribute blood flow from the periphery to the central circulation to meet the physiological demands. During exercise, blood flow is diverted away from tissues that are less metabolically active, such as internal organs, and redirected to the active muscles. In fact, depending on the intensity of the exercise, as much as 88% of the blood flow is directed to the muscles during exercise.(6)

5. Increased Extraction of Oxygen

Not only is the body capable of directing blood flow to the active tissues, but the ability to extract oxygen from the blood increases with exercise. Oxygen extraction at the capillary level increases from an average of 25% at rest to as much as 85% during exercise—another amazing adaptation.

6. Vital Capacity

Defined as the greatest volume of air voluntarily moved in one breath, either during inhalation or exhalation and the sum of the tidal volume and inspiratory/expiratory reserve volumes. **Tidal volume** is the amount of air inhaled or exhaled in an average breath. **Reserve volume** refers to the excess volumes which may be used in forceful inspiration or expiration. Research suggests that vital capacity is primarily based on body size and is not significantly influenced by training.(1, 5) We do, however, increase the percentage of the vital capacity used during exercise. Figure 6-7 demonstrates the various lung capacities.

7. Increase in Respiratory Rate

The rate of breathing plays a crucial role in delivery of oxygen during exercise. At rest the adult averages 12 breaths per minute, compared to an exercise ventilatory rate of 35 to 40 breaths per minute or an unbelievable rate of 60 to 70 breaths per minute of the elite athlete.(7) Considering both volume of air and ventilatory rate, we can observe increases in minute ventilation from six liters/min to 100 liters/min with exercise (or more).

For a more complete description of the physiological effects of exercise, see "Developing and Maintaining Aerobic Fitness."

References

1. Anthony, C.P., & Thibodeau, G. (1984). *Structure and function of the body*. St. Louis: Times Mirror/Mosby College Publishing.
2. Astrand, P., & Rodahl, K. (1986). *Textbook of work physiology*. New York: McGraw-Hill.
3. Brooks, G., & Fahey, T. (1985). *Exercise physiology: human bioenergetics and its applications*. New York: Macmillan Publishers.
4. Cooper, P.G. (Ed.) (1987). Aerobics theory and practice. Costa Mesa, Ca.: HDL Publishing Company.
5. Frost, R. (1984). *Athletics and the heart*. Chicago, Ill.: Year Book Medical Publishers, Inc.
6. McArdle, W., Katch, F., & Katch, V. (1991). *Exercise physiology. energy, nutrition, and human performance*. Philadelphia: Lea & Febiger.
7. McClintic, J.R. (1985). *Physiology of the human body*. New York: John Wiley & Sons.
8. Noble, B. (1986). *Physiology of exercise and sport*. St. Louis: Times Mirror/Mosby College Publishing.

7 Training for Strength

Neil Wolkodoff, MA

Focus

Strength training is viewed by many as the best means to improve "tone" and definition, sports performance and resistance to injury. For example, ACSM currently includes strength training as part of its recommendation for quality exercise programs. As strength training gains popularity, the accomplished fitness and health professional will need to be equipped to deal with this rising interest. What has contributed to the popularity of strength training?

Gaining a better appearance, or "tone," without a scientific definition, continues to be a goal that many fitness enthusiasts pursue. Women now feel more comfortable in a strength training setting, a radical change from even five years ago. This powerful combination of factors will continue to increase the popularity of strength training. As we age, our fast-twitch, or explosive muscle fibers, atrophy at a faster rate than our slow-twitch, or endurance fibers. Strength training helps to maintain both fiber size and ability.

Physiological/ Neurological Factors of Strength

Strength qualities can be divided into three basic qualities. How training is approached is based upon the desired strength goal. Muscular endurance is the ability to perform moderate to low-level work for an extended period of time, such as a short cycling race. Muscular strength is the ability to generate maximal force irrespective of time, such as in wrestling. Muscular power is the ability to generate the most force possible within a short period of time, such as in tennis.

Strength qualities can also be further subdivided as pure strength or functional strength capabilities. **Pure strength** refers to strength developed outside of a sport or application context. Force generated during weight training is pure strength. **Functional strength**, or speed strength, refers to strength which has been developed or transferred to a sport or application context.(1, 2) The use of leg strength in tennis would be an example of functional strength. The little research done on the relationship between these two qualities indicates one should build pure strength first, then adapt that strength to the functional situation. For example, during the off season a tennis player would develop pure strength via resistance training, and then gradually begin to adapt that strength to tennis by playing tennis and possibly utilizing plyometric exercises. Resistance training should be a base before power is developed.(2)

The terms **tone** and **definition** are also important, if not from a scientific perspective, as a main focus of the fitness client. Tone, in reality, is dependent upon definition insofar as the muscle through work has become more uniquely and aesthetically shaped. Tone is the muscular state in which the muscle has greater than average definition, and the fat layer over the muscle is small enough to let that definition show.

Strength gains and other associated results are dependent upon the optimal manipulation of certain variables. Muscular work is only part of the issue: the manner in which it is performed will determine training adaptations. Strength adaptations are a combination of neurological and physiological factors. The means of performing muscular work affects which of these factors will benefit.

Two Basic Types of Fibers

Human muscle fiber falls into two types, fast twitch (FT) and slow twitch (ST). The FT fibers are very explosive in nature and can produce a great deal of force in a short time, but are easily fatigued. There are now believed to be two types of FT fibers: IIA which are slightly less powerful and will adapt somewhat to aerobic training, and type IIAB fibers, which are very powerful but will not cross adapt to aerobic training. The fibers have a greater capacity for endurance or aerobic work, but are not very powerful.

Aerobic or low-level activities will recruit the ST fibers, and explosive or high strength activities will utilize the FT fibers. ST fibers have more aerobic capability and will be used in these situations as a matter of energy efficiency. As the force or intensity increases, the IIA fibers are recruited or called upon, and finally the IIAB, or the most explosive fibers are used.(3) Intensity of force in most cases is the primary determinant of whether or not these FT fibers will be trained and accessed. Low-intensity aerobics activities will not produce strength gains after a minimal level because there is not sufficient intensity to recruit the FT units.

Coordination Gradually Increases

When one grows stronger as a result of resistance training, these strength increases are both physiological and neurological. The physiological changes due to resistance training include, most notably, hypertrophy, or increase in muscle size. However, there are some neurological changes which must occur first in most cases before the size of muscle will increase. As one begins a resistance training program, the first factor to account for an increase in strength is increased coordination.

At first, the muscles do not respond in a coordinated or efficiently directed fashion to move the resistance. After two to three weeks, the muscles involved in the movement finally learn to accomplish the activity in the most effective fashion. There is a more productive recruitment order, and more force is produced as well as an increased synchronization of the firing of the motor units. The additional use of more motor units or groups of fibers to move the increasing resistance is the next training adaptation. This phase generally lasts six to eight weeks, and then the muscle will probably grow in size to the stimulus. In most resistance programs, strength gains are, in reality, a combination of neurological and physiological factors.

Strength Training and Weight Loss

Strength training has become popular lately with an aging baby boomer population seeking more efficient ways to manage weight control. Pounds seem to creep on easier with age, and dieting, with its yo-yo weight gain/weight loss cycle, is proving to be not only ineffective but hazardous to overall health. As more research documents the sustained reduction in resting metabolic rate following

---

FT

• explosive

• powerful

• easily fatigued

ST

• endurance

• aerobics

calorie-restricted dieting, more overweight people are turning to weight training as a viable alternative to dieting.

As muscles grow in size, the amount of metabolically active tissue increases, leading to a higher rate of caloric burn especially in the period immediately following workouts. Body composition with an ideal amount of lean mass has long been recognized as a favorable proponent in weight management; however, confusion has centered on which type of exercise is really beneficial for weight-conscious individuals. Traditionally, aerobic exercise was viewed as the optimal choice for individuals desiring to lose weight. However, resistance training combined with aerobics has also proven to be highly effective—and for some, more effective, since the body-shaping advantages of weight training offer a visible improvement in appearance within a relatively short time period (less than one month), further encouraging the goal-oriented individual.

A discussion of strength training in relation to weight loss goals is included in this chapter because of the inherent conflict between the two objectives, of which many exercisers are unaware. Whenever aerobic training programs are introduced side-by-side with dedicated strength or resistance training, the net effect is less strength gains. Due to **competing physiological responses**, the magnitude of the strength improvements is reduced, which is why serious body builders and power lifters often avoid aerobic activities. If the objective is to lose weight and improve health in general, then the individual needs to be willing to postpone some strength gains until a dedicated program can be initiated.

Specialization

A basic strength training program will not provide increases in strength, power and endurance beyond an initial level. One may develop muscular endurance, while muscular power may not increase, or may actually decrease. At high levels of fitness, specialization strength factors become mutually exclusive. These three qualities of strength involve different energy systems, muscle fibers and associated changes. Thus, simultaneous development at elite levels will not occur.

This appears to be true as well in the relationship between aerobic fitness and strength. Research which essentially began with Hickson in 1980 (4, 5), has strongly suggested in the last few years that strength levels can be compromised by high levels of aerobic training. This appears to be true because of the enzymatic and associated changes that occur in the muscle cell with aerobic training. As little as three aerobic training sessions per week could compromise the power abilities of a highly trained, powerful athlete. From a recreational perspective, this could be enough to detract from muscular shape and size.

Training Systems

Periodization

A discussion of training systems should begin with a description of periodization. The basic premise of this concept states that **variation** of certain training factors will lead to greater gains than no variation. The basic concept is related to Selye's general adaptation syndrome. (2, 3) When presented with a new training stimulus, the body is "shocked," or there is some physiological discomfort and change. The body adapts to the stimulus, and performance capabilities improve after a brief rest period and repeated training sessions. In addition, periodization implies the training stimulus must be changed or variety of training utilized for gains to continue to occur.

Volume, Load and Intensity

Within these concepts are the key terms of volume, load and intensity. Volume refers to the total amount of training, or the total work accomplished during the training session, such as lifting 2,500 pounds of weight. Load refers to the actual amount of weight lifted or resistance used in comparison to one's maximum in that particular exercise. If a person could lift 100 pounds one time in the bench press, an 80%RM or **repetition maximum** would be 80 pounds. Actual definitions of training in periodization depend upon whether the perspective is American or eastern European (6), as the eastern Europeans tend to view psychological stresses as part of the periodization equation. When the variables of volume, load and intensity are manipulated or changed in an optimal fashion, then gains result which are much greater than if a constant training program is used for the same time period. Normally in resistance programs, volume starts the training cycle very high, while load and intensity are fairly low. As one moves through the training cycle, which generally lasts 8-12 weeks, the volume decreases and the load and intensity increase. It should be noted that as training load and intensity increase, volume must decrease to allow the individual to rest and recover in response to the more demanding training stimulus.

While periodization was originally modeled in terms of Olympic weightlifting, many of the concepts have direct application to a fitness setting. Most individuals respond much better if their training program is periodically changed according to these principles.

Types of Muscular Contractions

There are a variety of muscular contractions which can be used in a number of training systems. **Concentric** or positive contractions are used when one lifts a weight or resistance, wherein the muscle shortens in a dynamic sense. **Eccentric** or negative contractions occur when the muscle lengthens, as happens when lowering a weight. In some high intensity training situations, negative loads are used to shock the system and provide further gains. Excessive negative loads are rarely appropriate for the beginner in a recreational setting. A combination of concentric and eccentric contractions are used in most weight-training systems and are effective at building strength.

Isokinetic contractions or movements are those in which the muscle shortens at a constant rate. This occurs in the sport of swimming because the speed of movement is fairly constant. Training isokinetically will build strength at that particular speed and below. Thus, a tennis player would train at a speed which is just slightly faster than normal movements, which should have a positive transfer to the various speeds encountered in tennis.

Contractions of muscle can also be static or isometric. In this case, the muscle does not change length when exerted against a fixed resistance. Studies of strength developed isometrically show that strength is specific to the joint angle at which it was developed. Isometric strength does not have much correlation with dynamic strength.(7)

The types of muscular movements and their various uses can be another dimension which can be added to the periodization model. Additional training modes offer the ability to add extra variables during training, and therefore could produce better gains than a set system of contractions.

Strength Training Systems

The main choices in terms of strength training systems are body building, power lifting and Olympic weightlifting. Fitness and strength professionals have begun to mix training systems and use the various systems in different training phases.

Body-building methods emphasize building muscle mass and definition. Body building may refer to the methods of training as well as competition for muscular definition and mass. One of the keys to this system is to isolate individual muscle groups, and this is part of the reason competitive body builders train five or six days per week. Isolated muscle group training would include such exercises as bicep curls, calf raises and leg extensions.

Most repetitions are normally accomplished in the 8-12 range, which produces the greatest hypertrophy or size gains. By overloading a single muscular group, superior size and definition will generally occur. Body-building methods appear optimal when used on a split-routine basis in which different muscle groups are isolated on different days. For example, arms, legs and abdomen may be trained three days, while the other three days the chest, shoulders and back are trained. The loads used in body building combined with the relatively short rest periods tend to selectively hypertrophy the slow-twitch and not the fast-twitch fibers.

Power lifting is both a training method and a set of competitive events. The power lifts are the bench press, squat and deadlift. Traditionally, power lifts have been used with sports such as football and wrestling.

Most power lifting programs use a system in which the individual is continually building towards a greater maximum in each lift. Most power lifting routines advocate that a large percentage of training be performed in the one-six repetition range.(3, 8) There is a great difference between power lifting as a training method and the methods used to train for power lifting competitions. Using the lifts themselves does not mean one must train in the 1-6 repetition range, which is too intense for the novice exerciser.

Olympic weightlifting has received a good deal of attention in sport training circles over the last ten years because of its potential application to power or explosive sports. The Olympic lifts consist of two lifts: the snatch lift, in which the bar is moved overhead in one motion; and the clean and jerk, in which the bar is moved overhead in two motions. Training for competition generally uses near-maximal loads with fairly long rest periods to allow recovery. Olympic lifting programs are designed to train the athlete for a single, maximal lift, which is too advanced for the beginner.

The proponents of these lifting techniques note that the upward thrust of the hips in the Olympic lifts is very similar to the upward motion in such sports as football, basketball and volleyball.(1, 9) The use of these lifts and their derivations could possibly be used for someone training for a power-based sport who has developed a sufficient strength base and will observe strict form.

Which methods produce superior strength gains?

Body-building techniques are the best developers of hypertrophy, followed by power lifting and Olympic weightlifting, respectively. These exercises performed slowly stress the muscle and work it through the full range of motion, and thereby develop superior vascularization compared to other methods. Power lifting and Olympic weightlifting stress the entire system during the lift, and minimal definition is achieved. The Olympic lifts produce the greatest force per unit of time, followed by the power lifts. If one's goals are size and definition, body building and power lifting methods are best. If the goal of training is sport performance, especially in a power-based sport, then power lifting and Olympic weightlifting are the best choices.

The use of various loads, intensities and rest periods will determine the effectiveness of any of the basic methods. Muscle will make adaptations to training which can be both metabolic and physiological. The training load will determine to a great degree which changes will occur.

Sub-maximal loads 30-60% of one RM will produce adaptations which result in local muscular endurance and not strength. Cords, bands and light hand weights fall into this category.

| For endurance |
| 30-60% of |
| 1 RM |

Sub-maximal strength loads are generally 60-90% of one RM and generally correlate with repetitions which can be performed in the 6-15 repetition range. Loads in this range produce the best strength and definition gains, with only minor gains in muscular endurance or power. For individuals in a recreational setting, loads and subsequent repetitions in this 6-15 repetition range are probably the most appropriate. Rest periods of shorter duration such as 45-60 seconds will produce gains in hypertrophy when combined with loads in this range. As the rest periods lengthen, there is a greater potential for strength rather than hypertrophy gains because of the available ATP-PC.(3, 8, 9)

| For strength |
| 60-90% of |
| 1 RM |

Maximal loads are considered to be 90-150% of one RM. Training performed in this range and will consist of six repetitions or less. In a case such as eccentric or negative training, a load of up to 150% of one RM might be used. Training in these ranges will produce maximal strength gains, or strength which is useful in situations in which an all-out attempt may be needed. In most cases, training in this load range is not appropriate for the individual at the recreational level. Rest periods should be a minimum of two minutes for maximal strength development to allow ATP-PC to fully re-synthesize, which is necessary for maximal strength development.

Training Equipment Machines vs. Free Weights

The two basic choices in terms of resistance training are free weights or weight machines. Free weights consist of both dumbbells and barbells. Periodization and the variation of load, volume and intensity were modeled around free weights and multi-joint exercises rather than single joint exercises and machines. Most of the training methods involved in body building, power lifting and Olympic weightlifting revolve around free weights.

Free weights are relatively easy to use, lend themselves to a number of exercises and are relatively inexpensive. They can be used to train the joint/muscle group from a number of angles. Progress is easy to measure, and in the case of dumbbells, they don't require much space. Free weights can be used for single-jointed exercises such as the bicep curl and multi-jointed exercises such as the parallel squat.

Free weights have several disadvantages: They are cumbersome to store, limited in the types of contractions they elicit, and pose a safety risk. Safety can be a consideration for the novice, so proper instruction and supervision is critical. Because of their few disadvantages, free weights will continue to be a popular form of resistance training.

Weight machines can be **isotonic** or **dynamic** variable resistance, variable resistance, isokinetic resistance, or computerized. Isotonic or dynamic variable resistance machines are those in which the resistance is "constant" or fairly constant throughout the range of motion. In this sense, these machines are most like free weights in the form of resistance they provide. **Variable resistance equipment** is designed around the principle that the force a muscle is able to produce during a contraction is not constant. In fact, the muscle (because of the relationship of the fibers and the mechanics of the exercise) will produce the greatest force in the middle of the range of motion, and the least amount of force at either end of the range of motion. "Cam" equipment, which is so named because of the cam device which mechanically alters the resistance during the range of motion, attempts to utilize this force/length relationship to derive greater gains. While the theory of variable resistance equipment is appealing, most research indicates that it is no more or less effective than conventional isotonic methods and actually may not fully mimic muscular capabilities.(10) Some pneumatic equipment, such as Keiser, adjusts the force curve with air pressure, and may be more adaptable to the actual muscular force curve and potentially more effective than mechanical cams.

Isokinetic equipment functions on the principle of limiting the speed of the lever arm and therefore creating resistance. Most exercise machines of this genre use a positive-only resistance and therefore, may lose some training adaptations due to negative loading of the muscle. Negative loads occur in sports, and may be a key to hypertrophy gains. Therefore, resistance training should include preparation for eccentric loads and movements. However, this form of resistance is commonly used in rehabilitation with very good results and very little trauma to the joint or injury. Isokinetic equipment is the most suitable for circuit training because of potential metabolic gains, but tends to be a poor developer of strength.

Summary

Training for strength will continue to gain popularity over the next decade. Strength training will lead to better appearance, weight loss and weight maintenance, resistance to injury and better sports performance. To be fully effective at prescribing strength programs, one must understand the basic physiology of strength. From a physiological basis, one can determine the needs of individuals in terms of muscular endurance, strength or power. The concepts of periodization, and the manipulation of training variables can play a key role in program effectiveness, even for the recreational exerciser. To be fully effective, the strength program also needs to utilize equipment and modalities which promote the characteristics desired while providing variation of training stimulus.

References

1. Kurz, T. (1991). *Science of sports training*. Island Pond: Stadion.
2. Medvedeyev, A. (1989). *A system of multi-year training in weightlifting*. (Trans. Andrew Chamiga.) Livonia: Sportivny Press.
3. Fleck, S., & Kraemer, W. (1987). *Designing resistance programs*. Champaign, Ill.: Human Kinetics.
4. Hickson, R.C. (1980). Interference of strength development by simultaneously training strength and endurance. *Journal of Applied Physiology*. 58:492-499.

5. Dudley, G.A., & Djamil, R. (1985). Incompatibility of endurance and strength training modes of exercise. *Journal of Applied Physiology, Respiratory, Environmental and Exercise Physiology,* 59:1336-1451.
6. Bompa, T. (1983). *Theory and methodology of training.* Dubuque: Kendall-Hunt.
7. Clark, D.H. (1973). Adaptations in strength and muscular endurance resulting from exercise. *Exercise and Sport Science Reviews,* 1:73-102.
8. Kroll, W., & Stone, M.J. (1986). *Sports conditioning and weight training* (2nd ed.). Boston: Allyn and Bacon.
9. O'Bryant, H., & Stone, M. (1987). *Weight training, a scientific approach.* Edina: Burgess Press.
10. Harman, E. (1983). Resistive torque analysis of 5 nautilus exercise machines. *Medicine and Science in Sports and Exercise,* 15:113.

8

Training for Plyometrics & Power

Debbie Ban-Pillarella

Focus

"WALK 2, 3, 4 PLYO JUMP PLYO JUMP . . ." chants the fitness instructor in a Power Aerobics class. "Plyo," short for plyometrics, has become common terminology in aerobic classes that are implementing controlled jumps, leaps and bounds. A closer look at the actual execution and implementation of these movements will find the term plyometric being incorrectly referenced. What we are doing in class, however, are power moves. The focus of this chapter is to define the differences and offer guidelines for training.

Background Information

Plyometric training has been used by strength coaches to increase the explosive power capabilities of their athletes. These training methods have been around for over 409 years and have included depth jumping, bounding, hopping and leaping drills to produce gains in muscle power and reactive strength. Muscle power by definition is the ability to develop force over a certain distance as rapidly as possible, while reactive strength is the ability to quickly switch from an eccentric contraction to a concentric contraction (also known as the stretch-shorten cycle). Muscle power and reactive strength regulate performance in sports like volleyball, basketball, wrestling and sprinting.

Plyometrics is a form of training that uses fast eccentric contractions followed by concentric contractions in activities such as depth jumps, bounding and certain forms of medicine ball work. As a training method, plyometrics bridges the gap between pure strength training and speed strength training.

Physiology of the Plyometric Concept

Although little empirical research on the measurable effects of plyometric training is available, strength coaches observe that it does work. Available research states that the concept of plyometric exercises primarily involves the training of the nervous system and involves the stretch reflex mechanism and the storage of elastic energy.

In the typical depth jump (step off a platform and, upon contact with the floor, immediately jump up vertically with maximal effort), the athlete's involved muscle fibers, muscle spindles and Golgi tendon organs undergo a stretch or eccentric movement. This lengthening activates the stretch reflex. In theory, muscles that undergo rapid lengthening through an eccentric contraction just prior to a concentric contraction (vertical jump phase) will engage in a greater positive work contraction.

Additionally, research shows that a body movement that requires speed and power can best be achieved by starting with a movement in the opposite

Fig. 8-1. Plyometric depth jump

direction. If you observe a batter preparing to swing at a ball, he first moves the bat in the reverse direction of the forward swing. This reverse movement stretches the involved muscle groups. The stretch stores the elastic energy in the muscles involved which is immediately released as the bat swings forward. This pre-stretch is often referred to as "loading a muscle." In the plyometric depth jump, elastic energy is stored during the landing phase and immediately released in the subsequent, jumping up phase.

Power Moves Are Pseudo Plyometric Moves

Hops, leaps and jumps that are typically executed in an aerobic exercise class as plyometric moves do not meet the criteria of traditional plyometric movements. The following chart will help you understand the similarities and differences between true plyometrics and the plyometric derivative, the power move.

Table 8-1. Contrasting Plyometrics with Power Moves

Similarities

Athletic in nature
Anaerobic HR response
Hopping, jumping moves
Controlled eccentric landing followed by concentric upward move

Differences

Plyometrics	Power Moves
Maximal intensity	Sub-maximal intensity
Prerequisite: high level of strength	Prerequisite: moderate level of strength
Geared toward athlete	Int/Adv. general fitness population
Specific to sport	Overall fitness
Total rest needed between moves	No total rest between moves
Upper and lower body depending on sport	Lower body emphasis
Low repetitions	Moderate repetitions interspersed frequently

In summary, many of our power moves are plyometric in nature, but not in application. Like plyometrics, power moves require the body to use the storage of elastic energy to execute the upward jump; however, they are nowhere near the intensity level of true plyometric drills. Additionally, power moves are used for a much longer duration than plyometric drills and do not push the body to exhaustion. Scaled down versions of plyometric drills can be performed in aerobics classes as well as in sport-specific classes to follow an interval format rather than true plyometric training. In this sense, these pseudo-plyometric moves (power moves) can be beneficial and will add variety and challenge as long as they are preceded by a good warm-up, followed by a sufficient cooldown, and are executed with proper form, alignment and control.

Goals of Power Moves

Power moves can be used for a variety of purposes. Goals need to be set in order to properly utilize the benefits of power moves. Below is a listing of some classes and their possible goals.

Table 8-2. Specific Sport Skills and Related Class

Class	Goal
Sport/Specific	Increase specific sport skills (volleyball spike, basketball dunk)
High/Lo Step	Add challenge and variety to aerobic choreography
Aqua Interval	Add high intensity moves to increase anaerobic training systems

Appropriateness

Power moves are appropriate for the intermediate to advanced level exerciser looking for a way to challenge his or her current fitness program. The potential power client should possess moderate strength, good body control, proper alignment and execution.

Power moves are contraindicated for the following populations:
- pre/post natal
- seniors
- obese
- orthopedic problems (knees, back and joint limitations)
- hypertension
- cardiac problems
- back problems

Where and When To Power

The use of power moves in a fitness program is limited only by the fitness instructor's creativity. Power moves have successfully been included into class formats in funk, step, high/low and interval. The specifics for their implementation are as follows—

Where:
- In the aerobic/anaerobic segment of the class

When:
- Following a thorough warm-up (see AFAA Standards and Guidelines)
- Following a five minute, non-power aerobic movement segment (marches, jogging, etc.). (If implementing power moves in a step class, never jump down from the step.)

How To Power

The following recommendations will assist you in safely executing power moves.

PREPARATION PHASE
- Down/Up Rehearsal Moves: To prepare the body for the eccentric/concentric movements to come in the power moves, simulate the power rhythm by rehearsing the downward and upward movements without executing the jumps.
- Verbal Cueing: Direct the power clients prior to the execution of the power moves as to their body awareness in space. For example, "We're getting ready for power moves, remember to hold your abdominals tight, lift your torso and concentrate on your form."

THE UPWARD PHASE
- Feet always relaxed under the body (no kicking feet to buttocks; no lifting knees to chest)
- Jump upward (lateral jumping will cause stress to supportive knee ligaments)
- Coordinate arm moves (raise arms up when jumping into air to assist in upward lift)
- Limit number of consecutive power moves (no more than eight consecutive power moves to reduce risk of injury)

THE LANDING PHASE
- Land softly (verbal imagery cues: land as if you are landing on big white clouds of marshmallows)
- Bend knees (to act as cushioning shock absorbers)

- Full foot contact with floor (avoid landing on toes)
- Limit lag time (minimal pause/delay between power moves)

Related Concerns
- Music—The music bpm's for execution of power moves should be correlated to the bpm's of each class (i.e., Step: 120-125; High/Lo: 140-150).
- Floor Surface—Power moves should be executed on a safe and supportive floor surface, never on concrete.
- Footwear—Supportive aerobic shoes need to be worn at all times.
- Heart Rates—Due to the high intensity of power moves, the heart rate may elevate toward the anaerobic threshold region. Perceiving exertion levels throughout power moves is recommended.

Injury Prevention/ Overuse

Injuries can result if power moves are:
- executed improperly
- used with inexperienced clientele
- done with great frequency

The most common power move related injuries are tendinitis and ligamentitis. A combination of rest, ice, compression and elevation is recommended as a remedy. If pain persists in spite of rest and ice for more than two or three days, a medical professional should be consulted. Also seek care if there is a loss of joint motion, any joint swelling or feeling of "giving way," or the pain is sharp, and you are unable to use the joint due to pain.

Common Error Analysis

Instructor/Client Communication
Fitness instructors need to have a verbal repertoire of comments to use when communicating error corrections to their clients. Below are four common power move execution errors and suggested verbal correction cues.

Practical Power Moves Analysis
Power Leap. Begin on two feet. While jumping into air, shift body weight to right leg; land on right foot; tap left foot on ground next to right foot and immediately leap into air shifting weight and landing on left foot. (Verbal cue: Imagine you are Jack-be-nimble, leaping up and over a candlestick.)

Table 8-3. Communication Cues for Correcting Various Execution Errors

Error	Analysis	Correction Cue
Client leans forward	Abdominals lax	"Hold abdominals tight to raise center of gravity."
Client executing power moves with momentum (high impact style)	No eccentric lengthening moves occurring	"You need a split second pause when you land before jumping up . . . say this in your mind upon landing, 'pause, lift'."
Client hyperflexing knees when jumping	Feet not under body	"It's time to spot-check to make sure your feet are beneath you. Are they?"
Client lands forcefully	Lack of body consciousness	"Your landing should feel as if you are jumping into and out of a cloud."

Power Jump. Begin on two feet. Bend knees slightly and jump upward. Land on both feet, knees slightly bent. (Verbal cue: Imagine you are jumping up to slam-dunk a basketball.)

Power Heel. Begin with right heel into floor slightly in front of left foot; left foot planted flatly into floor. Jump up into air changing feet mid-air and landing so left heel is into floor slightly in front of right. (Verbal cue: Let's think of doing a traditional, low impact heel dig with a lift upward to change feet.)

Power Choreography

The following sample sequence can be used in a high/low power class:

- Jog forward 8 counts, 2 power jumps upward, 2 step touches (right and left)
- Jog backward 8 counts, 2 power jumps upward, 2 step touches (right and left)
- 2 grapevines (right and left), 4 power heels (turning around to back)
- 2 grapevines (right and left on back side), 4 power heels (turning around to front)

Summary

Power moves are a great way to challenge the avid exerciser. If executed properly, they can add that spice you've been looking for. The preceding checklist contains some important points to remember when executing safe power moves. Good luck!

References

Adams, T. (1984). An investigation of selected plyometric training exercises on muscular leg strength and power. *Track & Field Quarterly Review,* 84:1: 36-40.

Bosco, C. (1982). Store and recoil of elastic energy in slow and fast types of human skeletal muscles. *Acta Physiologica Scandinavica,* 116: 343-349.

Borkowski, J. (1990). Plyometrics and progress: a case study. *Coaching Volleyball.* 29-30.

Chu, D. (1983). Plyometrics: link between strength and speed. *National Strength Coaches Association Journal,* 4: 20-21.

DeVries, H. (1987). *Physiology of Exercise* (3rd ed.).

Grimsley, J., & Woolard, D. (1987). Application of plyometrics. *Texas Coach.* 44-47.

Hocmuth, G. (1974). Biomechanik sport licher bewugungen, as quoted in *Modern Athlete and Coach, 44-47.*

Kyrolainen, K., et al. (1990). Mechanical efficiency of locomotion in females during different kinds of muscle action. *European Journal of Applied Physiology,* 61: 446-452.

Lundin, P. (1985). A review of plyometric training. *NSCA Journal,* 7:3: 69-74.

Poliquin, C., & Patterson, P. (1989). Classification of strength qualities, *NSCA Journal,* 11:6: 48-50.

Verkoshanski, Y. (1969). Perspectives in the improvement of speed-strength preparation of jumpers. *Yessis Review of Soviet Physical Education and Sports,* 4:2: 28-29.

Wilson, G., Elliot, B., & Wood, G. (1991). Effect on performance of imposing a delay during a stretch-shorten cycle movement. *Medicine and Science in Sports and Exercise,* 23:3: 364-370.

Wilt, F. (1970). From the desk of fred wilt, plyometric exercise. *Track Technique,* 64.

Wolkodoff, N. (1991). Plyometrics. *IDEA today, 33-36.*

Yessis, M., & Hatfield, F. (1986). *Plyometric training: achieving power and explosiveness in sports fitness.* Systems Publishing.

Judith Gantz, MA, CMA

9 Training for Flexibility

Focus

FLEXIBILITY IS A BASIC FITNESS COMPONENT. Developing a healthy range of stretch allows us to move with greater extent of motion and keeps muscles supple and responsive to the demands of daily activities and exercise. Although stretching has long been associated with dancers and gymnasts, everyone needs "fitness flexibility."

Stretching and Flexibility

Stretching in moderation provides most people with a well-rounded fitness program. Stretching in excess is only needed by those who engage in dance or sports requiring high degrees of joint range.

There are two definitions of flexibility.

Static flexibility: the capacity to move a joint throughout its full range of motion (ROM).

Dynamic flexibility: having responsive muscles which are conditioned for their elastic properties in order to move a joint throughout full ROM at varying speeds with varying forces.

Both types of flexibility require stretching, but dynamic flexibility applies the stretch to movements using speed and force, such as in the high leg kick of a dancer. When teaching flexibility programs, it is important to consider the movement goals of your clients or students. Anyone involved with activities demanding high degrees of flexibility, such as a dancer, has an athletic requirement that goes far beyond normal fitness needs. The demands of dance result in over-stretching. Since over-stretching is linked to injuries, fitness flexibility should not force advanced stretch positions. Stretching moderately and following kinesiological guidelines will bring positive long-lasting gains. When it comes to flexibility, more is not always better!

Flexibility Benefits

There are many benefits attributed to stretching: improved movement function, reduced muscle tension, enhanced relaxation, improved posture and coordination, reduced stiffness and delay of the physical deterioration associated with aging. Most of these benefits are reported from clinical and empirical findings because science is still studying the various effects of stretching. The notion that stretching before exercising can prevent injuries is surrounded by controversy. On the other hand, medical science is supporting the benefits of stretching as it relates to stress reduction. Kinesiologically, there is large agreement that safe stretching improves movement function. Increasing flexibility improves the range of motion available to our joints and reduces muscle stiffness and tension. A common compensation for tight calf muscles is to allow the foot to roll in (i.e., pronate). Foot pronation places undesired stresses on the foot, ankle and knee. Excessive pronation can contribute to such common injuries as shin splints, Achilles tendinitis and knee cap problems (patella femoral arthalgra or patellar tendinitis).

Most experts favor stretching as a means of reducing muscle tension. Holding less tension in the muscles makes the body feel more relaxed. Incorporating visualization and breathing techniques while stretching can promote relaxation and alter neurological responses to stress.

Regular stretching can improve posture and enhance coordination, limbering the body for easier movement. A flexible muscle is believed to provide less internal resistance to stretch, potentially enhancing speed and efficiency during performance.

Some of the characteristics of aging, such as stiffness and reduced activity, are countered by stretching. Although the fastest growing age group in America is over 65, there are few studies on the effects of stretching on the older adult. To date, we know stretching increases flexibility, but we do not know how much change is possible when one starts stretching as an older adult. A limber body at age 70 is not the same as a limber body at age seven.

Research studies are not conclusive as to how stretching prevents injuries. Some evidence reveals that adequate flexibility may prevent injuries associated with activities that move the joints beyond normal range of motion at rapid speeds. In power lifting or dancing, flexibility is crucial to the movement demands of these activities. Flexibility- induced performance enhancement may also result from increased musculotendinous compliance facilitating the use of elastic strain energy. This may at least partially explain why athletes state they feel they can throw harder and faster with increased flexibility.

There are multiple benefits to stretching, but some are questionable benefits. Fortunately, science knows the factors that influence flexibility. Understanding these factors sheds light on how to evaluate and design effective stretch programs.

| Reduces muscle tension |

| Improves posture and coordination |

| Counters stiffness |

| Enhances performance |

Factors That Influence Flexibility

Many factors determine and influence our flexibility:
- Genetic bony and connective tissue structure
- Tight or loose ligaments
- Muscular fascial sheath, joint capsule
- CT structures
- Stress and muscular tension
- Injury, pregnancy, age

The first factor, genetic bony structure, is something we cannot alter. The shape and size of our bones and the type of connective tissue we have is mainly determined by our genetic inheritance, that is, the structure we are born with.

Knowing the natural limitations of our anatomical structure allows us to stretch safely. Every joint in the body has a different range of motion (ROM) dictated by shape, size and how the bones fit together. Different body types are built with varying degrees of joint range. For example, the pelvis and hip joints are often shaped differently in men and women. A wider pelvis allows for greater turn-out in the hip. Consequently, the range of motion at the joint is greater. If an individual is born with the anatomical disposition for greater external hip rotation, they will be able to develop a larger "stretch" at that joint. Each joint can have variations in structure that enhance or limit flexibility.

Although generally, everyone has the same basic joint design, these differences result in variations of mobility or stability.

Joints and Stability

The major joints responsible for movement are classified as **nonaxial**, **uniaxial**, **biaxial** and **triaxial**. The most stable joint types are uniaxial (move in one plane), such as the elbow. Joints that move in two (biaxial) or three (triaxial) planes are more mobile and rely to a greater degree on the surrounding connective tissues (ligaments/ fascia/tendons) and muscles for support. It is difficult to over-stretch a uniaxial joint because there is a natural feel for where the stretch will stop. When stretching a triaxial joint, such as the hip or shoulder, the quality of elasticity in the connective tissues (ligaments, fascia and the musculotendinous unit) has a tremendous influence on why some people appear "naturally" limber.

The second influence on our flexibility is the quality of connective tissues: ligaments, fascial sheath, joint capsule and the musculotendinous unit. Although muscles have the greatest elastic properties, the fascial sheath covering muscle is composed of connective tissue which is rather non-elastic. Muscle tissue can stretch and return to its original shape and size, whereas connective tissue (CT) remains extended once it is stretched. The role of CT is to bind and hold things together, as in the case of ligaments binding bone to bone. Each type of CT has varying degrees of elasticity. If our ligaments have a higher proportion of elastic fibers, it makes us appear "naturally flexible."

Ligament Laxity

The condition of ligament laxity results from being born with ligaments that have a higher degree of elastic properties. Ligaments attach bone to bone, providing joint stability through tensile strength. Tensile strength is the ability to withstand being pulled or drawn apart. A joint with ligament laxity is more mobile and can extend further. The term "double jointed" is often used to describe ligament laxity because of the extreme positions that can be manipulated and held, forcing joints beyond their normal range. People with ligament laxity can be more prone to injury if they do not have adequate strength to support their joints. Stretching with this condition is considered safe if the body is well-positioned in each stretch, and there is a balance of strength to flexibility. Moving a joint beyond the limit to which it can be actively controlled is a set-up for injury.

Stress and muscular tension keep muscles in a shortened, contracted state. When muscles relax, tension is released. High levels of muscular tension tend to decrease sensory awareness and can contribute to an elevation in blood pressure. Habitually tense muscles tend to cut off blood circulation. Reduced blood supply results in a lack of oxygen and essential nutrients and causes toxic waste products to accumulate in the cells, leading to fatigue and pain.

Many scientists believe emotional tension and muscular tension are related. Ailments from emotional tension include headaches, joint and muscle pain, even stomach ulcers. Chronic muscle tension (called contracture) causes a muscle to be continually in a shortened state, resulting in tightness and reduced strength.

Pregnancy, injury and age all influence the quality of our flexibility. During pregnancy, the hormone **relaxin** causes ligaments and connective structures to

Overstretching joints

Bone to bone attachment

increase in their elastic properties. Although it can be helpful for some women to stretch, caution should be followed not to overstretch areas of the pelvis. When seated with soles of the feet together, pregnant women should avoid pushing down and out on the inside of the knees . . . this (precaution) prevents unintentional injury of the softened cartilage and supportive tissues of the symphysis and hip joint.

Any musculoskeletal injury interferes with the functioning of our soft tissues. Often an injury, such as a sprained ankle, will result in a reduced range of motion. This is because there is a build-up of scar tissue function resulting from connective tissue repairing itself. Stretching can enhance or hinder an injury, so seek medical evaluation and advice before attempting any rigorous flexibility program.

> Scar tissue
> hinders function

The relationship between age and flexibility is surrounded by conflicting data. One thing science does agree upon is that as we age, connective tissue (CT), which is made up primarily of collagen fibers, forms cross-links in areas that have restricted motion. Age is often associated with a sedentary lifestyle. The older and less active an individual is, the more rapidly muscles and joints tighten up. If the joints are not extended through various ranges, collagen cross-links are laid down in the tissues. The build-up of cross-links in the CT surrounding muscles restricts our movement potential and makes our bodies feel stiff and less flexible. Stretching breaks down cross-links and research suggests that regular mobilization can decrease cross-link build-up.

Physiology of Stretching

Muscles are made up of a series of larger to smaller bundles encased in multiple layers of connective tissue. Every small muscle fiber is surrounded by a sheath called the endomysium. These small fibers are organized into bundles, called fasciculi which are surrounded by a sheath called perimysium. The whole muscle is made up of fasciculi bundles that are held together by a connective tissue sheath, the epimysium. To initiate movement, the force of a muscle contraction is transmitted from the smaller fibers through the connective tissues to the bones. The endo, peri and **epimysium coverings** form the fascial sheath and become the attachment of tendon to bone. This fascial sheath offers the greatest resistance to stretch. When we stretch, we must stretch muscle and fascia together. Fascia becomes more pliable when it is warm. Physiologically, long-lasting changes in flexibility are more easily accomplished when stretching is performed with an elevated body temperature.

The interplay of the nervous system and the muscular system produces movement through muscles shortening and lengthening. The mechanism responsible for muscles shortening or contracting is located in the small units of a single muscle fiber, the **sarcomere**. The sarcomere is composed of thin and thick filaments called actin and myosin. When an impulse is generated by the nervous system, it triggers the actin and myosin causing the two filaments to pull closer together. This is the "contractile mechanism" or "contractile theory" of how muscles change length.

Muscles are protected by neurological commands carried out by reflexes. A reflex is a response that bypasses the brain and is transmitted directly from muscles to the spinal cord and back to the muscles. Embedded in the musculotendinous unit are two intrinsic receptors, the muscle spindle and the Golgi tendon organ. The function of these receptors is to detect when a muscle has been extended or stretched and to respond by cueing the muscle to contract or release. Anytime a muscle is stretched, a signal is sent to contract that same muscle. This reaction is called the stretch reflex.

The muscle spindle lies parallel and between the contractile fibers in muscles. It is a very small receptor responsible for activating the stretch reflex. The spindle is sensitive to length changes (tonic response) in a muscle (such as when we stretch) and responds to the rate or speed (phasic response) at which the length occurs. Most spindles have two types of intervention. Primary afferent fiber (Type I) responds to the speed of a stretch. The faster you stretch, the greater the response. Stretching with fast, bouncing movements will cause the monosynatic stretch reflex to fire and immediately send a signal to the muscle being stretched to contract (and relax the opposing muscles). The secondary fibers (Type II) conduct impulses at a slower rate. They respond to the final stretch length and act to relax the prime muscle, thus facilitating the stretch. For example, when a stretch is done slowly, these Type II fibers become active. Stretching slowly and holding the stretch allows the muscle spindles to reset (to become sensitive at a longer length) and shuts off the stretch reflex signal causing muscle contraction. Resetting a spindle allows a muscle to be stretched further before it fires.

The Golgi tendon organ (GTO) is located at the musculotendinous junction. This receptor is a protective device detecting changes in muscle tension and length. The GTO responds by inhibiting muscle contraction; for example, when the elbow is extended and excessive loads are placed on the joint area, the GTO will respond by signaling muscles to release, thereby causing the elbow to flex or bend.

Knowing the physiology of muscle composition and nerve receptors is the basis for understanding the pros and cons of different stretching techniques.

Techniques of Stretching

The physiological aspects of muscles, connective tissue and the stretch reflex have influenced the controversy as to what stretching methods are the safest and most effective.

There are four major stretching techniques:

1. **Ballistic:** A high-force, short duration method relying on speed and body weight to stretch the muscle. The speed used in this method causes the stretch reflex to be activated very quickly. Two opposing forces act on the muscle group: the force generated from the fast stretch attempting to lengthen the muscle, and the reflexive contraction of that same group. Using fast bouncing, rhythmic motion, especially if there is a high degree of force, can and is associated with greater muscle soreness. "Pulsing" is also included in this category.

2. **Slow:** Involves a gradual lengthening of specific muscle groups. The stretch is performed at a very slow tempo and can be useful in warming up before static stretching or in preparation for movement activities. Slow stretching is often called "rhythmic limbering" and incorporated into a warm-up routine.

3. **Static:** This is the most popular form of stretching. A stretch is made and held in a terminal position from ten seconds to several minutes. This is the technique used in yoga. Holding the stretch allows the muscle spindle to rest, and the initial muscle contraction triggered by the stretch

reflex to diminish. The static position promotes long-term changes in passive flexibility because it is low force and long duration. This method is considered very safe and will not cause undue muscle soreness.

4. **PNF** (Proprioceptive Neuromuscular Facilitation): This is a currently popular method of stretching that originated from physical therapy as a clinical technique. Generally requiring a partner (although a wall or bar can be used for some positions) this method involves a series of steps alternating contraction, relaxation and movement of specific muscle groups. The steps are as follows:

1. Put the muscle group in an elongated position.
2. Gradually contract the stretched muscle group isometrically (without moving the joint) until near maximum effort.
3. Hold the contraction 6-10 seconds.
4. Relax the contracting muscles.
5. Contract concentrically the opposing muscle group, extending the stretch (the partner can aid this stretch with gentle pressure to move the limb).

Repeat the above process three to four more times to fully stretch the muscle groups.

Why PNF is effective is not totally clear. Physiologically, this technique takes full advantage of the muscle spindle, stretch reflex and GTO responses along with reciprocal inhibition. The one drawback to PNF is the need for a partner. PNF does not lend itself to a class situation but is very useful in one-to-one training.

Increasing Flexibility

Long-term changes in flexibility are not well documented, but most experts agree that permanent muscle changes are possible when tissue temperature is elevated and low force, long duration is applied. Studies have shown that raising the temperature of a tendon increases the amount of permanent length change. The viso-elastic properties of all connective tissues make them more pliable when warm. For this reason, warming up before you stretch should make stretching more productive and possibly safer.

Using stretch techniques that limit the involvement of the stretch reflex appear to reduce stretching soreness. To increase flexibility hold stretches for at least 20 seconds and move in and out of the stretch positions slowly.

The greatest resistance to stretch is provided by the fascial sheath that stretch at least 20 seconds and moves in and out of the stretch positions slowly.

The greatest resistance to stretch is provided by the fascial sheath that covers the muscle. For this reason, it is important to feel the sensation of stretch in the center portion of the muscle. If the stretch pulls on the attachment sites, such as the base of the kneecap (attachment of the patella ligament to the tibial tuberosity) undue strain can be placed on the ligaments. Concentrate on extending the muscles in positions that do not put stress on the attachment points where ligaments are connected to bones.

Stretching is a natural activity, but effective and safe conditioning for flexibility requires an understanding of kinesiological principles. As with all fitness components, flexibility is developed by following a consistent program.

TYPES
- *Ballistic*
- *Slow*
- *Static*
- *PNF*

Hold stretch at least 20 seconds

Structuring a regular time to stretch helps to maintain regularity. Because stretching is a time to slow down, it can be a time to increase body awareness and reduce stress. As the body becomes more supple, moving with greater range of motion will make all other exercising easier and more enjoyable.

 CHECKLIST

Stretching Guidelines

To insure quality training for flexibility remember the following:

1. Use stretch positions that are safe for the joints. Be aware of body alignment while stretching.

2. Stretch until you feel a mild tension but not terrible pain in the muscle. Monitor the pulling sensation in the belly of the muscle. Avoid discomfort around the ligaments of the joints.

3. Hold the stretches 30-60 seconds. Avoid bouncing and pulsing because they elicit the stretch reflex.

4. Breathe slowly without breath holding and with concentration. Create a relaxed mental state, and stretch in a comfortable environment.

5. Stretch when the body is warm. The best results occur when your muscles are warmed up. Consider jogging in place or stationary cycling for 5 to 10 minutes until you "break a sweat" before doing your stretch routine. Also do stretching after your cooldown at the end of exercise.

6. Keep your program simple, regular, painless, and soothing. Incorporate stretching into your exercise program at least three days or up to seven days/week.

References

Alter, M. (1980). *Science of stretching.* Champaign Ill., Human Kinetics.

Anderson, B. (1980). *Stretching.* California, Shelter Publications.

Buroker, K., and Schwane, J. (1989). Does postexercise static stretching alleviate delayed muscle soreness? *The Physician and Sportsmedicine,* 17: 6.

Clippinger-Robertson, K. (1987). Flexibility for aerobics and fitness, *Seattle Sports Medicine.*

Cornelius, W. (1990). Modified PNF stretching: improvement in hip flexion. *National Strength and Conditioning Association Journal NSCA,* 12: 44-46.

Etnyre, B., & Lee, E. (1988). Chronic and acute flexibility of men and women using three different stretching techniques, *Research Quarterly forExercise and Sport,* 59:3: 222-228.

Holstein, B. (1988). *Shaping up for a healthy pregnancy.* Ill.: Life Enhancement Pub.

Hortobagyi, T., Faludi, J., Tihanyi, J., & Merkely, B. (1985). Effects of intense "stretching" flexibility training on the mechanical profile of the knee extensors and on the range of motion of the hip joint. *International Journal of Sports Medicine,* 6: 317-321.

Larson, L.A., & Michelman, H. (1973). *International guide to fitness and health.* New York: Crown Publishers.

Perez, M., & Fumasoli, S. (1984). Benefit of proprioceptive neuromuscular facilitation on the joint mobility of youth-aged female gymnasts with correlations for rehabilitation. *American Corrective Therapy Journal,* 38:6: 142-146.

Rasch, P. (1989). *Kinesiology and Applied Anatomy.* Philadelphia: Lea & Febiger.

Roundtable (1984). Flexibility. *NSCA Journal,* August-Sept.: 10-73.

Ryan, A.J., & Stephens, R.E. (1988). *The dancer's complete guide to healthcare and a long career.* Chicago: Bonus.

Shellock, F.G. and Prentice, W.E. (1985). Warming-up and stretching for improved performance and prevention of sports-related injuries. *Sports Medicine,* 2: 267-278.

Wilson, G., Elliot, B.C., Wood, B., & Stretch, G. (1992). Shorten cycle performance enhancement through flexibility training. *Medicine and Science in Sport and Exercise,* 24: 116-123.

Wilson, G., Elliot, B.C., & Wood, G.A. (1991). Optional stiffness of the series elastic component in a stretch-shorten cycle activity. *Journal of Applied Physiology,* 70: 825-833.

Coordination
The Overlooked Fitness Component

10

Judith Gantz, MA, CMA

Focus

THE AEROBIC CLASS IS FULL OF BODIES bobbing up and down. Across the room, an exerciser is moving with grace and precision while another participant is struggling with what foot to use and what direction to go. What accounts for the dramatic difference in movement? The precise and controlled mover has mastered coordination, the component that is often underplayed and overlooked in fitness programs.

Training for strength or aerobic endurance requires moving in patterns that use specific amounts of speed and force. The ability to move with accurate form, fluidity and control is determined by our coordination. When coordination is poor, joint alignment suffers and a multitude of strains and tears can occur. To avoid injury, one must exercise with kinesiological precision. For this reason, coordination is actually the foundation for all other fitness components.

Responding Neuromuscularly

Human movement takes place only as a result of neuromuscular activity. The simple action of taking a step involves a series of neuromuscular commands. Muscles are programmed to work in concert, creating primary joint actions while simultaneously calling into play muscles to stabilize, neutralize and extend in their opposite directions. Although we often think of "working the hamstrings," the brain does not perceive single muscle commands. Bending the knee involves a series of neuromuscular changes that are learned, practiced and remembered in sequences and patterns.

When we exercise, our movements are learned as sequences of action. Holding a barbell and squatting up and down is not only developing strength but programming the nervous system in a particular coordination. Any error in our coordination produces faulty alignment, better known as improper technique. Moving with improper technique offsets bony articulation and places undue stress on the soft tissues and muscles surrounding the joints. Our soft tissues—ligaments, fascia, tendons—were not designed to withstand high degrees of compressive forces. It is our bones and, to a degree, cartilage, that have the capacity to withstand impactive loads. For this reason, having poor coordination, especially when moving strenuously, can contribute to injury.

Well-coordinated movement is characterized by minimal expenditure of energy, while simultaneously producing force and applying it in the most advantageous direction. In teaching aerobics, how often have you given students corrections to keep their lower backs from hyperextending when executing a routine? When lifting weights, people also need careful instruction in how to maintain form and avoid awkward positions that will stress the spine, knees or shoulders. Once we have mastered coordination and movement efficiency, our actions look controlled and graceful. For some, this comes naturally, for others it is a fitness component that must be learned, cultivated and practiced.

> *Coordination =*
> *Correct form and technique =*
> *Efficient movement*

Fitness instructors can play an important role in helping an exerciser move with greater precision. The attention an instructor gives to correcting body position in any exercise activity is the first step in teaching coordination.

Proprioceptive Feedback

Developing coordination demands learning how to sense and feel how the body moves through space. The "movement sense" or kinesthetic perception involves proprioceptive feedback which tells us where the joints are positioned and how muscles exert effort. The kinesthetic and proprioceptive mechanisms rely on an ebb and flow of information between the sensory and motor neurons of the nervous system.

Kinesthetic Knowledge

Our sensory system picks up data and sends this to the nervous system for processing. The response sent from the sensory information comes from the motor neurons responsible for muscle action and movement. Sensory feedback *detects errors* in coordination, for example, when someone feels their lower back hyperextending during an exercise. The motor system processes the response of how to *correct those errors,* and feeds into our "kinesthetic knowledge," educating the neuromuscular system for error correction. The interplay of how the sensory and motor responses are organized varies the degree of force, timing and muscular control.

Coordination has been defined by medical expert Hans Kraus as the "well timed and well-balanced functioning together of several muscles in a single movement." Coordination requires training the neuromuscular system through repetition and feedback so the chosen movement activity becomes efficient.

Efficient movement is impossible without the smooth function of the nervous system. In any movement all the systems of the body are brought into play and work through the nervous system to produce balance, timing and muscular control.

Elements of Coordination

The three main elements of coordination are:
- **Balance Control**—The ability to adjust the center of gravity effectively to any base, stationary or moving.
- **Timing Control**—Setting and following the rhythm of a motion.
- **Muscular Control**—The ability to relax and keep muscles uncontracted if they are not needed for the execution of a movement.

Developing balance, timing and muscular control is a complex learning process. When you are teaching adults, remember to provide: 1) awareness and conscious attention to various movement patterns; 2) feedback and instruction to gain kinesthetic skills in error detection and error correction; 3) successful practice to establish new and accurate coordination patterns.

Learning to move in new ways is a complicated phenomena. All elements of coordination work together, but for purpose of explanation, each area will be looked at individually. Suggestions will be given about how to incorporate coordination principles into teaching practices and warm-up routines.

Balance Control

Developing a kinesthetic sense for balance requires learning how to shift weight. Weight shifting is the ability to mobilize the center of weight (located in the pelvis in an upright position), for the purpose of changing spatial directions or levels. Weight shifting informs the mover what foot is bearing the body's weight. Many students who feel clumsy in aerobic dance lack the kinesthetic perception of knowing where and when their weight shifted. Mastering balance control makes picking up exercise combinations much easier.

The following methods will assist in teaching the skill of weight shifting:

1. Begin by having students focus awareness on the pelvis. The pelvis transfers weight through the legs, feet and ground surface.
2. Slowly transfer or shift weight from right foot to left foot in directions of front-back, side-side and diagonals front and back. Give feedback if the weight shifting is occurring with proper alignment through the spine, hips, knees and ankles.
3. Design routines that shift weight through space on two feet and in various directions. Include moves that shift from two feet to one and hold balance on one leg.
4. Observe how students perceive the accuracy of their movement. Do they know when and how the weight is shifting? Can they self-correct, or do they still need more feedback from the teacher?

Timing Control

All movement takes place in time with specific rhythmic structures. How quickly one shifts weight or the timing used to move up and down from a step is timing control.

The following methods will assist in teaching the skill of timing:

1. Clap the rhythm while standing in place. (This is similar to what some aerobic dance instructors do as a lead-in to warm-up.) Add clapping and step together in a slow weight shift pattern. Establish that the student can hear and perform the clap with accuracy.
2. Start with moves that are slow and even. Add speed and rhythmic complexity to increase skill level. Ask the students to count and observe if their tempo speeds up or slows down drastically.
3. Move the whole body in one rhythm. Do not split up body parts, having them move at different times to different counts.
4. Observe how students perceive the accuracy of their timing. Do they know when to initiate a move? Can they self-correct their timing to match the teacher's or do they still need more feedback and assistance?

Muscular Control

Coordinated moves always look effortless, even when they're not. The ability to engage just the right amount of muscular effort comes with practice and repetition. When extra muscles are contracted or holding tension without purpose, our coordination is impaired and we look tight or awkward. Learning how to relax unnecessary muscle tension is a very important aspect of coordination.

Muscle control also involves executing actions that integrate the body parts. When our trunk (spine and pelvis) and limbs (arms and legs) move as a whole, every part looks connected and the flow of motion produces fluidity and precision. Many deep muscles connect the limbs to the spine, and most often the spine is either the stabilizer or initiatory of the movement. When an exerciser lifts a weight overhead, the spine stabilizes the work of the arms. In a pitcher's throw, the spine and pelvis give mobilizing power and thrust to the arm.

The following methods will assist in teaching muscular control:

- Demonstrate how to initiate a move, emphasizing where the movement starts in the body and what areas stabilize. For example, when a person presses a weight overhead, the spine stays held in upright alignment while the arms lift and push upwards.
- Make corrections when extra muscle tension is used during an action. Give clear instructions to move or relax a joint area, such as, "Move the shoulders up when the weight is lifted." Telling a student not to use a single muscle, such as the trapezius, is not as useful as identifying the specific body areas. Check to be sure the feedback is understood by watching the student execute an action without instructions. It can be helpful to use various methods of feedback, such as touch (kinesthetic), verbal instructions (auditory) or a mirror (visual).
- Teach exercises that use the whole body in one action, then trade off with exercises that isolate body parts. For example, lead a warm-up that reaches high with the arms, torso and legs; and alternate with smaller, isolating actions for the shoulders, hips or trunk.
- For the student who carries a great deal of tension, additional relaxation exercises and body therapy techniques such as Bartrnieff, Feldenkrais, Alexander, or stretching and yoga will assist in developing the kinesthetic sense to identify muscle tension and learn how to release it.

Summary

Many skillful professionals already teach coordination principles without knowing it. Instructors who correct exercise form are addressing this fitness component but may need to consistently incorporate it into their classes or training sessions. As with all fitness elements, every person has genetic gifts that seem to enable them to excel in strength, aerobic endurance, flexibility or coordination. The challenge for a teacher or trainer is to create balanced programs that work on all areas of fitness development from the beginner to the advanced student. Each type of exercise—especially sport and dance—should provide knowledge of how to master correct form and movement efficiency while improving physical conditioning. Every fitness program stands to benefit from including instruction in coordination.

References

Broer, M., & Zernicke, R. (1979). *Efficiency of human movement.* Philadelphia: Saunders Pub.

Kraus, H. (1947). Therapeutic exercise in pediatrics. *Medical Clin. North America,* 31: 629.

Part 2

Safety Guidelines

Common Aerobic Injuries

11 *Prevention and Treatment*

Patti Mantia, MEd
Linda Mason, PT

Focus

Instructors sustain the majority of injuries

Probable causes of common injuries in aerobics:

- exercise or non-resilient floor surfaces
- use of improper footwear
- improper progressions
- poor body mechanics
- postural misalignments/deviations
- inadequate muscular strength/muscle symmetry
- improper or insufficient warm-up
- poor flexibility
- inferior choreography

THE FOCUS OF THIS CHAPTER is to create an awareness of injuries common to the aerobic/exercise class setting. Recognition of injury potential, common injuries and treatments may be instrumental in protecting our students, ourselves and our sport. The decision to teach exercise programs comes with inherent responsibilities. These responsibilities include, yet are not limited to, the ability to instruct participants through a safe and effective exercise session.

Background

In order to conduct a quality exercise program, the instructor must have a basic understanding of the exercise sciences (anatomy, physiology and kinesiology), the principles of fitness conditioning and, in addition, must be able to recognize the potential for injury. Additionally, the instructor must have the skills necessary to transfer this knowledge into a practical setting.

Since its origin nearly two decades ago, aerobic exercise programs have attracted millions of enthusiastic participants. The numerous benefits obtained from aerobic programs are well documented and demonstrate the validity of this sport. However, like any form of exercise, aerobic classes carry a certain potential for injury. Fortunately, the potential for injury can be minimized by the prudent instructor.

A review of the scientific studies performed regarding injuries in aerobic classes demonstrates similar findings. The majority of injuries sustained in aerobic classes are reported by the instructor. In fact, four times as many instructors than participants have suffered from the repetitive stresses of aerobics.[3] These findings concur with similar research in that overuse is most commonly associated with injuries in aerobic classes.[9, 3, 4] The injuries tend to occur in the lower extremities, with the majority reported in the lower leg and foot.[9, 3]

Floor Surface

The nature of aerobic classes provides movement patterns that multiply the gravitational forces on the body. Therefore, a resilient floor surface that will give and absorb impact is recommended. Instructors often prefer specific surfaces for various types of classes: wood for jazz, carpet over mats for high impact aerobics. Exercise on concrete or other hard surfaces is never recommended.

Footwear

See "Safe
Foundations:
Shoes and
Floors."

Proper footwear is the most valuable piece of equipment for the aerobic participant. An aerobic shoe that provides adequate cushioning will help protect the lower extremities from impact shock. A shoe designed specifically for the biomechanical actions of aerobics is preferred. That is, the shoe should provide support and cushioning in the metatarsal region where the initial impact lands. The longitudinal arch should be properly supported, and the heel counter should be firm and stable. Footwear must be carefully selected to accommodate the individual's foot structure and type of class activity. A width sizing is recommended for a broad foot.

Progressions

Improper progressions are often exhibited by the novice exerciser. Frequently, the overzealous participant will begin with and/or rapidly advance to a regimen that is beyond their physical capacity. The result is, as one might suspect, muscle soreness, fatigue and possibly injury. This is the primary reason that new participants drop out. A recommendation of muscle conditioning and low impact programs may be appropriate for the unconditioned participant. Certainly, the novice exerciser should begin with the minimum recommendations, i.e., 3 days per week, 20 minutes of aerobic activity performed at 55-60% of the maximum attainable heart rate. Progressions that follow should be limited to one variable at a time, never increasing by more than one variable per week. The prudent instructor will not hesitate to advise students in this regard.

Body Mechanics

Maintenance of proper posture and body mechanics are essential components of injury prevention. The body should be erect and a natural alignment should be maintained. Particular attention must be given to the knees and spine. Exercise selection should allow participants to maintain proper alignment and not place unnecessary stresses on vulnerable joints. For example, when weight bearing the hip, knee and foot should be facing one direction to avoid torque at the knee. Instructors should carefully monitor participants throughout the class for proper body alignment.

Postural Misalignments

Postural misalignments such as genu valgus (knock knees) or genu varus (bowlegs) may predispose participants to injuries. Students with known postural misalignments, who have had pain in the past, or who experienced injury that has not completely healed as a result of exercise should be referred to a physician or physical therapist.

Postural deviations of the spine may lead to difficulties in exercise performance and/or injury to the participant. A certain degree of deviation is common as no two individuals are exactly alike. However, excessive spinal deviations, such as scoliosis, lordosis or kyphosis may result in increased injury potential. The injury may be a direct cause of the deviation itself, or a result of postural compensation.

Scoliosis, a lateral curvature of the spine, usually occurs in the thoracic region. This deviation often prevents the participant from maintaining proper spinal alignment and may result in pain or injury.

However, not all individuals with scoliosis are symptomatic, as symptoms vary according to the degree or severity of the deviation. Although diagnosis should be made only by a medical practitioner, scoliosis may be recognized by observation of different shoulder heights of the individual when the individual bends forward and is observed from behind. The causes of scoliosis may be structural or functional.

Functional scoliosis is a result of a muscular imbalance between the right and left sides of the body. Exercise programs that address muscular imbalances are often used by the therapist to correct or alleviate functional scoliosis. Congenital, or structural, scoliosis is difficult to manage with exercise. Students with suspected scoliosis or who experience symptoms should be referred to a physician or physical therapist.

The low back, or lumbar spine, is designed to have a degree of curvature, known as posterior concavity. Excessive curve of this region, termed lordosis, is associated with an anterior tilt of the pelvis. Although lordosis may be congenital in nature, it is often a result of tight hip flexor and back extensor muscles and weak abdominals. Strengthening of the abdominal muscles and stretching of the hip flexors and back extensors may alleviate this condition. Individuals with lordosis who experience musculoskeletal or neurological pain or discomfort should be referred for medical evaluation.

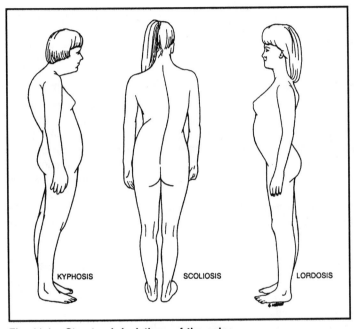

Fig. 11-1. Structural deviations of the spine

Normal curve of the thoracic spine is known as posterior convexity. Excessive curvature of this region is properly termed kyphosis. Kyphosis is often seen in older women and could be a result of osteoporosis or osteoarthritis.(8) Other common causes of kyphosis include muscular imbalances, inflammation of the spine and poor posture. Kyphosis may be identified with a rounded appearance of the shoulders, tight pectoral muscles and overstretched middle trapezius and rhomboid muscles. Kyphosis is often accompanied by a forward head (cervical lordosis) as the individual must compensate the cervical spine to look in a forward direction. Treatment administered by the physician or therapist will vary according to cause and severity.

A review of Figure 11-1 will help familiarize the instructor with common postural deviations. If the instructor suspects that any postural deviation or misalignment is compromising the safety of exercise for the individual, a medical referral should be given.

Inadequate Muscle Strength/Muscle Symmetry

Aerobic classes, by nature, present impact loads or stress to the body. Adequately developed musculature will help absorb and disperse the shock of impact throughout the body and will, therefore, reduce injury potential. It may be advisable for the novice exerciser to begin with a muscle conditioning program and/or low impact activities to decrease injury potential.

Instructors should include exercises to help develop muscular endurance/strength and be aware of the agonist/antagonist relationship. Imbalances between opposing muscle groups may predispose participants to injury.

Improper or Insufficient Warm-Up

The warm-up period is designed to prepare the body for the exercise that will follow. The combination of rhythmic limbering exercises and static stretching is believed to reduce potential for injury. Exercise selection for the warm-up period should mimic the work to follow and be appropriate for the group setting. (Modifications for some individuals may be required.) Students should be advised of the importance of the warm-up period and encouraged to arrive to class on time.

Poor Flexibility

Flexibility refers to range of motion and joint mobility and is specific to joint design. Although flexibility does not directly relate to health, it is a key component of fitness. The importance of flexibility exercises is sometimes ignored. Just as hypermobility may compromise stability within a joint, inflexibility of the musculotendinous structures may predispose participants to injury. Acute muscle injuries are more likely to occur when the muscle fibers or surrounding tissues are taut and incapable of withstanding sudden forceful stretches.

Instructors should include a carefully planned series of static stretches at the end of each class and encourage students to participate in this very important segment.

Inferior Choreography

Exercise selection should be carefully reviewed so that a training effect can be achieved with minimal stress to the body. This is, to some extent, specific to the population involved.

The experienced and prudent instructor will consider many factors to minimize injury potential in class:

- Choreography should be such that repeated stresses over one body part are avoided.
- Higher stress movements should be interspersed with lower stress activities.
- Movement patterns should be carefully choreographed to avoid sudden, rapid changes in direction.
- Modifications should be frequently included to accommodate all levels of fitness.

It is important to remember that the instructor's responsibility does not end with class design. Careful supervision and instruction is vital to ensure safety of exercise.

Even the most carefully planned and well executed exercise programs carry a certain potential for injury. It is important for the instructor to be familiar with the common injuries associated with fitness programs. The instructor must also recognize the limits of their training, and refer all injuries to medical professionals for evaluation and treatment.

If you strengthen the agonist, you must strengthen the antagonist.

See AFAA Standards & Guidelines for repetitive moves.

Acute Versus Chronic Injury

Overuse Syndrome

The most common type of injury in aerobic dance is chronic or long term in nature. When excessive, repeated stress is placed on one area of the body over an extended period of time, the tissue may begin to fail. This failure results in a chronic injury, often called "overuse syndrome." There is no specific trauma or incident that causes the injury and symptoms may persist for months with little change and/or frequent acute exacerbations.

An acute injury has a sudden onset due to a specific trauma, such as twisting your ankle. If the symptoms of an acute injury are ignored and the tissues continue to be stressed, the injury may become chronic. For example, a groin pull or hip adductor tendinitis can originate acutely from an excessive or fast lunging lateral movement. If it is not appropriately treated with RICE (Rest, Ice, Compression, and Elevation), the injury could become chronic.

Treatment

Providing a safe environment for exercising students is one of your primary responsibilities as an aerobics instructor. A safe environment includes the means to deal effectively with emergencies when they arise. The most basic of these means is a comprehensive first-aid kit for the treatment of minor injuries. The ideal kit can be purchased intact from Zee Medical Supply.

Treatment of an acute injury consists of RICE: Rest, Ice, Compression and Elevation.

Rest is necessary for proper healing to occur. Recommendations for rest depend upon the severity of the injury and vary from modifications of the exercise program to complete non-use.

Ice is used to decrease swelling and diminish pain. Ice can be applied directly in the form of ice cups or ice packs or indirectly through a plastic bag or towel. "Real ice" or a package of frozen vegetables such as peas are preferred over "chemical" ice which does not melt or freeze safely and may over-cool the tissues. Icing should be stopped when the skin begins to turn pink (usually no longer than 10-20 minutes) and can be applied repeatedly every 2-3 hours. Recommendations regarding the duration of ice therapy vary from 2-3 days, or until no further swelling is present.

Compression also helps to decrease swelling. Ace bandages and elastic wraps are examples of compression devices, and they may be used in conjunction with ice. The area above and below the injury should also be included in the wrapping to ensure even compression.

Elevation of the injured area helps to decrease swelling, as long as the afflicted area is raised above the level of the heart. For example, to sufficiently elevate the lower extremity, you must lie supine with the lower extremity elevated and supported versus sitting with the lower extremity at the same level as the hip.

For injuries that persist and/or increase in discomfort or swelling, see a physician as soon as possible. Also consult a medical doctor for any injury that involves joint pain or in which the effected area appears out of alignment.

Common Injuries

The following are the most commonly reported injuries in aerobic dance exercise. Possible treatment is suggested for each injury, but it is strongly recommended that all pain be evaluated and treated under a physician's care.

Patello Femoral Arthalgia is an overuse injury affecting the articular cartilage of the posterior surface of the patella, or kneecap. Common symptoms are:

- generalized pain that tends to increase with weight bearing knee flexion activities (such as squats), walking up or down stairs, or sitting for a long period of time with bent knees
- swelling
- grinding or grating noises

The exact cause is unknown and may be multivariable. Abnormal lateral tracking of the patella in the groove of the femur is a contributing factor. Excessive weight bearing during knee flexion, an abnormally positioned or shaped patella and ankle or hip deviations worsen the pateller tracking and

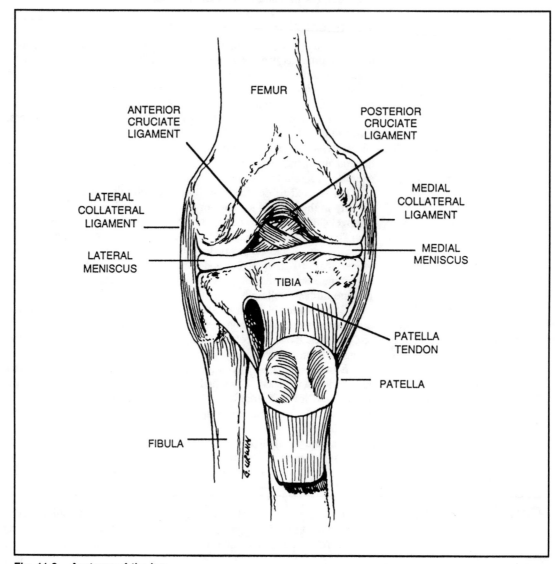

Fig. 11-2. Anatomy of the leg

cause inflammation. Prescription may include ice for acute exacerbations and a change of activity is usually required. Strengthening the quadriceps muscle and correcting abnormal foot motion may also help.

Shin splints is a catch-all term for pain occurring in the anterior or lateral lower leg and is the most frequently reported injury in aerobics. The majority of the pain is anterior tibialis muscle, tibial periostitis and/or stress fractures of the tibia. Treatment varies from RICE to immobilization with no weight bearing activity allowed. If any numbness or weakness occurs in the foot distal to the site of anterior tibial pain, a surgical condition called anterior compartment syndrome could be the cause. Clients with changes in sensation and strength of any body part should be referred immediately to a physician.

Anterior compartment syndrome is a very common injury in running. It is a condition involving the three muscles in the anterior compartment of the leg: the tibialis anterior, extensor hallicus longus and extensor digitorum longus. These muscles all perform ankle dorsiflexion. If these muscles are overworked, it will lead to swelling of the muscles and pressure to the fascia encompassing the muscles. This pressure may restrict blood flow to the muscle and lead to pain, numbness and paralysis. This condition can be a medical emergency. Treatment varies from RICE to surgical intervention.

Metatarsalgia is a term used for generalized pain and/or tenderness in the metatarsals, the heads of the long bones of the foot. Possible etiology is degenerative changes in the arches of the feet and/ or excessive or repeated

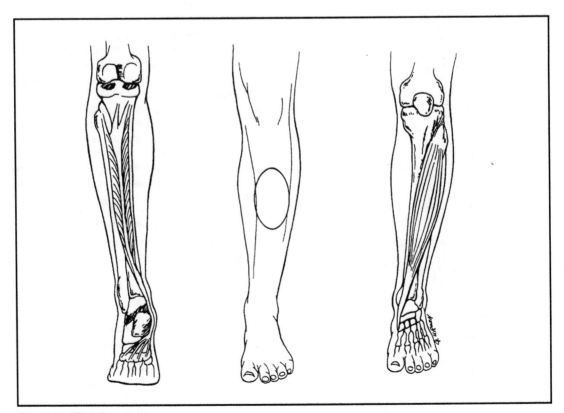

Fig. 11-3. Tibia/fibia pain

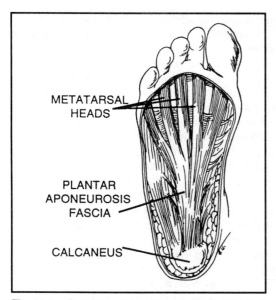

METATARSAL HEADS

PLANTAR APONEUROSIS FASCIA

CALCANEUS

Fig. 11-4.   Anatomy of the plantar aspect of the foot

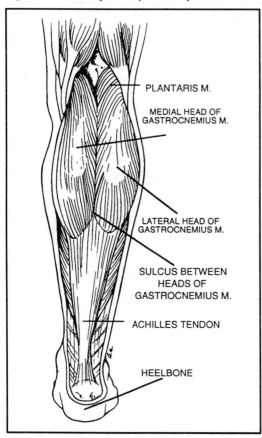

PLANTARIS M.

MEDIAL HEAD OF GASTROCNEMIUS M.

LATERAL HEAD OF GASTROCNEMIUS M.

SULCUS BETWEEN HEADS OF GASTROCNEMIUS M.

ACHILLES TENDON

HEELBONE

Fig. 11-5.   Anatomy of the Posterior Leg

force on the ball of the foot, as in jumping. RICE is recommended. Stress fractures must be considered.

Plantar Fascitis refers to inflammation of the fascia or connective tissue of the plantar or bottom surface of the arch of the foot. Pain commonly originates near the calcaneal insertion (heel) of the fascia and will progressively radiate towards the ball of the foot with increasing severity of inflammation. RICE, heel cushions and arch supports are possible therapeutic measures.

Stress fractures are microscopic fractures that occur usually to a weight bearing bone, such as tibia (leg bone) or metatarsals (foot bones). Pain is usually localized to one area and crescendos during activity. The fractures are usually due to repeated stress or overuse of the area. These fractures occur gradually and are not usually seen in X-rays during the early stages. Treatment may vary from a recommendation of modifications in impact to complete non weight bearing, by use of crutches. A stress fracture in the femur is a more serious form of stress fracture which may be present with diffuse hip pain.

Tendinitis is inflammation of the connective tissue that joins a muscle to a bone. The Achilles tendon is prone to this injury in aerobic dance. This is the common tendon of the gastrocnemius and the soleus muscles of the calf muscles. It inserts into the back of the heelbone. RICE and a cushioned heel lift is the recommended therapy. Stretching before and after exercise is key in prevention.

A **sprain** is a tearing or overstretching of a ligament. A ligament is connective tissue that connects bone to bone. Sprains are classified as first, second or third degree depending upon the severity. Recovery length can vary from days to months. Ligaments may be permanently deformed thereby increasing your potential for injury in future activities. Recommended treatment is RICE and assessment by a physician to determine severity and need for bracing.

A **strain** is an overstretching or tearing of a muscle or tendon. Severity can range from a minimum of torn fibers up to complete tearing from the bone called an avulsion. RICE is the recommended therapy, followed by early assessment by a physician.

> *For information on vocal injury, see "Voice Care & Injury Prevention."*

Summary

The injuries discussed in this chapter are the most prevalent in the aerobic class setting. The prudent instructor will regard this information as the basis for a medical referral and not diagnose injuries or recommend treatment.

References

1. Arnheim, D.D. (1985). *Modern principles of athletic training.* St. Louis: Times Mirror/Mosby College Publishing.
2. Cooper, P.G. (Ed.) (1987). *Aerobics: theory and practice,* Costa Mesa, Ca.: HDL Publishing Company.
3. Francis, L.L., Francis, P.R., & Welshons-Smith, K. (1985). Aerobic dance injuries: a survey of instructors. *The Physician and Sports Medicine,* 13:2: 105-111.
4. Garrick, J.G., Gillien, D.M., & Whiteside, P. (1986). The epidemiology of aerobic dance injuries. *American Journal of Sports Medicine,* 14: 67-72.
5. Gould, J.A., & Davies, G.J. (1985). *Orthopedic and sports physical therapy.* St. Louis: C.V. Mosby Co.
6. Moore, K.L. (1985). *Clinically oriented anatomy.* Baltimore: Williams and Wilkins.
7. Mutoh, M.D., et al. (1988). Aerobic dance injuries among instructors and students. *The Physician and Sports Medicine,* 16:12, 81-86.
8. Van Gelder, N. (1990). *Aerobic dance-exercise instructor manual,* San Diego, Ca.
9. Vetter, W.L., et al. (1985). Aerobic dance injuries. *The Physician and Sports Medicine,* 13:2, 114-120.

Arthur Siegel, MD

12 Medical Considerations of Aerobics

Focus

THE QUESTION IS NO LONGER "to exercise or not to exercise" but how much, how often and with what intensity to exercise in order to confer the maximum benefit in the promotion of health and fitness. Even medical patients are recommended to partake in regular physical activity, according to the latest United States Preventive Services Task Force Report, although discrepancies persist regarding specific guidelines.(1) The purpose of this chapter is to review the cardiovascular and other medical complications of exercise, and to recommend prudent actions for fitness instructors to take whenever they encounter clients with such complications.

Broadened Guidelines

The American College of Sports Medicine recently changed its exercise recommendations by lowering the intensity of range for target pulse from 60-90% of maximal heart rate in an effort to promote moderation and increased safety. In like fashion, AFAA has further expanded its training range from its original guideline of 70-80% to the present 55-85%. This recommendation translates into a strong mandate to counsel clients to introduce exercise slowly and incrementally. There are proven benefits for the cardiovascular system from regular, low intensity physical activity. The Centers for Disease Control and Prevention have made regular exercise recommendations similar to ASCM's in duration and frequency, but without intensity parameters.(2)

Recent research supports the conclusion that regular dynamic (isotonic) exercise has beneficial effects on cholesterol and blood pressure with energy expenditures as low as 40-60% of maximal heart rate. Sedentary subjects over the age of 40, individuals with coronary heart disease, and those with risk factors at any age are advised to undergo a physical examination and possibly an exercise electrocardiogram before starting an exercise program such as aerobic training. Once medical clearance has been obtained, exercise should be practiced incrementally and with low intensity to avoid musculoskeletal injury and cardiovascular strain.(3)

The acute circulatory effects of dynamic exercise in untrained persons are shown in Table 12-1. This low intensity exercise from moderate, paced walking to a conservative aerobic workout will progressively increase cardiovascular fitness from the cardiac and skeletal muscle effects shown. With dynamic exercise, systolic blood pressure is raised, but diastolic pressure usually declines, producing an increase in cardiac output, oxygen delivery and improved circulatory parameters. In addition to producing the healthful effects on cholesterol, body weight and body composition, exercise training has a

> **WITH EXERCISE**
> *Systolic BP Rises*
> *Diastolic BP Falls*

Table 12-1. Acute Hemodynamic Effects of Upright Dynamic Exercise in Untrained Persons.

Increased values	
Arteriovenous oxygen difference	2-3x
Cardiac output	2.5-4x
Coronary flow	3-5x
Ejection fraction	10%
End-diastolic volume index	5%-10%
Heart rate	2-3x
Oxygen consumption	10x
Stroke volume	20-50%
Systolic blood pressure	60-80 mm Hg
Decreased values	
Diastolic blood pressure	10-20 mm Hg
End-systolic volume index	5%-10%
Peripheral vascular resistance	60-80%
Systemic vascular resistance	60-80%

beneficial effect on coronary risk from modest hypertension by causing blood pressure to decline.(4)

As fitness improves from a regular exercise program, exercise intensity can be slowly increased with reduced injury risk and increased cardiovascular safety. Healthful exercise then becomes a part of an individual's life with a positive effect on physiological functioning as well as mental fitness and psychological sense of well-being. Both young and old can obtain these benefits with regular, moderate exercise.

Following the Exercise Prescription

A proper exercise prescription from a client's physician becomes even more important with advancing years given the underlying risk of cardiac, pulmonary, neurologic or musculoskeletal diseases which may make exercise difficult to initiate and potentially harmful if overexertion prevails.(5) Make sure the prescription for exercise from the client's physician includes recommendations for type, intensity, duration and frequency of exercise.

In some people with coronary artery disease (CAD), a target heart rate of 40-50% in an aerobic workout (once medically cleared) can provide cardiac and musculoskeletal conditioning with acceptable if not dramatic improvements in functional capacity. A modified Borg Scale of Perceived Exertion may be useful in regulating exercise intensity in low impact aerobics classes for the elderly with levels of 12-14 corresponding to a 50% of maximal heart rate level. Exercise should be initiated on the light or low end of the perceived exertion scale so that light conversation can also be conducted during workouts.

See Borg Scale in chapter on "Monitoring Aerobic Intensity."

Consistency over time maintains cardiovascular conditioning and may with adequate dietary calcium have a positive effect on bone by preventing **post menopausal osteoporosis**.(6) Moderation in intensity and consistency over time are dual pillars of an exercise program leading to health and well-being regardless of age and underlying medical conditions.

Hazards of Exercise

The professional fitness instructor needs to be fully aware of the following complications or hazards of exercise.

Heat Injury

Aerobic exercise involves the generation of internal heat through performance of muscular work. As the core temperature rises, an increased amount of cardiac output is delivered to the skin so heat can be dissipated in the form of sweating. Heat is lost principally through evaporation of sweat from the body surface, which cools the individual at the price of losing vital circulating fluids. Prolonged strenuous exercise invariably leads to dehydration, which may then lead to headache, muscle cramps, light headedness, fatigue, confusion, lethargy and persistent elevated body temperature. Advanced stages of heat exhaustion from exercise may lead to coma and even cardiac arrhythmias and sudden death. These rare and extreme hazards can be prevented by knowing ways to avoid dehydration and hyperthermia during exercise.

ACTIONS

1. Adequate hydration before exercise is the best prevention. Come to your exercise session well hydrated, passing clear-colored urine every two to four hours. Consume 8 to 10 ounces of water 10-20 minutes before beginning a light workout.

2. Insist on warming-up. The warm-up phase of exercise allows the muscles and tendons to adapt to the biomechanics of exercise while the blood flow increases to the exercising muscles. As body temperature rises, the sweating mechanism kicks into place with the perception of "second wind."

3. Prolonged exercise should involve breaks to consume additional water. Recommended intake is three ounces every 20 minutes.(4) For the overheated client, when appropriate, moisten the body surface by sponging or spraying to assist in the cooling process. Fans may aid evaporation. Such cooling measures provide a form of "external sweating," which helps to dissipate heat without using internal fluid resources for evaporation.

5. Avoid salt substitutes. Sweat is composed primarily of water lost from the tissues in a greater proportion than losses of sodium and chloride. This means that the body is under pressure to correct the imbalance. For this reason, salt substitutes are undesirable prior to strenuous exercise, and individuals should rely on the use of water alone to prevent heat injury or thermal stress.

6. Wear clothing that allows evaporation and ventilation. Appropriate dress during exercise is another important consideration in the prevention of heat stress. This involves dressing in light and loose-fitting clothing during hot weather exercise, especially on humid days when the sweating mechanism is less efficient.

7. On very hot days, stay indoors or in the shade. Exercising in full sun increases the risk of heat injury. Covering the head guards against the sun's radiant energy and protects one from dehydration as well as sunburn.

8. Avoid the use of saunas and hot tubs after exercise, which may compound the problem of fluid depletion. Fainting from orthostatic hypotension and heat-induced vasodilation are not uncommon in saunas after strenuous exercise sessions.

Cardiovascular Complications

In general, young healthy individuals require no medical clearance prior to undertaking an aerobic fitness program but would benefit from a general medical screening. Individuals at risk specifically for any cardiovascular disease, however, should have a prior medical clearance from a physician. Some of the major risk factors for development of coronary heart disease include hypertension, cigarette smoking and increased cholesterol levels. Uncontrollable factors include a positive family history, being male and advanced age. Women over 55 also have an increased risk for cardiovascular disease since they are no longer protected by high levels of estrogen.

In addition, certain conditions such as mitral valve prolapse may run in families and be associated with serious arrhythmias and even with sudden cardiac death. Individuals with any of these factors in their family history should have a systematic medical evaluation prior to undertaking a vigorous exercise program.

If a cardiac patient receives clearance from his physician to attend your class, maintain an open line of communication between the patient, yourself and his physician. If the patient is on cardiac or blood pressure medication, such as **beta blockers,** ask him to follow the target heart rate assigned by his physician, following a stress test. Beta blockers (i.e., Inderal) will neurochemically suppress the heart rate with an overall decrease in cardiac output, and prevent the patient from reaching normal training ranges for his age.

The following are some first-stage actions instructors can take in regard to preventing cardiovascular complications.

ACTIONS

1. Complete lifestyle questionnaires and fitness assessments. (See related chapters.)
2. Schedule a counseling session with the client and his physician.
3. Teach clients the importance of proper warm-up and cooldown and insist that they comply. The heart and circulation need a chance to accommodate slowly to the training range. Prevention of blood pooling in the lower extremities is of utmost importance during cooldown. Make sure clients keep walking as they take their heart rates.
4. Ask any individuals exhibiting irregular heart rate, light headedness, muscle cramps, perceived palpitations, chest discomfort or sudden, severe breathlessness to stop exercise and seek medical consultation immediately. Heart patients often describe symptoms such as a dull ache or pressure in the chest. All of these complaints warrant a halt in exercise and immediate referral to a physician, even if the individual does not describe these sensations as "pain." Extreme caution on the part of the instructor is recommended in these situations.

Exercise instructors should also be aware of the potential cardiovascular complications of exercise including the rare cases of sudden death during exercise. Studies in this area point to **silent congenital heart abnormalities** in the majority of cases of sudden collapse from heart arrhythmias during physical exertion. Such victims are young (aged 13-35) and often have a thickening of the heart muscle wall called hypertrophic cardiomyopathy. Individuals with a family history of sudden death during or even unrelated to exercise should have medical clearance prior to undertaking a progressive exercise program.

See AFAA Standards & Guidelines on Medical Clearance.

Beta blockers suppress heart rate.

Sudden collapse of young athletes

In contrast, victims of sudden death over the age of 40 usually suffer from atherosclerotic or coronary artery disease (CAD) as exemplified by the case of marathon runner Jim Fixx. Such individuals have advanced CAD and may be asymptomatic or denying symptoms prior to collapse from heart fibrillation. The absence of a recent myocardial infarction suggests that these deaths are arrhythmia induced. This emphasizes the importance of appropriate screening in older patients, especially with risk factors for underlying heart disease. The warm-up and cooldown phases of an exercise session are safety factors against the onset of such arrhythmia. The risk for sudden death has been calculated as one episode per 400,000 person-hours of jogging, which is minimal compared to the overall benefits. Exercise testing should be considered by all, but especially when risk factors, hereditary factors or symptoms are identified.

> *Warm-up and cooldown are essential for cardiac patients.*

Exercise-Induced Conditions

In spite of all its benefits, exercise is a stressor to the body, carrying a degree of risk. The following conditions—asthma, anaphylaxis and hives—can all be induced by exercise in susceptible individuals.

Exercise-Induced Asthma

The process of heat and humidity exchange from the lung space to the outside air can lead to condensation of moisture around the nose and throat, constriction of the bronchial tubes and symptoms of coughing and wheezing—the definition of exercise-induced asthma. Such individuals may have a background of allergies or be unaware of any respiratory symptoms except during exercise. Cold weather and dry air can also provoke coughing and the sensation of tightness in the central chest area.

Exercise-induced asthma is similar to the broncho-constriction experienced in "allergic" asthmatic bronchitis. Exercise-induced asthma is triggered, however, by the temperature and water exchange mechanisms described above and does not depend upon an allergic sensitivity. Symptoms may vary from day to day, may remain stable and then improve, only to worsen during the post-exercise period. Once again, symptoms may be chest heaviness with cough and, in severe cases, wheezing.

ACTIONS

1. Client brings aerosol to class. Exercise-induced asthma can be blocked and even prevented by pre-exercise treatment 20 to 30 minutes prior to exercise with aerosol medication. While several over-the-counter preparations are available, the most effective bronchodilators must be prescribed by a physician.
2. Client exercises in warm air only. Individuals can also diminish symptoms by warming inspired air, such as exercising with a surgical face mask in very cold weather. While this technique does not lend itself to the class setting, students may use these tips in other sports activities, such as cross-country skiing.

> *Bronchodilators*
> *Warm Air*

Persons susceptible to exercise-induced asthma should be examined, treated and encouraged to participate in full exercise activity for the benefit of physical conditioning. Lung function is maintained and preserved through such a program.

Exercise-Induced Anaphylaxis

Instructors should be aware of a rare but medically significant condition known as exercise-induced anaphylaxis. Some individuals may, during exercise, experience sudden facial swelling or a sense of tightness in the throat with difficulty in breathing. This reaction is similar to the type of reaction that can occur after a bee sting or penicillin exposure in a highly allergic individual. This condition requires emergency medical attention (injection of epinephrine should be administered immediately). Patients who have the unusual reaction should carry a bee-sting kit containing this medication so that attacks can be quickly treated. Anyone who develops a sudden difficulty in breathing accompanied by facial swelling should be suspected of having exercise-induced anaphylaxis. Fortunately, no fatalities have yet been reported.

> *Facial swelling is an early sign of anaphylaxis.*

ACTIONS

1. Call emergency medical personnel immediately.
2. Keep client as calm as possible until help arrives.
3. If client has a bee-sting kit (epinephrine), help him use it.

Exercise-Induced Hives

Instructor may note that some individuals develop a blotchy red rash, sometimes with itching, at the beginning of a workout. This is called exercise-induced hives, or urticaria, and results from histamine release in the skin due to rapid superficial temperature changes. The student should be assured that this condition is harmless. Low doses of antihistamines can be helpful in diminishing symptoms as long as the side effects of drowsiness are not more bothersome.

Basic mastery of the concepts of exercise physiology and the role of the cardiovascular system will better prepare the instructor to inform students. This in turn will enrich their understanding of the body's adaptation to regular exercise and the specific changes involved in promoting fitness. See references for more information on cardiovascular and other medical aspects of exercise which will enable instructors to provide sound advice and reassurance to their students.

ACTIONS

1. Determine if client has had this reaction before and knows about it.
2. Requires no emergency action. This condition is generally harmless.

Other Medical Considerations

Smoking Cessation and Exercise

Exercise training also improves the chance of becoming an ex-smoker for women participating in smoking cessation programs.[7] Women who stop smoking may experience minor weight gain including an increase in body fat, but lean body mass increases with regular exercise.[8, 9] Transdermal nicotine and a refocus on exercise may assist in the effectiveness of the smoking cessation programs. [10, 11] Smoking and sports do not mix, and the adverse effects of smoking may be greater in women than men.[12]

Estrogen and Exercise

Finally, careful studies have shown that post-menopausal estrogen treatment prolongs life and reduces coronary artery disease mortality. Other studies confirm that estrogens lower the risk of post-menopausal heart disease.(13, 14) While estrogens are safe and possibly protective in terms of coronary risk, anabolic steroids are atherogenic and hazardous.(15)

Exercise, calcium and estrogen are all helpful in preventing osteoporosis.

Exercise and Cancer Risk

While there is a great volume of literature on the beneficial effects of exercise in the primary and secondary prevention of coronary artery disease, little data exists on specific relationships between exercise and cancer. A recent study from the *Journal of the National Cancer Institute* reports a positive relationship between regular exercise and reduced risk of colon cancer.(16) The relationship between increased physical activity and decreased colon cancer rates do not prove cause and effect or a casual protective relationship, however. Low dose post-menopausal estrogen replacement does not appear to increase risk of breast cancer, but it does appear to facilitate safer exercise through the prevention of osteoporosis and reduction of coronary heart disease.(17)

Summary

Understanding the basic physiology of exercise and its benefits will enable instructors to guide clients toward sound exercise programs for health enhancement. On the other hand, knowledge of potential complications and exercise-induced hazards can help the instructor avoid pushing at-risk individuals to exhaustion. Whatever the potential for risk, there are certain common sense actions that instructors and their clients can take to avoid serious problems. Instructors should also read and be familiar with AFAA's Emergency Protocol in the Appendix.

References

1. Harris, S.S., Caspersen, C.J., DeFriese, G.H., et al (1989). Physical activity counseling for healthy adults as a primary preventive intervention in the clinical setting: report for the U.S. preventive services task force. *JAMA, 261:24: 3588-3598.*
2. Intensity of exercise now debate focus (1990). *MWN,* March 12: 20.
3. Taylor, P., Ward, A., & Rippe, J.M. (1991). Exercising to health—how much, how soon? *The Physician and Sports Medicine* 19:8.
4. Wood, P.D., et al (1991). The effects on plasma lipoproteins of a prudent weight-reducing diet, with or without exercise, in overweight men and women. *New England Journal of Medicine,* 325: 461-466.
5. Evans, W.J., & Meredith, C.N. (1989). *Nutrition, aging and the elderly.* (Eds. Hamish N. Munro & Darla E. Danford.) Plenum Publishing Corporation.
6. Nelson, M.E., Fisher, E.C., Dilmanian, F.A., et al (1991). An early walking program and increased dietary calcium in postmenopausal women: effects on bone. *American Journal of Clinical Nutrition,* 53: 1304-11.
7. Marcus, B.H., et al (1991). *American Journal of Cardiology,* 68: 406-07.
8. Williamson, D.F., Madans, J., Anda, R.F., et al (1991). Smoking cessation and severity of weight gain in a national cohort. *New England Journal of Medicine,* 324: 739-45.

9. Moffatt, R.J., & Owens, S.G. (1991). Cessation from cigarette smoking: Changes in body weight, body composition, resting metabolism, and energy consumption. *Metabolism,* 40: 465-70.
10. Daughton, D.M., & Heatley, S.A., Prendergast, J.J., et al (1991). Effect of transdermal nicotine delivery as an adjunct to low-intervention smoking cessation therapy; A randomized, placebo-controlled, double-blind study. *Archives of Internal Medicine,* 151: 749-52.
11. Hurt, R.D., Lauger, G.G., Offord, K.P., et al. Nicotine-replacement therapy with use of a transdermal nicotine patch: A randomized double-blind placebo-controlled trial. *Mayo Clinic Proceedings,* 65: 1529-37.
12. Chen, Y., et al (1991). Increased susceptibility to lung dysfunction in female smokers. *American Review of Respiratory Disease,* 143: 124-1230.
13. Egeland, G.M., Kuller, L.H., Matthews, R.A., et al. Hormone replacement therapy and lipoprotein changes during early menopause. *Obstetrics and Gynecology,* 76: 776-82.
14. Sullivan, J., Vnader Zwaag, R., Hughs, J.P., et al (1990). Estrogen replacement and coronary artery disease: Effect on survival in postmenopausal women. *Archives of Internal Medicine,* 150: 1925-1933.
15. Glazer, G. Atherogenic effects on anabolic steroids on serum lipid levels—a literature review.
16. *Journal of the National Cancer Institute,* Sept. 18.
17. Dupont, W.D., & Page, D.L. (1991). Menopausal estrogen replacement therapy and breast cancer. *Archives of Internal Medicine,* 151: 67-72.

Judith Baker, MEd

13 Lifestyle Questionnaire

Focus

THE FITNESS PROFESSIONAL is a facilitator of behavior change for clients and students. We have the important job of helping people improve their lifestyles. To help others with lifestyle changes, we need to understand how lifestyles develop, what lifestyle factors affect longevity, and how human beings change behavior. In this chapter, we will define lifestyle, identify health-enhancing behaviors, and discuss the use of lifestyle questionnaires to create awareness for both the fitness professional and the individuals we serve. It is not our job to be perfect specimens of mental and physical health, but we need to be aware of our own negative lifestyle behaviors and make positive changes so we can do our best to "walk the talk."

Why Complete a Lifestyle Questionnaire?

Lifestyle questionnaires serve to create and/or enhance awareness about behaviors and health habits of individuals, an important first step prior to making change. Many fitness enthusiasts concerned only with the cosmetic benefits of diet and exercise can be made aware of a "bigger picture" through the use of lifestyle questionnaires. Questionnaires are also useful in opening dialogue with individuals, identifying belief systems and focusing in on goals.

Lifestyle questionnaires are useful tools for the fitness professional in both group and individual settings. In group situations, students can fill out individual questionnaires and then share with a partner or small group about their positive and negative health habits and behaviors and needed changes.

Lifestyles

To find out how healthful a lifestyle you lead, take this simple test. The results will help you determine which of your health habits, if any, need improvement.

Alcohol Use *(If you do not drink check all 5 items.)*

___ 1. I drink fewer than two drinks a day.

___ 2. I never feel bad or guilty about my drinking.

___ 3. When I'm under stress or depressed, I do not drink more.

___ 4. I do not do things when I'm drinking that I later regret.

___ 5. I have never experienced any problems because of my drinking.

Tobacco Use *(If you have never smoked, check all 5 items, even though the last two items would not apply.)*

___ 1. I have never smoked cigarettes.

___ 2. I haven't smoked cigarettes in the past year.

___ 3. I do not use any other form of tobacco (pipes, cigars, chewing tobacco).

___ 4. I smoke only low tar and nicotine cigarettes.

___ 5. I smoke less than one pack of cigarettes a day.

Blood Pressure

___ 1. I have had my blood pressure checked within the last six months.

___ 2. I have never had high blood pressure.

___ 3. I do not currently have high blood pressure.

___ 4. I make a conscious effort to avoid salt in my diet.

___ 5. There is no history of high blood pressure in my immediate family.

Weight and Body Fat Levels

___ 1. According to height and weight charts, my weight is average for my height.

___ 2. I have not needed to go on a weight-reduction diet in the past year.

___ 3. There is no place on my body where I can pinch an inch of fat.

___ 4. I am satisfied with the way my body looks.

___ 5. None of my family, friends, or health care professionals has ever encouraged me to lose weight.

Physical Fitness

___ 1. I do some form of vigorous exercise for at least 30 minutes a day three times a week or more.

___ 2. My resting pulse is 70 beats a minute or less.

___ 3. I don't get fatigued easily while doing physical work.

___ 4. I engage in some recreational sport such as tennis or swimming on a weekly basis.

___ 5. I would say that my level of physical fitness is higher than that of most people in my age group.

Stress and Anxiety

___ 1. I find it easy to relax.

___ 2. I am able to cope with stressful events as well as or better than most people.

___ 3. I do not have trouble falling asleep or waking up.

___ 4. I rarely feel tense or anxious.

___ 5. I have no trouble completing tasks I have started.

Automobile Safety

___ 1. I always use seat belts when I drive.

___ 2. I always use seat belts when I am a passenger.

___ 3. I never drive an automobile after having more than two drinks.

___ 4. I never ride with a driver who has had more than two drinks.

___ 5. I have not had a speeding ticket or other moving violation during the past three years.

Relationships

___ 1. I am satisfied with my social relationships.

___ 2. I have a lot of close friends.

___ 3. I am able to share my feelings with my spouse or other family members.

___ 4. When I have a problem, I have other people with whom I can talk it over.

___ 5. Given a choice between doing things by myself or with others, I usually choose to do things with others.

Rest and Sleep

___ 1. I almost always get between seven and nine hours of sleep a night.

___ 2. I wake up few, if any, times during the night.

___ 3. I feel rested and ready to go in the morning.

___ 4. Most days, I have a lot of energy.

___ 5. Even though I sometimes have a chance, I never take naps during the day.

Life Satisfaction

___ 1. If I had my life to live over, I wouldn't make very many changes.

___ 2. I've accomplished most of the things I set out to do in life.

___ 3. I can't think of an area in my life that really disappoints me.

___ 4. I am a happy person.

___ 5. As compared to the people with whom I grew up, I feel I've done as well as or better than most of them with my life.

Scoring

Record the number of checks (from 0 to 5) for each area. Then add the numbers to determine your score.

Area	Subscore
Alcohol use	_____
Tobacco use	_____
Blood pressure	_____
Weight and body fat levels	_____
Physical fitness	_____
Stress and anxiety	_____
Automobile safety	_____
Relationships	_____
Rest and sleep	_____
Life satisfaction	_____

Interpreting Your Score

1. A score of 40 to 50 indicates a healthier than average lifestyle.

2. A score of 25 to 39 indicates an average lifestyle.

3. A score of 0 to 25 indicates a below-average lifestyle and need for overall improvement.

4. A score of less than 3 in any one area indicates a need for improvement in that particular area.

Lifestyle Questionnaire Source: Lifestyles, John M. Cavendish Ed.D. University of West Virginia, Morgantown, West Virginia, 1991.

Lifestyle Resources

1. Editors of University of California, Berkeley Wellness Letters (1991). *The wellness encyclopedia: the comprehensive family resource for safeguarding health and preventing illness.* Boston: Houghton Mifflin Publishing.
2. Russlanoff, P. (1988). *When am I going to be happy? how to break the emotional bad habits that make you miserable.* Bantam Books.
3. Ornstein, R., & Sobel, D. (1989). *Healthy pleasures.* Addison-Wesley Publishing Company Inc.
4. Borysenko, J. (1988). *Minding the body, mending the mind.* Bantam Books.

References

Mullen, et al. *Connections for health.* Dubuque, Ia: Wm C. Brown: 13

Knowles, J. (1977). *Doing better and feeling worse: health in the united states.* New York: W.W. Norton & Company.

Belloc, N., & Breslow, L. (1992). Relationship of physical health status and health practices. *Preventive Medicine,* 409-412.

Mullen, et al. *Connections for health*: 19.

Knowles, J., *Doing better and feeling worse: health in the united states,* 59.

Dishman, R.K. (1988). *Exercise adherence, its impact on public health.* Champaign, Ill.: Human Kinetics Publishing, 208.

Voice Care & Injury Prevention

14

Carol Swett, MA, CCC
Jo-Ann Ross, MA, CCC

Focus

ONE OF THE MOST IMPORTANT muscle systems of the body, the voice, tends to be severely neglected by the aerobic instructor population. Aerobic instructors depend upon their voices to provide appropriate directions and cues so that students can enjoy a smooth flow throughout the session. A voice that is clear, easily understood and carries well will be the most effective. Instructors, as professional voice users, must learn how to care for and condition their voices as they would any other major muscle group.

Anatomy and Physiology of the Vocal Mechanism

Vocalization involves integration and balance of the breathing apparatus, the spine, shoulders, neck, jaw and the articulators as well as the larynx, or vocal cords. The larynx, which is comprised of muscles, cartilage and connective tissue, houses the **vocal cords** (Fig. 14-1). These cords are a group of paired

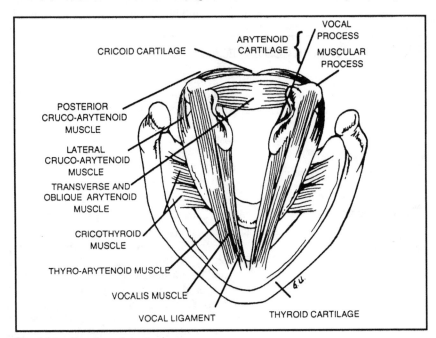

Fig. 14-1. Vocal cord anatomy

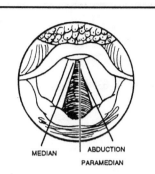

MEDIAN | ABDUCTION
PARAMEDIAN

Fig. 14-2a. Normal larynx phonation

Fig. 14-2b. Closed vocal cords

Fig. 14-3. Vocal nodules

muscles which create the movement necessary for swallowing protection, respiration, assistance in muscular mechanical advantage (Valsalva maneuver) and creating voice.

To be able to use the voice, appropriate breathing must first be considered. The muscles responsible for inhaling are the diaphragm, external intercostals, sternocleidomastoid and pectoralis major and minor. The muscles of exhalation work with the passive properties of torque, tissue elasticity and gravity and are the rectus abdominis, transverse abdominis, internal and external obliques.

During non-aerobic activities, the shoulders should not move up and down, and the upper chest should remain still. Movement is generally restricted to the abdominal area of the midsection, which moves outward and allows the body to relax and eliminate tension from the throat. The amount of time for inhalation and exhalation is about equal, except during vocalization when inhalation is rapid and exhalation is prolonged.

When working aerobically, the breathing rate is deeper, faster and heavier. The vocal cords are being forced apart in order to allow more space for the increase in oxygen supply (Fig. 14-2a). When we are voicing during this time we are actually working against the body's natural response to keep an open air space.

Excessive vocal use, vocal abuse or inappropriate use of the vocal mechanism may result in one or more warning signs. Inflammation of the vocal cords during an infection may increase your chance of having a vocal cord injury. **Sinus infection** and **nasal allergies** may worsen your chances of having a vocal cord injury. These warning signs may indicate that vocal injury has taken place. Injury to the vocal cords can be either traumatic or chronic depending upon the abuse that is occurring. Vocal injury can result in: swelling of the vocal cords, reddening of the vocal cords, laryngitis (illness-related or trauma-induced from extreme yelling or abuse), vocal nodules (Fig. 14-3) and contact ulcers.

Nodules are more prevalent among aerobic instructors and are characterized by calloused, benign growths on the vocal cord edges. They vary from the size of a pinhead to the size of a pea.

Symptoms of vocal injury:

Tired voice

Feeling a lump in the throat or need to clear the throat

Dry throat

Sore throat

Tightness or increased tension in throat

Symptoms that you or others might hear:

Hoarseness

Loss of voice or no voice at all

Squeaky, breathy or rough voice

Frequent coughing and throat clearing

Voice not heard clearly and worsens at night

Teaching Tips

1. Relaxation
   Keep the head, jaw, neck and shoulders tension free.
2. Posture
   Demonstrate abdominals or push-ups without speaking if you can, then move out of that position and continue to speak while instructing.
3. Projection
   Speak out, not down and up, not high or forced. Face your audience.
4. Pitch
   Use a natural pitch which allows you to speak comfortably without effort.
5. Cueing
   Incorporate gestural and visual cueing whenever possible.
6. Environment
   Keep music at a moderate volume. Move around the room to accommodate all students.
7. Microphones
   If your facility has one—use it! If not, insist that one is purchased. Be careful not to shout into the microphone or project unnaturally.

Summary

The voice is a muscle system that must be respected by the professional fitness instructor. Proper conditioning and using the voice correctly in class is crucial to good vocal health. If you experience any of these warning signs, consult an otolaryngologist. If a vocal injury has occurred, speech or voice therapy is recommended as it has proven to be effective in eliminating vocal injuries. Being aware of basic vocal functions, appropriate pitch levels, posture, and projection techniques, as well as the warning signs, will ensure a voice that is powerful, commanding and easily understood by your students.

 CHECKLIST

Voice Care Guidelines

1. Stay in good health.
2. Hydration.
3. Voice rest and pacing.
4. Avoid irritants such as smoke, smog, etc.
5. Avoid medications.
6. Avoid negative vocal behaviors.
7. Limit talking in noisy places.
8. Learn vocal and overall relaxation.
9. Focus your voice.
10. Avoid certain foods that have an irritating effect.
11. Warm up your voice.
12. Develop good breathing habits.
13. Avoid shouting or talking loudly.

Jeanette Dvorak

15 Safe Foundations
Shoes and Floors

Shoes

Focus

THE COMPETITIVE MARKET FOR ATHLETIC SHOES has spawned a wide variety of technically advanced fitness footwear. Extensive sports injury research has been conducted since the days when first-generation aerobics participants were allowed to perform high-impact exercise barefoot. Now there is more stringent safety cirteria. We know for a fact that instructors can significantly reduce the impact hazards of aerobic exercise by wearing proper footwear. They should insist their students wear proper shoes in class as well.

What To Look For

The most beneficial development in fitness shoes is that the wide variety of quality footwear available makes it possible to choose a pair with proper fit and sport-specific features. Nobody should wear an uncomfortable or unsupportive shoe for intense exercise. Not only is foot or ankle injury reduced by wearing proper shoes, but stress to bones and joints in the lower legs, knees and hips is dramatically lessened. Shock waves from even low-impact exercise can affect the lower spine and aggravate back muscles, according to research reports from Scholl, Inc.

Since the fitness research boom in the 1980s, athletic shoe manufacturers have continually invested in studies for shoe safety. Computerized analysis of foot strike and impact has led to more anatomically-designed shoes made of technically advanced materials. But overall, the most important elements for injury prevention are shock absorption, flexibility, stability and fit. Beyond those basic components, the array of other comfort and design features vary in importance according to a person's exercise activity.

Shock Absorption

Shock absorption—more accurately described as shock dispersion—is the most important reason to wear sports shoes. Shoe manufacturers have become so focused on this factor, many have patented devices and materials for cushioning. Shoes contain a three-layered sole for optimal cushion.

The outsole is made of rubber compound for durability as well as grip and traction. Certain outsole designs aid in shock dispersion, such as a hollowed or cantilever heel found in running shoes. For aerobics, a flat outsole is best.

The midsole provides most of the shock absorbency. Midsoles vary in shape from a full-length, molded piece to sectional padding beneath the ball and heel but cut away under the arch. Extra shock dispersion is often inserted

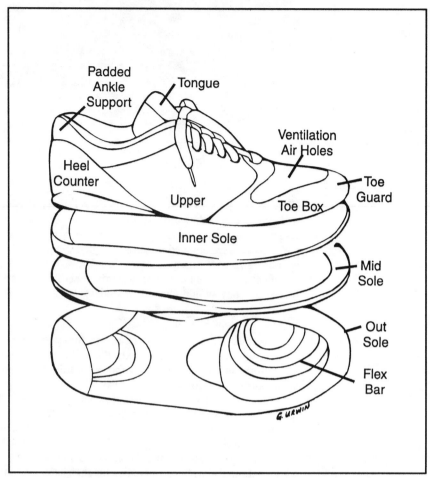

Fig. 15-1. Anatomy of a shoe

under the heel in the form of Hexalite™ air, gel, nitrogen or other type of material. Made of high-tech polymers—polyurethane, Hytrel® or EVA—multidensity midsoles can compress and regain shape throughout repetitive impact. However, shoes lose 50% of their cushioning capability after about 200-400 miles of use in running, and for instructors it's the midsole which breaks down before the outer shoe shows wear.

Above the complex midsole is an inner sole designed for comfort as well as cushion. The best form of inner sole, short of a custom-molded orthotic insert, is a removable sockliner. A sockliner or insert is convenient for washing and replaceable to extend the durability of a shoe. However, any recommendation for how long a shoe should last depends on a person's exercise regime, foot morphology and the exercise surface.

Flexibility

Multidensity polymers are used in the midsoles. Between the areas which need maximum shock absorption there is less dense construction, allowing the shoe to bend easily where the foot needs to bend. Give new shoes a flex test by holding them up and bending the toe box toward the heel. If the midsole is too thick to bend at the ball of the foot, muscle imbalance can occur during extended bouts of forward stepping motions. Muscle imbalance can eventually casue lower extremity pain or shin splints. On the other hand, if the shoe can be twisted excessively, it may be too flexible for multi-directional aerobics moves. But keep in mind the amount of torsional stiffness needed varies from activity to activity. In a high-top or midcut, also check for comfortable ankle flexion.

Flex grooves have helped rid aerobics shoes of fatigue and blister-causing stiffness. Cut into the outsole and midsole at the sides of the forefoot, flex grooves are a simple feature beneficial for step training and jump roping. Flex grooves are also prominent in running shoes. However the flared, or cantilever, outsole of running shoes make them inappropriate for dance style aerobics. Today's diversity of aerobics formats (step, slide, funk, etc.) calls for various balances of flexibility and stability. The choice of a more flexible versus a sturdier construction is based on personal preference and the particular aerobics activity.

Stability

Lateral motion, quick turns and stops make the requirements of an aerobics shoe much like a court shoe. However, due to the impact and repetition of aerobics, the shoe must also employ the cushioning of a running or walking

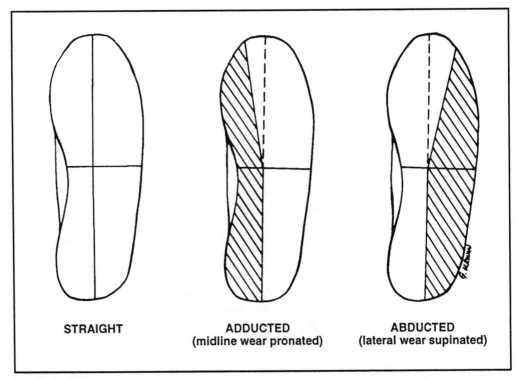

STRAIGHT

ADDUCTED
(midline wear pronated)

ABDUCTED
(lateral wear supinated)

Fig. 15-2. Sole wear

shoe. Like a court shoe, external support straps across the forefoot can help prevent the foot from rolling over to the side. As in a running shoe, a heel counter or heel wedge holds the rear foot in place. For support of the ankles and dorsal ligaments on top of the foot, look for a padded tongue and ankle collar with a notched achilles cushion. Make sure the heel counter is not too tight or stiff and won't pinch your Achilles' tendon. A toe guard is also practical for dance-oriented aerobics.

Different exercise styles have special shoe requirements. For instance, step training requires footwear that has effective all-around stability, yet is not too heavy. Many shoes have introduced a glove-like fitted tongue which wraps snugly around the foot. Made of ultra-lightweight materials like neoprene, this internal fit structure replaces bulky leather support straps. Funk or other dance-oriented aerobics also require a very stable but light, breathable fit in order to protect ankles from turning or twisting and remain comfortable throughout an intensive workout. The best choice is a high-top made of perforated leather or other ventilated material for comfort.

The Perfect Fit

Fit is a universal priority for sports shoes. People who exercise regularly, particularly aerobics instructors who participate for many hours per week, should learn what type of foot they have. To test for a high versus flat arch, stand barefoot on a flat surface and have someone try to place a finger under the arch of the foot.

The overall shape of a sole is called the last. The aerobics shoe category may not emphasize a variety of lasts as running shoes do. Yet you may find one particular manufacturer or shoe model fits better than others. Don't convince yourself an uncomfortable new shoe will be fine once it "gives a little" or "gets broken in." Over time, forcing a foot into the wrong shoe last can cause foot injuries such as tendinitis or bursitis.

Checklist

Buying Shoes

- *Don't insist on fitting into a certain shoe size, because sizes vary among manufacturers.*

- *Since most people have one foot that is larger than the other, have both feet measured and fit to the larger size.*

- *Stand during the fitting and be sure there is about 3/8 to 1/2 inch between the end of your toes and the shoe.*

- *Heels should fit with a minimal amount of slippage.*

- *The ball of your foot should fit comfortably in the widest part of the toe box.*

- *To be sure the overall fit is good, walk around in the shoe wearing the socks you normally wear during exercise.*

- *Try on shoes at the end of the day when feet tend to be larger.*

References

Copeland, Glenn, D.P.M., & Solomon, Stan (1992). *The foot book.* John Wiley & Sons Inc.

Rosenberg, Steven L., D.P.M. *Aerobic dance shoes: how to choose what to use* (1987). printed in Topics in Acute Care and Trauma Rehabilitation, Aspen Publishers Inc., October.

University of California at Berkeley, *Berkeley wellness letter,* (1992). Published by Health Letter Associates, New York, NY, January.

Getting an upper hand on lower back pain, published by Scholl, Inc., division of Schering-Plough Health Care Products, Liberty, NJ.

American Orthopedic Foot and Ankle Society (1992). Public Information Office, Seattle, WA, February, 1992.

"Adult Foot Structure," *Shoe Research Review,* August/November, 1990; "Lateral Ankle Sprains," July/August, 1989; "Athletic Shoe Cushioning," September/October, 1988. Shoe Research Review is a triannual report published by the NIKE Research Laboratory, Beaverton, OR.

"The U.S. Footwear Market Today," a report published by The Athletic Footwear Association, a division of Sporting Goods Manufacturers of America, North Palm Beach, FL, 1991.

Reviewed by Bob Rich of the Reebok Human Performance Lab, Stoughton, MA, 1993.

Floors

Focus

Types of Aerobic Flooring

- *padding over concrete*
- *layered padding covered with carpet or linoleum*
- *hardwood over padding*
- *wood suspended over springs or padding*
- *individual padded mats*
- *synthetic snap together tiles*

Because there is no standard criteria regarding the flooring of an exercise facility, instructors and frequent exercise participants need to be aware of the surface they are using. Safe aerobic flooring provides resilience for shock dispersion and the right amount of traction. When a well-padded, shock-absorbent floor is not available, be sure to compensate by wearing quality shoes and toning down exercise impact.

Reducing Injuries

Safe aerobic flooring should have a smooth, non-slip surface for safe motion, as well as resilience for shock dispersion. Exercise injuries related to flooring can be caused by impact and/or traction problems. Because cost and practicality also weigh into floor buying decisions, an ultimate floor is not necessarily guaranteed in a fitness club. Besides initial cost, durability and practical maintenance are factors to consider when buying flooring. Not all clubs can afford to install or maintain the most up-to-date, proven system. For instance a suspended wood floor has been rated most popular among instructors for its rebound action, according to a report by Scott O. Roberts, M.S. However,

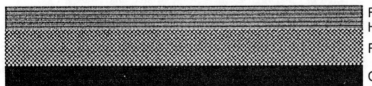

FINISHED HARDWOOD

RUBBER PAD

CONCRETE

Fig. 15-3a Suspension floor

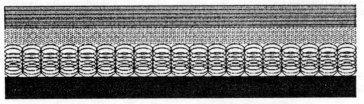

FINISHED HARDWOOD

SUB FLOOR

COILED SPRINGS

CONCRETE

Fig. 15-3b Spring floor

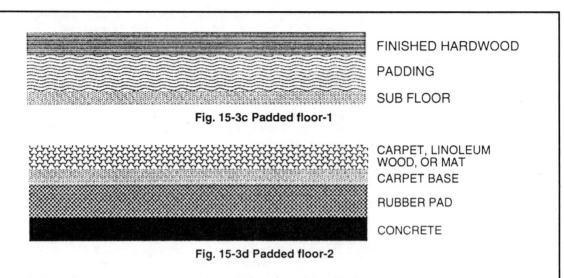

FINISHED HARDWOOD

PADDING

SUB FLOOR

Fig. 15-3c Padded floor-1

CARPET, LINOLEUM
WOOD, OR MAT

CARPET BASE

RUBBER PAD

CONCRETE

Fig. 15-3d Padded floor-2

CHECKLIST

Safety Practices

- *Avoid concrete or insufficiently covered concrete surfaces.*

- *Use appropriate choreography on carpet or rubber to avoid ankle or knee injury.*

- *Modify intensity, frequency and duration as needed.*

- *Beginners, pregnant women, senior participants or others who are sensitive to jarring of the joints should avoid hard surfaces altogether.*

- *Check flooring regularly for any defects and report them immediately.*

- *Keep an exercise log describing the type and duration of activity and the type of flooring being used. Training logs help evaluate the source of injury.*

a suspended wood floor is one of the most expensive, and there are no conclusive studies to date stating which floor is safest.

Below the Surface

There has been long-standing debate over which flooring system is most effective. So far, there is no standardized rating scale to easily identify the safety of flooring. And now that aerobics styles have diversified, so have the needs associated with floor surfaces. Non-slip surfaces are very important in step classes. Use of a step on gripping carpet or treaded surface is more ideal than on smooth wood, especially when sweat falling to the floor is a common factor. On the other hand, dance-based classes require a smooth surface for sliding and turning. When low-impact, sliding choreography is attempted on a carpeted or other high-traction floor, twisted ankles are a risk. In most cases, clubs have to rely on one floor to work for all class formats.

No matter what the style of exercise, the force exerted in an exerciser's foot strike can exceed three times his or her body weight. This pressure can cause stress fractures or other injuries to the lower extremities. Therefore, all exercise flooring—regardless of the top surface—must have a resilient, yielding subsurface. Concrete alone is the worst choice of exercise surface. Beyond that obvious caution, there is confusion over what floor provides the best cushioning. The truth is, cushioned flooring alone will not prevent injury. The best bet to protect yourself from stress and impact injury is a combination a well-cushioned floor, appropriate footwear and safe exercise instruction.

Floor Testing

In-depth research regarding flooring is continually conducted by the United States Surfacing Laboratories (USSL), a facility of the International Association for Sports Surface Sciences (ISSS). The USSL can provide more objective evidence and conclusions than private studies funded by flooring manufacturers. Standard surface testing measures safety factors such as force reduction, sliding coefficient and a floor's rigidity versus deformation. For further information on the science of surface testing, write to: ISSS, 214 N. Jefferson St., Suite 502, Richmond, VA 23220-4200.

Summary

Flooring is only a contributing factor to exercise safety. Shoes and safe technique must also be relied on for injury-free fitness. For instructors, exercise moderation is important to consider since overuse injuries are still common to the profession. Over a prolonged period, even the most up-to-date, high-tech flooring cannot safeguard against muscle fatigue and biomechanical imbalance, both of which can cause foot and leg injuries associated with repetitive impact. However, the importance of safe flooring cannot be disregarded. Quality flooring and shoes are the foundations of exercise safety.

References

Rosenberg, Steven L. (1987). Aerobic dance surfaces. *Topics in Acute Care and Trauma Rehabilitation*. Aspen Publishers Inc.
Kolitzus, Hans J. (1992). *USSL report*. Richmond, Va.
Roberts, Scott O. (May/June, 1992). Scratching the Surface. *American Fitness*.

Scott O. Roberts, MS

16 Low Back Protocol

Focus

APPROXIMATELY 80% OF THE POPULATION will develop back pain some time in their lives. In 80 to 90% of cases, low back pain is due to improper posture, faulty body mechanics, weak musculature, or a combination of these factors. In most cases, low back pain can be prevented and alleviated by proper body mechanics and regular exercise. Many physicians believe that the major cause of low back pain is simply physical deconditioning.

Faulty body mechanics is one of the leading causes of low back pain. By adhering to the exercise guidelines listed below, low back pain can be avoided.

Risk Factors For Low Back Pain

General—General risk factors include age, physical fitness, weight and height. The incidence of low back pain increases with age, excess body weight and poor physical fitness.

Postural/Structural—Postural or structural abnormalities are associated with a high incidence of low back pain. These abnormalities can be identified by physical examination and medical testing.

Occupational—The requirement for lifting in a twisted position is the strongest risk factor for future low back pain. Other occupational risk factors include twisting, bending, stooping, prolonged sitting, and poor work surfaces.

Environmental—Cigarette smoking is associated with low back pain.

Psychosocial—Depression and anxiety are associated with an increased incidence of low back pain.

Recreational—Although regular exercise is generally recommended as a preventive measure against low back pain, certain high-impact activities such as running, aerobic dance, and basketball may aggravate back problems.

Other—Multiple pregnancies have been associated with an increase in low back pain.

Exercise Guidelines for Low Back Pain

1. Always be aware of proper form and alignment.
2. Always maintain pelvic neutral alignment and an erect torso during any exercise movements.
3. Avoid head-forward positions in which the chin is tilted up.
4. When leaning forward, lifting, or lowering an object, always bend at the knees.
5. Avoid hyperextending the spine in an unsupported position.
6. Allow for an adequate warm-up and cooldown period during all exercise classes.
7. Most low back pain is caused by muscle weaknesses and imbalances including: tight hamstring and lower back muscle groups, tight hip flexor muscles, and weak abdominal and lower back muscles. Exercises should be routinely performed to improve muscle strength and flexibility.
8. Individuals who experience low back pain or have a history of chronic low back pain should be advised to consult with a physician and get specific recommendations for exercise.
9. If someone complains of low back pain following an exercise class, have them sit or lie down in a comfortable position and apply an ice pack to the affected area. Following a mild back strain, individuals should be encouraged to take several days off from exercise.

It appears that physical fitness combined with a healthy lifestyle may help prevent low back pain. More specifically, weakness of large muscle groups, particularly the back extensors, seems to put one at a greater risk of developing low back pain. Strengthening exercises for the low back should be performed on a regular basis to gain maximal benefits.

Exercises For The Low Back

Position: Supine with knees bent.
Activity: Slowly, pull one knee to chest and hold for five seconds, then do the same with the other knee.

Position: Supine, with knees bent and legs together.
Activity: Slowly rotate knees from side to side while keeping them together.

Position: Hands and knees.
Activity: Arch your back up like a cat, hold five seconds and relax.

Position: Hands and knees.
Activity: Slowly bring one knee to the chest then extend the leg straight out behind you.
           Repeat on the other side.

Position: Standing against the wall.
Activity: Squat down so that your lower back is pressed against the wall. Move your feet out
           from the wall and bend your legs to a "half-squat" and hold. Gradually straighten legs out and repeat.

Position: Lie on your stomach with legs and arms straight out.
Activity: Lift one arm, hold and relax. Alternate arms. Lift one leg, hold and relax. Alternate legs.
           Lift one arm and one leg on opposite sides, hold and relax. Alternate sides.

Position: Supine, with knees slightly bent.
Activity: Flatten your back against the floor by contracting your stomach muscles and rotating your
           hips backwards.

Additional Activities: Side stretch, abdominal curls, modified push-ups.

Prevention is the key to avoiding low back pain. Listed below are some common sense tips that are helpful in the prevention of low back pain.

Preventing Low Back Pain

1. Use back rests and lumbar supports when sitting.
2. Make sure seats offer optimal seating comfort and support.
3. Quit smoking.
4. Reduce stress and anxiety.
5. Change your position (for example, from sitting to standing) regularly.
6. Adjust table and work station to comfortable heights.
7. Avoid activities that are clearly associated with previous episodes of pain.
8. Always keep loads close to your body, and face the work using proper technique when lifting.
9. Allow for adequate warm-up and cooldown before and after exercise.
10. Always wear protective footwear and avoid exercising for prolonged periods of time on hard surfaces.
11. Strengthen abdominal muscles.
12. Follow AFAA Standards and Guidelines. Avoid harmful movements such as the plow
    and straight leg sit-ups.

Summary

Although low back pain is a common and costly problem, its precise causes are often elusive. There is still very little that medical science knows about back pain. Low back problems can be prevented by identifying risk factors associated with low back pain, by modifying work and recreation activities that cause low back pain, and by exercising on a regular basis.

References

Melleby, A. (1982). *The Y's way to a healthy back.* Piscataway, N.J.: New Century Publishers.

Frymoyer, J.W., Pope, M.H., Clements, J.H., et al. (1983). Risk factors in low back pain: an epidemiological survey. *Journal of Bone and Joint Surgery.* 65A: 213-218.

Imrie, D., & Barbuto, L. (1990). *The back power program.* New York: John Wiley & Sons.

Aerobics and Fitness Association of America. Lower Back Exercise Guidelines.

McQuade, K.J., Turner, J.A., & Buchner, D.M. (1988). Physical fitness and low back pain: an analysis of the relationships among fitness, functional limitations, and depression. *Clinical Orthopedic Research.* 223: 198-204.

Roberts, S.O. (April, 1991). Low back pain syndrome: newest findings about risk factors and prevention. *American Fitness Quarterly,* 18-19.

Roberts, S.O. (November/December, 1991). Back talk: conquering low back pain through exercise, education and stress reduction. *American Fitness Magazine,* 33-35.

Part 3

How to Teach Exercise

Monitoring Intensity

Class Format

Choreography

Training

Career Advancement

Equipment

Substituting

Motivation

Adherence

International Travel

Monitoring Aerobic Intensity

17

Denise Tucker

Focus

THIS CHAPTER WILL HELP YOU UNDERSTAND how to monitor intensity during endurance training for the cardiorespiratory system. Four factors influence how we train for any component of fitness:

- Frequency (how often)
- Duration (how long)
- Mode (type of activity)
- Intensity (to what degree of physiological stress)

In order to train the cardiorespiratory system, AFAA recommends that we train 3-5 times per week (frequency), for a minimum of 20-30 continuous minutes (duration), while performing activities that are rhythmical and aerobic in nature using large muscle groups (mode) and at 55-85% of maximum heart rate (intensity). The American College of Sports Medicine guidelines cover a wider range (60-90%), but it should be noted that the higher end of the range (i.e., over 85%), is for highly conditioned athletes and not the typical group exerciser.

Intensity can be measured for **maximal** and **submaximal** cardiorespiratory activity. Maximal intensity is measured in a controlled situation with trained personnel to monitor and administer the test. Specifically, a graded exercise test (GXT) is given either on a treadmill or bicycle ergometer, and the person being tested is measured for oxygen consumption (VO_2Max), heart rate and blood pressure and requires a voluntary effort to the point of exhaustion. In group aerobic exercise, we are working at submaximal levels and cannot use oxygen consumption or blood pressure to help us measure intensity.

The methods used for monitoring submaximal intensity during aerobic conditioning classes include **Heart Rate, Rating of Perceived Exertion** and the **Talk Test**. As a group exercise leader, you should be aware of how to use each of these common methods. The reason for monitoring intensity is to help participants successfully complete 20-60 minutes of continuous activity in order to increase and/or maintain the functional capacity of their cardiorespiratory systems.

> ### HEART RATE
>
> *A linear relationship exists between heart rate and exercise intensity—oxygen uptake. As the exercise workload becomes harder, an increase in heart rate occurs. Monitor heart rate to insure that a person is working at a safe and effective level.*

Definition of Terms

Resting Heart Rate (RHR)—The number of times the heart beats per minute while at rest. The best way to determine resting heart rate is to take a 60-second pulse for three consecutive mornings upon waking. The resting heart rate is the average of the three numbers. The average resting rate for women is 78-84 bpm, and the average for men is 72-78 bpm. People with a good level of cardiorespiratory conditioning generally have a lower RHR.

Maximal Heart Rate (MHR)—The theoretical maximum times the heart could beat per minute at a specific age. A graded exercise test would give an accurate measure of MHR. However, since this is not feasible for many people, the figure 220 minus (-) age is the general estimate, with 220 representing the maximum heart rate of a baby at birth. MHR equals 220 minus your age. Do not exercise at this level because it puts a tremendous stress on the body and produces extreme fatigue.

Training Heart Rate Range (THRR)—The range within which an individual needs to work for cardiorespiratory training to take place. AFAA recommends a THRR which is 55-85% of MHR. About 55% represents the lower end of the range and is generally recommended for beginners, heavy smokers or people recovering from an illness. The upper end of the range, 85%, is for the highly conditioned person who can comfortably work at this higher intensity. Working higher than 85% is only recommended for highly trained competitive athletes. It could be very dangerous for untrained people or people with known or undiagnosed cardiovascular disease to work at the higher end of their THRR.

There are several methods for calculating THRR including the Karvonen Formula and the Simplified Heart Rate Method.

Karvonen Formula

This formula is an individualized method of calculating THRR because it factors in an individual's resting heart rate. The formula is as follows:

1. Determine MHR (220 - age).
2. Subtract RHR from that number. This gives you your Heart Rate Reserve (HRR).
3. Multiply HRR by 55% and 85% to get the lower and upper ends of the THRR as recommended by AFAA.
4. Add RHR to the answers in item 3.

For example, Anne is an active 40 year-old with a resting heart rate of 65 bpm. Her Karvonen would be calculated as follows:

1. 220 - 40 = 180
2. 180 - 65 = 115
3. 115 x .55 = 63 and 115 x .85 = 97
4. 65 + 63 = 128 and 65 + 97 = 162

For Anne, 55% of her THR is 128 bpm and 85% is 162 bpm. Since she is already active, she would be working at the higher end of her THRR.

Karvonen THRR
(MHR - RHR)
x (% intensity)
+ RHR

Simplified Heart Rate Method

This method is more commonly used in the group exercise setting because participants are often unaware of what their resting heart rate number is and because reference charts reflecting norms for various ages and percentages within the THRR are widely available. It should be noted that this is the method recommended by AFAA for use in group exercise. Simply take 220 minus age to determine the MHR and then multiply first by .55 and then by .85 to determine the person's THRR.

Using Anne as an example:

220 - age = 180

180 x .55 = 99

180 x .85 = 157

Under this method, 55% of Anne's THRR is 99 bpm and 85% is 157 bpm. Compare this to the Karvonen formula, and you will notice the impact that resting heart rate has on determining an individual person's training range.

A reference chart is provided showing 60-second and 10-second heart rates for various ages at 55%, 70% and 85% of MHR.

Once a person knows his or her THRR, the working heart rate can be determined, by checking the pulse, either on the radial or the carotid artery.

Radial—If you are right-handed, locate the pulse on the thumb side of the left wrist, palm up. Place the index and middle finger, not the thumb on the artery. If you are left handed, reverse hands and wrists.

Carotid—This artery is located in the front of the neck. Place your index and middle finger on the outside corner of the eye and slide it straight down the neck, close to the "Adam's apple." Avoid pressing hard or placing the thumb on the opposite side of the neck at the same time because it could trigger a reflex to slow down the heart and could also impede blood flow.

When taking the pulse, AFAA recommends *beginning with the count of 1 and counting for 10 seconds*. Simply multiply this number by 6 to determine what the working heart rate is for one minute.

In order to effectively utilize heart rate as a measure of intensity, the pulse *must be taken immediately after vigorous exercise*. It is important to continue walking while taking the pulse in order to prevent blood-pooling in the extremities and to prevent lightheadedness. Ideally, AFAA recommends taking a pulse five minutes after the beginning of active aerobic work to determine if participants are working within their THRR. If this is not feasible, then a pulse check must be taken at the completion of the most intense aerobic work rather than not at all.

Recovery Heart Rate—This is an indicator of a person's fitness level. It indicates that speed at which heart rate returns to pre-exercise levels. As cardiorespiratory fitness improves, the speed at which the heart rate returns to normal also improves. Generally, recovery heart rate is taken two to five minutes after the completion of aerobic work and can indicate whether or not the cooldown period was sufficient.

> *AFAA recommends beginning with "1" and counting for 10 seconds.*

> HR = 10 sec. count x 6

> *AFAA recommends that the heart rate should be 55% or less of MHR five minutes after the completion of aerobic work.*

Methods

Rating of Perceived Exertion

Another way to measure intensity is for participants to pay attention to the way they feel. Exercise physiologists have found that perceived exertion, or how hard you feel you are working, can be a reliable guide to aerobic intensity. This method teaches people to listen to their bodies and can be used alone or in conjunction with heart rate.

In the early 1980s, Gunnar Borg introduced the Rating of Perceived Exertion, a scale of 6-20 roughly based on a resting rate of 60 and maximum heart rate of 200, as well as a second revised scale which goes from 0-10. Using the 15-point scale, a rating of 12 corresponds to approximately 55% of THRR and 16 to approximately 85% of THRR. On the 10-point scale, the corresponding ratings would be between 4 and 6. A sample of the Borg Scales are provided for your reference.

RPE
12-16
equivalent to
65-85%
THRR

Perceived Exertion can be useful for self-monitoring throughout an aerobic training session and can be very useful for helping beginners correlate their training heart rate with the way they feel while exercising at various intensity levels.

Talk Test

Another useful method for monitoring intensity in a group exercise setting is the Talk Test. If you are able to carry on a conversation while working out, then you are training aerobically. A sign of over-exertion is the inability to talk/count and indicates that the person is working too hard and should decrease intensity. The Talk Test can be used along with heart rate and perceived exertion to monitor intensity.

Table 17-1. Sample target heart rate ranges

Beats Per Minute & 10 Second Pulse

AGE	60% 1 MIN/10 SEC		70% 1 MIN/10 SEC		85% 1 MIN/10 SEC	
20	120	20	140	23	170	28
25	117	19	136	22	165	27
30	114	19	133	22	161	26
35	111	18	129	21	157	26
40	108	18	126	21	153	25
45	105	17	122	20	148	24
50	102	17	119	19	144	24
55	99	16	115	19	140	23
60	96	16	112	18	136	22

Equation: 220 - age = MHR
MHR x Intensity % = 1 Minute Heart Rate
Minute Heart Rate divided by 6 = 10 Second Count

Table 17-2. RPE		Table 17-3. RPE	
Original 20 Point Scale		**Revised 10 Point Scale**	
Rating	Description	Rating	Description
6		0	Nothing
7	Very, very light	0.5	Very, very light (just noticeable)
8			
9	Very light	1.0	Very light
10		2	Light (weak)
11	Fairly light	3	Moderate
12		4	Somewhat hard
13	Somewhat hard	5	Heavy (strong)
14		6	
15	Hard	7	Very heavy
16		8	
17	Very hard	9	
18		10	Very, very heavy (almost max)
19	Very, very hard		
20			

Note: Reprinted with permission from "Psychological Bases of Physical Exertion" by Gunnar Borg, 1982, *Medicine and Science in Sport and Exercise.* 14(5).

Summary

Utilize all three methods to help your students monitor their intensity and remind them that, in order to improve cardiorespiratory fitness, they should:

- Be *above the lower limit* of their THRR, otherwise there is no overload to the cardiorespiratory system.
- Be *below the upper limit* of their THRR, otherwise there is too much reliance on the anaerobic systems and an increased chance of injury.
- Feel they are working *somewhat hard* or *hard* (Perceived Exertion).
- Be able to *carry on a conversation* while working out (Talk Test).

References

Borg, G. (1982). Psychological bases of physical exertion. *Medicine and Science in Sport and Exercise,* 14:5.

American College of Sports Medicine (1991). *Guidelines for exercise testing and prescription* (4th ed.). Philadelphia: Lea & Febiger.

Howley, T.H., & Franks, D.F. (1986). *Health/fitness instructor's handbook.* Champaign, Ill.: Human Kinetics.

Golding, L., Myers, C. & Sinning, W. (1989). *Y's way to physical fitness* (3rd ed.). Champaign, Ill.: Human Kinetics.

Aerobics & Fitness Association of America (1992). *Standards & guidelines* (Rev. ed.).

McArdle, W., Katch, F., & Katch, V. (1986). *Exercise physiology—energy, nutrition and human performance* (2nd ed.). Philadelphia: Lea & Febiger.

The AFAA Board

18 Class Format

WITH THE CREATION OF SUCH DIVERSITY and variety in class content and style, it is no longer practical to offer one general recommendation for class format. Therefore, AFAA suggests that instructors adhere to the original recommendations for a general level high impact or low impact class. You must then expand this format to best meet the needs of a class that does not fit into a general aerobic class definition.

AFAA's Formatting Questions

When redefining your class format, consider the following:

1. What is your conditioning goal and how can you most effectively reach it?
2. What are the safety considerations in meeting your goal?
3. How much time are you allotted and how can the usage of this time affect the goal outcome?
4. How can your teaching environment, facility and equipment contribute to the effectiveness of your class content?
5. Who is this class most appropriate for and how can it be modified to appeal to others?

In addition to the guidelines offered within the AFAA Basic Exercise Standards and Guidelines, please refer to the specific class formats offered in this text under Part 9: Specialty Classes.

Building Aerobic Choreography

19

Lynn G. Brick, RN

Focus

AEROBIC FITNESS CHOREOGRAPHY is the coordination of music and movement through time and space. It is designed, developed, and created using methods similar to those in traditional dance choreography. Regardless of your level of experience or ability, it is essential to know and understand the basic principles of choreography. This chapter offers principles and techniques designed to help you develop an endless number of movements for your class participants.

The Basics

In traditional dance, movements and movement patterns with the following characteristics are artistically developed.

1. Movement patterns have a simple theme. Unrelated movements or themes are saved for other dance pieces.
2. Movement patterns are consistent.
3. Once a movement pattern is established, it is repeated throughout the dance piece. Either the movement is identical when repeated or just the movement qualities (i.e., elements of variation such as movement intensity, rhythm, tempo) are repeated.
4. Movement patterns are designed in a "bite-size" step-by-step method.
5. All dance movements have the following elements: design, dynamics, rhythm and motivation.

Design

Dynamics

Rhythm

Motivation

Remember these elements of developing traditional dance choreography as we review the basics of aerobic fitness choreography.

It is essential to understand the basic foundation of aerobic fitness choreography before you start to creatively develop and design new choreography. The basics of aerobic fitness choreography are divided into lower body movements (depending upon degree of impact of the foot on the floor) and upper body movements.

Low Impact Aerobics (LIA) is identified as keeping at least one foot on or as close to the floor as possible. For example, grapevines can be done in any of the following intensity options:

1. Step right, cross back left, step right, tap left foot. Step left, cross back right, step left, tap right foot. The dynamics of the height of the body remain the same while doing the three steps and the tap of the foot.
2. Knees bent low: Step right, cross back left, step right, straighten the body as you tap your left foot. Knees bent low: Step left, cross back

right, step left, straighten the body as you tap your right foot. There is a dynamic difference in the height of the body while stepping as compared to tapping the foot.

3. Knees bent low: Step right, cross back left, step right, hop as you bring your feet together. Knees bent low: Step left, cross back right, step left, hop as you bring your feet together. This is the highest intensity level which is referred to as a single impact action. In other words, out of four counts, three counts are low impact and one of the counts is high impact.

Moderate impact aerobics (MIA) is characterized by both feet staying on the floor, but the feet roll through a toe-ball-heel action every time. The body bobs up and down similar to high impact activity due to the heel lifting up and down. There are fewer impact forces to the feet because the whole foot is not leaving the floor.

High impact aerobics (HIA) is characterized by both feet leaving the floor alternately or at the same time. The impact forces on the foot are high and when executed continuously for extended periods of time can potentially cause physical injury.

The following basic movements are the simplest forms of impact which constitute the basic foundation of aerobic fitness choreography:

LIA	**MIA**	**HIA**
March	Skip	Jog
Step touch	Twist	Jump
Touch step	Plié/Releve (up on toes)	Hop
Squat/Plié	Any move between LIA & HIA	Jack
		Twist
		Splits
		Pendulum

Please note that most of these movements are bilateral (involving both sides of the body) and/or single count moves. For example, a knee lift is not a basic move. A knee lift is a two-count march which takes the leg through a higher plane of space. Also, a lateral lunge is a touch step with a planal variation which turns the body to alternately face the side walls. These basic moves, regardless of what form of impact you are teaching, are the moves which identify the beginning of a movement combination and lay the foundation for building, creating, and designing your movement combination.

Six of the above basic moves are ideal for transitioning. These basic moves are called "**neutral**" moves because both feet are on the floor and the weight of the body is centered. Any movement can follow these moves. Neutral moves are:

Squat/Plié	Twist
Plié/Releve	Jump
Skip	Jack

Upper body movements can be divided into basic movement types as well. They are:

Push/Abduction: Moves away from the center of the body.

Pull/Adduction: Moves in toward the center of the body.

Rotation (Internal or External): Twisting of the arms from the shoulder.

Circle: Forms a circular design.

Isolations: Moves only one part of the upper body at a time (i.e., shoulders or ribs).

Every move that we do in aerobic fitness is the coordination of lower body moves with upper body moves. Let's put these basic movements together. Choose one of the lower body basic moves to coordinate with any of the upper body basic moves. The following are just a few examples:

Lower Body with	Upper Body
March	Bilateral Chest Press
Touch-Step (Rear Lunge)	Posterior Deltoid Raises
Skip	Small Arm Circles At Chest Level
Splits	Bilateral Lat Pull Down
Twist	Alternate Arms Push Up
Jacks	Abduction (Lateral Deltoid Raises)
Step-Touch	Alternate Isolated Shoulder Circles

The following are factors which may influence the effectiveness of your teaching basic movements:

1. Know your participants' ages.
2. Know your participants' level of coordination.
3. Know your participants' level of experience.
4. Know if your participants have particular risks to develop injuries.
5. Know your comfort level of executing your basic movement.
6. Know your ability to teach basic movements, starting with lower body movements and gradually adding upper body movements.
7. Remember at all times whom the movement is **F.O.R.** This acronym refers to your participants' **Frame of Reference**. While you teach, try to have an out-of-body experience. See yourself teaching, and see yourself taking your class at the same time. Perceive your ability to teach your choreography the same way as your participants perceive your ability to teach.

Now you have laid the foundation and are ready to progress to create a movement combination. From this point, in order to build, develop, or change the move you have taught, it is necessary to know and understand the primary factors of smooth transitioning and the key elements of variation.

The Primary Factors of Smooth Transitioning

The skill of effective transitioning is essential for the following reasons. Transitioning techniques ensure the:

1. smoothness of class flow from one movement to another
2. effectiveness of your ability to teach
3. safety in movement execution
4. ability of your participants to follow you
5. control of all of the participants simultaneously

The following examples of cueing techniques will help you communicate to your participants:

For smooth transitioning:

1. Change one thing at a time.

2. Begin your second movement where your first movement ends.

3. Use conspicuous cueing.

1. **Footwork:** Refers to which foot you want them to move, right or left.

2. **Directional:** Refers to the direction you want people to travel, i.e., diagonal right front, half turn around, diagonal left rear, half turn around.

3. **Rhythmic:** Refers to the rhythm of the movement, i.e., slow-slow-quick-quick-quick-quick; single-single-double; 1-2-3, 1-2-3; step-ball-change, step-ball-change.

4. **Numerical:** Refers to the number of repetitions you want participants to execute, or the number of repetitions they have left. For transitioning purposes, avoid saying the number "1." If you take the time to say the number "1," you will not have the time to tell them what you want them to do next. Your numerical count down cueing should be this rhythm: "4-3-2-change." Please also note that you should always count down for transitioning purposes, never up. Why? When we countdown we never say 4-3-2-1-0-(-1)-(-2). They know once you get to one, the next beat of the music should be the next move. Counting up, on the other hand, has no finish or stopping point.

5. **Step:** Refers to the name of the step. For example, "Pony," "Chasse-Ball-Change," "Cha-Cha-Cha" are all examples of step cueing.

6. **Alignment:** Refers to body posture and placement throughout the entire class, not just during the muscle conditioning portions of class.

7. **Verbal and Nonverbal:** Refers to the "7-38-55" rule. This is the rule of communication. Seven percent of communication consists of the words that you say; 38% of communication is the way that you say those words; 55% of communication is body language. Never underestimate the power of communicating through your bodily gestures and posture. Let's face it. You may teach the most fabulous combinations, but if you don't believe in yourself or project a positive image, your class will not believe in you either.

8. **Visual:** Refers to cueing that is communicated through hand gestures and sign language. In other words, hand gestures indicate if the participants should move forward, back, right, or left, start from the top of the movement sequence or numerically prepare the class for the next move. These are just a few examples of visual cueing. Make up your own and use what is best for you and, most importantly, what is best for your participants.

The Elements of Variation

The elements of variation are the tools used to change, design, or develop movements from your basic movement. Knowing these elements will also help you to transition smoothly from one movement to the next. These elements are also known as the secondary factors which facilitate smooth transitioning.

Rhythm

Measured motion with regular recurrence of elements or features such as the beat of the music. The rhythm of movement is executed to every beat or in between every beat of the music. Half time, single time, double time, triple time, as well as syncopation are all examples of rhythm. Syncopation incorporates the "and" beat of the music. The following is an example of syncopation:

Do step-touch x 4 repetitions	Movement counts 1 through 8
In order to syncopate the rhythm, do 3 complete step-touches (right, left, right).	Movement counts 1 through 6
Hold the tap of the third step touch (left foot).	Movement count 7
Then lift your left foot, follow with your right foot as you do the last step-touch to the left.	Movement counts "and" 8

Most traditional aerobic fitness classes use music that is written in 4/4 or 4/8 time. In other words, there are eight beats per music measure or music phrase. Therefore, the movements we choose should also correspond to the same type of phrasing or eight movement counts. The first movement count should begin at the same time as the first musical count. In addition, the accents that we choose to use such as claps, snaps, or touches should correspond with the musical accents or the "up" beat of the music. This occurs on counts 2, 4, 6 and 8. This will help your class feel more motivated because the "up" beat of the music is a more driving beat.

The rhythm of movement can be varied regardless of the rhythm of the music through sound, look and feel. Claps, vocalizations and stomps are examples of rhythmic sound variations. Play around with the many ways to vary sound. For example: Do grapevine right and left (movement counts 1-8). Traditionally we clap on counts 4 and 8. Vary the rhythm by clapping on counts 4 and 7.

Adding or subtracting movement repetitions changes the look of the movement (i.e., the syncopation example above or single, single, double). Movements rhythmically feel different from one another when dynamics (i.e., strong vs. soft; staccato/short vs. lyrical/long) and other movement qualities are used (i.e., swinging, suspending, vibrating, sustaining, collapsing and percussing).

In addition, rhythmic variations can help to stylize your movements, especially when you are using music with a Latin beat.

Intensity

The degree of physical, emotional and psychological energy exerted to execute movements. Basically, the closer the feet and the hands are to the ground, the less intense the movement. The farther the feet and the hands are away from the ground, the more intense the movement during high impact aerobics. Also, if movements are long lever and are executed from the trunk (shoulders and hips) the intensity will increase. If movements are short lever and are executed from the knee or elbow joint, the intensity will decrease.

If your participants are under a great deal of emotional stress, the intensity level may be greater than or less than normal exertion, depending on each individual's coping capabilities.

Psychologically, the intensity may vary due to the participant's level of coordination and kinesthetic awareness. He/she may feel frustrated if movements that you choose are too complex or are too difficult to execute. The intensity level drops significantly when this occurs.

Suggested rules of thumb are:

1. Offer varied intensity options so people can choose which level is best for them.

   Option 1: Least intense

   Option 2: Intermediate intensity

   Option 3: Highest intensity

2. Be sure that all movements are broken down. Begin with basic movements, then gradually add one element of variation at a time, regardless of experience or ability. This is the "part-to-whole" method of teaching.

3. Have your participants leave every class that you teach feeling "successful." In other words, they should feel as if they can do all of the movements you ask them to do. This does not mean that they have to look like you as they exercise, but the "part-to-whole" method of teaching each move will enable your students to feel more successful each step of the way.

4. Alternate intense moves with less intense moves so that the body can expend calories more efficiently.

Direction

The floor pattern which the whole body travels. Think of the aerobic floor as a big stage. Then divide the stage into lines that your participants can travel. Forward and back, side to side, diagonal, up and down, lines, small circles, large circles and any combination of these are all examples of directional moves.

Particular movements are done most effectively in one direction. Jacks, skips and hops are usually most effective in a backward direction. The same movement can be done facing a different direction and can be perceived as a different movement.

Simple directional changes are a great way to add variety without creating too much complexity. It is important to cue your directional changes clearly and well enough in advance so that your participants will not be confused. Give your people landmarks to focus their eyes on or to move toward.

Symmetry

The similarity of form or arrangement on either side of a dividing line or plane of the body. In other words, symmetrical movement is bilateral movement. Novice or beginner participants feel best executing a symmetrical move because it is more balanced, more controlled and easier to do. A typical symmetrical movement is to do lateral arm raises as the feet do jumping jacks or touch-step.

For your participants who really enjoy a challenge, offer a variety of different types of movements. Asymmetrical moves, in which one side of the body does one thing and the other side of the body does something else, are a great way to challenge participants. For example, as the lower body does grapevine right and left, the right arm can push and pull when traveling right and both arms circle when traveling left. This not only offers variety to break up the monotony of doing the same moves all of the time but also may help to alter intensity level.

Spatial

The planes of space are basically vertical (up and down), horizontal, (side to side) and diagonal (up on one side and down on the other). I like to focus on all the parts of the body that are attached to the trunk and that have unlimited planes of space to use. In other words, with directional variations, the whole body moves. Spatial variations, however, refer to the planes of space in which the extremities, all joints, and the head move. In addition, these planes of space can form specific creative body designs as discussed in the Link Method with a Theme.

Style

Choose a variety of music styles. Encourage your participants to stylize their movements to the music.

The amount of individual personality or "attitude" that each participant applies while executing moves. Traditional HIA, MIA, or LIA may not require a particular style. Funk, Step, Latin, or Dynamic Stretching classes are best when each participant adds their own individual flair to the movements.

All of these elements of variation will help to create an endless variety of movements and movement styles. It is important to remember: **There is safety in variety.** In other words, the more you mix and match different types of movements, the more the safety factors increase due to altering impact stress factors to the feet and to the joints. For example:

Teach these moves in one combination:		
Right foot forward and back x 2 (the Mamba).	Arms alternately pump.	Counts 1-8.
Jack x 2.	Arms symmetrically lift laterally.	Counts 9-12.
Plié/Releve x 2.	Arms symmetrically press up.	Counts 13-16.

Reverse all with the left foot leading. Use the 32 counts total for the entire combination. As an advanced option, the second Plié/Releve can be one Power Jump.

As you can see, this combination uses all types of impact forces on the foot (LIA, MIA, HIA, and Power) and a variety of spatial upper body moves so as not to stress the shoulder joint.

The Link Method

Now you are ready to put movements together. In order to do this, I recommend that you use the Link Method which is the Part-to-Whole method of teaching. The Part-to-Whole method is a teaching tool which has been used by educators for quite some time. Educators found that people learn complex skills more easily when the "parts" of the "whole" skill are broken down and taught one step at a time, then linked together to make up the whole skill. This is also commonly referred to as the add-on method.

Start by teaching a basic lower body move. Then add a basic upper body move. You now have your choice of three options:

1. Keep your movement a simple movement, that is, a movement with consistent spatial and planal patterning.

2. You can change the lower body by using only one element of variation, and/or change the upper body by using only one element of variation. This will transform your original move to a new move.

3. You can combine the option one movement with option two movement to make a complex movement: two or more simple moves which involve multiple elements of variation. Establish a pattern of movement repetitions (i.e., step touch 4, march 8). Then you can make your movements travel (see Steps to Make a Combination).

Steps to Make a Combination:

	Lower Body	(then add)	Upper Body
Step 1	Step touch O-T-S		Abduct, then clap at chest level
Step 2	March O-T-S		Bilateral single count presses down
Step 3	Step touch x 4 O-T-S (establish the pattern)		Abduct and clap
	March x 8 O-T-S		Press down
Step 4	Step touch x 4 O-T-S (add the travel)		Abduct and clap
	March x 8 travel forward		Press down

Repeat the combination to be sure your participants can do it successfully.

Step touch x 4 O-T-S		Abduct and clap
March x 8 travel forward		Press down

PLUS

Step touch x 4 O-T-S		Abduct and clap
March x 8 travel back		Press down

EQUAL

32 counts of movement to music

The Link Method requires that each simple movement and complex movement is taught using the Part-to-Whole method. A new movement or a new element of variation is not added to the move until the participants feel comfortable executing the present move. This process is repeated for each new movement that you intend to teach. Each "whole" movement is linked together with the previous "whole" movements that you have already taught. Visually the Link Method looks like this:

Teach Movement A using the Part-to-Whole Method of teaching.

Teach Movement B using the Part-to-Whole Method of teaching.

Repeat "whole" Movement A; repeat "whole" Movement B.

Teach Movement C using the Part-to-Whole Method of teaching.

Repeat "whole" Movement A, "whole" Movement B, "whole" Movement C.

Teach Movement D using the Part-to-Whole Method of teaching. Repeat "whole" Movement A, "whole" B, "whole" C, and "whole" D.

Additional Link Method Principles

1. Take your time teaching each of the parts of your movements.

2. Make each of your movements consistent, whether they are simple or complex, each time that you repeat them.

3. Know your music.

4. Limit the number of simple "part" moves that comprise a complex movement to four.

5. Let the style of the music dictate the style of movements that you choose.

6. Remember, aerobics is the coordination of music and movement through time and space.

The Link Method is designed to help you to teach and create movements from the "parts" to the "whole" that transition smoothly from one to another, even if you are creating your combinations on-the-spot. However, often we make up a fabulous "whole" combination when we are in a creative mood (i.e., in the car, the bath tub, or just before we fall asleep). How do you break this combination down so that you can teach each "part?" The following are recommended steps to identify each of the "parts" so that you can get to your "whole."

1. Determine how many simple or basic lower body and upper body moves exist in the combination.

2. Identify the first basic lower body move.

3. Identify any elements of variation that are necessary to change the basic lower body move.

4. Add the basic upper body move.

5. Identify any elements of variation for the upper body move.

6. When you have completed the breakdown of the first part of the combination, identify the key components to transition from the first lower body basic move to the second lower body basic move.

7. Identify the key components of transition from the first upper body basic move to the second upper body basic move.

8. Link together the first lower and upper body moves with the second lower and upper body moves.

9. Repeat this process for the remaining identified basic moves.

10. Practice the best ways to break down your combination. Remember that a combination can be successfully broken down several ways. Choose the best way to break your combination down so that it is easiest for you to teach and, more importantly, so that your participants enjoy the most success.

The Link Method With a Theme

The Link Method with a theme focuses on movements and variations that have common traits. I am not referring to musical or holiday themes, but to movements and designs the body can make in the planes of space as well as in directional floor patterning.

Lower Body	Upper Body	
Movement A: (16 counts)	March forward 4 March O-T-S 4 (up and down dynamics) Repeat all back and O-T-S	Punch down x 4 Punch up and down x 2 Repeat
Movement B: (4 counts)	Alternate knee lifts (MIA)	Alternate bicep curls
Movement C: (16 counts)	Right knee up, walk 3 Repeat on other side Plié/Releve x 4	Press up and lower with curved arms Repeat With arms at both sides, raise and lower the fingers and shoulders x 4

The Link Method with a Theme is really an enjoyable way to design and create non-traditional types of movements for your classes. You may find that you are most creative with the body or floor pattern designs when you can visualize your "whole" combinations. Remember to focus on creating your Link Method with a Theme based on directional, rhythmic, spatial/planal, and symmetrical elements of variation. Another example of the Link Method follows with sample movement combinations for an asymmetrical theme:

	Lower Body	Upper Body
Movement A: (4 counts)	Right lead: Step-touch cross back	Left arm reaches up on a diagonal, Right arm reaches across body
Movement B: (16 counts)	"Zig Zag": 3 steps forward right diagonal, hop 3 steps forward left diagonal, hop Reverse traveling back	Right arm reaches laterally on right diagonal Arms circle at chest level Arms alternate punch up, left arm reaches laterally on left diagonal
Movement C: (4 counts)	Step Right: Left knee up Step Left ball change	Right arm punches up, left down, right arm punches across the lateral right body, left elbow pulls back at shoulder level
Movement D: (4 counts)	Step-touch right, Step & lift right knee	Both arms wrap waist toward left Left arm starts up and pulls down to waist

The Building Block Method

The Building Block Method is an effective free-form style of teaching. This method is an add on technique in which a new basic "whole" move is added on one at a time. All movements are basic "whole" moves, so that there are no "parts" to teach, and they are added on after a patterning of previously sequenced moves are done. The key element is to consistently add on the new move every time you direct your participants to the same location (i.e., one side of the room or one wall to face). They will anticipate your cues for the new move once this pattern is established. Visually, the Building Block Method looks like this:

Movement A	Jog (arms reach and clap)
Movement A + B	Jog (arms reach and clap) + Skip (circle arms low)
Movement A + B + C	Jog (arms reach and clap) + Skip (circle arms low) + Alternate knee lifts (bilateral bicep curls)
Movement A + B + C + D	Jog (arms reach and clap) + Skip (circle arms low) + Alternate knee lifts (bilateral biceps curls) + Splits + Alternate arm reach forward in opposition.

Basic "whole" moves usually have the following characteristics:

1. **Symmetrical**—Symmetrical moves are easy to cue and teach. Both sides of the body mirror one another.

2. **Balanced**—The arms move in opposition to the foot that is leading. The left arm reaches forward as the right foot steps forward, the right arm reaches forward as the left foot steps forward. An example is the HIA splits as the arms alternately reach forward in opposition.

3. **Centered**—All movements start from the center of the body, which is located in the center of the chest for men and in the center of the upper pelvic region for women. Centering refers to proper posture and alignment with a "pulled up" and controlled feeling. Some centered movements are both symmetrical and balanced. An example of a centered move is the releve/plié as the arms reach up and down. Often, participants will flop their upper body and their feet around as they do this move.

Teach control and focus on the movement as it extends from the center of the body.

As an option, one of the Building Blocks you have sequenced together can be a "whole" movement combination in a series of movements you are linking together.

The California Style

The California Style of teaching refers to directional variations as well as floor patterning. This technique is called the California Style because in the mid '80s, classes were often very full and held in small studios. In order to break up the monotony created by facing the same wall all of the time, the class turned to face different directions or different walls as the same movements were done. The perception of the participants was that the movements were not boring even though they were identical with each directional change.

Today, this concept still works quite well, but the moves take on any directional change. Here are just a few examples:

1. Jog 8 to the right front diagonal, 2 alternate knee lifts on-the-spot, skip 4 counts and turn around to face the left rear diagonal.

2. Forward 3 and hop to each diagonal corner.

3. Divide your class into six lines. Give each of the lines a different move to do. After several reps, have your class members power walk or jog forward and circle around within their line to face front. Then reassign each line a new move to do. (You can even use this technique as a circuit for muscle conditioning.)

4. Jack 4, kick 4, twist 8, jog 8 facing each wall.

The California Style helps to motivate your participants and gives you a technique to use your favorite moves with directional changes.

Summary

These principles and techniques of aerobic choreography may seem overwhelming. However, the more you practice and the more comfortable you feel using these step-by-step approaches, the more successful your teaching will be.

Most important, try to identify your own movement personality. Moves and movement styles that naturally click with your own personality will help you to be the best instructor that you can be.

Nancy Gillette, MA

20 *Instructor Training*

Focus

THERE ARE DOZENS OF WAYS in which future instructors receive training. Some programs meet national standards—others miss the mark entirely. How can instructors evaluate various training programs? What should they include? How important is it that they adhere to nationally accepted standards?

Background

Until about 1983, fitness instructor training was haphazard at best. No educational organizations or training associations existed purely for the benefit of the instructor and his/her training in the exercise field. Generally, an instructor entered the field as a star student filling in for an absent instructor, mimicking the exercises and style of the absentee instructor, obtaining what is referred to as "on the job non-training." Many found themselves with new part-time jobs. The only prerequisites for being an instructor in those days were a pair of athletic shoes, leotard and tights, and a music tape.

The field of aerobics and fitness has matured substantially since then. Now there are a variety of training options open for the instructor or would-be-instructor.

One of the major accomplishments within the exercise field in the past ten years has been the creation of training and certifying organizations. The accumulation of research and data on which to base standards, guidelines and proper content of such trainings has also served to put credibility and substance into these groups' criteria and curriculums.

However, because the exercise arena is still fairly new in terms of any substantiated evidence and information relating to aerobics, new studies are coming out that don't always comply with what was always thought to be "true" within the art and science of exercise. Because of conflicting or new information that disproves old studies and theories within the fitness field, selecting a club, organization or individual to act as a trainer for instructors is a difficult decision to make.

The group or individual should be as up-to-date on the latest research as possible. This isn't easy because information is constantly changing and being upgraded. A trainer should ideally be linked into a larger research or educational organization, for it's relatively impossible for one person to stay abreast of all that is happening within the exercise arena, no matter how conscientious he or she is.

How to Select a Trainer or Training Organization

When selecting a training organization or trainer, an instructor needs to look at the credentials and certifications of that individual or group. How long have they been in business? Who trained them? What is their reputation? Have they done any follow-up or continuing education after completion of the initial training? Were the trainees satisfied with it? Is that individual an outstanding or just a mediocre instructor? Will you have to travel to another city for the training sessions? What will be the expense incurred for the training? How many hours or days are included in the program? What will you receive upon completion of the program? Will you be certified? Is the certificate recognized locally? Regionally? Nationally or internationally? Is the certification a test of both theory and practical knowledge? There are many factors to consider.

Content of Instructor Training

The content of an instructor's training program will determine the future quality of that instructor-to-be. Both theory and its practical application within the class setting should be taught in conjunction with practical "how to's" of creating, instructing and demonstrating an appropriate fitness class.

The following should be included in a solid, complete training program:

Basic theory

- anatomy and kinesiology
- physiology
- nutrition
- injury prevention
- cardiorespiratory considerations

Practical application of theory

- class format
- risk factor assessment
- first aid and CPR
- medical responsibilities/emergency situations
- exercise selection
  - level of class skill
  - special population needs
  - local trends—steps, hi/lo, circuit training, funk, etc.
- cueing-alignment, safety, anticipatory
- choreography
- exercise evaluation
- transitions
- attire/shoes
- music selection—beats per minute guidelines
- professional conduct
- voice projection and protection—using a microphone
- relating to and motivating your students
- continuing education—post training

Any training program which does not include these components will leave gaps in an individual's skill or knowledge level, and will result in either ineffectual or unsafe teaching techniques.

Which to Choose?

Individual Trainer

An individual trainer who is well known in the field of exercise and has an outstanding reputation as being up-to-date, as well as personable and skilled in one-to-one training can be an excellent choice. Often clubs will hire instructors solely on the basis of having been trained by a certain individual, because the club then knows what to expect regarding the quality and style of the instructor. This is especially true in smaller cities throughout the United States where a trainer with a good local reputation has made a name for him- or herself. The drawback in selecting an individual, rather than an organization, is that the person may be teaching outmoded information or even incorrect information that could cause the instructor to injure a student, or even be sued and lose that lawsuit due to negligence or poor training.

Health Club Training

Many instructors-to-be select local training within a chain of clubs in their area. The advantage to this approach is that the club usually has instructor positions available for those who attend their trainings. Also, if you want to teach at more than one club, it is convenient if they are all owned or operated by the same individual or group.

Training Organization

One of the advantages of selecting a training organization, rather than an individual who owns their own training business, is the combined expertise and information the group shares among its members or partners. This is especially true if there is a board of advisors, an educational base to the organization, a newsletter or magazine for updating information to those who belong, or a research and data collecting department within the organization that will dispense the latest information to the trainers.

Another advantage is the networking opportunities that are available should you relocate to another city, state or country. Locating open positions and having certification or a training certificate from a well-established and respected organization can be an entree into a new locale or business. Having those credentials, or a resume that mentions a training organization by name, can insure your level of expertise as an instructor for those who have no previous knowledge of you.

Importance of Being Certified

Most health clubs or fitness studios require some sort of certification from their instructors prior to being hired. In addition to wanting to insure the expertise and quality of an instructor, owners/managers are also concerned with lawsuits and the club's reputation. For these reasons, an instructor who has certification from a training organization which requires both practical as well as theoretical knowledge assures the club/studio of the safety and effectiveness of the instructor's class formatting and instruction, both of which come under scrutiny during lawsuits from clients/students.

Summary

When selecting a trainer or training organization, look for quality of instruction, a good track record and reputation, a complete curriculum including both practical application as well as theoretical knowledge, and a personality that can provide assistance with motivational and adherence factors for your students. Seek out a training program which will supply the instructor with a certification that will provide future support, not just a temporary job.

Suggested Readings Collins, N.H. (1983). *Professional women and their mentors*. Englewood Cliffs, N.J.: Prentice-Hall.

Daloz, L.A. (1986). *Effective teaching and mentoring*. San Francisco: Jossey-Bass.

Gross, R. (1990). *Peak learning*. Los Angeles: Jeremy P. Tarcher.

Leonard, G. (1991). *Mastery, the keys to long-term success and fulfillment*. New York: Dutton Books.

Nancy Gillette, MA

21 Advancing Your Fitness Career

Focus

RESEARCH QUESTIONNAIRES FROM THE EARLY 1980s showed that the average fitness instructor had a "career span" of two and a half years, and that the instructor was generally a woman in her early twenties. As the field of fitness and aerobics matured, the career path for instructors has widened.

Career Choices

Once thought of as a "sideline," an "avocation" for most, fitness instruction has grown from a part-time, low paying job, to one with possibilities as broad as the minds that have created them over the past fifteen years. Credit for these new career choices is due in large part to the aging baby boomers who found that these "part-time" exercise teaching jobs were where their hearts were. As they chose to extend these avocations into careers, to take these second income sources and make them into their primary sources of revenue, some started their own small businesses while others took their accumulated expertise "on-the-road." Many of these new paths came from instructors who upon reaching ages 35 or 40, decided to become behind-the-scenes producers, rather than to remain in the fitness and exercise demonstration spotlight forever. The re-evaluation of preferences and strengths, skills and talents led instructors away and down a variety of career paths. Some moved into corporate boardrooms, others in front of cameras or behind podiums, rather than in front of mirrors.

Where to Begin

There are many career paths from which to choose, should an instructor want to diversify or specialize. Some possibilities depend solely on the instructor's inner motivations and goal orientation. The following checklist might help direct an exercise instructor toward the general path most suited to him or her. Does the instructor want:

- ( ) to be in the spotlight or behind-the-scenes?
- ( ) a paid position or a voluntary one?
- ( ) to work alone or with a group/association?
- ( ) to own their own business or work for someone else?
- ( ) to invest their own capital or have others support their endeavor financially?
- ( ) to work locally or have work that involves travel?
- ( ) to be responsible for moving and demonstrating exercises or remain behind a podium?

( ) to make presentations which are entertaining or strictly educational?

( ) to have local, domestic or international exposure?

Broad Options

In the past there were limited options for an individual who desired to instruct exercise or dispense fitness information to others. Today, myriad paths are available, depending upon an individual's desires, ability to travel, monetary goals, and group interactive skills. Once an individual enters a fitness career, usually as an exercise instructor, it is common for them to begin to specialize in one particular area or direction.

Many instructors have become:

- fitness/aerobics coordinators
- directors of aerobics/fitness for clubs
- managers
- owner/operators
- aerobics coordinators of a chain of clubs
- instructor trainers
- on-the-road workshop/seminar presenters

(a) lecture circuit (non-movement orientation)

(b) workshop circuit (lecture and movement)

(c) certification leaders (for a certifying body)

(d) certification examiners (for a certifying body)

(e) leaders of local/regional sites

(f) on-the-road domestic leaders on site

(g) international leaders on site

- choreographers
- music mixers for cassette tapes
- contributing authors of magazine articles
- contributing authors for books
- publishers of newsletters or informational brochures
- models for fitness/exercise oriented advertisements
- public service announcers for health and fitness on local cable or network TV, radio, or print media
- involved with the production of exercise video cassette tapes—as the script writer, consultant, choreographer, back-up principal, sponsor, fitness product rep
- stars/choreographers of own locally released fitness video
- stars/choreographers of internationally released fitness video
- resources to local business on wellness programs
- on-site coordinators or instructors for corporate fitness programs
- one-on-one personal trainers
- spokespersons for a product or facility
- representatives of a professional organization
- sales representatives for a fitness product

- coordinators of local charity events, 10K runs, triathalons, aerobathons, etc.
- aerobic competitors—regional, national or international winners
- public relations representatives or advertisers for local groups/events
- researchers for academic exercise/fitness studies at local universities and colleges
- volunteers in a research study or data collection activity
- involved with higher education—as a student, teacher's assistant, teacher, professor, or administrator
- school teachers—high school, junior high, elementary, pre-school or day care in physical education, health or recreation

Single ladder to climb?

In many career fields, there is a clearly defined ladder of success, a solitary hierarchy of money, power and status. For fitness professionals there is more of a horizontal branching of the tree's ladder, a diversifying or a specializing of focuses less clearly marked.

> *If instructors choose to associate themself with an organization that certifies or holds workshops/seminars, they will have their own ladder of expertise within that organization.*

Within each specialty, i.e., exercise video production, there will be those who create, produce and star in their own videos using a total individual budget of $5,000, or those who are hired as celebrities for $1.5 million up front plus a percentage of the sales revenue, not to mention incredible exposure worldwide. The financial success ladder is clear. Yet, in the fitness "profession," the celebrities are not the ones gaining respect, status, or credibility. The mentors, power holders and admired are the fitness educators and professionals with credentials, degrees and theoretical knowledge to match their success. To date, there seems to be a disparity between financial success and "fitness career" success within the inner circle of the exercise field.

Success in the fitness world must be measured individually. Since each step requires additional credentials, training, desire, skills or education, an instructor must be prepared to spend additional time and money to seek out appropriate conferences, workshops, books, individuals to meet, information to know, mentors, etc., in order to make the next move. With each new path ventured, additional information needs to be learned, assimilated and dispersed, which in turn creates additional jobs. It is this dynamic change that has kept the fitness industry in its growth phase.

AFAA's Ladder of Expertise

AFAA MEMBER

Individual who belongs to the 70,000-plus member association of fitness professionals worldwide, the world's largest fitness educator.

AFAA CERTIFIED PRIMARY INSTRUCTOR

Individual who has successfully passed both the written and practical components of the international Primary AFAA Certification, plus has a current CPR card. Certification to be renewed every two years through re-examination or continuing education.

AFAA SPECIALTY INSTRUCTOR

Individual who has successfully completed an AFAA Specialty program. Current offerings are Low Impact-a Second Look and Weighted Workout the Class Format Specialty, Teaching the Large Exerciser Specialty, Prenatal Specialty, Senior Fitness Specialty, Aqua Fitness Specialty, Youth Fitness Specialty, Step Reebok Certification, Personal Trainer and Fitness Counselor Certification and Weightroom Certification. Additional specialty programs are continually in development.

AFAA EXAMINER

Individual with an expertise in the examination process to score the AFAA Primary Certification Examination as one of three examiners for the Practical Examination component.

AFAA STEP REEBOK EXAMINER

Individual with an expertise in the procedures for scoring the practical component of the Step Reebok Specialty Certification.

AFAA ASSOCIATE CONSULTANT

Individual who has completed the application process successfully and has the expertise to co-lead the practical components of an AFAA two-day Primary Certification Workshop.

AFAA FULL CONSULTANT

Individual who has the expertise to co-lead the practical components of an AFAA two-day Primary Certification Workshop.

AFAA CERTIFICATION SPECIALIST

Individual who has the experience and expertise to lead an AFAA one-day Primary Certification Review without assistance.

AFAA LEAD/TRAINER CONSULTANT

Individual selected by the Board to lead both the practical and theoretical components of an AFAA two-day Primary Certification Workshop, a specialty workshop, or a 24-hour Instructor Training Program.

AFAA FITNESS PRACTITIONER

A degreed individual who has excelled in several Specialty Programs and Certifications and has demonstrated a professional mastery in providing wellness and fitness services. A liaison between health professionals and the public.

AFAA BOARD OF CERTIFICATION AND TRAINING MEMBER

By invitation, an individual who through seniority and/or excellence evaluates, develops, updates, and oversees the quality and content of AFAA's educational programs.

Summary

As with any specialty, additional training, education, research, networking, practice, time and energy are important to success. However, the most crucial step when contemplating a career is to evaluate the fitness instructor's strengths, goals and preferences.

Although a hierarchy does seem to exist among the more visible career selections, and especially among the most lucrative ones in which "celebrity" status comes into play, generally people do what they do because it meets their most basic needs, i.e. to help, to teach, to be in the spotlight, to have power, to control the purse strings, to lead.

Whatever motivates a person deep down inside and keeps them within the fitness field will lead them to the appropriate new career branch. Many instructors find their greatest joy is in the class setting and remain there long after most people in other careers have retired or moved into "administrative" positions. It's the love of what you do that keeps the newness and vitality in the path you choose, not the newness of the choice itself.

Suggested Readings

Blanchard, K., & Johnson, S. (1981). *The one minute manager.* New York: Berkeley Books.

Bolles, R.N. (1978). *The three boxes of life: and how to get out of them.* Berkeley: Ten Speed Press.

Bolles, R.N. (1970, 1992). *The 1992 what color is your parachute?* Berkeley: Ten Speed Press.

Dail, H.L. (1989). *The lotus and the pool.* Boston: Shambhala.

Peck, M.S. (1978). *The road less traveled.* New York: Simon and Schuster.

Peters, T. (1982). *In search of excellence.* New York: Harper and Row.

Peters, T. (1987). *Thriving on chaos.* New York: Knopf.

Pollan, S.M. (1990). *The field guide to starting a business.* New York: Simon and Schuster.

Kathy Stevens

22 Choosing Aerobic Equipment

Focus

AEROBIC EQUIPMENT INCLUDES all non-permanent items or props which are necessary or can be used to enhance the activities that take place within an aerobic room setting. Items can include stereo equipment, music, mats, charts, resistance products, cardio props and aqua aerobic or outdoor training equipment. Considerations include: locating manufacturers, costs, product quality and warranty, usage, storage and overall program enhancement.

Stereo Equipment

Typically, an aerobic setting needs some type of tape and/or CD playing system (preferably tape). A much appreciated feature is a speed or pitch control on the tape player. This is available in both fixed and portable units. An audio design company can advise you of necessary amplification and speaker needs based on the dimensions and acoustics of your room. Consideration should also be given to a microphone system; options include corded hand held, cordless hand held, cordless headset or cordless clip on. The corded microphone is the least expensive and most durable option, yet does not offer the ability to travel around the room or have freedom of arm movement. The cordless microphone is more conducive to the teaching situation, yet a high quality model is often very sensitive to abuse and can be quite expensive.

Music

Music may or may not be supplied by the club or organization. In most situations, tapes used should have professionally mixed music that will accommodate the beats per minute of specified classes. Some instructors choose to make their own tapes, but the pre-made tapes are much easier and cost effective (ranging from $15 to $50).

It is important that one checks with ASCAP and BMI (ASCAP: 1 Lincoln Plaza, New York, NY 10023 (212) 870-7576; BMI: 320 W. 57th St., 3rd Floor, New York 10019 (800) 872-2641) rules when purchasing or using recorded artists.

Mats

Mats are necessary if the exercise surface does not have adequate cushion for floor or body work. Mats are available in a variety of densities and sizes.

Charts

Charts are important as a training tool for class safety and education. They can be purchased laminated in a variety of dimensions. Popular charts are: muscle and anatomy guides, target heart rate (also available in children and older adult forms), rate of perceived exertion and CPR.

Resistance Devices

This category includes all types of light free weights (typically in the one to five lb. range), resistance bands or tubing, weighted bars, balls and gloves. Resistance devices are an optional type of equipment which can greatly increase the variety of classes that can be offered as well as allow instructors to continue to challenge students through basic principles of overload (see strength training chapter). Bands and weights have also been developed to work in conjunction with different stepping products. Storage is a consideration. Some type of shelf or box—preferably with a locking system—needs to be provided to keep equipment in order.

Cardio Props

Cardio props, which include all equipment that is used for cardiovascular training, support a growing market that is reflective of the need for variety and cross training. Cardio props include steps or benches, jump ropes (weighted and non weighted), slide boards and mini trampolines or spring boards. This type of equipment provides optional methods of adding variety and intensity to a program. Again, space and storage are major considerations. One must evaluate how many pieces can fit into the workout room and if this number will cost-effectively benefit the intended number of participants. Then, storage space must be provided in order to keep equipment in proper condition and out of the way of other activities.

Unique Items

Examples of these types of products are aqua equipment, kid fitness devices, therapy products, outdoor cross training equipment and specific products such as the Flo, Thigh-Toner, Slide Reebok, Abdominizer and Prostretch.

Summary

With the growing need for variety and specificity have come many innovative products that may or may not have a use in your program. When considering products, you need to compare the cost of each piece to the benefits it offers. Specifically, ask yourself what program or conditioning advantages the product offers and how they will benefit your club or personal situation. You also need to work firsthand with the product and evaluate its effectiveness before employing it with your class members.

Kathy Stevens

23 Substitute Teaching

Focus

SUBSTITUTE TEACHING CAN BE a very rewarding experience. By its very nature, it can offer an instructor a change of pace or serve as a training device to greater teaching and confidence skills. On the other hand, it can be an intimidating nightmare in which one feels rejected and incompetent for no controllable reason. This chapter will give you the insights and tools necessary to gain control of the sub situation and make it a positive experience.

Substitute teaching consists of those occasions for which an instructor covers a class which is not his or her own, particularly those classes with which they have not had a previous relationship and/or those that include devoted followers of the regular instructor. We will look at four factors which can influence the success of such a situation:

1. Evaluation of the situation
2. Establishing the right policies
3. Developing the proper attitude
4. Making the right connection

Evaluation of the Situation

There are two important elements to consider when evaluating a substitute teaching situation. The first is the technical information. You need to know what type of class you are covering, the intensity level, the time length of each portion of the class, the type of patterning preferred, the type of music appreciated and the start and end time of the class. The more specific and detailed this information, the greater the chances you will have of pleasing the students.

> Substitute teaching can add a new dimension to your teaching capabilities

The second element to evaluate is the psychological and physiological needs of the students. You need to know what kind of students you are dealing with. Are they a specialty population with specific needs (such as senior, beginners or pregnant women) or possibly an advanced group of aerobic diehards who need a highly motivating and driving routine. What is the existing relationship between the students and regular instructor? If this instructor is well received and followed by the group, you should find out what teaching characteristics he or she uses to motivate the class. Does the group respond well to a highly instructional teacher or do they prefer a high energy, driving teacher? Although you cannot completely change your style of teaching, you can try to adapt to the students with a mixture of your style and what they are accustomed to.

Establish the Right Policies

In establishing the correct substitute instruction policies, it is the responsibility of the club and instructors to set a clear and consistent method of dealing with substitute situations. The regular instructor must have a way of choosing a substitute who can meet the demands of the class. Often this method develops by trial and error, which can be avoided if the program director handles the decision. It is then the responsibility of the regular instructor to impart all of the previously mentioned information to the substitute. The substitute must be accountable for understanding the needs of the contracted class, and accept the commitment only if he or she feels able to meet those needs. The club can assist in this process of class clarification by offering an extended description of each class (scripted by the regular instructor) or by having a strict policy of format adherence, which dictates that classes be labeled by name and intensity so that all instructors teach a consistent format.

The club needs to have a method by which it can make the students aware of the substitute situation prior to the start of the class. Psychologically, students adapt more easily and have less negative reactions to controlled situations. When they are notified prior to an instructor change, they have the option to take class or opt for another scheduled time. This leaves the student with a sense of control. The earlier the knowledge is gained, the better the chances of acceptance for the club as well as the substitute instructor. Methods of notification can be verbal (by the regular instructor in prior classes, office staff or phone message) or written (in handout or posted form). Even in the case of last minute substitution, efforts should be made to post the change of events.

Developing Substitute's Self-Confidence

After evaluating the teaching situation and adhering to a constructive policy, the substitute teacher must consider his or her personal reaction to the situation. They themselves can create a level of acceptance or rejection through the attitude that they impart to the class. Of utmost importance is an attitude of self-confidence. As a substitute teacher, it is particularly important that you are certain that you can lead a proper and constructive class. This faith grows out of having the previously mentioned information as well as your overall teaching experience.

| Take requests and proceed with confidence. |

Secondly, the substitute instructor needs to be sensitive to the students' attitudes. Often students may feel disappointed or abandoned if they were not prepared for the instructor change. If students choose this psychological position, it is important for the instructor to recognize it without yielding her power as the class leader to those who may put it to trial. Often in these situations, substitutes will allow students to intimidate them with their negativism, which in turn creates an unfavorable class experience. The instructor needs to pacify the behavior of the students while ignoring the personal insult. In other words, take complaints with an accommodating attitude and move on.

Making the Right Connection

All teacher/student relationships depend on the interaction and ultimate connections made in class. Remember that the first few moments of interaction with others is when their attention spans and powers of retention are the highest. These are the things psychologists tell us that people notice first: 1) What they see (in fact, a surprising 55% of the meaning of your message is conveyed by facial expressions and body language); and 2) what they hear (38% of which is based on the characteristics of one's voice: rate or tempo, loudness, pitch, articulation and tone). You should be aware that the last thing people notice,

| Body language |

Tone

and therefore, the least important for a first impression are the words you are using (the words contribute only 7% of the meaning of your message). It is not that your words are unimportant. Yet, in order for them to be heard, the students must first like what they see and what they hear. Often their minds may be made up before you speak. Emerson wrote, "What you are speaks so loudly, I can't hear what you are saying." Therefore, it is easy to see how the first two to four minutes that you spend with a class may determine the rest of the hour.

Humor

Last, but not least, is the use of humor to increase your acceptance. Many successful businesses place a high value on humor. Top executives rely on their sense of humor to control their image and how the public views their company. This is especially true in a crisis situation. By using a bit of humor you can find a new perspective on a troubled, embarrassing or discouraging situation. Keeping an upbeat outlook gives you a sense of security in the middle of a disturbance. Using humor in the tense first minutes of a substitute class can help the students take a closer look at the temporary change that they may be taking too seriously. Both parties can then see the absurdity of the situation. This insight will lead to a greater self-awareness, which, in turn, leads to greater self-confidence and finally to improved acceptance and performance.

References

Anthony, R. (1988). *Magic power of super persuasion.* New York: Berkeley Books.

Hergenhahn, B.R. (1990). *Introduction to theories of personality.* Englewood Cliffs, N.J.: Prentice-Hall.

Magill, R.A. (1980). *Motor learning.* Dubuque, Ia.: Wm. C. Brown Company.

Motivating for Behavior Change and Exercise Adherence

24

Diana McNab, MEd

Focus

Motivation is an internal force that is born from the process of self-discovery. If you don't know who you are, how can you help your students come to know who they are? Success in teaching is derived from a basic understanding of the following:

1. Who am I?
2. What is my teaching philosophy?
3. How can I best deliver my passion?

Let's take a closer look at how a teacher can find the answers to these questions and become a true motivator.

Who Am I?

Self-discovery begins with your self-concept. This includes your ideal self (the person you would most like to be physically, intellectually, emotionally and spiritually); your self-image (how you see yourself); and self-esteem (how you feel about yourself). A motivating teacher has a healthy self-concept and a vision of what an ideal teacher is all about. She has pictured herself in front of her class as being calm, poised and ready for action. She can "see" the smile on her face and feel the energy and passion coming from her body. She is open and accepting of herself, and allows the energy of the music to flow through her to her class. This healthy self-concept leads to empowerment of self and others, and is a process that must be continuously worked on. Competent, consistent and committed teaching comes from constant surveillance and understanding of yourself. The self-discovery journey should always be challenged, reviewed and revised.

A logical way to begin this journey would be to examine the "Universal Laws of Our Being."(1) These are the basic laws of what it is to be human, encompassing how we think, act and feel. First, there is the law of control, which states that the more in control we are of our thoughts, attitudes and actions, the better we feel about ourselves. **Internal locus of control** is a sense that we are the captains of our own ships, have chartered a course and are in

> The "Universal Laws of Our Being"

control of the process. **External locus of control** is a sense other people are controlling our lives. This is a very disempowering feeling. The goal is to know who we are, what we want and how to get there. Peak performance teaching comes from internal locus of control, i.e. a feeling of inner competence and outer direction. Adherence to an exercise program will create these same feelings, and communicating this should be an important goal to any instructor.

The **law of cause and effect** states that thoughts are the cause of every result. Once we believe that we control our destiny through our thinking, we then have to concern ourselves with training the mind as well as the body. It is our thinking that creates possibilities in our lives. As an instructor, you plant positive thoughts in your head which create a positive attitude and lead to a positive result. You must then act in a way that reinforces that behavior. It is termed "fake it to make it." Exaggerated behavior, along with positive thoughts, facial expressions and encouraging words create an open and accepting atmosphere that enhances peak performance. Plant the seed of a positive thought, nurture it with a smile and watch it blossom. It works!

The law of expectations is a self-fulfilling prophecy: positive expectations lead to positive results. You determine your tomorrow by what you are thinking today. Believe in yourself and in your class, and watch the wonderful results. Your students will perform up to your level of expectations. The possibilities are limitless—reach for the stars!

The **law of attraction** says that people are drawn to your most dominant thoughts. Negative thoughts attract negative people, whereas a positive "being" opens up positive relationships. If you believe in yourself and in what you are doing, an aura of love and acceptance will be sent out. Just watch your classes fill up!

The final law enhancing the process of self-discovery is the **law of visualization and positive beliefs**. What you can perceive and truly believe, you can achieve. This is how it works: we think in pictures, therefore by surrounding a picture with positive beliefs and affirmations, it becomes deeply embedded in our psyche and the requested image will unfold. Get your class to visualize the results they wish to achieve, believe in the process and watch what wonderful things can happen. You get one-third of a neuromuscular contraction with each visualization, so watch your biceps grow as you visualize while you exercise.

The "Universal Laws of Our Being" help us to understand who we are, examine our interpersonal relationships and create an atmosphere in which optimum learning and performance takes place. Now let's talk about developing a teaching philosophy, starting with how intrinsic and extrinsic motivation can shape your teaching style.

The Thought Cycle
THOUGHT
"I love to exercise"
RESULT
"Positive!"
ATTITUDE
"I feel great!"
ACTION
"Loose, relaxed, ready"

What Is My Teaching Philosophy?

A philosophy consists of beliefs or principles that serve as guides to action. These principles help you cope with life's situations; however, a philosophy is useless unless you own it and nurture it. Consider these questions:

1. What is your philosophy of teaching and how is it being utilized in your classes?
2. Do your students come first?
3. What is your role in their fitness development?

4. Are you an educator, motivator and communicator in the area of health and fitness, keeping up with the latest skills, strategies and techniques?

5. Are you more interested in your own personal fitness and advancement than your classes?

The student must come first. Your responsibility is that of teacher, guide and coach. The role of a fitness instructor is to educate people about who they are, what their lifestyle choices can be and how to care for their bodies. This teaching format is both physical and intellectual, and encourages students to consciously take control of their lives.

Your success as an instructor is strongly related to your self-esteem, or how you feel about yourself. It is important to keep your public image in alignment with the real you, and not send opposing messages to your clients. Credibility and accountability are what people are seeking today. You, as instructor, must be constantly growing, learning and sharing new insights and ideas with your class. Knowledge is power, but only if you know how to use it.

A teaching philosophy should be centered around motivation. The best motivation comes from within. **Intrinsic motivation** emerges from a positive self-concept and is the ideal form of energy for pursuing dreams and goals. The key ingredient of intrinsic motivation is fun: do you feel alive and well? Or has working out become just that—work!

Intrinsic
Motivated from within

Intrinsically motivated people are pursuing the "pleasure principle" and strive to be competent and self-determining. They enjoy mastering a task and being successful and take pride in their exercise experiences. These clients work hard and are an instructor's dream.

In order to reinforce this type of motivation, the instructor must keep his or her classes enjoyable and creative, providing maximum involvement for everyone. She should educate students about the processes taking place during exercise, since the more knowledge, skills and understanding we have about why we are doing something, the more our desire to continue is increased. In addition, the instructor should bear in mind that socializing is a great intrinsic motivator. The comradely friendship and support we get from our "exercise friends" provides a wonderful form of self-acceptance.

Extrinsic motivation comes from outside of you, and the concern here is with the outcome, not the process. For example, exercisers who are extrinsically motivated have a certain body weight or percentage of body fat as their goals. They are working out—often in an addictive and compulsive way—to avoid the negative consequences of being overweight and out of shape. Too much, too soon and too often is usually their menu, and an instructor must be on the lookout for clients with this mindset. The instructor needs to find a way to turn the extrinsic motivation into intrinsic motivation. This can be accomplished by emphasizing enjoyment, moderation and variety; by creating a warm and supportive environment and the possibility of a positive experience; by rewarding personal achievements (attendance, weight loss, strength goals, attitude changes) and ignoring negative behaviors. Encouraging participants to compliment each other is frequently effective. Also, an instructor can further enhance a feeling of well-being with a smile, a gentle touch or warm eye contact. The sum total of these modifications is purely positive: fitness will soon be seen as a way of life, and the instructor as a facilitator.

Extrinsic
Outcome oriented

Another way to reach students is through *direct motivation*. This occurs when you appeal to a person's pride in the hope that he or she will work harder and more often to obtain the results wanted. Confronting students directly with positive *comments, praise* and *suggestions* helps to accomplish this. Establishing objectives in a progressive manner keeps students on track. Keep asking your clients, "What are your fitness and health goals?" and make them accountable for the answers.

Indirect motivation has to do with the class environment. The exercise space should be clean and bright, with good lighting and a great sound system. The atmosphere should be warm, friendly and positive. Make your studio a special place, and people will be drawn to it.

Clients who adhere to an exercise program usually have a strong internal locus of control, knowing that they are responsible for their lives and the choices they make. **Skill-oriented** individuals are drawn to new steps and choreography. **Socially motivated** clients come for the interpersonal connections and **end-result** clients just want to get fit, thin or strong. People are there for many reasons, so you want to keep all possibilities open for everyone.

True motivation also comes from meeting your client's *needs,* and addressing this issue adds an important dimension to any philosophy of teaching. Psychologist Abraham Maslow states that people attempt to satisfy their needs according to a system of priorities.(2) These needs can be divided into two categories: **deficiency needs**, such as hunger, thirst, sex, safety and security, and **growth needs**, such as love, self-esteem and self-actualization. Deficiency needs have the highest priority. According to Maslow, once a need is met or satisfied, it is no longer a need and that person can move up the hierarchy to the next one.

Following Maslow's theory, it would be interesting to put each client into their respective needs category. Exercise enthusiasts are usually exercising for fun, which meets their need for stimulation and excitement. They also want to be with people to satisfy social needs. And finally, they want to demonstrate competence and feel worthy.

Since people have a basic **need for stimulation**, they seek an optimum level of arousal. An ideal state of arousal is called *flow,* in which you are totally absorbed in your activity, feeling very much in control and experiencing extreme pleasure. There is also an endorphin release in *flow* state that enhances an exerciser's sense of well-being. As an instructor, it is very much within your control to set up a stimulating and energizing class.

Here are some suggestions for getting your class into *flow* state:

1. Fit the difficulty level of the class to the ability of the participants.
2. Keep the class stimulating by varying the activities and routines.
3. Keep everyone challenged and active.
4. Individualize certain routines and exercises.
5. Let participants demonstrate a skill or exercise.
6. Help clients set realistic body, health and performance goals.
7. Set up an atmosphere of unconditional acceptance.
8. Cooperatively teach the class, and ask for suggestions and ideas to involve your clients in the workout.
9. Visualize your routine beforehand, and set a personal goal as an instructor to keep you focused and intrinsically motivated.
10. Be willing to create and adjust as the needs change within your class.

As instructors, we want to emphasize to our students the following three points:

1. Set realistic goals.

2. Take personal responsibility for your actions towards those goals.

3. Learn to enjoy the process!

In addition to a need for stimulation, people have a **need for affiliation**. This need is one of life's great motivators and can be met in an exercise class. We are social beings who thrive on *acceptance, approval* and *appreciation*. Meeting people with similar interests is a strong bond and belonging to that group can add significant self-esteem to our lives. Once a feeling of acceptance has been established, we are willing to take risks and challenge our comfort zone. We need to feel secure to do this, and a great exercise instructor can make this possible by mingling with the students and showing true empathy and concern. This behavior is contagious, and serves to unify the group and create a class that, through affiliation, is self-stimulating and self-motivating.

Another very powerful need is the **need to feel worthy**. *Failure-oriented* clients see their results as flukes and do not believe in their ability to succeed. They often sabotage their fitness goals by overeating and not coming to class consistently. They do not see themselves as winners, and feel they do not deserve great bodies. Underlying issues of acceptance, approval and shame hinder these well-intentioned clients. One of our goals as instructors is to get our clients into *success-oriented* modes. These can be achieved through commitment, dedication and hard work. By using the law of control, they can actualize their fitness goals. We want them to affirm lifestyles of good nutrition, committed exercise and positive thinking, and feel worthy, competent and successful!

Become an effective communicator

There are three basic styles of teaching: command, submissive and cooperative. Each one affects students differently. The **command style** gives the instructor full responsibility for everything from the music, to choreography, to positions. He or she comes with a single game plan and follows it through, no matter what. This is a common, entry-level teaching mode. The class feels comfortable in the instructor's hands, but there seems to be a lack of spontaneity and individual attention because the instructor actually distances themself from the class. It becomes "the instructor" versus "the group," with no real empathy for what each person is going through. The **submissive style** has no game plan and no real class goals. There is a lack of organization. You are never sure if even the instructor knows what is coming up next. This leaves the class feeling insecure and unmotivated. Once a client has lost faith and trust in the instructor, it is only a matter of time before he/she drops out. An unprepared and unprofessional instructor is his/her own worst enemy.

The **cooperative style** combines the best of both worlds: it is organized yet not totally authoritarian. The instructor is creative, open to changes and suggestions, and involved in the flow of the class. He or she "sees" the needs of the class unfolding. The client feels a sense of belonging in this atmosphere.

The goal of good teaching is to encourage client independence and self-growth. We want our clients to incorporate what we teach them into their own lives. We aspire to be life skills managers who believe that our clients are more important than the workout. Helping students develop healthy lifestyles is a long-term objective, and can be done through subtle communication skills. The underlying message is that you, the instructor, care for them as human beings, and accept and trust them. This climate will allow growth to occur. Remember that each person in your class comes to you with her own agenda, and your job is to accept all your students the way they are, thus creating an opportunity for them to change.

Communication Skills

We communicate verbally and non-verbally, with words and with actions. To be an effective teacher, you must master certain skills so you can express yourself successfully, be a good listener, understand non-verbal communication and develop the ability to resolve conflicts. In the realm of **self-expression**, it is important to employ the following strategies:

1. Your messages should be clear and direct. Do not assume your class can read your mind. How strongly are you sending direct verbal messages?

2. Use "I" and "my" and own your thoughts. You disempower your messages when you say "we," "us," and "our." Stand behind your thoughts and words. *Accountability is powerful.*

3. Your messages should be complete, specific, clear and consistent. Avoid double messages and unstated intentions. Double messages are usually sent when you are afraid to tell a person something that might offend them directly. Be tactful, yet honest in your conversations.

4. Your messages should be supportive; directly state your feelings as soon as possible after an incident occurs. Timing plays a very important part in constructive communication.

> *Communicating begins with listening*

Active listening means that you are 100% focused on what the other person is saying to you. You use direct eye contact and reiterate any confusing portion of what they are saying to you. After class, it is imperative that you be available to your students to answer their questions and make them feel as if they truly count. Listening skills are probably one of teachings greatest motivators. How you attend to your students will determine whether or not they feel good and come back to your class.

Passive listening occurs when you are not fully present for what someone is saying to you, and you listen with half an ear, answering the question in your head before the speaker is even finished. This shows great disrespect for your student and also destroys your credibility as a teacher. Be "there" for your class before, during and after each workout, and if you are around the facility, be prepared to accommodate each participant. Here are some tips for active listening:

1. Listen with openness and empathy, trying to understand the other person's perspective.

2. Be mentally prepared to listen, face the person squarely, make eye contact, nod your approval and concentrate on what is being said.

3. Remind yourself not to pre-judge what the person is saying. Remove distractions and commit to being a better listener. Practice!

Proxemics is also an issue in exercise classes. It refers to the use of space between you and the class, between each class member, and also when communicating one-on-one. Exercise enthusiasts become very territorial when selecting a spot, so your role as motivator and teacher is to acknowledge their desire to be close to you, but to also respect the needs of the group. A few tactful adjustments could be in order, along with a friendly suggestion to certain aggressive students. Remember, your clients' first priority is to feel good.

Paralanguage is how you use your voice *(pitch, tone and resonance)*. Vary the tempo, rhythm, volume and pitch of your voice to keep your clients' attention. Articulate each word, and put *enthusiasm* into what your have to say.

Don't over-talk, and say only what is important to the class. Less is more when teaching exercise classes—*you* are the motivator, not what you say.

The final consideration regarding communication is **conflict resolution**. Whenever the action of another person prevents, obstructs or interferes in some way with your goals or actions, a conflict is likely. The key is to think before you speak, and make sure you are not too emotionally charged to make your point. It is often best to "cool down" and become rational before you confront a situation. *Role play* your response if it seems appropriate, and talk it over with your assistants to get a new perspective. Understand the issue before you verbalize any opinion and take care of the other person as well as yourself. Be tentative and proceed gradually—remember that everyone wants to be heard and feel understood and authenticated. Create a win/win situation if you can.

Summary

We can conclude that the choice of an appropriate teaching style coupled with finely-tuned communication skills can make becoming a true motivator possible. Once you have completed the self-discovery process and developed an inspirational teaching philosophy, what remains is the task of getting your message across in an efficient, professional, positive and caring manner. Motivation comes from within and is transmitted to others. It is actually the transfer of energy from one person to the next, and you, as instructor, are the vehicle facilitating this transfer. Great teaching is about empowering others to set goals and take risks, and then guiding them in their efforts.

A true sign of teaching success is selflessness: "I am here for you physically, mentally and spiritually. I unconditionally accept your presence within my class. Please watch me, listen to me and follow my actions. Let's hold hands and walk the path together."

Notes

1. Tracey, B. The psychology of achievement: six keys to personal power. Tape series. Chicago: Nightingale Conant, Inc.
2. Maslow, A.H. (1962). *Toward a psychology of being.* New York: Van Nostrand.

References

Burns, D. (1980). *Feeling good, the new mood therapy.* New York: Signet Books.

Crum, T. (1987). *The magic of conflict—Turning a life of work into a work of art.* New York: Touchstone.

Curran, D. (1985). *Traits of a healthy family.* San Francisco: Harper and Row.

Garfield, C. (1985). *Peak performance: Mental training techniques of the world's greatest athletes.* Los Angeles: Warner Books.

Jaffe, D., Jaffe, S., & Jaffe, C. (1984). *From burn-out to balance—A workbook for peak performance and self-renewal.* New York: McGraw Hill.

Jeffers, S. (1987). *Feel the fear and do it anyway.* New York: Fawcett Columbine.

Kellner, S. (1987). *Taking it to the limit—With basketball cybernetics.* East Setauket, N.Y.

Martens, R. (1987). *Coaches guide to sports psychology.* Champaign, Ill.: Human Kinetics Publishers.

Martens, R. (1981). *Coaching young athletes.* Champaign, Ill.: Human Kinetics Publishers.

Martens, R. ((1990). *Successful coaching.* Champaign, Ill.: Human Kinetics Publishers.

Maslow, A.H. (1962). *Towards a psychology of being.* New York: Van Nostrand.

Orlick, T. (1990). *In pursuit of excellence.* Champaign, Ill.: Leisure Press.

Orlick, T. (1986). *Psyching for sport: Mental training for athletes.* Champaign, Ill.: Leisure Press.

Orlick, T., & Partington, J. (1986). *Psyched—Inner views of winning.* Ottawa: Coaching Association of Canada.

Orlick, T., et al (1983). *Mental training for coaches and athletes.* Ottawa: Coaching Association of Canada.

Sinetar, M. (1989). *Do what you love and the money will follow.* New York: Dell Publishing.

Stranton, S. (1986). *The 25 hour woman.* New York: Bantam Books.

Tannen, D. (1980). *You just don't understand—Women and men in conversation.* New York: William Morrow & Co.

Tracey, B. The psychology of achievement: Six keys to personal power. Tape series. Chicago: Nightingale Conant, Inc.

Ken Alan

25 Exercise Adherence

Focus

IT IS ESTIMATED THAT 40% of Americans are inactive during their leisure time. Another 40% are periodically active at levels that are too low and infrequent to promote health and fitness gains, and 20% exercise regularly and intensely enough to meet ACSM's current guidelines for fitness. A professional exercise instructor knows that gaining the scientific knowledge base to develop an exercise program is only the first step in establishing a successful fitness business. This knowledge must be transferred to the public in an effective way, a way that keeps students coming back for more workouts. This chapter will focus on techniques that will bring students to your classes voluntarily!

Adherence and Compliance

Adherence generally refers to a voluntary action while compliance is mandatory. When students have to take an aerobics class to receive a passing grade in school, they comply by coming to class. When students choose to take an aerobics class for personal reasons, they adhere by coming to class. Adherence rates and patterns differ in various settings and types of programs. Although interest in the topic of exercise adherence has increased in the past few years, there are few published reports or studies that look specifically at the adherence rates and patterns in aerobic exercise classes.

Population Types

There are a number of factors that predict how a specific segment of the population will adhere to physical activity. Factors such as environmental conditions (cold, hot or inclement weather); cultural variables (how specific groups view particular activities); social and economic conditions (the availability of discretionary time and money that might be necessary to join a facility to exercise); educational status (those with more education are more likely to exercise); gender, race, age, religion, personality and general activity patterns all influence exercise adherence.

Aerobic fitness participants can be divided into three sub-groups: novices, intermediates and advanced students. Individuals who are already active have different requirements to maintain exercise motivation than irregular exercisers. Conversely, sedentary individuals need very different approaches to exercise than semi-active or regularly active participants. Interestingly, studies in exercise adherence have not yet been able to predict or explain exercise adherence with the preciseness or reproducibility required to design systematic interventions aimed at changing current physical activity and exercise patterns in the various population segments and settings in the fitness industry. In this chapter, you will find practical interventions to facilitate exercise adherence in ways that will promote healthy outcomes.

The population at large can be divided into four distinct categories, each with its own behavioral characteristics that require different action plans to facilitate exercise adherence. For discussion sake, these categories will be identified as Types A, B, C and D.

Type A Characteristics

Competitive

Potential for overuse

Two of the most significant Type A characteristics for instructors to be aware of are the following:

• May be willing to risk injury to work at very high levels of intensity.

• May be in the class for competitive reasons.

Type A individuals are the most advanced students who attend a group exercise class. If your fitness studio holds classes seven days a week, Type A students will be present seven days a week. If possible, Type As will stay and take two classes in a row. Or, they will come back later in the day to take a second class. Often active in other sports and activities, As are the ones who ride bikes miles and miles, pump iron for a few hours and engage in a fast five to ten mile run after dinner. Behavior characteristics of Type As include standing at the front of the room, having a favorite "spot" or place on the floor and frequently requesting louder music and faster tempos. They may be upset with substitute instructors. Some Type As become addicted to exercise to the point that other factors in their lives are shortchanged, such as work, family or friends. "Anorexic athletica" is a term used to describe the compulsive nature of Type As. Without megadoses of exercise, these individuals may perceive themselves as feeling fat, out of shape or just out of it.

Type A exercisers are frequently Type A individuals sociologically—hard-driven, success-oriented, highly motivated but short-tempered, hurried—and they bring these personality traits into the aerobics room.

A feeling of being invulnerable or immune to injury is not uncommon among Type A exercisers. It is doubtful that anybody in an exercise class wants to be injured, yet Type As are willing to take that risk to work at very advanced levels of fitness training. Most professional athletes are Type A. They are willing to risk injury to be the very best. Yet, unlike professional athletes, Type A exercisers generally are not making their livelihood in professional sports or athletics. What makes the aerobics industry unique is the Type As are more likely working out strenuously for appearance reasons than for performance. Athletes involved at the elite level know there is an inherent risk of injury associated with their high level of performance and take responsibility for the risk.

In spite of the non-competitive atmosphere that is associated with group exercise, it is possible that Type A exercisers are in class for competitive reasons. Many are ex-athletes, perhaps in amateur sports, and competing is common, natural and motivating for them. They enjoy the challenge of kicking higher than anyone else in the room, demonstrating a phenomenal stretch or proudly displaying their well-developed physiques. Competition is a major motivator for many people. Instructors should not discount this. The advent of aerobic competitions is a result of the competitive element that is inherent in any sport.

Action Plan

Professional instructors should encourage individuals with Type A characteristics to move into cross-training. Participating in only one activity with sufficient intensity, duration and frequency carries a risk of eventual boredom. It may be only elite athletes who can participate in one predominant activity at high intensities without getting bored or burned out over time. An innate quality that athletes are born with drives them to this level. For recreational athletes, however, one predominant activity may eventually lead to boredom over time. This has been evidenced in the past in other leisure activities, such as tennis, racquetball and running, in which popularity soared then waned.

Overuse syndromes or muscle imbalances commonly result from engaging in one activity only. In the aerobic dance-exercise industry, consider the possibilities for cross-training within program structure. High-impact, low-impact, step training and slide training are a few of the different kinds of programs that stress the musculoskeletal system in slightly different ways while still offering high-intensity training. Alternating high-impact with lower-impact activities on a daily basis is a prudent plan to help avoid overuse syndromes on a long-term continuum.

As people get older, reducing frequency and duration of aerobic activity, but not intensity, maintains aerobic fitness. Therefore, high intensity but lower-impact activities can satisfy the intensity needs of advanced students while minimizing the risk of accumulative trauma to the body. Of course, strength training programs help to maintain strength and reduce the opportunity of injury. This is why the American College of Sports Medicine has adopted a strength training recommendation. Unfortunately, ACSM guidelines do not address adherence.

Type As need to periodically assess their goals as to why they need to work out as often and as hard as they do. Is it for weight control, stress reduction, appearance, competition, performance? As professional instructors, we need to help our students achieve their goals in a safe and balanced way, so they can keep exercising for the rest of their lives.

| *Surveys point out, the higher the intensity of exercise, the higher the dropout rate.* |

Type B Characteristics

Type B exercisers are the students who come to class every other day instead of every day. The Type Bs who do work out every day alternate low-impact activities on one day with higher-impact activities on subsequent days, unlike Type As who tend to choose high-impact activities on a daily basis. Type Bs work at 65% to 90% of their predicted maximal heart rate. They wear appropriate shoes, drink lots of water, read up on fitness research. These are the "good guys!" Type Bs are individuals who exercise because they choose to, rather than because they have to. They are sensible rather than compulsive about exercise, and have affectionately embraced it into their everyday lives. This group is interested in the long-term outcomes of exercise as well as the short-term. Type Bs may exercise just as much as Type As but are satisfied with working at moderate levels to minimize the opportunity for injury.

| *Consistent* |

Action Plan

Most Type B exercisers require no special action plan to keep them exercising. Exercising itself is internally rewarding for them. This intrinsic satisfaction keeps Type B individuals in a moderate and balanced exercise program which can be maintained for a long period of time. Offering reinforcers, such as positive feedback and compliments, personal acknowledgements such as a phone call or note, or tangible rewards such as T-shirts, ribbons, certificates or other awards, are effective ways for you to recognize their consistent efforts.

| *Moderate* |

Type C Characteristics

Newcomers

Teaching Tip

Positioning new participants in an area in which they can see well and hear well enhances their opportunities for success. Grouping all new students together so they can all work at the same fitness level is another helpful technique. Doing this makes your job easier because it means you can give instructions to everyone together.

Type C individuals are those participants who are experiencing group exercise to music for the first time. Their previous history may include participation in other activities or a sedentary background.

Action Plan

Whatever the exercise history, the objective is the same: Get the new person to become a regular exerciser. A number of teaching strategies can be employed. First, after doing health, medical and fitness history screening, tell the individual what to expect in class. Explain the structure of the workout and give appropriate guidance as to what to do and what not to do based upon the information you received during the screening. By informing the participant that you will be assisting him/her during the workout, you avoid the risk of possible embarrassment or feelings of inadequacy on the part of the new student.

Avoid being concerned about students moving to the tempo of the music. Many new participants are busy concentrating on the exercises and may not hear the dominant accents in the music. The music may serve as background stimulation rather than the "move to the music" dominance that is traditional in aerobics classes.

Transitions with Type C participants are significantly less important than with more experienced exercisers. The fact that a student is moving at all may be more important than whether he changes movements when you want him to. Cue your participants for the transitions, but if new students are unable to master them, avoid making an issue out of the situation.

Demonstrate the intensity levels and exercise modifications that are appropriate for the new participants. You may have to be working at that level for much of the workout, since the new students may not know how to "work at their own levels" or "listen to their bodies." Since you are the role model, new students will try to emulate you. If you are working at a high level, they may try to do the same even if it is beyond their range. Therefore, if you work out at a low level, it gives them permission to work out at a low level, too. Verbally instruct intermediate and advanced students to work out at their appropriate levels, while you physically stay with the lower level option.

New participants need positive reinforcement not only during the session, but also immediately at the end of the workout. It is common for new people to feel as if they did not do well in class, so expect to hear comments like, "I couldn't touch my toes. I was going left when you were going right. I couldn't even do two aerobic numbers." Take any negative statement and turn it into a positive one, by establishing and reinforcing realistic and appropriate goals. For example, you might reply, "It may take many months before you are able to touch your toes. It takes a few workouts to figure out the aerobic patterns, and each week you should be able to do another few minutes of aerobic conditioning." Unfortunately, novices think that if they cannot complete everything the first time, then the program is not right for them. This misunderstanding increases the possibility of dropout.

Incentives

You may wish to set up incentive programs for Type Cs until they become Type B exercisers. Follow-up phone calls have proven to be effective for increasing adherence to programs. Periodic fitness assessments, establishing an

Incentives

exercise log, and specific rewards for achieving behavioral objectives can be created, such as a free workout pass after X-number of weeks of participation. Reward or acknowledge the behavior change rather than a fitness goal, such as losing X-number of pounds or inches. Reinforcing the behavior rather than the achievement of hitting the goal keeps new students from becoming disillusioned if they haven't "lost ten pounds in two weeks."

Type Cs will need positive reinforcements each time they work out with you for the first few months. This is a critical time for establishing a new behavior. Statistics show that around 50% of exercisers drop out after six months. This may be because it sometimes takes that long to reap the benefits of regular exercise. Type A and Type B exercisers get their reinforcement intrinsically. For them, the act of exercise is internally rewarding. For the new exerciser, extrinsic reinforcement by way of your interactive feedback is necessary until a level of training is reached at which exercise itself becomes the reward. Group exercise is different from other activities, such as walking or biking, that require basically one locomotor movement. Aerobic classes utilize a multitude of movement patterns that must be done to a certain cadence of music. This takes time for people to master. Not everyone is blessed with natural coordination to move to music. During this cognitive stage, extrinsic reinforcement from the instructor not only helps the participant to master correct form and technique, but also inspires the participant to endure until the movement and terminology become second nature.

Type D Characteristics

Individuals who are in this group are classified as physically inactive or sedentary. They can exercise but are prone to start and stop type of exercising or actually never partake in regular exercise at all, due to time constraints, expense, convenience, other obligations such as work or family or simply because there is no interest in their own fitness level. Interestingly, studies have shown that there is no relationship between physical activity and other health behaviors. Educational campaigns have changed people's diet and smoking habits, but have had no effect on activity habits. Data from surveys of both inactive and active populations that ask, "Why not exercise more?" suggest lack of time, willpower and apathy as chief reasons.

Non-Exercisers

Three Barriers to Exercise

The three main barriers to exercise seem to be time, effort and on-the-spot excuses. Physical activity requires much more time and energy than other health-related activities. Instructors need to consider appropriate program design and incentives to encourage Type Ds to begin and maintain a regular exercise program.

The health benefits of exercise are commonly promoted by the medical field as incentive to exercise. Psychological benefits and body image benefits are generally promoted by the private sector. Instructors need to help Type Ds overcome the obstacles that prevent them from participating in regular exercise, and secondly, develop programs to attract new populations to exercise.

	Active	Inactive
No time	51%	42%
No willpower	14%	18%
Don't feel like it	7%	13%

For Type Ds with no time for exercise, offer instruction and motivation to incorporate more exercise into daily life.

Advise students to walk flights of stairs instead of taking the elevator, stretch while watching television and walk to do more errands. Show non-exercisers that you care about them enough to offer these recommendations, even though they may not be able to attend your scheduled class.

A real key to success with the Type D population, however, is to develop and implement new programs in unconventional ways. For example, two or three daily stretch breaks at worksite locations may give people the opportunity to gain that important component of fitness in a convenient location. Shorter workouts appeal to those with limited time. Therefore, two lunch time classes of 30 minutes each may be more attractive than a 60-minute workout. Conditioning programs with weights tend to appeal to males who might not feel comfortable with more popular aerobic programming. In efforts to attract more males to group exercise, for instance, a program emphasizing strength conditioning may be more successful than a program that encompasses all three components of fitness.

| Stretch |

Once men have a successful experience with the workout, it may be more advantageous to then add aerobic and flexibility training. For seniors, having chairs available adds a measure of safety, security and comfort for those who may not have the ability to do a great deal of standing exercise. For teenagers, utilizing the current dance music and the latest dance moves makes the workout feel less like exercise and more like partying, something teenagers generally enjoy. Christian music is an alternative for those who are put off by contemporary music. "Oldies" music may attract baby-boomers, while Latin music is certain to appeal to those of Latino heritage.

Having special sessions in which T-shirts and sweats are required may be just the right cup of tea for those who are intimidated by the hard-bodies in revealing clothing. Step classes with simple choreography appeals to those who want the group exercise to music experience, but lack well-developed movement to music skills. Sport-specific classes can seduce sports buffs who don't attend regular classes.

Summary

Why do people avoid exercise? It may be a matter of unrealistic expectations, or that they can't postpone gratification. Frequently, it's the "too much too soon" syndrome which leads to soreness and discourages regular participation. Of course, the exercise habit is the opposite of the laziness habit. Loss of interest in exercise is compounded by time management issues. Why do people come to group exercise classes? The group energy, the social support, the music, the leadership and the motivation that working out with others provides are but a few of the reasons.

Why do people avoid group exercise? It could be for exactly the same reasons! Plus, the choice of music, the choice of exercises, inappropriate intensities, lack of personal attention, embarrassment, lack of coordination and perhaps ultimately, the fear of failure. Nobody wants to participate in an activity at which they are going to fail. People want to engage in activities at which they will be successful. Maybe that is why so many people in the United States lead sedentary lives. It is easy to be successful being sedentary. It is harder to be successful being active.

This, then, is our challenge as fitness instructors: To create programs that have more built-in opportunities for success than for failure, and to teach them in a way that is not only beneficial for the active individual who has affectionately embraced exercise, but also meets the needs of the inactive person who needs exercise even more.

References

Smith, D.H., & Theberge, N. (1987). *Why people recreate.* Champaign, Ill.: Life Enhancement Publications.

Dishman, R.K. (1988). *Exercise adherence.* Champaign, Ill.: Human Kinetics Books.

Schmidt, R.A. (1991). *Motor learning and performance.* Champaign, Ill.: Human Kinetics Books.

Davidson, P.O., & Davidson, S.M. (1980). *Behavioral medicine: Changing health lifestyles.* New York: Brunner.

26 International Travel for Instructors

Laura A. Gladwin, MS

Focus

AS FITNESS PROFESSIONALS BEGIN to broaden their horizons into international markets, practical protocol is a must. Understanding travel procedures and customs of foreign countries may help to reduce confusion and frustration as well as provide a competitive edge.

Checklist For International Travel

Refer to this guide before you go abroad.

1. **Passport:** A passport is a form of international identification and is necessary when traveling outside of the United States (with limited exceptions). It may be acquired through your local post office or State Department. Allow six to eight weeks for processing.

2. **Visas:** Visas are required in some countries for entry. There are different forms of visas (i.e., tourist or business) which allow the traveler certain rights and privileges within a country. To determine the appropriate visa required by the country or countries in which you will be working, contact the nearest consulate or embassy of those countries. Failure to secure the proper visa could result in a variety of unpleasant situations such as interrogation by local immigration officers. Processing may take as long as six to eight weeks.

3. **Immunizations/Vaccinations:** Some foreign countries advise specific inoculations to help assure healthy travel. Your travel agent can advise you of the countries which require certain inoculations prior to entry. Additional information regarding inoculations and other medical/health related concerns may be obtained by contacting the appropriate consulate or embassy.

4. **Contact Person:** Establish a contact person who will act as your guide and sponsor as soon as you arrive. This is very helpful when it comes to dealing with customs, food and travel within a particular country. Be sure to carry the contact's phone number and address with you.

5. **Translator:** In countries in which English is not the primary language, it is advisable to hire a knowledgeable, experienced and reliable translator, one who is familiar with the theory and practical application of health and fitness.

6. **Credibility:** To enhance your credibility with the country's inhabitants, it is helpful to learn local customs, greetings and salutations, and etiquette before your arrival.

7. **Assistance:** It is advisable to take with you the address and telephone number of the U.S. Embassy or Consulate in the countries in which you are traveling. These numbers may come in handy if any legal or political situations arise in reference to your presence within the country. Personnel at the local U.S. Embassy can assist you in understanding local rules, regulations, customs, etc.

8. **Business Cards:** And last but not least, take along your personal business cards. They will serve as an identification of your business, address and professional title. In some countries, it is customary to exchange business cards as a sign of respect as well as an actual ritual in opening business relations (i.e., Japan).

Summary

Work customs vary dramatically across the international scene. What may be appropriate in one country can be completely inappropriate in another. Therefore, it is important to arrange for a local contact, learn the customs, and check with as many knowledgeable sources about the country to which you will be traveling. Detailed preparation prior to your departure will help to insure the success and pleasure of your trip. In closing, one tip that may help you in any country—smile. It has the same meaning all around the world.

References

British Forsythe Travel. (1991). *TIM: Travel information manual.* Shawnee Mission, Kansas.

Cuffington, P. W. (November, 1991). Practical protocol. *Sky Magazine,* Delta Airlines.

Pan American Airlines (1984). *Pan am world guide: The encyclopedia of travel.* New York: McGraw Hill.

Part 4

Nutrition and Weight Management

General Nutrition

Sports Nutrition

Body Composition

Body Image

Weight Management

27 *General Nutritional Needs*

Laura Pawlak, PhD, RD

Focus

THIS CHAPTER ACQUAINTS THE INSTRUCTOR with a basic understanding of the type and amount of food fuel required for growth, development, exercise and survival. The human body relies on food as fuel for existence and utilizes nutrients for the positive growth, maintenance and work requirements of daily living. (For the nutritional needs during endurance and sports training, see the following chapter on "Sports Nutrition.")

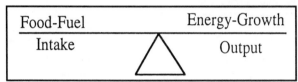

Food-Fuel	Energy-Growth
Intake	Output

Fig. 27-1. Intake - Output energy balance

Nutrients: The Food Fuels

Nutrients are chemicals necessary for the proper functioning of the body. There are seven nutrients essential for life: water, protein, carbohydrates, fats, vitamins, minerals and fiber.

Water

Function: Water, the most abundant body constituent, is also the most basic nutrient need. It performs three functions that are essential to life:

- Contributes to the structure and form of the body.
- Provides the liquid environment for cell processes.
- Aids in regulation of body temperature.

Intake is accomplished through three routes:

- water within solid foods (fruits/vegetables)
- liquids consumed (water, milk, other beverages)
- water generated within the cell through oxidation during normal metabolic processes

Water from foods and liquids is absorbed via the stomach, the rate depending on the temperature of the water. Although water can be absorbed throughout the small intestine, additional water absorption occurs mainly in the large intestine.

Intake of this nutrient should balance the output of water daily from:

- urine excretion
- stool excretion
- respiration losses through lungs
- losses from skin evaporation and sweat

Balance

Intake vs. Excretion

Requirement. Water losses through the skin and lungs can increase three to ten times during strenuous physical activity, especially when combined with exposure to high elevations or hot, dry climates. Water needs for the physically stressed person are discussed in the Sports Nutrition chapter. The standard of 1 ml/calorie for adults is adequate under non-sweating conditions. Stated in simpler terms, for each 1,000 calories consumed, one needs about one quart of water intake primarily from fluids.

Protein

Function and structure. Proteins make up the basic structure of all living cells and are essential for formation and maintenance of the organism. They are known as the building materials of the body. The individual building units are called amino acids. The quality of the protein as a building material is classified as complete or incomplete, depending on the type of amino acids and their percentage in the specific protein food. Therefore, the quality of the protein source can only be discussed in terms of the quality of the constituent amino acids.

Amino acids are categorized as essential or nonessential. The nine identified essential amino acids that cannot be manufactured by the human body are only available through food sources. Complete proteins are those that contain all essential amino acids in sufficient quantity to support life's maintenance and development needs. Proteins unable to fulfill this definition are categorized as incomplete.

Sources. Proteins of animal origin (meat, poultry, fish, milk, cheese and eggs) are complete. The quality standard for a complete protein containing the best ratio and quantity of essential amino acids is the egg albumin (egg white), although all the proteins stated are excellent. Incomplete proteins, those deficient in one or more essential amino acids, are of plant origin (grains, legumes, seeds and nuts), although together, they represent the full complement of amino acids.

Digestion and absorption. Although digestion begins in the stomach, the very long protein structure is only slightly decreased in size within this organ. Total digestion and absorption of the protein into its basic amino acid composition occurs within the small intestine. The amino acids then proceed via the blood system primarily to the liver for use as needed in building bodily structure. Proteins eaten beyond daily needs can be metabolized as an energy source at the rate of four calories per gram.

Protein

.4 gm per pound of body weight is recommended

Requirements. There is no set protein requirement for all persons since needs vary with the following three factors:

- Tissue growth and maintenance: Age-related growth spurts, pregnancy, lactation and tissue repair due to injury significantly increase protein needs. Although an individual with above average muscle mass requires more protein per day to maintain the tissue, requirements set for adults should more than adequately protect these persons.

- Illness and disease: Physical trauma dramatically increases protein requirements since protein is needed for repair and in addition, is often wasted as an energy source during these periods.

- Diet: True evaluation of the amount of protein required by the body is based on the quality of the protein source. Since all essential amino acids must be provided in sufficient quantities for construction of needed proteins by the body, a diet emphasizing complete proteins (animal foods) as the source provides acceptable levels of essential amino acids at a lower intake than a diet consisting primarily of plant sources of protein (incomplete protein).

Those persons choosing to eliminate all animal proteins from their diet can benefit from the following diagram to achieve the best combination of essential amino acids.

Assuming a variety of animal and plant proteins in the daily diet, a standard of 0.8 grams per kilogram of body weight is recommended for the healthy adult or about .4 grams per pound of body weight. It is easy to achieve one's protein requirement. For example, if a person weighs about 150 pounds, he or she would need about 60 grams of protein per day. If that person consumed two servings of dairy foods and two 3-ounce servings of meat, poultry or fish during the day, the protein allowance would be close to 60 grams. The addition of small amounts of protein contained in bread, cereals, legumes and vegetables would more than complete this individual's daily protein requirement. In most cases, the American diet contains two times the level of protein recommended for adults.

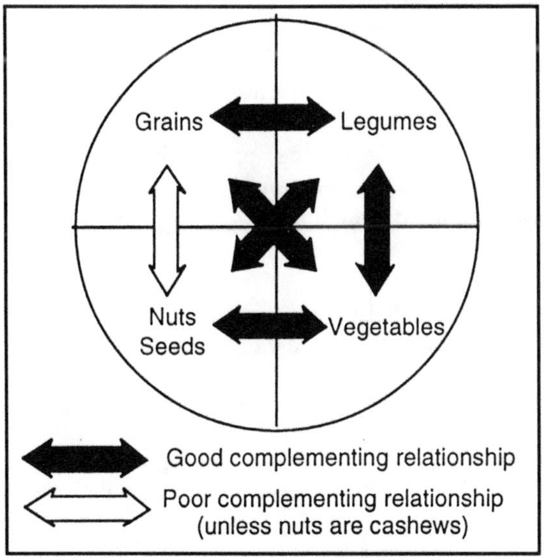

Fig. 27-2. Complementing relationships for vegetarian diets.

Carbohydrates

Function and structure. The fuel for body work is rapidly obtained from foods high in carbohydrates. Both instant and prolonged energy needs can be met by carbohydrates. Carbohydrates also spare proteins to perform their needed functions. When the diet is low in carbohydrates, protein must be wasted as an energy fuel.

The carbohydrates are classified by their structure and divided into the following three groups:

- Monosaccharides, called the simple sugars, are the smallest individual units of carbohydrate (glucose, fructose, galactose).
- Disaccharides are sugars composed of two monosaccharides (e.g., table sugar (sucrose) = glucose and fructose; milk sugar (lactose) = glucose and galactose.
- Polysaccharides are composed of many monosaccharide units, with chemical bonding between each unit, which may or may not be digestible as an energy source. For example, starch from plant food and glycogen from muscle digest into usable simple sugars. In contrast, fiber, though a polysaccharide, is not digestible by the human body.

Digestion and absorption. Very little digestion of carbohydrates occurs in the mouth. Stomach enzymes have no effect on them. Total digestion to monosaccharides is accomplished by the enzymes in the small intestine. These simple sugars are then absorbed into the blood stream and distributed to all organs for energy usage through the action of insulin, a hormone secreted by the pancreas.

> Carbohydrates isolated from foods, called refined sugars, should be limited to approximately 10% of the total carbohydrate intake since these sources have no nutrient value.

Sources. Carbohydrates of varying structure are part of plant foods such as legumes, nuts, grains, cereals, vegetables and fruits. They provide four calories of energy per gram weight.

Requirements. Current health standards recommend that approximately 55-60% of our daily caloric intake be consumed as carbohydrate.

Fiber

Function and structure. Dietary fiber is defined as the sum of indigestible carbohydrate and indigestible carbohydrate-like components of food. Fiber is categorized as soluble, that is, a fiber forming a gel in water, and insoluble, that is, a sawdust-like fiber that does not dissolve in water. Each type of fiber plays a distinctive role in body health as it is transported through the gastrointestinal tract, but in general fiber functions as:

- a bulk agent, easing elimination, decreasing appetite (insoluble)
- a chelating agent, decreasing the absorption of cholesterol and, in excess, vital minerals from the diet (soluble)
- an agent that decreases the rate of absorption of glucose from meals (both, mostly insoluble)

Digestion. Although defined as indigestible carbohydrate, some fiber can be metabolized by bacteria in the large intestine and thus are considered poor bulking agents.

Sources. All high fiber food, including fruits, vegetables, whole grains, seeds, nuts and legumes, contain mixtures of soluble and insoluble fibers.

> ### FIBER
> 25-35 gm per day recommended

Requirements. Although no requirement has been set for fiber intake, it is recommended that the American diet be drastically changed from the current approximation of 10-15 gm of fiber per day to 25-35 gm of dietary fiber. The fiber should be obtained in natural foods. It is not recommended that isolated fiber be consumed.

Fats

Function and structure. Fat combines with other nutrients to form important structural compounds, among which are blood lipids, steroids, cell membranes, bile and vitamin D. Stored body fat also aids in regulating body temperature since it insulates the body against rapid heat loss. Fat adds palatability and satiety to a diet and adds to the synthesis of vitamins by the body.

All fats are insoluble in water and are often called lipids. Lipids have the same structural elements as carbohydrate but are linked together very differently. When metabolized as an energy source, fats are then able to produce more energy, i.e., **nine calories per gram** of fat metabolized.

Lipids in foods can be divided into two types of basic components:

- animal fats—generally high in saturated fat, a source of cholesterol in the diet (cholesterol found only in animal foods)
- plant fats—higher in monounsaturated fats as in canola, olive and peanut oil
- higher in polyunsaturated fat as in safflower, sunflower, corn and soy oil
- low in saturated fat (exceptions: coconut, palm kernel, palm oils);
- devoid of cholesterol.

Digestion and absorption. Occurs primarily in the small intestine through the action of enzymes that break the complex fat molecule apart into simpler absorbable components. Bile salts act as emulsifiers in the digestive process. Small fatty acids are absorbed directly into the bloodstream while the longer chain fatty acids and cholesterol, due to their lack of solubility in water, must filter first into the lymph fluid for reorganization. When combined with water-soluble carrier proteins, the lipids can then enter the blood for transport to liver or adipose cells.

Sources. Unless removed by processing, fat is found in greater amounts in animal foods than in plant foods. Fat is hidden in processed food or visible as marbling in meat or as oils and spreads.

Requirements. As in protein nutrition, there are a few essential fatty acids that cannot be manufactured by the body and must be supplied by diet. However, there is no specific lipid requirement in the diet since the fat content of balanced food intake provides adequate amounts of the essential fatty acids. The average American ingestion of fat, especially animal fat, far outweighs the bodily needs. A current U.S. dietary goal is to reduce fat intake to no more than 30% of total calories, and to curtail saturated fat to no more than 10%. Unfortunately, the typical American diet often consists of a fat intake totaling 37-42% of daily calories, with some people reporting an intake as high as 60%.

FAT

Reduce to no more than 30% of total calories

Saturated fat no more than 10%

Vitamins

Function, food sources and requirements. The term "vitamin" is derived from the root word "vita," essential to life. Today, vitamins are defined as a group of organic compounds other than protein, carbohydrate and fat that cannot be manufactured by the human body yet are required in minute amounts for specific body functions of growth, maintenance, reproduction and repair. Vitamins are broadly classified solely on their solubility as water or fat soluble since each one is unique in its construction, properties, functions and distribution.

Digestion and absorption. Vitamins require no digestive process and are absorbed intact into the bloodstream. They are better absorbed when obtained through natural food sources than in tablet form. The fat soluble vitamins (Vitamin A, Vitamin D, Vitamin E and Vitamin K) can be stored in the liver; thus the potential exists for toxic effects from "mega" ingestion by supplementation. The water soluble vitamins, when absorbed in excess of needs, are quickly excreted through the kidneys. However, toxicity has been reported with "mega" doses of water soluble vitamins, such as vitamin C and vitamin B6.

Minerals

Function, food sources and requirements. Minerals are inorganic elements (metals) essential to man as control agents in body reactions and cooperative factors in energy production, body building and maintenance activities. The essential minerals are categorized into two main groups according to the amount used by the body:

- the major minerals present in large amounts
- the trace minerals utilized in lesser quantities

Digestion and absorption. Minerals require no digestion and are absorbed intact from the small intestine. Some minerals can be stored in the liver when ingestion exceeds need. It is therefore important to avoid intake above those values established as safe, especially when oral supplements are consumed.

Table 27-1. Fat Soluble Vitamins: Functions, Sources and Requirements

Vitamins*	Function (need for)	Sources	Adult Requirements (age 25-50)	
			Males	Females
A	Normal growth Normal vision Normal skin Formation of enamel	Liver, egg yolk, kidney Whole milk, butter Fortified margarine Fortified skim milk, yellow and dark green vegetables	5000 I.U.	4000 I.U.
D	Bone and teeth formation	Sunshine (absorbed through the skin), fortified milk	200 I.U.	200 I.U.
E	Healthy red blood cells (still being studied for a direct link with E)	Whole-grain cereals, salad oil, shortening, margarine, fruits, vegetables	15 I.U.	12 I.U.
K	Blood clotting	Green leafy vegetables, egg yolk, liver, cauliflower, tomatoes (Vitamin K is also produced by bacteria in the small intestines)	0.08 mg	0.065 mg

*Constant excesses of some vitamins can be harmful: Overdose of Vitamin A may cause dry, peeling skin, loss of hair, headache, loss of appetite, lumps on extremities, thickening of bones.
Overdose of Vitamin D can cause calcification of soft tissue, blood vessels, kidney tubules.
Vitamin E is an antioxidant that inhibits oxidation of Vitamin A.
Overdose of Vitamin K (in research with rats) has been found to cause rupturing of red blood cells.

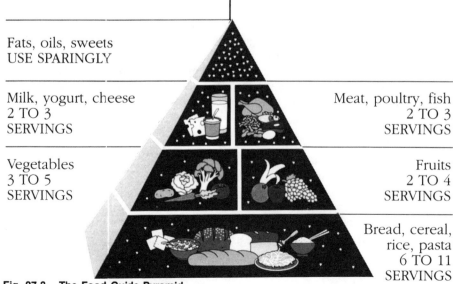

Fats, oils, sweets
USE SPARINGLY

Milk, yogurt, cheese
2 TO 3
SERVINGS

Meat, poultry, fish
2 TO 3
SERVINGS

Vegetables
3 TO 5
SERVINGS

Fruits
2 TO 4
SERVINGS

Bread, cereal, rice, pasta
6 TO 11
SERVINGS

Fig. 27-3. The Food Guide Pyramid

Food Guide Pyramid

How can you determine on a daily basis that all nutrient needs are met for optimum body function? The Food Guide Pyramid approved by the U.S. Department of Agriculture in 1992 emphasizes the priority you should assign to certain food groups in order to meet nutrient needs specified by the Recommended Dietary Allowances (RDA values). The Food Pyramid has replaced the "Basic Four" as a guide because it emphasizes that the lion's share of your calories should be from carbohydrates, which occupy the largest position at the base. As you climb the pyramid, serving size decreases until you reach the top category—fats, oils and sweets—which you should eat sparingly.

The Food Guide Pyramid shows a range of servings for each major food group. The number of servings that are right for you depends on how many calories you need, which in turn depends on your age, sex, size and how active you are. Almost everyone should have at least the lowest number of servings in the ranges.

Sugar and Fat Substitutes

Both saccharin (Sweet 'n' Low®) and aspartame (Equal/Nutrasweet®) are recognized as safe for human use in normal doses with one exception: Aspartame is a protein that breaks apart into its two constituent amino acids, aspartic acid and phenylalanine upon heating. Those persons with a rare disease called phenylketonuria are unable to consume aspartame safely.

Table 27-2. Major Minerals: Function, Sources and Requirements

Mineral	Function (need for)	Source	Adult Requirements (age 25-50)	
			Males	Females
Calcium	Formation of bone and teeth Clotting of blood Muscle function Nerve function	Milk and milk products, mustard, greens, kale, broccoli	800 mg	800 mg
Phosphorus	Energy production Nerve function Muscle function Bone and teeth structure	Cereals, meats, fish, legumes, eggs, milk, dairy products	800 mg	800 mg
Magnesium	Bone constituent Catalyst for chemical reactions in body; building of protein.	Brains, sweetbreads, liver, egg yolk, dark leafy greens, nuts, whole-grain cereals, beans, coffee, tea, cocoa	350 mg	280 mg
Potassium	Energy production Hair, skin, nails	Citrus juices, bananas Protein foods: meats, seafood, fish, poultry, eggs, cheese, legumes	—	—
Sodium	Muscle and nerve	Milk and milk products, meat, deep leafy greens, seafood, salt	1-3 gm estimate	1-3 gm
Chloride	Muscle and nerve functioning	Protein foods	—	—

Fat substitutes that attempt to trick the palate into sensing the smoothness and richness of fat, but without the actual fat molecule are being continuously improved as the demand increases for low-fat or non-fat yet tasty meals and desserts. Some food manufacturers are experimenting with altering egg white compounds and prune extract to simulate the taste of fat. Brands marketed today include Olestra and Simplesse.

Goal Weight Determination

The question always arises, "What is a healthy weight for me?" The Metropolitan Life Insurance Company actively researched those weights considered "ideal" since the 1940s. The newest table of weight for height is based on the industry's largest survey of weight vs. longevity (conducted in 1979 with approximately four million individuals over the previous 22 years). The standard divides each height per sex into three groups depending on frame size.

Weight standards provide no consideration to those physically fit persons with a high percentage of muscle tissue, and thus, less body fat. Muscle tissue is far heavier than fat tissue and becomes a significant variable when determining one's ideal or healthy body weight. The current terminology of "health" weight rather than ideal weight focuses on health not pounds. The terminology is a more positive, take-charge approach to wellness. However, the actual weight tables remain controversial among weight management authorities. The "healthy" weight standards condone the controversial principle that weight gain is acceptable with increasing age. Healthy weight should be defined as a healthy ratio of lean body mass to fat mass. Therefore, body fat measurement is a more accurate determination of true "health" than any height/weight table.

For a complete discussion of goal weight determination, see "Counseling for Body Composition" and "Trends in Weight Management."

Table 27-3. Acceptable Weights for Men and Women

Height	Weight in pounds	
	19-34 years	35 years and over
5'0"	97-128	108-138
5'1"	101-132	111-143
5'2"	104-137	115-148
5'3"	107-141	119-152
5'4"	111-146	122-157
5'5"	114-150	126-162
5'6"	118-155	130-167
5'7"	121-160	134-167
5'8"	125-164	138-178
5'9"	129-169	142-183
5'10"	132-174	146-188
5'11"	136-179	151-194
6'0"	140-184	155-199
6'1"	144-189	159-205
6'2"	148-195	164-210

References

1. *Healthy People 2000. National Health Promotion and Disease Prevention Objectives*. Nutrition Priority Areas, U.S. Department of Health and Human Services, Public Health Service, U.S. Government Printing Office, Publications No. 017-001-00474.
2. USDA. (1990). *Report of the Dietary Guidelines Advisory Committee for Americans*. Washington, D.C.: USDA.
3. National Academy of Sciences. (May, June, 1989). *Recommended Dietary Allowance* (10th ed.). Washington, D.C.: National Academy of Sciences.

4. Cooper, K.H. (1982). *The aerobics program for total well-being.* New York: Bantam Books.

5. Ardell, D.B. (1986). *High level wellness. Berkeley: Ten Speed Press.*

6. Anderson, L., et al. (1982). *Nutrition in health and disease.* (17th ed.). Philadelphia: J.B. Lippincott Co.

7. McGilvery, R.W., & Goldstein, G.W. (1983). *Biochemistry, a functional approach.* Philadelphia: W. B. Saunders Co.

8. Travis, J.W., & Ryan, R. S. (1983). *Wellness workbook.* (2nd ed.). Berkeley: Ten Speed Press.

9. *The vegetarian diet: Food for us all* (1981). Chicago: American Dietetic Association.

28 Sports Nutrition

Nancy Clark, MS, RD

Focus

THIS CHAPTER OFFERS PRACTICAL SPORTS nutrition information that addresses the nutrition questions fitness instructors, aerobic competitors and other athletes commonly ask. This information will help you guide your clients in the selection of a high quality sports diet that 1) fuels the muscles for top performance, 2) nourishes the body, and 3) contributes to current health and future longevity.

Carbohydrates—The Foundation of the Sports Diet

Athletes should eat a 60-70% carbohydrate diet on a daily basis to get adequate carbohydrates for both training and competing. These carbohydrates get stored 1) as muscle glycogen, needed to perform exercise, and 2) as liver glycogen, needed to maintain normal blood sugar level. Unfortunately, misconceptions about carbohydrates—what they are and what they aren't—keep many athletes from choosing the best carbohydrates.

Carbohydrates include both sugars and starches. Both get stored as glycogen but have differing abilities to nourish the athlete with vitamins and minerals. The carbohydrates in sugary soda pop or sports drinks get stored as glycogen but provide no vitamins or minerals. The carbohydrates in wholesome fruits, vegetables and grains also get stored as glycogen plus provide vitamins and minerals—the spark plugs that help the athlete's "engine" to perform at its best.

The average 150-pound active male has about 1,800 calories of carbohydrates stored in his liver, muscles and blood in approximately the following distribution:

Muscle glycogen	1,400 calories
Liver glycogen	320 calories
Blood glucose	80 calories

These carbohydrate stores determine how long an athlete can exercise. Depleted muscle glycogen results in "hitting the wall" and the inability to exercise energetically; depleted liver glycogen results in low blood sugar and causes the athlete to "bonk" or "crash," feeling lightheaded, uncoordinated, unable to concentrate and overwhelmingly fatigued. Proper pre-exercise nutrition includes adequate carbohydrates and can reduce the likelihood of becoming glycogen depleted.

Carbohydrates are important for all athletes regardless of the sport. Both runners and body builders alike need this fuel for performing their desired type of exercise. Weight-conscious athletes such as runners and figure skaters often try to "stay away" from carbohydrates, believing them to be fattening. Carbohydrates are *not* fattening. They supply only four calories per gram, as compared to fats that offer nine calories per gram. Carbohydrates can become fattening if eaten with fatty foods, such as butter on bread, gravy on potato and mayonnaise on a sandwich. Since carbohydrates are likely to be burned off

Hitting the Wall

rather than stored as fat, even weight-conscious athletes can and should include them as the foundation of their sports diet.

These menus are sample sports meals that offer at least 60% carbohydrates. Some of the food items (i.e., soft drinks, milk shakes) are not generally recommended as part of an optimal daily diet, but they can be incorporated into a fast-food meal on the road from time to time. The purpose of these sample meals is simply to offer the concept of what a 60+% carbohydrate diet "looks like," so that athletes can use it to guide their food choices. The menus are appropriate for active women and men who need 2,000-2,600+ calories per day. Food portions may be adjusted to suit individual needs.

TABLE 28-1. Sample High-Carbohydrate, Fast-Food Meals

	Total Cal.	CHO Cal.
Breakfast		
McDonald's Fast Food		
Orange juice, 6 oz.	85	80
Pancakes, syrup	420	360
English muffin, jelly	155	120
Total	660	(85% CHO)
Muffin House, Bakery		
Bran muffin, large	320	205
Hot Cocoa, large	180	100
Total	500	(61% CHO)
Family Restaurant		
Apple juice, large	145	145
Raisin Bran, 2 sm.	220	200
Low-fat milk, 8 oz.	110	80
Sliced banana, medium	125	120
Total	600	(91% CHO)
Lunch		
Sub Shop		
Turkey sub, no mayo	655	340
Fruit yogurt, Dannon	260	200
Orange juice, half-pint	110	105
Total	1025	(63% CHO)
Wendy's Fast Food		
Plain baked potato	240	200
Chili, 1 cup	230	100
Chocolate shake	390	220
Total	860	(60% CHO)
Salad Bar		
Lettuce, 1 cup	15	10
Green pepper, 1/2	10	8
Broccoli, 1/2 cup	20	15
Carrots, 1/2 cup	20	17
Tomato, large	50	45
Chick peas, 1/2 cup	170	120
Feta Cheese, 1 oz.	75	0
Italian dressing, 2 T.	100	0
Bread, 1" slice	200	180
Total	660	(60% CHO)

TABLE 28-1. Sample High-Carbohydrate, Fast-Food Meals, Cont'd

	Total Cal.	CHO Cal.
Dinner		
Pizzaria		
Cheese pizza, 4 sl. 13"	920	520
Large cola, 12 oz.	150	150
Total	1070	(63%CHO)
Italian Restaurant		
Minestrone soup, 1 cup	85	60
Spaghetti, 2 cups	400	320
Tomato sauce, 2/3 cup	120	60
Parmesan cheese, 1 T.	30	0
Rolls, 2 large	280	240
Total	915	(74% CHO)
Family Restaurant		
Turkey, 5 oz. white meat	250	0
Stuffing, 1 cup	200	160
Mashed potato, 1 cup	95	65
Peas, 2/3 cup	70	60
Cranberry sauce, 1/4 cup	100	100
Orange juice, 8 oz.	110	105
Sherbet, 1 scoop	120	110
Total	945	(63% CHO)

Abbreviations: CHO = carbohydrates, cal. = calories, oz. = ounces, sm. = small, mayo = mayonnaise, T = tablespoon, sl = slice.

To consume a daily sports diet that gets 60-70% of its calories from carbohydrates, the athlete should opt for more grains and starches and fewer fatty, greasy foods. By working with a sports nutritionist, the athlete can learn the appropriate food choices, such as bagels instead of croissants, pancakes instead of eggs, pasta instead of steak. Food labels, which list the grams of carbohydrates per serving can assist with appropriate food selection. Some dedicated athletes "count carbohydrates" to reach their daily quota. For example, an athlete who eats 3,500 calories each day should eat at least 60% of those calories in the form of carbohydrates: 60% x 3,500 = 2,100 calories of carbohydrates = 525 grams CHO (@ 4 calories/gram CHO).

Fat

For both cardiovascular health and optimal sports performance, athletes should reduce their intake of fatty, greasy foods such as donuts, pastries, butter, mayonnaise, french fries, and ice cream. These foods tend to fill the stomach but leave the muscles unfueled. In addition, they also may contribute to elevated blood cholesterol. Since the typical American diet is about 40% fat but only 45% carbohydrate, the athletes need to trade in fat calories for more carbohydrates to bring their sports diet to 25% fat, 60% carbohydrate—i.e., eat two plain bagels (400 calories of primarily carbohydrates) as opposed to one bagel with cream cheese (400 calories, 50% from fat).

Although eating *too much* fat is the standard problem among athletes, overly compulsive personalities commonly try to cut *all* fats out of their diet. They often become extremely restrictive with their food choices, eating only

Eat more but less fat

Instead of having one baked potato drenched with butter and sour cream (400 calories), eat two plain potatoes (400 calories).

fat-free foods such as rice cakes, broccoli and nonfat yogurt. This restrictiveness, at times, may border on an eating disorder. Since 20-25% of the calories in a sports diet can appropriately come from fat, this entitles the athlete to a small amount of fat, which is easily consumed in the hidden fats in wholesome muffins, lean meats and other popular foods.

Athletes with high caloric demands who severely restrict their fat intake may have trouble consuming adequate calories and maintaining their weight if they don't replace the deleted fat calories with adequate carbohydrates.

Sometimes the sheer volume of food poses a problem because one may tire of chewing before being adequately fed. By working with a sports nutritionist, the athlete can be taught how to include appropriate amounts of heart-healthy fats, such as peanut butter and olive oil, into their 60-70% carbohydrate sports diet.

Protein

Traditionally, athletes have eaten high protein sports diets, believing that if they eat extra meat, they'll build extra muscle. Excess protein does not build muscle; exercise does. To bulk-up, the athlete needs to perform resistance exercise, such as weight lifting and push-ups, in addition to eating a wholesome diet. To have adequate energy to perform the muscle-building exercise, the diet should be approximately 60% carbohydrate, 15% protein.

Strange as it may sound, both body builders and marathon runners should eat the same sports diet. Since body builders have comparatively more muscle mass than runners, they generally eat more calories and hence larger protein servings:

- 15% of the 2,600 calories a 140-pound marathoner might need is 390 protein-calories, or 97 grams protein, the amount in about 13 ounces of meat.
- 15% of the 3,600 calories a 170-pound body builder might need is 540 protein-calories, or 135 grams protein, the amount in about 18 ounces of meat.

It's hard to specify the exact protein requirement for athletes, because their needs vary according to type of sport (endurance athletes need more protein/kg than body builders), total calorie intake (dieters need more protein/kg than athletes eating their full complement of food), and level of growth and training (athletes rapidly building muscles have higher protein needs).

To help you calculate a client's protein needs, some safe protein recommendations are:

Active adult—1.0-1.5 gm/kg body weight

Growing athlete—1.5-2.0 gm/kg body weight

When it comes to protein intake, athletes seem to fall into two categories: *Protein pushers*—the body builders, weight lifters, football players who think they can't get enough protein; and *protein avoiders*—the runners, triathletes, dancers who never eat meat, in their efforts to bolster their carbohydrate calories as well as eat a low fat, heart-healthy diet. Both groups can perform poorly due to dietary imbalances. Protein pushers, such as high school athletes who frequently eat fast-food burgers and french fries, generally consume a high fat, high cholesterol diet that not only leaves their muscles unfueled but also contributes to heart disease. Protein avoiders, such as runners who think that meat is bad for their health, tend to be deficient in not only protein, but also iron and zinc, two minerals important for top performance. The trick is to teach athletes how to get *adequate* but not excess portions of *lean* protein. If you suspect a protein imbalance, you might want to refer the client to a sports nutritionist who will evaluate the current protein intake and teach the athlete how to make appropriate adjustments.

Vegetarian athletes who eat no meat tend to differ from the "protein avoiders" in that they make the effort to incorporate adequate vegetarian sources of protein into their diet. Rather than simply avoiding meat, they conscientiously include beans, lentils, tofu, nuts and other vegetarian proteins to fulfill their protein needs. Yet, their diets are still likely to be deficient in iron and zinc, two minerals found primarily in animal proteins, and particularly in red meats. Iron is important for preventing anemia; zinc is important for healing.

Iron

Athletes who become anemic due to an iron deficient diet are likely to experience needless fatigue upon exertion. Those at highest risk of suffering from iron deficiency anemia include female athletes who lose iron through menstruating, athletes who eat no red meats, marathon runners who may damage red blood cells via "footstrike hemolysis," endurance athletes who may lose a significant amount of iron through heavy sweat losses, and teenage athletes who are growing quickly and may consume inadequate iron to meet their expanded requirements.

To boost and/or maintain a high iron intake, an athlete can eat:

Women need almost twice as much iron each day (18 mg versus 10 mg for men) due to menstural blood loss.

1. Lean cuts of beef, pork and lamb (4 ounce portions) and the dark meat of chicken and turkey 3 to 4 times per week. (The heme-iron in these animal proteins is more bioavailable than the iron found in vegetable foods such as spinach and raisins.)

2. Enriched and fortified breads and cereals (by reading the food label, the athlete can determine if the product has added iron), as well as whole grains, beans and legumes. (The non-heme iron found in these plant foods has poor bioavailability.)

3. A food rich in vitamin C with each meal, such as a glass of orange juice or a vegetable, since Vitamin C enhances iron absorption from both heme and non-heme iron sources.

4. Foods cooked in cast iron skillets, particularly acidic foods such as spaghetti sauce, since the acid attracts the iron and significantly increases iron content of a food.

Athletes who do not eat meat or iron-rich foods may wish to take an iron supplement as a "health insurance" to possibly reduce their risk of becoming anemic. They should be educated that the iron from a supplement may be poorly absorbed compared to that found in animal proteins, and that they are likely to still have a diet that's deficient in zinc, since the two minerals tend to be found in similar foods. Hence, a supplement that contains both iron and zinc is the better choice, but nevertheless, an imperfect solution.

Vitamin/Mineral Supplements

The vitamin business is big business among athletes and Americans in general. For example, 90% of the nation's top female runners take supplements, as do 40-60% of the general population. The reasons for taking supplements vary. Some take supplements to compensate for poor eating; others as "health insurance." Many athletes swallow the advertising claims that promise enhanced athletic prowess. Unfortunately, they don't realize that if a claim sounds too good to be true, it probably is!

Calcium is an especially important mineral for active people that is often lacking if they avoid dairy and red meat. Women with regular menses need 1000 mg/day. Women with irregular menses need 1500 mg/day. Calcium supplements along with regular exercise may be helpful in maintaining strong bones to prevent osteoporosis.

Supplement takers often fail to understand that they still need to eat a well-balanced diet, regardless of the amount of vitamins they take. A pill may contain only 8 to 12 of the more than 50 nutrients needed for top performance. Many athletes spend significant amounts of money on assorted pills and potions, when they could spend the money on wholesome foods. If clients are taking supplements because they question the adequacy of their diet, they should have a nutrition check-up with a registered dietitian who can teach them to get the nutrients they need from the foods they eat.

Although it seems logical that an active person would need more vitamins than a sedentary person, the research to date shows no evidence of dramatically increased vitamin needs that cannot be met through a wholesome diet. An athlete who takes extra vitamins is unlikely to notice increased performance, strength or stamina, unless she/he was nutritionally deficient to start with, or perhaps experiences a placebo effect.

Most athletes easily consume more than enough vitamins with 1,500-2,000 calories of a variety of wholesome foods. Hence, the hard-training athlete who consumes 4,000+ calories can easily get more vitamins than needed. For example, the cyclist who drinks a 6 oz. glass of orange juice gets 100% of the RDA for vitamin C. If the exerciser is extremely thirsty, such as after a workout, she/he is likely to drink 24 oz. of juice—and get 400% of the RDA for C from this snack alone, to say nothing of what is consumed in other fruits and vegetables throughout the day.

Amino Acid and Protein Supplements

Athletes who strive to develop muscles and increase strength often look to amino acid pills and protein supplements for beneficial effects. To date, there is no evidence that the consumption of these preparations results in greater muscular bulk. Exercise, not extra protein, is the key to building bigger muscles. Athletes who want to bulk up should spend time lifting weights and performing other forms of resistance exercise, rather than spending their money on expensive amino acid supplements.

Table 28-2. Amino Acids: Food Versus Pills

Food or protein Supplement	Amount	Arginina (mg)	Tryptophan (mg)	Amount Needed for 25g Protein	Approx. Cost $
Chicken breast	4 oz.(raw)	2100	400	3 oz.(cooked)	0.30
Eggs	2	780	200	4	0.35
Skim milk	1 c	300	120	3 c	0.55
Amino Fuel	1 svg	20	75	7 wafers	1.45
Coach's Formula	1 svg	410	170	5 T	1.10
Dynamic Muscle	1 svg	680	240	4 T	0.70

This table compares the milligrams (mg) of two amino acids, arginina and tryptophan, as available in food and in several popular protein supplements. The second part lists the approximate cost for 25 g of protein. Abbreviations: oz = ounces, c = cup, svg = serving, T = tablespoon, g = grams *Note: Nutrient data adapted from Pennington J. Church H: Bowes and Church's Food Values of Portions Commonly Used, ed 14. Philadelphia, JB Lippincott, 1985; with permission. Protein supplement data is taken from product labels.*
From *Nancy Clark's Sports Nutrition Guidebook*. Champaign, IL, Leisure Press, 1990; with permission.

The amount of protein or amino acids found in the special powders or pills is far less than that obtained from foods. For example, an athlete would have to eat five tablespoons of one popular brand of protein powder (@ $1.10) to get the same amount of protein in a small (3.5 oz) can of tuna at half the price.

Fluids

Drinking adequate fluids is essential for top sports performance. Fluids transport nutrients to and from the working muscles, dissipate heat and eliminate waste products. Unfortunately, many athletes neglect this aspect of their sports diet and consequently hurt their performances. To maintain optimal hydration, athletes should:

Prevent dehydration during training by drinking adequate fluids on a daily basis—lots of water, juices. Athletes can determine whether or not they're drinking enough fluid by monitoring their patterns of urination: the urine should be clear colored and copious, and they should be urinating frequently. Dark colored, scanty urine is a sign of dehydration during a workout and a signal for the athlete to consume more fluids.

To increase awareness of sweat losses during exercise, athletes should weigh themselves before and after a hard workout.

Before an event, athletes should drink extra water, juice and other fluids to be sure the body is well hydrated. They should drink two to three large glasses of fluid up to two hours before the start of the event. Since the kidneys require about 90 minutes to process fluids, this allows sufficient time to empty the bladder. Five or ten minutes before start time, athletes should drink *another one or two cups of water or sports drink.*

During hard exercise, athletes should drink as much as they comfortably can, ideally 8-10 ounces every twenty minutes. Since they may be sweating off three times this amount, they may still have a water deficit. They should start drinking early in the event *before* they are thirsty, to prevent dehydration.

After exercise, athletes should drink enough fluids to quench their thirst, plus more. The thirst mechanism inadequately indicates whether the body is optimally hydrated; monitoring urination is safer. If several hours pass before an athlete has urinated, she/he is still dehydrated.

For the recreational athlete, water is always an appropriate fluid replacer before, during and after exercise. For endurance athletes and those exercising for more than 90 minutes, a sports drink or diluted juice that contains 60-100 calories per 8 ounces is best during exercise, because it will help to maintain normal blood sugar levels. The best recovery fluids include juices, because the juice replaces not only fluids but also the carbohydrates and electrolytes. Commercial sports drinks are generally better suited for consumption during the event.

Coffee is often used as a pre-exercise "perk me up." For some athletes, coffee seems to make the effort easier. It makes others needlessly nervous and jittery, plaguing them with a "coffee stomach" and excessive trips to the bathroom. Although the original research studies suggested that caffeine might have an ergogenic effect that enhances endurance performance, more recent studies challenge this finding (1). If an athlete is well fed, rested and nutritionally prepared for competition, coffee is unlikely to have any beneficial effects.

> *Each pound of weight lost represents two cups (16 ounces) of sweat. Athletes should replace this accordingly, and strive to lose no more than 2% of their weight during a workout (i.e., 3 lbs, 6 cups, sweat for a 150-lb athlete). If they become 2% dehydrated, they have reduced their work capacity by 10-15%.*

If athletes ask about caffeine, they should be reminded that every person has a unique reaction to caffeine. Some "perk up" with a cup or two; others don't want to touch the stuff. Hence, each athlete has to experiment with pre-exercise caffeine to determine if she/he experiences any ergogenic benefits. Athletes should also be reminded that caffeine has a dehydrating effect and is a drug banned by the Olympic Committee.

Precompetition Nutrition

Since one single precompetition meal inadequately compensates for a poor training diet, athletes should eat a carbohydrate-rich sports diet every day to enhance daily muscle glycogen storage. The precompetition meal should be simply an extension of the tried-and-true daily training diet.

The goals of the precompetition meal are to:

1. Help prevent hypoglycemia with its symptoms of lightheadedness, blurred vision, needless fatigue and indecisiveness—all of which can interfere with top performance.
2. Abate hunger feelings, help settle the stomach and absorb some of the gastric juices.
3. Provide energy for the muscles.
4. Provide adequate fluids to fully hydrate the body.

In preparation for competition, an athlete should eat a 60-70% carbohydrate-rich diet (ideally, this is the same as their daily training diet) and drink additional fluids both the day(s) *prior to* the event and the *day of* the event, in combination with tapering off from exercise in order to allow the muscles the opportunity to store the carbohydrates as glycogen.

Athletes participating in endurance sports that last for longer than 90 minutes, such as marathoning or long distance bike racing, should reduce exercise and emphasize carbohydrates for *three* days prior to the event.

Athletes participating in events that last less than 90 minutes can store adequate glycogen with one or two rest days and a carbohydrate-rich diet.

Meal timing. When planning the time of the precompetition meal, the athlete should allow adequate time for the food to empty from the stomach, so that she/he can exercise comfortably without feeling weighted down. Since high calorie meals take longer to leave the stomach than lighter snacks, the general rule-of-thumb is for an athlete to allow:

- 3-4 hours for a large meal to digest
- 2-3 hours for a smaller meal
- 1-2 hours for a blended or liquid meal
- less than an hour for a light snack, as tolerated.

Since fatty foods delay gastric emptying, the meal should focus on carbohydrates, with small portions of lean protein also being appropriate as an accompaniment, such as spaghetti with a little bit of extra lean hamburger in the tomato sauce, or a turkey sandwich with thickly sliced bread and a thin layer of turkey.

The night before **morning events**, athletes should eat a hearty, high carbohydrate dinner and bedtime snack. That morning, they should eat a light snack/breakfast to abate hunger feelings, replenish liver glycogen stores and absorb some of the gastric juices. For example, a runner who is going to participate in a 10 a.m. road race will want only a light breakfast (such as a small bowl of cereal with lowfat milk @ 300 calories), since the primary fueling was done the night before by the hearty carbohydrate-rich dinner. Before **afternoon events**, athletes should plan a hearty carbohydrate-rich dinner and breakfast, to be followed by a light lunch. A runner racing at noon can enjoy a heartier breakfast (such as four or five pancakes @ 600 calories), as compared to when he races earlier in the day. Before **evening events**, athletes should plan a hearty carbohydrate-rich breakfast and lunch, followed by a light snack one to two hours prior to the event. In addition to basing the meals on carbohydrates, athletes should also consume an additional glass of fluid with each meal, as well as between meals, to insure complete hydration. Water, lowfat milk and juices are the recommended choices, although the less nourishing soft drinks and sports drinks are also popular, acceptable choices.

Liquid meals. Since liquid foods leave the stomach faster than solid foods, the athlete may want to experiment with blenderized meals to determine if they offer any advantages. Reports of one research study (2) indicate that a 450-calorie meal of steak, peas and buttered bread remained for six hours in the stomach. A blenderized version of the same meal emptied from the stomach in four hours. Before converting to blenderized meals, the athlete should keep in mind anecdotal reports that too much liquid may "slosh" in the stomach and contribute to a nauseous feeling. Hence, any new meal should be experimented with during training to determine if it settles well.

Pre-exercise sugar. Historically, athletes have been advised to stay away from sugary foods prior to exercise, with the belief that the "sugar high" will trigger a rebound hypoglycemic effect that will hinder performance. More recent studies suggest that pre-competition sugar may actually enhance stamina and endurance. According to one report, cyclists who ate about 1200 calories of carbohydrates three hours prior to 95 minutes of intermittent exercise improved their performance. Another study (4) similarly reports that subjects who ate about 280 calories of carbohydrate 45 minutes prior to hard exercise (73% VO_2 max) improved their time to exhaustion by 12%.

> The best advice regarding pre-exercise sugar is to avoid the need for a quick energy fix by consuming appropriately timed meals prior to the event.

For some athletes, pre-exercise sugar does result in a negative hypoglycemic feeling with lightheadedness, confusion and fatigue. Hence, athletes who perceive themselves as being sugar sensitive should abstain from concentrated sweets and rely more upon hearty meals than sugary snacks for energy.

Psychological value of food. Precompetition food may have beneficial effects both physiologically and psychologically. If an athlete firmly believes that a specific food/meal (such as the traditional steak and eggs) enhances performance, then it probably does. The mind has a powerful effect upon the body's ability to perform at its best. Athletes who believe in a "magic food" that assures competitive excellence should take special care to be sure this food/meal is available pre-event. This is particularly important for athletes who travel. They should bring along tried-and-true precompetition foods, such as a favorite cereal, muffin or sandwich. By doing this, the athlete will be worry-free about what she/he's going to eat and will be better able to focus on performance.

Eating During Exercise

Athletes who exercise for more than 90 minutes will have greater stamina and enhanced performance if they consume carbohydrates *during* the event. These carbohydrates help to maintain a normal blood sugar level as well as provide a source of energy for the exercising muscles. Trained cyclists (150 pounds) can metabolize about one gram of carbohydrate per minute which equals 240 calories of carbohydrates per hour of endurance exercise. This breaks down into 60 calories per 15 minutes (about 8 ounces of sports drink)—much more than most athletes are likely to consume.

The harder an athlete exercises, the less likely she/he is to want to consume food. During intense exercise (>70% VO_2 max), the stomach may get only 20% of its normal blood flow (2). This slows the digestive process; any food in the stomach may feel uncomfortable or be distastefully regurgitated. Sports drinks or sugar solutions (5-7%) tend to be most readily accepted. Other popular choices include diluted juices, tea with honey and defizzed coke taken along with water.

During moderate intensity exercise, the blood flow is 60-70% of normal; the athlete can still digest food (2). Hence, the solid food snacks, such as bananas, fig bars and bagels, that recreational skiers, cyclists and ultra-runners eat during exercise do get digested and contribute to lasting energy during long-term, moderate intensity events.

Postcompetition Eating: Recovery Foods

Many of the same athletes who carefully select a high-carbohydrate diet prior to competition neglect their recovery diet. Since muscles are most receptive to replacing muscle glycogen with the first two hours after a hard workout, a low-carbohydrate post-event diet can hinder optimal recovery. This, in turn, limits the athlete's readiness to compete again, an important factor in the case of repeated events in the same day, which occurs with swimming or track meets. A poor recovery diet can also delay the athlete's ability to return to intense training.

A carbohydrate-deficient recovery diet is selected by athletes who eat:

- Too much protein, which may happen at a post-event dinner that centers on steak as a change from the precompetition pasta meal.
- Too many greasy foods, such as cheeseburgers and french fries that are popularly eaten by athletes who frequent fast food restaurants.
- Too many sweets, when the "sweets" are actually fat-laden cookies, ice cream and brownies that get at least half their calories from butter or margarine.
- Too few calories, such as may happen with diet-conscious athletes who skimp on carbohydrates (thinking that carbohydrates are fattening) and instead sustain themselves on protein-rich cottage cheese, tuna and chicken.

Examples of 300 calorie snack/meals include:

- *two cups (16 oz) of orange juice and a banana*
- *an average sized bowl of cereal with fruit for breakfast*
- *a dinner with generous servings of starch and vegetables*

To optimize the recovery process after a hard workout, an athlete should eat 200-400 calories of carbohydrates within two hours of the exercise bout, then repeat this another two hours later (5). This "dose" comes to about 0.5 grams carbohydrates per pound of body weight. For a 150-pound person this would be the equivalent of 300 calories of carbohydrates (75 gm) in a post-exercise snack (such as juice) followed by a carbohydrate-rich meal after stretching, showering and recovering from the workout.

Weight Gain

When thin athletes seek advice regarding weight gain, remind them that light athletes can be swift, skilled and effective, and caution them that with age, they'll undoubtedly bulk up. Efforts to gain weight by eating large portions of steak, french fries and ice cream may have negative future effects in terms of not only heart disease but also food preferences. Many once thin high school

TO GAIN WEIGHT

Add 500+calories/day to the baseline diet. This can be done by incorporating:

- *An extra snack, such as a bedtime peanut butter sandwich with a glass of milk.*

- *Larger-than-normal portions at meal time, such as two potatoes instead of one.*

- *Higher calorie foods, such as cran-raspberry juice instead of orange juice.*

athletes grow into obese businessmen with heart disease who love to eat fatty foods. Recommending healthful, high energy diets in addition to appropriate exercise and a weight lifting program is by far preferable to encouraging the consumption of fatty, fattening diets.

Many athletes who desire to gain weight simply need to *consistently* eat three meals per day plus additional snacks. Thin athletes commonly are "too busy" to eat adequately to support their calorie needs for growth and training. With regular meals and snacks that include generous portions of wholesome foods, they can consume adequate calories to resolve this problem.

Some athletes do indeed have trouble gaining weight, despite their abundant food intake. In theory, athletes who eat an additional 500 calories per day will enjoy one pound of weight gain per week. In reality, some people are "hard gainers" and need to eat far more calories than that (6). For them, food becomes a medicine, and they must eat even if they don't feel hungry.

A sports nutritionist can suggest quick and easy snacks and meals that will help the busy athlete accommodate the higher calorie intake.

Weight Loss

Many athletes—and not just those in weight-related sports such as running, dancing, and gymnastics—strive to lose weight. They believe that a lighter body will enhance performance and self-image (7). However, they commonly hurt their performances with crash diets and inappropriate weight reduction techniques.

"Diets" typically don't work. The best approach for successful weight loss that allows the athlete to lose fat and maintain energy for training is to incorporate appropriate portions of healthful, high carbohydrate, low fat foods. Strict diets based on sheer willpower result in feelings of denial (to say nothing of poorly fueled muscles).

A first step to successful weight reduction is for the athlete to keep greater food records and become aware of what, when and how much they eat. Typically, weight-conscious athletes "diet" during the day, then "blow it" at night. They are likely to have greater success if they eat the majority of their calories during the day so that they have energy to train, and then "diet" at night. The higher daytime caloric intake prevents feelings of fatigue, to say nothing of the ravenous hunger that often results in overeating in the evening. Generally speaking, once dieters become too hungry, they don't care about what they eat—nor how much—and can too easily overeat.

Gradual weight loss (1-2 lbs/week for women; 2-3 lbs per week for men) offers greater long-term success.

A second step is to know how many calories/day are appropriate to eat. To roughly estimate caloric needs for weight maintenance, multiply the desired weight by 12-15 calories per pound for moderate activity; 15-20 calories per pound for higher levels of activity. This number offers a very rough estimate of daily calorie needs; the actual requirements will vary greatly, depending upon individual metabolic differences.

From this estimate of calories needed to maintain weight, the third step is to determine the number of calories appropriate for weight reduction by subtracting 300-1,000 calories per day (subtract fewer calories for smaller athletes). Divide this number into three, and you'll have a calorie target for each meal. For example, a 110 lb female runner who's moderately active with daily activities plus runs five miles per day may need 110 (lbs) x 17 (cal/lb) = 1,870 calories per day to maintain weight. To create a calorie deficit for weight loss, subtract about 350-400 calories, bringing the total to 1,500 calories per day or 500 calories per meal. Weight loss should be no more than one-half to two pounds a week.

Special Nutritional Needs of Women

Female athletes should be particularly aware of their intake of iron (to replace menstrual losses) as well as calcium (to optimize bone mineralization). Unfortunately, many females are overly weight-conscious, think of food as the "fattening enemy" rather than a nourishing fuel, eat a very restrictive diet and cheat themselves of important vitamins, minerals and protein. Females who severely restrict their diets to the point of becoming amenorrheic place themselves at a much higher risk of suffering stress fractures and premature osteoporosis (8).

Although there's no proof that the thinnest athlete will be the best athlete, most American women—athletes included—think of themselves as being too fat. This social problem has particularly detrimental effects upon female athletes, as evidenced by the surveys which suggest that about one-third of female athletes struggle with some type of pathogenic eating problem (7). To help reduce the incidence of eating disorders, sports nutrition counseling (which includes discussion of body image and differences in body types) should be an integral part of women's athletics, to help women determine their healthy weight (as opposed to a self-imposed ideal weight) and to fuel themselves optimally.

Summary

Since each athlete is metabolically unique and has personal food preferences and special "magic foods," it's hard to make specific rules and regulations regarding sports nutrition. During training, the athlete should experiment to determine the foods and fluids that settle best and contribute to top performance.

To insure optimal sports nutrition among your athletes, I recommend that you work with a registered dietitian/sports nutritionist who has the time and expertise to educate the athletes about their nutritional needs and answer their nutrition questions with practical "how to" food suggestions. This sports nutritionist should be available for individual counseling with weight-conscious and eating-disordered athletes, and for group discussions with teams. The job of the sports nutritionist is to teach the athletes how to eat to win. Your job, as a fitness professional, is to reinforce that information and remind the athletes that everyone wins with good nutrition.

To find a local sports nutritionist, contact the American Dietetic Association (800-877-1600) and ask to be referred to a member of SCAN (its Sports and Cardiovascular Nutrition practice group). Or, ask for a referral from your state's dietetic association or your local hospital's nutrition department. For referral to a local sports nutritionist, call The National Center for Nutrition and Dietetics at 800-366-1655.

References

General

1. Weir, J., Noakes, T., & Myburgh, K. (1987). A high carbohydrate diet negates the metabolic effects of caffeine during exercise. *Medicine and Science in Sports and Exercise,* 19: 100-105.

2. Brouns, F., Saris, W., & Rehrer, N. (1987). Abdominal complaints and gastrointestinal function during long-lasting exercise. *International Journal of Sports Medicine,* 8: 175-189.
3. Sherman, W., Simonsen, J., Wright, D., & Dembach, A. (1988). Effect of carbohydrate in four hour pre-exercise meals. *Medicine and Science in Sports and Exercise,* 20: S157.
4. Gleeson, M., Maughan, R., & Greenhaff, P. (1986). Comparison of the effects of pre-exercise feedings of glucose, glycerol and placebo on endurance and fuel homeostasis in man. *European Journal of Applied Physiology,* 55: 645-653.
5. Ivy, J. (1988). Muscle glycogen synthesis after exercise and effect of time of carbohydrate ingestion. *Journal of Applied Physiology,* 64: 1480-1485.
6. Sims, E. (1976). Experimental obesity, dietary induced thermogenesis and their clinical implications. *Endocrine Metabolic Clinics of North America,* 5: 377-395.
7. Rosen, L., McKeag, D., Hough, D., & Curley, V. (1986). Pathogenic weight control behavior in female athletes. *The Physician and Sportsmedicine,* 14: 79-86.
8. Clark, N., Nelson, M., & Evans, W. (1988). Nutrition education for elite women runners. *The Physician and Sportsmedicine,* 16: 124-135.

Additional Professional Reading

American Dietetic Association (1986). *Sports nutrition: A manual for professionals working with active people.* Chicago, Ill.
Belko, A. (1987). Vitamins and Exercise—an Update. *Medicine and Science in Sports and Exercise,* 19: S191-S196.
Evans, W., & Hughes, V. (1985). Dietary carbohydrates and endurance exercise. *American Journal of Clinical Nutrition,* 41: 1146-54.
Lemon, P. (1987). Protein and exercise: Update 1987. *Medicine and Science in Sports and Exercise,* 19: 5157.
Williams, M. (1984). Vitamin and mineral supplements to athletes: Do they help? *Clinics in Sports Medicine,* 3: 623-637.

Sports Nutrition Books

Clark, N. (1981). *Nancy clark's sports nutrition guidebook.* Champaign, Ill.: Leisure Press.
Clark, N. (1981). *The athlete's kitchen.* Boston, Ma.: New England Sports Publications. (Available by mail order only, P.O. Box 252, Boston, 02113, $7).
Coleman, E. (1987). *Eating for endurance.* Palo Alto: Bull.
Williams, M. (1985). *Nutritional aspects of human physiology and performance.* Springfield: Charles C. Thomas.

This chapter has been adapted with permission from *Sports Medicine,* Ed. R. Strauss, Philadelphia: W. B. Saunders, 1993.

Evaluation of Body Composition

29

Frank I. Katch, PhD
Victor L. Katch, EdD

Focus

See also "Body Composition Counseling" and "Trends in Weight Management."

THE PURPOSE OF THIS CHAPTER is twofold: 1) to present three indirect procedures to assess body composition, and 2) to illustrate how these assessments can be combined with computer technology to help individuals achieve goals for body composition and nutrition and implement aerobic exercise programs.

The scientific measurement and evaluation of body composition permits accurate quantification of the major structural components of the body—fat, muscle and bone. This knowledge is crucial to the successful completion of any fitness regimen. Our experience indicates that, in their search for a simple way to measure body composition, fitness practitioners frequently sacrifice validity in favor of expediency. Although height-weight tables are still used to assess the degree of "overweightness" based on age and body frame size, such tables do not permit an assessment of the relative composition of the body. A person may weigh much more than the average weight for height standards based on insurance company standards, yet still be underfat in terms of the body's total quantity of fat. The so-called "excess weight" could simply be additional muscle mass. A more desirable alternative to the height-weight tables is to determine the body composition by reliable and valid indirect measurement procedures.

Techniques of Measuring Body Composition

Two indirect procedures for assessment of body composition are recommended. The first type applies Archimedes' principle of hydrostatic weighing. With this method, percent body fat is computed from body density (ratio of body mass to volume). The other kinds of procedure use fatfolds and girths to estimate aspects of body composition. The girth technique provides a more sophisticated opportunity for incorporation with computerized outputs.

Body Density Determined by Hydrostatic Weighing

According to Archimedes' principle, if an object weighs 75 kg in air and 3 kg when submerged in water, the loss of weight in water of 75 kg is equal to the weight of the displaced water. Because the density of water at any temperature is known, the volume of water displaced can easily be computed. In this example, 75 kg of water is equal to 72 liters or 72,000 cubic centimeters (1 gram of water = 1 cubic centimeter or cc in volume). The density of the person, computed as weight/volume, would be 75,000/72,000 cc, or 1.0417 g/cc. In the laboratory, the following procedure is used to determine body density.

The subject's body weight is first determined in air on a balance scale accurate to 50 grams. A diver's belt is usually secured around the waist of fatter-appearing subjects to ensure that they do not float upward during submersion. The underwater weight of this belt and chair is determined beforehand and is subtracted from the subject's total weight under water. The subject, who wears a thin nylon swim suit, sits in a lightweight, plastic tubular chair suspended from the scale and submerged beneath the surface of the water. A swimming pool can serve the same purpose as the tank, and the scale and chair assembly can be suspended from a support at the side of the pool. In the tank, water temperature is maintained at about 95 degrees F, which is close to the subject's skin temperature. Water temperature is recorded to correct for the density of water at the weighing temperature.

The subject makes a forced maximal exhalation as the head is lowered under water. The breath is held for about 5 seconds while underwater weight is recorded on a sensitive scale accurate to 10 grams or on a force transducer system with digital readout. The underwater weighing procedure is repeated 8 to 12 times because subjects "learn" to expel more air from their lungs with each additional underwater trial.

Measurement of Subcutaneous Fatfolds

The rationale for fatfold measurement is based on the assumption that approximately one-half of the body's total fat content is located in the fat deposits directly beneath the skin. The procedure for measuring fatfold thickness is to grasp a fold of skin and subcutaneous fat firmly with the thumb and forefinger, pulling it away from the underlying muscular tissue following the natural contour of the fatfold. Constant tension is exerted by the pincer arms of calipers at their point of contact with the skin. The thickness of the double layer of skin and subcutaneous tissues is then read directly from the caliper dial.

Fig. 29-1. Underwater weighing procedure for a former All-Pro quarterback

The most common areas for taking fatfolds are at the triceps and subscapula, and at the suprailiac, abdominal, and upper thigh sites. All measures are taken on the body with the subject standing. A minimum of two or three measurements are made at each site and the average value is used as the criterion score. When fatfolds are measured for research purposes, the investigator has usually had considerable experience and is consistent in duplicating values for the same subject made on the same day, consecutive days, or even weeks apart. The anatomical locations for the five most frequently measured fatfold sites are:

1. Triceps—a vertical fold is measured at the midline of the upper arm halfway between the tip of the shoulder and the tip of the elbow.
2. Subscapula—an oblique fold is measured just below the bottom tip of the scapula.

How to convert body density to percent body fat

The percentage of fat in the body can be computed from the following equation that incorporates body density:

Percent body fat =
$$\frac{495}{Density - 450}$$

See pages 274-277 for fatfold measurement

3. Suprailiac—an oblique fold measured just above the hip bone. The fold is lifted to follow the natural diagonal line at this point.

4. Abdomen—a vertical fold is measured one inch to the right of the umbilicus.

5. Thigh—a vertical fold is measured at the midline of the thigh, two-thirds of the distance from the mid-kneecap to the hip joint.

Although the use of fatfolds to predict percent body fat is widely used, a major drawback is that the person taking the measurements must have considerable experience with the proper techniques to obtain consistent fatfold values. Because there are no standards by which to compare the results between different investigators from diverse geographic regions, it is almost impossible to determine which sets of data are in fact "correct." Thus, prediction equations developed by a particular researcher (which may be highly valid for the sample measured) may be almost useless to predict accurately the body fat for an individual when another person takes the fatfolds.

> *The error in predicting body fat from fatfolds could be plus or minus 200% or higher*

Measurement of Girths

A cloth or plastic measuring tape should be used. The tape is applied lightly to the skin surface so that the tape is taut but not tight. This procedure avoids skin compression, which could reduce lower girth scores. Duplicate measurements should be taken at each site, and the average used as the criterion circumference score.

The anatomic landmarks for the various girth measurements are as follows:

1. Shoulders—maximal protrusion of the bi-deltoid muscles and the prominence of the sternum at the junction of the second rib.

2. Chest—for men about one inch above the nipple line; for women at the axillary level. Note: in men and women, the tape is placed in position with the arms held horizontally. The arms are then lowered and the measurement recorded at the mid-tidal level of respiration.

3. Abdomen—The average of the following two circumferences: (1) the conventional circumference of the waist just below the rib cage at the minimal width and, (2) level with the iliac crests at the umbilicus.

4. Buttocks—maximal protrusion and, anteriorly, the symphysis pubis—keep heels together.

5. Thighs—crotch level at the gluteal fold.

6. Biceps—maximal circumference with the upper arm fully flexed (not 90 degrees) and fist clenched.

7. Forearms—maximal circumference when the arm is extended with palm up.

8. Wrists—the circumference distal to the styloid processes of the radius and ulna.

9. Knees—the middle of the patella with the knee relaxed in slight flexion.

10. Calves—maximal circumference.

11. Ankles—minimal circumference, usually just above the malleoli.

Practical Use of Fatfolds and Girths

When the purpose is to evaluate changes in total body fat, fatfolds can be used to assess such changes in body composition. This is done by summing the individual fatfolds. For example, if triceps = 10.5, scapula = 12.0, iliac = 14.0, abdomen = 13.0, and thigh = 15.0, then the sum of fatfolds = 64.5 mm. If the person successfully follows a diet and exercise program, and fatfolds decrease to 50.0 mm, then the decrease in fatfolds of 14.5 mm translates to a percentage change in sum of fatfolds of 22.1%.

The same procedure used with fatfolds can be used with girths to determine changes in body compositions. The "fat" regions on the body are the two abdominal sites, buttocks, and thighs. Besides the summations of individual girths, simple equations that use three girths can be used to predict body fat to an accuracy of about 3.5%. The girth equations are valid for men and women ages 18-60 years old. For simplicity, a computer-generated report can be obtained that provides the results for percent body fat, lean body mass, lean-to-fat ratio, and optimal body composition.

For information about body composition and computerized meal planning, write to Fitness Technologies Press, 1132 Lincoln Street, Ann Arbor, MI 48104.

Body Image and Self-Esteem

30

Ronda Gates, MS

"Mirror Mirror on the wall . . . who's the thinnest one of all?"

Focus

THE OLD ADAGE THAT BEAUTY IS ONLY SKIN DEEP has taken on an air of quaintness in these health and appearance conscious times. We've become a nation obsessed with how we look. Whether we're seven or seventy, the results of a body fat measurement, a number on a bathroom scale or a distorted reflection in a mirror can push us into paroxysms of shame and guilt about our body image.

Two out of three women have mixed feelings or become depressed when they see themselves nude in a full-length mirror. Inaccurate body images interfere with a sense of self worth. At worst, our bodies become something we're inflicted with. "Mirrors can trigger negative thoughts about the body and arouse guilt or shame over inadequacies," writes Rita Freedman, author of *Bodylove* (Harper & Row, 1988).

The distorted view in the mirror is an apt metaphor for the way our body image shapes our life. If anything obsesses Americans, it's the way we look. "Thin is in" is what we read and hear in the mass media. It's what we teach our children. Our culture's relentless insistence that only the slim are beautiful and that thinness is a visible sign of virtue places a heavy burden on society. These messages and our distorted eyes and ears become a core part of our identity. The inner conflict aroused can interfere with our feelings of self worth and lead to low self-esteem.

The Interrelation of Self-Esteem and Body Concept

Self-esteem is how I feel about myself. It's a whole body concept—not just my body; not just my mind. It is the awareness of self that separates us from other animals. It is such a critical issue in our development that enhancing the self-esteem of school children has become a priority in some states. Self-esteem is about love, validation, affirmation and empowerment. We engage in a full range of behaviors that compromise our ability to actualize to our full potential when these basic needs are not filled.

Body image problems have their origins in childhood. Each of us is born lovable and full of self. We have the potential to take risks that enable us to make a contribution to the world. Early messages from significant others and caretakers toward appropriate body size and shape can form our reality. If we live in an environment in which we hear, "You can never be too rich or too thin," we will strive to achieve that elusive perfection that will make our caretakers love us more. An inability to measure up, especially when we are compared to others, can damage us to the core. As a result, American five-year-olds know it's bad to be fat, eight-year-olds are preoccupied with their appearance and by age nine many children are on a self-imposed diet.

Adolescents feel preoccupied with their changing bodies. Some girls experience the increase in fat deposits that comes with normal development as unwanted weight gain. In our teens, we see perfectly proportioned magazine models and TV stars who send out the message that it takes a great body to be successful. Fitness professionals are not immune to the agony of being in a line of work they believe requires a slim image—an image that too many strive for, cannot achieve and therefore, suffer the self-imposed, adverse consequences.

Warning Signals for Poor Body Image

Losing Weight Will "Fix" Us

There are clues to warn us when our body image may be compromising our self-esteem. If we perceive overweight as a character flaw and believe "fixing it" will make us a better person, we are setting ourselves up for disappointment. All-or-nothing attitudes about appearance should set off alarms. Comparing ourselves to others, especially male or female models who represent only 5% of our population predisposes us to low self worth.

Magical Thinking

Magical thinking is the belief that happiness, love, satisfaction and life fulfillment will be attained only if pounds are lost, body fat is lowered, thighs are firmed or a lean muscular appearance is achieved. Magical thinking may also be coupled with "black-or-white" thinking often expressed as a belief that food is good or bad and that a person is good or bad depending on the foods he or she eats. We can also pay attention to whether we are spending an increasing amount of time trying to perfect our body or working out harder or longer in order to feel different about ourselves.

Changing Our Attitudes First

The good news is that we can change our attitudes about who we are in relation to our bodies. We can learn to accept the body we have. The challenge is to acknowledge that our body is not an enemy and to treat ourselves more compassionately. Notice, without judgment, how your body image changes from day to day. Discover the role your physical, emotional, social and intellectual health play in shaping how you feel about yourself. Seek ways to help you feel good about yourself from within by focusing on your good traits. If necessary, find resources to guide you through the process of becoming less critical of your appearance and less preoccupied with mirrors, scales, body fat measurements, calories and clothing size. This course of action includes facing the issue of loving and trusting ourselves more fully.

Making A Difference As Instructors

As fitness professionals, we can begin by making a decision as to how we will deal with the national preoccupation with thinness. Everything we do as a representative of the fitness industry affects other people. We have become significant role models for society. We can refrain from justifying behavior that lowers self-esteem by avoiding statements like, "let's work off your ugly fat," or referring to a meal eaten the night before as a "pig out." We can stop complaining in our classes about our own bodies and put more emphasis on the feel-good aspects of a workout.

---

10 Skills for Developing a Healthy Body Image & Self-Esteem

Excerpts from The Body Image & Self-Esteem Workbook by Lauve Metcalfe, MS

#1: Honor your personal story.
Past events and experiences "shape" our perception of body image. By acknowledging your personal story, you become more conscious of past positive and destructive lifestyle patterns and are more receptive to choosing healthier behaviors.

#2: Accept yourself the way you are.
Developing an acceptance of your body image in the present form allows you to channel your energies into modifying behavior, rather than struggling with negative "woulda, coulda, shoulda" thinking.

#3: Create a positive mental outlook.
The attitude that you bring into a situation greatly determines the outcome. Creating, nurturing and sustaining a positive attitude is the key to feeling good about yourself.

#4: Develop positive self-talk skills.
Self-talk is composed of the messages you give yourself in an ongoing basis. By developing positive statements and affirmations you reinforce qualities, skills and attributes that exist within you. Regular use of affirmations will make an impression on your unconscious mind and have a major effect on the way you view yourself.

#5: Guide away from comparisons.
A healthy body image challenges the "picture perfect" images that the media and advertisers encourage people to emulate. Beauty is a multi-dimensional ever-changing combination of a variety of aspects of an individual. Celebrating the differences in hair texture, body build, skin color, energy level, attitude, age, and inner beauty creates individual expressions of beauty that make each person unique.

#6: Build your self-reliance.
Each time you challenge yourself and attempt a task or skill that is outside of your comfort zone, you will experience increased confidence in your abilities. By creating daily, mini mental, physical, emotional and spiritual challenges, you strengthen your mind, body and spirit resourcefulness.

#7: Live in the now.
To enjoy life fully, it is important to remember to stay in the present and experience life from moment to moment. What is needed is a healthy balance of looking forward to the future with anticipation, while respecting the past for its insight and, most importantly, living in the now.

#8: Reward yourself.
Creating rewards and positive incentives to keep you on track with your body image program is essential for long-term maintenance. Develop daily, weekly and monthly incentives that recognize the effort you are putting into your personal body image wellness program.

#9: Give yourself praise.
Acknowledge the positive steps you make in taking care of yourself. Be open to the praise of others and regularly give and receive compliments.

#10: Be connected.
Honoring the role that other people play in your life is important to staying on track with healthy behaviors. Take time out to be in touch with nature and the environment. Plant a garden, nurture a pet, visit an elder, and learn something from a child today.

The fitness goals for the '90s are broadening our standards of attractiveness, demanding more realistic models in the media, learning to cherish our differences, maximizing the many benefits of an aerobic or strength training workout and finally, accepting our bodies.

Summary

Self-esteem is significantly lowered due to the bombardment of body image messages one receives from negative self-talk as well as those messages transmitted by the media and the culture. Reversing this epidemic of poor body image for women and men can begin with fitness professionals—all it takes is our commitment to actively counter it. We can help our students acknowledge their body types, define realistic personal standards, then compliment them for their effort and progress. Beyond that, we can recommit to enjoying fitness as its own reward rather than the way it makes us look.

References

Brownell, K.D. *The LEARN program for weight control.* University of Pennsylvania School of Medicine.

Brownell, K.D., & Foreyt, J.P., eds. (1986). *Handbook of eating disorders.* New York: Basic Books, Inc., 301-27.

Davies, E., & Furnham, A. (1986). The dieting and body shape concerns of adolescent females. *Journal of Child Psychology and Psychiatry,* 27: 417-28.

Freedman, R. (1988). *Bodylove—Learning to like our looks and ourselves.* New York: Harper and Row.

Snow, J.T., & Harris, M.B. (1986). An analysis of weight and diet content in five women's interest magazines. *The Journal of Obesity and Weight Regulation*, 5: 194-214.

Gail Johnston

31 Trends in Weight Management

Focus

IT SEEMS CLEAR THAT DESPITE the $40 billion being spent on weight loss every year, our current methods are not producing lasting results. In addition, it seems reasonable to assume that 95% of chronic dieters who desire weight loss in order to get their lives on track are filled with frustration and despair as they watch every pound return—and then some. The question we're left with is: Are we doing more harm than good when we demand that fat people try every weight loss program until they find the "one" that will work for them? Whether a person wants to lose weight for cosmetic or health reasons, the truth remains: we don't have a stock formula for weight loss that works for every person.

By standing back to gain perspective on the state of weight management in the '90s, we note a few startling facts:

- Dieting is a way of life for 63 million Americans.
- Diets have a 5-10% success rate.
- Grocery shelves house more low-fat, sugar-free, low-calorie diet foods than ever before.
- The average weight of Americans is on the upswing even though total food intake has decreased.
- Eating disorders are at the highest levels in history.
- Weight cycling (yo-yoing) leads to a greater risk of heart disease.
- Overweight people are forming political and social advocacy groups.
- The practices of the weight loss industry are under public scrutiny.
- Class action suits are being brought against certain weight loss companies.

An anti-diet backlash began erupting in the early 1980s. Since that time, a variety of non-diet approaches have sprung up to entice consumers away from traditional weight loss regimens. And while none of these newer strategies promise thinness, they do offer happier alternatives such as higher self-esteem, a healthier relationship with food, a greater ability to live life to its fullest, self-acceptance and a more respectful body image. Weight loss is viewed as only a possible by-product of these changes.

Pioneers in this arena include, among others, Geneen Roth, Carol Munter, Jane Hirschmann, Susan Kano, Ellyn Satter and Susie Orbach. Some of these "pioneers" are hardly new faces on the scene, but they are practitioners who are suddenly finding an eager audience among the millions of frustrated dieters. They do not all agree on what is the most appropriate approach. They do, on the other hand, share a common goal of developing programming that is free of feelings of failure, shame and self-blame.

The Language is Changing

Much of the language of dieting was judgmental, rigid and hinting of Puritanism. In an effort to establish a new, safe, psychological environment for changing eating behavior, this old language has been one of the first elements to go.

Dieting and weight loss are tied into the old dream that sticking to a deprivation diet will bring us the thin body we desire. Changes in eating behavior more accurately describe the process that is taking place when we restructure our eating habits, whether by reducing fat in our diets or decreasing emotional eating.

We go on a diet when we feel frustrated with our weight. Lifestyle changes, however, are not temporary. These are the habits we can change for our lifetime because they fit our belief system, our lifestyle and our food preferences.

> Diets deprive us of the foods we love.
> Unfortunately, some diets also deprive us of the foods we need.

Until recently, we used to think of binging as the opposite of deprivation. But studies of people who deprive themselves of food reveal that binging is the result, not the opposite, of deprivation. The most straightforward way to avoid a binge is to be sure we have a sufficient amount of food. Restrained eating leads to feelings of helplessness and loss of control. Freedom of choice leads to feelings of satisfaction and empowerment.

When we label foods such as fruit and vegetables as good and foods such as dessert and candy bars as bad, we tend to absorb that same morality whenever we eat the food. "I was a good person today because I had a salad for lunch." "I was a bad person today because I had french fries." By putting pleasure back into eating, we classify all foods as equal in value. Some foods taste sweeter, creamier, crunchier, saltier, milder, etc. Some foods are higher in fat, while others are healthier choices. And if we have a normal appetite, we'll probably have cravings for all of these foods at some point.

The Process is Changing

In the past, the scale was the all-powerful determinant of how well you were doing on your diet. A high number on the scale decreed that you were an unworthy person. A low number on the scale proclaimed you as a deity. An individual's weight is insignificant as a milestone of success. Now people have the option of throwing away the scale and letting their bodies give them regular reports on their progress.

Most of us were taught to eat in response to external eating cues such as a clock signaling meal time, others telling us to eat or our work or leisure schedule. When we listen only to **external cues**, however, we eventually begin to lose our true instinct for hunger so that every emotion, physiological reaction (including thirst) and physical sensation is mistaken for hunger. The new eating behavior encourages people to recognize hunger and concede that they have a right to be hungry. Then they learn to eat when they're hungry, quit when they're full and eat the foods they want to eat. Their desirable and eventual goal is to do this *most* of the time.

> The new process of changing eating behavior forfeits external tools for internal tools.

People today answer questions such as "Did I eat the foods I really wanted today?" "Did I eat when I was hungry and quit when I was full?" "Did I do any unconscious eating today?" "What was going on for me that caused me to eat unconsciously?" This way they can look at the reasons they are turning to food instead of blaming themselves for failing to adhere to some unforgiving

Looking at the reasons for emotional eating is not the same as saying that fat people are emotionally handicapped or psychologically inferior to thin people. Looking at the reasons for emotional eating allows people to acknowledge that food is not the enemy, but rather a functional coping mechanism. Eating is the symptom, not the problem.

food plan. (Note: Looking at the reasons for emotional eating is not the same as saying that fat people are emotionally handicapped or psychologically inferior to thin people.)

Self-acceptance has also been difficult to achieve because individuals have struggled against yet another external cue: the societal message that you are only acceptable if you are thin. To counter that message, people are advised to live their lives "as if" they are okay just the way they are. This "living in the present" urges people to take actions that they would normally have put off until they attained a perfect body.

Perhaps the most significant change, however, has been the shift away from food and onto exercise. Movement helps break through the invisible wall that separates the mind and the body of many large people. And movement is not being viewed as another diet to be approached with the same old diet mentality and the accompanying guilt, shame and rigid language. It is seen, rather, as a tool to befriend the body. And, in a symbolic sense, muscle strengthening becomes a route to empowerment.

Summary

With increasing evidence that a predisposition toward a larger body may make thinness more of a dream than a reality, what results can be expected? While some weight loss does seem to accompany these "dump the diet" approaches, the greatest benefits seem to come from the freedom of living a life in harmony with food instead of in battle with it.

Where does education about healthy eating fit into all of this? First of all, the knowledge that a low-fat, low-sugar, low-salt and high-fiber diet contributes to a healthy body has not successfully motivated many people to change the way they eat. But once people have completed the process of diet withdrawal and are living in a world of unrestricted food choices, they tend to celebrate their new freedom of choice by selecting all kinds of food for all the right reasons.

One Size Does Not Fit All: Size Acceptance in the Fitness World

Pat Lyons, RN, MA

When I teach my class there are always a few women who snicker and make comments about the size of my thighs. It makes me feel so bad. I know I'm a good instructor, and I teach lots of classes every week but I just can't seem to make my legs smaller. I wish I knew what to say to these women who are so critical.

Sandra, age 24, size 10 aerobics instructor

Every time I've gone to an aerobics class I have always been the largest one there. It seems like you already have to be really thin and fit to even go to a class without being humiliated. All these little women talking about their awful fat thighs and how "sinful" they were the night before, saying they ate like pigs and really have to work it off today. And there I stand bigger than any of them. It's just too toxic for me. I'll never go back to one of those classes.

Judy, age 35, size 22 hopeful fitness beginner

Sandra and Judy represent two sides of the same body shame coin. While different in age, size and exercise experience, both were drawn to aerobics to become stronger and healthier and feel better about their bodies and themselves. But their experience was marred by pain. Unfortunately, their experience is repeated daily in aerobics studios around the country. The degrading language that women routinely use to describe their own bodies and to ridicule others would be shocking if we had not all become so accustomed to being insulted by the media.

American women have been convinced by Madison Avenue and the weight loss industry that until they are "perfect" they cannot rest, but must keep striving for thinness to be acceptable. The "perfect" body size for women is smaller than it has ever been in history; only 5% of women can be this size naturally. Our culture seems to expect the other 95% to keep trying until they "succeed" regardless of substantial research data that shows the strong influence of genetics on the development of body size. Most obvious is the fact that simply being thin is no guarantee of either success or health.

Have We Really Come a Long Way, Baby?

The social and psychological environment of many aerobics classes reminds me of my high school gym classes in the early '60s, and makes me wonder whether things are really that much better for women today. While boys ran around and played different sports in every season, we girls were indoors wearing identical gym suits and doing calisthenics. Week after week, we lined up in straight rows, repeating the same exercises at the same pace. In a voice heavy with criticism, our PE teacher repeatedly reminded us how important it was to work on our figures. (A curious concept: Boys have bodies; girls have figures.) I was ashamed of my "figure" because I didn't have one. I was fat, which automatically meant ugly, particularly in a gym suit.

Although I'd always loved and been good at sports growing up, I became too embarrassed about my body to continue being active and dropped out of sports completely by age 15. I began smoking and dieting in earnest, and spent most of the next 15 years on the sidelines inactive. Gym class was supposed to help me learn about my body and enjoy activity. Instead, it was a place where I learned to be self-conscious and ashamed.

Unfortunately, many women learn that same lesson when they try aerobics classes. Rather than exploring body awareness and self-expression, women line up in front of endless mirrors and focus instead on losing hated cellulite. Rather than being encouraged to laugh and play and learn to accept and nurture themselves in the bodies they have, they are exhorted to go to any lengths to "lose that ugly flab." Scantily clad instructors are viewed as role models for health, but underneath the physical appearance of "perfection" many may be living a life of emotional terror, fearful of gaining an ounce of fat.

One has to ask: Have we really made the joy of sport and movement more accessible to women as a group, or have we simply established an environment that legitimizes and encourages women in their relentless and scathing criticism of their bodies? To what extent has the focus on becoming "fit and trim" undermined women's health and self-esteem rather than improved it?

In an effort to escape the social stigma attached to fatness, last year Americans spent $30 billion on weight loss products and programs, including fitness programs. But statistics tell us that nine out of ten fail to maintain losses and risk their health in the process.(1, 2) Dieting, which precedes the development of frank eating disorders, now affects as many as 80% of fourth grade girls. In some surveys as many as 90% of women say they believe they are too fat, and girls as young as five say they are too ashamed to wear a swim suit. (3) We can look with alarm to ever-growing numbers of women with anorexia and bulimia; especially those whose bodies are on display in their professions are particularly vulnerable to these disorders. (4) Compulsive exercise, which can be part of an eating disorder, is now being identified as a disordered condition in itself. (4) Large women experience the most social censure, are under the most pressure to lose weight, and are told repeatedly to exercise to improve their health. But when they try to begin, they experience tremendous ridicule and embarrassment as well as unrealistic expectations for weight loss.(5, 6) Somewhere along the way we have lost our focus on health, and have succumbed to social pressure to "look good" regardless of what it costs.

If the goal of fitness professionals is to help people become healthy, then it is time to seriously address the issues of appearance and size prejudice. We need only look at who dominates the ranks of current fitness participants and instructors—young, thin, middle class, educated whites—to know that we have not done enough to make the benefits of physical activity readily accessible to all who might wish to dance and play. We must revamp our programs so that everyone can experience success. We must welcome instructors and participants of all sizes and help them learn to enjoy activity, rather than use it as punishment for the "sin" of eating or the "failure" of genetics. We must find ways to nurture self-esteem and self-acceptance, rather than continuing to crack the whip of compulsive self-improvement over peoples' heads.

Size Acceptance in Practice

Physical and emotional well-being go hand in hand, but do not blossom in a highly critical environment. Creating a safe, nurturing environment frees people to take risks and learn to trust themselves and their bodies regardless of size, age, limited mobility or lack of experience. When the focus is on finding their own strengths, rather than comparing themselves to others, individuals are free to feel good about their progress without holding out for "perfection" to feel success. Fitness is for everyone, not just those whose bodies happen to meet the current, socially accepted form.

Ironically, many aerobics instructors who are seen as the perfect size role model are often written off outside of the gym as bimbos. This damaging stereotype denies the difficulty involved in teaching and is simply one more example of size and appearance prejudice. Once instructors realize they do not have to live up to unrealistic standards of perfection, or measure their competence by society's stereotypes, they will likely find more joy in both professional and personal lives. Size acceptance benefits everyone.

The following are specific suggestions to put size acceptance into practice:

- Strongly discourage "toxic talk" about diets, body shame, self-degrading name calling, and other methods of criticizing oneself or others. When someone starts on a diatribe of this sort, one might say: "It's interesting that you're being so hard on yourself. Would you like to talk about the feelings or fears you have about your size?" or "It makes me both sad and angry to hear you talk like that about yourself. I'm trying to stop worrying so much about how I look, but when you talk like that it really hurts and makes me self-conscious about what you must think about me."

- Focus on the pleasure of movement in the present, rather than assuming a goal of weight loss as the necessary and expected outcome and measurement of success.

- Hire or train instructors of all shapes, sizes, ages, and ethnic groups to reflect the diversity inherent in the population and to enhance the value of role modeling fitness and health. Offer classes especially for large people taught by large instructors, so they can be paced safely and incorporate appropriate movement.

- Use a variety of movement and music, encourage self-expression and avoid rigidity.

- Teach people about "perceived exertion" rather than encouraging them to drive themselves to maintain a target heart rate for a certain number of minutes for it "to do any good." As work at the Cooper Institute for Aerobics Research in Dallas has shown, all movement "does some good," and people can learn to value many forms of activity as both enjoyable and healthful.(7)

- Teach skills to focus on internal body awareness, rather than just external appearance and form. As people learn to listen to internal cues, they begin to experience their bodies in much fuller, mind-body integrated ways. They learn that all bodies can become stronger and more flexible, as well as learn how to protect their bodies from injury or overuse.

- Encourage a variety of clothing styles as acceptable—the less revealing the better on the part of instructors—so that loose, flowing comfortable clothing is acceptable as dancewear.

- Improve the atmosphere of social support by creating opportunities for class participants to introduce themselves to each other, interact, laugh, play and have fun rather than competing with each other for the thinnest body.

- For the truly brave: remove the scales and body fat measuring from fitness programs. Develop evaluation methods to focus on functional health status and quality of life rather than external appearance and attaining "ideals."
- Perhaps most important, every time you look into the mirror, give yourself the benefit of total self-acceptance. Learn to stop any inner voices of self-criticism, and replace these messages with positive affirmations. You can role model size-acceptance in yourself as you encourage it in others.

Summary

As fitness professionals incorporate concepts of size acceptance into their personal and professional lives we will make physical activity more accessible and more enjoyable for more people. After returning to an active life of tennis, softball, running, skiing and backpacking in my early thirties, I learned to love sports again and became healthy and strong. But I never became thin. Now at 46, after writing a fitness book for large women and teaching classes for them, I believe even more strongly that life is too short and too precious to live it on the sidelines waiting to become thin. Life is a dance to which everyone is invited. As fitness leaders, we can all do our part to make sure everyone feels welcome.

References

1. NIH Technology Assessment Conference Panel. (1993). Methods for voluntary weight loss and control: Technology Assessment Conference Statement. *Ann. Internal Med.,* 119:7: 764-770.
2. Lissner, L., Odell, P., D'Agostino, R., Stokes, J., Kreger, B., Belanger, A., & Brownell, K. (1991). Variability of body weight and health outcomes in the Framingham population. *New England Journal of Medicine,* 324:1839-44.
3. Wolf, N. (1991). *The beauty myth.* New York: Wm. Morrow, 184-186.
4. Yates, A. (1991). *Compulsive exercise and eating disorders.* New York: Brunner-Mazel, 20-21.
5. Lyons, P., & Burgard, D. (1990). *Great shape: The first fitness guide for large women.* Palo Alto, Ca: Bull Publishing.
6. Packer, J. (1989). The role of stigmatization in fat people's avoidance of physical exercise. In Brown, L., & Rothblum, E. (Eds.) *Overcoming fear of fat.* Binghamton, NY: Harrington Park Press.
7. Blair, S. (1989) Physical fitness and all cause mortality, a prospective study of healthy men and women. *JAMA:* 262:17.

Part 5

Personal Training

Professionalism

Fitness Assessment

Weight Counseling

Client Dependency

Paula Besson, MEd

Focus

THE AFAA PERSONAL TRAINER/FITNESS COUNSELOR Certification program is designed to provide the fundamental theoretical knowledge and the practical skills necessary for instructors to advance to the role of personal trainer and fitness counselor. It is not within the scope of this section to prepare instructors for that field, but rather to offer many of the highlights of AFAA's program.

Background

Personal training is not a new concept, but it used to be a service associated with only movie stars or wealthy patrons. It has steadily made its way across both demographic and socio-economic barriers to emerge as a service that is currently used by more individuals than ever before. In so doing, it has provided new opportunities for those working within the fitness industry. And by all immediate indicators, growth is expected to continue for both those seeking and those providing services. Long term success of the service of personal training may be contingent, however, on where it places its emphasis. Personal training may have already been stereotyped as a service that focuses its attention on, and places value on the cosmetic benefit rather than the health benefit of regular exercise. This emphasis on "cosmetic athletics" is primarily a function of the media's relentless bombardment and seduction.

Many Americans are obsessed with their physical appearance. And although there seems to be enormous enthusiasm for exercise as evidenced by a diet and fitness industry that boasts billion dollar yearly profits, Americans seem to be more interested in the pursuit of the magic bullet of beauty rather than the day-to-day lifestyle behaviors that may profoundly affect the quality and longevity of their lives.

Beyond Appearance: Emphasizing Health

If personal training is to be a viable and enduring service, its scope should not be limited to the ever-prevailing emphasis on personal appearance. The personal trainer may in fact be in a highly favorable position to greatly influence the most serious health problems in America. The need for guidance has certainly never been clearer. Consider this: coronary heart disease remains the number one killer in America. Approximately 750,000 Americans die of heart disease each year. (1) This high number of deaths occurs despite the constant flow of information provided by the medical community, telling us that regular exercise along with dietary and lifestyle choices may dramatically reduce this number.

*Dr. Kenneth Cooper of the
Cooper Institute for
Aerobics Research
estimates that 80% of the
American population would
fall in the very poor, poor
or fair category after
performing his standard
12-minute cardiovascular
field test. (4)*

Become a Health Advocate

In fact, as little as three hours of brisk walking per week may reduce heart attack risk by 64%.(2)

Despite this encouraging information, the situation remains unchanged: Americans do not exercise regularly and are not choosing to live in a way that increases their chances for health and survival. In 1988 the U.S. Centers for Disease Control and Prevention reported that 80-90% of the American population did not participate in regular aerobic exercise, and at least 60% of this population did not do any exercise at all. (3) In a report published in 1993 jointly by the American College of Sports Medicine and the U.S. Centers of Disease Control and Prevention, in cooperation with the President's Council on Physical Fitness it was determined that only 22% of American adults engage in leisure time physical activity at the level recommended for health benefits, 24% of adult Americans are completely sedentary and 54% are inadequately active to receive health benefits. (5)

Getting Americans moving and keeping them moving is a critical challenge for the service of personal training, as well as the whole fitness industry. Even among the small percentage of regular exercisers, statistics indicate that those who do exercise regularly are expected to drop out within three to six months. (6) Clearly, although our fitness industry has thrived, it has failed to provide programs and services that keep Americans exercising.

Helping clients make food choices and understanding the mechanism of weight loss is another important challenge for the personal trainer. Although the American Heart Association and the American Cancer Society recommend limiting dietary fat to 25-30% of the diet, the typical American diet may be as high as 42%.(7) This, along with lack of exercise, contributes to obesity and high blood pressure conditions, which continue to be significant health risks in America. Approximately 60 million Americans are hypertensive and of that 60 million, approximately 60% are obese.(8)

Broadening the scope of personal training to include health concerns rather than just cosmetic concerns may define the profession in a way that will dramatically increase its growth, and enable it to make a highly significant contribution to the health of America. As the field of personal training grows, standards for effective procedures and services will have to be carefully examined and established. Finding our place within the allied health professions will be critical. Following the guidelines of industry research organizations and staying abreast of information and methods of education will also be crucial areas of concern. If the industry is to establish guidelines and define necessary areas of competence, certification seems logical.

Although, not without controversy, certification for aerobic instructors has certainly improved the quality of group exercise classes in terms of safe and effective training. The process of certification tends to encourage dialogue and controversy. This, for the most part, results in the consumer being the ultimate beneficiary.

Expanding Your Knowledge Base

The personal trainer will be required to be on the cutting edge of exercise science information. Given that most Americans get a fair amount of their fitness information from places like the checkout line of their local supermarket, their belief system is often based on misguided information about exercise and nutrition, inert substances and ineffective programs. Bringing credible information to clients is a necessary and important first step. Behavioralists know, however, that knowledge does not equal behavior change, and the act of giving information does not insure that clients will adopt or adhere to the program that has been developed for them. Issues of human behavior and mechanisms of learning will have to be examined if we are to do better than our predecessors. In defining the scope of services, personal trainers would benefit from learning methods of leadership that help facilitate behavioral compliance, without crossing the boundary between our area of expertise and that of clinical psychology. The personal trainer may be a powerful influence in the facilitation of health behaviorial change.

Professionalism and Ethics

As the service of personal trainer matures, many professional and ethical questions are surfacing. The personal trainer has a responsibility as a fitness counselor in his or her relationship with both clients and colleagues.

Summary

Finally, and with some irony, the ultimate goal of the personal trainer is to teach skills that lead to behaviors which result in client self responsibility, and the eventual termination of the client-trainer relationship. Success for the personal trainer may in fact be achieved when the client doesn't need a trainer anymore. Working with this goal in mind is what enables the personal trainer to help Americans live longer and healthier, and at the same time, to experience enormous employment possibilities. It is the hope of many within the fitness industry that personal training will accept both the challenge and the responsibility that has been offered.

References

1. University of California, Berkeley (1991). *The Wellness Encyclopedia.* Boston: Houghton Mifflin, 54, and (2), 19.
2. Beasley, J. (1991). *The betrayal of health.* New York: Random House, 149.
3. *The Wellness Encyclopedia*, 216.
4. *The Wellness Encyclopedia*, 216.
5. American College of Sports Medicine (October/December, 1993). *Sports Medicine Bulletin,* 7.
6. American College of sports medicine resource manual for guidelines for exercise testing and prescription (1988). Philadelphia: Lea and Febiger, 335.
7. Howley, E., & Powers, S. (1990). *Exercise physiology: Theory and application to fitness and performance.* Dubuque, Wm. C. Brown Publishing, 406.
8. *The Wellness Encyclopedia*, 52.

Fitness Assessment and Testing

33

Mary Yoke, MA

Focus

WHY SHOULD YOU, THE FITNESS PROFESSIONAL, be knowledgeable about fitness assessments? What does a fitness assessment consist of? How is it administered and what do you do with all the information you collect? This chapter will answer these questions and more: it will specify exactly how to perform many of the more basic and widely used tests, and will serve as an introduction to more advanced fitness assessment and exercise prescription.

Why Perform a Fitness Assessment?

All health club facilities, exercise studios and personal fitness trainers should, at the very minimum, request that clients complete a medical history form or risk factor check, an informed consent, and, depending on the client's health status, request a signed physician's release form. This basic health screening should be an essential part of any client's entry procedure because it will help to identify individuals at risk for cardiovascular, musculoskeletal or other health problems. A basic health screening helps protect the client and is important for the club or trainer from a legal and insurance perspective. The other components of a thorough fitness assessment may not be considered essential but will nevertheless yield a great deal of useful information.

CHECKLIST

Benefits of a Fitness Assessment

(1) Helps establish the client's current health status and provide you with baseline information.

(2) Provides extremely useful information for comparison later as the client progresses and improves.

(3) Serves as a powerful and educational motivating tool, thus increasing the likelihood of adherence.

(4) Demonstrates your professional prudence and knowledge, which can be helpful if potential legal issues arise.

How Do You Assess Physical Fitness?

Exercise scientists have agreed that a physically fit person has adequate to high levels of cardiorespiratory endurance, muscular strength and endurance, flexibility, and an appropriate body composition. A person who is physically fit can perform a great deal of work or exercise without excessive fatigue. Therefore, fitness tests measure an individual's ability to perform physical work. In addition, a thorough fitness assessment will screen the client for injury prevention and risk factors and will help the client evaluate related lifestyle and wellness issues. After the fitness assessment, there should be an interpretation and counseling session with the client prior to formulating the client's program and exercise prescription.

Components of a Fitness Assessment

A. Medical history form

B. Analyze risk factors

C. Request physician's clearance form if necessary

D. Informed consent form

E. Give preliminary information about the actual fitness test

Step One: Initial Screening

A. MEDICAL HISTORY FORM

As mentioned above, the initial screening and paperwork are an essential step prior to your work with any member or client. These forms should be collected at your first meeting, and if your client has risk factors which require medical clearance, you will want to postpone further testing and/or exercise until their physician has signed, stamped and returned the Physician's Clearance form to you. A sample medical history form is included in this chapter.

B. ANALYZE RISK FACTORS

By definition, a risk factor is any factor which makes it more likely that an individual will have a disease. The more risk factors a person has, the greater the likelihood that they will have or develop a particular disease. Two important organizations have identified major risk factors in the development of the number one cause of death in the United States, coronary heart disease.

Risk factors identified by the American College of Sports Medicine are:

- diagnosed high blood pressure greater than or equal to 160/90 mmHg, (or on blood pressure medication)
- total cholesterol levels greater than or equal to 240 mg/dl
- cigarette smoking
- diabetes mellitus
- family history of heart disease or sudden death in parents or siblings prior to age 55
- sedentary lifestyle

Risk factors identified by the American Heart Association are:

Alterable

- high blood pressure greater than or equal to 140/90 mmHg
- total cholesterol greater than or equal to 240 mg/dl
- cigarette smoking
- sedentary lifestyle

Unalterable

- male sex
- age
- family history of heart disease or sudden death in parents or siblings prior to age 50

The medical history form should inquire as to whether your client has any of these risk factors, has known cardiac, pulmonary or metabolic disease, or has any symptoms which might suggest that they have coronary or metabolic disease.

What is a symptom? According to the ACSM, major symptoms which suggest cardiopulmonary or metabolic disease are:

- chest pain
- unaccustomed shortness of breath
- dizziness or fainting
- ankle swelling
- palpitations or irregular heartbeats

- cramping pains in legs or feet
- known heart murmur(1)

C. PHYSICIAN'S CLEARANCE

After noting your client's responses to the medical history form, as well as their age and sex, the ACSM recommends that you require a Physician's Clearance if:

- There are two or more risk factors present.
- There are symptoms of cardiopulmonary or metabolic disease.
- There is known cardiac, pulmonary or metabolic disease.
- They are male and age 40 or over.
- They are female and age 50 or over.(1)

The physician may also recommend or perform a diagnostic exercise stress test at this time.

In addition to observing the ACSM recommendations for obtaining medical clearance, the American College of Obstetricians and Gynecologists recommends that all pregnant clients be cleared for exercise by their physician prior to starting an exercise program.(2) It is also advisable to request a Physician's Clearance from clients who have been recently hospitalized for any reason, who have chronic or acute muscle or joint injury, or who are on prescription medications. A sample Physician's Clearance form is included on page 286.

If a client does not fall into any of the above categories, they are then classed as apparently healthy and do not need medical clearance prior to fitness testing or exercise. In the event that a client has several risk factors, known disease, or medical complications or injuries, you may decide that your level of knowledge is insufficient for providing the safest monitoring and exercise programming for their condition. Know your limitations. It may be more prudent to recommend a cardiac rehabilitation facility or a physical therapist depending on the nature of their problem.

D. INFORMED CONSENT

Prior to beginning the actual fitness test your client/member should read and sign an informed consent form. This form should briefly explain the exercise test procedures, any risks or discomforts that may be involved, benefits that can be expected from the fitness assessment, and the responsibility of the client to ask questions or report unusual feelings or symptoms if they arise during the assessment. A sample informed consent is included in this chapter.

See chapter with
"Lifestyle Questionnaire"

Lifestyle/Wellness Evaluation. A lifestyle or wellness evaluation may be part of the initial screening, or may be administered later in the program. It may include an assessment of the client's smoking, dietary, drinking, drug and exercise habits, as well as providing insights into an individual's social, emotional, and intellectual health.

Exercise Attitude Profile. This brief questionnaire may help uncover any roadblocks or resistance to exercise, and may help identify client misconceptions about physical fitness.

E. PRELIMINARY INFORMATION TO BE GIVEN TO CLIENT

Prior to the actual exercise tests, the client needs to be informed about appropriate footwear and clothing and instructed to avoid drinking caffeinated beverages, smoking, or consuming a heavy meal for at least two hours before the fitness assessment. Cigarettes, a large meal, and caffeine can all alter resting and exercising heart rate and blood pressure responses. Conversely, not eating anything for several hours prior to testing may cause a drop in blood sugar levels after the tests, leaving the client feeling dizzy, lightheaded or nauseous. (For example, it would not be advisable to skip breakfast and then perform vigorous exercise just prior to lunch.)

Finally, if the client/member is ill or has recently had a viral infection, it is probably best to postpone the physical assessment.

Step Two: The Fitness Assessment

After the initial paperwork is completed, Physician's Clearance form is returned (if necessary), and preliminary instructions have been given, the actual fitness assessment begins.

A. RESTING VALUES

An assessment of resting values may include the resting heart rate, resting blood pressure, and, in a diagnostic stress test administered by an Exercise Test Technologist or Physician, a resting ECG.

Resting Heart Rate. A true resting heart rate is obtained first thing in the morning when the body is completely relaxed but conscious, before getting out of bed. Since even a "true" resting heart rate fluctuates, it's best to measure on three consecutive days and take the average. In the fitness assessment setting, try to get as accurate a resting heart rate as possible by having the client sit quietly for 5-10 minutes prior to palpation.

Resting heart rate may be palpated at the radial artery at the wrist for a full minute or for 30 seconds (multiply by two for the minute value). It is normal for some individuals (especially athletes) to have respiratory sinus arrhythmia at rest, which means that pulse speeds up during inhalation and slows during exhalation. For this reason, counting for 30 or 60 seconds at rest is more accurate than counting for 6, 10 or 15 seconds. It is also acceptable to palpate the pulse at the carotid artery at the side of the larynx on the neck, although it may not be as accurate if too much pressure is applied. Baroreceptors in the carotid artery detect pressure and may reflexively cause the heart rate to decrease. As a result, many professionals prefer that heart rate measurement be taken at the radial pulse.

Resting Blood Pressure. Since high blood pressure, or hypertension, is one of the three primary alterable risk factors for coronary heart disease, and since an estimated one third of American adults, or 60 million, have borderline or high blood pressure(4), routine measurement of resting blood pressure is very important. It is recommended that all fitness professionals, particularly personal trainers, learn to monitor blood pressure. This becomes increasingly important should you decide to work with higher risk clients. During the fitness assessment, if your client has high resting blood pressure readings after three measurements, and has another risk factor (i.e., family history of heart disease), then they are classified as higher risk (see ACSM guidelines above), and further testing or exercise should be postponed until they are cleared by a physician.

Resting blood pressure can be affected by the same factors as resting heart rate (caffeine, stress, time of day, etc.). In addition, many clients become anxious

---

A. Resting Values

B. Body Composition Assessment

C. Cardiorespiratory Fitness Assessment

D. Muscular Strength and Endurance Assessment

E. Flexibility Assessment

F. Other

Normal: 120/80

Borderline: 140/90

High: 160/90

about having their blood pressure measured, so relaxing quietly for 5-10 minutes prior to measurement is advised.

What is considered normal blood pressure?

Normal, or average, blood pressure is usually thought to be around 120/80 mmHg. A person is not considered to have borderline hypertension until the values exceed 140/90 mmHg. ACSM defines diagnosed hypertension as systolic blood pressure >160 or diastolic blood pressure >90 mmHg on at least two separate occasions, or on high blood pressure medication(1). The top number or higher value is referred to as the systolic pressure, or the amount of pressure or force exerted against the arterial walls immediately after the heart has contracted. The bottom number or lower value may be thought of as the "run-off" force, or the amount of pressure still remaining against the arterial walls as the heart relaxes before the next contraction.

B. BODY COMPOSITION ASSESSMENT

Evaluation of the client's body composition is an important part of the fitness assessment. Although many clients may be interested in learning about their estimated percent body fat for cosmetic reasons, one of the primary reasons for assessing body composition is to educate your client about the health risks involved with excessive body fat.

Many medical authorities believe that too much body fat is a health hazard and increases the risk of heart disease, diabetes, high blood pressure, some forms of cancer, low back pain and other musculoskeletal problems. New research points to the ravages of diet-cycling among overweight individuals as perhaps the primary culprit, adversely affecting overall health and longevity statistics.

Body composition refers to the percentage of body weight that is fat and is based on the assumption that body weight can be divided into fat mass and lean body mass. (Lean body mass is assumed to include muscles, bones, organs, internal fluids, etc.). The equations that the norms for body composition are based on also assume that the densities for fat and lean body mass are the same for everyone. Therefore, the norms that you choose to use in estimating your client's percent body fat ideally should have been developed on a population with your client's age, gender, race, and physical activity level.

AFAA's recommendation for healthy percent body fat in men is 12-17% and in women is 18-22%. Note that this is healthy, not average.

The location where excess body fat accumulates is significant for health reasons. Studies have shown that when a greater amount of fat is stored in the abdominal area relative to the extremities, a person is at higher risk for heart disease, diabetes, and metabolic disorders. A method for assessing this risk is the **waist to hip ratio**: simply divide the waist circumference by the hip circumference.(5) If the ratio is greater than .95 for men or greater than .85 for women they are considered to be at higher risk.

There are several methods available for estimating your body's composition. Following is a list of the most common techniques and the advantages and disadvantages of each.

1. HYDROSTATIC WEIGHING

This underwater laboratory method is considered to be the "gold standard," or most accurate technique, for estimating body fat percentages. In this procedure the subject is seated on a chair attached to a scale suspended over a

---

Healthy Body Fat Levels

WOMEN   18-22%

MEN   12-17%

special tank. The subject is asked to forcefully exhale completely (excess air in the body increases the tendency to float), and is submerged underwater as the examiner records the subject's weight on the scale. Several attempts should be made as the subject becomes more proficient at completely exhaling underwater. Body volume is then determined by subtracting the underwater weight from the individual's body weight in air. (Underwater weight must also be corrected by subtracting the weight of the chair and the subject's estimated residual volume, or air trapped in the lungs and gastrointestinal tract.) Body volume is then used to calculate body density; and body density is then used to estimate percent body fat using an appropriate population specific equation. The advantage of hydrostatic weighing is its high rate of accuracy, validity and reliability. Disadvantages include the fact that it is not widely available in commercial and corporate settings, is expensive, time consuming, and necessitates highly trained laboratory examiners. In addition, some clients are uncomfortable in the water and/or have difficulty completely exhaling underwater.

2. BIOELECTRICAL IMPEDANCE

In this method electrodes are attached to the subject's hands and feet. A painless mild electric current is then passed through the body and the time it takes to course from the hands to the feet is recorded. Since lean tissue contains a high percentage of water, the bioelectric current is passed more quickly through a person with a greater lean body mass.

Advantages of the test are that it is fast, easy, painless, and the person examining requires minimal training. Disadvantages are that the subject's level of hydration must be controlled (recommendations are no eating or drinking within 4 hours of the test, no exercise within 12 hours of the test, no alcohol consumption or diuretics within 48 hours of the test, and that urination must take place within 30 minutes prior to the test)(6), the equipment may be quite expensive depending an the manufacturer, and research has not firmly established the accuracy of this method.

3. INFRARED INTERACTANCE

This technique, perhaps best known by its widely used brand name, Futrex 5000, is based on the fact that the ability of a body tissue to absorb and reflect infrared light depends on its composition. A fiber optic probe is placed on the skin (usually at the biceps) and a near infrared beam penetrates the underlying tissue to a depth of 4 cm. The probe collects any reflected energy and returns it to the spectrophotometer.

Advantages of the method include its easy portability, non-intimidating nature, and the fact that it is very easy to administer. Disadvantages are its expense and the lack of conclusive studies establishing this technique's reliability and validity.

4. ULTRASOUND

Portable ultrasound meters estimate body composition by emitting high frequency sound waves that penetrate the skin surface at five different sites. The sound waves are reflected back from the fat-muscle interface, producing an echo that is picked up by the ultrasound unit which then measures the distance between the skin and fat-muscle layer.

The primary advantage of this system is its portability. Disadvantages are that this method is costly and not yet scientifically validated.

5. CIRCUMFERENCES AND BONY DIAMETERS

A variety of equations predicting body fat percentage have been developed using circumferences (girths), measured with an inexpensive tape measure, and/or bony diameters, measured with a device called a skeletal anthropometer. (For a detailed listing of bony diameter sites see the Anthropometric Standardization Reference Manual, pp 27-38.)(8)

Some of these equations also utilize skinfold measurements taken with skinfold calipers. Body fat estimations using circumferences have been shown to be relatively accurate if the appropriate equations and constants are used. For example, to estimate percent fat on a 21-year-old male, weighing 174 lbs:

    a. Upper arm, abdomen, and right forearm circumferences are measured to the nearest 1/4 inch.

    b. The upper arm value is converted into Constant A, abdomen value converted into Constant B, and right forearm value converted into Constant C utilizing published conversion constants.(7)

    c. Substitute these constants into the formula appropriate for young men: Constant A + Constant B - Constant C - 10.2 = % body fat.

Advantages of the circumference method are the low cost and lack of special training required. In addition, taking girth measurements over a period of time simply to monitor body build and weight changes due to an exercise and diet program can be useful and motivating to your client. On the data sheet included in this chapter, note the space provided for circumference as well as skinfold measurements. Disadvantages of the circumference method include the potential for incorrect tape measure placement as well as the inconsistency involved in pulling the tape measure too tight or not tight enough. Special cloth tapes, known as Gulick tapes, are available to help standardize tension; and adhering to correct tape measure placement for circumference sites listed below will help ensure repeated accuracy.

    1. Abdominal: horizontal measure at level of umbilicus.

    2. Waist: horizontal measure taken at the level of the narrowest part of the torso.

    3. Hips: maximum posterior protrusion of the buttocks.

    4. Thigh (proximal): Just below the fold of the buttocks.

    5. Upper arm: midway between the acromium and olecranon processes.

    6. Forearm: maximum circumference with elbow extended and palm supinated.

    7. Calf: maximum circumference between knee and ankle (8).

6. SKINFOLD (FATFOLD) METHOD

The skinfold method of body composition assessment has been widely used and validated; when properly performed by experienced examiners it is relatively accurate. Special calipers are used to measure the skin and subcutaneous fat thicknesses at selected sites (sites vary depending on the equations used). Calipers range in price from $15 - $350 with the more expensive models being more accurate and long lasting.

The major disadvantage and source of error in the skinfold method is incorrect technique and/or lack of experience on the part of the examiner. It takes a great deal of time and practice and proper training to develop the proper technique. Always adhere conscientiously to the standardized guidelines below (from the Anthropometric Standardization Reference Manual, pp. 55-70) (8) to help ensure accuracy.

How is body fat calculated from skinfold measurements?

1. All measurements should be taken on the right side of the body.
2. Carefully measure the appropriate sites 2-3 times each.
3. Find the average value for each site and then add all the sites together.
4. Find the appropriate table (Percent Fat Estimations) included in this chapter and note where the sum of the skinfolds and your client's age intersect. This is the estimated percent body fat.

Essential Fat and Storage Fat

The total amount of fat weight in the human body can be categorized under two areas or sites depending upon the function.

Essential Fat

The first site where a small amount of fat is stored is in the bone marrow, heart, liver, lungs, intestines, spleen, kidneys, cell membranes, nerve tissue and certain tissue in the spinal cord and brain. This fat is commonly termed essential fat. This fat is required for normal physiological function of the various organs. In men and women, this essential fat accounts for about 3% of the total body weight. However, in females the essential fat also includes what is known as sex-specific or sex-characteristic fat. This sex-specific essential fat usually accounts for an additional 9-12% of body weight in a woman. Its development is related to normal sex-hormone control. The mammary glands and the pelvic region are the primary areas of storage of this fat. In one recent study it was found that the weight of the breasts only accounts for about 4% of this sex-specific fat in a group of women who varied in percent body fat between 14% and 35%. (24) The majority of this sex-specific fat is probably located in the hip, thigh and pelvic regions and is under sex hormone-related influence.

Storage Body Fat

The second major site of the body fat is the fat that accumulates in the subcutaneous tissue between the muscle and skin-storage body fat. This storage fat or adipose tissue serves several bodily functions. First, it serves as a shock absorber to cushion and protect bones, muscles and internal organs from injury. Storage fat also functions as an insulator against hot and cold environments. It can help maintain a somewhat constant core body temperature while at rest. However, it should be pointed out that excessive storage fat acts as a hindrance in regulating body temperature while exercising. During exercise the body has a decreased ability to transfer heat to the periphery, which is generated as a result of an increased muscle metabolism, through excessive amounts of stored adipose tissue. In addition to interfering with heat transfer through the subcutaneous layer, excess body fat directly adds to the metabolic cost of aerobic activities in which the body weight must be moved. The overfat person in an aerobic exercise class is at a distinct disadvantage in terms of heat regulation and physical performance.

Skinfold Measurements
(JACKSON AND POLLOCK)

Males

Chest (pectoral): A diagonal fold taken one half the distance between the anterior axillary line (underarm crease) and the nipple.

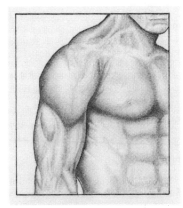
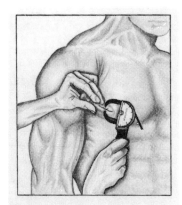

Abdomen: A vertical fold taken at a distance of 2 cm. (1 inch) to the right of the umbilicus.

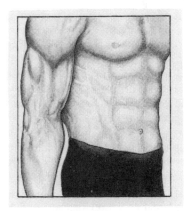

Thigh: A vertical fold in the midline of the anterior aspect of the thigh, midway between the inguinal crease (fold in the hip during hip flexion) and the proximal border of the patella. The body weight should be placed on the opposite leg so that the right thigh is relaxed.

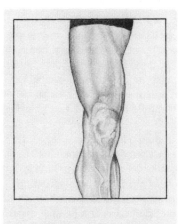
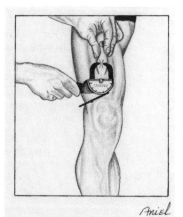

Aniel

Skinfold Measurements

(JACKSON AND POLLOCK)

Females

Triceps: A vertical fold measured in the midline of the posterior arm over the triceps muscle. Anatomical landmarks are the lateral projection of the acramial process and the inferior border of the olecranon process with the elbow flexed at 90 degrees. A tape measure should be stretched between these two landmarks and the midpoint located on the lateral aspect of the arm. The actual site is at this level on the posterior aspect. During measurement the right elbow should be extended and relaxed.

Suprailiac: A 45-degree angle diagonal fold immediately above the iliac crest along the anterior axillary line.

Thigh: A vertical fold in the midline of the anterior aspect of the thigh, midway between the inguinal crease (fold in the hip during hip flexion) and the proximal border of the patella. The body weight should be placed on the opposite leg so that the right thigh is relaxed.

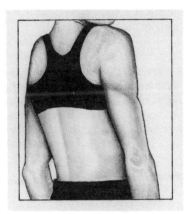
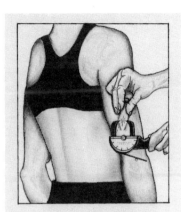

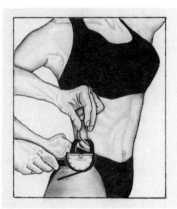
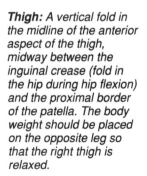
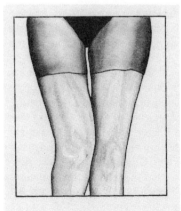
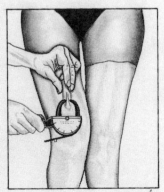

C. CARDIORESPIRATORY FITNESS ASSESSMENT

Cardiorespiratory endurance, or aerobic capacity, is one of the most important components of fitness. Low levels of cardiorespiratory endurance have been associated with increased risk of premature death from all causes, most specifically from cardiovascular disease. In addition, greater aerobic fitness usually means that an individual is more habitually active, and this has been linked with many health benefits. (11)

Aerobic or cardiorespiratory fitness is defined as the ability to perform repetitive, moderate to high intensity, large muscle movement for a prolonged period of time. VO_2 max (also known as maximal oxygen consumption or **maximal oxygen uptake**) is often considered by exercise physiologists to be the most important measure of a person's aerobic fitness. It refers to the maximum amount of oxygen able to be consumed and utilized by the body during an all-out effort to exhaustion (such as during a maximal exercise test). It is assumed that this measurement represents a person's maximal capacity to resynthesize ATP aerobically. The more aerobically fit an individual is, the greater the ability to resynthesize ATP, and the higher the VO_2 max or ability to consume and process oxygen. VO_2 max is measured in either liters of oxygen consumed per minute (an absolute value), or in ml of oxygen consumed per kilogram of a person's body weight per minute (a relative value).

Another important indicator of a person's cardiorespiratory fitness may be their **anaerobic threshold,** also known as the onset of blood lactic acid. This is the point during exercise (or exercise testing) in which the work becomes so intense that muscle cells cannot produce the additional energy aerobically, and so begin to rely more and more on the anaerobic glycolytic pathway (lactic acid system) to produce ATP. At this level, lactic acid begins to accumulate and the anaerobic threshold has been reached.

When a person is aerobically fit, they can exercise at high levels of intensity without reaching this point, since the body has been trained to comfortably consume and utilize large quantities of oxygen. Consequently, we can say that the anaerobic threshold, or level where lactic acid begins to accumulate, is also quite high. Both VO_2 max and the anaerobic threshold increase with aerobic endurance training.

How is cardiorespiratory fitness assessed?

Cardiorespiratory fitness can be evaluated with either **maximal** or **submaximal** exercise tests and can be assessed either directly (with oxygen consumption equipment) or estimated (no oxygen consumption equipment is used).

1. **Maximal exercise tests** fall generally into two categories: diagnostic and functional. In a diagnostic exercise test (sometimes called a "stress" test or GXT), the purpose is to diagnose the presence and/or the extent of coronary heart disease in addition to evaluating the patient's ability to perform work. (This is the type of test that a physician may recommend be performed on one of your higher risk clients). The patient will be continuously monitored during exercise via a multi-lead ECG and may or may not be using oxygen consumption equipment. This test usually takes place on a treadmill or cycle ergometer and the patient is pushed to achieve their maximum work effort. By evaluating the ECG (especially at higher intensities) the physician or technologist can discern heart function abnormalities as well as cardiorespiratory endurance.

Obviously, this kind of exercise test should only be administered by highly trained personnel in a clinical setting.

The purpose of a "functional" maximal exercise test is simply to assess cardiorespiratory fitness. This kind of test is often used to evaluate athletes and is valuable for research purposes. It is frequently performed and taught in university exercise physiology labs as well as some commercial and corporate fitness settings. The subject's VO_2 max is usually directly measured with oxygen consumption (metabolic) equipment as they exercise to exhaustion on a treadmill or cycle ergometer. When viewing the metabolic equipment during such a test, physiologists assume that VO_2 max has been achieved at the point where the oxygen consumption plateaus even though the subject is able to perform increased work prior to exhaustion.

2. **Submaximal exercise tests.** There are many types of submaximal tests. Here the purpose is *not* to diagnose heart disease (ECGs are rarely used), but to assess the client's functional aerobic fitness and to enable you to prescribe an appropriate level of exercise intensity for each individual client. Submaximal tests may be used to predict or estimate VO_2 max, but the tests are concluded when a predetermined submaximal level has been reached (usually 85% of your client's estimated maximum).

In this kind of testing, oxygen consumption equipment is rarely used or available; instead, information is gathered using the client's heart rate, perceived exertion, and in many tests, their blood pressure response to exercise. Submaximal tests are based on two major assumptions:

1. That there is a linear relationship between a person's oxygen consumption (or VO_2), and their heart rate; in other words, if VO_2 increases, expect the heart rate will also increase in a corresponding fashion, especially at the intensities necessary for exercise.

2. That an individual's maximum heart rate can be predicted from the formula 220 - age = **Maximum Heart rate.** In fact, this commonly used formula is accurate for only about 75% of the population. In the remaining 25% maximum heart rate can vary from the formula by as much as 10-15 bpm, resulting in either an under or over prediction of max.

Bicycle ergometer test. At many commercial and corporate fitness facilities, the submaximal cycle ergometer test is the preferred form of aerobic fitness assessment. Advantages of the test are that the ergometer is easy to calibrate, relatively inexpensive and portable (as compared to a treadmill), non-intimidating to clients, and heart rate and blood pressure are easier to assess during cycling exercise than during walking or running exercise. Also, since most cycle protocols are multi-stage, more information can be obtained than during the single stage 3-minute step test. Disadvantages are that it may be difficult for your client to maintain a constant speed or workload, (they may slow down or speed up), they are more likely to experience localized muscle fatigue which may limit their performance. Also, the examiner needs some specialized training to administer the test properly, (i.e., at a university, or through the ACSM or YMCA certification programs).

The submaximal bench step test. If you don't have the training or equipment to perform a cycle ergometer test, a suitable alternative is the 3-minute step test used by the YMCA(3). Advantages of the step test are that it is less time consuming and less expensive, more portable, non-intimidating to clients, and takes less training to administer. Disadvantages include the fact that there is only one workload, which means less information about how your

Submaximal exercise tests are most often performed on treadmills, cycle ergometers, or bench steps. Several different protocols (testing formats) are available.

client responds to various intensities. In addition, heart rate, blood pressure, and rate of perceived exertion are not monitored during exercise, all of which makes the step test less useful for exercise prescription. It is also less accurate in predicting VO_2 max than the cycle ergometer test.

The premise underlying the step test is that if a client has a low recovery heart rate one minute after stepping, they are in better physical condition and therefore will have a higher VO_2 max.

Aerobic dance exercise tests. In an effort to overcome problems associated with specificity of training during testing, (i.e., testing aerobic dance participants on a cycle), researchers have recently devised exercise tests using aerobic dance movements (13, 14). These tests (one maximal, the other submaximal), need more scientific validation before they can be recommended.

Field tests. A number of field tests, both maximal and submaximal, have been developed to predict VO_2 max, assess cardiorespiratory endurance, and evaluate performance. Advantages are that they are inexpensive, can be used for large groups, and are easy to administer. Disadvantages include the lack of control involved and the difficulty in measuring heart rate, blood pressure, rate of perceived exertion, and other physical responses during the test.

Running field tests. Several endurance run tests are available, including the one mile walk-run test for ages 5 to 18 years (15), and the Balke 15-minute run (16). Perhaps the tests most widely used by schools, universities and the military are the 12-minute run and the 1.5-mile run tests popularized by Kenneth Cooper (17). The idea behind all run tests is for the subject to run as fast as possible in a maximal effort for the specified time or distance. The faster the time, the higher the estimated VO_2 max. These tests are only appropriate for healthy individuals or for those whose risks have been completely evaluated.

D. MUSCULAR STRENGTH AND ENDURANCE ASSESSMENT

Muscle strength, the ability of a muscle or muscle group to exert maximal force for one repetition, and **muscle endurance,** the ability of a muscle or muscle group to exert submaximal force of several repetitions (or to hold a contraction for a sustained length of time), are both important components of fitness for your client's physical well being. Without adequate muscle strength and endurance clients are more likely to suffer from low back pain which afflicts 3 out of 10 Americans at some point in their lives, and/or poor posture, as well as other musculoskeletal problems. The development of muscle strength and endurance leads to an increase in lean body mass and an improvement in body composition, which in turn causes an elevation in resting metabolic rate. In addition, maintaining muscle strength and endurance is an important factor (especially for elderly clients) in performing everyday essential tasks adequately and without injury.

Static strength tests are usually performed on either cable tensiometers or dynamometers. Cable tensiometers are more often used for rehabilitation purposes as they allow strength measurement of 38 different muscles at specific joint angles (a goniometer is necessary to measure the joint angle). Test protocols and norms are available. (19) **Dynamometers** are available to assess hand grip strength and back and leg extensor strength, with the hand grip dynamometer being most widely used. The procedure is simple: After adjusting the hand grip size for your client, have them stand holding the dynamometer in one hand with the elbow flexed. Instruct them to exhale while squeezing as hard as possible (maximal voluntary contraction) for 2-3 seconds. Allow 3 trials for each hand and compare to the published norms. (20)

Muscular strength can also be assessed **dynamically** by the one-repetition maximum (1 RM) test. Perhaps the most frequently performed 1 RM test is the **1 RM Bench Press,** which assesses the strength of the pectoralis major, anterior deltoid and triceps muscle groups. The person's maximum amount of strength for one repetition is formed through trial and error.

Researchers have found that the 1 RM Bench Press (as well as the 1 RM Military Press) is the most valid measure of upper body strength.(22) The test is relatively safe (especially when performed on a bench press machine). The equipment is readily available in most fitness facilities, and the test is easy to administer. Disadvantages include the potential for injury that exists with any maximal effort, the fact that clients may perform the Valsalva manuever (holding their breath to "bear down"), the lack of portability of the equipment, and the "intimidation factor" for clients unfamiliar with weights. Norms also exist for the 1 RM Leg Press which tests the muscle strength of the upper leg muscles.(22)

How is muscle endurance assessed?

The most commonly performed tests for muscle endurance are calisthenic in nature, which means that the client lifts his own body weight. These tests assume that your client's body weight is a submaximal weight that they can lift many times. In fact, for some deconditioned clients doing just one push-up or one sit-up requires a maximal muscular effort. (Obviously, this would show that they are in the poor category for muscle strength and endurance.) In addition, other tests for muscular endurance exist which use an external, standardized weight, such as the bench press test developed by the YMCA. Here, women lift a 35-lb barbell and men lift an 80-lb barbell to a metronome count of 60 bpm. The test is concluded when the client can no longer keep the pace, breaks form, or cannot complete another repetition. Published norms are available for ranking your client's upper body muscle endurance on the bench press.(3)

The push-up test also measures upper body endurance and is easier to administer than the bench press and needs no special equipment.

> *Muscle strength can be assessed either statically (isometrically), or dynamically (isotonically).*

1. Have your client assume the appropriate position: men are on hands and toes (regular push-up), women are on hands and knees (modified push-up).

   Instruct them to breathe with each repetition and to do as many as they can with good form. As with all fitness tests, assure your clients that they should stop if they feel any pain or discomfort.

2. Count the number of push-ups they can perform correctly. The spine should remain in good alignment (supported by the abdominals), with the neck continuing as a natural extension of the spine. The chest should come within 3 inches of the floor (you may use your fist as a guide or use a 3-inch Nerf-type ball that they need to touch with each repetition).

3. The test is over when they can no longer maintain form or complete another rep. Again, compare the score with that of published norms in testing manuals.

The crunch test has been recently developed as a safer modification of the sit-up test. (20) It is important to include some assessment of abdominal

The sit-up test has been criticized because it involves not only the rectus abdominis but the iliopsoas muscle group. The client is asked to perform as many full sit-ups (elbows touching the knees) as possible in one minute while the feet are held in place. This test may aggravate existing low back pain and relies on an exercise (the full sit-up), that is not recommended for training.

endurance when evaluating your clients, since weak abdominal muscles with poor endurance have been linked with the development of low back pain. Here is the protocol:

1. Have your clients lie supine with the knees comfortably bent, arms at the sides with the fingers pointing towards the feet. Be sure the low back remains pressed to the floor at all times. Instruct them to curl up with head and shoulders off the floor and to slide their hands a distance of 6 inches forward on the floor. (You may use a ruler, a marked piece of tape, or your own hands as a guide.) Allow one or two crunches for practice.

2. Begin the timer, and count how many crunches they correctly perform in one minute. Remind them to exhale with each repetition.

3. Compare their score with the norms for their age and sex.

Back tests. Since low back pain affects 80% of the population, many tests have been devised to assess the strength, endurance, and flexibility of the contributing muscle groups. A relatively safe test for assessing abdominal endurance was presented above. Other tests, such as the National Back Test and the Kraus-Weber test used by the Y's Way to a Healthy Back Program are available. (23)

E. FLEXIBILITY ASSESSMENT

Flexibility is defined as the range of motion possible around a joint. Like muscle strength and endurance, flexibility is specific, and there is no single test which assesses total body flexibility. Flexibility assessment may provide crucial information for your clients. When range of motion is limited around a joint due to muscular tightness, that joint is more susceptible to injury. This is especially evident for proper functioning of the spine.

How is flexibility assessed?

Flexibility can be evaluated either directly or indirectly. Direct measurements are more accurate but unfortunately, the equipment necessary is not widely available in most commercial and corporate fitness facilities. Instruments for direct measurement include the goniometer, a protractor-like device, and the Leighton flexometer, consisting of a dial with a weighted pointer. These tools actually measure the individual joint angle in degrees that are achieved during various stretches.

There are many indirect tests of flexibility. Perhaps the most widely performed is the **Sit and Reach** test used by the YMCA. (3) This test primarily measures the flexibility of the hamstring and erector spinae muscles, as well as the calf and upper back muscles. The flexibility of all these muscle groups is important for healthy low back functioning. Advantages of the test are that it is easy to administer, requires a minimum of equipment, and has widely validated norms. Disadvantages include the slight risk of injury due to the position required (seated unsupported forward flexion), and the fact that a person's score may be influenced by the length of their body segments (for example, a long trunk and short legs). The procedure for the Sit and Reach test:

1. After explaining the purpose of the test to your clients, have them actively warm-up (if they are not already warm from the cardiorespiratory assessment), and perform some static stretching, particularly of the hamstrings, low back and calf muscles.

Tight erector spinae, hamstring and iliopsoas muscles have all been implicated as a possible cause of low back pain.

2. Instruct them to remove their shoes and to sit on the floor with their knees straight (pressed to the floor) and the feet approximately 12 inches apart. The heels should be in contact with the Sit and Reach box with the ankles dorsiflexed. If no Sit and Reach box is available, a tape measure or yardstick may be used. The heels should be aligned at the 15-inch mark on the tape, with the zero end towards the body. (You may want to secure the yardstick or tape measure to the floor using some masking tape at the zero and 15-inch marks.)

3. Have your clients place their hands on top of each other with fingers aligned, and slowly exhale and stretch out over the box, tape, or yard stick without bouncing. Allow them to relax and then perform 2 to 3 more trials.

4. Taking the farthest distance reached as the score, compare it to the norms in the Y's Way to Physical Fitness Program.

F. OTHER POSSIBLE FITNESS ASSESSMENT COMPONENTS

Assessment options for the major components of fitness have been presented above; however, depending on time, financial and equipment factors, as well as your skill and knowledge base, there are many other optional tools developed by physiologists and wellness professionals that you may want to include in assessing and guiding your clients.

1. In addition to the Lifestyle Questionnaire, you may want to include a specific questionnaire to evaluate your client's **level of stress** and/or ability to use coping strategies. Excessive negative stress has been linked to many diseases and disorders such as hypertension, coronary heart disease, cancer, ulcers, insomnia, back pain and headaches.

2. Many wellness professionals like to include some sort of **nutritional assessment** or dietary recall when counseling clients. Although a full nutritional analysis and dietary recall is beyond the scope of this chapter, a food frequency assessment is quick, easy to administer, and can be educational for your client.

3. Several types of **cholesterol tests** are available. Some facilities offer their clients relatively inexpensive, fasting blood lipid profiles performed by an outside laboratory. This is the most accurate test, as it requires the subject to fast for 12 hours, and the blood is returned to the lab for LDL, HDL, triglyceride and total cholesterol analysis.

Step Three: The Interpretation/Counseling Session

Depending on time factors, you may or may not decide to present the results of the fitness assessment at the same session as the actual testing. When you do decide to go over the results, be sure to present them in a positive manner. No matter how your clients scored on a particular test, encourage them not to focus on a specific numerical score, but instead to focus on the fact that if they adhere to their exercise program they will change and improve over time. Review the five components of fitness and the importance of reducing their risk factors, and encourage them to develop a larger view of health and wellness. Remember, part of the purpose of performing fitness testing is to educate and motivate!

In this session you need to help your client have reasonable expectations about their exercise program and its expected results. Preparing them for a realistic experience and establishing achievable goals have both been proven to help with exercise adherence and long lasting behavior change. When discussing goals, ask your clients to pinpoint their first priority or number one fitness goal. Be sure that this goal is specific (avoid such loose statements as "getting in shape") and achievable. Short term goals of 2-4 weeks are more effective than long term goals.

At the end of each goal period re-evaluate your client's progress and give appropriate feedback. During this session create a "game plan" as to exactly how your client will reach their goal. Specify exercise dates, times, places, attire, dietary modifications, etc. Since the goal's progress should be measurable, specify the date for fitness test re-assessment (allow three months for measurable benefits such as decreased resting heart rate, increased aerobic capacity, decreased percent body fat, etc.). Be sure to also encourage the less quantifiable internal reinforcements of progress such as awareness of enhanced self-esteem and increased energy. In addition, a behavioral contract may be used during the counseling session. Based on your client's feedback during this session, the next task is to formulate an appropriate exercise prescription.

References

1. American College of Sports Medicine (1991). *Guidelines for exercise testing and prescription* (4th ed.). Philadelphia: Lea & Febiger.
2. American College of Obstetricians and Gynecologists (1985). *Exercise during pregnancy and the postnatal period*. Washington, D.C.: ACOG Home Exercise Programs.
3. Golding, L.A., Meyers, C.R., Sinning, W.E. (1989). *Y's way to physical fitness: Complete guide to fitness testing and instruction*. (3rd ed.). Champaign, Ill.: Human Kinetics Pub.
4. National Heart, Lung & Blood Institute (Sept., 1986). *A guide to heart & lung health at the workplace*. NIH Publication No. 86-2210, Bethesda, Md.
5. Bray, G.A., Gray, D.S. (1988). Obesity, part 1—Pathogenesis. *Western Journal of Medicine,* 149: 429-441.
6. Caton, J.R., Mole, P.A., Adams, W.C., & Heustis, D.S. (1988). Body comp analysis by bioelectrical impedance: Effect of skin temperature. *Medicine & Science in Sports & Exercise,* 20: 489-491.
7. McArdle, W.D., Katch, F.I., & Katch, V.L. (1990). *Exercise physiology, energy, nutrition & performance*. (3rd ed.). Philadelphia: Lea & Febiger.
8. Lohman, T.G., Roche, A.F., & Martorell, R. (Eds.) (1988). *Anthropometric standardization reference manual*. Champaign, Ill.: Human Kinetics Pub.
9. Durnin, J.V.G.A., & Womersley, J. (1974). Body fat assessed from total body density and its estimation from skinfold thicknesses: Measurements on 481 men & women aged 16-72 years. *British Journal of Nutrition,* 32: 77-97.
10. Jackson, A.S., Pollock, M.L. (1978). Generalized equations for predicting body density of men. *British Journal of Nutrition,* 40: 497-504.

11. Blair, S.N., Kohl, H.W., Paffenbarger, R.S., Clark, D.G., Cooper, K.H., & Gibbons, L.W. (1989). Physical fitness and all cause mortality: prospective study of healthy men & women. *Journal of the American Medical Association,* 262: 2395-2401.

12. Pollock, M.,L., & Wilmore, J.H. (1990). *Exercise in health & disease, evaluation & prescription for prevention & rehabilitation.* (2nd ed.). Philadelphia: W.B. Saunders Co.

13. Reeves, B.D., & Darby, L.A. (1991). Comparison of VO_2 and MR responses of college females during graded exercise tests: Treadmill vs dance exercise (Abstract). *Medicine and Science in Sports and Exercise Supplement,* 23:4.

14. Mcintosh, M. (1990). *Lifetime aerobics.* Dubuque, Ia.: Wm. Brown Pub.

15. McSwegan, P., Pemberton, C., Petray, C., & Going, S. (1989). *Physical best: The AAHPERD guide to physical fitness education and assessment.* Reston, Va.: AAHPERD.

16. Balke, B. (1963). *A simple field test for the assessment of physical fitness.* CARI Report 64-6. Oklahoma City, Civil Aeromedical Research Institute, Federal Aviation Agency.

17. Cooper, K.H. (1968). *Aerobics.* New York: M. Evans & Co. Pub.

18. Kline, G.M., Porcari, J.P., Hintermeister, R., Freedson, P.S., Ward, A., McCarron, R.F., Ross, J., & Rippe, J.M. (1987). Estimation of VO_2 max from a one mile track walk, gender, age & body weight. *Medicine and Science in Sports and Exercise,* 19: 253-259.

19. Clark, D.H. (1975). *Exercise physiology.* Englewood Cliffs, N.J.: Prentice Hall.

20. *Canadian standardized test of fitness operations manual* (3rd ed.). Ottawa, Ontario, Canada: Fitness & Amateur Sport.

21. Jackson, A., Watkins, M., & Patton, R. (1988). A factor analysis of twelve selected maximal isotonic strength performances on the universal gym. *Medicne and Science in Sports and Exercise,* 12: 274-277.

22. Gettman, L.R. (1988). Fitness testing. In Blair, S., Painter, P., Pate, R., Smith, L., & Taylor, C. (Eds.) *Resource manual for guidelines for exercise testing and prescription,* Philadelphia: Lea & Febiger, 168.

23. Melleby, A. (1992). *The Y's way to a healthy back.* Piscataway, N.J.: New Century Pub., 23.

24. Thiel, J.E. (1985). Body composition. In Aerobics and Fitness Association of America (Ed.), *Aerobics: Theory & Practice,* 70.

Sample Informed Consent

PLEASE READ THE FOLLOWING CONSENT FORM AND IF YOU WISH TO PROCEED WITH YOUR EXERCISE TEST, SIGN WHERE INDICATED.

The exercise test which you will perform consists of either riding a specially designed bicycle ergometer, or stepping on a 12-inch step. The purpose of this test is to examine the response of your heart and lungs to submaximal exercise and recovery. In this way we hope to determine how much work you can do and what can be done to improve your physical condition.

Complications have been few during exercise tests, especially those of a submaximal nature. If a person exercising is not tolerating work well, it usually becomes apparent and exercise is stopped; however, you are urged to report any unusual symptoms during the test. You may request that the test be stopped at any time. Mild lightheadedness and even fainting may occur, and there is a slight risk of cardiovascular complications such as abnormal blood pressure or a heart attack. Every effort has been made to minimize these risks by evaluation of your medical history form. If you have any health conditions, especially related to heart or lung function, please be sure to let us know before testing begins.

My questions have been answered concerning the fitness test, I have read and understand the above statements and hereby consent to participate.

_____
(Name, please print)

_____
(Signature)

_____
(Date)

_____
(Witness)

Sample Physician's Clearance Form

Please return this form to: wellness director / personal trainer

Address _____Phone_____

I have examined _____ on _____
                        (client's name)   (date of last exam)

I have found the following:

_____She/he may participate fully in a physical activity program consisting of cardiovascular, strength and flexibility training without limitation.

_____She/he may participate in a physical activity program with the following limitations (please include a brief description of any medical condition which might affect his/her program).

If your patient is on any medication which may affect the heart rate or blood pressure response to exercise (elevating or suppressing) please indicate:

Physician's signature_____ Date_____

Please note: This record must be stamped with physician's official stamp or be accompanied by a typed letter on a physician's letterhead, documenting that a medical evaluation has been performed on the named client. The physician's clearance form will not be accepted without such proper verification.

Sample Medical History Form

Name _____ Date_____

Telephone_____

Date of birth_____age_____height_____weight_____

In case of Emergency, contact:_____relationship_____

Address_____phone_____

Physician _____Specialty _____

Address _____phone_____

Are you currently under a doctor's care? ☐ Yes ☐ No

If yes, explain:_____

Date of last physician check-up: _____

Have you ever had a stress test? ☐ Yes ☐ No ☐ Don't know

If yes, were the results: ☐ Normal ☐ Abnormal

Do you take any medications on a regular basis? ☐ Yes ☐ No

If yes, please list medications and reasons for taking _____

Have you been recently hospitalized? ☐ Yes ☐ No

If yes, please explain:_____

Do you smoke?	☐ Yes	☐ No
Have high blood pressure	☐ Yes	☐ No
Have high cholesterol	☐ Yes	☐ No
Diabetes	☐ Yes	☐ No

Have parents or siblings who prior to age 55 had a:

Heart Attack	☐ Yes	☐ No
Stroke	☐ Yes	☐ No
High blood pressure	☐ Yes	☐ No
High cholesterol	☐ Yes	☐ No
Have known heart disease	☐ Yes	☐ No
Rheumatic heart disease	☐ Yes	☐ No
Heart murmur	☐ Yes	☐ No
Chest pain with exertion	☐ Yes	☐ No
Irregular heartbeat or palpitations	☐ Yes	☐ No
Lightheadedness or fainting	☐ Yes	☐ No
Emphysema	☐ Yes	☐ No
Other metabolic disorders (thyroid, kidney, etc.)	☐ Yes	☐ No
Epilepsy	☐ Yes	☐ No
Asthma	☐ Yes	☐ No
Back pain: upper middle lower	☐ Yes	☐ No
Other joint pain (explain)	☐ Yes	☐ No
Muscle pain or injury (explain)	☐ Yes	☐ No
Are you pregnant?	☐ Yes	☐ No

I attest that the above information is true to the best of my knowledge.

Signature _____Date _____

Table 33-2a. Percent Fat Estimations For Women

Age (years)

Sum of three skinfolds	18-22	23-27	28-32	33-37	38-42	43-47	48-52	53-57	>57
8-12	8.0	9.0	9.2	9.4	9.5	9.7	9.9	10.1	10.3
13-17	10.8	10.9	11.1	11.3	11.5	11.7	11.8	12.0	12.2
18-22	12.6	12.8	13.0	13.2	13.4	13.5	13.7	13.9	14.1
23-27	14.5	14.6	14.8	15.0	15.2	15.4	15.6	15.7	15.9
28-32	16.2	16.4	16.6	16.8	17.0	17.1	17.3	17.5	17.7
33-37	17.9	18.1	18.3	18.5	18.7	18.9	19.0	19.2	19.4
38-42	19.6	19.8	20.0	20.2	20.3	20.5	20.7	20.9	21.1
43-47	21.2	21.4	21.6	21.8	21.9	22.1	22.3	22.5	22.7
48-52	22.8	22.9	32.1	23.3	23.5	23.7	23.8	24.0	24.2
53-57	24.4	24.4	24.6	24.8	25.0	25.2	25.3	25.5	25.7
58-62	25.7	25.9	26.0	26.2	26.4	26.6	26.8	27.0	27.1
63-67	27.1	27.2	27.4	27.6	27.8	28.0	28.2	28.3	28.5
68-72	28.4	28.6	28.7	28.9	29.1	29.3	29.5	29.7	29.8
73-77	29.6	29.8	30.0	30.2	30.4	30.6	30.7	30.9	31.3
78-82	30.9	31.0	31.2	31.4	31.6	31.8	31.9	32.1	32.3
83-87	30.0	32.2	32.4	32.6	32.7	32.9	33.1	33.3	33.5
88-92	33.1	33.3	33.5	33.7	33.8	34.0	34.2	34.4	34.6
93-97	34.2	34.4	34.5	34.7	34.9	35.1	35.2	35.4	35.6
98-102	35.1	35.3	35.5	35.7	35.9	36.0	36.2	36.6	36.8
103-107	36.1	36.2	36.4	36.6	36.8	37.0	37.2	37.3	37.5
108-112	36.9	37.1	37.3	37.5	37.7	37.9	38.0	38.2	38.4
113-117	37.9	38.9	38.1	38.3	39.2	39.4	39.6	39.8	39.5
118-122	38.5	38.7	38.9	39.1	39.4	39.6	39.8	40.0	40.0
123-127	39.2	39.4	49.6	39.8	40.0	40.2	40.3	40.5	40.7
133-137	40.5	40.7	40.8	41.0	41.2	41.4	41.6	41.7	41.9
138-142	41.0	41.2	41.4	41.6	41.7	41.9	42.1	42.3	42.5
143-147	41.5	41.7	41.9	42.0	42.2	42.4	42.6	42.8	43.0
153-157	42.3	42.5	42.6	52.8	43.0	43.2	43.4	43.6	43.4
158-162	42.6	42.8	42.0	43.1	43.4	43.5	43.7	43.9	44.1
163-167	42.9	43.0	43.2	43.4	43.6	43.8	44.0	44.1	44.3
168-172	43.1	43.2	43.4	43.6	43.8	44.0	44.2	44.3	44.5
173-177	43.2	43.4	43.6	43.8	43.9	44.1	44.3	44.5	44.7
178-182	43.3	43.5	43.7	43.8	44.0	44.2	44.4	44.6	44.8

Table 33-2b. Percent Fat Estimations For Men

Age (years)

Sum of three skinfolds	18-22	23-27	28-32	33-37	38-42	43-47	48-52	53-57	>57
8-12	1.8	2.6	3.4	4.2	4.9	5.7	6.5	7.3	8.1
13-17	3.6	4.4	5.2	6.0	6.8	7.6	8.4	9.1	9.9
18-22	5.4	6.2	7.0	7.8	8.6	9.3	10.1	10.9	11.7
23-27	7.1	7.9	8.7	9.5	10.3	11.1	11.9	12.6	13.4
28-32	8.8	9.6	10.4	11.2	12.0	12.8	13.5	14.3	15.1
33-37	10.4	11.2	12.0	12.8	13.6	14.4	15.2	15.9	16.7
38-42	12.0	12.8	13.6	14.4	15.2	15.9	16.7	17.5	18.3
43-47	13.5	14.3	15.1	15.9	16.7	17.5	18.3	19.0	19.8
48-52	15.0	15.8	16.6	17.4	18.1	18.9	19.8	20.5	21.3
53-61	17.8	18.5	19.3	20.1	20.9	21.7	22.5	23.3	24.1
63-67	19.1	19.9	20.6	21.4	22.2	23.0	23.8	24.5	25.4
68-72	20.3	21.1	21.9	22.7	23.5	23.8	25.1	25.8	26.6
73-77	21.5	22.3	23.1	23.9	24.7	25.5	26.3	27.0	27.8
78-82	22.7	23.5	24.3	25.0	25.8	26.6	27.4	28.2	29.0
83-87	23.8	24.6	26.4	27.2	28.0	28.8	29.6	30.3	31.1
88-92	24.8	25.6	26.4	27.2	28.0	28.8	29.6	30.3	31.1
93-97	25.8	26.6	27.4	28.2	29.0	29.8	30.5	31.3	32.3
98-102	26.7	27.5	28.3	29.1	29.9	30.7	31.5	32.3	33.4
103-107	27.6	28.0	29.2	30.0	30.8	31.6	32.4	33.2	33.9
108-112	28.5	29.3	30.1	30.8	31.6	32.4	33.2	34.0	34.8
113-117	29.3	30.0	30.8	31.6	32.4	33.2	32.0	34.8	35.6
118-122	30.0	30.8	31.6	32.4	33.1	33.9	34.7	35.5	36.3
123-127	30.7	31.5	32.3	33.0	33.8	34.6	35.4	36.2	37.0
128-132	31.3	32.1	32.9	33.7	34.4	35.2	36.0	36.8	37.6
133-137	31.9	32.7	33.4	42.2	45.0	35.8	36.6	37.4	38.2
138-142	32.4	33.6	34.4	35.2	36.0	36.8	37.6	38.4	39.2
143-147	32.9	33.6	34.4	35.2	36.0	36.8	37.6	38.4	39.2
148-152	33.3	34.1	34.8	35.6	36.4	37.2	38.0	38.8	39.6
153-157	33.6	34.4	35.2	36.0	36.8	37.6	38.4	39.2	39.9
158-162	33.9	34.7	35.5	36.3	37.1	37.9	38.7	39.5	40.3
163-167	34.2	35.0	35.8	36.3	37.4	38.1	38.9	39.7	40.5
168-172	34.4	35.2	36.0	36.8	37.6	38.4	39.1	39.9	40.7
173-177	34.6	35.3	36.1	36.9	37.8	38.5	39.2	40.1	40.9
178-182	34.7	35.4	36.2	37.0	37.8	38.6	39.4	40.2	42.1

Source: Jackson and Pollack, 1985. Reprinted from the May 1985 issue of *The Physician and Sportsmedicine* by special permission from McGraw-Hill, Inc. Copyright 1990 by McGraw-Hill, Inc.

Table 33-3. Standard Values For Bench Press Strength In 1-RM Lb/Lb Body Weight

Rating	20-29	30-39	40-49	50-59	60+
		Age (years)			
WOMEN					
Excellent	>0.78	>0.66	>0.61	>0.54	>0.55
Good	.72 - .77	.62 - .65	.57 - .60	.51 - .53	.51 - .54
Average	.59 - .71	.53 - .61	.48 - .56	.43 - .50	.41 - .50
Fair	.53 - .58	.49 - .52	.44 - 47	.40 - 42	.37 - 40
Poor	<0.52	<0.48	<0.43	<0.39	<0.36
MEN					
Excellent	>1.26	>1.08	>0.97	>0.86	>0.78
Good	1.17 - 1.25	1.01 - 1.07	.91 - .96	.81 - .85	.74 - .77
Average	.97 - 1.16	.86 - 1.00	.78 - .90	.70 - .80	.64 - .73
Fair	.88 - .96	.79 - .85	.72 - .77	.65 - .69	.60 - .63
Poor	<0.87	<0.78	<0.71	<0.64	<0.59

Reprinted with permission from the Cooper Institute for Aerobics Research, *Physical Fitness Specialist Manual*, 1980.

Table 33-4. Norms For Abdominal Crunch Test (1 Min)

Rating	20-29	30-39	40-49	50-59	60+
		Age (years)			
WOMEN					
Excellent	53-66	48-59	41-50	35-43	29-36
Good	42-52	37-37	32-40	27-34	23-28
Average	30-42	25-36	22-31	17-26	15-22
Fair	16-29	13-24	12-21	8-16	6-14
Poor	0-15	0-12	0-11	0-7	0-5
MEN					
Excellent	58-71	53-64	47-57	41-50	35-43
Good	47-47	41-52	37-46	32-40	28-34
Average	35-46	28-40	26-36	22-31	19-27
Fair	20-34	14-27	14-25	12-21	10-18
Poor	0-19	0-13	0-13	0-11	0-9

Counseling for Body Composition Changes

34

Paula Besson, MEd

COUNSELING AND SUPPORTING THE CLIENT who wishes to significantly reduce body fat is a great challenge for the personal trainer. The statistics pointing to long term maintenance of weight loss are not very encouraging. But by keeping the focus on achieving health rather than slimness, the personal trainer may be in a most advantageous position to positively impact an overfat client's physical and emotional well-being.

The Quest to Lose

The quest to lose body fat is a topic of great interest to a wide audience ranging from elite athletes to severely obese individuals at significant risk of developing a variety of obesity related illnesses. In response to this interest, the past decade has produced a weight loss industry which has experienced a steadily increasing growth. In 1989, approximately 65 million Americans spent an estimated 32 billion dollars on products or services related to losing weight. (1) This estimate is expected to increase to 51 billion dollars by 1995.(2) In spite of the thriving weight loss industry and the continued high interest in losing weight, approximately 60-70 million American adults and 10-12 million American teenagers are considered overfat.(3) Also discouraging is the fact that most dieters who do manage to lose weight often regain the lost weight in a few years.(4)

Obesity is defined by the American College of Sports Medicine as the percent of body fat that increases the risk of disease.(5) Although moderate excess fat is not harmful, values considered to be excess relative to health risk are values that exceed 20% body fat for men and 30% body fat for women respectively.(6) Obesity can be a dangerous medical condition which increases the risk of coronary heart disease through its influence on blood pressure, diabetes, blood lipid and lipoproteins levels.(7) Other diseases associated with obesity include stroke, gallbladder and renal disease.(8)

To address these health risks, trainers will need to develop weight loss programs that are based on current scientific research, as well as reflect an understanding of the dynamics of human behavior the past 10 to 12 years, Americans have been trying to achieve weight loss through programs that emphasize cheap, quick and easy methods. De-emphasizing short term goals, and encouraging patience, may be necessary prerequisites regardless of the type

---

NOT FAIR

Although research has provided much credible information on successful methods of weight loss, as yet there is no unifying theory to explain human variability, and why some people become too fat, while others who eat more calories do not. (9)

of program implemented. Early focus needs to be placed on the repetition of positive behaviors rather than the amount of weight lost.

The Energy Balance Equation

Although much research is still needed, and numerous controversial issues exist, there is general support for the Energy Balance Equation. The Energy Balance Equation states "Body mass will stay constant when calorie intake equals energy expenditure," (10) There are, of course, several variables that influence this equation, and the manipulation of those variables are ultimately what will determine the loss (negative energy balance) or gain (positive energy balance) of body fat.

Creating a "Negative Energy Balance"

To create a negative energy balance equal to one pound of lost fat, 3500 calories must be used in the form of energy expenditure. To understand ways to best influence a negative energy balance, we must look at the function and variability of resting metabolic rate. Simply stated, resting metabolic rate (RMR) is described as the rate of calorie expenditure while at rest. Understanding the influence that eating and exercise exert on RMR is a key component to developing a successful weight loss program. The recommendations that follow discuss the interrelationship and influence of the many variables that have been shown to affect RMR and subsequent weight loss. RMR can be influenced by both caloric restriction and caloric expenditure. It is recommended that a negative energy balance be shared equally between diet and exercise.(11)

To Gain One Pound of Fat

Ingest—and don't use—3500 calories

Counseling Recommendations for Effective Weight Loss

1. Avoid restrictive calorie diets and fasting.

Although seemingly a logical approach to creating a negative energy balance, scientific investigation has repeatedly shown that restrictive calorie diets produce a rapid reduction in RMR.(12) This reduction may be as dramatic as 45%.(13) RMR accounts for as high as 70% of daily energy expenditure. This reduction, therefore, represents a significant decline in daily caloric need. During periods of low calorie intake the energy production of the various systems within the body decrease energy production in their attempt to adapt to the lower caloric intake.(14) This adaptation occurs in an attempt to conserve energy for future needs.(15) This of course is counterproductive in attempting to lose weight.

2. Avoid quick weight loss.

Quick weight loss results in little or no fat loss. The weight lost by a quick weight loss program represents a loss of mostly carbohydrate and water. One gram of carbohydrate requires 2.7 grams of water for it to be stored in the body. (16) Lean body mass is also lost as a result of a quick weight loss program. This diminishment in lean body mass results in a decreased need for calories.(17)

3. Perform aerobic and strengthening exercise regularly.

Many studies have shown that the adoption of a physical activity program is the best predictor of long term weight loss and subsequent maintenance.(18) Since RMR is directly related to the ratio of lean body mass, (19) resistance

---

Research has shown that as body fat decreases, RMR increases. (21)

training should be highly recommended as an essential component of the weight loss program. Resistance Training has been perhaps the most underemphasized component of the comprehensive weight loss program. Aerobic activity has long been recommended as a way to significantly increase energy expenditure. The body uses large amounts of fuel in aerobic activity. The exact amount of calories used is highly variable but may represent between 20-40% of daily energy expenditure. (20) Aerobic activity also influences weight loss by its use of fat as fuel.

4. Follow a diet high in carbohydrate and low in fat.

Americans consume between 37% (22) and 42% (23) of their daily calories from fat and some report intakes as high as 60%. Fat supplies more than twice the calories of carbohydrate and protein and provides a lower thermogenic effect during digestion. The thermogenic effect refers to the net amount of calories assimilated by the body after the process of digestion. As much as 28% of the calories of carbohydrate is used in the process of digestion, as opposed to about 7% for digesting dietary fat. (24)

Summary

There is clearly no single cause of obesity, (25) and the degree of body fat that may be lost and maintained involves the manipulation of many factors. Weight loss is influenced to a high degree by human variability and genetic predisposition. (26) Increases in the amount of calories burned through regular aerobic activity, participating in progressive resistance training exercise, and eating a moderate calorie, low fat diet, are probably the most important factors in losing and maintaining fat loss.

Initially, clients should be reinforced for their exercise behaviors rather than the amount of weight lost. Integration of these new behaviors over time may be the key to weight loss success.

References

American College of Sports Medicine (1991). *Guidelines for exercise testing and prescription* (4th. ed.). Philadelphia: Lea and Febiger, (5) 171, (18) 195.

American College of Sports Medicine (1988). *Resource manual for guidelines for exercise testing and prescription.* Philadelphia: Lea and Febiger, (7) 355, (19) 357.

Howley, E., & Powers, S. (1990). *Exercise physiology: theory and application to fitness and performance.* Dubuque, Ia.: Wm. C. Brown Publishing. (11) 404, (14)(15)(16)(17)(20)(21) 395-400, (23) 377, (25)(26) 391-392.

Katch, F., & McArdle, W. (1988). *Nutrition, weight control and exercise.* Philadelphia: Lea and Febiger, (3) 155, (6)(8)(10) 138-139, (13) 167.

35 Overcoming Client Dependency

Sheila King, MS

Focus

ONE OF THE CHIEF LONG TERM GOALS that personal fitness trainers work toward with their clients is the acquisition of independently driven healthy lifestyle behaviors. That is characterized by clients learning to perform their workouts for themselves, not for their trainers. Up to that point, it is not uncommon for clients to grow overly dependent upon their trainers. As a result, it is up to professional trainers to alert themselves to dependency warning signals and intervene with some positive changes.

What is Dependency?

Consider this situation: as a personal trainer you've been working with a female client for six months. She is making great progress in losing weight and achieving her fitness goals. There is one problem: if either you or she goes on vacation, she doesn't exercise. Nor does she exercise between sessions with you. When you question her about this she replies, "I just can't do it without you; you're so great, I really need you here to motivate me."

As complimentary as these words are, they signal trouble. Although she may be doing well as far as exercise is concerned, this client suffers from trainer dependency (see Checklist).

Trainer dependency is the unrealistic expectation on the part of clients that their personal trainer is solely responsible for their fitness. Without the motivation and supervision provided by their trainer, many clients will not follow through on their commitment to exercise. They have not learned one of the most important lessons fitness instructors can teach and that is self-responsibility for their own health behaviors.

Self-responsibility means that the client, and only the client, must take credit for success and setbacks. A self-responsible person has internalized the knowledge and skills provided and is able to implement an exercise program with little external motivation provided by the trainer. Without self-responsibility, the client is ultimately destined to fail, and so are you. There will always be someone or something else the client can blame for lack of progress toward personal health goals. That someone might turn out to be you.

It is tempting to think we as trainers have all the answers to our client's health problems. This is a common attitude among inexperienced trainers or veterans who think that their approach to training is somehow unique and different providing the ultimate edge for their clients. Other trainers profess to be fitness gurus possessing a unique ability to understand the client or be totally available to them.

Rescuer

These attitudes and beliefs can only engender in clients a perception of the trainer as a "rescuer" on whom they can depend to solve their myriad of health and fitness problems. In reality, it is the client who is ultimately responsible. Positioning yourself as the primary agent of change for the client will have negative effects. (1) Trainers in this situation will become distressed at their lack of control over the situation and begin blaming themselves for the lack of progress in the program. They may question their skills and program strategies. This involvement can lead to "burnout" rapidly. It is unlikely that any one trainer or program will provide the client with lifetime success. As health and fitness professionals, our long term objective is to teach the client the skills and knowledge they will need to continue pursuing a lifetime habit of exercise.

Burnout

Examine Your Role as Health Facilitator

A facilitator is someone who frees a situation of difficulties or obstacles and makes the process of behavior change easier. As a health facilitator the trainer will assist the client in the process of behavior change as related to exercise.

The first step in teaching a client self-responsibility is for the trainer to be very clear about his or her role. The responsibility of the personal trainer is to provide a client with skills, knowledge and motivation to achieve and maintain exercise-related fitness goals. This includes developing a program that will instill in the client a sense of self-efficacy which is important for relapse prevention (1). In doing so, the personal trainer provides the client with the tools for maintaining a life-long habit of exercise. In essence, you are preparing the client from the outset for the time they will no longer need your full-time assistance to maintain their exercise habit. If you are very clear about your role in this relationship, the client can begin the process of behavior change with a mindset toward self-reliance. They can begin seeing the big picture and start the program with an independent attitude. Goals should be specific, clearly defined and realistic to enhance the feelings of self-accomplishment and success (2).

Self-Reliance

Fostering Self-Management Behaviors

It is very important to involve the client in the exercise prescription process from the beginning (3). Instead of the trainer designing the program it should be the client who designs the program with your guidance. They can then take ownership of the program and begin to learn the valuable skill of exercise prescription. Begin homework assignments immediately. Have the client practice some form of exercise like stretching by themselves between sessions. Reinforce their independent exercise behavior by asking them how they enjoyed the exercise and if they want to review any of the techniques.

Designing the program

Emphasize that the goal for the program is to assist the client in achieving and maintaining life-long fitness. Since it is unrealistic to think that you will be with that person to motivate them for the rest of their lives, it is prudent to develop a plan for reviewing your involvement in the program and your role in assisting them. Three months often works well from a physiologic and behavioral point of view.

Three month review

First evaluate progress toward goals stated in the initial interview, providing reinforcement for positive changes. Then in planning the next stage, re-evaluate your role in assisting them. Be sure not to give the client the impression that you are trying to get rid of them or are abandoning them. Always let them know you are available to them and that you will not leave them before they

Group support

are ready to implement the program on their own. Slowly decrease the number of sessions per week and then plan periodic checks. Clients may need to seek additional help with their exercise programs throughout their lifetimes and you may give them clear guidelines as to when they might seek additional help (i.e. they haven't exercised in a month or they've gained five pounds). Periodic phone calls from you to check on their progress is also a nice touch. Long term compliance may improve if clients feel they haven't failed when they seek additional help with their program.

Be aware of the dialogue between you and your client. If clients make comments about how instrumental you are in their success, acknowledge the praise and reinforce the concept that *they* are the one making all the changes and should receive the accolades. Responses such as "Thanks, I'm glad I can help but remember *you* are the ones making changes and becoming more fit. You deserve the praise."

Assist the client in developing a network of exercising companions. Consider a "two for one" session to orient a friend to the exercise program. Don't be afraid to encourage your client to join a group exercise program if you feel they need group support and motivation. Groups have been found to be a powerful means of motivation and encouragement for long term behavior change. Get to know other professional trainers in your area whom you trust and respect and consider exchanging clients once in a while to allow the client to see fitness from another professional's perspective. For example you may be a specialist in interval training techniques. Clients may benefit from the additional knowledge and skills obtained while you may benefit by introducing variety and avoiding burnout. This type of approach will reinforce in the client that there is no one person who can "do it for them" but that with help they can "do it themselves."

CHECKLIST

Symptoms of Trainer Dependency

You may need to re-examine your role if your client:

- *Refuses to exercise if you are on vacation or ill.*

- *Won't work with a substitute trainer.*

- *Attributes their health improvements to your involvement.*

- *Looks to you for more than basic psychological support or nutrition education.*

- *Expresses a need for more rather than less of your involvement as the months progress.*

References

1. Foster, G.D. (Jan./Feb., 1992). Reasonable expectations for clients and practitioners. *The Weight Control Digest,* 2:1: 133-136.
2. Rejeski, W.J., & Kenny, E.A. (1988). *Fitness motivation: Preventing participant dropout.* Champaign, Ill.: Life Enhancement Publications.
3. Blair, S.N., Painter, P., Pate, R.R., Smith, L.K., & Taylor, C.B. (Eds.) (1988). *American College of Sports Medicine, Resource Manual for Guidelines for Exercise Testing and Prescription.* Philadelphia: Lea & Febiger, 323-344.

Part 6

Business and Leadership Skills

Basic Skills

Personnel

Marketing

Legal Considerations

Directing Programs

Basic Business Skills

36

Managing a Fitness Facility

Penny Reeves-Goff

Focus

THIS CHAPTER IS DESIGNED TO GIVE YOU an overview of basic business skills. Meeting with business leaders in your community, reading business publications including books and magazines, and consulting with other business persons in the fitness industry are highly recommended.

Beyond Survival: Making Your Business Thrive

In one of my favorite business books, *The E Myth,* author Michael Gerber writes about a "Fatal Assumption" that people make when they decide to start a business: "If you understand the technical work of a business, you understand a business that does that technical work." In the fitness industry we see this "Fatal Assumption" played out time and time again. The sheer number of aerobics or fitness businesses that close their doors each year is proof. In other words, because you are good at teaching aerobic classes and enjoy working with people to improve their fitness levels, doesn't mean you understand the business that provides aerobics and fitness instruction. Many fitness professionals make the jump from instructor or trainer to management or ownership without considering the basic skills necessary to run a business effectively.

As a business owner or manager, you may be responsible for class scheduling; hiring and firing; training (instructors, front desk, baby sitters, etc.); making and enforcing policy; marketing; promoting; advertising; financial aspects like payroll, bill paying, tax filing; budgeting; cleaning the facility or making sure someone else does it correctly; and a myriad of other general office duties that may pertain to your business. Even if you hire someone to do some of these jobs, you will oversee each area because you are ultimately responsible.

It is extremely important to make a realistic assessment of your individual skills before embarking into management or ownership. This will enable you to devote your energies and talents to those jobs you are good at and enjoy. Teaching eight classes a week is a far cry from directing a program or owning and operating a business. While all that teaching experience helps, when you own or manage a business, you may find that you no longer have time to teach. You're too busy cleaning bathrooms, working the front desk, babysitting when the sitter doesn't show up, working on budgets . . . you get the picture? The experience you have now as an instructor will enable you to be good in that one area of operation, but you'll need to either become well-versed in the other areas or hire people who are.

Personal Skills

- *Recognize your weaknesses.*
- *Capitalize on your strengths.*

A "mission statement" can help you chart your course in the business world. A mission statement is a short paragraph or sentence that describes what the business is all about—the vision of what the business is and will become. The mission statement of the business must be compatible with your own personal goals and standards. Mission statements are important because every decision you make, every policy you create, everything you do in the business, must contribute to that vision. If your personal goals and standards are different from those of your business, whether it's your own business or a business you're managing, you'll find your job is suddenly at odds with what's important to you. Being in harmony with the long term goals of a business means quality job performance, an enjoyable work environment and great personal satisfaction.

Components of a Successful Business and Necessary Skills

1. Customer Skills

We are in a service business and that means we need a keen understanding of just who our customers are, what their needs are and what we can do to continue to meet those needs. Too often owners and managers get so involved in the day-to-day running of a business that they overlook the very reason for the business. Viewing the customer as an obstacle to work around will not bring success. Customers are the purpose of our business. Stay close to your customers; take time to listen to them after class. Work at the desk; answer the phones; be available when they want to talk to you.

Make information available

Give your customers information about your business. Operating policies, class schedules and descriptions, methods of membership payment, other services offered like babysitting or personal training, all help your customers. Most problems arise from misunderstandings. An informed customer will be less likely to have problems with the policies of your business. Keep records of all transactions with customers in alphabetical files. Include membership payments, complaints, bounced checks, problems, etc. If a customer is habitually causing a problem or violating rules or asking you to bend the rules, you'll have a record of it and will be able to discuss it with him or her in private.

Be consistent in the way you treat customers. Don't fall all over them during their first visit and then rarely speak to them after they sign up. Consider every company procedure/policy from the viewpoint of a customer. Try and make the process hassle-free. If the experience with your business is not consistent—if customers can't depend on getting what they've paid for every single time—they'll go somewhere else.

2. Leadership/Communication Skills

As an owner or manager, it is imperative that you develop effective leadership and communication skills if your business is to function successfully. Your primary job as a business owner or manager is to lead and create a desirable working environment. Lead by effective communication and example. What you do and what you say, how you do it and say it, communicates your ideas, philosophies, policies, expectations, dreams, dissatisfactions, disappointments, concerns, and caring.

3. Planning Skills

Planning is done before, during, and after a business operation has begun. Planning and follow through are critical to the long-term success of a business. What is most difficult is taking the time to plan. Often the best way to make certain planning gets done is to "get away." It may take a whole day or a whole week. Planning meetings must include key personnel and management and business owners.

Business Plan. Short term and long term: Your business plan reflects your mission, your long-term vision of what the company is trying to become. The plan should contain your specific objectives and the operational strategies or courses of action needed to get there.

Operational Plan. Must be specific within each department: front desk, instructor training, main office, weight room, retail. It should include the specific action that needs to be taken in each department to meet the objectives. What you'll do next month, next week, tomorrow, right now. Operational planning consists of all the big and small details that can't be overlooked if you're to meet your specific objectives.

Financial Plan. Reflects the financial mission: The financial plan is your long-term vision of what your company is trying to become in financial terms. It consists of the specific objectives and the operational strategies or courses of action needed to get there. How much money do you want to make? How much do you need to make each day, week, month to achieve that goal? How many customers do you need/at what price per membership? What will it cost to get and service those members? Are there any other sources of income? In any business, income is the bottom line. Regardless of the quality of instruction or the high tech equipment or the spacious locker rooms, if your business doesn't make enough money, you simply can't stay in business.

Even if you don't enjoy working with numbers, you must understand the budgeting process, and you must get involved in budgeting. Many software companies have computer programs that actually make budgeting easy! These programs let you run numbers and create a budget for any department. Let's say you want to see clothing at your facility. You set up a budget and run your numbers to see how long it's going to take you to break even or to make a profit. Then compare numbers: your "Pro forma" or projected budget to your actual monthly **Profit and Loss** statements and make adjustments. Is clothing profitable for your business? The numbers don't lie! Looking at the monthly P and L statements (a list of monthly income versus the expenses) can tell you if something is making money or costing money. It can show expenses that are increasing, expenses that are holding the line, trends in revenues and expenses, etc.

Marketing Plan. Who are your customers and what do they want? Marketing starts, ends, lives and dies with your customer. What you want is unimportant. It's what your customer wants that's important, and sometimes what your customer wants is different from what you think. Your Marketing Plan will reflect how you are going to tell your customers about your business. What is the position of your business in the marketplace? What image do you want your company to project? This image must also reflect the perceived needs of your customers. Your services must be marketed to customers with a position and image that lets them know you'll be meeting their needs. Differentiate yourself from your competitors by emphasizing your unique strengths and benefits.

Many new businesses fail because of insufficient capitalization or working capital. If you are just starting a business, make sure you borrow or have the ability to borrow enough funds to see you through initial growth stages. If you are borrowing money from a lending institution, they will want to see a detailed financial plan including projections of income and expenses, as well as an ability to pay back the loan if things don't turn out as projected.

Budget and Advertising Plan. Create a budget for advertising and be picky about where and how often you advertise. Advertising can be expensive, but if it reaches your target market and causes them to take action, it's well worth the dollars spent. Don't forget the free mileage your business can get through good public relations. Effective public relation skills include establishing contacts with the various media (TV, radio, newspapers, magazines) in your community. Establish positive connections with area businesses and prominent community organizations. Make yourself or a staff member available as a speaker for these businesses and organizations. These media contacts and speaking engagements help to create high name identification for your business. In addition, they reinforce your company's "expert" and "service" image in the eyes of the community.

Remember that the best form of advertising is word of mouth, and your best advertisers are your current customers. Look at all promotions from the viewpoint of regular customers and analyze each promotion before initiating it. Make your promotions easy to understand, for the customer and your staff. If your marketing plan includes sales promotions and incentives for staff, again look at these promotions from the viewpoint of a staff member and analyze before beginning the promotions. Make staff promotions easy to understand and easy to do.

Summary

This brief overview of business skills is just a start. I encourage you to further your business knowledge and skills through reading, attending business classes, consulting with business leaders and asking questions. It is these skills that will enable your fitness business to stay fiscally fit while you keep your customers physically fit!

Penny Reeves-Goff

37 *Personnel Management*

Focus

ACCORDING TO STATISTICS, one of the main reasons people continue to go to a club or aerobic facility is the staff: the instructors, the front desk person, the babysitters, the weight room staff. It's not the price that keeps customers coming back. It's not the expensive equipment or the suspended floor. It's the people servicing your customers. The staff is responsible for the ultimate success of any fitness business. They are responsible for that all important, one-on-one contact with each person who walks in your door.

In business, you may have heard the phrase "moments of truth." Each business has hundreds of them daily. A moment of truth occurs every time one of your staff interacts with a customer or potential customer. As owner or manager, you are the one who ultimately controls how your staff handles these moments of truth. The following chapter offers tips to help you manage in ways that make every moment of truth a positive, rewarding experience.

Hiring

If you hire the right person for each job, half of your responsibility is met. Never underestimate the importance of the hiring process. Take your time when looking for the right person to fill a position with your company. In addition to an in-depth interview, check references. Ask the reference to give you the names of some co-workers of the applicant and call them for additional testimonials. Find out as much as you can about the person you are interviewing. Ask him or her to explain how they would handle a dissatisfied customer. Ask questions that pertain directly to the position you're trying to fill. Give each applicant a written description of the job they are applying for, and make certain they understand what the job entails. The hiring process must be objective, not subjective. A job description that lists the responsibilities of a particular position enables you to hire the right person to fit the job. Too often, businesses hire a person (usually a friend) and then try and create a job description based on that person's abilities or lack thereof. Never create a job to fit the person.

Salaries, Benefits, Bonuses

Salaries. If you market your facility as a place where clients can receive high quality instruction then you must be ready to pay for highly qualified, competent fitness professionals. Be competitive with fitness instructor salaries in your area. You don't have to pay the highest, but good pay along with other benefits will keep the top instructors and fitness staff committed. I've never heard of a business going broke because they paid their fitness staff too much. If an instructor attracts and keeps customers and is in tune with the philosophy of your company, then he or she is worth a competitive salary.

The right person at your front desk can more than earn his/her salary by the manner in which they handle potential customers who call for information

Your front desk staff is the first contact most people have with your business, either by phone or in person.

or come in to pick up information about your facility. Your front desk staff probably has more "moments of truth" on a daily basis than any other member of your staff. Be willing to pay these people what they are worth!

Benefits and Bonuses. In addition to salaries, your staff may expect benefits and bonuses which are both tangible and intangible. Tangible benefits include workman's compensation insurance; health insurance; paid vacation time; cash bonuses; free in-house workshops for continuing education; music, shoe and clothing discounts at local stores; facility memberships for spouse/children; babysitting during class hours; etc.

Intangible benefits and bonuses include praise, support, and recognition. The intangible benefits are so simple to list, yet they are often the most overlooked. Be generous in your praise to employees who are outstanding in the performance of their jobs. If a member tells you something positive about an employee, pass it along to the employee immediately! Positive feedback encourages more of the behavior that prompted the favorable report. Immediate recognition reinforces and supports that behavior. Publicly recognize employee accomplishments on a staff or facility bulletin board.

Expectations. In playing the board game Monopoly, every participant likes to know the rules. Understanding the rules of the game not only makes the game enjoyable, it also gives it a sense of order. Business is no different. Employees want to know the rules of the game at your business. They want to know exactly what is expected of them. A written job description should be given to each staff member. It should outline the specific responsibilities of the job as well as the compensation for that position. In addition, each employee should receive an employee handbook which includes policies of your company that you and your employees live and work by. Each staff member receives a copy of his or her job description and employee handbook when you hire them. At the job interview, you review both. If an applicant has a problem with any policy, it's better for both of you to know before you hire him.

The organizational chart of your business will accompany the employee handbook. If your business is small, you may have only two or three names filling all the positions, but the organizational chart will describe all the work that's going to be done or is being done when your company is at its full potential. It describes what a particular position is responsible for, what operational duties fall under that position, and who the person in that position reports to—"the buck stops here" theory. Most importantly, the organizational chart lets each member of the staff know who they need to report to in specific areas of the company. Changes in the employee handbook, job descriptions and organizational chart are certain. You need to make sure that all employees receive copies of changes as they occur.

Training. Employee training is a must in the competitive fitness industry. From service training for your front desk staff and national certification for your fitness staff, to child care training for your babysitting staff, more smart businesses are offering in-house training programs and continuing education opportunities to their staff members. Providing opportunities for your certified instructors to receive CEU credits at a reduced cost without having to travel is a wonderful employee benefit. Many fitness facilities offer a scholarship for one instructor to attend an industry convention at the facility's expense. That instructor then reports back to the group as a whole with a mini-workshop on what she/he learned, (new choreography, etc.). It's an opportunity to reward a

| Positive feedback |

| Employee handbook |

loyal, productive instructor and encourage all staff (knowing they may be next to be awarded a scholarship).

Leadership and Communication. The written communication tools you use include the employee handbook, facility operation procedures, service guidelines, job descriptions, and the organizational chart. What you say in these pieces and how you say it conveys your philosophy. Read them from the perspective of your staff or customers and then rewrite them if necessary. Another very effective written communication tool is a weekly or monthly newsletter for employees only. In addition to department updates, the newsletter can let employees know what's going on: news of upcoming promotions, who's doing what, who's had a baby, etc. A simple newsletter of this sort can help create and maintain a team atmosphere even though the morning shift and the evening shift only see each other at staff meetings.

Staff meetings. All employees must be addressed if not monthly, then bimonthly or quarterly. The written agenda for the meetings should include department reports, membership updates, announcements of facility promotions and upcoming trainings, and perhaps even a social hour which enhances team spirit. Staff meetings with key employees or department heads should be held weekly. Be available when an employee calls you. Get back to them within 24 hours if they called and you were unavailable to talk. In all dealings with staff, whether one-on-one or in group meetings, owners and managers must be effective listeners. When listening to staff concerns or problems, repeat what you hear to see if you understand. Ask staff members for input and get them involved. Very often you have a wealth of talented individuals on staff in areas you wouldn't imagine.

> *Schedule creative sessions with your staff to brainstorm new ideas for your business.*

Through your staff newsletter ask for assistance on a project or problem if you need it. Then, act on suggestions you get. Don't ask for advice if you don't plan to use it.

Summary

There is a "pride of ownership" that develops if your staff has regular input. Pride of ownership translates directly into better service given enthusiastically by a staff who knows they are a valuable asset to your business. Better service and involved staff members translate directly into higher revenues and a healthy business environment in which all employees can prosper.

Marketing and Promoting Your Business

38

David Essel, MS

Focus

THIS CHAPTER OUTLINES KEY MARKETING and promotional concepts for instructors and business owners. The question so often asked by fitness professionals worldwide is "How can I continue to grow and watch my business succeed with all the competition that pops up daily?" The answer, which may sound too simple to be true, lies in creating a sound product based on one's abilities and then obtaining consistent and forceful publicity. The ideas that follow have proven to be true whether one is looking to promote one individual or an entire business.

Consistent Positive Publicity

The key presented here is to pay strict attention to how to approach and then work with the media. In many cases there may not be a great difference between the services that two facilities offer or the talents of two people. The difference may be dramatic, however, with regard to who will obtain a consistent amount of coverage for their business. The following three keys can help you design a relationship with the media that will virtually guarantee success for your career.

I. Planning Success with Promotions

A common mistake made by many people in business today is never examining the real strengths of their operations. Without this knowledge and a plan of action, it is almost impossible to consistently sell the media on how you can help them.

    A. Company strengths—List all of your attributes, education, abilities, equipment and staff in short, detailed sentences. Examine this statement and then get feedback from your associates. By doing this, you can formulate a plan with which you can assist the media and their customers.

    B. Plan of action—Locate the various media in your immediate area and state. Obtain names of contact people (including addresses and phone numbers) who can benefit from your knowledge and services. Include electronic (radio, TV) and print (magazines, trade journals, newspapers) representatives. Decide whom to contact and begin today.

C. Publicity calls—call to introduce yourself and/or your business to the right contact person in each area and ask how you can be of assistance. Ask questions concerning the demographics of their clients. Be prepared for some very short answers. Always be courteous and follow up with a letter including suggestions as to how you can help their customers.

D. Financial planning—Set aside a monthly promotional budget to pay for calls, mailing, etc.

II. Promotional Strategies

A. Charity events—By helping others, you always help yourself. Have your name associated with worthwhile charities at least two to four times a year.

B. Press releases—Make certain they are newsworthy and contain a message or facts that are of benefit to the media followers. It is important to know the demographics of each media vehicle you contact. Issue releases on a monthly or quarterly basis.

C. Express Mail—If the message is critical to your business, attract the attention of the press with express mail or a certified letter.

D. Respect deadlines—Upon contacting the media, learn and then jot down the times and days when it would be most effective to call.

III. The Final Plan

A. Ask for help—Involve your staff in planning promotional events that will attract the media's interest. Plan ahead for several months or even an entire year.

B. Feedback from the pros—After forming a relationship with the media, ask for their input with regard to the impact of your press releases and press kits.

C. Be persistent, but polite—It may take months or years for the media you really want to pay attention to you and to respond. Hang in there!

References

Wright, H. (1990). *How to make 1,000 mistakes in business and still succeed.* Illinois: Wright Track.

O'Brien, R. (1977). *Publicity—How to get it.* New York: Harper & Row.

Sara Kooperman, JD

39 Law and Exercise

Focus

THE PURPOSE OF THIS CHAPTER is to give aerobic instructors, personal trainers, fitness facility managers and club owners an overview of legal issues concerning the exercise industry. Legal status, taxes, insurance, standards of care, negligence, incident reports, waivers of liability, informed consent forms, legal music sources, AIDS and discrimination, employment manuals and written employee evaluations will all be addressed. This chapter is in no way meant to substitute for legal advice. It should, however, provide a broad overview of issues surrounding the fitness community.

Legal Status: Employer/Employee/Independent Contractor

Determining your legal status as a fitness professional is extremely important when identifying your legal liability, insurance status and tax responsibilities.

To determine if someone is considered an employee or an independent contractor, the courts look at the theory of "respondent superior." This theory analyzes whether an employee's activities are directly monitored or supervised by his or her employer (i.e., when an employee "responds" to his or her "superior"). The activities looked at include: who actually collects money from the clients, whether the instructor is on the schedule regularly, how the employer controls the work performed by the employee/independent contractor. Does the employer "train" the employee?

When Is An Instructor An Employee?

If a club collects all membership dues and training fees, and the club has the instructor teach specific classes or sessions at regular times, and the club manager regularly trains the staff periodically, the aerobics instructor or personal trainer is identified as an employee. The club or fitness center is liable for injuries surrounding the aerobic instructor's and the personal trainer's activities during his or her job-related activities. This means that the employer would be responsible for paying all legal fees and damage awards should an injured client sue the club/instructor and win. If the club carries insurance, the insurance company would have to pay the legal fees and the damage awards, depending upon the extent of the coverage. Therefore, the club should carry insurance on this employee.

An employer is also responsible for taking taxes out of an employee's paycheck and submitting the funds to the government. Should the club fail to do this and the instructor fail to declare income earned when paying taxes, the government may sue the club for the undeclared funds and appropriate penalties. Thus, the club could be held liable for the government fines, back taxes, and back workers' compensation fees.

Employment Manuals

- *Set policies regarding employee discipline and termination.*

- *Notify the owners, managers and employees of standards and expectations.*

- *Define company policies and set guidelines that involve the law. It is recommended that a lawyer be consulted when a club is drafting its manual.*

Taxes

What Are The Responsibilities of An Independent Contractor?

A fitness professional who is an independent contractor is responsible for carrying his or her own insurance policy, responsible for all liability surrounding his job performance and responsible for declaring income and paying taxes to the government. The legal status of an independent contractor is much more tricky than an employee's status. An employee's activities are directly monitored or supervised by his employer; while an employee "responds" to his or her "superior," an independent contractor acts independently of his or her employer. The independent contractor need not respond to his or her superior (the employer) for job direction.

For example: A house painter does not ask the house owner who has hired him or her what brush to use, how to apply the paint or what ladder the painter should employ when painting. The painter monitors his or her own activities. In the scenario of an aerobics instructor who teaches in a corporation, the aerobics instructor would be an independent contractor and the corporation would be the employer. Since the corporation (AT&T for example) knows nothing of aerobic training techniques and the instructor collects his or her own funds or is paid by AT&T, the aerobics instructor is considered an independent contractor and the corporation is considered the employer. The aerobics instructor should carry her own insurance and make sure to declare income from the classes in her tax return. For if the instructor is tax audited for any reason and has not declared this income, she could be liable for penalties starting at $3,000.

If, as a fitness professional, you are unsure of your legal relationship with your employer, it is recommended that you clarify it for insurance and tax purposes. Often employers have their instructors sign independent contractor/employee relationship contracts to outline their legal statuses. Assuming that both parties understand the ramifications of these contracts, the courts will honor these arrangements.

Standard of Care: Reasonable and Prudent

To determine if a fitness instructor is liable for an injury felt by a client, the courts ask: "What would a reasonable and prudent exercise professional do in a similar situation?" Basically, determining if a fitness instructor is liable means determining if a fitness instructor is negligent. There are four elements that must all be present before an injured student (a plaintiff) can recover damages from an instructor (a defendant).

(1) Duty

The "duty" that the courts place upon a fitness instructor is "to respond as a reasonable and prudent exercise professional in a similar situation." The first element of this duty is that the instructor must act "reasonably and prudently." Instructors must maintain an industry-wide standard of what is **"reasonable and prudent."** Since more and more fitness professionals are seeking certification and are continuing their educations, it is important, if not imperative, that fitness instructors be certified to teach aerobics or personal training and recertify when necessary.

Fitness instructors in Illinois are required by statute to maintain their CPR certification. There is a push for the legislature to statutorily require fitness instructors to be certified to teach aerobics and personal training as well. While

The four elements of negligence are:

1) Duty

2) Failure to perform that duty

3) Proximate cause

4) Damage

> All "reasonable and
> prudent" instructors are
> now certified.

**Written Employee
Evaluations**

*When a club does
terminate an employee's
job, an employee manual
provides documentation
that the employee's
behavior did not meet
legitimate company
policies. Yet, it is very
important to enforce the
company policies
even-handedly and
consistently. Should an
employee's behavior be
inconsistent with company
policy, this behavior should
be written up and given to
the employee's superiors
and the employee.*

---

this is not a state requirement as of yet, it is a recommendation that instructors and club owners should not take lightly.

The second element of this "duty" requires that the instructor act "reasonably and prudently" in a **"similar situation."** A "similar situation" means that if someone were injured in one of your classes seven years ago because they were doing high impact aerobics on a cement floor, the instructor may not be held liable. The reason would be because seven years ago, low impact aerobics was not as prevalent and research surrounding exercise surfaces was not readily available. A "reasonable and prudent" exercise instructor seven years ago would teach high impact aerobics on a cement floor. Today, of course, we know that this would be completely dangerous to both our students and instructors. But, the courts look at what was "reasonable and prudent" in a "similar situation" seven years ago when the injury occurred.

While I used an example of a student suing an instructor, or club, for an injury which occurred seven years prior, this situation is most unlikely to occur. All states have *"statutes of limitations."* These statutes require that an injured party sue within a certain time frame. For example, Illinois civil procedure requires that a person must sue within a two-year time period for certain types of personal injuries. This means that if a student gets injured and decides to sue three years later on the injury, the courts prohibit him or her from doing so. The reasons for this are that most likely after several years, the people who would be testifying in the suit may forget some of the incidents surrounding the litigation. The injured party, the witnesses, the instructor and even the attending physicians' memories get faulty after time. Further, the courts are so glutted with litigation that if people could sue after indefinite time periods our legal system would grind to a halt from overuse.

(2) Failure to Perform that Duty

The second element of negligence would be the failure to respond as a reasonable and prudent exercise professional in a similar situation. To prove that an instructor or club **failed in some way to respond reasonably,** the court would look towards industry-wide standards. The courts would seek expert testimony regarding the safety standards that are set by the industry. The courts would analyze what the certifications require, what fitness manuals recommend and what workshops out on the market prescribe. Industry standards must be met. This means that instructors must remain abreast of new research, new training techniques and updated standards. It is our legal responsibility to act as "reasonable and prudent exercise professionals in a similar situation."

(3) Proximate Cause

The third element of negligence is proximate cause. This requires that the **injury actually be caused by the fitness professional.** This means that the instructor can either "do" something to encourage an injury or "fail to do" something to encourage an injury. If the instructor is leading an antiquated exercise that is bad for the knees and fails to look around the room to spot if any participants are in danger of injury, the instructor could be found liable. The instructors actually "did" something to cause the injury by using an old exercise that was unsafe and "failed to do" something by not looking around the room.

See information on health history in the chapter on "Fitness Assessment."

If a client has a pre-existing injury and the exercise that the instructor leads simply triggers this injury, the courts may still find the instructor liable for this injury. The courts are very lenient with the requirement of proximate cause. It is recommended that all instructors, clubs or studios do health history forms on their clients.

If during a health history form questionnaire a student fails to indicate a pre-existing injury and the court discovers this pre-existing injury, most likely, the court will not hold the instructor liable. This is because the instructor requested the information from the student and the student failed to inform the instructor, or hid the information of this injury from the instructor. It therefore would appear that the instructor did not proximately cause the injury, as he or she was not made aware of any susceptibility toward injury on behalf of the student.

(4) Damage

Right about now in this chapter, I am sure that you as instructors are ready to quit teaching. Please remember that you cannot be sued if there is no damage! Yes, a sprained ankle is an injury, but where is the true damage? There probably are no doctor bills because the student treated the injury himself or herself with R.I.C.E. The student did not have to miss work; the student did not have to get a babysitter for his or her children; nor did the student have to go to a psychiatrist to recover from the emotional damage of the sprain. There were no out-of-pocket expenses spent on the sprained ankle. To support a lawsuit, a court must find that there were actual damages arising out of the injury.

Damages are calculated by **adding up the expenses relating to the injury,** as the above descriptions describe: doctor bills, loss of income, babysitters, etc. In California, if a student is injured as the result of an instructor's touch, for example the instructor pushed the student to enhance a stretch and the student tore a muscle as a result, the court can award treble damages. This means that because the instructor physically handled (or mishandled) a student, the student can recover for three times the amount of actual damages that he or she incurred.

It is therefore recommended that instructors do not touch their students. Instead, invade the space of your clientele by piercing that invisible bubble that Californians call "my space." Additionally, an instructor may wish to teach by pure demonstration. Show the exercise as it should appear. Then copy your student, demonstrating the student's poor technique, and finally visibly correcting the student's poor technique with proper technique.

Incident Reports and Adaptations

If an instructor sees a student using hand weights during the high impact section of class and fails to stop that student from performing this unsafe exercise, the instructor could be found liable. This is a failure to act as a "reasonable and prudent exercise professional in a similar situation." Specifically, if the instructor approaches the student and recommends and requests that the hand weights be put down until the sculpting section of class, the instructor must make sure that the student follows through and actually puts the hand weights down.

It is not recommended that the instructor start a fight with the student to ensure that the hand weights are released, but it is recommended that the instructor take his or her position of teacher seriously and understand that *he or she is liable if that student is stubborn and fails to put down the hand weights.* The instructor should call or get one of the managers on duty for the club to come into the classroom and take charge of the situation.

Quickly explain to the manager that this student will not comply with safety standards in your (the instructor's) classroom. Then you (the instructor) have complied with the duty to act as a "reasonable and prudent exercise professional." If no manager is on duty, and the instructor does not wish to interrupt the class, the instructor should ask the hand weight exerciser to sign an incident report (directly after class) stating that the instructor informed the student fully of the dangers of doing high impact aerobics with hand weights, and that the student assumes the risk of the injuries that can result from this type of activity and will not sue you or the club as a result of such possible injuries. This serves two purposes: It assures the club, studio and/or instructor that they will not be held liable should the student sue for a resultant injury. It also informs the student that you are serious about safety in your classroom. While this approach seems quite severe, please remember that lawsuits are equally severe. Further, the instructor need not be demanding, condescending or intimidating when requesting that the form be signed. A calm and considerate explanation that for legal and insurance reasons, this type of form must be completed usually appeases the client's feelings of aggression. The instructor should be as polite and accommodating as possible, even explaining that this form is required by our lawyers and our insurance carriers. By placing the blame, or requirement, on someone other than yourself (the instructor) the student is much more willing to comply happily. The instructor should use the above language and fill out this form either on a club or studio incident report form.

An easy (but expensive way) to deal with this type of situation is to document that certain behavior is not permissible under the club's published rules and regulations. (Members must adhere to instructor's requirements during fitness classes.) Members should be required to read these regulations, which should be subject to periodic renewal and change, and members should be subject to losing their membership privileges if they violate the rules and regulations. But remember, a revocation of membership privileges not only causes a loss of immediate income, it may subject the club to additional losses of income due to the bad press surrounding the disgruntled member.

Health History Forms

Health history forms are now the norm in the fitness industry. These forms are quite valuable because they can actually reduce the number of injuries that may occur. When a club and an instructor are made aware of a pre-existing condition that makes a student subject to injury, the club or the instructor can make allowances for the student and better accommodate individual needs. It is probable that fewer injuries will result. However, *health history forms are a double-edged sword because the more you know, the more you are liable.* This means that if you, the club or the instructor, is made aware of the possibility of injury due to a pre-existing condition, the club and/or the instructor is voluntarily assuming the responsibility to specifically prevent against this tendency to injure. Therefore, it is imperative that clubs, and specifically instructors, utilize the information that they gather in the health history forms.

CUSTOMIZE

All clubs should create their own incident report form. These forms should contain the spaces for the names, addresses, and telephone numbers for the injured party(s), the instructor(s), the witness(es) and the club supervisor(s) on duty. Dates, times and locations should all be reported. Comments should be thoroughly and completely written down surrounding the incident, answering who, what, where, when and how the incident occurred.

Actively using all of the data collected in these forms is virtually impossible. The instructor cannot be expected to know each and every fact about each and every participant that comes into the club. Therefore, it is important that clubs cover themselves against this Pandora's box of liability.

Firstly, the club should only ask questions in the health history form that the person conducting the initial interview knows how to work with.

Do not inquire about medical prescriptions, unless the person conducting the interview has been specifically trained in this area. Secondly, the club should limit the usage of the information collected from the health history form to the initial interviewer. This is important because club managers, individual instructors and substitute instructors cannot possibly read and remember every individual member's health history information.

Waivers of Liability

In May of 1987 the Illinois Supreme Court decided a very important case for the fitness industry. This case, Larsen v. Vic Tanny International, confirmed that an individual 1) who knew of the dangers which may cause an injury in a health club, 2) who realized the possibility of injury and 3) who entered into a contract not to sue a health club voluntarily, can waive the right to sue a health club if they become injured. Simply, this means that if you require your clients to sign a waiver of liability (specifically, an informed consent form) prior to their beginning an exercise program with you, and they injure themselves in your program, they may not be able to sue you.

When I first read that Larsen v. Vic Tanny International would come before the Illinois Supreme Court, I was ecstatic. I imagined the wonderful effects: More clubs would become aware of the fact that they can protect themselves from suit via a correctly worded informed consent form, the cost of insurance would plummet, and droves of attorneys would contact their health club clients and redraft their old waivers of liability. Unfortunately, I have not seen this forecasted trend. What I continue to see are the tired and incorrect statements that "Waivers of liability are not worth the paper that they are written on." While in the past this blanket statement was true, it may not be true anymore.

Waiver of Liability v. Informed Consent Form

A waiver of liability is an agreement between the club and the client that if the club permits the client to exercise in its facility, the client blanketly agrees not to sue the club should the client become injured. An informed consent form documents that the client has been fully informed of the risks and possible discomforts involved in a physical fitness program. The client assumes the risk of injury in contract form and cannot sue the club should he or she become injured. The difference between a waiver of liability and an informed consent form is that in an informed consent form, the client has been informed of the possible injuries that could occur to him or her prior to contractually waiving the right to sue. Currently, there is a trend in the law to uphold waivers of liability if they comply with certain standards. The most important of these standards is that the client/member must have "assumed the risk" that the injury may occur to him or her.

The client must have entered into the contract "voluntarily." This means that they signed the contract without being forced into it. In some states, the client must also have been informed of the possible injuries or discomforts they may incur such as muscle tears or strains, broken bones, heart attacks, etc. Courts reason that if a client voluntarily assumes the risk of an injury, the club should not be held liable. This means that if a contract specifically describes the injuries that may occur, and the client signs the contract, the courts will uphold the contract and not hold the club liable if such a designated or sufficiently alike injury occurs.

In other states, where such a waiver specifically sets forth in clear language the range of activities to which it applies, the court will enforce the contract. Newmann v. Gloria Marshall Figure Salon, Illinois Appellate Court, Second District, 149 Ill. App.3d 824,500 N.E.2d 1011. The key words in this phrase are "range of activities." In these states, a contract need not specifically state particular injuries such as "heart attacks, muscle tears or strains" that a client/member can incur. The court may still uphold the contract if the waiver merely mentions an activity in which the client was injured. No longer does the seller/club need to articulate specifically the injury sustained. The only restriction on this rule is that the client/member must have been able to reasonably contemplate that he or she assumed the risk of injury resulting from the specific activity.

SEE YOUR ATTORNEY

Please note that this waiver is only to serve as a guideline. Remember, the rules for waivers of liability vary from state to state. One should not expect this particular waiver to hold up in their state court. See your individual attorney, and feel free to take along this chapter.

Even if your attorney discovers that waivers of liability are not upheld in your state, still redraft your waiver to comply with these recommendations. You never know when the law may change. Should your attorney discover that waivers of liability/informed consent forms are upheld in your state, negotiate with your insurance carrier to reduce your rates. The trend in the law is clear. It's up to us to use it!

Sample Waiver of Liability/Informed Consent Form

"I, _____, have enrolled in a program of strenuous physical activity including but not limited to aerobic dance, weight training, stationary bicycling and various aerobic conditioning machinery offered by Sara's City Workout, Inc. I hereby affirm that I am in good physical condition and do not suffer from any disability which would prevent or limit my participation in this exercise program.

"In consideration of my participation in Sara's City Workout, Inc.'s exercise program, I, _____ for myself, my heirs and assigns, hereby release Sara's City Workout, Inc., (its employees and owners), from any claims, demands and causes of action arising from my participation in the exercise program.

"I fully understand that I may injure myself as a result of my participation in Sara's City Workout, Inc.'s exercise program and I, _____, hereby release Sara's City Workout, Inc., from any liability now or in the future including, but not limited to heart attacks, muscle strains, pulls or tears, broken bones, shin splints, heat prostration, injuries to knee, lower back, foot and any other illness, soreness or injury however caused, occurring during, or after my participation in the exercise program.

I hereby affirm that I have read and fully understand the above.

_____
Signature

_____
Date

Legal Music Sources

The definition of the 1976 Copyright law states that "the copyright owner has the right to charge a fee for the use of his or her music in public performance." Public performance is defined as "a place open to the public or as any place where a substantial number of persons outside a normal circle of family and its social acquaintances are gathered." Health clubs, studios and even church basements where fitness classes are offered fall into these categories. Licensing fees must be paid to each of the two major performing rights organizations ASCAP and BMI. When you buy a legally produced music tape from one of the many companies listed at left, your ASCAP and BMI rights are not covered. You are still required to pay ASCAP and BMI companies for the right to play the music in your facility. While you should contact ASCAP and BMI as soon as you are playing music in a public place, currently, there are no late penalties or retroactive fees charged when the company contacts you. Do not ignore ASCAP or BMI contacts, pay your fees according to their charts quickly and quietly.

If you are planning to get into music tape production and sales, you should investigate the legal responsibilities carefully. The copyright owner, the composers, lyricists and publishers of the songs should receive remuneration for their talent. To make sure that the talent that produced the songs receives their just monies, music tape companies and video production businesses are required to pay for each and every song that they use. The music tape companies pay for the right to use the music from the record labels (like Virgin Records) directly. While this can be quite expensive, fines for using unlicensed music run as high as $10,000, and not less than $250, for each song. Currently, the record labels are suing illegal music tape distributors. Fines and actual jail sentences are being imposed by the courts. Should someone decide to copy and sell a legally produced music tape that they have purchased from one of the companies listed, they are subject to the same legal punishment.

AIDS And Exercise

It is a very difficult situation dealing with members who have AIDS. There is absolutely no documented case which finds that AIDS can be transmitted due to health club activities. AIDS is viewed as a "disability" by courts in most jurisdictions. Therefore, health clubs should treat members who have AIDS as they would treat any other client who has a disability, "even-handedly."

A club should establish a disability policy and enforce that policy. This means that if you would require any other member who has a communicable disease to supply a note from a physician stating that it is all right for the disabled person to exercise, it would be perfectly legal to require a member who has AIDS to supply similar physician approval. Further, if a health club has a rule that members with open sores may not exercise in the facility, the health club must enforce this policy. This means that the club should enforce this policy even when a member has a scratch as well as when a member has an open sore due to AIDS.

Many problems are currently arising due to clubs revoking member's privileges simply because a member was diagnosed with AIDS. Singling out a member because they have AIDS might be found discriminatory. If the club has a rule that says that members who contract communicable diseases may temporarily lose their membership until the remission or cure of that disease is documented and such a rule is enforced by a club in situations other than AIDS victims, the courts may find that enforcement of this rule in the situation of a member with AIDS might be all right. The even-handed enforcement of this rule is what the courts examine. Other clients' memberships have similarly been revoked because of similar communicable disease contraction.

Therefore, it is recommended that clubs set up standard policies regarding communicable diseases. This policy should be in posted rules and regulations for the facility. In the membership contracts that clients sign (or in the informed consent forms that members sign) the members should be notified that they are responsible for adhering to all rules and regulations regarding membership privileges. A sample rule and regulation of this type may read: "Membership privileges may be temporarily or permanently revoked should a client contract a communicable disease, whether it be curable or not, whether the source of communicability be known or unknown." Another policy may read: "All membership privileges may be temporarily or permanently revoked if a member has an open sore."

According to the Americans with Disabilities Act, club owners must reasonably accommodate those with disabilities unless they can establish "undue hardship" on the operation of their business. This relates to club owners who cannot accommodate members with disabilities such as AIDS. If club owners demonstrate that they are financially crippled as a result of accommodating a member with AIDS, the courts may find that under the Americans with Disabilities Act, the club has demonstrated an "undue hardship." For example: If a substantial number of members are leaving and potential clients are not joining because of an existing member who has AIDS has open sores and regularly uses the whirlpool and pool, the courts might find the financial strain an "undue hardship."

However, this is a difficult test to pass. The courts may also examine the fact that other financial opportunities may open to a facility which accommodates members with AIDS or HIV positive individuals. This may actually open up new financial possibilities. This is a very complicated issue with heavy constitutional overtones that must be dealt with in a delicate manner. I highly recommend that all clubs facing issues of members with AIDS that are financially impacting their business consult a lawyer in their state immediately.

References

Herbert, D. L., & Herbert, W. G. (1992). *Legal aspects of preventive and rehabilitative exercise programs* (2nd ed.). Canton, Oh.: Professional Reports Corp.

Herbert, D.L., & Herbert, W.G. (Eds.) *The Exercise Standards and Malpractice Reporter* (Full Series). Canton, Oh.: Professional Reports Corp.

Directing a Fitness Program

40

Cynthia Shields McNeill

Focus

AS A FITNESS DIRECTOR, YOU WILL FIND yourself playing a variety of roles. Although you will be interacting with people at all levels—staff, members, peers, general managers and club owners—all of your relationships will require the same commitment to high quality care.

Roles and Responsibilities

To command respect in the fitness industry, fitness directors must meet the challenge of offering the highest quality fitness program to members. The fitness instructors are the crucial link to that success. When hiring instructors, first go through a detailed interview. An instructor must be certified by a nationally recognized certification program as well as be certified in CPR. Be careful not to rely solely on credentials, however. A seasoned fitness director will also be able to obtain, through the interview process, such important information as self-worth, as reflected in personal appearance, attitude, professional conduct and communication skills. A good instructor knows the difference between being a class leader and being an educator. Educate your class members—students do not want to play follow the leader; they are in class to learn.

Develop a **mission statement** at your club and inform your instructors of it. For example, "The Athletic Club's mission is to provide and maintain a standard of excellence in service to its members and a quality working and learning environment for its staff."

The goal of providing professional quality programming and instruction as well as customer service should be shared by all staff members in order to establish a unified team effort. An **instructor manual** is helpful in outlining needed information concerning the club and its policies and procedures.

Even the most talented instructors need **feedback** and encouragement to grow professionally. Offering workshops for continuing education purposes informs the staff of your high standards. Clear communication is essential to a high level of performance. Monthly meetings help establish a sense of unity among the instructors. These meetings also give the director a chance to discuss any policy changes, exercise updates or expected goals for the program. A brief business meeting followed by a workshop keeps instructors informed. Even clubs with a small to non-existent budget for instructor education can offer **staff training** workshops.

Invite presenters from local universities to your facility in exchange for guest passes. Area professionals are often eager to speak in order to obtain visibility and contacts. Speakers could include orthopedic surgeons, physical therapists, podiatrists, psychologists, and nutritionists, to name a few. Don't

---

 CHECKLIST

For Successful Directing

There are four elements which are essential to the operation of a successful fitness program:

1. Establish clear goals for the staff by providing a mission statement, job descriptions and open communication.

2. Hire knowledgeable and competent staff and build a high performance team.

3. Nurture your staff by providing a learning environment and genuine respect.

4. Be flexible.

See chapter on "Law and Exercise."

overlook the talent of your staff. Ask your instructors to research topics of interest and make presentations to the group. A choreography exchange is another excellent way to promote professional growth. For fun, try a tape exchange followed by a covered-dish supper. Your staff is the backbone of your program, and it is crucial that they know how valued they are to the success of the club. Let them know they make a difference.

Establish a strong sense of pride. Set a tone for high standards, not only through the mission statement, but also in the way you present yourself as Director. High employee morale motivated by a sense of pride is essential to the overall success of a program. Build a team with the reputation of being an elite group of fitness professionals. Nurture and support continued **professional growth**. Acknowledge excellence through instructor awards and verbal and written praise. A strong sense of pride often makes the difference between an instructor staying with your program as opposed to going down the street to a club that pays $5 more per class.

Communication is the key! This is often a problem for Directors with large programs running from 6 am-9 pm. It's true you can't be at the club all the time but do try to vary your schedule. Instructors like it when you take their classes; it shows them that you care about the program, the club, the instructors. Another important key to good communication is providing a **mailbox** for each instructor. This could be a special file or a memo box, but each instructor should have his or her own space. Fill these mailboxes, not only with memos, but also with articles promoting professional growth and notes of appreciation. Let the instructors know how valuable they are to the program.

Open Door

Allow the instructors to share any concerns or questions regarding their classes. We all become frustrated at one time or another and often frustration can lead to instructor burnout. The more support you offer your staff, the more support you will get in return. A unified staff is a more polished staff with less employee turnover. Everyone is a winner when staff morale is high!

Listen to your staff and listen to your members. Develop a system to receive member comments complete with name and phone number. A "help keep us in shape" comment form encourages members to voice their opinions. Always follow up a comment with a phone call. This type of personal attention helps build a loyal member base. This also demonstrates that you care about member needs and that their opinions matter.

An important role for a fitness director is designing and maintaining a fitness class schedule to best meet members' needs. This is probably one of the most challenging tasks on your agenda because of the difficulty involved in pleasing everyone. When developing a schedule, keep the following guidelines in mind: To meet the fitness and time needs of the members, offer a balance and variety of classes. Schedule a mixture of classes during the same time slots to ensure cross training. Present educational FYIs and list profiles, plus a detailed description of classes. Be sure to include the focus of the class and for whom it is appropriate. The most effective presentation for class format is the grid system. It makes finding classes and times quick and easy, especially if your club has more than one studio. Ask the members what they would like to see on the schedule, but keep in mind that you are the professional with the fitness knowledge to provide a safe, well-balanced program. You would do a great disservice to the members if you offered only one type of class because it was the most popular. Educate your members on the importance of cross-training.

Summary

Being a fitness director is a challenging and rewarding career. If you love to teach, but want to be part of upper management, you can do both in this position.

Ask your supervisor for advice if you are currently a fitness instructor and would like to advance to a fitness director position. Let your career goals be known. Find out what training you need and go for it! You will find that those in the fitness profession do it because they love their work, and because of that passion, you can usually find an enthusiastic mentor to help you climb to the next rung.

Aerobic Director Responsibilities

Daily
- Observe and report any mishap or clientele feedback.
- Resolve or develop an action plan to resolve all problems and questions that arise on a daily basis.
- Check floors, mirrors, mats, equipment and stereo system.
- Post all necessary interstaff communications.
- Be available by phone or by pager.
- Substitute in case of last-minute cancellations.
- Assist with class coverage.
- Keep instructors aware of relevant information.
- Be a positive influence and proactive trouble shooter.

Weekly
- Check weekly cleaning schedule.
- Make contact with management to discuss any of above items or problems.
- Meet with other department heads at facility if appropriate.

Monthly
- Coordinate staff meeting.
- Provide regular opportunities for continuing education.
- Provide regular performance evaluations.
- Account for instructor payroll.
- Help with club promotions.
- Follow through on promises and commitments.

Ongoing
- Establish and update the aerobic schedule and class descriptions.
- Recruit and train new instructors or substitutes. Include interview, audition, job description. Establish class and instructor policies. Include pay rates, substitution policies, performance standards.
- Acknowledge and consider all staff suggestions.
- Organize new employee folders, tax records, aplications, schedule availability, certification and CPR records.
- Maintain miscellaneous forms such as phone list, aerobic schedules, payroll sheets, daily logs, time cards, evaluation forms, aerobic program questionnaires, complaint forms, incident report forms.
- Continue to create and develop new programs.
- Create a supportive working environment.
- Sponsor team events and fund raisers.
- Network within the fitness profession and industry.

—Kathy Stevens

Part 7

Mind/Body Considerations

Holistic Fitness

Wellness

Debbie & Carlos Rosas

41 Holistic Fitness

Focus

TODAY THE SINGLE DIMENSION of "physical" fitness and health is joined by dimensions of "mind" and "spirit" to feed the needs of the whole person. This new dimension is creating a new paradigm in fitness called "holistic fitness." It is a new era that taps into one's inner life, blending conscious thought and action to bridge the gap between the mind, the body and the emotional spirit. As an instructor, you can learn to "dance" with the multidimensional aspects of human functioning. This chapter marks the first time that holistic movement has been addressed in a fitness textbook. Instructors can venture into this exciting field by following the principles outlined here, as well as pursuing their independent studies into the holistic life.

A Holistic Philosophy

The philosophy of holistic fitness is based on **holism**, meaning that everything exists in relationships and that we cannot change any part without affecting the whole. The basic premise of a holistic fitness program is that there is a heightened level of wellness and fitness that exists when we consider human beings more than the mere sum of the physical parts, when we consider all that the body, mind and spirit offer.

In class, the whole of each student is considered, including his or her physical health, mental, emotional, social, environmental, spiritual and nutritional habits. All exercises, principles and concepts in a holistic fitness environment offer a way for the student to safely and continually improve and change.

FOUNDATION

Although the concepts in this chapter may sound complex and new to you, the actions on the exercise floor are beautifully simple, and simply beautiful. Filtering down into mainstream fitness are movements and principles from the once "higher consciousness" body arts such as Feldenkrais, the Alexander technique, yoga, tai-chi, tae-kwon-do, and aikido.

Holistic Learning

There are many ways to learn movement. Holistically, we place this psychophysical learning into two categories, rational and intuitive—the emphasis on blending these two to encourage systemic and conscious movement. In this way, we positively integrate the sensory, motor body and the thinking body, using both the left and the right sides of the brain, using both the intellectual and creative selves.

Rational learning is the Western, more scientific way of embodying information, a way of processing information that discriminates, divides, compares, measures and categorizes. While this process is effective in learning, it is not the only way to learn and should not be relied upon solely for gathering information. You can use your rational thinking to absorb information from books, to question, to observe, divide and disseminate information. It is a useful tool, but not the only tool available to you.

Intuitive learning is an approach using the physical body in a much more sensate, non-intellectual way. This is developed by observing the body from a place other than through the five senses, opening yourself up to the feelings and sensations that come through to you from your body. You can perceive this as your sixth sense. Drawing on your inner resources, this process enables you to hear more, see more, and remember more, creating a "body seeing," a "body wisdom" that goes along with "right knowing." It is here that you gain access to hidden images, ideas, sensory based memories, and conscious creativity.

Systemic learning takes place when the learning modes of the mind, the body and the spirit collaborate. It combines intuitive and rational learning and allows us to become more fully integrated and alive. In fitness, it is the safest, most thorough and energy efficient way to learn.

The Two Learning Groups

Rational learners are very good at responding to verbal directions and love to be told exactly how to do the exercise. They like to "think" about how to do the exercise. Actually, they love to think! Unfortunately this slows down their response time. They grab onto each command with their eyes and ears and follow step by step, hoping that this will help them to integrate body parts and follow the sequences in class. They can follow various rhythms when logically presented, counted out loud and given a precise place and time. They are generally more comfortable with structured classes and may get agitated if there is not a form or structure to hold on to. They are best guided from precision and form into feeling and expression.

Intuitive learners more readily trust their body's other wisdoms and actually have an easier time with spatial awareness. They easily adjust to different rhythms and movements, and flow in and out of change easily. They love to "feel" their way through an exercise. They prefer not to think about "how to do it" and they enjoy the freedom of spontaneous, "freer" movement. Their down side can be a lack of focus and inability to structurally organize movements in a precise way. They have a tendency to get confused and irritated when too many verbal and visual directions and commands are given. They are best guided from feeling and expression into form and precision.

Steps In Creating Awareness

To develop and enhance extended body/mind/spirit awareness, apply this four-step process to sharpen your own awareness perception:

1. Focus on a particular body part and its action.
2. Ask yourself a question about it that will elicit thinking and observation.
3. Recognize what is true for you based on your physical and mental questioning and observations.
4. Acknowledge where you are and create a change based on what you can do to comfortably and safely move to another level, to another space. When balance and harmony are restored, you're on track.

Energy follows intention and attention.

As you gain in awareness-perception skills, you'll be ready to teach awareness to your class members. The following awareness principles should be reinforced whenever necessary:

- Slow down and be "present" in the moment, blending the senses of your body, mind and spirit to feel and help direct your choices of action.

- Find a focus such as your hand or elbow to help you direct your attention and energy. Stay with that focus until you feel you have begun to move in new ways, from new places that are natural and spontaneous.
- In a non-judgmental atmosphere, stay fascinated in your process.
- Remain process oriented over goal oriented.
- Make small adjustments that keep you moving in the direction of change.
- Be willing to remain on a plateau, what you may consider a no change place. Remember that changes are always occurring. Often we are incapable of sensing the smaller, minute changes as they are developing.
- Respect the wisdom of your body, mind and spirit. Be willing to go slower, take two steps back, work less, start over, and re-examine and be patient should there be some small amount of physical, mental and emotional discomfort as the changes occur.
- Every day evaluate how you are feeling relative to your growth and fitness. Observe yourself in and out of class. Make adjustments that support the all-gain, no-pain theory.
- Awareness is about being conscious. Change takes time. Replace frustration and anxiety with patience and love.
- Choose one thing that you would like to change. Be aware of that part, that quality or action. Send loving energy to that area and create action in and around it.

In Class

1. Look for and feel for a sense of balance while everyone is executing motions.
2. Look for and feel for ease and receptivity in your body and in others. Observe the overall physical, mental and spiritual energy moving through the class.
3. Notice what everyone can easily do and build from that place of safety and security.
4. Make adjustments that will create a natural flow in all of the movements.

Movement Forms

FLOW

Flow of energy is interrupted by the following: mechanical repetition, unnatural and painful action, one speed compartmentalized movement, and the dismemberment of body from mind and spirit.

Choose one concept at a time from any of the movement forms and begin to integrate that principle into your workout and your life. Focus your energy and attention by using your chosen concept to keep you directed. Notice how this focus changes everything about your movement, from alignment to speed. By focusing on one concept for an entire workout, you will allow the necessary time for your body/mind/spirit muscle memory to pick up the new information and a new way of moving.

Tai-Chi: The Slow Dance

On a sensory and visual level, tai-chi is a slow dance. Because of its slow speed, tai-chi is efficient and comfortable while conditioning the body-mind and the spirit. Moving freely, joints spring-loaded, relaxed and ready, the fluidity of tai-chi circular motions gives definition to the body without the use of external

- *Lead with the heel out.*
- *Work with a lower center of gravity.*
- *Shift body weight.*
- *Move from center or tan-tien.*
- *Blend the body-mind and the spirit.*
- *Keep grounded.*

- *Eliminate all unnecessary force when executing a technique.*
- *Stay alert and prepared for the next movement.*
- *Work on the timing of your technique and the correct use of power, swiftness or slowness in executing the movement.*

- *Maximize effect with the minimum effort.*
- *Shift the weight over each foot.*
- *Energy follows attention.*

weights. Unintentionally, flexibility and range of motion increase. As the joints are lubricated, the muscles are massaged with the bones from the inside out, in an elegant and pain-free way.

Another element easily added to your workout from tai-chi is *"moving from center,"* your tan-tien. This powerful place is located two inches below the navel in the center of your body. Imagining a white ball of energy in this area can help you develop awareness and a balanced relationship of your body to the space around you. This awareness makes it much easier for you to coordinate arm and hand motions to your whole body.

Tae-Kwon-Do: The Dance of Precision

It can be a fitness culture shock to experience a martial art discipline such as tae-kwon-do. It can also be a great awakening to the power of discipline, balance, chi and precision based on survival and function. Consciously using chi, the life-force energy, you become grounded and able to deliver powerful kicks or punches and to gracefully change linear movement into efficient, circular movement. One discovers the power and efficiency of the spiral and circle as a safe way to direct movement and energy. With this movement form, precision becomes a challenge, a feeling, a dynamic. Different speeds—slow, moderate and fast—are tamed to become tools that deliver aerobic or anaerobic workouts. Breath supports all initial movement and provides the power behind every motion. Sounds evoke abdominal work and spinal support when exertion is needed. The stances, the leg positions of tae-kwon-do, become cornerstones for leg work, providing support, grace, agility, speed, groundedness, strength, flexibility, balance and power. Effort is replaced by ease with the simple action of sinking and rising and moving about the earth in a grounded way. Begin by adding these concepts into your class and discover the power of tae-kwon-do.

Aikido: Harmonious Spherical Motion

This gracious movement form will provide you with an education in the use of energy, connectedness to yourself, others and to your environment. The basic concept of aikido is to meet all conflict with resolution through blending to create harmony. This principle alone can keep you going for a long time when it is applied to fitness.

Aikido uses the body, mind and the spirit with an emphasis on spirit energy. Focusing on blending with what is around at all times, you develop body/mind fitness and enhanced awareness. Aikido's use of spiral motions and on "blending" and moving in harmony, helps you develop a sensible and natural wisdom from within the intuitive thinking body. You can begin to add a basic aikido principle by focusing GRACE. G-grounding, R-relaxation, A-awareness, C-centering and E-energy.

Jazz: Fun, Showmanship and Expression

Jazz is a unique manifestation of gestures and of your own feelings expressed through dance. It is the jive, the jiggle, the bump, the pulse and the sway. Jazz is as much a part of each and every one of us as eating, breathing and sleeping. We all have our own jazz walk, our interpretation of isolated body parts with added expression. By adding rhythm steps to your class, such as the cha-cha-cha, your choreography can take on the quality of jazz, with syncopated body motions replacing stiff, holding motions. The shake, the

- *Move as a whole unit.*
- *Express syncopated beats and movement.*
- *Become expressive.*

shimmy, the snake, the hip bump—all of these gestures condition different parts of the body, mind and spirit. Begin to add jazz to your workout for fun and awareness of muscle balance and imbalance. Focusing on detail, isolation, syncopation, patterns and theatrics will help you develop the ability to think of and do many things at one time. This kind of multi-thinking and multi-moving integrates the use of your left and right brain.

Duncan Dance: Spirited, Honest Movement

Isadora Duncan knew there had to be a better way. A radical in her time, she threw aside the constricting corsets and ballet shoes to create natural body, mind and spirit movement. Unrestricted and uninhibited, free from holding and free from shoes, she turned rigid motion into fluid, graceful motion with emotion. Using full body expression, extension and play, Duncan Dance develops grace, strength, flexibility and balance. Begin by adding these concepts to your class to get the feeling of Duncan Dance.

- *Connect to earth, using the feet.*
- *Reflect what you are feeling.*

Modern Dance: Playing With Balance, Shapes and Space

Visually and mechanically, the human body can create and become many fascinating shapes in space. Modern Dance provides a foundation for creating many shapes through technique, improvisation and playful discovery. This kind of dance discovery becomes a way for you to tap into your own body language, freeing your spirit and creativity, creating profound effects on the body, mind and spirit. The free, expansive movement changes increase strength and flexibility in the whole body. Incorporating on- and off-balance motions, balance becomes something to play with. Losing it one moment and finding it the next. Space becomes something you can feel, with a texture and a temperature. Creating shapes and lines with your body, the breath quickens as you expand your body into a circle, a square and into a soft sculpture that can be molded into any shape. Changing directions, falling and recovering, modern dance is an elegant way to load and unload muscles to gain additional strength and flexibility. The play and creativity of this movement form is an endless stimulation to the right brain.

- *Vary the tempo of circular motions.*
- *Permit gravity to pull you down into a collapse.*
- *Change the focus of your head and eyes.*
- *Maintain awareness of the center of a circle.*

Yoga: The Conscious Dance of Alignment and Posturing

Yoga is a way to make space in and around your joints and to become flexible. It encourages you to look inward, developing awareness by feeling and sensing. Focusing on conscious, purposeful bone alignment, yoga postures create new alignment and the proper functioning of the body and its organs. The movements of yoga help you to develop muscle balance and movement stability, as well as flexibility and relaxation. There are many styles of yoga that are applicable to any fitness program, but as a knowledgeable and certified instructor, you should know how to safely modify yoga postures for any population. (For example, AFAA does not recommend the plough for the non-yoga practitioner. Instead, substitute a modified abdominal stretch, and teach proper breathing during the sustained hold.)

- *Regular practice is more important than trying advanced postures.*

Feldenkrais: The Conscious Feeling of Movement

Renewed physical and mental health is obtained by developing sensory awareness. Moshe Feldenkrais has developed exercises for the posture, the

- *In every action we take exists movement, sensation, feeling and thought.*

eyes, the imagination and the body parts that dramatically change the way we pattern our body and its habits. He taught that nothing is permanent about our behavioral patterns, those patterns that create our form.

Feldenkrais exercises focus on feeling the body in action to create permanent changes in the body. Through this method we can change, improve and build better body habits to feel more alive on a daily basis.

The Alexander Technique: Movement From the Top

- *The goal is to apply the process of non-interfering (inhibition) and consciousness reasoned intention (direction).*

In the Alexander Technique, *process*—the steps to get to an end and not the end itself—is the way. Therefore, results come easily and in a less stressful way. By paying attention to the quality of movement, changes occur effortlessly. When you discover the way you use your body, you can change your approach to develop ultimate effectiveness. The essence of this technique is as follows: As you begin any movement or action, move your whole head slightly forward, upward and away from your whole body, and allow your body to lengthen and follow that upward direction.

Rolfing

- *Resilient and elastic muscles are important pumping mechanisms to ensure proper metabolism.*

Ida P. Rolf has created for us a practical and meaningful form for integrating our human structure that induces change toward balance. While the structural integration of Rolfing deals with deep manual intervention of the elastic soft tissue structure, the myofascia of the body, the goal of this treatment is to balance the body in the gravity field. In brief, Rolfers believe that if tissue is restrained, and balanced movement demanded at a nearby joint, tissue and joint will relocate in a more appropriate equilibrium. The process of Rolfing is one of progression towards a more efficient, balanced body. A few of the benefits from Rolfing are proper alignment, ease of motion, comfort in the body, wellness and heightened energy levels.

Somatics

Thomas Hanna, the developer and founder of a field called somatics, suggested to us that our sensory motor systems, the mechanism fundamental to all human experience and behavior, often had malfunctions that he called sensory-motor amnesia. These malfunctions of the sensory-motor system can cause fundamental deterioration in our lives. Somatics presents exercises and approaches that show us how to avoid and reverse this aging process. The belief that as we grow older, our bodies and our lives can continue to improve, right up until the very end, is real.

- *Remain supple.*

Systemic Movement: Moving as a Unit

Most students come into class as a whole person, only to quickly be dissected into parts once they begin moving. Top parts moving without bottoms. Bottoms moving without the tops. Incorporating whole body motions that use the body as a unit is a safe and intelligent way to move. Even when isolating one body part, feel for the integration of the entire body as a support for motion and movement. This approach is important in the warm-up, aerobic, cooldown, relaxation and stretch aspects of your class. Add systemic motion to your movement using these concepts.

The Three Body Weights—Head, Chest and Pelvis

Many times in exercise, the core of the body, your spine, the head, chest and pelvis are neglected. Arms move, legs move, yet the core remains motionless, adding stress and rigidity to the spine and to the movement. You can properly organize your movement and safely add agility motions by thinking of these three body parts, one in relationship to the other. This concept is very helpful in adding flexibility and strength to your spine. By focusing on the movement, alignment and relationship of your head, chest and pelvis, you can avoid stress and strain and add natural motion to your exercise.

As a beginner, keep your three weights lightly and loosely balanced over each other while you move. To prevent strain to your neck, shoulders and upper and lower back, maintain movement around and through these areas. Focusing on the alignment of these three body weights, feel the downward pull and lengthening from your tailbone toward the floor, your chest directly above your pelvis, the upward alignment of energy out the top of your head and along the back of your neck. In this way, you'll gain extension of your spine and alignment for safety and proper postural integration.

Breath: Airwaves of Motion and Sound

Breathing is an internal ebb and flow of energy and oxygen. A steady and natural rhythm of breath, in through the nose and out through the mouth, provides you with the fuel necessary to work out and to maintain a relaxed body and mind at all times. It is most essential to wellness, holistic fitness, relaxation and life!

In holistic fitness, incorporating a variety of speeds in your movement class will help you develop different approaches, exercises and ways of breathing. The slower you move, the deeper you can breathe and the more you increase your lung capacity and spinal flexibility. Ideally, diaphragmatic breathing is the best. However, in faster, more powerful moves, a shorter faster breath may be required. Be aware of your breath. Notice how it changes and adapt it to fit your movement and speed.

Resources

Music

Music has the power to foster good health, peace and harmony in our bodies. Whether it is our voice, an instrument or a song, it is a powerful ingredient in the formula of "holistic fitness." Health maintenance, wellness in the body, mind and spirit is promoted and maintained by using music at the proper volume, choosing songs with positive lyrics and with mood enhancing sounds. The right kind of music and the proper use of sound can promote relaxation, motivation and internal fitness to keep us well.

Certain sounds and rhythms, even though we may enjoy them, are harmful to our bodies. The ill effects of these sounds are cumulative, and strong vibration from excessive noise wears out the sensory cells of our ears. Even muscular strength can be reduced by excessive sound. We can change the mood of a movement and the muscle response through various kinds, speeds and rhythms of music. Working with the music, the up and down beats, the speeds and rhythms, helps unite body, mind and spirit with movement and sound.

The bottom line is health and well-being! Choose wisely. Think positively. Listen wisely. Following are some music suggestions to help you approach your class using "holistic" sounds and rhythms.

- **New Age—up beat**
  Kitaro, Ray Lynch, Steven Halpern, Peter Buffett, Teja Bell, Mannheim Steamroller
- **New Age—mood music**
  Mike Rowland, Lazaris, Aeoliah, Windham Hill, Paul A. Sutin
- **Jazz**
  Artful Balance, Herb Alpert, Alan Parsons Project, Chris Spheeris, Tom Scott, Dan Siegel
- **Primal and Ethnic**
  Gabrielle Roth, Paul Winter, Bertha Egnos and Gail Lakier, Gino d'Auri, James Galway
- **Movement Provoking**
  Enigma, Azuma Tri Atma, Raphael, Bobby McFerrin, Mickey Hart
- **Dance**
  UB4O, Gloria Estefan, Curtis Salgado, Lisa Stansfield, Simply Red, Seal, The Commitments, Carlos Santana, Mariah Carey, movie soundtracks

Visualization and Imagery

Begin to add visualizations into your class by offering various movement suggestions that are visually and systemically focused. Below are a few examples to get you started.

- Feel like a willow tree swaying in the wind to work your abdominals and to loosen your spine.
- As you exhale, imagine that you are squeezing water out of a sponge to create a natural contraction.
- Shake coins loosely in your hands to feel agile in your arms.

Summary

The goal is to teach in ways that provide positive results in which we encourage non-judgmental learning and free expression of the self. It is important to guide students into their own discovery rather than demanding that they follow you, the teacher. Give yourself permission to be real, express emotion. In this way, your students have permission to be themselves, too.

Because "holistic fitness" is feeling based, it can be very emotional for students as they connect to various psychophysical parts of themselves. Often these parts arise unexpectedly. Personalities such as the child within, the adolescent, the adult, the warrior, the nurturer, the leader, the follower, etc. For many, this can be the first time they experience a new self, their own emotions and their own power to act and make decisions based on what they feel and think. Go slowly and remain compassionate and loving throughout your process.

John Travis, MD, MPH
Meryn G. Callander

42 *Wellness*
The Big Picture

Focus

WHILE MANY PEOPLE THINK OF WELLNESS only in physical terms (nutrition, fitness, stress reduction) its originators envisioned it as a multidimensional concept, incorporating the mental, emotional and spiritual aspects of a human being.

At its core, wellness reflects a paradigm which stands in direct contrast to the prevailing **treatment model**. The **wellness model** promotes self responsibility, compassion, and cooperation between client and practitioner. With the practitioner's help, the client recognizes "dis-ease" as a message drawing attention to an aspect of life that needs healing, rather than something to be overcome, rejected, or *fixed*. The wellness model then empowers individuals to continue developing their unique potential as growing human beings.

This chapter assists the fitness professional in broadening his or her thinking on health and disease, offering a vantage point from the wellness paradigm.

Addressing the Underlying Attitudes and Behaviors

The word *wellness* caught on in the hospital and corporate worlds in the '70s and '80s, but at the cost of its proponents' watering down of the original concept in order to fit wellness into the existing medical/treatment model.

Similarly, many fitness programs are based on a modified treatment (dominator) model, focusing on preventing problems/symptoms or attempting to overpower them. Great attention is placed on human *doing* (action/behavior change), but little attention is placed on human *being* (the underlying beliefs/feelings). The present emphasis on quick results/easy fixes falls short of addressing the fundamental issues which lead to despair and self-destructive behaviors (that in turn have driven our illness-care system to bankruptcy).

Sustainable well-being requires addressing the underlying self-destructive attitudes and behaviors rampant throughout society. Popular definitions of wellness need to be expanded beyond their narrow focus on individual fitness or nutrition. Without addressing the underlying causes of dis-ease, such programs are only Band-Aids, providing no more than symptomatic relief.

The wellness of an individual cannot be addressed in any meaningful way unless viewed within the context of the prevailing consciousness of our world. The impact of this consciousness is universal, manifesting in every realm of our society—the medical, economical, environmental, psychological, and the spiritual. It is inseparable from our well-being.

From Discountability to Accountability

The treatment model mirrors the prevailing cultural norms. It is rooted in a **Paradigm of Discountability**. The roles open to us in this paradigm are the *oppressed,* the *dominator,* and (of special interest to the helping professions) the *rescuer* (a driving need to "fix" people/problems). Even the language of the treatment model: compliance, regimen (or more revealing: "regime," "battling," "overcome") reveals its fundamentally adversarial mindset.

This approach is also perpetuated through many professionals' desire for only tips and practical tools, with minimal questioning of the underlying assumptions inherent in the system in which they operate. This system is bankrupt, financially and emotionally. Frustration and burnout among practitioners is at an all time high. Clearly something major has to be changed. The Wellness Model offers a fundamentally different approach to disease and health.

Sustainable well-being, personal and planetary, calls for a shift into a **Paradigm of Accountability**. The roles available in the paradigm of accountability focus on life as a learning experience full of endless possibility. The results are self-responsibility with love/compassion, cooperation, and conscious co-creation (see *Wellness for Helping Professionals,* Travis & Callander, 1990).

Here are three key concepts vital to an appreciation of the multidimensional nature of wellness. You can find these in more detail in the *Wellness Workbook* (Travis & Ryan, 1988).

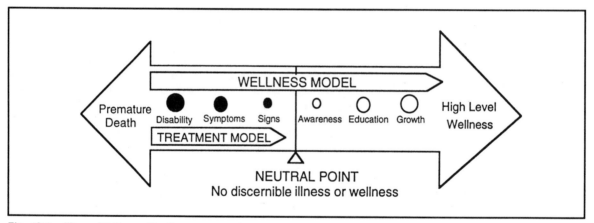

Fig. 42-1. Illness/Wellness Continuum

What is Wellness?

- A choice—a decision you make to move toward optimal health.
- A way of life—a lifestyle you design to achieve your highest potential for well-being.
- A process—a developing awareness that there is no end point, but that health and happiness are possible in each moment, here and now.
- A balanced channeling of energy—energy received from the environment, transformed within you, and returned to affect the world around you.
- The integration of body, mind and spirit—the appreciation that everything you do, and think, and feel and believe has an impact on your state of health.
- The loving acceptance of yourself.

Most people think in terms of illness and assume that the absence of illness indicates wellness. There are actually many degrees of wellness, just as there are many degrees of illness.

The Illness/Wellness Continuum

High-level wellness involves giving good care to your physical self, using your mind constructively, expressing your emotions effectively, being creatively involved with those around you, and being concerned about your physical, psychological and spiritual environments.

The Illness/Wellness Continuum (see Fig. 42-1) illustrates the relationship of the treatment model to the wellness model. Moving from the center to the left shows a progressively worsening state of health. Moving to the right of center indicates increasing levels of health and well-being. The treatment model (which is designed to overpower unwanted conditions) can bring you up to the neutral point where the symptoms of disease have been alleviated. The wellness model, which can be used at any point on the continuum, helps you move toward higher levels of wellness. The wellness model is not intended to replace the treatment model, but to work in harmony with it. If you are not well, treatment is important, but don't stop at the neutral point. Use the wellness model to move toward high-level wellness.

While people often lack physical symptoms of illness, they may still be bored, depressed, tense, anxious, or generally unhappy with their lives. Such emotional states often set the stage for physical and mental disease. Even cancer can be brought on through the subsequent lowering of the body's resistance from excessive stress. The same feelings can also lead to abuse of the body through smoking, overdrinking, overeating and not exercising. But these symptoms and behaviors represent only the tip of the iceberg. They are usually substitutes for other more basic human needs such as recognition from others, a more stimulating environment, caring and affection from friends, and greater self-acceptance.

The Iceberg Model

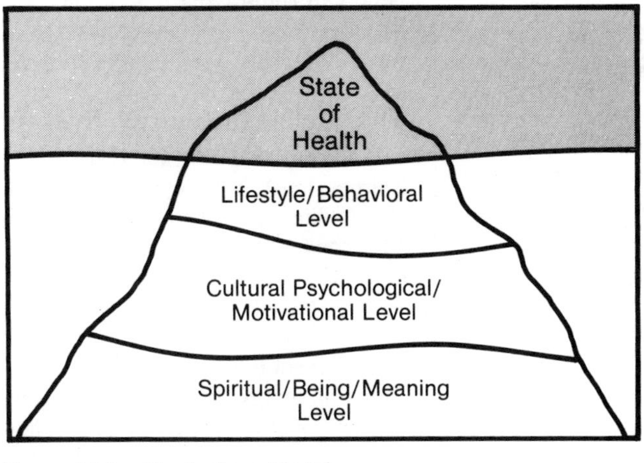

Figure 42-2. The Iceberg Model

The "well" being is not necessarily the strong, the successful, the young, or even the illness-free being. A person can be living a process of wellness and yet be physically handicapped, aged, in pain, imperfect. Conversely, he or she can be physically healthy and still functioning from an illness mentality—

constantly worrying and judging themselves. Regardless of where on the Illness/Wellness Continuum a person assigns himself/herself, what matters most is the direction he or she is facing.

The Iceberg Model

Icebergs reveal only about one-tenth of their mass above the water. The remaining nine-tenths remain submerged. Your current state of health—be it one of disease or vitality—is just like the tip of an iceberg (see Fig. 42-2). This is the apparent part—what shows. If you don't like it, you can attempt to change it, do things to it, chisel away at an unwanted condition. But, whenever you chip some off, more of the same comes up to take its place.

To understand all that creates and supports your current state of health, you have to look under the surface. The first level is the **Lifestyle/Behavioral** level—what you eat, how you use and exercise your body, how you relax and let go of stress, and how you safeguard yourself from the hazards around you.

Many people follow lifestyles that they know are destructive, both to their own well-being and to that of the planet. Yet, they may feel powerless to change them. To understand why, you must look still deeper, to the **Psychological/Motivational/Cultural** level. Here lies what moves you to lead the lifestyle you've chosen. You can learn what payoffs you get from being overweight, smoking, driving recklessly, or from eating well, being considerate of others, and getting regular exercise.

Exploring below the Psychological/Motivational level, you encounter the **Spiritual/Being/Meaning** level. (It is really more of a realm than a level because it has no clear boundaries.) It includes the mystical and mysterious, and everything else in the unconscious mind, and concerns such issues as your reason for being, the real meaning of your life, or your place in the universe. How you address these questions, and the answers you choose, underlie and permeate all of the layers above. Ultimately, this realm determines whether the tip of the iceberg, representing your state of health, is one of disease or wellness.

The Wellness Energy System

Energy Input. Imagine yourself receiving energy from three major sources: breathing (oxygen), sensing (stimuli in your environment) and eating (food which is oxidized by cells and is used to build and repair body tissues). You convert some of the energy you take in to maintain the channel—your body—by generating heat and nerve impulses, replenishing and distributing blood, nutrients and hormones, and repairing tissues.

Energy Output. Now think of your body as a pipeline or conduit of energy. You channel this energy through your body, mind and being, converting it to forms of energy before returning it to the environment around you. Wellness results from the balanced flow of these energies through you.

The following represent the nine different outflows of energy to the environment.

- **Self-responsibility and love**. This is a form of energy which manifests as the attitude you choose toward your life. Wellness is enhanced by living your life with self-responsibility and love.
- **Moving**. Not only do you move your body through your external environment (exercise and fitness), but you move internal muscles to provide blood circulation, digestion, reproduction, etc.

Energy Check

The presence of disease is a message that some form of energy is not flowing smoothly in your life. You are in some way blocking, overusing or ignoring one or another form of energy.

- **Feeling**. Energy is also used for expressing emotions.
- **Thinking**. The brain is a major user of energy for thought processing, intuition and dreaming.
- **Playing/Working**. How you spend most of your waking hours.
- **Communicating**. A complex form of energy encompassing many of the preceding forms of energy.
- **Sex**. Covers the whole spectrum of life-energy, not just genital feelings.
- **Finding Meaning**. Seeking purpose and direction to the above forms of energy.
- **Transcending**. Beyond the rational and connects us with all-that-is.

Putting together the input and output, we have the complete Wellness Energy System of a human being. This system is an alternative to the usual piecemeal way of looking at health. It offers an integrated overview of all human life functions, seeing them as various forms of energy. The harmonious balancing of these life functions results in good health and well-being.

Summary

Small changes have a ripple effect because of the interdependence of all aspects of life. You can't wear tight shoes for very long before you start to notice that everything about your world feels cramped. When you are worried about something, you're likely to have an upset stomach, too. What may appear to be separate events or individual symptoms are really interconnected aspects of a much larger and more complex system. Since there are many of us, and we are all interacting and exchanging energy with each other and everything else in our environment, the picture is *very* large. Taken together as a whole, our picture can be no smaller than the whole planet. But remember that small changes can have big results. Through small changes, we can heal ourselves and our world.

References

Travis, J.W., & Regina, S.R. (1991). *Wellness: small changes you can use to make a big difference*. Berkeley, Ca.: Ten Speed Press.

Travis, J.W. & Callander, M.G. (1990). *Wellness for helping professionals, creating compassionate cultures*. Mill Valley, Ca.: Wellness Associates Publications.

Part 8

Special Populations

Large Exerciser

Prenatal

Senior

Adaptive

Accessibility

Youth

Additional Populations

Teaching Fitness to the Large Exerciser

43

Gail Johnston

The information presented in this chapter is consistent with AFAA's Specialty Certification "Teaching Fitness to the Large Exerciser." Only a portion of the related Standards and Guidelines are summarized below.

Focus

THE PRIMARY GOAL OF ANY EXERCISE PROGRAM should be to improve or maintain the health of the individual who is exercising. Many instructors have lacked the knowledge and confidence to provide safe and effective fitness programs for the large exerciser. Coupled with the embarrassment and anxiety many large exercisers feel when they begin exercising, the number of programs suited for this special population's needs has been rather small. New approaches and programming alternatives are being developed all the time as we expand movement options for the large exerciser.

Destroying the Myths

Because of the pervasive fat bias that exists in this country, it is important to dispel some myths at the start.

Fat people are all at health risk. Health risk is determined by poor lifestyle habits, not the number of pounds recorded on the scale. Obesity is a contributing risk factor for heart disease, not a major one. It is the correlation with such conditions as hypertension, hyperlipidemia and diabetes that links obesity with heart disease.

Fat people should exercise. To exercise is a matter of choice. While exercise is a healthy habit to adopt, large people do not deserve to feel that they have an obligation to society to exercise.

Fat people are all inactive. Dancers, exercisers and athletes come in all sizes. Celebrities Nell Carter, Lynne Cox, John Goodman and any number of football players role model the larger perspective on this issue because they have all won acclaim for their active performances. The more permission we give to large people to enjoy movement and not undertake it as punishment for their body size, the more large people we will see indulging in sports and exercise programs.

Fat people are all uncoordinated. The size of the body is not the determinant of grace, coordination or physical ability. While each person brings his or her own physical limitations to the activity, physical ability is also enhanced by repetition and practice.

Thinness is the goal of exercise. As long as this myth continues, there will be an enormous number of people who will not be able to succeed at exercise. Finding pleasure in movement is the process, and the process of integrating pleasurable exercise into a healthy lifestyle is the ultimate goal.

Guiding Your Clients Toward Success

As a fitness professional, your job is to support your client through his or her process of changing from an inactive lifestyle to an active one. This requires a variety of attitudes and skills.

A non-judgmental attitude sets up a psychologically safe environment. Only harm can come from evaluating an individual's worth according to his or her size, lifestyle, speech, appearance, color, ethnicity or gender. Lectures, criticism and reprimands have no place in this process of positive change.

Effective listening skills help to facilitate the change process because your clients feel as if they're being heard. Active listening takes practice because it requires total concentration. It places a greater importance on hearing what other people say than on what you feel the need to say to them. This skill helps your clients develop a bond with you based on the assurance that your listening is proof that they are worthy human beings.

Support your clients as they move toward their goals. Don't project your own goals onto your clients. Let them determine the exercise intensity that is comfortable for them. Give them time to decide which exercises give them pleasure and to determine their own level of satisfaction with their performances. Allow them to feel successful for just being there with you.

Role modeling healthy lifestyle practices shows your clients that the lifestyle they are struggling to achieve is possible. It also gives you an opportunity to practice what you preach. In your life, do you give as much attention to your spiritual and emotional health as you do to your physical health? Are you forgiving of yourself when you aren't perfect? Do you totally accept and appreciate your body as it is? Are you patient with yourself when you're learning something new?

An ongoing hunger for knowledge helps you avoid fads, educate your clients and maintain a full array of options for problem-solving.

Participant Screening

A current health assessment and health risk appraisal is essential for all clients. Please refer to the AFAA Standards and Guidelines regarding pre-class procedures and medical clearance. The guidelines are appropriate for large individuals. Anyone with a pre-existing medical condition or family history of risk factors should be screened by his or her physician prior to beginning an exercise program.

The primary responsibility for the individual's overall health management should lie with the individual and his or her physician. Requiring physician approval may be one of the first barriers to fitness for your large clients. Many large people are reluctant to approach their physicians for an exercise recommendation for fear that the medical approval will be wrapped in prejudicial language such as "Of course you should exercise. You'll lose that weight and look a lot better." To help your clients past this barrier, maintain a list of names of physicians who are "fat-friendly" to whom you can refer.

Fitness testing (e.g., body composition, step tests, muscular strength, flexibility and endurance tests) is commonly offered prior to beginning an exercise program as a motivational tool for the client. Some clients, however, will push beyond their current fitness levels in order to "pass" the tests. Also, it may not be inspiring for a client to learn that his or her body fat is over 30%. Because fitness testing may be demotivating for some and uncomfortable for others, it should be administered only on an individual basis as your clients request it.

Monitoring Intensity

Fatty deposits in the area of the wrist and neck make pulse monitoring the least effective method of evaluating exercise intensity. The preferred method is the Borg Rated Perceived Exertion (RPE) Scale.

The goal is to exert to the degree that the exercise feels moderate to strong, or within the range of "moderate" to "strong." This is more of a "whole body" perception, as opposed to the feeling in a certain area of the body (e.g., legs or chest). See chapter on "Monitoring Aerobic Intensity" for Borg Scale of Rated Perceived Exertion.

Five Questions for the Large Client

There are no specific exercises that can or should be done by the person possessing a larger body. The key to appropriate fitness programming is to learn how to modify exercises for each individual client based on the answers to the following five questions for that individual.

- What is the most effective position to work this muscle group considering the weight distribution?
- Is the spine protected?
- What is the leverage to be considered?
- What is a reasonable speed of movement?
- What is a reasonable range of motion?

Exercise Considerations

Don't limit the movement options. Without your assistance, your clients are successfully navigating a wide range of daily activities that includes standing, sitting, bending, lifting, climbing stairs, and getting in and out of cars. Your role is to expand on these movements. Don't put your clients in a chair unless non-weight-bearing exercise is recommended.

Four elements of a safe and effective exercise class should be integrated in the following order:

- Safety first because pain or injury is one of the most common reasons for dropping out of an exercise program.
- Motivation next to help the exerciser focus on the social and pleasurable aspects of movement.
- Alignment is next because most new exercisers feel as if they've done something wrong when their alignment gets corrected.
- Education is last, not because it is unimportant but because education does not usually motivate new exercisers to stay with their programs.

When clients are ready for education, they usually start asking questions.

Include movements that open the body such as stretches for the pectoralis group. Because of the fat bias in our society, it is common for the posture of larger individuals to close down as if they are trying to hide their bodies.

Consider the speed of the movement. Moving too quickly may cause an exerciser to use momentum to keep up. Backed by substantial body mass, a movement executed too quickly could lead to injury.

High impact exercise is contraindicated. A compression of three times body weight on the lower leg could lead to injury over time.

Exercises that teach kinesthetic awareness are helpful for individuals who are out of touch with their bodies. For example, place a hand on the working muscle to feel for the contraction.

Balancing exercises help clients find their center of gravity to assist with grace and confidence in movement. These exercises should be done with the option of a ballet barre, wall or other support.

Adapt exercises to allow body mass to move for greater range of motion. For example, when an individual with greater abdominal body mass is performing spinal flexion in a seated position, one or both legs should be in a straddle position so range of motion is not limited by the abdomen contacting the thighs.

The supine position is recommended only for limited periods of time. Compression of internal organs from large torso body mass may inhibit breathing if the position is held for long periods of time.

Last, but certainly not least, don't forget the fun factor. The actions of stretching and contracting are not necessarily fun for someone who has been inactive for a long time. You can add fun to your class through music, movement, instruction, versatility, personality and a little craziness.

Criteria for Discontinuing Exercise

Shoulder, chest, arm discomfort

Fainting (syncope)

Dizziness

Fatigue

Nausea

Shortness of breath (dyspnea)

Orthostatic hypotension

Uncontrolled, spastic movement (ataxia)

Summary

Movement options for the large exerciser are constantly expanding as our knowledge of this special population increases. A comprehensive exercise program will meet the needs of the large exerciser by providing safe and effective fitness activities.

44 Pregnancy and Fitness

Bonnie Rote, RN, NACES

Focus

THIS CHAPTER WILL DISCUSS the anatomical and physiological changes that occur in pregnancy that affect exercise, with particular emphasis on the muscles most stressed by pregnancy and childbirth. Pertinent adaptations to a basic exercise program will also be discussed as they relate to each of these changes.

The Fit Pregnancy

Pregnancy is finally starting to be recognized as a modified state of health rather than a state of illness. As a result, more women are continuing their daily regimens, including exercise, throughout their pregnancies. In addition, women who become pregnant are more aware of the positive benefits of exercise and may elect to start a program, despite not having exercised for many years prior to becoming pregnant. Both the beginner and the experienced exerciser have the same anatomical and physiological changes which will affect their ability to exercise. However, some guidelines may differ for these two groups, as the experienced exerciser is more fit and has much more kinesthetic awareness than her beginning counterpart.

> Quicker labor?
> No.
>
> Quicker recovery?
> More likely.

Instructors of pregnant exercisers are responsible for educating their students as to how the changes of pregnancy will affect their exercise programs, and how to safely modify routines to reduce the chances of physical injury to themselves and to the developing fetus. Ongoing prenatal care and close communication with their caregivers on the type, frequency and intensity of exercise is a must for the pregnant student. Students often place unrealistic expectations on the effect that exercise may have on the outcome of their pregnancies, labors and deliveries. Research on exercise and pregnancy in humans is slight, and often conflicting. It has been shown that exercise during pregnancy can enhance energy level, self-esteem, and mood, while reducing some of the physical discomforts of pregnancy. A speedier recovery after delivery and a quicker return to the prepregnant state have also been documented.(1) Some research studies have also shown shorter second stages of labor and reduction in Cesarean section rates,(2) however other studies have shown no correlation to this. Although the instructor can have a positive influence on a pregnant woman's psychological as well as physical preparation for childbirth, it is also important that they keep a realistic perspective on the role exercise will have.

Physiological Changes

Hormonal Changes

Increased levels of the hormones relaxin, elastin, estrogen and progesterone soften the connective tissue surrounding the joints.(1) This is to allow the pelvic joints to expand to accommodate the baby passing through the pelvic inlet during birth, but unfortunately, all the weight bearing joints are affected too—especially the knees, ankles and hips. Stretches should not be taken to maximal resistance, just mild tension. Stretches for the adductors should be done with special caution, as forceful stretches of the inner thighs may place undue stress on the symphasis pubis (pubic bone) potentially causing separation. Warm-ups will need to be a little longer (8-12 minutes) and somewhat less vigorous to allow the joints to warm up adequately. Exercises which involve **deep knee flexion**, such as deep lunges or squats, should be modified so the hips do not drop below the knees. Activities that involve balance, forceful movements or extreme jarring should also be avoided to reduce the risk of orthopedic injury to the mother. The use of weights or rubber tubing for lower body strengthening of the abductors and adductors is cautioned due to the potential joint stress on the hip.

Hip abduction exercises in the side lying position, with the leg at a 45-degree angle with a long lever, may cause a feeling of instability in the pelvic joints for some women and should be modified to a shorter lever, or by bringing the leg in line with the pelvis. Supine hip adduction exercises should be done so that the legs go no wider than the shoulders to avoid stress on the groin muscles.

> *Longer warm-up*
>
> *Protect joints*

Cardiovascular and Hemodynamic Changes

The blood volume may increase as much as 30-50%.(3) Plasma volume increases more than the red blood cells, resulting in a tendency toward lower hematocrit levels. However, during exercise, plasma volume shifts resulting in hemoconcentration and improved oxygen carrying capacity in the blood.(1) This is considered to be a protective factor for the fetus. Heart rate and cardiac output are elevated at rest. The resting heart rate may elevate as much as 15 beats per minute during pregnancy.(4) As a result, pregnant women reach their maximal capacity at a lower level of physical work than when nonpregnant, especially with weight bearing exercise.(5) Cardiovascular responses to exercise are even more variable during pregnancy, therefore close monitoring of the heart rate is recommended.(1)

Exercise also causes a **redistribution of blood flow** to the working muscles and away from the splanchnic organs which include the uterus. Animal studies have shown that at least 50% of the blood flow must be shunted away from the uterus before the fetus appears to be affected.(6) Other animal studies have also shown that the blood that does flow to the uterus tends to favor the area where the placenta is attached, therefore the blood flow to the fetus is not as compromised.(7)

A beginning prenatal student should keep the duration of her cardiovascular workout to 15-20 minutes with heart rate checks at approximately five minute intervals. Although perceived exertion is a better indicator for a pregnant woman to determine proper intensity, a beginning student lacks the body awareness to rely on this completely. The experienced exerciser who is accustomed to exercising longer may continue to do so, provided her intensity level during that time period is reduced. Training at the same perceived physiological strain is recommended.(9) Heart rates should be monitored also with checks at least at ten minute intervals. Training heart rates should be 60-70% of heart rate maximum, with a more advanced exerciser at 75%. Exceeding 144 beats per minute is not recommended due to lack of research beyond this range. Training

> ### The "144" Rule
>
> *A meta analytic review of the existing research on pregnant exercisers has shown that an exercise program using a variety of exercise modes performed for an average of 43 minutes per day, three times per week at a heart rate of up to 144 bpm appears to be safe.(8) The authors also caution that the application of these findings should be approached very carefully until further research is available.*

60-70% = THR

but not > 144

at Resting Heart Rate + 1/2 Heart Rate Reserve (220 - Age - Resting Heart Rate) has also been recommended.(10) In addition, an overly vigorous rhythmic warm-up may elevate the heart rate too quickly, so it is recommended to be aware of how much of the rhythmic movements involve keeping the arms above shoulder level.

Recovery from the cardiovascular workout is an excellent indicator of exercise tolerance, and should be monitored closely. When women reach their third trimester, they tend to have more variability in their ability to recover from vigorous activity (see side bar on recovery pulse rates, p. 349).(11)

The weight of the uterus and fetus may also compress the **inferior vena cava** when the mother is in a supine position. This compression decreases the venous return from the legs to the heart and head. Symptoms usually include dizziness, lightheadedness, nausea and restlessness. Students who suffer from these symptoms should avoid this position, and supine exercises will need to be modified. Symptoms will usually occur after the fourth month of pregnancy, and students should be encouraged to roll to their left sides if they are uncomfortable on their backs. If a student does not have any symptoms, exercises in the supine position should be limited to four to five minutes at a time to allow for optimal circulation.

Modifications for supine abdominals might include standing, upright positions or reclining on two pillows. Modifications for supine buttocks work might include standing, side lying pelvic tilts or all fours positions if tolerated. It should be noted that there is no documented research that links any fetal problems or defects at birth to a mother being in a supine position after the fourth month of pregnancy; however, a conservative approach to this issue is still recommended.

Respiratory Changes

Fetal oxygen demands may increase a pregnant woman's resting VO_2 as much as 16-32%.(12) Pressure on the diaphragm from the enlarging uterus reduces the height of the pleural cavities as much as four centimeters, causing a feeling of dyspnea or difficulty taking a deep breath.(1) The **decreased functional reserve capacity** and residual volume is compensated for by an increase in tidal volume and lateral expansion of the lungs. Pregnant women tend to breathe deeper, not faster to meet the increased oxygen requirements of pregnancy. Research indicates that mild to moderate levels of exercise appear to be well tolerated in relation to increases in oxygen consumption, but research on oxygen consumption during strenuous exercise and weight bearing versus non-weight bearing exercise is conflicting.(4)

Metabolic Changes

The needs of the growing fetus increase the basal metabolic rate of the mother. Body core temperature also increases. Animal studies have linked neural tube defects to high body core temperatures during the first trimester of pregnancy.(13) Some human studies corroborate this, but the studies have been on women who ran high fevers during their early pregnancies.(13) The exact level of intrauterine temperature that is potentially harmful to the fetus is unknown; however, studies done on pregnant exercisers have shown that exercise in moderation was well tolerated with no resultant hyperthermia.(14)

Since the neural tube is developing at three to four weeks of pregnancy,(15) this appears to be the most vulnerable time period for hyperthermia. **Dehydration** during exercise could have a very harmful effect and is a known cause of premature labor later in pregnancy. Pregnant women should be encouraged to drink before, during and after exercise and cautioned not to exercise when they are febrile, or in hot, humid weather, when their own mechanisms for heat dissipation are compromised.(1)

Hot tubs, saunas and Jacuzzis should be avoided to minimize the possibility of overheating.

Endocrine Changes

Due to the demands for glucose from the fetus, blood glucose levels, particularly fasting blood glucose levels tend to be lower. Pregnant women also tend to use carbohydrates at a greater rate during exercise.(1, 4) Hypoglycemia may occur during prolonged exercise. Morning exercisers who suffer from morning sickness and working mothers who exercise immediately after work may be at risk due to prolonged periods of not eating prior to their workout.

Epinephrine and norepinephrine levels increase significantly during physical activity. Norepinephrine increases the frequency and amplitude of uterine contractions.(1) The progesterone and estrogen tend to negate these effects. However, individuals who are susceptible to premature labor may be cautioned not to exercise too vigorously to avoid the risk of initiating contractions.

Eat or drink a snack rich in complex carbohydrates and protein at least one to two hours before exercising.

Anatomical Changes

Lordosis

As the uterus increases in size and weight, it pulls the pelvis into a forward tilt, causing stress on the lumbar sacral ligament and lower back muscles. This causes constant shifting of the center of gravity, hence the concern for doing activities requiring balance. The abdominal muscles tend to stretch and weaken while the lower back muscles tend to shorten resulting in a "sway back" or lordotic posture. Students should concentrate on strengthening the abdominal muscles, buttocks and quadriceps, and stretching the lower back and hip flexor muscles.

Maintaining proper pelvic alignment throughout all exercises will help stabilize the torso and reduce the risk of lower back strain. Gentle rocking of the pelvis while concentrating on tightening the buttocks, quadriceps and abdominal muscles in standing, all fours and supine positions will help strengthen these areas. Hip flexor and lower back stretches should be included in the warm-up and cooldown sections of the workout. Due to the natural tendency to assume a lordotic posture, pregnant students need to be constantly reminded to maintain a neutral pelvic alignment, especially in non-weight bearing positions, as they are often unaware of their lower back posture in these positions.(16)

Tilting the pelvis back into correct neutral alignment will help avoid lower back pain.

Kyphosis

The weight of the enlarging breasts tends to pull the shoulders forward resulting in a slouched posture of the upper back (kyphosis). The pectoralis muscles shorten while the upper back muscles (trapezius and rhomboid) stretch and weaken. Upper body work should focus on strengthening the upper back muscles in order to avoid a permanent postural imbalance.(17) If a student is accustomed to using low weights and executes proper alignment, she could continue using them as long as she doesn't increase the weight load. Deconditioned or unfit pregnant students who are beginners are not advised to use more than one to three pounds, provided they can execute the exercises

Use of weights

properly. Strengthening of all the upper body muscles is recommended to prepare women for carrying their infants and baby equipment (strollers, diaper bags, etc.) and to reduce strain on their backs.

Carpal Tunnel Syndrome

Edema associated with pregnancy can cause swelling in the wrists resulting in compression of the median nerve.(18) Symptoms include numbness and tingling when the wrists are in a flexed position. Exercises such as the all fours position, wall push-ups, or flexed wrists during certain arm movements may cause these symptoms of carpal tunnel syndrome. Use of rubber tubing for upper body strengthening is not recommended due to the tendency of students to "break" the alignment of their wrists and potentially exacerbate the condition.

Round Ligament Syndrome

The uterus is suspended in the abdominal cavity by ligaments. Two ligaments run diagonally down the pelvis from the hip bones. After a fetal growth spurt, women may notice a dull, pulling sensation in these ligaments for two to three days until the ligaments adjust to the stretching. Sudden turns or sharp movements may illicit a spasm in these round ligaments. Bending slightly forward, taking deep breaths, and massaging the area gently will usually help. Movements which involve turns, or lateral movements which don't keep the hips facing front, may irritate the round ligaments. Anticipatory cues for directional changes in the cardiovascular workout are extremely important to avoid sudden turns. The round ligaments may also bother some women in the all fours

Sudden turns

position when the leg is fully extended behind for hip extension. This exercise may need to be modified to keep the leg lower and use a short lever position.

Pelvic Floor Muscles

The pelvic floor or pubococcygeal muscles are probably one of the most stressed muscles groups during pregnancy and childbirth. They are located between the legs and are attached to the pubic bone in front and coccyx in back. This muscle group is responsible for supporting the weight of the pelvic organs (uterus, bladder and bowel) and encircles the urinary opening, the outer vagina and anus. During pregnancy, the weight of the uterus and growing baby places tremendous stress on these muscles. During childbirth, these muscles undergo tremendous stretching in order to allow the baby to pass through the birth canal. In addition to helping control urination, exercising the pelvic floor muscles is helpful for:

1. Increasing the tone and elasticity of the muscles which allows them to stretch more easily during birth.
2. Restoring muscle tone in the vagina after childbirth.
3. Increasing feelings of sexual arousal during foreplay and sexual intercourse.
4. Increasing circulation to the genital area.

To locate the pelvic floor muscles, students should be told to sit on the toilet, and try stopping and starting the flow of urine, by tightening up inside, without moving their legs.

The simple Kegel exercise is an excellent way to strengthen the pelvic floor muscles. This exercise can be done in several different ways.

1. Tighten the muscles used to stop the flow of urine, hold for a count of ten, and release.

Include Kegels

Prenatal classes should always include Kegel exercise. Students in regular classes should be encouraged to "Kegel" during any exercises which involve a vulnerable position for the pelvic floor, such as modified squat and lunge work, and at any other appropriate time in class.

2. Rapidly tighten and relax the muscle.
3. "Elevator" exercise—gradually tighten the muscle slowly to the count of three, pulling up and holding at each "floor"; then relax slowly to count of three, stopping at each "floor."
4. When doing the "elevator" in preparation for giving birth, allow the muscle to totally relax or "bulge" slightly (the "basement") after relaxing to the count of three. This very relaxed state is used during pushing to ease the baby down the birth canal and through the pelvic floor muscles.

Students should be encouraged to try to build up to five to ten sessions of ten repetitions throughout each day. After delivery, students often forget these muscles since they are not visible. Rehabilitation of this muscle group is crucial to avoid long-term problems such as stress urinary incontinence and sexual dysfunction from weak pelvic floor muscles.(17)

Diastasis Recti and Abdominal Strengthening

As stated previously, the enlarging uterus stretches and weakens the abdominal muscles. Maintaining strength and tone in these muscles is critical for lower back support and pushing. It should be noted that pregnancy is not the time to expect or train for significant strength gains. Abdominal strengthening should be conservative and relative to the incoming strength level of the participant.

Exercises should be done in a slow, controlled manner (pulsing or rapid contractions should be avoided) to avoid undue stress on the linea alba. The **linea alba** is the fibrous seam which connects the two rectus muscle sheaths in the center of the abdomen. Positions for abdominal strengthening may need to be modified if a mother cannot lie supine. It is also extremely important for students to exhale on the effort phase to avoid the Valsalva maneuver. The Valsalva maneuver involves holding the breath and straining or bearing down during effort. This can result in a rapid increase in blood pressure and intra-abdominal pressure.

The muscle used most in childbirth is the **transverse abdominis**. Particular attention should be paid to strengthening this muscle group. Pulling the abdominals inward and holding them in with forced exhalation in a supine or an all fours position is a very good exercise.(17) However, they should avoid doing a Valsalva maneuver. Pregnant women should be reminded to pull in with their transverse muscles during all exercises, and to use and strengthen this muscle group as much as possible. They tend to forget to hold their abdominal muscles in once they begin to "show."

The hormones secreted during pregnancy also relax the linea alba. Women may notice a thicker waistline as a result of the decreased tone very early in pregnancy. As the uterus expands, the forces may cause the linea alba to separate (diastasis recti), like a zipper under too much stress.

Since the oblique muscles insert into this seam, once separation occurs, oblique exercises which involve trunk rotation should be avoided.(17) This separation, considered very normal during pregnancy, is painless and often goes unnoticed. It may happen gradually or occur suddenly as with a bout of excessive vomiting or constipation. See side bar for checking for separation and modification of abdominal exercises.(17)

Students beginning an exercise program in their last trimester should stick to maintenance exercises such as standing pelvic tilts and abdominal contractions inward with exhalation.

Safety Concerns

The safety of the mother and her unborn child is the primary concern during exercise. Students should be told to stop exercising and consult their physicians should any of the following occur:

Pain

Dizziness

Pubic Pain

Back Pain

Bleeding

Faintness

Tachycardia

Palpitations

Shortness of Breath

Difficulty Walking

Recovery Heart Rate

1. Exercise at your normal aerobic workout intensity.
2. Count your pulse for 10 seconds immediately after stopping the exercise (post exercise pulse rate).
3. Multiply the number by 6.
4. Allow 1 minute to pass and count your pulse again for 10 seconds (1 minute pulse rate).
5. Multiply the number by 6.
6. Subtract 1 minute pulse rate from post exercise pulse rate to get recovery pulse rate.
7. Divide recovery pulse rate by 10 for score.

Interpretation:
5-6 = highly efficient recovery rate
4 = average untrained recovery rate
1-3 = low recovery rate indicating least efficient cardiac output

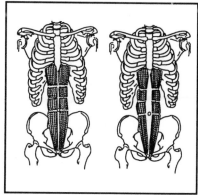

Fig. 44-1. Diastasis Recti (4 and 9 months)

Diastasis Recti

Check for diastasis

1. Have student lie on her back with knees bent.
2. Gently but firmly place 1-2 fingers perpendicular to the linea alba, at a 90-degree angle to the abdomen, approximately 1-2 inches below the naval.
3. As the student slowly raises her head and shoulders, check how many fingers you can insert into the gap.
4. You may observe a bulge in the central abdominal area as the head and shoulders are raised.

Results

1. Separation of 1/2 inch or 1 finger is considered normal.
2. If separation is 2 fingers: (a) eliminate any oblique work involving trunk rotation, (b) splint the muscle by crossing the hands over the abdominal area. Slowly raise the head and exhale. Do not elevate the shoulders or raise the head to the point where the bulge appears. (See Fig. 45-2.)
3. If separation is more than 2 fingers: (a) eliminate head raises. Do not do leg lowering type exercises. (b) Do abdominal contractions with outward breaths and pelvic tilts using abdominal muscles to tilt the pelvis in various positions.

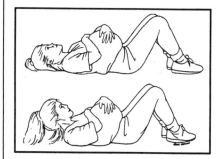

Fig. 44-2. Splinting the abdominal muscles

References

1. American College of Obstetricians and Gynecologists (1985). *Exercise during pregnancy and the postnatal period.* Washington, D.C.: ACOG home exercise programs, 1-6.

2. Hall D., & Kaufman D. (1987). Effects of aerobic and strength conditioning on pregnancy outcomes. *American Journal of Obstetrics and Gynecology,* 157: 1199-1203.

3. Metcalfe, J., McAnulty, J. H., & Ueland, K. (1981). Cardiovascular physiology. *Clinical Obstetrics and Gynecology,* 24: 693-710.

4. Wells, C. L. (1985). *Women sports and performance.* Champaign, Ill.: Human Kinetics.

5. Ueland, K., Novy, M., Peterson, E., et al (1969). Maternal cardiovascular dynamics IV. The influence of gestational age on the maternal cardiovascular response to posture and exercise. *Amerian Journal of Obstetrics and Gynecology,* 104: 856-864.

6. Lotgering, F.K., Gilbert, R.D., & Longo, L.D. (1985). Maternal and fetal responses to exercise during pregnancy. *Physiological Reviews,* 65: 1-36.

7. Bonds, D. R., & Delivoria-Papadopoulos, M. (1985). Exercise during pregnancy—Potential fetal and placental metabolic effects. *Annals of Clinical and Laboratory Science,* 15: 91-99.

8. Lokey, E,. Tran, Z.V., Wells, C., Myers, B., & Tran, A. (1991). Effects of physical exercise on pregnancy outcomes: A meta analytic review. *Medicine and Science in Sports and Exercise,* 23: 1234-39.

9. Cummings, S. (Jan., 1986). The pregnant pause. *Health Magazine,* 68-73.

10. Shangold, M., & Mirkin, G. (1985). *The complete sports medicine book for women.* New York: Simon and Schuster.

11. Kattus, A.A. (1972). *Exercise testing and training of apparently healthy individuals: A handbook for physicians.* New York: American Heart Association Committee on Exercise.

12. Gorski, J. (1984). Exercise during pregnancy: Maternal and fetal responses. A brief review. *Medicine and Science in Sports and Exercise,* 17: 407-416.

13. Goodlin, R.C., & Buckley, K.K. (1984). Maternal Exercise. *Clinics in Sports Medicine,* 3: 883-894.

14. Jones, R.L., Botti, J.J., Anderson, W.M., & Bennett, N.L. (1985). Thermoregulation during aerobic exercise in pregnancy. *Obstetrics and Gynecology,* 65: 340-345.

15. Nilsson, L. (1986). *A Child is born.* New York: Dell.

16. Rote, B., & Sekine, K. (1987). The educational needs of the prenatal patient who participates in dance exercise. *Topics in acute care and trauma rehabilitation,* 22: 67-82.

17. Noble, E. (1982). *Essential exercises for the childbearing years.* Boston: Houghton Mifflin.

18. Artal, R., Freedman, M., & McNitt-Gray, J. (1990). Orthopedic problems in pregnancy. *The Physician and Sports Medicine,* 18:9: 93-105.

45 Senior Fitness

Laura A. Gladwin, MS

Focus

THIS CHAPTER WILL REVIEW the importance of screening the senior participant as well as developing a safe and effective total body conditioning program for our older population. It will also discuss senior exercise adherence and give an example of a workable class format.

Today, Americans are growing older and living longer, with those individuals over sixty being the fastest growing age segment of the United States. By the year 2030, approximately 21% of us will be over 65 years of age. Because of this extension in longevity, health professionals are looking for ways to improve and maintain the quality of life in the elderly. Researchers and gerontologists have been investigating the effects of exercise on the senior population and have found excellent results. Evidence indicates that exercise is an important factor in preventing or at least slowing down many age-related declines in physical functions and performance, such as cardiovascular and pulmonary functions, muscular strength and endurance, balance and flexibility and bone mineral density. Now with increased interest in exercise prescription for improved quality of life for the elderly, trained professionals in the field of senior fitness are becoming more in demand.

Programming for the Elderly

As in any age group, senior fitness levels vary from individual to individual. Therefore, it is important to screen your senior participants with a medical history questionnaire. In addition, tests of functional capacity (treadmill test or one-mile walk test) are recommended, since as people age they display higher incidences of heart disease, arthritis, neuromuscular dysfunction, diabetes, muscular atrophy, pulmonary insufficiency, orthopedic limitations, and possible cerebral atrophy, all of which can limit exercise capacity. In 1992 over 12% of the American population was 65 years or older. This group consumed over 30% of all prescription drugs dispensed, and as much as 40% of all nonprescription drugs purchased annually. Cardiovascular medications, diuretics, sedatives, and tranquilizers represent about half of these drugs and can affect exercise tolerance. For example, beta blockers such as Inderal, Pindalol, Corgard, and Tenormin may cause slowing of the heart beat, low blood pressure, drowsiness and orthostatic intolerance during exercise. The fitness professional should be aware of each of the above conditions and how each may limit exercise capacity.

Importance of Screening

It is also important to understand that most individuals 65 and over can participate safely in regular physical activity, both endurance and strength training. Therefore, when developing senior fitness programs, refer to the exercise guidelines set forth by the American College of Sports Medicine (ACSM), and the Standards and Guidelines of the Aerobics and Fitness Association of America for Senior Fitness. During program development, incorporate all aspects of fitness, such as aerobic conditioning, muscular strength, muscular endurance, and flexibility.

Cardiovascular Conditioning

For the average, healthy, mature adult (over 50) AFAA and ACSM recommend beginning aerobic exercise at a low to moderate intensity, three to five times per week for a minimum of 20 minutes. A more frequent, longer duration activity, at a low to moderate intensity, will produce positive physiological changes within an aging body with less injury occurring. Activity-related injuries may occur more frequently among elderly people due to poor flexibility, osteoporosis, or other musculoskeletal disorders. Therefore, aerobic exercises such as walking, swimming, stationary bicycling, low-impact aerobic dance, and seated-chair aerobics are recommended along with an adequate warm-up and cooldown period.

An inadequate heart rate response to exercise may be found in the senior participant. Because of this, the use of rated perceived exertion (RPE) may be a better indicator of exercise intensity than a heart rate. However, Andrew Ostrow in his book, *Physical Activity and the Older Adult,* suggests that older adults may not be accurate in their ability to rate exercise exertion levels. It may be advisable to use both a target heart rate and RPE when determining exercise intensity in the senior participant.

> *Initially, include both RPE and THR.*

Muscular Strength and Endurance

With normal aging, a general reduction in muscle mass occurs. The **loss of muscle mass** is thought to be due to atrophy from disuse resulting in a decrease in the number of muscle fibers and in the diameter of the remaining fibers. The loss of muscle fiber has been reported to be as high as 30% between the ages of 30 and 80. The good news is that it is never too late to gain strength through exercise. Fiatarone, Marks, Ryan, Meredith, Lipsitz, and Evans (1990) studied ten men and women, all 90 years of age, relative to their strength development potential. After completing an eight-week, high intensity weight-training program (focusing on the quadriceps) results showed a 174% strength gain in the right legs of the subjects. The lower extremity strength gain ranged from 61 to 374%, demonstrating a three- to four-fold increase in strength overall.

> *ACSM (1990) recommendations for strength training in the healthy senior participant are as follows: A training frequency of two times per week minimum, a minimum of one set per muscle group and 8 to 12 repetitions per set at moderate to slow speed, exercising 8 to 10 different muscle groups.*

Circuit training using light weights and high repetitions is the most recommended program for older adults. Resistance training utilizing isotonic exercises are preferred over isometric exercises since isometric exercises have a tendency to elevate blood pressure leaving the older adult at possible risk. However, individuals suffering from arthritis may be an exception. Isotonic strengthening of muscle groups at inflamed joints can aggravate tenderness and pain. In this instance, employment of slow stretching and very conservative isometric exercises help to prevent muscle atrophy.

Low weight/high repetition resistance exercise (which can easily be incorporated into group fitness classes) is less risky for older exercisers, and it increases muscular endurance significantly. Muscular endurance is considered to be more useful than absolute muscular strength in the day-to-day activities of older individuals. Furthermore, low-resistance work has resulted in improved absolute strength in older individuals. The use of elastic bands and exercises performed in water, with the water acting as the resistance, are also very effective in developing muscular strength in older adults.

Balance and Flexibility

Balance, a physical performance variable, is typically found to decrease with age and is thought to be an important factor relative to the prevention of falls.(22) The chances are about one in three that individuals who have reached the age of 80 will suffer an injurious fall.(23) Exercise and/or activity has been found to significantly reduce the loss of balance in the elderly, particularly elderly women. It is extremely valuable, therefore, for you to discuss proper body mechanics as they relate to balance as well as to develop exercises which focus on improving balance.

Flexibility is another area of concern. Flexibility tends to be lost due to connective tissue stiffening and a decrease in mobility with age. However, regular exercise can help reduce the loss of flexibility.

In a study by Rikli and Edwards (1991) 31 previously sedentary, female volunteers ages 57 to 85 were measured for flexibility over a three-year period while participating in an exercise program which included static stretching and range of motion exercises (i.e., overhead arm reaches, hamstring stretches, shoulder stretches and rotations, and trunk and hip flexion and extension). Results showed significant gains in shoulder flexibility and improvement in the sit and reach flexibility test during the first year with flexibility levels maintained over the second and third years.

Exercise Adherence

Exercise adherence for the elderly participant is a key toward positive physical results. Factors that influence exercise adherence include changes in fitness and health status of the participant, increased feelings of competence and personal growth and commitment and goal setting. Exercise programs specifically designed for the older adult that are enjoyable and offer tasks which are easily completed may create a positive effect on exercise adherence as well.

Active fit vs. sedentary unfit

Physiological adaptations come about more slowly in older adults, so implementation of an exercise program should start gradually and then progress at a slower rate than would be implemented for younger adults. There are exceptions to this rule, however. The young active seniors (60s and 70s) are sometimes more apt to attend fitness classes designed for 20 to 50 year olds (i.e., step aerobics, low impact aerobics and conditioning classes). They do not consider themselves "old." They are healthy, very active, and very alive individuals. Placing them in a senior fitness class supposedly designed for their aging needs may actually be interpreted as an insult instead of a positive gesture on the instructor's part.

Keep in mind that a very active senior participant in his 70s can demonstrate the fitness level of a moderately-fit 30-year-old.(30) The senior fitness class may be more appropriately named for the sedentary, unfit mature adult (60 to 90). This individual may feel more comfortable exercising among his/her peers or in the privacy of his/her own home. (Personal trainers should be alert to this potential market.)

Class Format

As a suggested format for the healthy, sedentary, mature adult (60-90), begin the class with an easy warm-up, followed by a 30-minute, low-to-moderate walking program. The time element will vary because of the variety of fitness levels and physical disabilities. Some participants may walk for 15 minutes, others for 30. Let them know that they should keep walking as long as they feel comfortable and are welcome to stop at any time. Then take approximately 30 minutes for stretching all the muscles in the body, working from head to toe. This is a wonderful time to work on posture, breathing, body awareness and kinesthetic awareness (body movements in relation to space). Include muscle stimulation and stretching exercise for the fingers and wrist as well as the foot and the ankle. A seated-chair position is recommended to allow novice participants to fully concentrate on each stretch without losing balance.

Upon completion of the stretching segment, allow approximately 30 minutes for major muscle strengthening. This can either be performed in a chair, on the floor (when not contraindicated) or in a standing position. Start your participants out by performing exercises that work the limb(s) against gravity as the only resistance. Once they have demonstrated proper form and body alignment, gradually progress them to mild resistance bands (Dynabands or other elastic bands) then up to hand-held weights. Do not forget abdominals! Seniors can get down onto the floor for abdominal work when not contraindicated. The few who feel more comfortable in a chair can remain in the chair and still perform abdominal exercises. We realize as professionals that this is not the most effective way to work abdominals, yet, for these participants, it is the safest. This is also a good time to demonstrate how to go from a standing position to the floor without injury. Use the chair as a support mechanism as much as possible, until participants have gained the necessary strength and confidence to do it on their own. Complete major muscle strengthening exercises with a final total body stretch.

End the class with a 30-minute, low-impact aerobic segment, including a simple warm-up and cooldown, using music and movement patterns that senior participants can relate to and enjoy. Keep the intensity low to moderate. Take a heart rate and RPE several times during this portion of the class and prior to class dismissal.

Class formats may differ, but the pattern described above seems to work when a variety of ages and fitness levels are present. The older senior participant enjoys the mild walking, stretching, and strengthening activities while the younger seniors and the ones who want more of a challenge will stay for the entire two-hour program. Remember, since each group is different, it is important to be objective and flexible and use the class format that works best for the individual group.

Walking

Muscle strengthening

Enjoyable and Pain-Free

Always remind participants that they are welcome to stop whenever discomfort arises or they feel tired and fatigued. Gradually build intensity and develop enjoyable, but realistic challenges in order to maintain interest.

Summary

As researchers continue to look at the process of aging, we see that everyone ages differently. And, the human body, no matter what age, can respond to and receive positive effects of training through regular exercise. With America growing older, exercise will play a major role in maintaining health and independence among the elderly. As a fitness professional, you can make a major contribution by providing safe and effective exercise programs.

References

1. Spence, A.P. (1989). *Biology of aging.* Englewood Cliffs, N.J.: Prentice Hall.

2. Shephard, R.J. (1981). Cardiovascular limitations in the aged. In E.L. Smith & R.C. Serfass (Eds.), *Exercise and aging: The scientific basis.* N.J.: Enslow Publishers.

3. Zadai, C.C. (1985). Pulmonary physiology of aging: The role of rehabilitation. *Topics in Gerontolgy Rehabilitation,* 1:1: 49.

4. Laforest, S., St. Pierre, D.M., Cyr, J., & Gayton, D. (1990). Effects of age and regular exercise on muscle strength and endurance. *European Journal of Applied Physiology,* 60: 104-111.

5. Rikli, R.E., & Edwards, D.J. (1991). Effects of a three-year exercise program on motor function and cognitive speed in older women. *Research Quarterly for Exercise and Sport.,* 62:1: 61-67.

6. Bennet, P.H. (1967). Report of work group on epidemiology. *National Committee on Diabetes,* 3:1.

7. Serfass, R.C., et al (1985). Exercise testing for the elderly. *Topics in Gerontology Rehabilitation,* 1:1: 58.

8. Shephard, R.J. (1984). Management of exercise in the elderly. *Canadian Journal Applied Sport Science,* 9:3: 109.

9. Williams, B.R. (March, 1992). Avoiding medication misadventure. Seminar: California State University, Fullerton.

10. Tanji, J.L (1990). Hypertension: Part I: How exercise helps. *The Physician And Sports Medicine,* 18:7: 77-81.

11. Cooper Aerobics Center (1989). Senior Fitness. Presented at the IDEA Educational Convention, San Diego. CA.

12. American College of Sports Medicine (1990). Position statement on the recommended quantity and quality of exercise for developing and maintaining cardiorespiratory and muscular fitness in healthy adults. *Medicine and Science In Sports And Exercise,* 22:2: 265-274.

13. Aerobics & Fitness Association of America (1990). Standards and Guidelines of the Aerobics & Fitness Association of America for Senior Fitness. Sherman Oaks, Ca.: AFAA.

14. Ward, A., Taylor, P., & Rippe. J. (1991). How to tailor an exercise program. *The Physician & Sportsmedicine,* 19:9: 64-74.

15. Ostrow, A. C. (1984). Physical activity and the older adult. Princeton, N.J.: Princeton Book Co.

16. Fiatarone, M.A., Marks, E.C., Ryan, N.D., Meredith, C.N., Lipsitz, L. A., & Evans, W.J. (1990). High intensity strength training in nonagenarians: effects on skeletal muscle. *Journal of American Medical Association,* 262:22: 3029-3034.

17. Dewitt, J., & Roberts, T. (September, 1991). Pumping up an adult fitness program. *JOPERD,* 67-71.

18. Anderson, T., & Keamey, J. T. (1982). Effects of three resistance training programs on muscular strength and absolute and relative endurance. *Research Quarterly for Exercise and Sport,* 53:1: 1-7.

19. Biegel, L. (1984). *Physical fitness and the older person: a guide to exercise for health care professionals.* Rockville, Md.: Aspen Systems Corporation.

20. Aniansson. A., & Gustafsson, E. (1981). Physical training in elderly men with special reference to quadriceps muscle strength and morphology. *Clinical Physiology,* 1: 87.

21. Eckert, H.M., & Espenschade. A.S. (1980). *Motor development* (2nd ed.) Columbus, Oh.: Charles E. Merrill Publishing Co.
22. Eckert. H.M. (1987). *Motor Development* (3rd ed.) Indianapolis, In.: Benchmark Press.
23. Gryfe, C.I., Amies. A., & Ashley. M.J. (1977). A longitudinal study of falls in an elderly population: 1. Incidence and morbidity." *Age & Ageing*, 6: 201-210.
24. Rikli, R.E., & Busch, S. (1986). Motor performance of women as a function of age and physical activity level. *Journal of Gerontology*, 41:5: 645-649.
25. Roberts, S. (March/April, 1990). Active aging: Exercise and the older athlete. *American Fitness*, 51-62.
26. Wankel, L.M. (1984)/ Decision making and social support strategies for increasing exercise involvement. *Journal of Cardiac Rehabilitation*, 4: 124-135.
27. Dishman, R.K. (1981). Prediction of adherence to habitual physical activity. In F. Nagle & H. Montoye (Eds.), *Exercise in Health and Disease*. Springfield, Ill.: Charles C. Thomas.
28. Martin, J.E., & Dubbert, P.M. (1984). Behavioral management strategies for improving health and fitness. *Journal of Cardiac Rehabilitation*. 4: 200-208.
29. Shephard, R.J. (1987). Human rights and the older worker: Changes in work capacity with age. *Medicine and Science in Sports and Exercise*, 19: 169-173.
30. Chinnici, M. (April, 1991). How to protect your body from time. *Self Report*, 128-129.

Sample Workout for Active Seniors

Janie Clark, MA

Warm-up for approximately 10 minutes with:
1. Rhythmical limbering movements (such as shoulder shrugs, hip shifts, and arm circles)
2. Gentle activity designed to increase circulation (such as walking in place and easy-does-it arm swings)
3. Conservatively-executed stretches (including mild stretches for the back, the hamstrings, and the calves)

Aerobics for approximately 20 minutes. Develop creative patterns by combining the steps shown below (as well as other low impact movements).

1. **March in place with arms active**

2. **"The Twist" (gentle versions only)**

3. **Knee lifts with arm reaches toward the front**

4a. **(Start) Side steps with claps (two steps to the side, then back)**

4b. **Repeat side steps with claps on other side**

5. **Toe touches to the front with arm reaches overhead**

6. **Aerobics performed in circle formation**

7. **The traveling conga line**

Observe a **post-aerobic cooldown** period for 5 to 10 minutes using non-strenuous movements similar to those performed during the warm-up. Gradually decrease the intensity level with light activity that engages the lower body along with gentle stretches.

Strengthening exercises for approximately 15 minutes. The following senior-specific modality considerations apply:

8. **Initially, senior should practice exercises without the use of resistive devices**

9. **As strength and confidence increase, easy-tension bands may be introduced**

10. **Upon further conditioning, light handweights may be employed**

11. Additional accessories (such as dowels, neckties, scarves, towels and foam-type balls) may be used

12. Floor work is appropriate when well tolerated. When getting up and down for floor work is difficult, chair routines may be developed

13. A viable alternative may be to combine seated, chair activity with standing exercise

14. Standing knee extension exercise for lower body strengthening

Below is a sample list of well-known, standard strengthening exercises appropriate for most older adults:

1. OPEN AND CLOSE HANDS
2. BICEPS CURL
3. TRICEPS EXTENSION
4. UPRIGHT ROW
5. SINGLE-ARM BENT OVER ROW (with spinal support supplied by placing the opposite hand and knee on a weight bench)
6. STANDING PUSH-UP WITH HANDS AGAINST WALL (pushing away from a wall is easier on delicate wrists than the traditional floor push-up)
7. MODIFIED BENT-KNEE SIT-UP (include forward curls as well as curls toward both sides)
8. REVERSE CURL

9. HAMSTRING AND GLUTEUS CONTRACTION
10. KNEE FLEXION
11. KNEE EXTENSION
12. LEG LIFT ENGAGING THE OUTER THIGH (abduction)
13. LEG LIFT ENGAGING THE INNER THIGH (adduction)
14. CALF LIFT (raise onto toes)
15. SHIN STRENGTHENER (With heel on floor, energetically tap toe to floor at a steady pace.)

Enjoy a **cooldown stretch** for 5 to 10 minutes. Below is a sample stretch routine suitable for almost all older adults. With reference to well-conditioned seniors, the chair stretches shown here may be modified for safe execution on the floor or in a standing position:

15. The backward reach

16. The upward reach

17. The gentle pull

**18. The forward stretch
with continuous hand
contact for spinal
support**

19. The turn

20. The leg hug

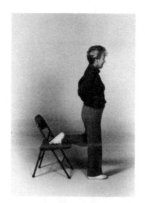

21. The quad stretch

22. The leg-out stretch

23. The leg-over stretch

24. The point

25. The flex

References

The Aerobics and Fitness Association of America (1990). *Standards and guidelines of the aerobics and fitness association of america for senior fitness*. Sherman Oaks, Ca.

Clark, J. (1992). *Full life fitness: a complete exercise program for mature adults*. Champaign Ill.: Human Kinetics Publishers.

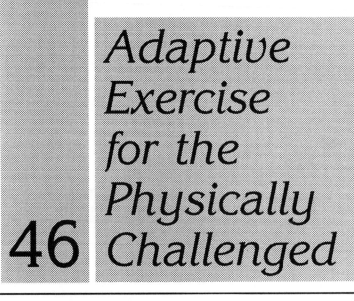

Adaptive Exercise for the Physically Challenged

46

Kathy F. Normansell, MS

Focus

NOT ALL PERSONS CAN READILY JOIN and receive benefits from a traditional aerobics class. The recognition of unique needs has increased the offerings of "specialty classes" for seniors, persons who are overweight, pregnant women, and those with cardiac problems. However, the specific needs of those with physical disabilities have not been fully addressed by any of these classes. The purpose of this chapter is to outline some of the physiological implications and related concerns of specific disabilities, to provide practical tips to aid instructors in integrating disabled members into their classes and to motivate instructors to seek additional training so that they can provide successful aerobic classes for participants who are disabled.

Physiological Responses to Exercise

Without a basic understanding of how disabilities can affect physiological responses to exercise, the aerobic instructor has no way of judging whether the aerobic needs of the disabled participant are being met. While both acute and chronic physiological responses to exercise can be predicted for able-bodied men and women, such responses cannot necessarily be generalized for the disabled person. Depending upon the extent and the type of disability, the degree of physiological response possible will vary from the able-bodied norms.

The rationale for an aerobic workout is to exercise the body hard enough to create a demand for a targeted amount of oxygen to be consumed (VO_2), thus positively stressing the cardiovascular system. It is the role of the cardiovascular system to deliver oxygenated blood to the working muscles and remove the waste products of the energy metabolism from these muscles. With the able-bodied population, the limiting factor during aerobic workouts usually involves the efficiency of the cardiovascular system. In simple terms, conditioning (training) strengthens the heart muscle, allowing it to pump more blood per stroke and improves the efficiency of the skeletal muscles in extracting and utilizing the oxygen.

During exercise, arterial circulation redistributes blood and oxygen from inactive organs to active muscles to support aerobic metabolism. If the oxygen

Compromised cardiac response.

demands exceed the ability of the heart to supply oxygenated blood, then the aerobic metabolism will be limited, resulting in fatigue and diminished work capacity. Thus, any disability which affects the control of the heart rate (HR), blood pressure, or myocardial contractibility can reduce the cardiac output response and the overall ability to perform aerobic exercise.

In some cases of spinal cord injury (SCI) above the sixth thoracic vertebrae, the autonomic nervous system (ANS) may be damaged to the extent that the heart rate cannot be stimulated above 100-110 bpm, obviously impairing the ability to distribute large quantities of oxygenated blood in a timely manner. Additionally, lack of sympathetic nervous control affects the maintenance of blood pressure through improper regulation of vasodilation and vasoconstriction. With any lower body paralysis, the skeletal venous pump is absent, resulting in venous pooling and edema which further limits the circulating blood volume.

The amount of oxygen utilized during exercise, and ultimately the degree of stress to the cardiovascular system, is determined by the amount of muscle activity. The more muscle mass working, the higher the demand for oxygen, the more "aerobic" is the activity. If a person is limited in the amount of functioning muscle available, then a large oxygen demand cannot be created and the cardiovascular system will not be fully stressed. Such conditions which limit functional muscle mass include full or partial paralysis, such as with spinal cord injury, spina bifida, polio or cerebral vascular injury (CVA), muscle denervation as with multiple sclerosis (MS), atrophy as with muscular dystrophy (MD), muscle spaciticity, common with head injury (HI), CVA or cerebral palsy (CP), or amputation. In these cases, both the acute and chronic responses to an exercise session would be limited.

If a reduced muscle mass is attempting to do the work of what is normally conducted by a larger muscle mass, then the energy cost of the relatively high work load on the remaining musculature may actually result in an anaerobic rather than an aerobic response. Because of the relatively smaller muscle mass involved, the physiological responses to maximal exercise are less for upper body work than for whole body or even lower body work. While the maximal, aerobic potential from exercise may be limited, research has shown that even spinal cord injured quadriplegics can benefit with increases in their cardiac output from an upper body training program.

Assuming that enough muscle mass can be utilized to create an aerobic demand and that there is no damage to the ANS, then long-term physiological responses/improvements will be dependent upon adherence to training principles. When a progressive disability is involved, long-term improvements in fitness level may not be seen. To date, no definitive research has indicated that exercise participation either increases or decreases the speed or severity of the rate of progression.

While exercise may not directly affect the progressive nature of the disability, it may help the person cope with the progression.

If an individual is slowly losing muscle functioning due to MD, exercise should at least prevent added loss caused by deconditioning. It is important to remember, however, that a temporary worsening of the condition may occur in cases such as MS and MD if the muscle is worked to total fatigue. Thus, resistance work should be submaximal and not to fatigue. With rest, complete recovery should occur. In almost all cases, medical associations have supported the participation in regular exercise programs for persons with progressive physical disabilities.

Fit Principles

To achieve a training effect from exercise participation, the FIT (Frequency, Intensity, Time) overload principles are generally prescribed. For apparently healthy adults, the American College of Sports Medicine (ACSM) recommends a frequency of three to five times a week, at 55-85% heart rate max (HR max), for 20-30 continuous minutes.

While the frequency of exercise should not be affected by most disabilities, the recommended intensity levels will be changed with many. Typically, the target heart rate for exercise is determined using a percentage of the maximal heart rate, estimated by the formula of 220 minus age. Because the upper body is not capable of working to the same maximal levels as the lower body, the ACSM recommends using the adapted formula of 200 minus your age to determine the maximum heart rate for upper body work rather than the traditional formula.

The heart rate may not always be a reliable guide to use with some disabilities. The use of the target HR during aerobics classes is based on the linear relationship between HR and VO_2 established during lower and full body work. With upper body work, when the arms are raised above shoulder level for prolonged periods, the heart rate may be inflated relative to VO_2 due to the increased stress on the heart, which is not coincident with an increased oxygen demand. Thus, the use of the rate of perceived exertion (RPE) may be more accurate than the HR in most seated aerobics classes. Consider using the Borg scale in the chapter on "Monitoring Intensity."

The RPE is recommended for use with persons with a spinal injury above the sixth thoracic vertebrae, for persons who have limited tactile sensation, persons with attention deficits and for persons with coordination difficulties which cause them problems in finding their pulse. The use of the RPE should be carefully explained before it can be utilized effectively. With patience and practice, persons who are mentally retarded can also successfully use the RPE scale.

Regardless of whether the HR or RPE is used, persons with MS and MD should be encouraged to work at the lower end of their target zone. If they begin exercising at too high an intensity, fatigue may develop early and preempt the remainder of the workout. At other times, they may not realize that they have over-exerted until several hours later when total exhaustion occurs causing a temporary worsening of their condition. With rest, recovery will occur; therefore an added rest period may be required on days of exercise.

The time and duration of aerobic exercise is recommended to be 20-30 continuous minutes. The ACSM recommends beginning a new exercise program for sedentary, deconditioned adults using discontinuous intervals of "hard" to "easy" exercise bouts. Since the sedentary, disabled person will likely be even more deconditioned than the sedentary, able-bodied person, an exercise program should be started conservatively. Over time, the length of the "hard" phase should be increased while the length of the "easy/recovery" phase is reduced until a continuous period can be achieved. When muscle paralysis or weakening, or a progressive disability is involved, a continuous period may never be achievable and intervals may always be the best option. Further discussion on intervals will be addressed later in the section on movement adaptations.

THR for Upper Body Work

200 - Age = Y

Y (55-85%) = THR

Use of RPE

Importance of rest

Associated Concerns

Other associated concerns may accompany some disabilities. The prevention of most of these problems is the responsibility of the participant; however, an instructor should be aware of the potential for such occurrences. Exercising in **high heat and humidity** can be dangerous for anyone, especially persons with injury to the ANS, which might occur with a spinal cord injury or MS. Such individuals may have a reduced ability to sweat. The production of sweat and its evaporation is one of the ways the body rids itself of excess heat to maintain the core body temperature.

Another source of heat dissipation is the radiation that occurs as vasodilation and blood flow diversion bring the heat to the body surface. With ANS damage, both of these sources of heat reduction may be absent or reduced, thereby increasing the risk of heat exhaustion or heat stroke. Overheating may also increase the fatigue level for persons with MS and limit their endurance and ability to work hard. Conversely, working out in **cold environments** can tighten arthritic muscles or the spastic muscles of someone with cerebral palsy, making fluid movement even more difficult.

> Guard against friction and skin irritations

Persons with impaired circulation need to be cautious of creating skin irritations which can take a prolonged time to heal. If impaired sensation is involved, the individual may be unaware that an abrasion has developed until a large sore appears. Persons with amputations can develop irritations from sweat increasing friction against the prosthesis. If severe enough, such sores can prevent the ability to wear the prosthesis until healing occurs.

Pressure sores from prolonged sitting are serious problems for wheelchair users who should relieve the pressure with frequent chair "push-ups." A full bladder may increase the heart rate and/or blood pressure of someone with a spinal cord injury. Emptying the bladder or catheter bag before exercising may also help prevent an accident. Should a bladder accident occur, the aerobic instructor should try to minimize any embarrassment to the participant and call as little attention as possible to any necessary clean up.

Seizure disorders may be an associated condition with many disabilities. While medication controls the majority of seizures, the aerobics instructor should be aware of any class members who have a history of seizures. Seizures are not medical emergencies and do not require medical attention unless they continue for prolonged periods (10-15 minutes) or seem to be following one after another. Long-term exercise tends to reduce seizure activity. Seizures during exercise itself are rare, but post-exercise seizures are fairly common. Multiple seizures may also occur. Following a grand mal seizure, an individual will likely be tired and need rest. Therefore, the instructor should discourage the person from leaving the facility immediately and alone. It is not uncommon during a grand mal seizure for an individual to lose control of the bowel and bladder. The most important intervention during a seizure consists of protecting the individual from injury without restraining him/her. Remove any objects nearby that could cause injury. Help protect the head from banging on the floor, but again, do not restrain. The instructor can also play an important role in helping relieve any embarrassment that a seizure may cause.

Pre-Class Instruction

The more an instructor knows about his/her participants prior to the start of a class, the better prepared the instructor can be to help meet the participants'

See AFAA Standards and
Guidelines for Medical
Clearance.

Balance

*Even though an individual
may walk unassisted or
even with the use of
canes, he or she may not
have good enough
balance to perform aerobic
movements to tempo while
standing. Many
ambulatory persons who
have had a stroke, head
injury or who have CP
may not be able to control
their balance while
attempting to perform the
aerobic routines. Thus,
sitting for at least part of
the class may provide
better stability, allow freer
movement and contribute
to a more aerobic workout.*

needs. While it is time consuming, a pre-class interview with a new participant
is very beneficial.

Do not assume that a physical disability causes a person to be unhealthy
or at unusual cardiovascular risk. Many disabilities are stable, non-progressive
and cause no more inherent risks than occur with an able-bodied person. Follow
the guidelines established by AFAA to determine when a physician's clearance
is needed. Increased liability should not be a concern provided instructors are
trained and follow established guidelines.

A **medical history/health risk screening** should be required of all new
fitness class participants. A few extra questions may elicit helpful background
information on a disability. Questions might address whether any special
assistance is needed in class or in the locker room, whether or not the individual
can transfer in and out of their wheelchair independently, and/or whether the
individual is currently under a therapist's treatment. The usage of medication
should be noted and any possible effects related to exercise, over-exertion or
heat should be determined.

A **pre-class interview** is a good time to check the degree of balance and
stability of the person while standing or sitting. Although the participant may
be active in other sports activities, the aerobics class may involve many new
movements. A seat or chest belt may provide an added measure of security,
provided the material has some give and is not constrictive. Immobilization of
a wheelchair may or may not be desirable depending upon personal preference.
Certainly the power switch to an electric chair should be shut off before exercise
is begun.

Many movements in an aerobics class will easily adapt—almost
automatically—to fit someone who is exercising while sitting down, while other
movements will need special adaptation. At the pre-class interview, alternative
moves can be explored. Any movement in which the majority of the
power/aerobic demand is being created by the lower body will need adjustment
for someone exercising while seated.

Movement Adaptations

Traveling moves. Effective in a traditional aerobics class, traveling moves
are difficult for those who are seated to perform. On a level surface, a wheelchair
is very efficient, even several pushes would not likely be very aerobic for most
wheelchair users. Additionally, most classes incorporate traveling moves in
sets of four to eight counts. Such short duration travels consist of only one or
two pushes on the wheelchair before breaking to reverse the movement direction.
Such stop and start moves will be anaerobic at best. During traveling moves,
the seated participant will need to find an upper body alternative. Similarly,
many low-impact classes utilize power moves which involve flexion/extension
of the knees and hips to work the body up and down against gravity. It is not
recommended that someone seated attempt to mimic this type of move by
raising up and down with the trunk—a move which would undoubtedly
compromise the back.

Intervals. The use of intervals is an important part of most adapted routines.
Because the upper body musculature is relatively small, even when unaffected
by disability, overuse of the muscles can easily result in fatigue. If a disability
is involved, over fatiguing the muscles could result in an inability to complete
the workout and obtain the cardiovascular benefits. This is especially a risk

with muscle weakness and muscle paralysis. Interval usage of the muscles will help reduce the fatigue risk. Repeated moves with the arms raised overhead should be followed by moves in which the arms are kept low, allowing the deltoid muscles to relax. Intervals of repeated bicep curls could be followed by tricep work. Large movement patterns should be followed by smaller patterns, fast moves by slower. The important point is to avoid prolonged repetition using the same muscle group.

Balance and coordination. A different problem occurs with ambulatory and non-ambulatory persons with balance and coordination problems, such as found with CP, HI, and CVA. Transitioning from one movement pattern to the next can be quite difficult. Often persons with balance/coordination problems will lag a few counts behind the rest of the class due to their difficulty in coordinating all the components of the movement. If the movement pattern is changed every eight counts, the reaction delay and slowness in coordinating the new movement may make it very difficult for the person to keep up. Thus, prolonged repetition is more appropriate. Persons with balance/coordination problems may also have trouble with any intricate foot patterns, dance moves, or multi-part combinations. Simplicity of movement patterns is the key to a successful workout.

Warm-up and cooldown. During the warm-up when lower body limbering or static stretching is being conducted, seated individuals who will not be doing any leg work may substitute arm/shoulder stretches. Many classes incorporate floor work near the end of class before the final cooldown. If a person does not have any voluntary movement in the lower body, he or she may want to leave class when the floor work begins. If this occurs, the instructor has a responsibility to explain to the participant the importance of a full cooldown and encourage him/her to conduct some stretching out on the wheelchair at home. Most wheelchair users have chronic tightness from prolonged sitting and are vulnerable to contractures of the hip and knee flexors. Additionally, many paraplegics and some quadriplegics have some active abdominal muscles and should be encouraged to do as much of a curl-up as possible, even if the shoulders can just barely be lifted off the floor.

Most wheelchair users can benefit from some floor work, but many need some assistance in **transferring in or out of their chairs**. Proper technique must be followed in assisting in a transfer to prevent injury to the disabled participant or to the person conducting the transfer. Body mechanics in a good lift include using the leg muscles (not the back), keeping a wide base of support, keeping a firm grasp on the individual, and keeping the weight close to the body. For safety of the individual being assisted with the transfer, care should be taken not to scrape the body against the wheelchair or drop the person on the floor. Transfers should be done on soft (matted) surfaces.

The disabled individual should give the directions and feel comfortable with the transfer. There are several different ways transfers can be conducted, utilizing partial to total assistance. Before attempting to give assistance in a transfer, proper training and practice is important. Consult with a physical therapist at a local hospital for instruction in how to safely perform a transfer.

Within a traditional aerobics class, much concern is given to **proper postural alignment** in order to prevent undue stress and injury. Malalignment is a symptom of some disabilities, thus postural deviations may be seen and need to be accepted. It is not the role of the aerobic instructor to try to correct

Use of Wheelchair

Not all persons who exercise seated do so because of paralysis. Weakness, lack of coordination or amputation may cause some persons to use a wheelchair. In these cases, the seated exerciser should be encouraged to incorporate leg movements to increase the aerobic demand. Such leg moves could include marching, small kicks, toe taps, step-outs and knee lifts. Those who do not have functioning leg movement should be encouraged to use trunk movement when possible to increase the aerobic demand. Gentle side-to-side or forward and back rocking can be done.

such deviations, rather the instructor should help the participant get as effective and safe a workout as possible. For example, a person with a quadriplegic SCI may need to lean back in the chair for stability due to lack of trunk and abdominal muscles. Toe walking due to excessive tightness in the achilles tendon and internal rotation of the legs due to tightness in the hip adductors are common with CP. Therefore, many people with CP will not be able to stand in "proper alignment" during class. An aerobic instructor is not a therapist and should not attempt therapeutic intervention. On the other hand, the instructor must be aware of contraindicated movements which could have adverse results.

Administrative Concerns

Several issues which are not directly related to the instructor's abilities can affect the success of an integrated program. Such issues include facility accessibility, advertising/promotion, and the type of class taught. Accessibility is discussed in the next chapter.

Advertising and promotion. Spreading the word that a program is open to persons with physical disabilities can be an arduous task. Many may feel intimidated to attend a club that is perceived to be a place for "perfect bodies" only. Others may not wish to attend if they think it is going to be a "special" segregated class. Probably the best marketing approach to take is a varied one. Use as many different media as possible. If instructors attend a National Handicapped Sports (NHS) Adapted Fitness Instructor certification workshop, publicize it. If one or two disabled persons are already interested in the class, arrange to have them involved in a photo with the instructor. A resource for participant referrals includes local physical, occupational or recreational therapists and any local affiliate of NHS or the Veterans Administration. If there is a rehab center nearby, offer to conduct several free sample classes for the patients who are nearing discharge. Some facilities have had success in recruiting by doing demo classes in area malls. As with any new program, word of mouth will probably be one of the best advertisers.

Type of class. If a special, segregated class is going to be offered, careful consideration must be given to the time and day it is scheduled. Most facilities' "down time" is also the time that is most inconvenient for working adults.

Once the participant is ready, the type of class he/she enters will affect successful integration. For obvious reasons, step classes will probably be the hardest to adapt for persons who are lower body mobility impaired. Similarly, a class which utilizes a predominance of traveling moves will put the disabled member at a disadvantage when it comes to achieving a good workout. Classes consisting of movements which stay in one spot and offer variety in arm and leg moves are more easily adapted for disabled participants. A circuit class may be the best alternative, with a few of the stations modified specifically for the disabled members. Such stations could include arm cycling (with a bicycle secured to the top of a table and the pedals turned by hand) or a rower machine (with the seat stabilized).

If a large number of class members are disabled, a team teaching approach would be beneficial, fun and initially easier than teaching solo. While the main instructor is teaching class as usual, the co-instructor can make modifications for the disabled class members where necessary. Team teaching can allow for a much more individualized approach, as well as increase motivation and excitement in the class. The ideal technique would be to utilize a properly

Team Teaching

trained disabled person as the co-instructor. To promote the feeling that all participants are equal members of the class, the lead may be changed at times; i.e., have the main instructor teach seated, with the co-instructor providing alternatives for those standing. Over time, as the participants learn to make adaptations on their own, the co-instructor may be phased out.

Instructor Attitude

An instructor can make or break any class. An instructor can make a workout fun, motivating and challenging or make it an hour of pure sweat and strain. Likewise an instructor's attitude can determine whether a person who is disabled participates successfully in an aerobics class. Disabled persons are not "special" or amazingly brave just because they carry on in life with a disability. Persons with disabilities are not always friendly, just as those who are able-bodied are not always friendly. The instructor needs to be relaxed and comfortable and treat a person with a disability as he treats any other class member.

The bottom line is that a person is a person first, the disability is secondary. A specific comment does need to be made regarding persons with communication problems. If an instructor does not understand an individual's speech, the instructor should say so. Pretending to understand is condescending and will not be appreciated by the individual.

Summary

It would be difficult in this chapter to describe all the specific concerns and adaptation suggestions for various disabilities. The instructor is encouraged to learn as much as he or she can about the disability, think through the implications, and most importantly, seek additional training. Since 1984, National Handicapped Sports has been conducting adaptive instructor training courses, and now offers a certification course in conjunction with AFAA. Providing adapted classes can be rewarding for both the instructor and the participant. Proper training can help ensure that it is also safe and effective.

References

American College of Sports Medicine (1991). *Guidelines for graded exercise testing and prescriptions*. Philadelphia: Lea & Febiger.

Arthritis Foundation of America (1983). *Arthritis: The basic facts*. New York: Arthritis Foundation of America.

Bleck, E., & Nagel, D. (1982). *Physically handicapped children: A medical atlas for teachers*. (2nd ed.). New York: Grune A. Stratton.

Borg, G.A.V (1982). Physiological basis of perceived exertion. *Medicine and Science in Sports and Exercise,* 14: 377-381.

Cantu, R. (1982). *Diabetes and exercise*. New York: E.P. Dutton, Inc.

Clark, K.S. (1966). Caloric costs of activity in paraplegic persons. *Arch Phys Med Rehab,* 47: 427-435.

Fasko, P.M., & Knopf, K.G. (1988). *Adapted exercises for the disabled adult*. Dubuque, Ia.: Eddie Bowers Publishing.

Figoni, S.F. (In press). Perspectives on cardiovascular fitness and spinal cord injury. *Journal of the American Paraplegia Society.*

Franklin, B. (1985). Exercise testing, training and arm ergometry. *Sports Medicine*, 2: 100-119.

Glaser, R., Sawka, M., & Laubach, L. (1979). Metabolic and cardiopulmonary responses to wheelchair and bicycle ergometry. *Journal of App Physiology,* 46:6 :1066-1070.

Miller, P. (Ed.) (in press). National handicapped sports. In *Adapted Fitness Instruction: A Manual for Group Exercise Leaders.* Champaign, Ill.: Human Kinetics Books.

Pimental, N., Sawka, M., Billings, D., & Trad, L. (1984). Physiological responses to prolonged upper-body exercise. *Medicine and Science in Sports and Exercise,* 16:4: 360-365.

Sawka, M.N. (1986). Physiology of upper body exercises. In K.B. Pandolf (Ed.), *Exercise and Sports Sciences Review.* New York: Macmillan, 14:175-210.

Shephard, R.J. (1990). *Fitness in Special Populations.* Champaign, Ill.: Human Kinetics Books.

Sherrill, C. (1986). *Adapted Physical Education and Recreation.* (3rd Ed.). Dubuque, Ia.: W.C. Brown Publishers.

Zwiren, L.D., Huberman, G., & Bar-or, O. (1983). Cardiopulmonary functions of sedentary and highly active paraplegics. *Medicine and Science in Sports and Exercise,* 5: 63.

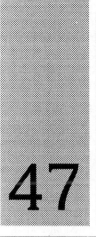

Accessibility Guidelines for Fitness Clubs and Programs

47

Bob Choquette
Lisa Ericson

Focus

IN JULY 1990, THE LANDMARK Americans with Disabilities Act was passed, extending and enlarging the provisions of the Rehabilitation Act of 1973. The new ADA mandates accessibility for virtually every amenity offered to the public by any entity. The only organizations specifically exempt from ADA are those that employ less than 15 people. Even for these however, the Act and resultant publicity has provoked America's conscience enough that most service-oriented persons are asking themselves what they can do to assist this unprecedented societal overhaul.

Because the law is new, it is open to interpretation and detailed implications have yet to be seen in many sectors of our service economy. The fitness world represents one such sector. This chapter represents the visions, recommendations and current techniques of the leading fitness professionals representing the hearing impaired, mobility impaired, and sight impaired.

Foster Accessibility

The following outline can be used by a club or company to ensure fitness accessibility.

I. RESEARCH YOUR LOCAL COMMUNITY RESOURCES.

    A. Which organizations currently provide services to your disabled citizens?

    B. What are the known demographics for each group; i.e., number of persons, age, gender, residential area, degree of involvement with fitness or recreation?

    C. Who are the leaders and/or the more independent among the disabled citizens?

    D. What services are available for each major disability group to support your efforts?

        1. Transportation for mobility access

        2. Interpreters for communication access

        3. Sign language classes for staff

        4. Relay services for telephone access

        5. Readers for blind persons

6. Mobility aids for wheelchair and blind persons

7. Other

E. What community-based funds are available for such services and/or to support your efforts?

II. BRING YOUR DISABLED ADVISORS INTO PARTNERSHIP WITH YOU.

III. PREPARE YOUR PROPOSAL FOR MANAGEMENT (OR YOURSELF IF YOU ARE MANAGEMENT).

A. Who will you serve?

B. What mix of self-contained (designed for a specific disability group) and integrated activities will you offer at the start and at the completion of your process?

C. What funds are needed and where will they come from?

D. Which staff persons will require what level of training?

E. What physical changes will be needed in your facility?

F. What kind of orientation program will you offer for your current (nondisabled) clientele?

IV. CONDUCT IN-SERVICE TRAINING AND ORIENTATION PROGRAMS UTILIZING DISABLED LEADERS.

V. HOST AN OPEN HOUSE/KICKOFF EVENT.

VI. PROVIDE FOLLOW-UP SUPPORT TO BOTH DISABLED CLIENTS AND YOUR STAFF.

It is imperative to not announce your accessibility until your disabled advisors are able to substantiate your claims. Nothing can hurt your credibility more with the disabled community than eagerness to serve without commitment to your own enlightenment and involvement of your disabled community leaders.

Fitness Programming for the Visually Impaired

If an individual has a visual impairment, this usually means that she/he is legally blind. Most people are not totally blind; they have varying degrees of vision and may be able to detect lightness and darkness, for example. The needs of these people will vary.

Generally needed are braille maps of the facility, braille and raised markings and signage where required, and recessed hooks along the lower walls outside the showers and within various fitness areas for the leashing of guide dogs. It is important to know that now most blind people read braille. Some can read large type with a special piece of equipment, and some prefer raised letters and other information.

Prior to participation in a program, any visually impaired participant should obtain a letter from a physician. The letter should be given to the fitness facility during the health and fitness evaluation in order to determine if any special considerations are required. It is very important for the fitness staff to know how to deal with a medical emergency should one arise. During the evaluation, the staff person should ask if there are any special things the individual desires in an emergency. There may be things related to the visual impairment even the physician may not know.

Specialized training. Fitness staff members will require training for interacting with and instructing visually impaired clients. These new clients are "just like everyone else" and generally desire to be treated in the same manner as other clients. The specialized instructional techniques required can be beneficial to the general membership as well. Thus, established programs will be enhanced by the inclusion of visually impaired persons.

Fitness staff members should be certified, have CPR training, and a thorough understanding of their students' visual impairments and medical considerations. The instructor must also be willing to undertake an entirely new method of teaching. Patience, understanding and precise verbal communication are critical. The education of visually impaired exercisers generally requires a tactile element (i.e., the visually impaired person will need to "feel" what the instructor or other aide is doing.) Often it can be quite challenging to explain verbally what a sighted person perceives as a simple movement.

Specialized classes. A self-contained class (a class designed for a specific disability group) is generally required to orient visually impaired persons to exercise and movement. These classes do not represent a philosophy of segregation, but merely a recognition that a specialized educational method is needed; a prerequisite so to speak. Visually impaired clients should be encouraged to participate in any facility programs where they feel comfortable. They should also be encouraged to remain in the self-contained class for as long as they desire. Additionally, general membership should be welcomed and encouraged to join the self-contained class. The nature of this specially designed class is such that it can be very beneficial to sighted beginners because they will learn the basics from a whole new perspective.

A person who has been blind their entire life perceives movement with feeling and in relation to space around them. This type of perception can be quite foreign to a sighted individual.

Open access classes. Actual instruction of visually impaired persons in a group exercise setting entails a refined skill that generally requires specialized training. Application of these techniques have proven successful and can be used with other special populations and with the general membership. The techniques involve an understanding of spatial awareness and specialized verbal cueing, both of which have been developed in close consultation with experienced blind persons and thus reflect the perceptions that only a visually impaired person can provide.

Enhanced socialization. Perhaps the most important aspect of a program for visually impaired persons is that it must provide a social environment. Because overall opportunities for socialization are usually limited by transportation issues, membership in a health club offers the visually impaired person a much appreciated chance to meet, chat, and share with old friends and new friends, both visually impaired and sighted. This element of enhanced camaraderie is noticed by the general membership and can have a very positive impact on perceptions and attitudes toward visually impaired persons and toward disabled persons in general.

Improved self-acceptance. An additional related benefit is that the fitness staff most involved with the visually impaired program will gain new friends and an enhanced feeling of self-acceptance. This will contribute to the continuation of the program. Visually impaired persons as a group have been frustrated in the past by programs that start and stop within a short time. As stated earlier, systematic and sensitive planning can ensure this special program's incorporation into the ongoing life of the facility.

If a fitness professional uses this step-by-step guide and involves visually impaired leaders from the start, it will not be long before success is evident. Seeing the sense of joy and accomplishment on the faces of new clients will be a natural barometer.

—Bob Choquette

Seated Aerobics

Historically and with a few exceptions (swimming, rowing and hand ergometer), cardiovascular fitness has been dependent upon the function of the lower extremities. The market for seated aerobics, however, is far from limited to persons with disabilities or to those who cannot walk. There are many reasons why a person might want to get a cardiovascular workout from a seated position, and seated aerobics classes can meet the needs of a variety of persons, not just those who use a wheelchair as their primary means of ambulation.

Any number of things can go wrong with the lower extremity. Many articles have been written about clients who experience "aerobic withdrawal" when put on the injured reserve list by a sprained ankle or a knee injury. As we baby boomers age, such injuries become both more frequent and more likely to impose permanent limitations; indeed most of us are likely to blow out a knee, a hip, or an ankle well before we are ready to passively assent to that first coronary.

Variety. A person might choose to do a workout sitting down because of insufficient coordination to do a standing workout confidently; perhaps the individual will develop enough confidence to do a standing workout at a later date. One might also be motivated by a simple desire to develop better posture, isolate back and abdominal muscles, or build slow twitch muscle mass in the upper body to balance what we customarily develop more in the legs. Pregnancy, weight problems, shin splints, plantar warts, and good old vanity are just a few more reasons we might want to have a bit more musculature above the waist. Many clients are stepping up to the challenge of bench classes, but many others for a variety of reasons find it attractive to use the same bench as a seat!

Music and choreography. In addition to the normal requirements of any good class, teaching a seated class requires a higher beat per minute in the music (up to 170 bpm) in order to provide a high enough heart rate from moving a shorter, lighter lever than the leg. Double timing may be necessary for some moves. This puts rather stringent demands on the choreography. It must be well cued and easy to understand. Rapid changes are needed not only to prevent boredom but to avoid overusing specific muscles. Compensations for differences in students' strength and abilities can be achieved by adjusting the elevation of the arms, thereby allowing a whole class to do similar movements at the same tempo at individual levels of exertion.

Heart rate. Many students in such a class may be on medications, such as beta-blockers, which can affect the heart rate. Therefore they need to be encouraged to measure their performance by perceived exertion rather than by pulse rate, though many appear unduly fascinated by the arithmetic. The subject of hand weights is frequently raised. Although weights could certainly have applications in a strength and toning class, they are more contraindicated for the aerobic portion of a seated class than for a standing class due to the potential consequences of shoulder joint injury to a wheelchair user.

Instructor training. Although one's students may not all have disabilities, it is imperative that the instructor of such a class have more than a nodding acquaintance with the various forms of paralysis, multiple sclerosis, post-polio syndrome, traumatic brain injury, stroke and other conditions which might simultaneously incline a student toward a seated class and provide contraindications or complications affecting performance and safety. There are certain problems, such as hyperreflexia, which can be experienced by these individuals and an instructor must be able to recognize and deal with them in order to prevent a potentially life-threatening situation. Even with a good grasp of these elements, one should accept people with significant physical problems into an exercise program only with a physician's approval and supervision. This serves to not only limit instructor and facility liability exposure, but protects the student as well.

It is important at this point to distinguish physical therapy and rehabilitation from fitness for the healthy disabled. An exercise class is no place for a recently injured or disabled person to be working on basic functions. Physical therapists, occupational therapists and others train for years to learn how to assist people at this stage, and we do not need to compete with them. We should instead be conferring with them about their patients who do attend our classes, and utilizing the knowledge we have to help those students become stronger and healthier through exercise.

—Lisa Ericson

Summary

It is important for fitness professionals to be aware that disabled persons by and large wish to be self-directed. They live with limitations, but they live for their potential. They have survived what many able-bodied persons dread to experience and are worthy of profound respect. The way to show this respect is to ask them to guide you in the process of developing your program to meet their needs. You must have an "advisory council" even if the council is one person, a disabled friend or friend-to-be who wants your class or facility to be accessible. This person is the key to your enduring ability to offer fitness programs to the disabled peer group.

Instructors and managers should become familiar with the sections of the Act that apply to the fitness industry. These are included in the reference pages, and refer to accessibility in health clubs and recreation entities, to credentialing bodies and processes, to transportation for those with mobility impairments, and telecommunications access for those with hearing impairments.

Exercise Guidelines for Children

48

Scott O. Roberts, MS

Focus

WITHIN THE LAST DECADE, a great deal of research has focused on the effects of exercise training in children, and it appears that both young and older children respond to training much the same way as adults do. Educators, parents and fitness professionals can help children get in better shape by teaching children positive attitudes, making children aware of the benefits of exercise at a young age, and most of all, making fitness enjoyable for them. The following chapter offers fitness instructors a range of programming considerations consistent with AFAA's Youth Fitness Guidelines.

BENEFITS

- *Improved ability to meet the demands of daily physical activities*
- *Improvement in physical performance test*
- *Improved self-image and self-confidence*
- *Improvement in motor skills*
- *Reduction of anxiety, depression and tension*
- *Lower risk for developing chronic health conditions than sedentary children*

Effects of Endurance Training On Aerobic Capacities

There is convincing evidence that prepubescent boys and girls can improve their aerobic and anaerobic capacities following exercise training. The average improvement in VO_2 max in most studies is 10 to 15%, depending on the mode of training, the intensity of the exercise and the length of training program.

Exercise capacity, performance and maximal oxygen uptake increase throughout childhood, regardless of training. Young children, however, have distinctly lower anaerobic capacities when compared to adolescents and adults. It appears, though, that children can improve their anaerobic capacities by following a training program.

Effects of Resistance Training On Strength Development

Numerous scientific studies have demonstrated that prepubescent children can gain significant strength following structured, supervised resistance training. In addition to improvements in muscular strength, resistance training can increase flexibility, improve physical performance, prevent injuries, increase lean body mass and reduce the percentage of body fat. It appears that the benefits of supervised resistance training for prepubescent children outweigh the potential risks.

Safety Considerations

- **Medical clearance.** Children with a pre-existing medical or musculoskeletal limitation condition should have a medical examination before starting any form of exercise program.

- **Proper supervision.** Proper supervision is the most important variable in reducing potential injuries.
- **Training programs.** Training programs need to be matched to the age, interests and maturity level of the child. Although free-weight and aerobic dance exercise training have been shown to be safe and effective, such training may not be appropriate for some children.
- **Intensity of training.** Children should never perform single maximal lifts or sudden explosive movements when exercising. These exercises may cause problems at the growth plates of the long bones.
- **Proper breathing.** Children should be taught to breathe properly during exercise.
- **Thermoregulation.** The risk of thermal injury is much greater in children than in adults, since children have a smaller ratio of weight to body surface area to dissipate heat. Exercise sessions should be reduced or curtailed when the relative humidity exceeds 90% and/or when the air temperature exceeds 85°F.
- **Acclimitization.** Children can acclimatize to hot conditions, but the process takes considerably more time (repeated exposures) than with adults. The intensity of the exercise should be gradually increased over a 10- to 14-day period when moving to a warmer environment.
- **Hydration.** Children should always be fully hydrated prior to exercising in any type of environment (hot or cold). Children should be encouraged to drink during exercise (8 ounces every 20 minutes), since at least one study has shown that children will voluntarily dehydrate themselves during exercise.

Special Populations

- **Asthma.** Several investigations have demonstrated that children with asthma can improve their fitness level without adverse effects. The benefits of such training may lead to a lowering of the intensity and frequency of exercise-induced asthma attacks.
- **Diabetes.** Children with controlled diabetes should be encouraged to exercise in an effort to expend energy, reduce body fat, and improve diabetic control.
- **Obesity.** In addition to weight loss, other benefits of exercise in obese children include improved self-image, reductions in blood pressure and reductions in serum lipids.

Recommendations For Aerobic Training

Sufficient evidence exists that children physiologically adapt to endurance training. Lacking, however, is a general consensus on the quality and quantity of exercise required to improve and maintain a minimum level of fitness in children. The American College of Sports Medicine states, "until more definitive evidence is available, current recommendations are that children and youth obtain 20-30 minutes of vigorous exercise each day."

Several investigators have recommended that adult standards be used when establishing the intensity of exercise, as well as the frequency and duration of children's fitness programs.

- **Type of activity**. Children should be encouraged to participate in sustained activities that use large muscle groups (e.g. swimming, jogging, aerobic dance, etc.). Other activities, such as recreational, sport and fun activities that develop other components of health and performance (speed, power, flexibility, muscular endurance, agility and coordination) should be incorporated into a cardiorespiratory fitness program.
- **Intensity**. Exercise intensity should start out low, and progress gradually. There are no recommendations available on the use of training heart rate during exercise for children, although some recommend the use of adult standards for children. Another way to monitor exercise intensity is with the use of the Borg scale of perceived exertion.
- **Duration**. Since children will be involved in a variety of activities during and after school, a specific time should be dedicated to aerobic and strength conditioning activities. These exercise sessions should last between 20 and 30 minutes, but it may be necessary to start out with less time initially.
- **Frequency**. Two to three days per week of endurance and strength training will allow adequate time to participate in other activities, and yet be sufficient enough to cause a training effect.
- **Group exercise classes**. Use only four-inch steps with young children. Make sure all dance movements are slow and controlled. Training programs need to be matched to the age and maturity level of the child. Try to avoid combining very young and old children in the same class.

Typical age and skill categories

Infancy
  0 to 1 years

Early Childhood
  2 to 6 years

Mid-Childhood
  7 to 11 years

Early Adolescence
  12 to 15 years

Late Adolescence
  15 to 18 years

Recommendations For Resistance Training

- **Resistance training**. Children should be encouraged to participate in a variety of activities that involve repetitive movements against an opposing force.
- **Free weight training**. Proper lifting technique and safety are the two most important factors to consider. Start with small 1/2 to 1-pound dumbbells to start. Perform a variety of upper and lower body exercises.
- **Weight training machines**. With the exception of several companies that manufacture weight training equipment specifically for children, most exercise equipment is designed for adults. If children cannot be properly fitted for the machines, they should not be used.
- **Manual resistance training**. With manual resistance training, resistance is provided by a partner. Children take turns applying resistance during different movements. Example: Hip Abduction: one child lies on the ground while the other child applies resistance to the leg being raised (abducted).
- **Isometric training**. Isometric training occurs when muscles are contracted but do not change in length. Example: Bent Over Lateral Raises: one child bends at the waist and tries to raise his/her arms up, while the other child applies the resistant force. These exercises can also be done individually.

- **Tubing exercises.** Exercise tubing can be purchased in different resistances, or made from scratch. All resistance exercises should be performed in a slow, steady, sustained manner. Use a specific count during the initial movement and the hold phase and then return to the resting phase.

Additional Programs

- **Pulling activities.** Tie a rope to a wall and have children pull themselves toward the wall while sitting on a piece of carpet, or pull a weighted sandbag toward the body.
- **Pushing activities.** Push-up; throwing a medicine ball.
- **Hanging.** Child hangs from a bar and swings; child slowly releases from an assisted pull-up (eccentric work).

Summary

The degree to which prepubescent children can improve physiologic measures depends upon growth and maturation rates and the exercise stimulus during the training program. There is sufficient existing literature which provides convincing evidence that prepubescent children are capable of adapting physiologically to training. However, until more conclusive guidelines and recommendations are available on designing and leading safe and effective exercise for children, fitness instructors should always use conservative strategies when working with children.

References

1. Roberts, S.O. (1992). The effectiveness of selected strength training methods on developing strength in prepubescent children: A critical analysis. Paper presented at the 58th Annual SW-AAHPERD Meeting, Phoenix, Az.
2. Roberts, S.O. (1992). Trainability of prepubescent children: current theories and training considerations. In M. Leppo (Ed.), *Childhood physical fitness: A multidisciplinary approach.* Washington, D.C.: ERIC Clearinghouse on Teacher Education.
3. Roberts, S.O. (1993). *Developing strength in children: A comprehensive approach.* Reston, Va.: National Association of Sport and Physical Education.
4. Roberts, S.O., & Staver, P. (1992). Fit kids. *American Health Magazine,* 9.
5. Roberts, S.O. (1992). Child's play. *American Fitness Magazine.*
6. Roberts, S.O. (1993). AFAA home study program on youth fitness.
7. Roberts, S.O. (1993). AFAA youth fitness guidelines.
8. Munson, W.W., & Pettigrew, F.E. (1988). Cooperative strength training: A method for preadolescents. *JOPERD,* 2: 61-66.
9. Sale, D.O. (1989). Strength training in children. In Gisolfi, C. V., & Lamb, D. R. (Eds.), *Perspectives in exercise science and sports medicine.* Carmel, In.: Benchmark Press.
10. Rowland, T.W. (1989). Oxygen uptake and endurance fitness in children: A developmental perspective. *Pediatric Exercise Science,* 1: 313-328.

Scott O. Roberts, MS

Working with Additional Populations

49

Focus

General Guidelines

- *Review the medical history questionnaires before the first exercise session.*

- *Know the emergency procedures of your facility.*

- *Use the Borg RPE scale and be able to teach clients how to use it.*

- *Don't pretend to know everything; ask questions. If you don't feel comfortable working with certain individuals, explain why, and have them get specific exercise recommendations from their doctors.*

- *Remember the team approach—physician, client or patient and instructor. All work together to make the exercise training safer and more effective.*

THE NUMEROUS BENEFITS OF EXERCISE for healthy individuals have been recognized for individuals diagnosed with certain chronic diseases. Many of the individuals who have been advised by their physicians to exercise will choose to do so in a health club setting. For this reason, and in order to lead safe and effective exercise sessions, fitness instructors need to understand some of the special precautions for working with individuals with either a known or suspected chronic disease. The following discussion is intended to provide a brief overview of this topic since comprehensive treatment is not within the scope of this manual. For more detailed information regarding exercise and special populations, consult the various references listed at the conclusion of this chapter.

Asthma

Asthma is a respiratory problem characterized by shortness of breath, coughing and wheezing. It is due to constriction of the smooth muscle around the airways, a swelling of the mucosal cells and increased secretion of mucous. Asthma can be caused by an allergic reaction, exercise, infections, emotion or other environmental irritants. Approximately 80% of asthmatics experience asthma attacks during exercise, a term referred to as exercise-induced asthma (EIA). Asthma is not a contraindication to exercise; however, before starting an exercise program, asthmatics should develop a plan for exercise with their physicians.

EXERCISE GUIDELINES FOR ASTHMA

1. Before starting an exercise program, the client should have a medication plan to prevent EIA attacks.
2. The client should have a bronchodilating inhaler with him or her at all times and be instructed to use it at the first sign of wheezing.
3. The exercise intensity should be kept low at the beginning of the session, and gradually increased. Longer warm-ups may be necessary.
4. If the client uses an inhaler several minutes before exercise, the possibility of an EIA attack may be reduced.

Heart Disease

Heart disease continues to be the leading cause of death in the United States. Although there are several different forms of heart disease, atherosclerosis, the narrowing of the coronary arteries, is by far the leading contributing factor. Aerobic exercise plays an important role in the prevention and treatment of heart disease. Physical inactivity is now considered by many experts to be a primary risk factor for heart disease, along with cigarette smoking, hypertension and high cholesterol.

EXERCISE GUIDELINES FOR HEART DISEASE

1. Clients should be screened for heart disease risk factors. Clients with two or more risk factors, and/or symptoms suggestive of heart disease should have a physical exam and exercise test prior to beginning an exercise program.
2. If a client has heart disease or has recently had open heart surgery or a heart attack, additional information will be needed (i.e., medical clearance from a physician).
3. Make certain the guidelines from the physician regarding physical activity are followed.
4. Be sure the client stays within his/her heart rate or RPE range.
5. Instruct the client to inform you of any abnormal signs or symptoms before, during or after exercise.
6. The exercise intensity should be kept low at the beginning of the session, and gradually increased.

Arthritis

Although there are over 109 different forms of arthritis, the most common forms are rheumatoid and osteoarthritis. Osteoarthritis is a degenerative process caused by the wearing away of cartilage, leaving two surfaces of bone in contact with each other. The majority of people with osteoarthritis have little pain or stiffness. Rheumatoid arthritis is caused by an inflammation of the membrane surrounding joints. It is often associated with pain and swelling in one or more joints. The benefits of exercise include stronger muscles and bones, improved cardiorespiratory fitness, and improved psychosocial well-being. Exercise is contraindicated during inflammatory periods of arthritis because exercise can worsen the process.

EXERCISE GUIDELINES FOR ARTHRITIS

1. Clients with arthritis should be encouraged to participate in classes in which quick or excessive movement can be avoided, such as low-impact or water exercise classes.
2. Exercise sessions should be frequent and low intensity.
3. Exercise intensity and duration should be reduced or avoided during periods of inflammation or pain.
4. Arthritic clients may need an extra warm-up and cooldown period.
5. The exercise sessions should be modified in terms of intensity and duration according to how well the client responds, changes in medication and fluctuations in the disease and pain levels.

Diabetes

There are two forms of diabetes—insulin dependent (Type I) and non-insulin dependent (Type II). Type I diabetes generally occurs in childhood, and regular insulin injections are required to regulate blood glucose levels. About 10% of all people affected with diabetes have Type I. Type II diabetes is the most common form of diabetes, affecting 90% of all diabetic patients. Type II diabetes typically occurs in adults who are overweight. Type II diabetics are not able to use the insulin they produce. Treatment of Type II diabetes varies, and may include a change in diet, medication and exercise therapy. Exercise plays an important role in diabetic control, primarily for Type II diabetics. Some of the benefits of exercise for diabetics include: increased insulin sensitivity, weight loss/control and reduced heart disease risk.

EXERCISE GUIDELINES FOR TYPE I AND TYPE II DIABETICS

	Type I	Type II
Type:	Aerobic	Aerobic
Duration:	20-40 minutes	40-60 minutes
Frequency:	5-7 days/week	4-5 days/week
Intensity:	Low to High	Low

Special Precautions for Diabetics

1. Insulin should not be injected into primary muscle groups that will be used during exercise.
2. Blood glucose levels should be monitored frequently.
3. A rapid-acting carbohydrate to correct hypoglycemia should be carried at all times.
4. Exercise sessions for diabetics should be scheduled at the same time of day for better control.
5. Exercise should be avoided during peak insulin activity.
6. A carbohydrate snack should be consumed before and during prolonged exercise.

Hypertension

For additional information, see chapter on "Medical Considerations of Aerobic Exercise."

Hypertension is a condition in which the blood pressure is chronically elevated above levels which are considered healthy and desirable for an individual's age. Hypertension is defined as 140/190 mmHg for individuals younger than 60 or greater than 160/95 mmHg for those older than 60. Hypertension is considered a major risk factor for coronary artery disease. Exercise training is now recognized as an important part of therapy for controlling hypertension.

EXERCISE GUIDELINES FOR HYPERTENSION

1. Low-intensity dynamic exercise is recommended.
2. Clients should be encouraged to exercise at least four times per week.
3. Isometric exercises should be avoided.
4. If weights are used, the resistance should be kept low and the repetitions high.

5. Exercise intensity may need to be monitored by the RPE scale, since medications can affect the heart rate during exercise.

6. Have the client report to you any changes in medications, and/or any abnormal signs or symptoms during exercise.

7. Encourage the client to monitor and track his/her blood pressure and pulse before and after exercise.

8. Client should use proper breathing technique and avoid Valsalva maneuver.

Summary

Because exercise is becoming a widely accepted form of therapy for certain chronic diseases, fitness instructors should expect to be working with individuals who have been so diagnosed in the future. Instructors are encouraged to learn more about working with special populations by attending workshops and reading from some of the references listed below. For information on certification programs and workshops in this field, contact the American College of Sports Medicine.

References

Blair, S.N., Painter, P., Pate, R.R., Smith, K.L., & Taylor, C. (1988). *Resource manual for guidelines for exercise testing and prescription—American college of sports medicine.* Philadelphia: Lea & Febiger.

Horton, E.S. (1988). Exercise and diabetes mellitus. *Medical Clinics of North America.* 72:6: 1301-1321.

Pate, R.R., Blair, S.N., Durstine, J.L., Eddy, D.O., Hanson, 0., Painter, P., Smith, L.K., & Wolfe, L.A. (1991). *American college of sports medicine—guidelines for exercise testing and prescription.* Philadelphia: Lea & Febiger.

Pollock, M.L., & Wilmore, J.H. (1990). *Exercise in health and disease* (2nd ed.). Philadelphia: W.B. Saunders Company.

Part 9

Specialty Classes & Trainings

Low Impact

Muscular Endurance

Step Training

Fat Burning

Tubing

Bands

Aquatic

Deep Water

Circuit

Interval

Funk

Sports Conditioning

Slide

Competitive Aerobics

Low Impact Aerobics

50

Merrily Smith

Much of the information presented here is a condensed adaptation of AFAA Standards and Guidelines.

Focus

INSTRUCTING A SAFE AND EFFECTIVE low impact aerobics class that benefits everyone from the high impact "die-hards" to the aerobic novice is a definite challenge for instructors. Clearly, we now have the advantage of several years of practical application and biomechanical expertise to draw from as we design enjoyable and effective LIA classes.

Impact and Intensity

Low impact is a form of exercise in which all of the movement patterns are performed with at least one foot in contact with the floor at all times. By keeping one foot grounded, the amount of stress associated with the floor impact is significantly lessened. Some common examples of LIA moves are marching, step touches, heel digs, grapevines, lift steps and lunges.

Low Impact Aerobics does not necessarily imply that the class is performed at low intensity. Because LIA has less impact, it is often perceived as lower intensity than it actually is. New participants are often surprised when they monitor their heart rates to learn that their heart rate is indeed within or above their target training heart rate ranges. The intensity varies from beginning to advanced levels, depending on exercise selection, exercise sequencing and movement patterns. Indeed, there are many benefits for all fitness levels, from improved health to desired body composition changes.

By contrast, a high impact class contains primarily movements of a high impact nature, in which one or both feet can leave the floor, such as jogging, hopping, skipping and jumping. Both techniques are valid and effective depending upon individual needs and body types. Many participants prefer a combination of the two styles of impact. Today we define this "combo" class as high-low aerobics. "Hi-Lo" ranges from moderate to high intensity and includes balanced impact intensity forces. Biomechanically, Hi-Lo can be easier on the joints than a traditional high impact class.

According to research performed by Drs. Peter and Lorna Francis of San Diego State University, the softer landings in a low impact class can reduce the vertical force on the ball of the foot to about one-and-one-half times the weight of the body. This is a considerable improvement over the jumps and hops in a conventional high impact class which create a force that can exceed three times the weight of the body.

But Is LIA Actually Safer?

The good news is there is less pounding and fewer aches and pains associated with low impact aerobics than with high impact. The bad news: this new exercise program, like any other form of exercise, is not without its problems. Research shows that if you eliminate the impact of repetitive jumping, you reduce the risk of stress on the articular surfaces of the joints and decrease the chance of tendon overuse injury or shin splints.

But if workouts are not choreographed and taught effectively, the muscular stress of low impact movements may strain participants in some unexpected way. (3) An example of this is faulty choreography that requires a sudden change of direction causing unexpected excessive torque to the knee.

Conditioning Principles and Recommendations

As in any aerobics class, improvements in cardiorespiratory endurance are dependent on the intensity, duration and frequency of the program.

How do you influence intensity?

Simply understanding the conditioning principles is not enough to teach an effective low impact class. Intensity will vary depending on the following factors: exercise selection, elevated movement, movement patterns and sequencing speed and lever length. The instructor must understand how to manipulate the factors, particularly if very fit participants are going to be challenged.

For a complete discussion of conditioning principles and recommendations, please refer to the AFAA Basic Exercise Standards and Guidelines.

1. EXERCISE SELECTION

The variety of movements used and the choice of exercise appropriate for an individual's fitness level will be a determining factor in raising or lowering exercise intensity as well as maintaining a consistent intensity level throughout the aerobic portion of the class.

Moderate to higher intensity low impact moves require the body to be lifted and lowered vertically against gravity. The legs have 4 to 5 times the muscle mass as the upper body. Arm patterns help to increase intensity, but the bottom line is full range of motion and movement that includes the moderate to larger leg muscles is the best way to increase cardiovascular conditioning.

2. ELEVATED MOVEMENTS

Intensity of a particular movement is also influenced by the elevation at which it is performed. For example, the intensity of performing bicep curls with the elbows raised out to the sides of the body at shoulder height is greater than when the same movement is performed with the elbows at waist level. This is because the gravitational pull is stronger when the body or limbs are in an extended, raised or long lever position as compared to a short lever, lower position.

3. MOVEMENT PATTERNS AND SEQUENCING

In a low impact class, the intensity can be increased by varying the elevation of arm and leg combinations. Traveling across the floor in a continuous pattern that elevates both arms and legs will further increase the intensity of the workout. Following this pattern with a similar pattern will maintain or further increase the intensity. Sequence of movement patterns is another controlling factor of intensity in a low impact workout.

For example:

1. Combine 3 marching steps with knee lift, and repeat.
2. Add a traveling variation and move towards the front, then towards the back 4 times.
3. Add an arm pattern that includes a combination of elevated movements. (i.e., shake hands down 3 times below the waist, then clap above the head.)
4. Repeat 2-3 and change the knee lift to a skip.
5. Repeat 2-4 and add on 4 alternating lunges.

Compare the above example with the next example:

1. March in place 3 times and knee lift, repeat.
2. Add below the shoulder, shake the hands down 3 times and clap.
3. Add on side to side, step R, touch L 4 times.
4. Change arms and reach both out shoulder height (count 1) clap (count-and).

This last example produces a lower level of intensity, compared to the first example, because the movement patterns and sequence selected are all similar lower intensity moves. It is critical for the instructor to pay attention to selection of movement patterns and sequencing.

4. SPEED

Speed of movement during a lower impact class will have a direct effect on elevation of heart rate. Movement either in place or in traveling patterns across the floor should be performed through a full range of motion with control. Speed at which movement across the floor is correct if momentum and alignment are controlled.

5. LEVER LENGTH

Arm or leg exercises that use extended levers, for example straight arms in a horizontal position as opposed to bent elbows in the same position, will increase the workload or intensity of the movement due to the amount of force required to move the lever—in this case, an arm against gravity. It is also more difficult to control movement without momentum through a full range of motion and maintain proper body alignment with the use of longer levers. Long lever movements should be modified for beginners or interspersed with short lever movements in sequencing patterns as a means of controlling intensity.

Summary

Low impact aerobics is virtually suited for every healthy individual if instructed and performed safely according to recommended training principles. It is an ideal activity for those who must restrict stress to the knees, feet, lower legs and hips. Low impact aerobics was never intended to replace high impact aerobics, but its growing popularity cannot be ignored.

51 Muscular Endurance Training

Susan O. Cooper, MA

Focus

THE CHAPTER WILL SHOW YOU how to transform your weighted workout into a class that addresses muscular endurance training. Most fitness programs train the cardiovascular system and include some type of muscular strengthening routine, however, muscular *endurance* is often overlooked. Yet as we go about our daily activities, it's muscular endurance that plays a crucial role in how well our physical bodies meet a variety of demands and resist injury.

Setting Realistic Goals

Successfully establishing any new fitness program means helping your students set realistic fitness goals for their bodies. This is especially important in a muscle sculpting class. Frequently, students will describe an "ideal body" that is genetically impossible for them to develop. There are two ways to help a student set obtainable fitness goals. The first method includes identifying body types through a procedure called somatotyping.

Longer Classes

Weighted workouts designed to increase muscular endurance should be a vital part of a total fitness program. Unfortunately, current typical hi-low impact aerobic classes provide a maximum of 10-15 minutes of muscular sculpting activity and muscular endurance training requires a dedicated 30-40 minutes. As a result, muscular endurance training is passed over—but it needn't be.

1. Determine body type from the following descriptions:

- **Endomorph.** Round, softer shape, short heavy legs, narrow shoulders and a large chest, weight usually concentrated in lower body (hips and abdomen), body fat above ideal ranges, has difficulty losing body fat and sculpting for definition.
- **Mesomorph.** Muscular, stocky shape, chest larger than waist, broad shoulders, body fat within and often lower than ideal ranges, no difficulty losing body fat or sculpting for definition.
- **Ectomorph.** Leaner, more frail shape, long arms and legs and short trunk, round shoulders, indistinct buttocks, body fat varies, no difficulty losing body fat, difficulty in bulking or acquiring muscular definition without heavy weight training.

Many individuals can have the characteristics of a combination of two body types such as **endo-meso** or **meso-ecto,** but it is impossible to be ecto-endo. The most important principle here is genetics. Your parents' body types dictate your body type. For example, if your mother was an ecto-meso and your father was an endo-meso, then your chances of having predominantly mesomorphic characteristics are very high.

Once we help our students realistically determine their body types and accept the bases from which they must work, we can consider the second factor in determining results from a muscle sculpting class. **Muscle belly length,** or the length of the belly of the muscle in comparison with the length of the tendons that attach the muscle to the bone, will also dictate the realistic potential for muscular hypertrophy. If the muscle belly length is longer than the tendon length, then the muscle has potential to grow larger. If the muscle belly length is shorter than the length of the tendon, then the muscle will not be able to grow as large. There are two simple tests for determining muscle belly length for the upper and lower body.

2. Estimate Muscle Belly Length

UPPER BODY

Contract the bicep of the right arm so that it forms a right angle. Take the fingers from the other hand and see how many fingers can fit between the angle of the elbow and the end of the bicep muscle.

1. one finger = long muscle belly
2. two fingers = medium muscle belly
3. three fingers = short muscle belly

LOWER BODY

Stand on one foot with heel off the ground and the gastrocnemius contracted. Place a finger on the point of the muscle closest to the heel. Relax the muscle and compare the distance between the end of the muscle and the back of the knee and the end of the muscle and the heel.

1. knee to gastrocnemius > gastrocnemius to heel = long muscle belly
2. knee to gastrocnemius < gastrocnemius to heel = short muscle belly
3. knee to gastrocnemius = gastrocnemius to heel = medium muscle belly

If we add these two genetic factors: body type and muscle belly length, we should be able to design a more effective muscle sculpting program that will produce realistic results! For example, if a person enters your sculpting class with obvious endomorphic tendencies and after measuring, exhibits short muscle bellies, a program designed to reduce body fat and lift heavier weight is recommended. On the other hand, if a student exhibits mesomorphic tendencies with long muscle bellies, a program designed to reduce or maintain the present body fat level as well as tone and define the musculoskeletal system through a muscular endurance type regimen is appropriate.

Physiology of Muscular Strength and Endurance

Understanding the physiology of muscular strength and endurance will also help you develop effective sculpting sequences in class. There are five basic training effects for programs developing muscular strength and endurance:

1. **Muscular power**—strength x speed
2. **Muscular strength**—maximum strength / 1 repetition
3. **Muscular endurance**—repeated force / many repetitions
4. **Muscle tone**—partial contraction of muscle due to strong neuromuscular facilitation
5. **Hypertrophy**—increase in muscle size

To accomplish these training effects, the program design will definitely vary. For example, in a muscle sculpting class that uses three-pound weights with continuous motion along with some non-weighted power movements, the focus is on muscular endurance and power with some definite improvements in muscle tone. There will be slight strength gains and some hypertrophy, although these two training effects would be accomplished more quickly in a weight room with heavier weights and less repetition.

Muscle Fiber Types

Another factor to consider when designing a results-oriented, muscle sculpting class is muscle fiber types. The two basic types of muscle fibers are fast twitch and slow twitch. **Fast twitch** muscle fibers are anaerobic, easily fatigued, use quick, forceful contractions, bulk at a faster rate, and are involved in stop and go activities. On the other hand, **slow twitch** muscle fibers are aerobic, fatigue-resistant, react with slower, less forceful contractions, bulk at a much slower rate and are utilized in endurance activities.

Most individuals are born with approximately 50% slow twitch fibers and 50% fast twitch fibers. There are many studies being done that indicate slow twitch fibers can be trained to act like fast twitch fibers. However, genetic properties determine how many of each type of fibers you have at the outset. The type of muscle fibers you have will dictate the type of sculpting program your body will respond to quickly. A medical procedure, which consists of taking some tissue from your muscle belly, can determine the percentages of fast twitch and slow twitch fibers.

A less expensive, practical method is to think of the types of activities at which you excel. If you like to run, is your strength in running short distances quickly (fast twitch), or long distances slowly (slow twitch)? In an aerobic class, do you like to take classes in which the exercises seem to stay about the same intensity (slow twitch) or do you like the type of class in which the exercise intensity increases dramatically, then decreases and continues with that type of roller coaster effect (fast twitch)?

Muscle Contractions

To begin to understand how to sequence a muscle sculpting class, it is important to understand how a muscle works. There are two types of muscle contractions that are primarily used in sculpting classes: isometric and isotonic. An isometric contraction is one in which the muscle exerts force, but does not change in length. Isotonic contractions cause the muscle to change in length with varying tension while moving a constant load.

There are two types of isotonic contractions:

1. **Concentric.** The muscle exerts force, shortens and overcomes resistance (lifting).
2. **Eccentric.** The muscle exerts force, lengthens and overcomes resistance (lowering).

Neuromuscular Facilitation or "Muscle Smart"

Performing a muscle contraction with correct form and total fiber participation is a learned process. Muscle contractions are actually controlled by the brain. Simply put, the brain sends a message to the bicep to contract. If the message does not reach the bicep, then the muscle does not contract and the action is usually performed with momentum and little fiber participation. The act of training the brain and the muscle to work as a team is called neuromuscular facilitation or, as I prefer to label this condition, "muscle smart."

Most aerobic instructors enjoy steady state activities, which indicates that their bodies respond well to slow-twitch activities. If your fitness goals cannot be met by just doing slow-twitch activities, then you must include some fast-twitch activities such as power moves and muscle strengthening into your fitness program.

For additional information, see chapter on the "Musculoskeletal System: Structures and Functions."

Primary Movers

In every joint action, there is a muscle that contracts and acts as the primary mover or **agonist.** To allow this joint action to occur, there is another muscle that acts in opposition to the agonist called the **antagonist.** In some joint action, there is also a **stabilizer,** which is a muscle that usually stabilizes the position so the agonist and antagonist can perform the movement with full contraction. For example, in a bicep curl performed at shoulder level, the bicep is the agonist, the tricep is the antagonist and the deltoid acts as the stabilizer of the movement.

Muscle Balancing

Muscle balancing is the steady state zone of muscle sculpting. Think of the body as the center pole of a tent. There are ropes attached to the center pole (muscles) that will pull the tent one way or another depending on which rope is the tightest and strongest. To create a well stabilized tent, all ropes must be equally tight.

If working	Be sure to also work
Biceps	Triceps
Serratus Anterior	Latissimus Dorsi
Abdominals	Erector Spinae
Pectorals	Trapezius/Rhomboids
Iliopsoas	Gluteus Maximus
Abductors	Adductors
Quadriceps	Hamstrings
Gastrocnemius/Soleus	Tibialis Anterior

The same is true of the human body. All the muscles of the body work in pairs to create movement. If one part of the pair is stronger than another, a muscular imbalance is created, which leads to improper body alignment and the possibility of injury in exercise classes. For example, if the pectoralis and abdominal muscles are very strong and the back muscles are very weak, a postural condition is created called kyphosis or "hump back." To correct this condition, from a strengthening viewpoint, the pectoralis must be stretched and the back muscles strengthened. In order to prevent muscular imbalance, all muscle sequences must focus on working muscles in opposing groups.

Fatigue vs Failure

In order to see the results from the contractions of muscles, it is important to work opposing muscle groups to fatigue but not to a point of failure. This means the muscle feels tired, but you are able to complete the movement without the muscle shaking or cramping. When the muscle feels fatigued, it is time to move to the opposing muscle group. Muscle soreness which occurs during the workout is known as **acute muscle soreness.** This can be relieved by changing to a different muscle group or stretching the muscle.

Another type of muscle soreness is called **delayed onset of muscle soreness**. This usually happens two days after a workout. There is still much controversy over what causes this condition and how it can be relieved. Some theories state that there is an actual tearing of the muscle during the workout and that warming up and stretching the muscle before the workout along with using lighter weights will help to alleviate this soreness.

Amount of Weight vs Repetition

The amount of weight used and the number of repetitions completed dictate the type of results that can be expected from a sculpting program. To obtain a larger muscle mass, heavier weights with less repetitions must be included.

This will also promote greater muscular strength gains. Smaller weights and more repetitions are used to develop greater muscular endurance and muscular tone.

Injury Prevention

One common cause of injury in a muscle sculpting class is movements that are executed too rapidly and with incorrect body alignment. Many students have undeveloped neuromuscular responses, so they are unable to complete an exercise with the proper control and correct contraction. Students frequently start muscle sculpting classes with weights that are too heavy or progress to a heavier weight when they feel the class is too easy. Sometimes a class will seem too easy if the student is not executing the move with a full contraction of all muscle fibers. By using a larger weight and having an undeveloped neuromuscular response, a student is more likely to incur some type of injury.

The most common types of injuries that occur in a sculpting class involve the joint areas. Bursitis, tendinitis, or ligamentitis—all inflammation problems caused by overuse—are prevalent in sculpting classes. The number of squats and lunges used in combination work may cause some knee problems to occur. Less common injuries include muscle strains or ligament sprains.

A complete warm-up along with proper body alignment and the use of appropriate weights are the most important factors in injury prevention. Training students how to facilitate effective neuromuscular response also aids in decreasing injury.

If injury does occur, please use the RICE method—rest, ice, compression and elevation—for immediate relief. If pain is consistent after this treatment, advise your student to see a physician.

Bicep Curl

For Muscle Strength

REPS	WT
1 set of 8-12	50 lbs

For Muscle Endurance

REPS	WT
4 sets of 8-12	5 lbs

See chapter on '"Common Aerobic Injuries and Treatment."

In addition, see AFAA Standards and Guidelines on Class Format.

Class Sequence

The format for a muscle sculpting class can vary depending upon which muscle groups you plan to highlight that day. A general outline of a typical, total body sculpting class might follow this sequence:

Warm-up (7-10 minutes). Include a balanced combination of rhythmic and static stretching with specific attention applied to the shoulder joint and shoulder girdle area.

Upper Body (10 minutes). Work opposing muscle groups with combinations featuring non-specific legs. Focus on specific upper body work.

Lower Body (10 minutes). Work the opposing muscle groups of the lower body in fatiguing combinations with little or no arm work.

Combination Upper and Lower Body Work (10 minutes). Reach the peak in intensity with combinations utilizing both the upper and lower body in specific muscular fatigue sequences.

Upper or Lower Body only (5 minutes). If the upper body is the focus in this section, the lower body would be worked more specifically on the floor.

Standing Cooldown (3-5 minutes) Include non-weighted combination of rhythmic and static stretching before going to floorwork.

Floorwork (5 minutes). If the focus on the last weighted segment was the lower body, then work the upper body using push-ups because the pectoralis major and minor are worked so little in a standing position. If the upper body was the focus of the last weighted section, then work the lower body in this section.

Cooldown Stretch (5 minutes). Provide a final static stretch with special attention given to all muscle groups specifically worked.

Types of Equipment

The equipment you choose for the muscle sculpting segment of class can vary from day to day because the array is always increasing. Hand-held weights, tubing, rubber bands, poles, weighted balls and benches are just a few of the products on the market. Once you understand muscle sequencing or fatigue, then adding different types of resistive equipment to your methods will only enhance the effects. Remember to instruct your students as to the appropriate ways to use each new piece of resistive equipment so as not to cause injury.

Music

120 - 130 bpm

The music you choose for the muscle sequencing segment of the class can help motivate your students to complete this part of class with appropriate form and concentrated contractions, or it can cause them to watch the clock, counting the minutes before the class is over. Music within the 120-130 bpm range works very well to continuously motivate students as well as to allow the instructor to complete work with proper form and full range of motion.

Muscle Sequencing: Putting Brain and Muscle Together

Introduction

The basics of anatomy and musculoskeletal movement must be understood before any muscle sequences can be put together for safe and effective muscle sculpting. **Neuromuscular facilitation** (the message system from the brain to the muscle which initiates contraction) must be learned before correct form and complete contractions can occur.

Once this system is learned, quick and complete fatigue of the muscle will occur with appropriate sculpting sequences. At this point, the student becomes "muscle smart." He or she knows where the muscle is, how to contract it completely and how to fatigue it by using correct form and alignment. The sequence is find the muscle, contract, then allow the joint to move.

The Sequence

Muscle sequences are put together just as you would sequence movement for aerobic exercises. The three basic movement patterns that are used in muscle movement are:

- **arm combinations.** 2 arm movements and 1 leg movement
- **leg combinations.** 2 leg movements and 1 arm movement
- **units of movement.** 1 leg movement combined with 1 arm movement

The format for creating muscle sequencing follows:

1. Choose the muscle group.
2. Pick the appropriate equipment.
3. Select movement pattern—arm combination, leg combination, or units of movement.

Combine movements using several variables of change:

1. contractions—isometric, isotonic-concentric, isotonic-eccentric

2. speed of movement

3. lever change

4. direction

5. elevation

6. use of gravity

7. traveling

Designing the Muscle Sculpting Sequence

Let's design a sample muscle sculpting sequence for a class that meets two days a week. It is Thursday, and your focus in Tuesday's class was the pectoralis and trapezius muscles. Since both of these muscles surround the shoulder girdle and shoulder joint, an exercise sequence focusing on the muscles surrounding the elbow joint would be appropriate.

After choosing the muscle group, you must decide which muscle of the group you will work first. Let's say you choose the bicep/tricep muscle group, and you decide to work the bicep first. Following the steps for creating an effective muscle sequence identified earlier would produce this format:

1. muscle group—biceps
2. type of equipment—weights
3. movement pattern—units of movement

Now, review the elements of change listed above and decide which you will use. Remember to decide on directional changes. Your bicep sequence might look like this:

Unit 1—Biceps curl in front of the body with a lunge (Fig. 51-1.)

Unit 2—Biceps curl on the side of the body with a squat side to side (Fig. 51-2.)

Unit 3—Biceps curl with the arms turned to the center of the body, a stationary squat (Fig. 51-3.)

Unit 4—Biceps curl with the arms turned to the center extending left, center, then right (Fig. 51-4.)

You would repeat this pattern of four units for three or four sets (a set would be repeating all four units one time).

At this point, the biceps should be fatigued. It will be time to move to the tricep group. A suggested sequence for the tricep is listed below:

Unit 1: Alternating lunges forward with full isotonic back tricep extensions

Unit 2: Triceps extension with a focus on eccentric contraction and speed variation 1,2,3 pulse (on count "four," elbow comes back to a

Fig. 51-1.

Fig. 51-2.

Fig. 51-3.

Fig. 51-4.

flexed position for a finish focusing on triceps (concentric phase). Legs lunge back with three count, hold, and step in on count "four."

Unit 3: Hold a stationary lunge with arms behind back. Triceps are in an isometric contraction with a focus on the concentric phase as arms lift up straight.

Unit 4: Full range of motion isotonic contraction with the palms facing away from back. Pull palms toward scapula bone and then lower toward lower back. Legs alternate lunges backward.

To superset this muscle group making sure that the muscle is totally fatigued, you might choose to repeat the biceps sequence with the same weight, a heavier weight or a different piece of equipment. This same supersetting sequence would work for the triceps. At this point, the biceps/triceps muscle group should be completely fatigued, and it would be appropriate to switch to a lower body muscle group to allow the upper body to rest before more work is completed.

Cross-Training The Muscle—Advanced Sequencing

The aerobic fitness level of our bodies is further enhanced by cross-training activities, such as walking on Tuesday, jogging on Wednesday, aerobics on Thursday, bench stepping on Friday and an interval class on Saturday. These same principles of changing activities and stressing the body at different levels also apply to muscle sculpting.

Within a regular aerobics class we have trained our cardiovascular system to work efficiently under steady state conditions. When we include interval training, which works on the principle of moving in and out of steady state activities, our body feels and reacts differently. The work seems harder and more demanding. The same rules apply to a sculpting class. If the movement of the muscle constantly stays at the same speed with the same intensity or weight, the muscle will train efficiently in this "muscle steady state zone." On the other hand, if each muscle sequence changes the level of movement, using all types of contractions and a variety of equipment, the muscle must adapt quickly to the different variations. This is what I call "muscle cross-training."

In a beginning muscle sculpting class the sequences will include more full range of motion and isotonic contraction. This allows the student some time to make the brain to muscle connection and become "muscle smart." Once this connection takes place, it's time to challenge the muscle by using sequences that involve different contractions, different ranges of motion and different types of equipment. This more involved muscle sequencing would lead to the cross-training effect for the muscle with faster results.

Summary

Muscle sculpting classes that train the body for muscular endurance activities should be included in a total fitness program. The most important focus of the program is teaching students where the muscle is, how to contract the muscle completely and how to allow the joint to move—all with correct body alignment. Once this is accomplished, we must help our participants set realistic goals for their bodies, goals that are in keeping with their genetic makeup. With all these factors in place, we should be able to develop a muscle sculpting program that will give fast and effective results.

References

Aerobics and Fitness Association of America (1985). Chapter 2. *Aerobics: Theory & practice.* Costa Mesa, Ca.: HDL Publishing Company.

Aerobics and Fitness Association of America. (1989). *Standards and gulidelines of a Weighted Workout.*

Costill, D.L., & Wilmore, J.H. (1988). *Training for sport and activity* (3rd ed.). Dubuque, Ia.: Wm. C. Brown Publishers.

Kapit, W., & Elson, L. (1977). *The anatomy coloring book.* New York: Harper & Row.

McArdle, W., et al. (1981). *Exercise physiology—energy, nutrition, and human performance.* Philadelphia: Lea and Febiger Co.

Thompson, C.W. (1978). *Manual of structural kinesiology.* G.P. Norris.

Westcott, W. (1990). *Strength fitness: physiological principles and training techniques* (3rd ed.). Dubuque, Ia.: William C. Brown.

Wilmore, J.H. (1986). *Sensible fitness* (2nd ed.) Champaign, Ill.: Leisure Press.

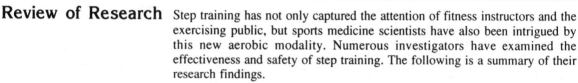

52 Step Training

Lorna L. Francis, PhD

Focus

ONE OF THE RECENT DEVELOPMENTS within the fitness industry is step training (also known as step aerobics, bench aerobics, bench stepping or aerobic stepping). Created and popularized by Gin Miller in the late 1980s, step training is an aerobic modality that consists of stepping up and down on a platform while performing creative choreographic movements to music. The predominantly low impact, high intensity nature of this athletic activity has attracted both men and women of all ages interested in a simple yet challenging aerobic workout.

Review of Research

Step training has not only captured the attention of fitness instructors and the exercising public, but sports medicine scientists have also been intrigued by this new aerobic modality. Numerous investigators have examined the effectiveness and safety of step training. The following is a summary of their research findings.

1. The energy cost of step training increased steadily as step height was raised from 4 to 12 inches. Lower step heights produced energy costs similar to those of walking briskly while higher step heights produced energy costs equivalent to those of jogging at speeds of five to seven mph. All step heights produced sufficient cardiorespiratory demands for improving aerobic fitness within ACSM's guidelines (1, 2, 3, 4).

2. Propulsive or airborne step patterns in which both feet are off the floor or step at the same time required greater energy expenditure than non-propulsive step patterns in which one foot is in contact with the floor or step at all times. However, all non-propulsive step patterns that were studied including the basic step (up, up, down, down) produced sufficient cardiorespiratory demands for improving aerobic fitness (1, 2, 3, 4, 5, 6).

3. Music tempos between 120-128 bpm were sufficiently demanding to improve aerobic fitness although increases in energy cost were minimal (4% to 5%) when music tempo was increased from 120-128 bpm (3).

4. There is no significant difference in the energy cost when stepping with and without one-pound hand-held weights on an eight-inch step. However, subjects perceived the intensity of exercise to be higher when using one-pound hand weights. The addition of two-pound hand-held weights while stepping did result in a marginal increase (6.7%) in energy cost (5).

5. The vertical impact forces for non-propulsion steps were similar to those of walking at three mph (6). Propulsion movements on top of the step such as jumping up onto the platform produced vertical impact

forces between 2-2 1/2 times the weight of the body (4). While these vertical impact forces were higher than those of non-propulsion steps, they were considerably lower than those of running at seven mph.

Step Training Guidelines

On the basis of current step training research and knowledge of exercise physiology, biomechanics and kinesiology, the following guidelines have been developed by **Step Reebok**, the premiere educational provider for step training information.

Step Height

The appropriate height of the step is dependent on the experience, skill and fitness level of the participant (Table 52-1) as well as the degree of knee flexion when the knee joint is fully loaded. Participants with healthy knees should never allow the knee joint to exceed 90 degrees of flexion when the knee is fully loaded (all of the body's weight is placed on the leg performing the first upward step onto the platform).

Participants with a history of knee pain or injury should not exceed 60 degrees of loaded knee flexion (assuming they have permission from their physicians to participate in a step training program). To reduce the risk of knee injury, it is wise to choose a relatively low step height that will sufficiently challenge the cardiorespiratory system to produce aerobic benefits.

For more information on step training, attend the AFAA/Step Reebok Certification Workshop.

TABLE 52-1. Determining Appropriate Step Height

Level of Stepping Experience, Skill and Aerobic Fitness	Step Height*
Deconditioned and inexperienced stepper	4 inches
Conditioned but inexperienced stepper	up to 6 inches
Conditioned and regular stepper	up to 8 inches
Conditioned, well skilled and regular stepper	up to 10 inches
Highly conditioned, highly skilled regular stepper (level of an elite athlete)	up to 12 inches

*Regardless of experience, fitness level or skill, do not use a step height that causes the knee joint to flex beyond 90 degrees.

Stepping Posture

When stepping up and down on a platform, maintain good body alignment by keeping the head up, the shoulders back, the pelvis in a neutral position, and the knees relaxed (neither flexed nor hyperextended).

Do not bend from the waist when stepping up. Instead use a full body lean from the ankle joints.

Stepping Technique

When stepping up onto the platform, contact the top surface with the entire sole of the foot (this helps to absorb shock) and center the foot on the platform so that the heel does not hang over the edge of the step (keeping the heel on the step will reduce the risk of Achilles tendinitis). When stepping down from the platform, step close to the platform and allow the heels to contact the floor (this helps to absorb shock). Exception: *Do not press the heel to the floor for any step pattern which requires participants to step a significant distance from the platform, such as during a lunge step or repeaters.*

To minimize vertical impact forces step gently (quietly) up and down from the platform. Participants must keep their eyes on the platform periodically especially if they are learning a new step or are inexperienced.

Do not perform any choreography that requires participants to step down with their backs to the platform. Vertical impact forces can be increased by as much as 25%.

Choreographic Considerations

Step Patterns

To avoid stress to the leading leg, do not perform single lead steps for more than one minute before changing the lead foot (a single lead step occurs when the same foot leads each time the step is repeated).

To reduce stress on the support leg, do not perform more than five consecutive repeaters on the same leg (a repeater occurs when the non-weight bearing phase of the movement is repeated, such as consecutive knee lifts).

To reduce the risk of impact-related injuries, many propulsion step patterns such as lunges and jumps are limited to a maximum duration of one minute before changing to a less stressful step pattern. However, depending on the fitness level and skill of individual participants, it may be prudent to perform lunges or any other stressful step pattern for less than one minute.

Arm Movements

Do not add arm movements, especially complex arm patterns, until participants have mastered the foot work.

To reduce stress on the shoulder girdle, do not maintain the arms at or above shoulder level for an extended period of time. Frequently alternate between high, mid and low range arm movements.

It is easier for beginning step training participants to perform bilateral arm movements in which both arms perform the same movements, such as arm curls, than to perform unilateral movements in which the left and right arm perform different movements such as alternating arm curls.

Be cautious of arm movements that could result in improper alignment during specific step patterns such as lifting the arms above shoulder level on a diagonal lunge. This arm pattern can encourage forceful back hyperextension.

Use of Weights

The increase in energy expenditure is marginal when light hand-held weights are added while performing step training. In addition, light weights contribute little to muscle hypertrophy or muscle definition. The risk of injury to the shoulder girdle, however, is increased significantly when a weight is rapidly moved through a large range of motion, especially if the lever is long (straight arm versus a bent arm). Since the physiological benefits are minimal and biomechanical risks for injury are possible, the use of hand-held weights during the aerobic stepping portion of the class is not recommended until further biomechanical research has been conducted.

To provide adequate resistance for strength development, the use of weights and elastic resistance is recommended during the isolation portion of a step training class.

Music Cadence

Select music tempos between 118-122 bpm for the aerobic portion of a step training class. While faster music tempos increase energy expenditure slightly, body alignment and stepping mechanics are seriously compromised when performing step training to fast music tempos.

If using music tempos above 122 bpm during the warm-up phase of the class (usually performed off the step), do not begin the aerobic segment of stepping up and down on the platform until the faster warm-up music has finished.

Not recommended during aerobics.

Additional Considerations

Progression

A slow progression is important to help minimize the risk of overuse injury. Beginning step training participants should perform no more than 10 minutes of step training during the initial conditioning phase of exercise. Step heights should not be raised until participants have increased their stepping skills and level of cardiorespiratory fitness.

Hydration

Step training results in significant water losses. Water should be replenished frequently both during and after step training classes.

Summary

Step training is an exciting aerobic modality that has been widely adopted by the exercising population. By carefully following the guidelines presented in this chapter, participants can continue to enjoy step training as a safe and effective aerobic activity for many years to come.

References

1. Calarco, R.M., Wygand, J., Kramer, J., Yoke, M., & D'Zarnko, F. (1991). The metabolic cost of six common movements patterns of bench step aerobic dance. *Medicine and Science in Sports and Exercise,* 23: S140 (abstract).
2. Olson, M.S., Wiliford, H.N., Blessing, D.L., & Greathouse, R. (1991). Cardiorespiratory responses to "aerobic" bench stepping exercise in females. *Medicine and Science in Sports and Exercise,* 23: S27 (abstract).
3. Stanforth, D., Velasquez, K., & Stanforth, P.R. (1991). The effect of bench height and rate of stepping on the metabolic cost of bench stepping. *Medicine and Science in Sports and Exercise,* 23: S143 (abstract).
4. Copeland, C., Francis, L., Francis, P., & Miller, G. (1992). *Power step reebok.* Boston: Reebok International, Ltd.
5. Blessing, D.L. (1991). The Energy Cost of Bench Stepping With and Without One and Two Pound Hand-Held Weights. *Medicine and Science in Sports and Exercise,* 23:528 (abstract).
6. Francis, L., Francis, P., & Miller, G. (1991). *Introduction to Step Reebok.* Boston: Reebok International, Ltd.

The author wishes to acknowledge Gin Miller and Reebok for their invaluable input and support.

Madeleine Lewis

53 The "Fat-Burning" Class

Focus

FAT-BURNING IS WHAT YOUR CLIENTS clamor for—so give it to them the best you can. This chapter sifts fact from fiction regarding a genuine fat-burning class.

When Do We Burn Fat?

An often-heard phrase in aerobics classes is "Slow down! Work at a lower rate— you'll burn more fat," but sadly, it's a popular notion derived from grabbing bits and pieces of research with the end result being rather misleading. True, there is some physiological research that suggests when exercising at the lower end of the training heart rate (approximately 60% of maximum), the human body obtains a somewhat larger percentage of its fuel from fat stores than it does when exercising at any other intensity level. But in the long run, if a fairly fit person consistently worked out in the lower end of the training zone, she/he would not be burning as much fat as in a higher intensity workout. It's a question of total calories burned per minute—and how many minutes one can last!

Longer duration

Working out at a lower intensity by definition implies burning a lower number of *total calories per minute*. Therefore, even though lower intensity exercise burns a slightly higher *percentage* of fat, in order to make lower intensity exercise as effective overall, it's necessary to exercise for a longer period of time.

Consequently, the structure of a "fat-burning" class differs from a standard aerobics class in one important aspect—in a fat-burning class the "aerobic" segment of the class is lengthened from the standard 20-25 minutes to anywhere from 40-50 minutes. This strategy is intended to provide the maximum opportunity for *total calorie burning*—and thus fat consumption—within the structure of a one-hour class.

Although our bodies burn the largest percentage of fat at the lower end of the training heart rate, moderate intensity choreography (approximately 75% of maximum) is recommended during the aerobic portion of a fat-burning class for two very practical reasons. First, working out at moderate intensity will still burn a significant number of fat calories—with the added bonus of burning a larger total number of calories. Secondly, moderate intensity exercise is sufficiently challenging to provide beneficial *training effects* that would not necessarily be obtained working at only 60% of your training heart rate. At the same time, moderate intensity exercise is not so strenuous as to make exercising uncomfortable over such a long period of time.

These guidelines are simple and easy to follow, but they also present a real challenge for your choreography skills: creating 35-50 minutes of no more than moderate intensity choreography that's not so dull and boring that your students lapse into a coma.

Many instructors may think they don't have enough creative moves to fill the whole time with enjoyable and interesting choreography. The trick is to modify moves and lengthen and layer combinations you already have.

Tips For Fat-Burning Sucess

Combine High, Low and Moderate Impact Moves

One of the primary safety concerns with regard to the lengthened aerobic section of a fat-burning class is overuse injuries. Using moves with a variety of impacts can really help prevent such injuries. Also, combining these three different movement vocabularies provides three times the variety of moves from which to choose.

Add Jumps and Hops

Instead of doing four side-to-side steps, try doing three side-to-side steps and a jump, jump. Another example would be three marches and a jump. Not only can this technique easily turn a low intensity move into a moderate intensity move, adding a jump at the end of a move leaves you in a "neutral" position with your weight on both feet. From there, it is a very smooth transition to move in any direction or to add on any move.

Polish Up on Turns

A cleverly placed turn can simply and easily give your old choreography a whole new look—while allowing you to teach the same combination for a longer period of time. Turns can be added to stationary moves as well as traveling moves. Keep in mind that turns can be scary for some people, so it's important to clearly establish the move first by repeating it several times before you ask your students to perform it while turning.

Try a Combo Within a Combo

This is another great choreography extender: establish your combination, then graft an arm combination onto it. Without requiring any new steps, this technique allows you to lengthen the amount of time you can spend on one combination as well as provide an additional mental challenge for the more advanced student.

Teach Power Moves

Pliés, lunges, squats, leg extensions and plyometric-type moves conducted during the standing section provide additional muscle-strengthening opportunities for the legs and buttocks. However, power moves will quickly raise heart rates and exceed lower-end training ranges for many participants.

And finally—have fun! Remember, you want your students to have the most successful experience possible, and to come back to your class again and again. If you're having fun, they will too!

References

Astrand, P.O., Rodahl, K. *Textbook of Work Physiology*, 3rd edition, New York: McGraw-Hill, 1986.

Resistance Tubing

54

Class and Guidelines

Connie Love, MA

Focus

RESISTANCE COMES IN MANY FORMS such as machines, free weights, basic body weight, manual resistance, bands and tubing. The focus in this chapter will be on the use of tubing in a class environment or in a one-to-one personal training situation.

Building in Progression

CHECKLIST

Action Steps For Designing A Resistance Program

- *Identify specific joint actions to isolate targeted muscles.*
- *Identify the agonist, antagonist and stabilizer muscles to properly sequence and muscle balance.*
- *Determine the types of contractions.*
- *Choose the number of sets and repetitions.*
- *Find the optimum speed of the exercises.*

Progression is the key element to the success and effectiveness of any resistance training program. Simply stated, this means the resistance or force is increased gradually as one's strength increases and adapts to the load or the intensity of the exercise.

With tubing, the load or the intensity of the exercise can be varied in different ways. There are different strengths of tubing. However, if only one strength of tubing is used, ways of altering the intensity is by foot placement. While standing on the tube, if the feet are close together or if only one foot is used, the intensity is lighter. Moving the feet further apart increases the intensity. (Figure 54-1)

In performing unilateral exercises, or using one arm, the intensity is altered by the foot placement and the length of the tube from the foot to the handle. The shorter the distance from the foot to the handle, the greater the intensity. The longer the distance from the foot to the handle, the lighter the intensity. (Figure 54-2)

The recommendations for a resistance tubing training program is that at least one set of 8-12 repetitions be performed. For deconditioned clients or to further enhance muscular endurance, 12-20 repetitions is recommended. One exercise for each major muscle group, or 8-10 exercises performed a minimum of two times a week, will ensure basic strength development. The major muscle groups are quadriceps, hamstrings, hip adductors, hip abductors, pectoralis major, latissimus dorsi, deltoids, biceps, triceps, abdominals and low-back. Exercising to mild muscle fatigue with proper form and control is recommended for effective strength development.

Full Range of Motion

It is important to exercise each muscle through the full range of motion to ensure the use of the greatest amount of muscle fiber. Working through the full range of motion will also strengthen the primary mover muscle and stretch the antagonist muscle. While performing a total body workout, it is advisable to sequence from the larger muscle groups to the smaller muscle groups. This works the most demanding muscles first before fatigue occurs.

Slow and Controlled

Safety and form are of major concern in any resistance training program. Therefore, all exercises should be performed in a slow, controlled manner. Fast, explosive movements can place excessive stress on the muscles, joint structures and connective tissues. Movement speed is most effective when exercises are performed with two seconds on the lifting phase (concentric contraction), a pause at the most contracted position, and four seconds on the lowering phase (eccentric contraction).

Breathing Through Resistance

Breathing also plays an important role in resistance training. It is advisable to exhale on the exertion of the lifting phase and inhale on the lowering phase. Holding the breath will create muscle fatigue at a faster rate and will illicit the Valsalva maneuver. This is a condition causing the glottis to close and the abdominal muscles to contract, forming an unequal pressure in the chest cavity, reduced blood flow to the heart and insufficient oxygen to the brain. Dizziness and temporary loss of consciousness may occur.

The Value of Rest

Rest and repair is necessary for muscle growth and recuperation. Generally, 48 hours is sufficient for this process to occur. Three consecutive days of resistance training (Monday, Wednesday and Friday) with cardiorespiratory training on the alternate days is an adequate schedule for the average person. Also, a rest period of 60-90 seconds between exercises is sufficient for immediate muscle recovery.

Plateaus are Normal

After the initial months of resistance training and when adequate strength levels have been attained, it is common for a plateau to be reached. At this time it is important to vary the exercises, the intensity, increase to multiple sets and vary the angles of the exercises. This will further enhance the development of muscular strength and endurance.

Training Format

Warm-up—rhythmic movement and gentle static stretches emphasizing muscles to be involved in the workout.

Workout—at least one exercise for each major muscle group (8-10 exercises) performed for 8-12 repetitions.

Cooldown—rhythmic movement and static stretches held for a minimum of 10 seconds and targeted at the muscle groups stressed during the workout.

Sample Workout #1

Day 1: Chest, back, shoulders, biceps, triceps, quadriceps, hamstrings, hip abductors/adductors, lower leg, abdominals and low back

Day 2: Rest

Day 3: Repeat Day 1 Workout

Sample Workout #2

Day 1: Upper body: Chest, back, shoulders, biceps, triceps, abdominals and low back

Day 2: Lower body: Quadriceps, hamstrings, hip abductors/adductors, lower leg, abdominals and low back

Day 3: Rest

 CHECKLIST

Tubing Tips

1. Prior to using, check all tubing for holes or tears.
2. Avoid pulling the tubing toward the face.
3. Select appropriate resistance to maintain proper form and alignment.
4. Avoid gripping the handles too tightly as not to elevate blood pressure.
5. Maintain wrist alignment so the hand is in line with the forearm.
6. Maintain continuous tension in the tubing whereas movement can be controlled.
7. Maintain the same rhythm on the lifting and lowering phase.

Fig. 54-1. Two-foot position on tube.

Fig. 54-2. One-foot position on tube.

Fig. 54-3. Chest press (pectoralis major, anterior deltoid, triceps).

Fig. 54-4. One-arm row (latissimus dorsi, posterior deltoid, biceps).

Fig. 54-5. Lateral raise (deltoid group).

Fig. 54-6. Overhead press (deltoid group, trapezius, triceps).

Fig. 54-7. Biceps curl (biceps, brachial radialis and brachialis)

Fig. 54-8. Reverse curls (biceps, brachial radialis and brachialis)

Fig. 54-9. Overhead triceps press (triceps)

Fig. 54-10. Hip abduction (hip abductors)

Fig. 54-11. Hip adduction (hip adductors)

Fig. 54-12. Squat (gluteals, quadriceps, hip flexor, and hamstrings)

References

Aerobics and Fitness Association of America (1985). *Aerobics: Theory & practice.* Costa Mesa, Ca.: HDL Publishing Company.

Wescott, W.L. (1990). *Strength fitness: physiological principles and training techniques* (3rd ed.). Dubuque, Ia.: Wm. C. Brown, Publishers.

Body Contouring with Elastic Bands

55

Karen Andes-Carcamo
Diahanne Bedortha

Focus

WHETHER YOU TRAIN ONE PERSON or a hundred, using elastic bands for resistance means you can carry a whole gym in your workout bag. This chapter addresses the most effective ways to contour and sculpt through the use of elastic bands.

Bands: An Introduction to Weight Training

Bands are simple, low tech, very effective body sculpting tools for all body types and body parts. Elastic resistance can provide a non-intimidating introduction to weight training, stand alone as a thorough workout or supplement regular weight training. Many students actually prefer the bands over weights because the stretchability helps them feel their muscles.

Variety

Many students tend to use weights that are either too light or too heavy. With very light weights, the effect on muscle fibers may be minimal and may not inspire results. With heavy weights, inexperienced exercisers often use too much momentum, lose form and sometimes even fail to effectively work their targeted muscles. In a classroom, it's much easier to accommodate different fitness levels and stronger/weaker muscles with bands than with several pairs of dumbbells. Simply double the bands and/or supply two or three per person to suit various needs.

There are several types of elastic bands on the market. Dynabands, or Therabands are three or four feet long pieces of Latex sheeting. On the plus side, they can be used in a huge variety of ways: you can stand or sit on them, double or triple them up, loop them around a step or tie them in a circle. Some exercisers find them uncomfortable, since they don't have handles. But an overhand grip and/or gloves can solve this problem. Spri tubing does have handles but the length of the band limits you to certain ranges of motion, unless you "choke up" on the tubing itself, to increase resistance.

There are also Step Straps which fix the tubing under a bench. Rubber bands are excellent for leg work, such as abduction (standing or lying), hamstring curls, leg extensions and some upper body work. However, the range of motion isn't great. The exercise choices are limited and the bands break easily. Finally, sport cords or Lifeline Gyms are excellent in that they can be

> This chapter offers another perspective on resistance training. For additional discussions, see "Resistance Tubing: Class and Guidelines" or "Muscular Endurance Training."

anchored around a doorknob, so your resistance can come from you. The problem is, compared to the other choices, they are expensive. All bands come in various strengths.

Basic Recommendations

1. When creating exercises, try translating movements that you do with free weights, cable equipment and machines. The form you teach with bands should be the same when done with a weight.

2. As with weight training, good posture will create good form (which in turn, creates good physique). Work with the spine's natural curve (i.e., "neutral spine"). Do not pelvic tilt when you do any standing band (or weight) work. Stabilize the spine with tight abs and lower back muscles held in a slight contraction. Also keep the chest open, shoulders down and back.

3. Avoid the "dead zone" of the band, or where it goes slack. Try to adjust it so there is resistance through the full range of the lift. In some classes, this will not always be possible. However, to provide intensity, add some partial reps where the pull or resistance is greatest and when the muscle is in peak contraction.

4. Anchor the band opposite the muscle you want to work. For instance, when you do a shoulder press, the band can be secured under your feet, a step or bench, or, if sitting, under your buttocks so that when you raise your hands, the line of force goes directly over your working muscle.

5. With bands, you can actually draw the lines of force. Keep those lines as clean and straight as possible. When you use two arms at a time, make sure those lines are parallel and/or symmetrical.

6. Beware of snapping the bands on the eccentric or negative part of the movement.

7. Avoid using momentum.

8. Consciously squeeze the working muscles with every rep.

9. Work slowly and go for "the feel." A 2-count lift and 2-count lower works well.

10. Try super slow motion moves in 4-count or 8-count. Save your single counts for partial reps.

Determining Reps

The amount of reps an individual can do depends on the thickness of the band and a person's strength. About 8-12 is a good number for increasing strength and building lean tissue. The workload should be getting difficult by 8, very, very hard by 12. If the workout is still too easy by 12, have people start the set with two bands and finish with one. (In bodybuilding, this is called a descending set.)

Higher reps can be good, too (16-24) when working with stubborn muscles like calves or abs or when incorporating partial reps at the end of a set. But high reps with bands for most upper body exercises will simply build muscular endurance if the work is too easy and not add lean muscle. If the workout is too hard, people will tend to lose form. To vary the number of reps, think of doing 8 or 12 "working" reps, then add on perhaps 8 more partial reps or even 8 counts of just holding the contraction. Always remind your students to keep their form.

Adding Variety to Your Angle

Try to vary your exercises and "angles of attack." Always working with the same reps, exercises and the same amount of resistance will "bore" your body and won't inspire improvement. Create an atmosphere in which students enjoy extending their reach—even if that means they do one or even one-half a rep with more resistance. Acknowledge their strength gains.

As with weights, verbal cues don't always work here. You may need to touch your students to help them achieve or maintain proper form. Try breaking down exercises. For instance, when teaching "lat" exercises, have them start a pull-down to the front, just with straight arms, so they get the feeling of engaging the lats before the arms. Band work can sometimes be like one-to-one training in a group. You may need to walk around the room for an entire class period. It's your opportunity to teach muscular awareness. It's also your great challenge to make certain your students understand what they're supposed to feel.

The number of exercises that can be done with bands is limitless. Here are three basics:

1. **Chest press.** Sit or lie on a step. Place band or bands around upper back (or under step if using a long cord). Hold ends of band. Press arms forward (or upward if lying down) so arms straighten and hands come together. Keep chest lifted as you contract. Arms and bands should form an "A" shape.

2. **Squats.** Stand on the center of one or two bands. Hold ends either down by hips or up over shoulders for more resistance. When you squat, be sure to sit back in the hips, maintain neutral spine and press up with heels as you lift.

3. **In-place lunges.** Step on the center of band with front foot. As you lower and lift back leg, make sure front knee stays over ankle, not over the toe. Again, press up with the front heel.

Summary

Very portable, easily adaptable bands offer instructors a lightweight alternative to heavier weights for resistance training. By varying the intensity and number of repetitions, you can "stretch" a band's effectiveness and create a variety of great workouts.

56 Aquatic Exercise

Sandra K. Nicht

Focus

AQUATIC EXERCISE HAS ENJOYED a tremendous growth in popularity and professionalism in the past few years. Instructors should consider the expanding market of individuals seeking the non-impact aerobic/conditioning benefits of working out in water.

Benefits of Working Out in Water

Water aerobics can provide an effective cardiorespiratory stimulus even though the heart rate may be lower than it would be during weight-bearing exercise. Toning exercises become more isokinetic due to increased water resistance as speed of movement increases. In water, muscles must work against the body's own natural buoyancy rather than the force of gravity, and it becomes possible to work opposing muscle groups easily as momentum is virtually eliminated.

Aquatic therapy, per se, is still the realm of the medical professional. Whether a patient is recovering from a specific injury, surgery, or learning to live with a limiting medical condition, it is recommended that a specific program be prescribed and supervised by the physician or therapist in attendance. Once released from rehabilitation, the recovering person must continue on his or her own. Frequently the patient does not have the will to persist. An opportunity awaits the knowledgeable aquatic instructor who is willing and able to develop and present a carefully designed program that accommodates the needs of persons with physical limitations and disabilities, or those who are recovering from injury or illness.

Training and Certification

Basic aquatic instructor training and certification is provided by organizations such as Aquatic Exercise Association, American Aerobic Association International, and ExerSafety Association on the national level, and groups such as the Aqua Society of Atlanta on the regional level. Many of these programs also offer Continuing Education Units to AFAA Certified Instructors. Many water exercise instructors with years of teaching experience also take time to train new instructors.

Continuing Education Providers for various organizations present shorter training programs that can help instructors prepare for certification as well as gain new ideas for their classes. YMCA and Red Cross programs emphasize water safety and rescue techniques, important skills for anyone working in and around pools or open water areas. Emergency Water Safety Certification should be considered a teaching prerequisite for aquatic instructors in addition to CPR and first aid training. Specialty aquatic certifications such as the Arthritis Foundation/YMCA Arthritis Program (created to provide relief to those suffering the pain and limitations of the different types of arthritis) or the new program offered by the National Multiple Sclerosis Society (developed to improve MS sufferers' ability to perform daily tasks) are an excellent way for qualified aquatic instructors to begin working with the disabled.

Target Class

Program/class design is dependent upon the specific market targeted. A water exercise class for active adults would be very different from a class geared toward seniors with arthritis. Instructors should carefully consider their own interests and professional goals when learning to teach aqua classes. A mismatch between the goals of the instructor and those of the participants could result in injuries or a drop-off in interest. The facility where classes are held (indoor, outdoor, community center, health club, hospital-based, etc.) and its mission statement will also help determine the market with which an instructor will be working.

Many instructors choose to teach without music due to poor acoustics in pool areas or because of competition from other programs occurring simultaneously. However, music can make the class more enjoyable and give a theme or style to the workout. Music tempos generally range from 124 to 136 beats per minute, although more vigorous classes may be able to work with faster music. Experienced instructors take into consideration many factors when selecting music: participant preferences, physical strength, and type of workout desired; overall water depth and at what depth participants choose to work; and the style or type of movements selected. Ideally, the music should allow for both fast and slow movements. Quicker tempos increase resistance while slower movements allow for longer levers and greater range of motion at the joints. A mix of both provides tremendous variety and evenly distributes stresses to different areas of the body.

Specific markets

124-136 bpm

Requirements

Pool depth should be fairly shallow, approximately three to five feet deep, to allow for participants to stand in water reaching their waists or chests. Lower heart rates occur in deeper water possibly due to the lower demands on the cardiorespiratory system to pump blood against gravity as well as to the greater ability of the body to shed heat to the water. Shallower depths result in higher heart rates, but may also increase the risk of injury due to the higher impact involved and may not confer greater cardiorespiratory benefits.

Research is needed on the effects on VO_2. Deeper water allows for more buoyant movements and greater resistance for the upper body when arms are kept under the water's surface. It also reduces the heat stress to the body by allowing more skin contact with cool water and less exposure to hot, humid pool air. Greater depth also cushions the impact of jumping. As many participants choose not to wear protective shoes during class, it may be safest to encourage them to work at chest depth.

Water temperature will affect the target population for any potential aquatic class. A competition pool, with its colder temperatures, would be an inappropriate location for arthritis classes but would be ideal for vigorous aerobics or programs for persons with multiple sclerosis (who fatigue easily in warm temperatures). A **therapy pool** could be disastrous for aerobics, due to the risk of heat stroke, but classes emphasizing gentle range of motion exercises and stretching would flourish in such an environment.

Class Types and Guidelines

The general structure of many aquatic aerobics classes follows the same cardiorespiratory stimulus, cooldown, strength-conditioning exercises, and final stretching. Minor differences in warm-up and cooldown are due to the unique nature of the aquatic environment. Cooler water temperatures preclude static stretching as the body would be chilled. Any stretch needs to be balanced with vigorous movement in other parts of the body so that the core temperature remains elevated. Alternative body positions are a must, as it would be difficult to perform many of the stretches commonly demonstrated in the studio. Fortunately, stretches in a standing position in water are easier than on land due to the support of the water as well as the increased buoyancy of the body.

Toning exercises are also more easily performed in a standing position, with participants using the pool's edge as a ballet barre. Many instructors use the added buoyancy of external flotation (kickboards, swim buoys, etc.) to create exercises which are fully suspended. Care must be taken to avoid excessive stress to the shoulder girdle if the arms remain in an abducted position for long periods. Careful sequencing of exercises not only provides variety to the class but prevents fatigue for vulnerable joints and muscles.

Types of Aquatic Classes

In the interests of providing increased programming variety, and thus broadening a facility's attraction to a wider number of potential members, additional class formats have been developed and refined by innovative aqua instructors to take advantage of the unique properties of the pool environment. Walking and running programs, classes which combine aerobics with traditional swimming techniques, and adaptations of classes found in aerobic studios (such as bench-stepping and circuit training) all demonstrate the diversity of the medium.

Water walking has become an increasingly popular class format for many seniors, allowing for the cardiorespiratory benefits of walking and the muscular toning provided by the water. The loose structure of these classes also allows for greater socialization among participants, a tremendous drawing card for many older adults.

Deep water running allows the runner or jogger to duplicate the motions of running without the impact. Once used only for rehabilitation purposes, instructors now teach entire classes devoted to suspended movements. More information on this topic is contained in the chapter on deep water exercise.

Aquatic bench/stepping is a recent variation of step aerobics. Beginning with the same movements found in step classes and progressing to actions which could potentially be unsafe in the studio (but now take advantage of buoyancy and cushioning) aquatic step is finding its place among other aqua classes as both a separate class and as a component of other classes by using the resistance that water provides rather than the elevation of the body's center of gravity to boost intensity. Aquatic classes incorporating the step are now being taught across the country to children (as part of a circuit-style class), persons with multiple sclerosis (with dramatic improvements in overall endurance and leg strength) and arthritis, as well as to active adults.

See the chapter on "Step Training" for more information on basic step technique.

Bench/steps of high-density plastic or reinforced fiberglass are used so that a stable platform is provided for the activities performed. Choreography for these classes must take into account the possibility that bench/steps may move slightly due to turbulence created by the movements. It is strongly recommended that instructors not only obtain training in both step aerobics and aquatic exercise, but also attend an aquatic step seminar to take advantage of the expertise of instructors currently teaching this technique.

Circuit-style classes run the gamut of programs following the traditional format (separate stations for each exercise) to classes which use enjoyable activities to subtly teach coordination or movement skills. The basic principle is to change the activity performed after a set interval, concentrating on a particular muscle group or movement skill. This keeps the class focused on a particular goal and running smoothly from beginning to end. Time seems to pass more quickly in a circuit class.

Use of Resistance/Flotation Devices

Commercially available flotation or resistance devices can increase the intensity of movements performed underwater and allow for the addition of fully suspended movements in the deep area of the pool. Equipment has been ergonomically designed for use in certain water activities that will localize resistance to specific areas of the body without strain. Aqua boots and cuffs, flotation belts and "dumbbells" and webbed gloves are all effective devices for increasing the challenge to the muscles of the upper or lower body, or increasing buoyancy for deep water workouts.

See next chapter, "Deep Water Workouts."

Attire

Footwear is strongly recommended since abrasions may occur to bare feet, resulting in discomfort or infection. Proper aqua shoes also provide traction on potentially slippery surfaces in and around the pool area. Some shoes also provide a measure of support and resilience, cushioning the impact of jumping on hard concrete and tile pool bottoms. Many instructors recommend wearing washable aerobic or cross-training shoes as long as they are only worn in the pool area (not also used for aerobics or street use).

The type of **swimwear** worn depends on individual preference. Most participants wear regular swimsuits, others prefer to wear leotards and tights, feeling that they are better covered and supported. Generally, clothing made of Lycra will support better than cotton or nylon fabrics and will hold up better to chlorine and other pool chemicals. Hand washing immediately after wear also extends the life of any fabric exposed to harsh disinfecting chemicals.

Swimcaps have been a controversial issue in the aquatic-aerobic industry. Many pools still require the use of swimcaps in an attempt to keep pool filters from being clogged with hair. Participants may prefer to keep their hair from becoming wet or just wish to keep it out of their faces. Some instructors feel that caps prevent body heat from being dissipated during vigorous exercise. In colder water temperatures this may be an advantage (preventing chilling during the cooldown portion of class) but in warmer pools excess heat retention could cause health problems. One compromise, for participants who don't mind getting their hair wet, is to wear a Lycra cap which allows heat to escape (and can also be soaked if one gets too warm) while keeping the hair out of one's face. Seniors have also pioneered the use of hair nets and shower caps to keep their hair from being crushed or soaked. Regardless, it is advisable for the more fashion-conscious to schedule their salon appointments *after* class.

Summary

Aquatic exercise is a growth industry for instructors. As our population ages, active adults search for alternatives to traditional studio exercise programs that will offer an opportunity for vigorous work but also be gentle to their joints. As instructors continue to advance their knowledge and seek new challenges in teaching, pool facilities will be looking for those who can add a splash to their programs.

Resources

Aquatic Exercise Instructor Education

American Aerobic Association International
Aqua Society of Atlanta
Aquatic Exercise Association
The Arthritis Foundation, National Chapter
ExerSafety Association
The Multiple Sclerosis Society, National Chapter
The Red Cross, National Chapter YMCA

Aquatic Exercise Equipment

Aerobic WorkBench
Hydro-Fit Inc.
HydroTone Therapy Equipment, Inc.
Spa Bells

Sprint-Rothhammer
Speedo

Swimwear and Footgear
Hind
Omega
Ryka

Thanks to Donna Richardson, owner of StayFit Plus and Helen Tilden, founder and past president of Aqua Society of Atlanta.

Deep Water 57 Workouts

Karen Anges-Carcamo
Diahanne Bedortha

Focus

THANKS TO THE INVENTION of the flotation belt, it is now possible to exercise in deep water, suspended in a vertical position. The sensation is somewhat like flying—except that you're not moving through air—you're pushing through a viscous mass, as if dancing in a vat of jello. This is the ultimate no-impact workout. Actually, it can be three workouts in one. Aerobic and muscle conditioning plus flexibility can be achieved simultaneously. All this and you don't even get your hair wet!

How to Work in Water

Increased resistance through vertical position.

To appreciate why deep water training works so well, first it helps to understand the unique properties of water. In the water, you have almost no gravity. You're relieved of 90% of your body weight, thus, you become buoyant. This frees you to move in a whole new way, supported by the water. Then you have a choice: you can either float and bob (which is relaxing but isn't a workout) or you can push and pull the water to work with its resistance. Water is 12 times more dense than air, so when you use it, it's like having weights all around your body!

Working with this resistance is crucial to getting an effective workout. Thus, your ultimate aim is to find the path of *most* resistance. Be sure to keep all exercises **below the water line,** where it counts. Waving arms in the air is not an intelligent use of water. And beware of simply using **buoyancy assisted moves,** like jumping up and down.

With your body in this vertical position, you increase your resistance 75% over swimming! When your body is horizontal, your aim, in fact, is to **minimize** drag and cut through the water. Vertically, your aim is to **maximize** drag and push the water. Since the range of motion in your legs is much larger, a great gluteal workout is possible. Also, there's much greater arm movement variation than with swimming. More muscles get involved and toned!

With bent arms and legs (i.e., "short levers"), resistance and intensity are easier; with straight arms and legs ("long levers"), resistance is greater. However, if you bend the limbs just a little, you can make it harder still. This affects the width of the lever and is known as "eddy drag." Speed will affect resistance and your workload, too. Any time you double your speed in the water, you increase the intensity four times.

The muscle conditioning that takes place with deep water training can be instrumental in creating good muscle balance. When you consciously move limbs with equal force, going both forward and back, up and down, or out and in, you apply equal forces to opposing muscles. The key word here is consciously. Although gravity in water is greatly minimized, gravity is still in effect—heavy objects sink. Therefore, when you lift your knee, lower it with equal force to work muscles on the back of your leg. In other words, work it both ways. (Note: Water is forgiving, but it still has resistance. If a movement hurts, don't do it or vary the movement so it's pain free.)

Aerobically, deep water training is quite a challenge. What's interesting is that your heart rate will always be about 10 to 15% lower in the water than it is on land. But you still get a great workout, burn fat and calories and exercise your cardiovascular system. All that really needs to be adjusted is your mind. Here's why it takes less energy to get the job done in the water.

1. The force of the water surrounding your body actually acts as an auxiliary heart pump lowering your heart rate. The water pressure aids blood flow back into the heart (the venous return). Thus, your heart receives a little outside help and therefore works more efficiently. Meanwhile, you still get all the aerobic training benefits.

2. Because of the lessened gravity in the water, there's also less effort put on the limbs, which results in a lower heart rate.

3. In water, your body dissipates heat four times faster than in air. Also you cool down more quickly in the water. A cooler body temperature means a lower heart rate.

4. Heart rates will be a little lower in cool water, a little higher in warm. Ideal water temperature is 83-86 degrees F.

So, if your heart rate is 140 in the pool, add 10 to 15% to find your equivalent heart rate on land—about 154 to 161 bpm. When you are teaching a class, the Perceived Exertion Scale may provide a more accurate way to monitor intensity. Since your body loses heat so fast, stopping to check the pulse can give you an inaccurate reading. As on land, remember to slowly nudge the intensity forward. Steady progress brings results.

Table 57-1. Water-Adjusted Heart Rate Chart		
Age	Min HR	Max HR
20-29	124	179
30-39	119	161
40-49	114	152
50-59	108	143
60-69	103	134
70+	98	125

Your lungs get a workout during deep water training. Because the water pressure compresses the lungs slightly, you have to work harder to expand your lungs in order to get breath down there. This effort works the muscles around the rib cage and increases your overall respiration.

Your flexibility increases in water, again because gravity relieves you of body weight. Thus, your range of motion is much larger than it is on land, both in motion and in static stretches.

One final benefit that water provides is a psychological boost, a feeling of well being, although no one fully understands why.

Form and Posture

Aim for a good vertical position, with chest lifted and expanded, abdominals tight, buttocks slightly tucked under and squeezed together. At first, some students might bend forward at the waist. That's because the center of gravity shifts out of the hips and into the chest, which becomes your center of buoyancy. A slight flutter kick will help maintain proper body position.

Your objective with movement is a nice fluid, counterbalance between the arms and legs, as takes place when you walk. Here are three basic moves to get you started. Incidentally, if you teach or do this to music, use a bpm of 120 to 150. (You can also listen to a Walkman with a waterproof "Aquatunes" belt.)

Cross Country

Move arms and legs, like scissors. The motion should come from hips and shoulders, not elbows and knees. For more resistance, point toes and cup hands, palm up on the up stroke, down on the down. For variation, try smaller, faster moves, with hands in a sculling motion down by your hips. Good for buttocks, hips, shoulders, back and chest.

Sit Kicks

Sit as if in a straight back chair, knees at hip level. Keep quads still as you extend one leg and bring the other heel under the buttocks. Point toes. Work arms with a bicep curl and tricep kickback motion. Good for hamstrings, quads, biceps and triceps.

Straight Leg/Toe Touch

Again, try to keep legs straight and remember vertical posture. Alternate kicking forward. Try to make the water surface "boil" with a flick of your toes. But don't compromise your body position to do so. It's not how high you kick, but how hard. Reach for your toe with opposite arm and stretch the other behind you, like a hurdler. This is the ultimate toner for buttocks and also works chest, back, shoulders and arms.

Try varying your workouts with shorter "interval" days. Try 30-45 minutes, alternating one to two minute hard and very hard intervals with somewhat hard and moderate resting intervals. This increases aerobic capacity and provides overall conditioning.

For endurance and fat-burning workouts, work at a steady, more moderate pace for 45 minutes to one hour.

Summary

Originally conceived as an excellent form of rehabilitation, deep water training works for anyone seeking an energizing, challenging but gentle form of fitness—one that can be practiced for a lifetime.

 CHECKLIST

Who Benefits From Deep Water Workouts?

1. Anybody gets a challenging workout that's gentle on the body.
2. Runners add mileage without adding impact.
3. Cross trainers add variety and get a full body workout.
4. Overweight individuals burn body fat in a safe environment.
5. Injured people maintain and gain fitness during rehabilitation.
6. Bodybuilders get aerobic exercise that also helps heal overtrained muscles.
7. Pregnant women maintain a lower heart rate for baby's safety. Also minimize all impact on "opened" joints.
8. People with multiple sclerosis maintain a lower core body temperature and train in safety.
9. Arthritis sufferers experience a rejuvenating joint workout in deep water.
10. Non-swimmers work comfortably in the deep water.

Tere Filer, MA

58 Circuit Training

Focus

SOME INSTRUCTORS WHO TEACH circuit training at clubs have a dedicated room with a variety of equipment permanently installed at strategic stations. But you can also transform any room into a circuit training class using portable equipment. Instructors can develop a loyal following by providing clients with an extremely time-efficient workout that addresses muscular conditioning along with cardiorespiratory training.

Developing the Circuit

Circuit training, not to be confused with interval training, is considered one of the basic systems of weight training. Typical weight training workouts are conducted in what is called a priority system, which involves working one muscle group or performing one type of exercise to completion, and then going on to the next exercise and so on. By contrast, circuit weight training involves repeating exercises and muscle group work through a **series of stations.** Each station may be set up to include muscle isolation exercises, a cardiovascular activity, or stretching. It is important to design the circuit so that the principle muscles used alternate from station to station in order to keep moving and maintain a consistent heart rate. The circuit method's purpose is to develop both muscular strength gains as well as cardiovascular improvement.

For many years, circuit training was used in schools and athletic facilities to accommodate large volumes of participants in the shortest amount of time with a limited variety of equipment. In fact, expensive equipment or large, bulky machines are not necessary to perform an effective workout. Circuit training provides the flexibility of modifying each station to the needs and limitations of the participant's fitness level and space available. From beginner to advanced, circuit training is considered one of the most efficient modes of accomplishing a complete workout in a short period of time.

Numerous studies have been conducted to compare the effects of circuit weight training on cardiovascular fitness and the CVD risk factors. Studies evaluating circuit weight training (weight training using moderate weights for 10-15 repetitions with 15-30 second rest intervals between bouts of activities) show an average improvement in VO_2 max of 6%. This compares to an average improvement in VO_2 max of 18% during typical steady rate aerobic activities such as running, cycling or jogging.

It may be concluded from this information that circuit weight training should not be the only method used when one of your goals is to improve your cardiovascular fitness. Circuit weight training will, however, sufficiently maintain cardiovascular fitness. To better understand the role of circuit training in your fitness program, it is important to describe the actual format of a typical circuit weight training workout and some of the variations that could be applied.

Goals of circuit training

1. Improved cardiovascular fitness

2. Improved muscle strength and endurance

3. Reduced body fat levels

4. Increased flexibility and injury prevention

5. Improved glucose tolerance and insulin sensitivity

6. Improved serum lipid levels (total cholesterol, total cholesterol/HDL, and LDL/HDL ratios)

7. Improved self-esteem and emotional fitness

Circuit weight training usually involves resistive devices such as variable resistance machines, pulleys, cables, and/or free weights (barbells and dumbbells). The circuit would include as few as 5 or as many as 15 stations which could be repeated several times. The timing of the sequence would require one minute per station with only 15-30 seconds of rest in between. The intensity, or amount of resistance to be used at each station, should be moderate (40-60% 1RM). The goal is to complete as many repetitions (usually 15-20) as possible within each station in order to fatigue the specific muscle or muscle group being worked.

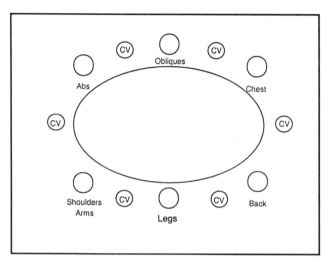

The next station would work a different muscle or group of muscles so that the overall energy output can be maintained throughout the session. Since each station is performed with maximal effort in a very short period of time, the major energy system being used for this format would be the anaerobic glycolytic pathway. The major energy source being utilized would be muscle glycogen or stored carbohydrates. The energy cost for a 20-minute workout has been shown to average approximately 200 kcal (less for women than for men). It is an excellent means of burning calories, but stored fat does not play a significant role. Because many exercisers have a concern for weight control, the circuit may take on a variety of changes that will affect the energy pathways utilized as well as the energy sources.

Fig. 58-1. 12-Station Circuit. This circuit plan includes six CV stations, which is an optional feature. These could include steps, mini-tramps, treadmills, stair climbers, etc.

Super circuit formats include a cardiovascular type of station incorporated within the circuit of weight training exercises. Equipment such as a stationary bicycle, stair climber, treadmill, or stepping platform may be used, or the participant may choose to jog in place, jump rope, perform calisthenics (jumping jacks, high kicks, etc.) as the aerobic component. As long as the overall intensity of the workout is maintained, the resulting cardiovascular improvement will be accomplished. By altering the time sequence, the energy pathways utilized will also allow for increased usage of stored fat as an energy source. A common pattern used would be one minute of muscle conditioning activity followed by two to three minutes of cardiovascular activity. This format could be adapted, with careful planning, to a group exercise class.

Peripheral Heart Action System. A training session using this system is divided into several sequences of exercises. A sequence is a group of exercises, each for a different muscle group. The number of repetitions per set of each exercise may vary, but usually 8-12 repetitions is the norm. An exercise may combine several muscles or muscle groups or may isolate only one. All of the exercises in the sequence are repeated three times in a circuit fashion before moving on to the next sequence which will involve doing different exercises for the same muscles. The number of sequences may vary from four to six per session.

The goal of the peripheral heart action system is to keep blood moving from one body part to the next. It is an extremely fatiguing program if a major goal of your workout is to increase cardiovascular endurance. The short rest periods and maintenance of a relatively high heart rate make this program very similar to normal circuit weight training. A cardiovascular station could also be incorporated between the exercise sequences. There is no specified time interval for the exercise sequence as long as the rest periods between exercises is kept short. The following shows a sample four-sequence peripheral heart action session.

	Sequence			
Muscle group	**1**	**2**	**3**	**4**
Chest	push-ups	bench press	incline flys	cable flys
Back	bent-over rows	seated rows	lat pull-down	chin-ups
Legs	reverse lunges	leg extension	leg press	squats
Shoulders	overhead press	lateral raise	front press	upright row
Abdominals	sit-ups	reverse curl	Roman chair	crunches
Obliques	lateral sit-ups	crunches	variation	variation

Summary

Whether in an aerobics classroom or in the weight room, you can design a fun, intense, and motivating circuit workout. Be creative by using hand-held weights, tubing, bands, or partner resistance. You may want to set up stations around the room, or if there is enough equipment for each participant, everyone can work simultaneously doing the same exercise. Decide what muscle groups you wish to work and what exercises will best accomplish the goals. Check form and alignment and practice the exercises without weights or resistance before starting.

Remember, circuit training is done quickly. In order to achieve the strength training and cardiovascular benefits, the rest periods are kept brief. Emphasize posture, full range of motion, and control through muscle resistance. Circuit training can be an exciting addition to your present workout schedule, especially if you are interested in the benefits of cross-training.

References

American College of Sports Medicine (1990). 1990 Position stand, The recommended quantity and quality of exercise for developing and maintaining cardiorespiratory and muscular fitness in healthy adults.

American College of Sports Medicine (1990). *Guidelines for exercise testing and prescription.* Philadelphia: Lea & Febiger.

Fleck, S.J., & Kraemer, W.J. (1989). *Designing resistance training programs.* Champaign, Ill.: Human Kinetics Publishers, Inc.

Garhammer, J. (1987). *Strength training: your ultimate weight conditioning program.* New York: Time, Inc.

Howley, E.T., & Franks, B.D. *Health/fitness instructor's handbook.* Champaign, IL: Human Kinetics Publishers, Inc.

McArdle, W.D., Katch, F.I., & Katch, V.L. (1981). *Exercise physiology.* Philadelphia: Lea & Febiger.

Pearl, B., & Morgan, G.T. (1986). *Getting stronger.* New York: Random House, Inc.

Stone, M., & O'Bryant, H. (1987). *Weight training: a scientific approach.* Edina, Mn.: Burgess International Group, Inc.

Wilmore, J.H., Parr, R.B., Ward, P. et al. (1987). Energy cost of circuit weight training. *Medicine and Science in Sports and Exercise,* 10: 75-78.

Wright, J.E., Patton, J.F., Vogel, J.A., et al. (1982). Aerobic power and body composition after 10 weeks of circuit weight training using various work: rest ratios. *Medicine and Science in Sports and Exercise,* 14:170.

Troy DeMond, MA

59 *Interval Training*

Focus

INTERVAL TRAINING COMBINES HIGH AND LOW intensity intervals in a single workout. By incorporating interval training into their existing exercise progams, instructors can discover an effective means for training both aerobic and anaerobic systems. Class members can maximize desired fitness results through this unique approach.

Working Aerobic and Anaerobic Systems

The ultimate goal of interval training (I.T.) is to push both the aerobic and anaerobic systems to their maximum limits. Alternating brief periods of **high intensity** work with **low intensity** recovery periods (commonly referred to as the intervals) results in overloading both energy systems. It is important to understand that during steady state exercise, sufficient oxygen is supplied to and utilized by the working muscles. Hence, there is a balance between oxygen available for the body's use and the intensity level of the activity.

However, as the exercise intensity is increased to the point that oxygen demands can no longer be met, anaerobic metabolism contributes to the energy requirements of the activity. An example of this would be a sprinter running a fast 440-yard dash and then "actively" recovering with a slow one. Or, an aerobic student might perform a series of high intensity power moves for three minutes followed by one minute of body conditioning work combined with low intensity squats. Continually incorporating this type of work/rest program into any existing aerobic training program will enable your students to reap the many benefits of interval training.

Why I.T. Works

Unlike a program that strictly trains the aerobic system, interval training allows your students to train both the aerobic and anaerobic systems. The greatest concentration for increased oxygen and carbon dioxide exchange occurs during the high intensity portions. It is at this level of intensity that the accumulation of lactic acid tends to be the greatest. This continual build-up of lactic acid will eventually hinder muscular contraction and overall physical performance. However, by decreasing the intensity for a brief period of time, active recovery can occur because the body's ability to utilize oxygen and deliver nutrients to the working muscles is then increased.

During this decreased intensity portion, the incorporation of weights, exercise bands, tubing, or even calisthenics are excellent ways for your students to increase muscular strength and endurance and to help eliminate toxic byproducts such as lactic acid. Hence, the participant pushes to an anaerobic state, promotes muscular strength and endurance while actively recovering and still remains in an aerobic state. It is crucial to remember this important point: The participant remains in an aerobic state if—and only if—the heart rate stays

Active Recovery

above the training threshold. If the heart rate drops below this level during the active recovery period, the aerobic state is not maintained.

Making I.T. Work

2 to 3 times per week

HR at Low Intensity

During active recovery periods, the optimal intensity is 60% age-predicted maximum heart rate. Do not let the heart rate drop below this level. Not only does this level maintain blood perfusion through the heart and liver to facilitate the removal of lactic acid, but it also allows for optimal muscular strength and endurance work through movements that are slow, controlled and isolated.

Frequency

Research indicates that significant physiological improvements occur if interval training is implemented two to three times per week. However, this will vary depending on the present fitness level of your students and the exercise goals. For example, an individual concerned with improving his/her general fitness level will reap minimal "interval" benefits by participating in interval training only one time per week.

A highly trained athlete will gain significant "interval" improvements by participating more times per week. However, as effective instructors, you must remember that interval training can be very stressful at any level of participation. Therefore, be aware of the possibilities of overtraining related injuries and monitor your programming accordingly. Providing your students with a safe and effective workout scenario is your number one priority.

Work/Active Recovery Ratio

The work interval is known as the high intensity portion of the workout. The active recovery interval consists of low intensity movement. Both combine to make up what is called a **cycle.** Generally, the number of cycles in a workout is once again dependent on your students' current fitness levels and exercise goals.

Intensity

In attempting to increase the exercise intensity to or slightly above an anaerobic threshold for a brief period, have your students select an intensity of 85% age-predicted maximum heart rate. However, it is important to assess individual fitness levels when determining intensity levels. An extremely fit student might reach a threshold at 85% maximum, whereas an individual new to exercise might cross the threshold at 70% maximum. Without metabolic testing, it is virtually impossible to determine at exactly what heart rate intensity level an individual will cross the threshold. Therefore, inform your students that there are other indicators that the threshold point is near: dramatic increases in heart rate signals, increases in breathing depth and frequency, possible hyperventilation, and even muscle fatigue. Remember, safety is the first concern, and for most, prolonged exercise at high intensity levels is too demanding and dangerous.

Work-To-Recovery Ratio

How long your students participate with high intensity movement and recover with low intensity body conditioning segments is dependent upon their exercise goals, present fitness level, and the primary energy system (aerobic vs. anaerobic) they want to train. Let's examine two extreme examples of interval workouts. First, a track athlete is likely to work with intervals of a one-to-one ratio—sprint for one minute and actively recover for the next. Or, another athlete might do what's known as "mile repeaters"—running a "hard" mile, followed by an "easy" mile.

Conversely, a long distance person will work with intervals of a two- to-one ratio—recovering only half the time he/she works. Remember, the long distance runner's goal is to push hard for longer periods of time than the track athlete (who needs short bursts). That is why it is critical for the effective instructor to tailor the interval workouts to the goal of the student if at all possible.

Taking I.T. To The Class

Begin your class with a 10-minute warm-up that will prep the joints and begin to increase core body temperature and prepare it for more strenuous exercise. Design the warm-up so that the heart rate begins to reach 50% to 60% maximum near the end of the warm-up period.

Once this is accomplished, the interval segment begins. Each interval is four minutes in duration and consists of three minutes of high intensity power moves; jumping jacks; knee lifts; and plyometrics, immediately followed by one minute of active recovery body conditioning. During the three minute high intensity period, encourage your students to work at 85% maximum.

Three minutes is an optimal time because those participants who are extremely fit may challenge themselves for the entire time, or newcomers to this type of training may be encouraged to stay "more aerobic," working up to 85% in the latter portion of the cycle. A music fade for five seconds is essential between work and recovery periods. It cues your participants that change is about to occur. Then, the active recovery portion begins incorporating tubing, bands, weights, or calisthenics to promote body conditioning. During this period, your students' exercise intensity should be decreased to 60% maximum. This is the optimal intensity for increasing blood perfusion and removing lactic acid while remaining in an aerobic state. (1) This three minute—one minute format should be followed for six sets, completing the interval period in 24 minutes.

A post-aerobic cooldown in which the movement lowers the heart rate to below 60% maximum should follow the interval segment. A 10-minute abdominal section to isolate eccentric (lengthening) contractions follows the cooldown, and a super stretch completes your students' workout.

Now that you have a basic understanding of the physiological responses of interval training and a general format of implementation, following several guidelines will allow you to make your students' first interval class a success. First, while making your interval music tapes, include a five second music fade between each work and recovery period. As mentioned earlier, this cues participants that change is about to occur and is also a great place to begin a heart rate check if needed. It also serves to educate the participants as to how their bodies are responding to the varying intensities.

Several ideal body conditioning moves make the interval class format a success during active recovery periods and promote muscular strength and endurance: shoulder press/power slide; shoulder press/power knee; chest cross/power squat; upright row/power calve raise; bicep curl-tricep press/power

Table 59-1. The Interval Training Workout	
Rhythmical Warm-Up/Stretch	10 min
Interval Training (6 sets)	24 min
4 minute cycles	
3 minutes of high intensity activity	
1 minute of body training	
Post interval cooldown	5 min
Abdominal work	10 min
Super stretch	5 min

MUSIC

Beats per minute during the high intensity portion should be from approximately 150 to 160. Music for the active recovery periods should be 120 bpm. This allows for muscle isolation.

slide. These combinations of upper and lower body movements provide total body conditioning while the body actively recovers from each work segment.

Summary

Remember, interval training is peaks and valleys in exercise intensity. I.T. not only improves all three energy systems, but also helps promote muscular strength and endurance. If you want to maximize student results and literally provide them with the key to achieving success in any personal fitness program—try interval training.

References

McArdle, W., Katch, F., & Katch, V. (1993). *Exercise physiology: energy nutrition, and human performance*. Philadelphia: Lea & Febiger.

Victoria Johnson

60 *Funk*
The Aerobic Evolution

Focus

AN INSTRUCTOR SHOULD NOT NEED years of technical dance training to take and/or teach a funk class. What is needed, however is "attitude" and patience. Funk does not happen overnight. Instructors are challenged by this new form of aerobics because it provides a fresh new look for their class. Students enjoy it because of the freedom and exhilaration experienced in meeting a high-style challenge.

What is funk?

Funk is a form of movement that incorporates disciplined dance techniques, including ballet, jazz and modern dance with African movement. First, dance technique gives the body strong lines and originates movement from the body center, which creates balance and drama. Secondly, African movement relates to "raw" dance steps in which upper body isolations and stylized accents dominate. With funk, the two—dance technique and African movement—meld together, joined by powerful leg moves to create an overall aerobic effect. The downbeat-centered movement is the beat of the street, a challenge for many students, but also an exhilarating experience for those who need a change of pace from traditional aerobics.

To interpret and implement funk moves, you must develop a base level of dance savvy. Start with a repertoire that you can expand upon by integrating dance moves and funky patterns into your class rather than just starting a funk class from scratch. If you prefer to teach free style, then it is best to implement funky moves into the warm-up and after the high cardio phase of the cooldown portion of the class.

Since most of the funk moves are low impact, it is an easy transition for your low impact clients to learn funky marching, jazz squares and syncopated jazz squares. Funk can also be easily translated into a body sculpting format simply by utilizing funky foot patterns in the warm-up or cooldown. Since this class format is slower and more methodical, there is an opportunity to focus on alignment technique and verbal cues, such as plié, releve, turn out, close, and first or second position feet placement. Lower body level cueing includes: demi (semi) grant, parallel. For chest and back, cue to contract and expand. The idea is to incorporate these cues into the routine to allow for more fluid movement.

> *Teaching Methodology*

> **Funky Step**
>
> *Use arm patterns in the beginning such as waves, snaps, jazz hands, claps and Vogue arms. Then incorporate funky floor combinations and step combinations in intervals.*

Suggested Funk Class Format

1. Warm-up (7-10 minutes)

Active warm-up, limber and loosen: upper body, torso isolations, rib cage, side to side, neck, shoulder rotations, hip isolations.

Stretches: neck, shoulders, hamstrings, calves, soleus, quadriceps, upper and lower back.

2. Aerobic Segment (40 minutes)

First 3-5 minutes: Begin by marching in place and using a variety of arm patterns.

12-15 minutes: The base moves that you will be using to build combinations.

12-15 minutes: Build your combinations based on the moves you have been teaching. Now is when you add personal style. You can change the accent in the music. You can perform a particular move in a double-time rhythm, add a hand accent or just plain add a little "attitude!"

5-6 minutes: Now perform your combinations for the finale. Allow the student to break loose and get creative.

3. Cooldown (4-6 minutes)

Cooldown with walking motions such as the hustle, grapevine or light marching. Next, stretch the same muscle group you stretched in the warm-up.

4. Stretch and Floorwork (7-10 minutes)

Do a series of crunches as well as oblique work. Low back strengthening should also be done because of the rib cage motion forward and back, and side to side. End the class with long, slow static stretching. Hold for at least 20-30 seconds per stretch.

The key to a successful funk class is progression, not intimidation. Start with a basic move and build upon it. Offer encouragement throughout the entire workout. Most of the funk moves are unfamiliar to the average students so they need to feel they are on the right track.

 CHECKLIST

Funk Safety

- Warm up longer (at least 12 min.) and isolate neck, shoulders, upper torso, rib cage, ankles and calves.
- Practice your dancer's turnouts (external rotation of the hips in order to protect the knees).
- Don't let your knees overextend your toes.
- During the first 3-5 minutes of pre-cardio work, concentrate on movement that travels front and back in order to give the ankles and knees more time to warm up.
- When marching, don't bend far forward at the waist (sustained forward flexion).
- When teaching combinations, keep the class moving. Maintain an aerobic heart rate as you demonstrate.
- Let your entire class rehearse combinations, not just the front row.
- Wear proper aerobic footwear, not the fashionable heavy boots.

Fig. 60-1. Plumb line alignment. Pelvis tucked, chest and shoulders upright, elbows bent.

Fig. 60-2. March. Begin your march on down beat. Land toe, ball, heel.

Fig. 60-3. March

Fig. 60-4. Keep the body centered over the feet, the spine remains straight with the pelvis in a neutral position (not back, not forward). The feet must be securely placed, with the arches supported so they do not roll. Movement should be smooth and slow.

Two core movements of dance/funk training include the march and the plié. Both are demonstrated above.

Funk Guidelines

Charles Little and Donna Richardson

1. Style Variations.

The most popular form of funk music is rap, in which the lyrics are spoken and the bpm ranges from 100-125. Another variation is hip hop, which is characterized by musical downbeats with rhythm changes and tempos at the same bpm as rap. The other styles, such as reggae and gospel, are adopting the rhythms and syncopated lyrics of rap music to enhance their style.

2. Rhythm Variations.

Music is measured in four 1/4 beats at a time, and two measures of music equal a phrase of movement (8 counts). The most commonly used rhythms incorporate 1/2 beats allowing for up to eight different movements per phrase. Most funk choreography incorporates a slightly more complex rhythm with the use of 1/8 beats (twice as quick as 1/4 beats).

A phrase of 1/8 beats would be counted as follows:

1+2+3+4+, 5+6+7+8+

This allows up to 16 different movements per phrase, which can be combined to create endless variations of choreography.

3. Rhythm Accents.

Denote changes in movement dynamics by placing a greater attack on certain movements to create a contrast between movements. For example, when doing a step touch, place little emphasis on the first step, then embellish the second step by placing two times the force along with a planal change in the leg to increase the dimension of the movement.

4. Directional Changes.

Provide contrast to choreography by changing focal points, thus providing greater possibilities of variations.

5. Stylization.

Base moves can also be transformed into funk choreography by adding trendy dance gestures. (Michael Jackson's Egyptian style arms or Vogueing.)

6. Range of Motion.

Gauge movements by their speed. Quicker movements require smaller range of motion.

7. Muscular Control.

Each individual movement should be executed with a focused contraction of the primary muscle group involved in the joint action. Momentum movements should be avoided.

8. Correct Alignment.

The skeletal alignment should be stacked for optimal support. Imagine a center midline running from head to toe. All joints should be relaxed, avoiding hyperextension or locking of the joints. Muscular support should be given by the rectus abdominus and erector spinae muscles.

9. Movements to Avoid
   - hyperextension of the spine, neck and knee
   - unsupported forward spinal flexion
   - pivoting on a loaded knee joint and knee hyperflexion

Jill Boyer
Sandy Greger, MEd, ATC

61 Sports Conditioning

Focus

BEFORE PARTICIPATING IN ANY SPORT, it is important to become involved in a conditioning program. Pre-season conditioning will improve performance, increase skill, and help to prevent the injuries most common to that sport. Accidents occur frequently when muscles tire and reflexes slow. Strong muscles won't tire as quickly, so we can spend more time playing and less time recovering.

Learn the Sport's Physical Requirements

Although there are similarities in all conditioning programs each sport is unique unto itself, as is its training program. These differences must be recognized and defined. As an exercise instructor you must learn the physiological requirements of each sport. Since each activity stresses the body in a slightly different manner, specific exercises need to be developed in order to improve performance. If you are unfamiliar with a sport, watch the game or event carefully to see what muscles are involved and how their movements are utilized during actual performance. This will give you valuable clues as to what exercises to select for training.

In any conditioning program, certain factors need to be addressed. They are strength, flexibility, and endurance.

Strength is the maximum amount of force that a muscle is able to exert in a single contraction. By selecting strengthening exercises specific to the chosen sport, you can greatly enhance muscular efficiency and reduce the possibility of injury.

See Chapter on "Interval Training"

Flexibility is the maximum range of motion available at a joint. Increased flexibility decreases risk of injury to joints and muscles by increasing available range of motion. It helps to improve the quality of performance by reducing muscle tension which allows for freer more fluid movements. It is important to note that different sports have different flexibility requirements.

The term endurance pertains to the muscular as well as cardiorespiratory systems. Muscular endurance is the ability of a muscle to contract repeatedly over a long period of time. The cardiorespiratory system is the pathway our body uses to get oxygen and other nutrients out to the working muscles. The more efficiently the heart can pump blood, nutrients and oxygen to the muscle, the greater the cardiorespiratory endurance of the body. Maintaining a 55 to 85% maximum heart rate for a period of no less than 20 minutes will help to achieve this goal. However many sports require a high anaerobic capacity as well. This refers to the body's ability to function for a short period of time in a state of oxygen debt at a high intensity. For these sports, some form of interval training should also be considered.

Alpine Skiing Pre-Conditioning Program

As an example in designing a sport-specific training program, we will look at the demands that downhill (Alpine) skiing puts on one's body and develop a program to meet these special needs.

Alpine skiing is technically difficult and potentially very dangerous. Being in shape for skiing can make these difficulties easier to overcome and help reduce the risk of injury. Gone are the days of skiing your way into shape. "Hitting the slopes" will be far more enjoyable if done figuratively not literally.

Skiing is a sport that demands tremendous muscle strength and endurance, good flexibility and a well developed aerobic and anaerobic capacity. Balance, agility and coordination as well as muscular power, are also prime factors that must be taken into consideration when developing a training program for this physically demanding sport.

By examining the energy demands of skiing, one can see quickly that it is important to train both the aerobic and anaerobic energy systems. The Alpine skier must be a long distance runner as well as a sprinter. One method of training both systems is Fartlek training or Swedish speed play. In this form of interval training, constant pace periods (submaximal) are interspersed with shorter periods of increased speed (maximal). Movement is continuous, thus placing an anaerobic stress within the context of aerobic training.

To design a sports conditioning program, you must:

1. **Assess the physical demands.** Alpine skiing demands the development of power, strength and endurance of the legs, thighs, gluteals, hips, abdominals, and lower back. One way of achieving this goal is through circuit training, which emphasizes strength training within an aerobic format by moving rapidly from one exercise to the next using low resistance and high repetition, achieving not only muscle hypertrophy but a significant increase in aerobic capacity as well.

2. **Match the appropriate exercises.** The ability to sustain isometric contractions of the thigh, calf, buttocks, abdominal and back muscles to maintain position and control while skiing are necessary, but intermittent bursts of power and dynamic contraction are also required to carve turns. Exercises that stress these muscles isometrically as well as isotonically should be considered along with some form of plyometric training, which will help to develop greater muscular power.

3. **Look for the specific challenges.** In Alpine skiing, we are constantly subjecting our bodies to quick changes of direction and variations in terrain then recovering lost balance. Sometimes, we are successful in overcoming these challenges; sometimes we are not. If we do not meet the challenge, we may find ourselves hurtling through the air, landing in the infamous "face plant." We increase our chances of surviving these falls without injury if we have good flexibility. When our muscles are tight, the range of motion available at the joint is limited, predisposing us to injury. It is important to keep in mind that flexibility is joint and direction specific and will differ with each individual. One's flexibility is determined by lifestyle, past athletic history and genetics. For Alpine skiing, an overall flexibility program is recommended.

4. **Determine the total components.** Having examined the physical requirements of our sport, we have determined that the following components need to be addressed:

a) aerobic and anaerobic energy systems

b) muscular strength, power and endurance, primarily for the lower legs, thighs, hips, back, abdominals, and gluteals

c) flexibility for the total body

The class that follows has been designed specifically to meet these needs.

Tuned to Ski Circuit

1.   Slalom Running. Develops the ability to shift the body's weight rapidly while moving forward. Fine tunes turning ability. Proper foot landing is heel, ball, toe.

2.   Lateral Slides. Develops the ability to shift the body's weight laterally rapidly. Fine tunes turning ability.

3.   Air Squats. Conditions the legs to act as shock absorbers over uneven terrain, i.e., moguls, etc. Avoid hyperextension of the knees.

4.   Wall Sits with Heel Raise. Strengthens the quadriceps, hip flexors and calf muscles. Sitting position is held for the one minute time limit. Heels are raised and lowered in time with music. Never drop the buttocks below the level of the hip.

5.   Step-ups. Strengthens the hip and knee flexors. Enhances climbing ability. Bench can be 8-12 inches high depending on participant ability. Angle of step should never exceed 90 degrees from the hip.

6.   Rope Jumping. Stabilizes the forearm and conditions the wrists for poling. Promotes independent leg action, calf, quad and hip extensor strength and endurance.

7.   Pole Hopping. Promotes independent leg action and lateral hip movement.

8.   Push-ups. Strengthens upper body, abdominals and back muscles. Hips should be slightly piked to avoid low back strain.

9.   Standing Lunges. Strengthens knee musculature. Weight should be centered in the heel of the front foot during lunge. Do not allow knee to exceed the tip of the toes.

10.   Box Jumping. Plyometric training helps develop muscular contraction and extension of the legs, as well as power and quickness. Bench may be 8 to 10 inches depending on participant ability.

Step-Tap   Step-Tap

Summary

In conclusion, our world as a whole is becoming more competitive as evidenced by the aggressive approach many of us take to our chosen leisure time activities. George Sheehan, world renowned physician and runner once said, "Every individual is an athlete whose event is getting through a 16-hour day." Getting through the rigors of a normal work day and having enough energy and strength left over to play our favorite sports is a goal everyone can work toward. Achieving and then maintaining physical fitness, we enable ourselves to play longer, harder and ultimately better in any sport we choose.

We would like to thank Sam Greger, our devoted uncle and father for his patience and dedication to the sport of Alpine skiing.

References

American College of Sports Medicine (1988). *Resource manual for guidelines for exercise testing and prescription.* Philadelphia: Lea & Febiger.

Buxbaum, R., & Micheli, L.J. (1979). *Sports for ltfe: Fitness training, their prevention and nutrition.* Boston: Beacon Press.

Lamb, D.R. (1982). *Physiology of exercise: responses & adaptations* (2nd ed.). New York: MacMillan.

Noble, B.J. (1986). *Physiology of exercise and sport.* St. Louis: Times Mirror/Mosby College.

Pearl, B., & Moran, G. (1986). *Getting stronger: Weight training for men and women.* Bolinas: Shelter.

Sheehan, G., (March 10, 1988). Lecture delivered at The Academy of Osteopathic Academy of Sports Medicine Clinical Conference, Palms Springs, Ca.

Southmayd, W., & Hoffman, M. (1981). *Sports health: The complete book of athletic injury.* New York: Perigee.

United States Ski Team, National Alpine Staff (1977). *Alpine training manual.* Park City: U.S. Ski Team.

Kathy Stevens

62 Slide Aerobics
Lateral Movement Training

Focus

SLIDE TRAINING IS A NEW FORM of aerobic and anaerobic conditioning which involves the use of LMT or lateral movement training. In order to perform this movement, it is necessary to have a type of exercise equipment which allows one to slide in a side-to-side motion similar to speed skating. Opportunities for sports conditioning, personal training and fitness instruction abound for the slide enthusiast.

How To Get Started

More than abductors and adductors

The necessary equipment is generally referred to as a lateral movement trainer (LMT) or slide board. Slide boards were developed over a century ago by European speed skaters. Since that time a variety of competitive and Olympic athletes have found slide training to be a remarkable way to increase lateral speed, power and agility. Originally constructed with wood, today's models usually have a six to ten feet long plastic sliding surface with end ramps or blocks. Board width is approximately two or three feet.

Some units have biomechanically-angled end pieces or end pieces that can be adjusted for length. These boards come in stationary or portable roll-up models. Special slide socks are worn over one's fitness shoe to reduce friction and provide a smooth sliding movement across the length of the board.

The basic slide movement begins with feet together against one of the end bumpers. By pushing against the end bumper with the adjacent leg, one's body is moved laterally in a gliding fashion to the opposite bumper. You then push off in the opposite direction and repeat this movement over and over again. With practice, one can master lateral movement with ease and will find the boards to be simple and fun to use.

Lateral movement is an integral part of many of our favorite recreational and competitive sports such as racquet sports, basketball, soccer, volleyball, skiing and skating. When working on a lateral movement trainer, the hip abductor and adductors are more directly involved in a strength capacity. Also EMG studies have shown that the quadriceps and hamstrings work almost continuously though the push-off and glide phases of the movement as well as the core muscles (including the abdominals) which are used to maintain proper positioning. A similar action takes place in the muscles of the lower leg and foot. The type of contraction will vary between concentric, eccentric and isometric as in most sports activities. For many athletes and lesser conditioned individuals, lack of lateral movement and stabilizing strength is a primary cause of lower back and knee injury (2). LMT's develop stabilizer muscles as well as the proprioceptive and kinesthetic needs for enhancing **dynamic balance,** which has made these devices very popular in rehabilitation circles. The key factor in the LMT's successful usage in therapy is its ability to return an injured patient to functional levels at or above pre-injury status.

With the introduction of slide training to the aerobic and fitness industry has come a variety of movements and combination patterns that can be performed in a classroom setting. The slide class provides a **non-impact** (vertical) option for cross-training with our traditional forms of aerobics. It can be used aerobically or anaerobically. For a good aerobic workout and calorie usage, this activity is comparable to treadmills, stairclimbers or cross country ski machines.

Slide board studies were conducted over a six-week training period by Peter A. Harmer, Ph.D., Sports Medicine at Willamette University in Salem, Oregon. Heart rate measures indicated that slide board training without adjunct resistance elicits training heart rates meeting or exceeding values recommended to produce a cardiovascular training effect. Workouts can also be more plyometric in nature to develop leg power and quickness. According to the same studies, statistical analysis of pre-post test differences on standardized measures of cardiovascular performance (Queens College Step Test) and agility (SEMO Agility Test) indicate a significant improvement in both areas over the course of the study. According to sports training specialist, Suzanne Nottingham, "Slide training, from a sport-specific point of view, adds elements of lateral conditioning comparable to no other mode of exercising. My personal favorite uses are for cross-training for Alpine and Nordic skiing, in-line skating and hockey."

Summary

Slide training is an age-old concept yet a new direction in fitness for the athlete, rehabilitating individual and exercise enthusiast. Slide training is based on research and knowledge of physiology, biomechanics and kinesiology. This lateral wave of the future is quickly changing the way that we train in the aerobics room as well as on the playing field of life.

References

1. Markland, J. (1991). Benefits of the kneedspeed slideboard program. Research References information provided by Kneedspeed Inc., Gresham, Or.

2. Osbourne, R. (1990). Slide-em cowboy! The new lateral movement trainer. *American fitness quarterly,* 9:4: 10-13.

3. Reese, S. (1991). Slide boards: A conditioning and rehabilitative tool. *National Strength and Conditioning Association Journal,* 13:5: 22-24.

Petra Lansner-Robinson
Marti West

63 *Competitive Aerobics*

Focus

TRADITIONALLY, AEROBICS CLASSES have promoted the concept that each individual should participate at a level of exertion and difficulty based on their personal degree of fitness and experience. Competition has never been a primary motivator in the aerobics class. After all, there is no inherent impetus to perform faster, longer, jump higher, or score points. Aerobics is not based on subjective measure—it originates in dance and the desire to move.

How then, do we make a sport of aerobics? Most sports are based on the achievement of a goal that can be quantified. Many sports, such as track and field events, and downhill skiing, are predicated on speed, distance and height. Ball sports, such as baseball, tennis, golf, and soccer, are built on scoring points. Combative sports, such as wrestling or boxing are designed around the awarding of points or matches based on one opponent physically overpowering and/or mentally outwitting the other opponent. Other sports, such as figure skating, gymnastics, and diving, are classified as artistic sports which means the judging is based on how one individual performs particular movements in comparison to an established standard of performance. Competitive aerobics falls into this category.

Standards for a New Sport

Unlike many other artistic sports that have standardized and easily recognized movements, such as a flip, jack-knife dive, or toe-loop jump, competitive aerobics is a new sport. The movements of aerobics are only now becoming standardized according to internationally recognized performance criteria, thanks to organizations such as AFAA and the International Aerobics Federation.

Competitive aerobics is also distinctive in that it is the only sport based on fitness. For example, push-ups and sit-ups are normally regarded as training methods for general fitness or specific sports. However, in competitive aerobics, they become part of the actual movements to be judged.

The goal of competitive aerobics is to synthesize the traditional, 60-minute aerobics class into a **short representative routine** which allows the athlete to demonstrate highly refined skills that are integral to the performance of an aerobics class. Since the goal of an aerobics class is to provide a total fitness training opportunity, competitive routines mirror the extension of the components of physical fitness, i.e., cardiovascular conditioning, muscular strength and endurance training, and flexibility. Aerobics classes are designed to deliver this type of comprehensive training in an enjoyable, creative format. Representative competitive routines include:

1. Aerobic Choreography

Demonstration of repeating 8-count combinations that are performed to music with 4/4 timing. Aerobic choreography is distinguished from dance by its limited use of pauses and stylistic hesitations. The movement is continuous and normally there is one movement or step per beat. This type of continuous movement represents the basic fitness goal of an aerobics class, which is to maintain the heart rate at a level sufficient to obtain a training effect.

2. Upper Body Strength

Presentation of exercises demonstrating upper body strength. This would include compulsory exercises such as push-ups.

3. Abdominal Strength

Demonstration of abdominal strength, as evidenced by the presentation of abdominal curls.

4. Lower Body Strength

Presentation of exercises demonstrating lower body strength. This includes exercises such as lunges, squats, and to a certain extent, jumping jacks and high kicks.

5. Non-Aerobic Choreography

Presentation of the muscular strengthening exercises in a creative manner which would differentiate the performance of these exercises from a standard fitness test.

6. Flexibility

Demonstration of specific movements which require muscular flexibility, such as high leg kicks, and splits.

Other criteria, such as use of music is important, and in some competitions, body development based on appearance versus performance is also judged.

Competition Overview

The three main competitions in the United States are:

1. The Aerobics & Fitness Challenge, produced by AFAA, the Aerobics and Fitness Association of Amenca.
2. The National Aerobic Championship, produced by Howard Schwartz Associates, Inc.
3. The AAU-USAASF Aerobics Championships, produced by local and national AAU-USAASF affiliates.

The Aerobics & Fitness Challenge, produced by AFAA is a multi-tiered competition, beginning within the health club in a Club Challenge event open to everyone. No advance preparation of routines, music, or costumes is necessary at this level. Competitors are judged as they participate in a nationally consistent routine, on their execution, ability to pick up the routine, and their performance quality.

Part 10

Appendices

Amanda J. Beaudin

BECAUSE EMERGENCY PROTOCOL TECHNIQUES CHANGE often, the contents of this protocol are for reference and review purposes only. Observing the following basic procedures will give you a jump start on any emergency situation:

Every fitness instructor should be current in both Adult CPR and standard first aid procedures.

- Post accurate telephone numbers for all available assistance. Make certain all staff members know where the numbers are posted.
- Purchase and have on hand a comprehensive first aid kit. Review the contents and add any items you feel are missing. Be sure everyone knows where the kit is stored.
- Meet with all staff members and determine individual responsibilities during any emergency. Go over each procedure in detail to assure understanding.

In most emergencies, you will need to activate the EMS System or Emergency Medical Services System which is usually a team of paramedics and EMTs. In many areas, the phone number for EMS is 911. However, to be safe, check your local listings for the appropriate phone number. Run a practice drill in your setting and make sure everyone knows the correct procedure.

Listed below are potential emergencies followed by the appropriate reactions.

Victim is not breathing, but has a pulse (rescue breathing).
Reaction

- Check for unresponsiveness.
- Shout "Help" to attract the attention of bystanders.
- Open the airway using head-tilt/chin-lift method (Figure A-1a and A-1b).
- Look, listen, and feel for breathing for three to five seconds.
- Give two full breaths, pinching the victim's nose and sealing your mouth around his (Figure A-1c).
- Check pulse for five to ten seconds. Check for severe bleeding.
- Call EMS.
- Begin rescue breathing by giving one breath every five seconds for one minute (about twelve breaths) and then recheck pulse. If pulse is present, continue rescue breathing. If pulse is not present begin CPR.

Fig. A-1a.

Fig. A-1b.

Fig. A-1c.

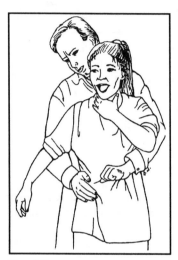

Fig. A-2a.

Fig. A-2b.

Victim is conscious and choking.
Reaction

- Ask "Are you choking?"
- Ask "Can I help?"
- Begin abdominal thrusts (Figure A-2a and A-2b). Repeat until the object is expelled or the victim becomes unconscious.

Victim is unconscious and choking.
Reaction

- Check for unresponsiveness.
- Shout "Help" to attract the attention of bystanders.
- Open the airway using head-tilt/chin-left method (Figures A-1).
- Look, listen, and feel for breathing for three to five seconds.
- Give two full breaths, pinching the victim's nose and sealing your mouth around his.
- Retilt head (maybe it wasn't tilted far back enough).
- Give two more full breaths.
- Call EMS.
- Straddle legs and give five abdominal thrusts (Figure A-3).
- Come back up to mouth and do a finger sweep (Figure A-4a and A-4b).
- Give two full breaths (unless victim is breathing on own) to see if airway is clear. If air goes in, check pulse and breathing to determine if you need to do rescue breathing or CPR. If air does not go in, repeat abdominal thrusts, finger sweeps, and breaths until breaths go in.

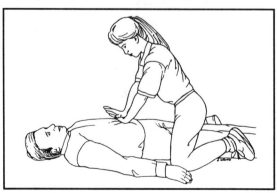

Fig. A-3.

Victim has no pulse and no breathing (CPR).
Reaction

- Check for unresponsiveness.
- Shout "Help" to attract the attention of bystanders.
- Open the airway using head-tilt/chin-lift method (Figure A-1).
- Look, listen, and feel for breathing for three to five seconds.
- Give two full breaths, pinching the victim's nose and sealing your mouth around his.
- Check pulse for 5-10 seconds. Check for severe bleeding.
- Call EMS.
- Begin CPR by giving 15 compressions, 1.5 to 2 inches deep (Figure A-5).
- Give two full breaths.
- Repeat 15 compressions and two breaths cycle three more times (approximately 1 minute).
- Check pulse.
- If there is no pulse, continue CPR, checking pulse every few minutes. If there is a pulse, stop CPR and begin rescue breathing if needed.

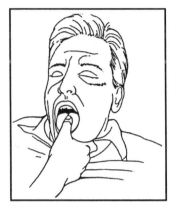

Fig. A-4a

Victim is bleeding externally.
Reaction

- Call EMS.
- With a barrier (if possible) between you and the victim, apply direct pressure.
- If the bleeding continues, add more gauze (if available) and elevate the limb above the level of the heart.
- If the bleeding continues, apply a pressure bandage using gauze and a roller bandage (Figures A-6a through A-6c).
- If bleeding continues locate brachial (arm) or femoral (leg) artery and press against bone until bleeding is under control (Figure A-7).
- Treat for shock.

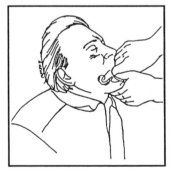

Fig. A-4b

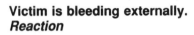

A pressure bandage is not a tourniquet; instead, it is tied snugly and is not meant to cut off all circulation.

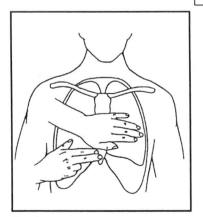

Fig. A-5a

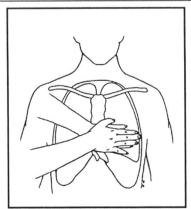

Fig. A-5b

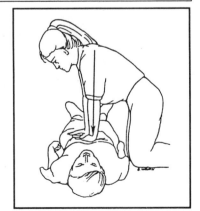

Fig. A-5c

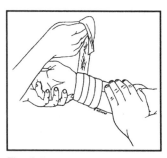

Fig. A-6a

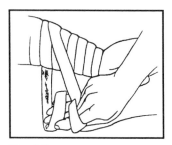

Fig. A-6a

Victim is in shock or may go into shock.

The victim may be confused, have very fast or very slow heart and breathing rates, trembling and weakness in the arms and legs, cool and moist skin, pale or bluish skin, lips and fingernails, or dilated pupils. Shock will lead to death if untreated.

Reaction

- Call EMS.
- If you do not suspect head injuries, spine injuries or leg fractures, place victim on his back and elevate legs 8 to 12 inches. If you do suspect head injuries, spine injuries, or a leg fracture, do not move the victim.
- If the victim vomits, lie him or her on one side.
- If the victim is having trouble breathing, have him sit in a semi-reclining position.
- Maintain the victim's body temperature by using blankets (cold victim) or providing shade and loosening clothing (hot victim).

Fig. A-6c

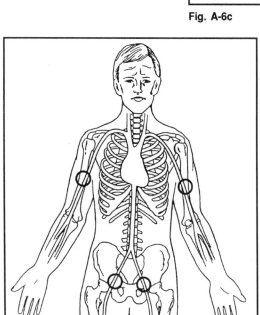

Fig. A-7

Victim has a fracture, strain, sprain, or dislocation.
Reaction

- Call EMS.
- If the injury is an open fracture (bone has broken through the skin and bleeding is present) control bleeding with pressure points only (Figure A-7).
- If the injury is a closed fracture, dislocation or sprain, splint in the position found, and only when you must transport the victim. Do not splint if it causes further pain to the victim or if you do not need to move the victim.
- To keep the victim comfortable, have him or her rest, use an ice pack, and elevate the injured area (if no further pain is incurred).

Victim has a head or spine injury.

The victim may have a change in the level of consciousness, severe pain or pressure in the head, neck, or back, tingling or loss of sensation in the extremities, partial or complete loss of movement of any body part, unusual bumps or depressions on the head or spine, blood or other fluid in the nose and ears, profuse external bleeding of head, neck, or back, seizures, impaired breathing or vision as a result of injury, nausea, vomiting, persistent headache, loss of balance, or bruising of the head, especially around the eyes and behind the ears.

Reaction

- Call EMS.
- Minimize movement of the spine and head by supporting the victim's head in the position found.
- Maintain open airway.
- Monitor consciousness and breathing.
- Control any external bleeding.
- Maintain normal body temperature.

Victim has a nosebleed.

- Nosebleeds may be an indication of head injury. Refer to the above symptoms to evaluate the possibility of a head or spine injury. If you suspect a head or spine injury, do not try to stop the flow of blood or liquids. Follow the directions above. If you do not suspect a head or spine injury, follow the directions below.

Reaction

- Have the victim lean forward. Pinch nose until bleeding ceases.

Victim has a diabetic emergency.
Reaction

- Call EMS.
- Provide care for any life-threatening conditions.
- If the victim is conscious, give him sugar (candy, soda pop, fruit).

Victim is experiencing a stroke (Cerebrovascular Accident).
Reaction

- Call EMS.
- Maintain open airway.
- If victim vomits, and you can tell that one side of the body is paralyzed, position the victim on the paralyzed side and allow fluids to drain.
- Stay with victim. Monitor pulse and breathing, and reassure the victim until help arrives.

Victim is having a seizure.
Reaction

- Call EMS.
- Move objects away that may cause injury.
- Protect the victim's head by putting a thin cushion under it.
- Position victim on side if there is fluid in the mouth.
- When the seizure is over, check breathing and pulse. Treat any injuries. Reassure and comfort the victim.

Victim is having a heat emergency.
Reaction
- Call EMS.
- Cool the body.
- Give cool liquids if the victim is fully conscious.
- Minimize shock.

Victim is experiencing hypothermia.
Remember, hypothermia can occur at any temperature and does not necessarily involve the victim falling into cold water. Hypothermia may occur any time there is a drop in body temperature.

Reaction
- Call EMS.
- Gradually warm the victim.
- Give warm liquids (not alcohol or caffeine) if the victim is fully conscious.
- Minimize shock.

Summary

Review this protocol frequently and keep your CPR and First Aid certifications current. You must be prepared for emergencies so you can react quickly and appropriately.

References

American Red Cross (1991). *Standard First Aid Instructor's Manual.* Washington, D. C.: American Red Cross.
American Red Cross (1988). *Standard First Aid Student's Manual.* Washington, D. C.: American Red Cross.
American Red Cross (1991). *First Aid Responding to Emergencies.* St. Louis, Mosby-Year Book.
American Red Cross (1993). *First Aid and CPR Instructor Manual.* St. Louis, Mosby-Year Book.

Reprinted with Permission from the American Red Cross, *Standard First Aid Instructor's Manual,* 1991, 1988, and *First Aid Responding to Emergencies,* 1991.

Appendix B

AFAA Video Review Criteria

AFAA offers assistance to any individual or company interested in producing fitness videos. AFAA Video Consultation includes everything from scripting, technical direction, pre-video consultation and post-edit advising to program consultation. Once a video is approved by the AFAA Board, the box cover may be labeled with the AFAA-Approval logo.

The following review criteria are used to ensure that exercises are consistent with the Basic Exercise Standards and Guidelines.

INSTRUCTOR TECHNIQUE

cues
choreography
exercise selection
transitions
sequencing
positioning
alignment
warm-up, stretches
aerobics
calisthenics
upper body
lower body
abdominals
cooldown stretches
use of equipment

TECHNICAL PROFICIENCY

camera angles
sound quality
music and beats per minute
set
supporting talent
graphics

SAFETY INFORMATION

precautions
adaptations
benefits
intensity measurement
equipment recommended
written material included

OVERALL EFFECTIVENESS

as a motivator
as a cardiorespiratory workout
as a musculoskeletal
    conditioning program
as a progressive training tape
meet its target market

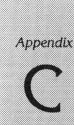

Linda Shelton

abduction	Movement away from the midline of the body.
acidosis	Too much acid in the blood and body fluids.
actin	A contractile protein of muscle fiber.
acute	Having a sudden onset, characterized by sharpness, severity and brief duration.
adaptive shortening	Shortening of muscle fibers and decreased range of motion due to inactivity.
adduction	Movement toward the midline of the body.
adipose tissue	Connective tissue in which fat is stored.
adolescent onset obesity	After puberty, when an individual acquires too much fat due to the sudden increase in the number of fat cells.
adrenaline (epinephrine)	A hormone secreted by the medulla of the adrenal glands, especially under conditions of stress that induces physiologic symptoms such as accelerated heart rate, increased arterial blood pressure and increase in blood sugar concentration.
adult onset obesity	After age 18, when an individual acquires too much fat due to the increase in the size of fat cells.
aerobic	Means literally, with oxygen, or in the presence of oxygen.
aerobic capacity	The ability of the body to remove oxygen from the air and transfer it through the lungs and blood to the working muscles; related to cardiorespiratory endurance.
aerobic exercise	A method of conditioning the cardiorespiratory system by using a variety of activities that create an increased demand for oxygen over an extended period of time.
agonist	A muscle that is a prime mover, directly responsible for a particular action.
alkalosis	When the blood has a lower hydrogen ion concentration than normal and an excessive base (bicarbonate ions) in the extracellular fluids.
all-or-none law	A muscle contracts to its fullest potential or not at all.
amenorrhea	Absence of menstruation.
amino acids	Building blocks of protein; organic compounds containing nitrogen, hydrogen, and carbon.
amphiarthrodial	A type of articulation joined by hyaline cartilage, classified as either permanent or stationary joints and slightly moveable.
anaerobic	Requiring no oxygen; usually short spurt, high energy activities.
anaerobic threshold	The point at which the body can no longer meet its demand for oxygen and anaerobic metabolism is accelerated.

anemia	A condition in which there is a reduced number of erythrocytes or decreased percentage of hemoglobin in the blood.
angina pectoris	Chest pains caused by insufficient supply of oxygen to the heart muscle.
anorexia nervosa	A psychological eating disorder, usually seen in young women who intentionally starve themselves.
anoxemia	A deficiency of oxygen in the blood.
anoxia	A deficiency of oxygen, most frequently occurring when blood supply to any part of the body is completely cut off.
antagonist	A muscle that acts in opposition to the action produced by a prime mover.
anterior	Front side of an organ or part of the body.
aorta	The largest artery in the body that delivers oxygenated blood from the left ventricle to the entire body.
aortic stenosis	A narrowing of the valve opening between the lower left chamber of the heart and the aorta.
arrhythmia	An abnormal rhythm of the heart beat.
arteriole	Small arteries that regulate the flow of blood into the capillaries.
arteriosclerosis	Abnormal thickening or hardening of the arteries that causes the artery walls to lose their elasticity.
artery	Large vessels with middle smooth muscle layer which carry oxygenated blood away from the heart to the body tissues.
arthritis	Inflammation of the joints.
atherosclerosis	A type of arteriosclerosis in which the inner layer of the artery wall becomes thick and irregular due to fat deposits, decreasing the inner diameter of the artery.
ATP (adenosine triphosphate)	Intracellular carrier of chemical energy produced by the body for muscular work.
atrophy	A reduction in size or wasting away of any organ cell, resulting from disease or disuse.
autonomic nervous system	Division of the nervous system that functions involuntarily and is responsible for innervating cardiac muscle, smooth muscle and the glands.
axial skeleton	The bones of the head and the trunk: skull, vertebral column, thorax and sternum.
ballistic	Bounce or explosive movement, unsustained.
basal metabolic rate	The energy requirements necessary for maintenance of life processes such as heart beat, breathing, and cell metabolic activities; referred to as BMR.
bilateral	Affects both sides of the body equally.
blood pooling	A condition caused by ceasing vigorous exercise too abruptly so that blood remains in the extremities and may not be delivered quickly enough to the heart and brain.
blood pressure	The pressure of the blood in the arteries.
bradycardia	Abnormally slow heart rate.

bronchus	One of two large passageways between the trachea and the lungs.
brown fat	Believed to be a more concentrated energy source that can be utilized more efficiently than other forms of fat.
bulimia nervosa	A psychological eating disorder characterized by food gorging then induced vomiting after eating, as a means of weight control.
bursa	A fluid-filled sac or cavity, located in the tissue at points of pressure or friction, mainly around joints.
bursitis	Inflammation of the bursa sac, can be an overuse syndrome.
calisthenic exercises	Part of a workout that emphasizes specific muscular work, utilizing resistance.
calorie	The amount of heat necessary to raise the temperature of 1 gram of water 1°C.
cancellous bone	Inner, spongy portion of bone tissue.
capillary	Small, thin-walled blood vessels connecting arterial and venous blood systems that allow the exchange of materials between blood and tissues.
carbohydrate	Organic compounds containing carbon, hydrogen, and oxygen; when broken down, the main energy source for muscular work and one of the basic foodstuffs.
cardiac	Pertaining to the heart.
cardiac cycle	The contraction/relaxation pattern produced in the heart by the ventricles.
cardiac output	The volume of blood pumped by each ventricle in one minute.
carotid pulse	Pulse located on the carotid artery down from the corner of the eye, just under the jawbone; used for taking heart rate.
cartilage	White, semi-opaque fibrous connective tissue; cushions and prevents wear on articular surfaces.
catecholamine	A hormone that is a neurotransmitter, released under conditions of stress includes epinephrine and norepinephrine.
cervical spine	Refers to the neck; the first seven vertebrae of the spine.
cholesterol	A chemical compound found in animal fats and oils; higher levels of cholesterol are often associated with high risk of atherosclerosis.
chondromalacia	Softening of condral cartilage on patella (backside); first symptoms usually clicking or grating sound in knee.
chronic	Persisting for a long period of time.
circumduction	Movement in which the extremity describes a 360° circle.
compact bone	Hard portion of bone that forms the diaphysis and epiphysis.
concentric contraction	Isotonic movement in which the muscle shortens.
condyle	A rounded projection at the end of a bone that articulates with another bone.
connective tissue	Primary tissue characterized by cells separated by intercellular fluid that supports and binds together other tissues and forms ligaments and tendons.
coronary arteries	Two main arteries, arising from the aorta, arching down over the top of the heart and carrying blood to the heart muscle.

couch potato	A side-lying position with head resting in palm of support arm causing a misalignment of the cervical spine.
coronary thrombosis	An obstruction, generally a blood clot, within a coronary artery which hinders the flow of blood to a part of the heart.
CPR	Cardiopulmonary resuscitation. First-aid measure to aid an individual who is not breathing and without a pulse.
cueing	Verbal technique using small words or phrases that describe upcoming exercises or body alignment positions.
dendrite	Nerve-cell process that transmits impulse to cell body.
diabetes	A hereditary metabolic disease, characterized by an inadequate activity of insulin, affecting the regulation of normal blood glucose levels.
diaphysis	Shaft of a long bone, consisting of a hollow cylinder of compact bone that surrounds a medullary cavity.
diaphragm	Dome-like sheet of skeletal muscle that separates the thoracic and abdominal cavities; contraction during inspiration expands the thoracic (chest) cavity.
diarthrodial (synovial)	Freely moveable joint with movement limited only by ligaments, muscles, tendons and adjoining bones.
diastolic pressure	Blood pressure within the arteries when the heart is in relaxation between contractions.
distal	End of any body part that is further from the midline of the body or from point of attachment.
diuretic	A drug that stimulates increased renal water excretion.
dorsal	Pertaining to the back.
dynamic flexibility	Having responsive muscles which are conditioned for their elastic properties in order to move a joint throughout full range of motion at varying speeds and forces.
dysmenorrhea	Painful menstruation.
eccentric contraction	Muscle lengthens while contracting, developing tension as when the muscles oppose the force of gravity.
ectomorph	Body type, characterized by frail and delicate bone structure, lean musculature and usually very little fat.
edema	An abnormal accumulation of fluid in body parts or tissues; swelling.
electrocardiogram	A graphic record of the electrical activity and heart beat pattern; EKG, ECG.
electrolyte imbalance	Inappropriate concentration of ions in body fluids.
embolism	Sudden blocking of artery or vein by a clot brought to its place by the blood current.
empty calories	A term used to denote food contributing calories that are void of nutrients, protein, vitamins and minerals, i.e., alcohol, sugar, fat.
endocrine glands	Ductless glands that empty their secretions directly into the blood stream; these secretions contain specific hormones that influence growth, reproduction.
endomorph	Body type characterized by a large block-shaped body, wider at hips and abdominals, a predominance of fat tissue but not necessarily obese.

endorphin   A natural substance that can be produced by the body during extended exercise periods that may exhibit "morphine-like" pain inhibiting qualities.

enzyme   A protein catalyst that stimulates and accelerates the velocity of chemical changes in the body.

epicardium   Thin, transparent outer layer of the heart wall.

epiphysis   Enlarged ends of bones where growth centers for long bones are located (epiphyseal plate).

ergometer   An apparatus for measuring workloads by an individual, e.g., bicycle.

essential amino acids   The eight amino acids that the body cannot manufacture in sufficient amounts to meet physiologic need.

eversion   Rotation of the foot, turning the sole outward.

extension   A motion of increasing the angle between two bones; straightening of a muscle previously bent in flexion.

fascia   Layer of fibrous tissue under the skin or covering and separating muscles.

fascicule   Bundles of nerve, muscle or tendon fibers, separated by connective tissue.

fat   Stored as adipose tissue in the body, it serves as a concentrated source of energy for muscular work; a compound containing glycerol and fatty acids.

fatigue   A diminished capacity for work as a result of prolonged or excessive exertion.

fatty acid   See triglyceride.

fibril   Fine thread-like structure which gives cells stability.

fibroblast   Connective tissue cell located near collagenous fibers which develop into fibers.

fibrous joint   See synarthrodial.

fixator   A muscle acting to immobilize a joint or bone; fixes the origin of prime movers so muscle action occurring is exerted at the insertion.

flexion   Bending of a joint between two bones that decreases the angle between the two bones.

frequency   As related to exercise, how often work is performed.

frontal   A plane, vertical to the median line that divides the body into anterior and posterior parts.

fructose   A monosaccharide, sometimes known as fruit sugar, that does not stimulate insulin production.

glottis   Opening between the vocal cords, entrance to the larynx.

glycogen   Form in which digested carbohydrates are stored in the muscles and liver and utilized as energy for aerobic activities.

glycogenolysis   Body's breakdown of glycogen to glucose.

glycolysis   The breakdown of glucose to simpler compounds such as lactic acid; occurs in muscle.

glucose   A simple sugar; form in which carbohydrates are transported in the blood and transported in tissues; other sugars are converted into glucose by enzymes in the body before they can be used as an energy source.

HDL	High-density lipoproteins that return unused fat to the liver for disposal; HDL levels are raised by aerobic exercise; are beneficial due to their "removal" effect on harmful lipoproteins.
heart attack	Damage (tissue death) of the heart muscle due to blockage of a coronary artery by either an embolus or thrombus.
heart failure	Congestion or accumulation of fluid in various parts of the body result from the inability of the heart to pump out all the blood that returns to it.
heat exhaustion	The collapse of an individual, characterized by prolonged sweating and inadequate replacement of salt and fluid without failure of the body's heat regulating system.
heat stroke	Acute medical emergency characterized by rectal temperature at 105° or higher and no sweating, caused by failure of the body's heat-regulating system.
hemoglobin	Oxygen-carrying protein of red blood cells.
herniated disc	A condition that occurs when the nucleus pulposus distends outside of the intervertebral disc, usually quite painful.
homeostasis	A state of equilibrium and internal balance of the body.
hormone	A chemical agent secreted by the endocrine glands; each affects a specific organ and elicits a specific response.
hyaline cartilage	Translucent bluish-white cartilage with a homogeneous matrix, present in joints and respiratory passage, and forms most of the fetal skeleton.
hyper	Beyond normal limits, excessive.
hyperextension	To increase the angle of a joint past the normal range of motion.
hyperplasia	Increase in the number of cells produced in an organ or body tissues.
hypertension	High blood pressure; unstable or persistent elevation of blood pressure above normal ranges. 140/90 is in general a high normal blood pressure.
hypertrophy	Increase in size of tissue, organ, or cell, independent of general body growth.
hyperventilate	Excessive rate and depth of respiration, leading to abnormal loss of carbon dioxide from the blood; can cause dizziness.
hypo	Less than normal.
hypoglycemia	An abnormally low blood glucose concentration, characterized by a number of symptoms such as dizziness, nausea, headache, heart palpitations, confusion, forgetfulness.
insertion	The place or mode of attachment of a muscle; the moveable part of a muscle during action.
insulin	The hormone produced in the pancreas which regulates carbohydrate and fat metabolism and causes increased cellular uptake of glucose.
intensity	Degree of strength, energy, or difficulty; as related to a workout: the class level.
intervertebral disc	Fibrocartilage cushion between the vertebrae.
inversion	To turn inward.
ischemia	A local, usually temporary decrease in blood supply in some part of the body resulting from obstruction of arterial flow.

isokinetic — Contraction in which the tension developed by the muscle while shortening at constant speed is maximal over the full range of motion.

isometric — Movement against an immovable force; static; a muscle contraction in which the tension increases, but muscle length remains the same.

isotonic — A contraction in which a muscle shortens against a force, resulting in movement and performance of work; also referred to as a dynamic or concentric contraction.

ketone — A compound formed during the incomplete oxidation of fatty acids.

ketosis — An abnormal increase in ketone production and accumulation in the blood; occurs especially in protein-sparing diets or fasting.

kinesthetic awareness — Body sense; ability of individuals to "feel" where their bodies are in relation to space.

Krebs cycle — A series of chemical reactions occurring in the mitochondria, during which energy is produced from metabolism of carbohydrates, fats and amino acids and the complete oxidation of acetyl CoA is accomplished.

kyphosis — Abnormal rounding of the thoracic portion of the spine, usually accompanied by rounded shoulders.

lactic acid — The byproduct of anaerobic metabolism of glucose or glycogen in muscle.

lactose — A disaccharide composed of glucose and galactose; milk sugar.

lateral flexion — Movement of head and/or trunk, bending to either side.

lateral movement — Any side-to-side movement away from the midline of the body.

LDL — Low-density lipoproteins; manufactured in the liver, they circulate throughout the body, making their fat available to all body cells; contain 45% cholesterol.

ligament — Bands or sheetlike fibrous tissues that connect bone to bone and reinforce joints from dislocation; they are nonelastic and have limited range of motion.

lipid — Fats; organic chemicals made up of carbon, oxygen and hydrogen that are insoluble in water.

lordosis — Sway back, increased or excessive lumbar curve.

lumbar spine — The largest five vertebrae between the thorax and the pelvis, the area that needs the most protection during exercise.

maintenance — When dieting, caloric intake equals caloric expenditure.

marrow — A soft, highly vascular and specialized connective tissue found in the medullary cavity of most bones; capable of producing blood cells.

maximum heart rate — Theoretical maximum rate at which your heart can beat at your age; in a healthy individual, 220 minus your age is a formula used to calculate the maximum heart rate; do not exercise at this rate.

maximum oxygen consumption — The highest level of oxygen an individual can consume and utilize per minute.

medial — Toward the midline of the body.

meniscus — Crescent-shaped fibrocartilage within a joint, i.e., shock absorbers in the knee. A common knee injury caused by trauma or fast rotation movements.

mesomorph — Body type characterized by a solid muscular build.

metabolism	The chemical reaction of a cell or living tissue that transfers usable materials into energy.
metatarsalgia	Pain in the forefoot in the region of the heads of the metatarsals.
mitochondria	Spherical or rod-shaped organelles, found outside the nucleus, that produce energy for cells through cellular respiration.
monosaccharide	Simple sugar, i.e., glucose, fructose, lactose, found in fruits, vegetables, milk, honey and cane sugar; end-product of all digestible forms of carbohydrates.
Morton's syndrome	A condition where the second toe is longer than the first throwing more weight on the third and fourth toes, causing irritation of the nerves.
muscle spindle	A type of receptor, located among the fibers of a skeletal muscle that responds to muscle contraction (stretch).
muscular endurance	The ability to perform repetitive work over a prolonged period of time.
myelin	Fatty, white substance forming medullary sheath around nerve.
myocardial infarction	The damaging or death of an area of the heart muscle, resulting from a reduction of blood supply to the area, also called a "heart attack."
myocardium	The thick, muscular layer forming the heart wall.
myofibril	The longitudinally arranged contractile elements, composed of actin and myosin of a skeletal muscle.
myotatic stretch reflex	The body's automatic protective mechanism against severe injury and abuse. If a muscle is stretched too quickly or with force, the reflex causes the muscle to contract; stretch threshold.
negative balance	In weight control, caloric intake is less than caloric expenditure.
neuromuscular	Pertaining to the relation between nerves and muscles.
neuron	Nerve cell that transmits messages throughout the body.
oxygen debt (recovery oxygen)	The oxygen required in the post-exercise period (above resting level) to provide energy for restoring the body to its pre-exercise condition.
oxygen deficit	A period in which the level of oxygen consumption is below what is necessary to supply appropriate ATP production required of any exercise.
periodization training	Cyclic training that rotates specific workout components throughout various periods of a training program.
plyometrics	A form of training that uses fast eccentric contractions, followed by concentric contractions to increase muscular power.
pressor response	The heart rate and blood pressure are elevated disproportionately to the oxygen cost of the activity.
pronation	Shifting the body weight to the inside of the foot.
proprioceptors	Sensor receptors in muscles, joints and tendons which give information concerning movement and postion of the body.
pulmonary ventilation	The rhythmic movement of air in and out of the lungs.
pulse pressure	The difference between the systolic and diastolic blood pressures.
radial pulse	Pulse found on the inside of the wrist on the thumb side near the wrist bone.

RDA   Recommended Dietary Allowances; percent or amount of calories for proteins, fats, carbohydrates, vitamins and minerals that should be included in the daily diet.

reciprocal innervation   A stretching technique in which an individual contracts the opposite muscle he wants to stretch.

recovery heart rate   Heart rate taken at the end of class after a stretch cooldown to gauge when the heart rate has returned to pre-exercise pulse.

red blood cell   Erythrocyte; blood cells responsible for oxygen transport.

residual volume   The volume of air that remains in the lungs after the deepest possible expiration.

respiration   Interchange of oxygen and carbon dioxide between an organism and its environment.

resting heart rate   Pulse rate while still lying down in the morning before arising.

rhythmic limbering   Low intensity exercises, performed at a low to moderate pace that help prepare the body for more vigorous exercise by providing an increase in the flexibility of tendons and ligaments, raising muscle temperature and stimulating muscle function.

RICE   Immediate injury treatment: rest, ice, compress, elevate.

risk factors   Factors known to be related to disease but cannot be proven to be the actual cause.

ROM   Range of motion.

rotation   Movements around an axis.

sagittal   Plane that divides the body into right and left parts.

SAID principle   "Specific adaptations to imposed demand;" training must be relative to the activity for physiological change to take place.

saturated fat   A fatty acid carrying the maximum possible number of hydrogen atoms.

scanning   Teaching technique of observation; looking for incorrect body alignment and positioning in your class.

scoliosis   Abnormal lateral twisting or rotating of the spine.

shin splint   Delayed pain on the front or sides of lower legs caused by inflammation of the fascia connecting to the leg bones or muscle tears.

side stitch   Sharp pain in the side, thought to be caused by a spasm in the diaphragm, due to insufficient oxygen supply and improper breathing.

smooth muscle   Involuntary muscles consisting of nonstriated, spindle shaped muscle cells, found in the walls of hollow viscera.

specificity of training   To improve muscular endurance and strength, applied resistance and range of motion must be specific to the muscle or muscle groups being worked; also applies to endurance training.

sphygmomanometer   Instrument used to measure arterial blood pressure.

spirometer   Instrument used for the collection, measurement or storage of gas.

spot reducing   A popular but false assumption that an individual can "burn" fat only in desired areas.

sprain	Wrenching or twisting of a joint in which ligaments are stretched past their normal limits.
stabilization	Static contraction of a muscle(s) that maintains a stable position so that joint action occurs by the primary mover.
static flexibility	The capacity to move a joint throughout its full range of motion.
static stretch	Held, non-bounce muscle contraction in which muscle tension is sustained throughout the stretch.
steady state	After the first 3-4 minutes of exercise, oxygen uptake has reached an adequate level to meet the oxygen demand of the tissue; heart rate, cardiac output and pulmonary ventilation have attained fairly constant levels.
strain	"Muscle pull;" a stretch, tear or rip of the muscle or adjacent tissue, such as fascia or muscle tendon.
strength	Maximum force or tension that a muscle or muscle group can produce against resistance.
stress fracture	Fracture caused by stress, overuse or pathologic weakness of the bone in the foot or leg.
strength plateau	A period of time that usually follows significant physical gains in which progressive increase in strength training effects ceases.
striated muscle	Skeletal voluntary muscle that attaches to and moves the skeleton.
stroke volume	The volume of blood ejected by each ventricle of the heart during a single systole.
subluxation	Dislocation or disarticulation of a joint.
submaximal work	Workload performed below maximum heart rate; aerobic exercise is submaximal.
supination	Shift the body weight to the outside of the foot.
supine	Lying face up.
synarthrodial joint	All articulations in which bones are held together tightly by fibrous connective tissue in a nonmoveable fashion, i.e., sacroiliac.
synergist	Muscle that combines with another and aids in its action.
synovial joint	(See diarthrodial joint).
systolic pressure	The highest level to which arterial blood pressure rises, following the systolic ejection of blood from the left ventricle.
target heart rate range	The rate at which the heart is beating to get the optimum aerobic effect; formula for obtaining a target heart rate equals 220 minus your age times 55-85% is reasonable for a healthy individual to use.
tendon	Band of dense fibrous tissue forming the termination of a muscle and attaching muscle to bone with a minimum of elasticity.
tendinitis	Continuous, low-grade inflammation of a tendon, with pain on movement; can lead to partial or complete rupture of tendon.
thoracic spine	Twelve vertebrae from the neck to lumbar area.
tibial torsion	Twisting of the tibia, usually associated with supinated or pronated feet.

tonus	A slight, sustained muscle contraction.
torque	Amount of twist around an axis.
training effects	Physiologic adaptations that occur as a result of aerobic exercise of sufficient intensity, frequency and duration to produce beneficial changes in the body.
transverse	Plane that divides the body into upper and lower halves.
triglyceride	A compound composed of glycerol fatty acids; varies in degrees of saturation and stored in the body.
unsaturated fats	Contain double bonds between carbon atoms; usually are vegetable rather than animal fat.
Valsalva maneuver	A dangerous condition that can occur if an individual holds his breath, causing the glottis to close and stomach muscle to contract, forming an unequal pressure in the chest cavity, reduced blood flow to the heart and insufficient oxygen supply to the brain. Dizziness, temporary loss of consciousness may occur.
vasoconstriction	Narrowing of blood vessels as a result of smooth muscle contraction.
vasodilatation	Dilation of blood vessels due to the relaxation of smooth muscles.
vein	Vessel carrying blood toward the heart.
venous return	Venous return refers to the "pumping action" of the muscles in the extremities and respiratory system along with venoconstriction to move oxygen-poor blood back to the heart.
ventral	Towards the stomach; anterior or front.
ventricle	Blood dispensing chambers of the heart.
vertebrae	Bony or cartilaginous segments, separated by discs that form the spinal column.
vital capacity	The greatest volume of air that can be forcibly exhaled after the deepest inspiration.
vocal nodules	Growths that develop on the vocal cords due to overuse injury, resulting in severe, chronic hoarseness.
warm-up	A balanced combination of static stretches and rhythmic limbering exercises that prepare the body for more vigorous exercise.
working heart rate	Heart rate taken at the completion of the aerobic portion of a workout to determine if an individual is within her or his target zone and at proper intensity for age and physical fitness level.

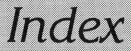

Index